W9-AZM-677

IN THE SHADOW OF WAR

IN THE SHADOW OF WAR

The United States Since the 1930s

MICHAEL S. SHERRY

Yale University Press   New Haven and London

This publication has been supported by a grant from the National Endowment for the Humanities, an independent federal agency.

Designed by Sonia L. Scanlon. Set in Bembo type by The Composing Room of Michigan, Inc.
Printed in the United States of America.

Library of Congress Cataloging-in-Publication Data

Sherry, Michael S., 1945–
  In the shadow of war
Michael S. Sherry.
       p.   cm.
    Includes bibliographical references (p.) and index.
    1. United States—Politics and government—1933–
1945. 2. United States—Politics and government—
1945–1989. 3. United States—Politics and
government—1989– 4. United States—History,
Military—20th century. 5. War—Social aspects—
United States—History—20th century. 6. National
security—United States—History—20th century.
I. Title.
E743.S53   1995
973.9—dc20   94-46849
                       CIP

    ISBN 0-300-06111-0

A catalogue record for this book is available from the British Library.
♾The paper in this book meets the guidelines for permanence and durability of the Committee on Production Guidelines for Book Longevity of the Council on Library Resources.

10 9 8 7 6 5 4 3 2 1

To my parents, John and Pauline Sherry

CONTENTS

ACKNOWLEDGMENTS

My primary debts are to a small group of friends and readers. Three—Marilyn Young, Lane Fenrich, and Leo Ribuffo—worked through a huge and frustratingly paginated manuscript to provide the kind of advice an author considers ideal. They were sympathetic to this book's purposes, shrewd about where it failed to meet them, and constructive about how to remedy the problems, even though some inevitably remain. All three made suggestions incorporated here but inevitably not fully reflected in citations. Lane Fenrich provided not only criticism but a sounding board for my ideas and a source of new ones, meticulous help in editing and shaping the final manuscript, and sustaining friendship. Laura Hein provided smart advice, important tips, and unfailing encouragement. George Chauncey and I traded stories and advice about the difficulties of finishing long books. Numerous graduate and undergraduate students responded helpfully to sections of this book or arguments in it delivered in other forums. Andrea Gregg provided prompt and precise research assistance at the final stage of this project. Charles Grench, the Yale University Press editor of all my books, provided the flexibility, quiet support, and timely advice for which he is rightly well known.

While most granting agencies were not forthcoming (perhaps because reviewers thought the book too "ideological," as I was told early on, or because works of synthesis still rarely get funded), Northwestern University gave essential support. A grant from its President's Fund for the Humanities provided a year's leave, an additional quarter's leave was given by the university, sympathetic department chairs allowed me to arrange my schedule to maximize time for writing, and the College of Arts and Sciences provided further funds to finalize the manuscript.

James Beal was once again indulgent of the absences, truncated vacations, and the like necessary for me to complete a book, and helpful in other ways as well. So too were other family members. I thank them all.

Lake Ann, Michigan
September 1994

PREFACE

Since the late 1930s, Americans have lived under the shadow of war. This is their history under that shadow and a reflection on its legacy—the story of America's militarization and how it changed the nation.

To say that Americans lived in war's shadow is to indulge in a metaphor, but one appropriate to their sensibilities. A 1941 advertisement (see fig. 2) displaying a bomber's shadow darkening a suburban home offered a metaphor apt for a half-century of anxiety about the nation's safety. It showed both the ominous shadow cast by war and the still untouched scene beneath it—both hovering danger and lingering tranquility, external threat and domestic innocence.

For that was how most Americans perceived the threat of war. To them, war came from outside America to intrude upon their lives and to wrest them from their pacific ways (*War Comes to America* was the title of a famous World War II propaganda film). And war itself seemed a murky phenomenon. Enemies were distant and elusive, and the proper response to them hard to define. Larger dangers—to life as the nuclear dilemma emerged, to liberty as the "garrison state" grew—defied measurement still more. Even films and photographs often left war in the shadows: Americans saw the mushroom clouds of nuclear explosions but rarely the destruction unleashed beneath them. And of course war's destruction almost never came to America. War's shadow hung over the nation, but its substance was hard to grasp.

Both regrettable hypocrisy and laudable idealism were involved in Americans' perceptions of war's sources. Regarding military vigilance and action as imperatives imposed upon them by external forces, they rarely acknowledged that their immersion in those imperatives arose also from their own values and ambitions. They talked about how war changed America, as if they were its passive victims, but less about how, deliberately or inadvertently, they changed themselves through war and changed war making itself. In the understandable but simple moral drama they saw, bad guys—Nazis, Japs, Commies, Russians—made them take up arms. But that outlook, by shoring up their self-image as a pacific people, also granted only tenuous legitimacy to the vast apparatus of national security they built, for if war's shadow receded, the apparatus might itself wither. National myth thus provided space for other pursuits—of profit or equality or moral perfection—to persist, even as they were yoked to war's demands. Viewed as an imposition upon the nation, the demands of national security held compelling urgency but lacked fundamental legitimacy.

The metaphor of this book's title suggests how Americans perceived their transformative experience, and also how we might now interpret it, for its effects on our history were often as shadowy as they were far-reaching. Some results were trivial though telling: a French fashion designer designated his new women's bathing suit the bikini, after the Pacific island where the United States tested atomic bombs in 1946. (Scantily clad women were, after all, regarded as "bombshells.") Some results were grandly apparent though poorly reckoned with: once an intermittent and often unimportant concern, national security assumed permanent and paramount importance in American life, so that much of the nation's treasure was devoted to it, its armed forces spread over much of the globe, and its science and industry were profoundly reoriented. The fortunes of politicians also hinged on their relationship to war, as when Lyndon Johnson's 1964 campaign portrayed opponent Barry Goldwater as itching to start a nuclear war. And every social group found its fate altered or at least reconceived amid hot and cold war; it was no coincidence that at the end of this era one of the most esteemed black Americans was a general, Colin Powell.

Other results were hard to pin down, in part because the weighty demands of war were in persistent tension with war's remoteness for most Americans. Nuclear weapons embodied that tension most dangerously, their cataclysmic potential paired with their virtual invisibility and total nonuse in war after 1945, but that tension cut through most of American life. Perhaps most insidious and hard to pinpoint, war defined much of the American imagination, as the fear of war penetrated it and the achievements of war anchored it, to the point that Americans routinely declared "war" on all sorts of things that did not involve physical combat at all.

Thus militarization reshaped every realm of American life—politics and foreign policy, economics and technology, culture and social relations—making America a profoundly different nation. To varying degrees, almost all groups were invested in it and attracted to it—rich and poor, whites and nonwhites, conservatives and liberals (the last more so than is usually recognized today). Certainly, all were changed by it.

Any book analyzing broad patterns leaves out a great deal. This book emphasizes war as agent of and rationale for the nation's transformation, as the blank screen on which unrelated concerns were often projected, and as the paradigm in which Americans defined themselves, pursued change, or resisted it. It is impossible to cite all instances of those phenomena, however, and foolish to suggest that militarization was determinative of all of this era's history. Divisions involving race, class, and gender, for example, like the nation's much-touted decline in economic vitality, all had autonomous dynamics as well as connections to the forces of militarization. As with terms for other periods, the label "Age of Militarization" is a creative oversimplification. Militarization did not define or cause everything that happened. It simply loomed large and persistently enough to give unity to a half-century of history, to make of it something of a common piece, distinct from the history that preceded it and possibly from the next half-century.

Other labels have been devised to describe aspects of that history: "the national security state" and "the warfare state," for institutions; the "Cold War," for the dominant conflict of this period; "hegemony" or "imperialism," for the global power that the United States exercised. But these terms, though unavoidable at times in a work like this, tend to posit a static condition and fail to capture both the breadth and the partiality of America's militarization. The federal government never became a "national security state" with the singlemindedness that term implies, for it was too chronically in disarray and too challenged by other tasks to give national security sole priority. "National security" itself is a slippery term; it long ago acquired a neutral, timeless, objective quality, when in fact the term is a politically constructed artifact of the period under study. Nor did the nation quite become a "warfare state," for it never celebrated or entered war wholeheartedly enough for the term to do it justice. "Cold War" describes the great rivalry between the Soviet and American spheres of influence, but that rivalry flowed in part from a deeper revolution in international relations and American consciousness, and "Cold War" obscures the hot wars that occurred under its aegis. And while America's role in the world was often "imperial," the term hardly accounts for much else in American culture and politics.

Hence I use the broader term "militarization" to capture the historical process that the United States entered in the 1930s. Militarization bears a close relationship to an older term, "militarism," but the latter is more politically charged—evocative of Prussia, Nazi Germany, or imperial Japan—and it refers more to a static condition than to a dynamic process. Militarization can be defined as "the contradictory and tense social process in which civil society organizes itself for the production of violence."[1] I use the term more broadly to refer to the process by which war and national security became consuming anxieties and provided the memories, models, and metaphors that shaped broad areas of national life.

Caveats about this term are in order. First, militarization was not a uniquely American experience, nor was the United States alone responsible for its global scale in the twentieth century. Second, a militarized nation need not be dominated by military institutions and elites: America's civilian leaders often pursued national security and embraced military values more fervently than military officers. Third, such a society need not be warlike, in the sense of relishing war; in the American case, countervailing emotions, like dread at the prospect of war and desire to enjoy affluence, prevented a war ethos from fully developing. Finally, though obviously expressed in the "production of violence," militarization may have sources and outlets far removed from violence and military power. Although overlapping phenomena, war and militarization did not march in historical lockstep. In fact, intense involvement in war absorbed energies, while diminished involvement often released them into other outlets for militarization, as when metaphors of war spread widely in American politics and culture during the 1980s.

Those caveats also suggest that the concept of militarization "is a little blurry around the edges."[2] But what it lacks in precision it makes up for in breadth. Since militarization, like industrialization, was a varied and changing rather than uniform historical process, it makes sense that the term for it embraces varied, even discordant, phenomena.

If not already clear to readers, it will become obvious that I view America's past half-century critically, but I seek no scapegoats among individuals or institutions. Presidents, and others who influenced or challenged them, receive much attention because their record is a common and plausible way to give coherence to a crowded history, because they did exercise much power, and because they shaped the moods and opinions of Americans. Their role in history was as much illustrative as determinative, however, and their responsibility for its outcomes was shared with others. Criticism of individual leaders remains appropriate, but the United States and its leaders were not alone responsible for the Cold War, the arms race, or other evils of our time—or for their passing. The forces militarizing America were deeply embedded, as are those which will establish a different path.

Regarding the methodological and theoretical issues that now vex historians, I have, through conscious choice and force of training and habit, taken an eclectic approach. Attentive to new approaches that "decenter" American history and dismantle its traditional narrative forms, I have nonetheless posited a center for this story, the national state and the political culture which it helped to construct and express. But I see that center as unstable, disrupted by tensions within and challenges from without, ones substantial enough to defy rigid notions of "center" and "margins." And I see a narrative focused on that center as a compelling, though not the only, way to organize this history. In turn, this narrative usually follows but sometimes challenges the chronological divisions Americans generally see in their past.

This book draws on my previous scholarship and teaching, on limited primary sources (generally of an accessible sort), and on the work of other scholars. Anyone in the field realizes that this scholarship is voluminous and ever-growing, and knows useful titles that I have not cited. At the same time, precisely because of its groaning volume, this scholarship now warrants a synthesis, one other scholars will test, refine, or reject, since the task of making sense of America's age of militarization is just beginning.

PROLOGUE: WAR IN AMERICAN HISTORY

War created the United States. Although many Americans professed genuine hostility toward it, war was central to their history, the instrument by which they forged and expanded their nation and often defined themselves.

The American Revolution was itself a war, often a nasty one. It broke out in part over military issues—the fiscal burdens, intrusive presence, and ideological threat many Americans perceived in English military ambitions and institutions. It presented the rebels with a dilemma that would persist in American history: How could they wage war against the evils of militarism without creating them in their own midst? And it left Americans in a tenuous military condition; despite their victory, reliable defense of the nation's borders was in doubt for three decades.

Politics and folklore sustained the centrality of war for Americans long after the Revolution. No figures loomed larger in political mythology than George Washington, the warrior President, and Abraham Lincoln, the war President. From Washington through Teddy Roosevelt, former military officers seized the presidential nominations of their parties and often the presidency itself. The Revolution and the Civil War remained touchstones of national memory, their meanings repeatedly plumbed and refashioned. A nation born in war, threatened by invasion, expanded through conquest, and finally reconceived in civil war, owed much to Mars.

True, it paid its debt grudgingly. Americans often celebrated what war gained them, but rarely war's institutions and burdens. Their distrust of professional "standing armies"—of their origins in a decadent Europe, of their power to corrupt or overawe the Republic—was deep. The new nation sanctioned only a bare-bones, decentralized military force. It relied on the voluntary enthusiasm of amateurs—men Washington described as "just dragged from the tender Scenes of domestick life" and all too "ready to fly from their own shadows"[1]—and hence also on the coercion of ideological fervor rather than the compulsion of the state to wage its wars. And although military service added attractive plumage to a political candidate, military officers as a class did not gain great social prestige or telling political clout. From the outset, then, a deep ambivalence pervaded American attitudes toward war and its institutions: dependence on both matched distrust of each.

The armed forces nonetheless played a telling role in defending, expanding, and building the new nation. As if to resolve their ambivalence, Americans liked their military forces best when they undertook decidedly unmilitary functions. President Thomas Jefferson established the United States Military Academy at West Point less as a schoolhouse in destruction than as an academy of science and engineering, the role it played for decades in a nation hell-bent on internal development but lacking institutions with the requisite expertise. Army officers like Meriwether Lewis and William Clark surveyed the West and searched out its scientific secrets. Academy graduates, either in uniform or after entering private business, helped to build bridges, canals, harbors, and railroads. They were happy to do so, seeing in that role, rather than in war making, their main hope for gaining social prestige and economic security. Their efforts forged a lasting link between the armed forces and the nation's economic and technological development. That link went further. The army's Harpers Ferry and Springfield arsenals pioneered standardized mass production. In the 1840s, Congress debated how development of iron-clad warships might nourish the iron industry. Later, businessmen and technical experts gleaned the Civil War's record for lessons on how to rationalize the burgeoning corporate economy.

During the nineteenth century, Americans also developed their particular, though not unique, style of imagining and waging war. American officers favored a "strategy of annihilation"[2] entailing head-on assaults against an enemy's armed forces or productive capacity, rather than limited campaigns of movement, surprise, or attrition. It was a brutal style of war waged against Native Americans and in the Civil War, when many Americans embraced war's destructiveness as an instrument of higher causes and took "flight into unreason: into visions of purgation and redemption, into anticipation and intuition and spiritual apotheosis, into bloodshed that was not only intentional pursuit of interests of state but was also sacramental, erotic, mystical, and strangely gratifying."[3] Wars of annihilation drew on such attitudes, and on the capacity to mass produce weapons and war materiel and the locomotives and ships to move them. The system was synergistic, if rarely seen as such: the armed forces spurred economic development, which in turn enhanced American military power.

Some Americans carried this vision further. Developing the "cult of the superweapon," they imagined stunning new weapons enabling the nation to usher in a Pax Americana by smashing its enemies or by making war too hellish to be waged, so that "war shall cease to desolate the world nor burning cities mark its dreadful track," as the inventor Robert Fulton hoped.[4] By century's end, the notion was commonplace that submarines, airships, or other devices might deter or humanize war, despite doubts about what would happen if the magical weapon belonged instead to an enemy, or got used in a civil war among Americans, or made killing too easy rather than too horrific. Mark Twain savagely mocked the vision of American weapons making peace in *A

Connecticut Yankee in King Arthur's Court (1889), a comic nightmare of auto-
mated butchery in battle. But dreams of triumphal American technology continued to hold sway. They tapped Americans' ambivalence about war, promising that the nation could gain what it wanted from war through superior
technology rather than through the dreadful leviathan of large standing
armies.

Imagining future wars, Americans also continued to plumb the meaning of
past ones—above all the Civil War, which gripped the American imagination
so long in part because a half-century went by before another major war. Americans judged politicians by their wartime heroism and waved the "bloody
shirt" in political campaigns. They employed war as a metaphor for other
struggles, as in one scholar's *History of the Warfare of Science and Theology in
Christendom*. They compared the Civil War's attractive model of idealism, discipline, and self-sacrifice to the rank materialism, squalid corruption, and corporate giantism of post–Civil War America. Few Civil War veterans wanted another war or joined Oliver Wendell Holmes, Jr., in urging Americans "to pray,
not for comfort, but for combat." But many Americans joined Teddy Roosevelt
in celebrating the strenuous and democratizing virtues of wartime service. Or
they tried to extract the virtues of war from war itself. Champions of civil service reform drew on an "ideal of military professionalism." Social reformers
saw charity work as akin to enlisting in an army at war, now "with vice and
poverty as the enemy." Edward Bellamy's *Looking Backward* (1888) imagined a
utopia at peace but operated by a disciplined army of workers. In 1910 came the
crowning appeal to exploit war's virtues in peacetime, William James's "The
Moral Equivalent of War." James proposed to rekindle the Civil War spirit by
drafting youth into an "army against nature" whose soldiers would dig coal,
wash dishes, erect skyscrapers, and generally "get the childishness knocked
out of them"—a proposal often seen as a precursor to the New Deal's Civilian
Conservation Corps and John Kennedy's Peace Corps. Views like James's, although easily seen as opposed to the bellicose militarism of a Teddy Roosevelt,
in fact only bent similar assumptions to different purposes. James, too, believed
that "militarism is the great preserver of our ideals of hardihood."[5]

Reflections on the Civil War also emerged amid fears of a new war (for which
the Paris Commune of 1871 served as a frightening model) that might pit the
nation's social classes, racial or ethnic groups, or ideological factions against
each other. Indeed, military forces repeatedly intervened on the side of the new
corporate giants to subdue striking workers, just as embattled workers saw
themselves as "industrial armies" and marched in 1894 as "Coxey's Army."
Afraid of the enraged masses, prominent Americans proposed an expanded
army to garrison cities—arguments more successfully used for modernizing
state militias, or the National Guard, as collectively they came to be called.
From a different vantage point, authors of apocalyptic visions—Twain in *Connecticut Yankee*, Ignatius Donnelly in *Caesar's Column* (1890)—cast war as a civil

conflict harnessing dreadful new weapons to internal passions. Although fear of class war abated after the century's turn, champions of preparedness claimed that universal military service would close the fissures of class and ethnicity by giving all boys a common discipline and training in democracy's virtues.

For Americans fearing domestic strife, the Civil War had resonance. It loomed over succeeding generations just as World War II did over later generations fearing another international war. The great class war never erupted, just as World War III never broke out, but in both cases skirmishes in the imagined war—conflicts with labor in the late 1800s, the "limited wars" of Korea and Vietnam—kept the specter alive. In such ways, war occupied a central place in America's earlier history, as in our own times.

But the similarities cannot be pushed very far. Above all, after the War of 1812 the new nation enjoyed remarkable immunity from attack, though not the "free security" that nostalgic Americans in the mid-twentieth century imagined. Border disputes, threats to trade, Native Americans' resistance to conquest, and growing imperial ambitions offered real challenges. But it was with reason that young Abraham Lincoln could ask in 1837, "Shall we expect some transatlantic military giant to step the ocean and crush us at a blow?" and answer boastfully, "Never! All the armies of Europe, Asia, and Africa combined . . . could not by force take a drink from the Ohio or make a track on the Blue Ridge in a trial of a thousand years."[6] The only serious threat to the nation, Lincoln recognized, came from within it.

A term like "national security," implying broad and continuous efforts to defend a country, as yet had no place. The United States maintained a *War* Department (and a Navy Department)—not yet a Defense Department and a National Security Council—a designation suggesting that war was an episodic event, not the object of sustained anxiety. War intruded only occasionally into the lives of Americans, and when it did occur, its circumstances (except for the Civil War) allowed leaders great latitude about whether to participate. The Civil War loomed over the American imagination, but as a site of contested memories about a bitter division, not as the touchstone of national unity against a foreign threat. It therefore lacked the resonance with world events that World War II would hold for Americans. Few nineteenth-century Americans saw their nation's fortunes as bound up with distant wars in a seamless world and as dependent on massive military power. What became war's constant shadow was then only a passing eclipse.

By the same token, war and defense rarely dominated national politics. The Spanish-American War, the difficult war to conquer the Filipinos that followed, and the simultaneous modernization of the armed forces all reflected a higher priority on military force and more intense debate about it. But as late as the raucous debate on military preparedness in 1915–16, no credible, immediate threat to national safety could be invoked; bellicose advocates of preparedness were "more interested in polishing the fire engines than finding the blaze."[7] Instead, that debate pivoted on almost everything else: trade, national pride, the internal cohesion of a polyglot and class-riven nation.

Too, the armed forces only slowly became a truly national instrument of power wielded by a centralized state. The navy's ships were dispersed among far-flung stations, only starting to join in a battleship navy in the 1890s. The army remained broken into small units long after major activity against Indians ended. The National Guard was largely a creature of state governments. Wartime recruitment of soldiers and sailors lay mostly in the hands of states and localities. The professional training of soldiers and officers remained in infancy. Except for the President, no central authority knit together this hodgepodge. Given its fragmented structure, most soldiers in the Spanish-American War, many even in World War I, marched as a unit from the same locality, which held their loyalties and scrutinized their progress for signs of local pride or grief. They were Milwaukee's finest or Ohio volunteers, not homogenized instruments of Washington's impersonal authority, which they often keenly resisted.

Above all, the armed forces lacked the size to drive the nation's economy and politics. In select areas, as with their technological contributions, their role was critical to the nation's development. And telling precedents for the future did emerge: the "very extensive and expensive old-age assistance program for [Civil War] veterans" constituted the first major federal welfare program, one that foreshadowed the powerful linkage between welfare and military service in the twentieth century. But that precedent was not immediately followed up. By century's end, universities had also displaced service academies as the premier engineering schools and "the day of the soldier-technologist, well versed in science and committed to its peacetime uses, had largely disappeared." Britain's "military-industrial complex" was already the unstable fulcrum for its economy and a leader in the global arms trade. In contrast, arms contracts were significant in turn-of-the-century America (President Grover Cleveland warned in 1894 that "if no new contracts are given out, contractors must disband their workmen and their plants must lie idle"), but the nation had at most only the "keel of a navy-industrial complex."[8]

Spending on the armed forces reflected their modest place in the nation's political economy. Until well into the twentieth century, military expenditures in peacetime took 0.4 to 0.9 percent of gross national product annually. National defense did comprise 20 to 25 percent of federal spending from the 1880s through the 1920s, and far more if payments to veterans and on the federal debt—obligations largely acquired in war—are also counted. But the federal budget comprised so small a share of GNP (less than 3 percent before the 1920s) that defense spending still commanded few national resources. Moreover, debt service and veterans' payments, primarily reflecting the episodic burdens of war rather than the ongoing costs of national defense, are often excluded in broad chronological and cross-national comparisons. Judged by direct expenditures on armed forces, peacetime military spending before the 1930s paled in comparison to the post–World War II era, when it seized about 10 percent of GNP (itself far larger than a half-century earlier).[9]

The armed forces did grow, not only in costs but in manpower. Contrary to Cold War mythology, which held that the nation had foolishly disbanded its armed forces after each war, those forces increased sharply in the wake of all wars after 1848, tripling after the Spanish-American War to some 150,000 personnel and nearly doubling again by the mid-1920s. Still, these forces were only 10 to 20 percent of what nations like France and Britain maintained at the turn of the century. Active-duty military forces comprised less than 0.1 percent of America's population in the 1890s, and under 0.2 percent in the 1920s, but from 1.3 to 1.8 percent of the total population in the 1950s and 1960s. The cadre of civilians working for the armed forces was also modest—less than 20 percent of total federal civilian employment through the 1920s (when such employment exceeded 500,000), but roughly half of that employment in the mid-1950s (when total employment reached 2.4 million). Only by one critical standard, death in war, did the nineteenth-century record eclipse that of the twentieth. No other American war matched the Civil War in casualties, especially as measured against total population—over 600,000 military dead (one in every five white males of military age in the South, one in sixteen in the North), plus thousands of civilian dead—or in physical destruction to the nation.[10]

In sum, until well into the twentieth century national defense claimed only a minor part of the nation's resources. War imposed enormous burdens, but defense as an ongoing activity did not. Despite blood-curdling expressions of militaristic sentiment from some Americans, militarization as a grand historical process was at most incipient, well behind the stage it had reached in Europe.

The forces were nonetheless gathering to advance that process in America. War's democratization, industrialization, and professionalization were often seen in the nineteenth century as likely to make war more humane and less frequent, but those developments, tied as they were to that century's powerful nationalism and imperialism, only prepared the way for the titanic warfare of the twentieth century. Europe was caught up in an arms race bearing down on and sucking in the rest of the world.

Americans responded to that arms race with a confused and limited expansion of their own armed forces. Some chastised Old World militarism, but others were eager to join the race, especially its showy competition in battleship navies. No single ideological viewpoint or cluster of interest drove the growth of American arms. Because many anti-imperialists were also virulently anti-British, for example, they supported a big American navy able to challenge the world's largest fleet or expand American commerce. While industrialists pressed for contracts and scientists like Thomas Edison promised amazing weapons, their efforts to secure defense monies had only limited results in the absence of intense interservice rivalries or widespread alarms about the nation's safety. What drove military modernization and expansion at its critical stage during the Roosevelt and Taft presidencies was a small coalition of patrician civilians like Elihu Root, Henry L. Stimson, and Roosevelt himself, and reformers within the officer corps.

Still, their calculations of interest did not alone propel modernization and expansion. Only occasionally, and then not very plausibly, did reformers cite territorial safety as justification. They also wanted military power in order to support American hegemony over a world-capitalist economy, but that argument too was strained and episodic. Military institutions were "organic growths developing, as do most great social institutions, out of complex soils of vested interests, political and economic ambitions, unanalyzed fears and untested assumptions about historical causation." Like Roosevelt, many Americans believed that military power expressed more than it underwrote the nation's ascendancy: big nations needed big navies and the expansion that went with them, "or we are not great" and face only "stagnation and decay," so naval officers could argue. That view prevailed easily before World War I, when war, at least in its horrific forms, seemed remote, so that the nation's new engines of war "were thought of simply as beautiful pieces of machinery completely unconnected with the destruction of human life"—symbols of national pride and technological achievement. The growth of American arms also proceeded because the resources to realize it were abundant, and because Progressive reformers admired effective national government and saw armed forces as an expression of it.[11]

The ease with which the armed forces expanded allowed for substantial confusion about ultimate purposes. A convenient war, as with Spain in 1898, or a convenient war scare, as with Japan during Teddy Roosevelt's presidency, provided pretext but little compelling reason for the armed forces' growth. Economic and territorial imperialism, strategic anxieties, nationalism and racism, elitist longings to enhance the nation's internal cohesion, attraction to darkly determinist notions—such impulses behind expansion thrived in a climate where none was severely tested and at force levels still so low that few Americans needed to worry about joining Europe's powers in the abyss of war and militarism.

Americans did peer into that abyss during World War I, which marked a watershed in their relationship to war. Mindful of Europe's methods of total war, American political, business, and military leaders constructed a national machinery for harnessing resources. Manpower, industry, science, food, trade, and opinion were conscripted into service, as war's democratization yielded its paradoxical results: war in the name of the people sanctioned their mobilization and death at unimaginable levels.

All too often, it is true, the machinery of American war making jammed, its gears only beginning to mesh when the war ended. American forces remained surprisingly dependent on the British and French for airplanes, artillery, and other implements of war. Complicating America's mobilization was a volatile mix of antiwar fervor, idealistic war aims, repressive impulses, sectional division, and class conflict among Americans ("If you conscript men for war, conscript wealth for war," one congressman demanded). Perhaps most important was the persistence amid the new approach to war of an older ethic of voluntary, decentralized mobilization for war, evident when President Woodrow Wilson proclaimed the new Selective Service Act, though surely an act of state compulsion, as only a "selection from a nation which has volunteered in mass."[12] New federal agencies like the War Industries Board were as much the captives as the rulers of America's corporations. All too often, hesitancy about brandishing state power led only to its underhanded employment or to ugly vigilantism and popular hysteria to substitute for it. Voluntarism and compulsion, enthusiasm and efficiency, freedom and discipline—such dualisms, long familiar in American history, cut through the American war effort, framed how many Americans viewed it, and revealed their ambivalence about entering a world of mass slaughter and global power.

American leaders nonetheless built the rudiments of a national security state. These included agencies of economic mobilization; a capricious apparatus of internal security; organizations to enlist universities, scientists, and intellectuals into the cause; the battle fleet "second to none" long sought by ardent navalists; a mass and partially mechanized army; and a fledgling air force attracted to new doctrines of strategic bombing.

In another way, too, World War I illuminated America's future: as a massive if disappointing experiment in using war to serve political and social agendas. The desire to extract constructive change from war was hardly new to Americans in 1917, but no war exposed it so boldly, in part because the newly assertive state promised riper opportunities for action. In his famous formulation of war's opportunities, John Dewey, speaking for progressive intellectuals reluctant to enter the maelstrom, presented war as a "plastic juncture" in history that held out the possibility of securing "the supremacy of public need over private possessions."[13] Diverse interests shared Dewey's sense of war's malleability, though not his interest in liberal reform: businessmen keen on expanding trade, controlling the embryonic apparatus of economic regulation, or smashing organized labor; union leaders like Samuel Gompers, seeking to enhance labor's status and power; feminists and moral reformers, seizing the chance to push for woman's suffrage and prohibition; nationalists and nativists, yearning to purify a polyglot nation; blacks, hoping their contribution to victory would speed their full citizenship—and the list could go on.

Many of these groups were to be bitterly disappointed because they either failed to get what they wanted (as with black leaders) or found the price too high (as with progressive intellectuals). World War I reworked the basic fissures of American society, but in ways few groups could anticipate or control. Randolph Bourne's memorable barb at progressives applied to others as well: "If the war is too strong for you to prevent, how is it going to be weak enough for you to control and mould to your liberal purposes?"[14] The question would endure. Never again would Americans so brazenly champion the potential of war abroad to unleash beneficent change at home. The lure of that potential would persist, however, muted in future rhetoric but if anything more powerful in actuality.

Just as impressive as the speed with which Americans plunged into World War I and divined its meanings was the rapidity with which they discarded much of its legacy. As preparation for the age of national security, this war, in part because America's role in it was so brief, was a dress rehearsal after which the props were stored and even the stage sometimes abandoned. The jerry-built machinery to mobilize men and materiel soon was in shambles. As the Red Scare dwindled, the apparatus of internal security shrank, although legacies like immigration restriction endured. Wartime visions of seizing world markets, though partly realized, faded before the lure of a robust market at home.

The armed forces, it is true, were now enlarged, modernized, and innovative, developing some of the world's best weapons, studying the war's lessons about modern industrial warfare, and forging links to science and industry through new organizations like the National Advisory Committee on Aeronautics and the Army Industrial College. And on the West Coast there emerged the embryo of a "metropolitan-military complex" shaped less by authorities in Washington than by fledgling entrepreneurs, ambitious scientists, and local boosters tapping the imperial dreams of the West's fast-growing cities. But no orderly system of militarization was yet in place. Thus Congress, steeped in antistatist and anticorporate ideology and fearing "a powerfully independent military-industrial clique that would fleece the taxpayer and foment war," imposed rules that pitted the pace-setting aircraft companies savagely against each other and against the armed services, their primary market. Presidential parsimony, popular antagonisms, interservice rivalries, and weak institutional linkages curbed long-range planning in strategy and logistics. Whatever the lessons of World War I, they were at best partially implemented.[15]

War also taught lessons in the necessity of avoiding it as well as the means to wage it. Americans had already experienced the horrors of modern war in their Civil War, but that war's predictive value was not widely recognized here or abroad, its ferocity instead being seen as anomalous, due to the nature of civil war. World War I, however, as an international war that erupted amid growing anxiety about technological and economic change, made apparent the destructive and dehumanizing nature of modern warfare. Tentatively during the war, savagely after it, some soldiers, reformers, politicians, and writers exposed the mechanized madness and excoriated the civilization that produced it. World War I taught Carrie Chapman Catt, for example, that "war is in the blood of men; they can't help it. They have been fighting ever since the days of the cave-men" (such sentiments led the War Department to red-bait and harass antiwar feminists).[16] Indeed, war-borne visions of an armed American colossus fell vic-tim in part to the ideological pacifism and diffuse antimilitarism of the 1920s.

Yet the lessons touted by war's opponents triumphed no more clearly than those proclaimed by advocates of armed vigilance. War was rarely the main target of "disillusioned" postwar writers and artists, many of whom, like Er-nest Hemingway, were not pacifists. Instead, World War I was "a fabulously useful, if expensively purchased, metaphor for the corruption of the culture they had under siege." Besides, what dismayed Americans was less the war itself—brief, triumphant, and relatively inexpensive for them (116,516 Ameri-can personnel died, fewer than half in battle)—than its aftermath of revolution, greed, and stillborn treaties abroad, and inflation, hysteria, and squabbling at home. War's multiple legacies seemed less to coalesce than to cancel each other out.[17]

No simple retreat into isolation or "normalcy" accounted for the stalemate, for no such retreat was possible or even desired by most Americans. Wilson's Republican successors shared his vision of American leadership in a global capitalist system even as they shifted the tactics designed to achieve it. Despite the Senate's defeat of the Treaty of Versailles, the United States made vigorous diplomatic and financial efforts on the world stage. Those included arms con-trol treaties which capped the size of the great powers' fleets while encouraging the technological innovation in which the United States was emerging as preeminent—in essence, carefully balancing the conflicting lessons drawn from the war experience. Meanwhile, diverse political forces—feminists and other pacifists opposed to any war, populists and progressives suspicious of eastern capitalists, unilateralists opposed to alliances, conservatives more wor-ried about the domestic order—repeatedly assaulted the potent symbols of America's past or prospective involvement in world war. They defeated Amer-ica's entry into the League of Nations and the World Court; railed against the evils of chemical warfare; denounced the financiers and militarists presumed to thrive on war and weapons; embraced the Kellogg-Briand Pact to outlaw war; and attacked plans for a mass American army capable of once again storming Europe's battlefronts. Their efforts were linked to a widespread de-sire among Americans to gain the advantages of global economic power with-out sustaining its costs, including those of wielding military power. In Warren Cohen's phrase, they sought "empire without tears." That desire, seen during World War II as lamentably weak and hypocritical, made sense in the 1920s, when no credible threat to American interests existed to justify a firmer em-brace of military power.

But the pacific aspirations and antimilitarist politics of this era also obscured the nation's deepening involvement in the world and the growing military power used to underwrite it. American culture, particularly in its fascination with new technologies, also masked these changes. Heroes like aviator Charles Lindbergh were celebrated as exemplars of an old pioneer spirit, paragons of a modern scientific age, and creators of an international web of travel and communication that would smother the provincial forces of nationalism and war. Crusaders for air power like Gen. Billy Mitchell were seen not as proponents of a deadly new technology but as populist rebels against the forces of militarism. And the technologies themselves, above all the bomber, were celebrated as instruments for preserving the nation's immunity from war, not as a new means to wage it. In that fashion, the progress of American armaments between the world wars seemed indicative more of bygone virtues and peace-loving impulses than of new terrors and challenges.

Even those thinking about such terrors still held out hope. Many Americans remembered the scientific butchery of the past war and feared its resumption. They penned horrifying tales of the carnage made possible by recent or anticipated inventions—gas and bacteriological weapons, long-range bombers, even an atomic device. They glimpsed nothing less than mankind's ability to "accomplish its own destruction," as Winston Churchill put it, or to carry out a military and ecological "holocaust" in a matter of hours, as the American social critic Stuart Chase worried.[18] And yet such prophets offered a more hopeful message as well: precisely because another war was so horrific a prospect, nations led by rational leaders either would never allow it to occur or would tolerate it so briefly that it would reach a mercifully quick end.

In this dimension too, that of grand imaginings of the future, Americans did not yet have to anticipate constant peril to their safety and strenuous efforts to avert it. War's place in the nation's history was large, but its militarization—the large and sustained focus of anxieties and resources on military power—was evident only in teasing outline. Well into the 1930s, "the shadow of the future was already plain; but there was nothing with which to give it substance."[19]

PART ONE

THE MILITARIZATION
OF AMERICA

EMERGENCE, 1933–1941

As If "Invaded by a Foreign Foe"

On a gray and grim March 4, 1933, in a city that seemed like "a beleaguered capital in war time," President Franklin Roosevelt invoked war as a metaphor for the nation's economic crisis and a model for its solution. He proposed to solve unemployment "by direct recruiting by the Government itself, treating the task as we would treat the emergency of a war"; to follow "lines of attack" on the financial crisis; to summon Americans to be "a trained and loyal army"; to urge on them "a unity of duty hitherto evoked only in time of armed strife"; to assume "unhesitatingly the leadership of this great army of our people." Near the conclusion of his First Inaugural Address came his boldest challenge. If Congress failed to take effective action, he would ask for "broad Executive power to wage a war against the emergency, as great as the power that would be given to me if we were in fact invaded by a foreign foe." There followed the crowd's loudest cheer, a response Eleanor Roosevelt found "a little terrifying."[1]

On a day famous for his claim "that the only thing we have to fear is fear itself," the analogy to war was hardly Roosevelt's only theme, and too much can be made of it: he never explicitly asked Congress for "broad executive power." Still, war provided FDR his dominant metaphor, just as he explicitly rejected others ("We are stricken by no plague of locusts," he insisted).

The war analogy addressed multiple purposes and audiences. It was designed to revive the unity (exaggerated in memory) of World War I. Taking Americans back to 1917, it implicitly repudiated the 1920s, and with it the petty materialism and rigid economic dogma which many believed had caused the Depression. Treating the nation as if "invaded by a foreign foe," the war analogy vaguely imputed an external cause for economic disaster, diminishing American culpability for it. Invoking war, FDR also served notice that he would draw on the last war's models of bureaucratic and presidential action; its invocation was intended, and understood, to strengthen his legal and political claim to power. FDR also used the analogy at a time of international instability, with dictators on the march and the First World War's sour legacy of revolution, nationalism, and debt fresh to Americans. Above all, the war analogy reflected the felt gravity of the economic crisis and FDR's sense of what would best mobilize Americans behind his course of action.

Hardly confined to political rhetoric, war-related models and metaphors also suffused culture in the early 1930s. Film and fiction displayed contemporary fears (or hopes) that fascistic government, military measures like martial law, or war itself might be used to overcome the economic crisis or curb the predators and revolutionaries it bred. Released just after FDR's inauguration, *Gabriel Over the White House* had its cinematic president form an Army of Construction "subject to military discipline," use military courts-martial to try and execute racketeers, and display America's air power to force the world's nations to disarm.[2] Similar moods surfaced in nervous admiration of Mussolini's Italian fascism—far less often Hitler's version—and in recurrent speculation that FDR's New Deal or other forces (like Louisiana's senator Huey Long) might usher in fascism. There was no consensus that militaristic solutions were desirable—more Americans probably feared them than wanted them—but their mere mention indicated how hard it was to imagine solutions to the Great Depression that did not partake of war, revolution, or some mixture of the two.

These uses of the idea and the institutions of war drew them closer to the center of American politics and revealed that their emerging centrality derived from dynamics internal to the nation as well as from challenges beyond its shores. In particular, those uses of war exposed how much the nation's coming militarization owed to uneasiness about the growing size and power of national government. Passionate calls for federal action to cope with the Great Depression collided with persistent distrust of a powerful state, a distrust inscribed in the Constitution and linked to faith in individual responsibility, which strong government would presumably undermine. Sometimes expressed by FDR himself, distrust of the state impeded its authority to take large, effective action.

It required the sanction of war—as memory, model, metaphor, or menace—to sustain that authority. As William Leuchtenburg later commented, use of the "war analogue" during the 1930s exposed "both an impoverished tradition of reform and the reluctance of the nation to come to terms with the leviathan state," as if the nation could find no way "to organize collective action save in war or its surrogate."[3] Federal action to discipline corporations, employ the impoverished, or aid the elderly seemed of arguable necessity—useful, but rarely compelling to the nation's survival. The arena of war, on the other hand, presumably compelled action: nothing less than the nation's survival and honor were at stake. Borrowing from that arena, Roosevelt and others gained legitimacy for state action otherwise viewed suspiciously and tried to forge the unity that war presumably entailed—to override differences of class, ideology, race, and the like that supposedly hampered state action.

Enhancing the state's legitimacy, the war analogy also served the New Deal's conservative purposes. War, as Americans increasingly understood it, required centralized direction and executive supremacy. The New Dealers' "war approach," according to Leuchtenburg, "rejected both mass action and socialist planning" in favor of corporate-government cooperation. New Dealers most feared not "the opposition of the conservatives, who were discredited," but instead "the menace of antiplutocratic movements. Yet in damping the fires of popular dissent, they also snuffed out support they would need to keep the reform spirit alive." To be sure, the "war approach" was not consistently followed, FDR did sometimes stoke the "fires of popular dissent," and antistatism limited the New Deal's centralizing tendencies. But the war analogy, with all its connotations of emergency and peril, did presume entrusting national elites with extraordinary power.[4]

Although the metaphors and models of war enhanced the power and legitimacy of the state, few Americans consciously intended that result. The war analogy came too easily to require much calculation. Sometimes its use was simply trivial, a mere gloss on other rationales more deeply felt. And it did not lead directly to war or to the nation's militarization: only in concert with changing economics, politics, and technology on the international stage could those results occur. But use of war as metaphor and model did help prepare Americans materially and psychologically for war. And by allowing them to avoid the central dilemma of the state's legitimacy, it eased political conflict in the 1930s at the price of strengthening the habit, destined to reappear over the next half-century, of harnessing politics and state initiatives to the imperatives and models of war. In those indirect but powerful ways, it furthered the transition to a militarized America.

Roosevelt was ideally suited to preside over and speed along that transition. Few modern presidents had the background and temperament to move so comfortably in the arenas of both war and peace. His first major position, as assistant secretary of the navy during World War I, increased his knowledge of war abroad and politics at home. His gravest political crisis before his presidency—his 1919 investigation into homosexual behavior at the Newport Naval Training Station met a Senate subcommittee's harsh reprimand and a public outcry over his use of youthful sailors to entrap alleged offenders—came at the troubled intersection of military policy and domestic culture, where conflicts would arise repeatedly in the next decades. Rhetorically, FDR was gifted at employing the images of one arena in the other, as when domestic crisis led him to invoke the metaphors of war, and later when he translated war's demands back into the homefront's language of production. Most of all, he was comfortable with the demands of war and the power he exercised in it. He shared little of the era's fear of corporate-military institutions and their power to manipulate or corrupt the nation. He was instead in that tradition of elite easterners like Teddy Roosevelt and Henry L. Stimson, who championed preparedness and accepted the institutional demands that modern war seemed to make. At the same time, he was not awed by the romance of war or by the men and institutions that conducted it. He presented war's demands with a coolness appropriate to the modern temper and to a nation suspicious of the lofty idealism of 1917. It is true that his attitudes and talents did not always serve him well. It is also true that he alone did not guide the nation toward militarization, whose course he only partly intended and dimly foresaw. Lesser leaders might have taken that course. Roosevelt did so expertly.

FDR drew on an old tradition of using war politically and rhetorically. Amid the prosperity of the 1920s, few found war a useful metaphor for domestic crisis simply because few perceived a crisis. But as a model of national unity and state control of a chaotic economy, World War I loomed large even in prosperous times among "more advanced Progressives," who "looked back fondly toward the war mobilization which seemed to have drawn a blueprint for America's future."[5] The decade's bold initiative in prohibition also emerged out of wartime idealism, experimentation, and anti-immigrant feeling. Cautious reformers like Commerce Secretary Herbert Hoover, who saw government's role as catalytic rather than coercive, found wartime experience equally instructive.

Just how instructive emerged sharply after 1929, when hard economic times crippled Hoover's presidency. The common phrase "fighting the Depression" itself drew on military imagery, and analogies to war now flowed freely. *The New Deal*, Stuart Chase's widely read 1932 analysis, called for a "general staff" to direct the forces of economic recovery. The *Nation* compared the crisis of the 1930s to the Civil War. At one point, Hoover proclaimed, the nation had fought its "battle of Chateau-Thierry" and now had to regroup for its "battle of Soissons," referring to two key battles of World War I. Keenly aware of the national mood if inept at altering it, Hoover drew on the Great War's uses of propaganda in trying to lift the nation's spirits. He awkwardly compared the Depression to war: "We have the combats, if against an unseen foe of inestimable strength. We have our men and we have our casualties among them." Hoover saw himself as "the commanding officer at general headquarters," an aide recalled. "We have all been saying to each other the situation is quite like war," Secretary of State Henry L. Stimson observed.[6]

Proposals for economic recovery during the Hoover years also drew on wartime experience. General Electric's Gerald Swope urged a federal bond issue of wartime dimensions to finance public works. Economist Richard T. Ely sought an economic general staff to direct an army of the unemployed that would "relieve distress with all the vigor and resources of brain and brawn that we employed in the World War." Favorite legacies from the last war were its War Industries Board and War Finance Corporation, the latter a model for the new Reconstruction Finance Corporation.[7]

Remembered in different ways, World War I was inevitably used to diverse purposes in the 1930s. While some progressives saw in it a model for forceful action, Hoover used "the metaphor of war to serve a conservative function: that of draining internal antagonisms onto a common national enemy." Such uses of war were problematical, as some critics recognized: war's organizational machinery was designed to swell production, whereas during the Depression production far outstripped demand; and war sanctioned temporary improvisations, whereas many reformers sought long-term structural change. An effort to drain "internal antagonisms onto a common national enemy" was also risky, since war produced an identifiable enemy, but the foe now was an abstraction, the "Depression." For that reason among others, Hoover's effort to rally support did him little good. He did no better during the bleak summer of 1932, when the "Bonus Army" of World War veterans marched on Washington to demand early receipt of their service bonuses. Placards reading "Cheered in '17, Jeered in '32" symbolically linked the war and the Depression, but Hoover went far beyond symbols when he called in the army, under Gen. Douglas MacArthur, whose tanks and infantry expelled the veterans from Pennsylvania Avenue and torched their shacks at Anacostia flats.[8]

The problematic utility of the war analogy at such specific levels suggests that its appeal went deeper. War was invoked to sanction action itself as much as any specific action. Americans were told to "consider what would happen if the United States declared war today. Everybody knows what would happen. Congress would immediately stop this interminable talk and appropriate." As Roosevelt condemned Hoover in 1932: "Compare this panic-stricken policy of delay and improvisation with that devised to meet the emergency of war fifteen years ago." His claim that in 1917 "the whole Nation mobilized for war" also implied that a warlike unity against the Depression would override divisions among Americans. Of course, the Democratic Party, having held the White House during the Great War, more easily laid claim to its legacy.[9]

That was quickly apparent in the parade of agencies and actions improvised by the administration and Congress in 1933. FDR's first major step was to invoke the Trading with the Enemy Act of 1917 to declare a national bank holiday. Days later, he drew on the authority Congress had given Wilson during the war to ask for emergency powers to balance the budget—supported by congressmen citing "a state of war" and the necessity to "follow the flag."[10]

"There was scarcely a New Deal act or agency that did not owe something to the experience of World War I." Major organizations owed a debt, such as the Tennessee Valley Authority, whose anchor was a wartime government nitrate and power project at Muscle Shoals, and the Agricultural Adjustment Administration, inspired by the War Food Administration and headed by George Peek, for whom "this whole thing clicks into shape" because of "his war experience." Most New Deal agencies owed debts to the legal authority, programmatic example, bureaucratic shell, key personnel, or rhetorical inspiration of the Great War, and collectively to two grand wartime legacies, bureaucratic improvisation and deficit financing. Meanwhile, New Dealers fondly cast their jobs and goals in military language, whether they "volunteered" or were "drafted," served at "general headquarters in Washington, D.C." or in "the front-line trenches," worked as generals or as "noncoms," marched in "divisions" or as "shock troops." Indicating the grimness of their task, their metaphors invoked army duty, not more glamorous naval or air service. Implicitly, they also rendered the New Deal as men's work; women did not buy easily into military language.[11]

Few agencies revealed the debt to the last war more than the National Recovery Administration, set up in 1933 to regulate production, prices, and wages. It was modeled on the War Industries Board, inspired by "the great cooperation of 1917 and 1918" (as FDR called it), headed by Gen. Hugh Johnson, a West Pointer involved in wartime mobilization, and promoted by propaganda techniques borrowed from the World War.[12]

Those techniques exposed both the menacing and laughable possibilities latent when war's models are harnessed to domestic crusades. Johnson figured that he could speed economic recovery with a patriotic campaign designed to pressure businesses into signing agreements on wages, prices, and production. Plastered on thousands of storefronts, the Blue Eagle (critics thought it disturbingly similar to Nazi icons) and its slogan "We Do Our Part" became symbols of compliance with NRA codes and support for the New Deal. Women will "save our country," Johnson proclaimed, and achieve "as great a victory as the Argonne. It is zero hour for housewives. Their battle cry is 'Buy now under the Blue Eagle!'" Johnson likened failure to join "this great army of the New Deal" to wartime treason and dubbed anyone disloyal to the effort a "slacker," a World War I term for those who evaded patriotic duty. Roosevelt, no slacker at rhetoric himself, said the same thing less harshly. "In war, in the gloom of night attack, soldiers wear a bright badge on their shoulders to be sure that comrades do not fire on comrades," he noted in urging Americans to display the Blue Eagle. "On that principle, those who cooperate in this program must know each other at a glance." The hoopla climaxed in September 1933 with the biggest parade in New York City's history.[13]

A different thrust of the New Deal—to link recovery with rearmament—was less important at the time but telling in its implications. Military spending fell in the early 1930s, reaching a historic low as a percentage of total budgets, but began a sharp rise in fiscal 1935. Meanwhile, the official defense budget excluded the use of Public Works Administration funds to build aircraft carriers, bombers, attack planes, military airports, aviation research facilities, and army barracks. Those funds, $824 million over several years, were large, about equal to the official defense budget in any one year, and such imaginative budgeting generated controversy: Congress forbade it in 1935.[14]

As with much else in the New Deal, the close connection between military programs and economic recovery was not unique to the United States during the depression. Critics as diverse as business conservatives and the Communist Party's *Daily Worker*, and even some New Deal sympathizers, compared this and other practices to those of Nazi Germany and other nations. Military spending to promote recovery, work camps for the unemployed, and the state's use of martial rhetoric were among the similarities. Common to them all was a more assertive state responding to crisis or exploiting it. Too much can be made of such comparisons, however. They indicated less some ideological affinity than the manner in which economic crisis drove different political systems toward common responses (as often happens in war as well). In the American case, they also indicated again the impoverished tradition of governmental action, in which the military stood out as the oldest, biggest, best-trained bureaucracy for taking large actions, with its long record of building dams, coping with natural disasters, mobilizing men, and processing paperwork.

The warlike frenzy of 1932–1933 soon subsided, but some uses of war as metaphor and model sustained popular New Deal programs throughout the 1930s, most of all the Civilian Conservation Corps (CCC). Enlisting thousands of unemployed young men (and older World War I veterans), "Roosevelt's Tree Army" waged war on forest fires, floods, and soil erosion. Although Congress scaled back FDR's design for a more regimented program, mobilization of "Our Forest Army at War" unleashed memories of 1917, and the United States Army ran the corps (reluctantly, when other agencies proved unequal to the task). Boys received rigorous physical training, lined up for roll call by platoons, and got "dishonorably discharged" if they left the corps early. Admirers saw in the CCC virtues long attributed to universal military service—an "Americanizing influence" pulling boys loose from their local ties, familiarizing them with the nation's wholeness and grandeur, and forging a sense of nationhood out of diverse ethnic, regional, and class identities.[15]

The CCC also foreshadowed the military's troubled but pioneering role in race relations, for Congress included an extraordinary ban on racial discrimination in the corps's operation. Enforcing that ban was another matter. Especially in the South, but not only there, a chorus of protest, complete with shrill alarms about dangers to white womanhood, arose against racial integration or the encampment of blacks nearby. Roosevelt, seeing "political dynamite" in the issue, ducked it, and the CCC never effectively integrated blacks or placed them on an equal footing. They did eventually achieve equal representation in the corps, however, and the CCC's achievements in race relations, exceeding those of most New Deal agencies, were a rehearsal for the time when global crisis hitched the fortunes of African-Americans to the armed forces.[16]

Despite its record in race relations—or, for minorities, because of it—the CCC was the most popular New Deal agency. Not that Americans embraced it as a training ground for war. When the assistant secretary of war likened the corps to "economic storm troops" in 1934, or its civilian director boasted in 1937 that CCC boys could be "turned into first-class fighting men at almost an instant's notice," critics pounced hard, voicing widespread fear that the corps could become a vehicle for fascistic or bellicose impulses. Its popularity nonetheless remained overwhelming. The corps was celebrated as a way to channel constructively the explosive potential of thousands of young men and to impart direction to a nation battered by the Depression. That celebration could unfold despite the decade's intense antiwar spirit because the CCC fulfilled an old dream. It provided the virtues of military service without the vices of war, its attractive forms without its ugly substance. Americans could think of their army as almost a social service agency, not an instrument of war.[17]

The CCC nonetheless prepared Americans for war in ways mostly ignored at the time. It made the armed forces seem essential to national vitality. It accustomed a generation of young men to military service. And it gave the army political respect and useful experience in the logistics of dealing with large numbers of men. Not surprisingly, the CCC easily shifted function late in the 1930s, when polls showed overwhelming approval for introducing formal military training into the CCC. By 1940 "Roosevelt's Tree Army" had become a training ground for his real army.

The CCC was only a more pointed illustration of how the New Deal provided what Roosevelt would call "internal preparedness" for the coming world crisis. Recovery, not preparedness, was his primary objective in 1933, but by 1936, before threats from abroad dominated his agenda, FDR began putting a different twist on the New Deal. "National defense and the future of America were involved in 1917. National defense and the future of America were also involved in 1933," he announced.[18]

As he and other New Dealers suggested, the New Deal served national defense in ways broader and more profound than its specific military programs. It protected and developed natural resources, from rivers to forests to farmland, needed in war. Through programs like rural electrification and highway development, and through the administration's adroit use of the media, it pulled local communities and isolated Americans into the national grid of media systems, promoting national consciousness and loyalties. It reoriented corporations, unions, farm groups, and other powerful interests toward Washington and accustomed them to the power that government would have in wartime. It modernized the physical and organizational structures of government at all levels and its ability to function decisively in crisis. It sponsored artistic efforts that celebrated the nation's traditions and heightened national consciousness. It strengthened the health and morale of young workers who might carry war's burdens. Above all, it sustained the hopes of beleaguered Americans and their trust in government. Many of these achievements were intangible, but Roosevelt, no inconsiderable student of warfare, soon appreciated how those intangibles contributed to the nation's strength in war.

He did so vividly in his January 4, 1939, Annual Message, at a time when the global crisis was much on his mind. "Our nation's program of social and economic reform is therefore a part of defense, as basic as armaments themselves," he announced, offering illustrations. Almost conflating the New Deal with national defense, he grandly proclaimed: "Never have there been six years of such far-flung internal preparedness in our history."[19]

Wartime observers soon echoed Roosevelt's themes. The New Deal "stood us in good stead when war came upon us," one scholar argued, for "our American cities faced the call to war with greater unity, health, skills, and productive power, and understanding of what they are fighting for and against, than could possibly have been true otherwise." Dixon Wecter, historian and acute judge of wartime moods, argued in 1944 "that America's young leadership believed coolly—as France's, for example, had not—that their country held something valuable enough to be paid for by death." Wecter asked "whether America would have looked worth dying for . . . if it had been the nation of the Harding scandals, the Bonus Army, and the soup kitchens of Mr. Hoover's republic?" No, he answered firmly, for the Roosevelt era "went far toward curing the cynicism of youth growing up in the shadow of materialism, depression, and the bankrupt peace of their fathers."[20] Though partisan and contested, such interpretations of the New Deal captured an element of its success and the way many Americans perceived it.

Other developments besides the New Deal, notably the era's distinctive nationalism, also helped Americans to prepare materially and psychologically for war. The decade's dominant cultural and intellectual trends imparted an acute sense of American history and culture. Popular novels like *Gone with the Wind* (1936), ambitious projects like that at Williamsburg to reconstruct a physical past, and the artistic and historical endeavors sponsored by the New Deal built a new consciousness of history and tradition. It was evident, Warren Susman argued, in the striking popularity of Ruth Benedict's *Patterns of Culture* (1934) and, "for the first time, frequent reference to an 'American Way of life.' " This "effort to seek and to define America as a culture" gained energy from the insecurity that the Depression bred and the resulting desire to find an anchor in a common past.[21]

The development of nationwide media systems enhanced this cultural self-consciousness. The new art of opinion polling showed Americans "the core of values and opinions" that supposedly united them. Radio and movies helped to make for "the sharing of common experience, be they of hunger, dustbowls, or war."[22] FDR and his New Dealers proved adept at leading the new media (less so the print media) to provide symbols of national action. In popular culture, these developments were vividly demonstrated on October 30, 1938, in the wake of the Munich crisis, when Orson Welles's radio dramatization of H. G. Wells's *The War of the Worlds* triggered an infamous panic among listeners convinced a Martian invasion was actually taking place.

Though a distinctive nationalism resulted from these developments, it dictated no one political stance. Instead, Charles Alexander argues, it could embrace "internationalism and isolationism, socialism and conservatism, not to mention radicalism, liberalism, and even fascism." As Susman notes, "It was not . . . simply that many writers and artists and critics began to sing glowingly of American life and its past"—although, significantly, they did. More important was an acute though hardly uniform sense of the traditions and attitudes that presumably united Americans—of nationhood itself. The contest over how to define nationhood was sharp and unresolved, but the contest itself defined the era's nationalism more than particular stances taken. Its import lay not in making Americans more bellicose but in giving them a keener sense of what they might defend in war. It thus mirrored the New Deal's achievements in "internal preparedness."[23]

Those achievements in internal preparedness, and indeed the cleverness of the phrase itself, marked a final way in which Roosevelt borrowed from the arena of war to confer legitimacy on the state's role at home. Just because FDR was successful at such borrowing did not, however, guarantee him control over the nation's foreign and military policy. Exploiting war's models and metaphors was one thing. Charting a path for the nation in a growing world crisis was something else. In that effort, FDR was more cautious than he was in fashioning programs of economic order and recovery.

And for good reason. For one thing, the international arena was far less predictable and controllable by him than the domestic. For another, he was less sure about what to do abroad. Japan's expansion in China, Mussolini's fascism, Hitler's rearmament, the stagnant international economy—such threats to global stability FDR understood fairly well, but far less so how to deal with them. Moreover, the forceful exercise of foreign and military policy, whatever its content, could aggravate fears of state power and a dictatorial presidency already harbored by his opponents.

Although these factors compelled caution, others gave FDR elbow room. With the line between domestic and foreign policy more blurred than ever, action in one sphere could spill over into the other, as using rearmament as a recovery measure already had shown. Constitutionally, the president had a freer hand vis-à-vis Congress and the courts in foreign and military affairs than in domestic policy. Finally, many Americans were genuinely alarmed about the world crisis, if divided about how to deal with it. If external threats were perceived to be sufficiently menacing, many Americans were prepared to regard the state's action abroad as compelling.

They were hardly prepared to do so at mid-decade, however. Memories of World War I were a major reason. Participation in that war was viewed suspiciously by many Americans and war itself was bitingly portrayed in popular culture, as in the Academy Award–winning *All Quiet on the Western Front* (1930), the best of a new genre of antiwar films. Already viewed uneasily in the 1920s, World War I only seemed more tragic in the 1930s, since the economic disruption it had unleashed and the burden of debt it had left behind were often seen as causes of the Great Depression.

The backlash against participation in the war, including a keen sense that the nation had been snookered into it, climaxed at mid-decade with a congressional inquiry headed by Sen. Gerald Nye. Sensationally conducted, sensationally covered by the media, sensationally echoed in bestsellers like *The Merchants of Death*, that inquiry built on a decade's debate about the causes of the war, and on suspicions of corporate and military power long felt by populists, antibusiness progressives, socialists, and various radicals. Nye's committee found collusion on a national and international scale among financiers, arms makers, and government officials. The committee grasped how that collusion arose out of the complex demands of modern war and modern capitalism, but condemned how it had pulled the United States into war in 1917 and feared how it might do so again. It also warned that even in peacetime such collusion furthered the concentration of corporate and governmental power and the regimentation of American lives.

The Nye committee criticized the past more effectively than it shaped the future. It was partly responsible for the series of neutrality laws passed by Congress beginning in 1935 and designed to prohibit the economic entanglements that might suck the nation into another war, but its other proposals—to nationalize munitions industries and curb war profiteering—were never seriously realized. The issues it raised were deemed peripheral to debate over foreign policy at the decade's close and remained peripheral until resurrected in the 1960s. Controversy over the institutional underpinnings of militarization, it might be said, thus flared up and then died out in the mid-1930s, just when militarization was gaining momentum, and the Nye committee itself became the object of snickers from sophisticated quarters that ridiculed its sensationalism while overlooking its substance.

Still, the committee's deliberations were a reliable barometer of persisting revulsion against the last war and a mounting antiwar spirit. Historians provided another measure of that revulsion. In 1935, journalist-historian Walter Millis offered *Road to War: America, 1914–17*, a damning bestseller. Among professional historians, a sharp contest about the origins of World War I had climaxed in the 1920s, but they found a surrogate for it during the 1930s when they rehashed the causes and consequences of the Civil War, now labeled the "needless war," the "work of politicians and pious cranks," the product of a "blundering generation," and "the ghastly scourge."[24]

Many college students shared their mood, and only the 1960s would see comparable student antiwar activism. Students rallied against conscription and war, even though the United States was engaged in neither at mid-decade. On some campuses, they succeeded in ending requirements (still in force at many state schools) that male students take reserve officer training. They also attacked collegiate sports for inculcating warlike attitudes and with deadly humor created mock organizations like the Veterans of Future Wars, Future Chaplains of Future Wars, and Future War Profiteers.[25]

Antiwar students were part of a quarrelsome alliance of outright pacifists, activists from leading Protestant dominations and from the national YMCA and YWCA, women's groups, communists and socialists and labor organizers, and conservatives fearful of the power that war would give Roosevelt and the Democrats. That alliance had no stable ideological core, only an intense antiwar spirit. It embraced some people indignant about the horrors of Stalinist Russia and others more fearful of fascism, including some who joined the fight against it when the Spanish Civil War (1936–1939) pitted Franco's rebels, supported by Nazi Germany and fascist Italy, against Spain's constitutional government. It embraced others still searching for ways to use the League of Nations or private philanthropic organizations to make peace prevail. But this motley alliance was not far from the mainstream of American opinion, which, as pollsters showed, overwhelmingly repudiated entry into the last war. No less respectable a figure than Kansas publisher William Allen White bewailed the waste and futility of the Great War, writing in 1933 that "the boys who died just went out and died. To their own souls' glory of course,—but what else? . . . Yet the next war will see the same hurrah and the same bowwow of the big dogs to get the little dogs to go out and follow the blood scent and get their entrails tangled in the barbed wire."[26] Views like White's, though hardly universal, were widespread, even fashionable.

Those views generated much of the support for a far-reaching challenge to presidential power, a proposed constitutional amendment empowering Congress, except in the case of direct attack and a few other eventualities, to call a popular referendum to decide whether the nation would declare or engage in war. The amendment narrowly failed a key test in the House in 1938 after strenuous lobbying against it by the administration, and its proponents were dismissed thereafter as narrow-minded pacifists and isolationists, people with "no conception of what modern war . . . involves," as Roosevelt privately put it. The charge was inaccurate. The amendment drew support from diverse sources, including ardent internationalists and preparedness advocates, all united by a determination to democratize war-making policy. That determination did not disappear after 1938, but no such broad challenge to presidential power would reappear until the 1960s. As with the Nye committee's failure, the amendment's defeat marked the crest of resistance to a course only starting to accelerate.[27]

The movement for the amendment also exposed the role of women and gender in war and foreign policy. Its chief sponsor, Indiana Democrat Louis Ludlow, had long championed women's rights and appealed for support from women's groups. Overwhelmingly, they provided it, but they offered little distinctive feminist rhetoric in pressing for the amendment or for other planks in the peace movement's platform. Many women's organizations felt forced to devote energy to their longstanding interest in social welfare, now heightened by the Depression. Female professionals, like the journalist Dorothy Thompson and *Nation* publisher Freda Kirchwey, played a growing role as individuals in media debate and in the New Deal bureaucracy, but the most visible women in politics—Secretary of Labor Frances Perkins and Eleanor Roosevelt—both sympathized with the President's outlook and were constrained from challenging it. Cultural images complicated women's efforts to address issues of war and peace. The Great War, with its mass carnage among men pitted against its liberating effects for many women, had left an ugly implication in Anglo-American culture that women were war's beneficiaries and men its victims; a Pulitzer Prize–winning 1937 cartoon, for example, depicted war as a "syphilitic whore" tempting men to their dread fate (see fig. 2).[28] Modern warfare was changing women's place in politics and culture, but in charged ways that made women's voices both concerned and cautious.

Through all the debates on war and foreign policy, a kind of "isolationism" did persist. In 1944, British commentator D. W. Brogan remembered St. Louis on the eve of the war as "the calm, dead center of a tornado whose outer boundaries were too far away for comprehension or apprehension." The nation's localism struck him. "The United States is not and will not be a vast Metroland." Brogan recalled the mood sympathetically: "It took the actual shadow [of war], repeated again and again, to awaken Somerset [England]; Illinois had to awaken with far less help from the eye and ear." But the isolationism he described was more a mood than a political position, a lingering, desperate sense of insularity from the world's ills. Its strain of "belligerent nationalism" did threaten FDR's designs for collective security, but isolationism dictated few positions on other issues, like rearmament.[29]

More telling was how Americans considered the future of warfare and their nation's role in it. For the most part in the 1930s, they imagined a benign American armed force in a malign world of militarism and technological change. Japanese forces warred in China and Italians in Ethiopia, and German rearmament was ostentatiously displayed to the world. Lurid tales, given credence even by sober commentators, circulated in science fiction, pulp literature, and the popular press about future wars initiated suddenly by air attack with gas, biological, incendiary, or atomic weapons, decimating nations or civilization itself in hours. These fantasies of technological apocalypse made another war seem loathsome but also implied that war had become too horrible to occur, or that American technological superiority might prevail.

Against a backdrop of aggression abroad and fantasy unchecked, America's armed forces seemed modest, even stodgy, geared to defense and unlikely to wage major war. The army was small. The navy was powerful—alarmingly so to critics—but its mission remained defensive. The Army Air Corps was developing new bombers, but backers of air power portrayed them as defensive weapons designed to blast any forces crossing the oceans to invade America. When American B-17s intercepted an Italian liner in the Atlantic in a training exercise given live radio coverage, newspapers captured the defensive paradigm: "FLYING FORTS, 630 MILES OUT, SPOT ENEMY TROOP SHIPS."[30] In any event, the Air Corps's ugly struggle for independence from the army gained more attention than its capabilities in warfare. Meanwhile, use of American military power in Central America and the Caribbean was declining, and its commitment to defending the Philippines was in doubt. All in all, American military power in the mid-1930s seemed limited in size and mission, its potential reach obscured by the paradigm of defense, by the smoke generated in interservice rivalries, and by unflattering comparisons to more formidable powers.

In such circumstances, the foundations for global American military power could be strengthened without attracting much attention. Though keen to enlarge that power, military officers neither foresaw another world war nor wanted to enter it; they presented rearmament in modest terms, as a defensive measure. The gains in American military power, instead of involving gross increases in armaments and personnel, were generally subtle, low-key, or out of public view. The military's training and strategic planning became more sophisticated, as did its linkages with civilian authority, private industry, and science. Technological development proceeded all the more easily in a field like aviation, where key advances drew on or benefited a civilian transport industry that seemed to epitomize peaceful progress. Keen to guard against a repetition of 1917, politicians and journalists focused on neutrality legislation and warned against a mass ground army, but often overlooked the subtler developments or simply found them not threatening to the vague premises of isolationism.

At least until 1937, Roosevelt offered no signs that American military power would be used abroad in a major war, for he had no intention that it should be, or pressing need to change course. Much of Washington's attention went to matters of economic diplomacy rather than to problems of war and strategy. The intentions of potential enemies remained murky, though hardly comforting, and the ability of old-line powers like France and Britain to resist such enemies still seemed substantial. By 1937, FDR sought to expand the navy and took modest steps to explore how German, Italian, and Japanese advances might be resisted, but no sense of impending crisis gripped him and no forceful leadership ensued.

The waning months of 1937 and the opening ones of 1938 saw a shift both at home and abroad. Roosevelt's ill-fated attempt to "pack" the Supreme Court by enlarging its membership, strikes led by new industrial unions, and a sharp recession set off by cutbacks in government spending intensified the clash of economic interests, strained the New Deal coalition, and eroded FDR's prestige. "Middletown" (Muncie, Indiana) had earlier greeted federal aid like "manna direct from heaven," but by 1936 it displayed "a mood of anxious resentment toward those on relief," and toward federal power as well.[31] Abroad, Japan and China renewed full-scale war in the summer of 1937 and Germany gobbled up Austria the following spring.

Amid this "sea of troubles" for Roosevelt, issues otherwise of secondary importance became flashpoints at the juncture of foreign and domestic policy. FDR's request of Congress for power to reorganize executive agencies, coming after the Court-packing episode and just when Hitler seized Austria, unleashed wild charges (from conservative Roosevelt-haters among others) of dictatorship, allegations that "intensified worry that Roosevelt was importing European totalitarianism into the United States." At the same time, right-wing congressmen shrilly denounced the New Deal as a tool of the communist menace and a treasury for funding it.[32]

FDR was in trouble at home just as trouble escalated abroad, the twin crises merging in political rhetoric when opponents applied models of totalitarianism to Roosevelt and the New Deal. There was a logic to these connected crises, and indeed to the whole course of the New Deal and the Depression. Seen as a kind of war and modeled on efforts to wage the last war, the New Deal struggle against the Depression could logically blend into preparations to wage war. Just where, after all, did one "war" end and the next begin? Gaining legitimacy through the metaphors and models of war, the state might gain fuller legitimacy through war itself or through preparations to wage it. Roosevelt surely did not foresee such a transition, only muddling his way through it. He surely was not eager to expand the nation's defenses, the effort to do so carrying political risks. Just as surely, however, his notion of the New Deal as "internal preparedness" neatly straddled and conflated the two spheres of national action.

The Construction of National Security

Although played out in Europe, the Munich crisis of September 1938 marked a turning point for the United States as well. Hitler's demand for Czechoslovakia's Sudetenland, and his threat to go to war to get it, shook Europe's capitals, as panicked governments gave gas masks to their citizens and desperate envoys darted about trying to avert world war. British and French leaders felt they had a weak hand: their rearmament was in disarray, their friend across the Atlantic seemed disengaged, their other possible ally (the Soviet Union) scared them, their empires taxed their strength, their citizens dreaded war. Above all, they feared attack by the German Luftwaffe on their cities. "We cannot expose ourselves now to a German attack," one English general insisted. "We simply commit suicide if we do." British prime minister Neville Chamberlain resolved the crisis by giving Hitler the Sudetenland, although Hitler, yearning for military conquest, was disappointed that Germans seemed sullen at the prospect of war. For his part, Chamberlain took pride in gaining time for British rearmament. The evils of "appeasement" drummed into later generations as *the* lesson of Munich were not immediately apparent.[33]

Regardless, Roosevelt took instruction from German victory. Secretive, sometimes misinformed, often vague or fatuous, and buffeted by fast-changing currents, he nonetheless saw himself as fashioning a hard-headed view of the world and the role of power in it. For him, conventional indices of military strength mattered little—by that standard, Britain and France might have prevailed in the Munich crisis. What mattered more was Hitler's adroit mix of verbal intimidation, propaganda, and threats to unleash his air power, all brandished in a world where instant communications and deadly technologies intensified both real dangers and perceptions of them. As FDR saw it, these new forms of power heightened the peril to America but also, though he said less about it publicly, the possibility for exercising American power—if he could beat Hitler at his own game.

FDR wanted the tools of that power. In the pithy summary of Munich offered by one of his ambassadors, "If you have enough airplanes you don't have to go to Berchtesgaden" (where Chamberlain presumably caved in to the Luftwaffe's threat). Because of their power to intimidate and destroy, bombers seemed to Roosevelt the trump card in the new game. "Had we had this summer 5,000 planes and the capacity immediately to produce 10,000 per year," FDR told his advisors in November, "Hitler would not have dared to take the stand he did." Guns and barracks "would not scare Hitler one blankety-blank-blank bit!" one general paraphrased Roosevelt. "What he wanted was airplanes!" His attempts to get them were slowed by a conservative military bureaucracy and by suspicions that his plan to sell aircraft to Britain and France would ensnare American fortunes with those of weak-willed, duplicitous allies (whose steadfastness Roosevelt also doubted). Modest by later standards, the aircraft he sought were too few and came too late to carry off any Munich in reverse or to provide much help to allies. Nonetheless, he had taken a momentous turn by promoting the newest military technologies, by making national security his primary concern, and by advancing a new conception of it.[34]

Fond of playing schoolmaster to the nation, Roosevelt presented that conception with vigor. In August 1938, he had warned that "we in the Americas have become a consideration to every propaganda office and to every general staff beyond the seas."[35] By January, he was unfolding his new conception in depth and detail: the United States now resided in a seamless world of commerce, communication, ideology, and technology, all of which were tearing down the barriers that once had insulated America.

As always, Roosevelt's purposes were multiple—to challenge the neutrality laws, justify rearmament, and outline the evils of potential enemies and the threat to America of their economic nationalism. But as he saw it, the peril was less economic or ideological than technological and strategic. As he said on January 4, 1939, "The world has grown so small and weapons of attack so swift" that peace has become indivisible, war uncontainable, and "events of thunderous import have moved with lightning speed." Technological change, especially in aviation, had so shrunk space that even distant enemies could threaten America. Just as important, it had shrunk time, so that "survival cannot be guaranteed by arming after the attack begins," not when "the hour-glass may be in the hands of other nations."[36]

Although technological and strategic peril lay at the heart of Roosevelt's new conception of national security, he did not reduce it to a mere matter of weaponry. Magnifying the threat were dictatorships which "command the full strength of a regimented nation," conscript the many resources needed for total war, and wield new techniques of psychological and economic intimidation. Consequently, American security rested on all constituents of national power, not only on military force, and especially on the unity and morale of the American people—hence his frequent if futile injunctions to the nation's newspapers to report only the truth (as he saw it) and his recasting of the New Deal as "six years of such far-flung internal preparedness." Indeed, his January 4 address so wove together his domestic and national security policies that they emerged as almost indistinguishable.[37]

Many contemporaries suspected that Roosevelt was pursuing rearmament in order to revive the sagging fortunes of the economy, his presidency, and the New Deal. Privately, he sometimes gave that impression. Foreign orders for American airplanes "mean prosperity in the country and we can't elect a Democratic Party unless we get prosperity." Even publicly he pointed out that such orders "can give employment to thousands."[38] But Roosevelt poorly understood the economic stimulus of government spending and had not given up on advancing the New Deal further. While ambitions for American economic recovery and hegemony did shape his thinking (decisively so for those historians who see his course largely as a means to the end of that hegemony),[39] FDR had neither the temperament nor the circumstances to sort out means and ends so neatly. Whatever his long-term goals, the strategic crisis of the late 1930s, in which economic power loomed more as weapon than as goal, seemed more immediate, and it deeply fascinated and worried Roosevelt. He likely saw economic benefits as only a bonus to be plucked from the necessary evil of rearmament, and indeed that bonus was at first modest. Defense spending rose 50 percent between fiscal 1936 and fiscal 1940, but not until 1940 did it increase enough to drive the economy. Only if he foresaw in 1938 the far larger budgets of 1940–1941—for which there is little evidence—could he have calculated great advantage to rearmament.

Critics' narrow reading of FDR's intentions missed the deeper logic embedded in seeing the New Deal as "internal preparedness." Rearmament merely confirmed and amplified, albeit to great effect, the existing impulse to legitimate the state's role at home by linking it to the arena of war. Even early in the decade, some New Dealers had foreseen how agencies modeled on mobilization during the last war could be retooled for another; other New Dealers later embraced mobilization as a way to help make the New Deal permanent. When the Depression had been rendered as a war, war could seem almost a logical outcome of the Depression. "This country in a sense embarked upon some of the conditions of a war economy when we first undertook to fight the depression," one observer noted in 1941. "Now, in a vastly intensified fashion, we face industrial mobilization for a greater war."[40] Mobilization for defense was less a wholly new enterprise than a continuation of the earlier struggle on a different front, one with an identifiable enemy to replace the faceless foe of the Depression. FDR could link the New Deal and defense mobilization because of that logic, not just because of his silver tongue.

Critics then and later also charged that FDR foresaw and sought America's entry into a general war. FDR, however, although ruling nothing out, instead probably assumed a continuation of the bluffs, intimidation, and limited war that characterized Europe at the time of Munich and the Far East until Pearl Harbor. After Munich, he sought to wage a war of nerves, not of weapons. "There are many methods short of war, but stronger and more effective than mere words," he said on January 4, 1939, "of bringing home to aggressor governments the aggregate sentiments of our own people." In March, he lectured reporters about America's undeclared naval war with the French in the 1790s. "This business of carrying on a war without declaring a war, that we think is new, is not new." Even if war erupted, he mused during the Munich crisis, Hitler's enemies would resort to "pounding away at Germany from the air," perhaps with American help, a course "more likely to succeed than a traditional war by land and sea." After Europe's war began on September 1, 1939, he still sought to strengthen Britain and France as well as America's deterrence and industrial capacity. Although it slowly waned, his hope of keeping America's role in the war limited was finally crushed only by Pearl Harbor.[41]

Moreover, Roosevelt's public statements, though geared to the immediate crisis, also implied a revolution in national security that would outlast it. Hitler's aggression exemplified threats which FDR saw as rooted in lasting changes in technology and strategy, ones that stripped America of its geographic isolation and made preparedness a permanent task drawing on all sinews of national strength. War and defense, older terms for more occasional and narrowly military activities, were yielding to the expansive demands of "national security," a term FDR began using. Those demands were to become paramount and permanent.

It was a change that Roosevelt drove home again and again—only reiteration, by others as well as FDR, could effect the construction of national security. Germany's invasion of Poland prompted his reminder that "when peace has been broken anywhere, the peace of all countries everywhere is in danger." When German armies rolled into Western Europe and Norway in the spring of 1940, the frequency and vividness of FDR's formulations increased. He decried how "a false teaching of geography" created the illusion of "some form of mystic [American] immunity that could never be violated"—science's "annihilation of time and of space" destroyed that illusion. To the point of tedium, he rattled off the flight times of bombers over all sorts of routes—from Greenland to Nova Scotia, Africa to Brazil—to emphasize "the amazing speed with which modern equipment can reach and attack the enemy's country." Such changes, he argued on August 2, obliterated parallels to earlier American history: "We were [in 1917] completely free from any attack. Now, that will never happen again in the history of the United States." In a world where "no attack is so unlikely or impossible that it may be ignored," America's security was a global affair. It also presented limitless demands: "If the United States is to have any defense, it must have total defense. We cannot defend ourselves a little here and a little there." Cold Warriors would not view national security more expansively.[42]

Throughout 1940, Roosevelt stressed the nature of modern warfare more than the evil of fascism or the virtue of nations resisting it. Issuing little uplifting Wilsonian rhetoric, he instead offered a drumbeat about the cold realities of the world. That was the case again at summer's end, when Congress enacted the first peacetime draft: with only a nod to the older language of voluntarism and mixing "Americans from all walks of life," FDR focused on the harsh realities that prompted selective service and the complex, tedious, demanding training that men would undergo.[43]

The drumbeat continued during the bitter struggle between Roosevelt and Wendell Willkie for the presidency. Despite FDR's notorious vote-getting pledges—"Your President says this country is not going to war," he promised on November 2, 1940—he continued his alarms about shrinking space and time, "total defense," and the like. He offered homely details about the complexities of modern war production, deplored "the fatal errors of appeasement," and defended the New Deal as a tool of national security. Some emphases shifted in December, when he hammered harder on the necessities of production and opened his campaign for Lend-Lease aid to the British. But even though telegrams "begged me not to tell again of the ease with which our American cities could be bombed," as he told the nation, he continued to do so. Summing up the historical changes he had described for two years, on January 6, 1941, he starkly contrasted the current peril to a long, earlier era when "in no case had a serious threat been raised against our national safety or our continued independence."[44]

Outlining a new conception of national security, Roosevelt presented it as reactive to broad changes in the international environment. And it partly was. But he was shaping perceptions as well as offering them, seeking to mold a new world as well as to portray it. Rarely did he mention that in the closed world system he portrayed, American interests had been expanding outward just as other nations were impinging more on America. Rarely did he acknowledge that the changes he noted in commerce and technology were as much America's doing as that of other nations. Rarely did he suggest that just as an enemy's bombers might soon reach the United States, America's bombers might soon reach the enemy. Rarely did he note that new inventions which extended the reach of potential enemies also provided new means to counter them: Facing Anglo-American naval and air power in the Atlantic, Hitler could only envy the ease with which British armies had reached America in 1776.

By making technology central to a new conception of national security, FDR spoke to American preferences and priorities, for it was in technology that Americans excelled and perceived much that had transformed their lives. Since Americans had pioneered so much technology, how could it not be the decisive element of a changing world? To suggest otherwise diminished the American achievement and made the outcome of the world struggle hinge on other forms of power, in which the United States might not excel. Roosevelt did not merely perceive the importance of technology in modern warfare, he seized on it as fitting the nation's strengths, and he deepened the American impulse to achieve global power through technological supremacy. In short, his conception of national security was an ideological construction, not merely a perceptual reaction.

That conception also derived from particular anxieties in American culture. In many ways, Roosevelt and others took older views of technology and inverted them. In the 1920s, many Americans had celebrated how radio, aviation, and other devices were knitting together the nation and the world, leading countries and cultures to mix with and understand each other. In the 1930s, however, technologies once often viewed benignly seemed increasingly malign, at least when enemies controlled them.

That shift was evident in Americans' nervousness about technology's place in their lives. In films like Frank Capra's *It Happened One Night* (1934), the dominant iconography always involved transportation and communications—the railroad station, the Western Union office, the automobile, the phone booth, the airplane—and characters achieved happiness only when they escaped such contrivances. Such films conveyed uneasiness about "the inability of individuals to communicate privately in the world of such awesome, constant, universal public communications."[45]

A similar uneasiness arose about war and diplomacy. In its first serious foray into international newscasting, American radio covered the Munich crisis with a startling immediacy that did not diminish bewilderment at what occurred (or panic weeks later after the "War of the Worlds" broadcast). Roosevelt's public statements were peppered with references to technology—"the flood of mail and telegrams" he had received, the diplomat just dispatched by airplane, "the first train press conference since Germany moved into Denmark," the radio broadcast he just made to the Americas, the phone call just completed with an important personage, and the like. Though sometimes made in a celebratory vein—as if to suggest how the nation's leaders were abreast of the latest technology—such references also revealed a nagging anxiety that technology was inadequate for, even damaging to, an understanding of onrushing events. (One satirical novel featured a "phonoscope" that permitted moviegoers to watch a war as it was taking place.) Just as Capra's characters lived in a whirl of technology that impeded real private communication, national leaders seemed to operate in a whirl of international contacts (all the media emphasized that Chamberlain *flew* to Germany) that left them in despair of real public communication. Such anxieties further shaped the new conception of national security.[46]

Roosevelt, of course, hardly constructed that conception singlehandedly. Others paralleled his efforts. Surprisingly, however, leaders in government and the armed forces did not often do so. Many in those circles did support his policies, but few conceived national security so broadly or with such emphasis on technology. Leaders of key Cabinet agencies—State, War, Navy, and Treasury—tended to speak the older language of preparedness and to focus on the specific aspects of policy for which they were responsible.

Military officers in particular responded cautiously to FDR's conception of national security. Like him, they emphasized stern necessities rather than glamorous possibilities. "There is nothing romantic, dramatic, or satisfying in modern conflict," Gen. George C. Marshall told the American Legion. "It is all horrible, profoundly depressing; and now it carries with it a dreadful threat to civil populations." More bluntly than FDR, Marshall condemned Americans' alleged indifference to national defense. Air Corps officers, impressed like FDR by air power's role in the Munich crisis, pondered its lessons of "'Unwaged War,'" foresaw "future 'Munichs,'" and mused on how a globe-girdling American air force could "stop the aggressor nation from even planning the attack, through fear of retaliation." Marshall, the army's new chief of staff in the summer of 1939, also considered such possibilities. But he worried more about how air power "staggers the imagination," sensationalized public debate, and distorted the allocation of national resources (temptations to which he felt FDR sometimes succumbed). The caution of officers like Marshall was deeply rooted. They were inclined to view war's causes in narrow economic terms, given to seeing American interests beyond the hemisphere as limited, wary about a fickle public opinion and its fads, positioned still at the fringes of power, and constrained from speaking loudly in public. Skeptical about how much technology would change warfare—"We expect *too much of machines*," Marshall told the nation—most military leaders emphasized them less than the President. In all these ways, they followed more than led Roosevelt in the construction of national security, even as they labored to educate him and the public in its mundane realities.[47]

Other voices were at least as important. Academicians seeking a role in foreign policy began talking about "national security." The term was not new, but its earlier meaning had been narrower, suggesting military preparedness or (among strutting Americanists) defense against alien influences within the nation. Scholars now used the term to refer to the shrinkage of space and time and the consequent demands that FDR also summoned up. Self-conscious "real-

ists," they saw themselves as grounding American foreign policy in cold calculations of national interest and balances of power rather than in moral idealism
or political ideology. Less inclined than FDR to emphasize technological
change, they found more continuity between past and current dilemmas in the
nation's security, but their outlook broadly paralleled Roosevelt's. "Rearmament is not sufficient," wrote Princeton's Edward Mead Earle: all sources of
power must be harnessed to each other and to effective policy, and still would
not be useful "unless the iron of determination enters our soul." At the same
time, they agreed with Roosevelt that total war was not the only option: "The
totalitarian states wage covert war against the rest of the world," Earle argued
in the winter of 1941, implying that the United States might do likewise.
Largely based at elite institutions in the Northeast, they offered a kind of academic cachet for Roosevelt's outlook, and influenced commentators like Walter
Lippmann with a wide audience.[48]

Their outlook corresponded with a broader reorientation among American
intellectuals, many of whom "now renounced pacifism with the same fervor
with which they had previously denounced war." Intellectuals attacked moral
relativism in their "effort to rearm the West spiritually for the battle with the
totalitarians," arguing that such relativism "had morally disarmed the United
States for the coming struggle." Not all intellectuals grasped the cold calculations of power that attracted the new national security experts. Instead, some
defended the "ultimate truth of the debased 'liberalism' of our recent past" or
restated grand ideological claims about democracy or still grander religious or
philosophical values. But whether stressing harsh realities or lofty ideals, many
warned of fascism's inescapable menace and lashed out at opposing intellectuals "for weakening American fiber in its struggles with totalitarians." In 1938,
Charles Beard—the era's most prominent historian and intellectual opponent
of FDR's foreign policy—found himself berated for his "unfortunate influence
. . . from the point of view of keeping alive a necessary patriotic glow in the
juvenile breast." "Irresponsible" intellectuals, as poet Archibald MacLeish labeled them, were too "scientific, neuter [with that word's connotations of emas-
culation], skeptical, detached" to understand the world struggle, much less
wage it. In that vein, Lewis Mumford denounced "the arid pragmatism" that
left American liberals unable to understand "the basic issues of good and evil,
of power and form, of force and grace, in the actual world." These intellectuals,
helping to change notions of national security, were also changed in the process, inevitably prizing more their allegiance and service to the state.[49]

At first glance, intellectuals' summons to higher truths seemed at odds with
the thrust of foreign policy "realists," who claimed to eschew ideology and idealism. But realists themselves laid claim to universal truth: the hard realities of
international relations. And the intellectuals' reorientation paralleled the new
conception of national security by emphasizing the value of what was to be
protected from the fascist threat. It also replicated a key element of that conception, for by insinuating links between the insidious ideas of totalitarian systems

and the outlook of "irresponsible" Americans, it implied an intellectual seamlessness to the world: threatening ideas could leap great distances just as threatening weapons might. By the same token, intellectuals emphasized how broadly national security was now conceived—like Roosevelt, they regarded ideas as equal to weapons in importance. Indeed, Max Lerner entitled his 1940 tract *Ideas Are Weapons.*

This intellectual reorientation was complex, resisted, and incomplete before Pearl Harbor. By no means did it silence intellectual opposition to FDR's policy. Nor did it always single out Nazi Germany as the only enemy: the concept of totalitarianism was also applied to the Soviet Union (and Japan), especially after the 1939 Hitler-Stalin pact dividing Eastern Europe and again, more forcefully, after the war. Proponents of intellectual rearmament also seemed at times to admire what they claimed to condemn. MacLeish, for one, feared that totalitarians "were stronger in arms because they were stronger in heart."[50] Intellectuals' attacks on moral decadence, or the effort of someone like Mumford to restrict freedom of expression in the name of defending it, struck critics as disturbingly similar to totalitarian crusades, sparked by desire less to face enemies abroad than to cleanse culture at home. Despite its dissonances, however, intellectual reorientation was coherent enough to strengthen the new idea of national security.

In contrast to the leading role of intellectuals, businessmen played a lesser part in the construction of national security. To be sure, business was no monolith. Some of its cosmopolitan leaders and media (like *Fortune* magazine) saw grave economic and strategic issues at stake in the world crisis, and profits to be had from rearmament. But business's ties to government remained tense, and no cohesive "military-industrial complex" had yet emerged, especially since Congress rather than the armed forces still wrote the rules for defense contracts. Thus the aircraft industry, although technically advanced and dependent on military orders, was still so riven by competition, so violently antilabor, and so frustrated by its losses on government orders that it could forge no close alliance with New Dealers regarding national security. Other business leaders—some auto industry heads, for example—feared they would lose civilian markets and create excess productive capacity if they took defense contracts. They also feared the administration itself, until its rapprochement with Republicans and business began in 1940. Many businessmen joined the anti-interventionist cause, while others were compromised by their economic ties to Germany or other countries. Divisions in the business community inhibited articulation of a forceful message, as did its reluctance to wade into any controversy after the beating its public esteem had taken in the Depression. Too, until 1941 the economy still had too much "slack" to force a debate over the choice between "guns and butter" that might engage businessmen. For such reasons, they offered no clear leadership collectively, however powerful some individual voices were.

Women were also on the margins, though not for want of trying to play a role. Women's groups plunged into public debate—and split badly, even though women were more inclined than men to an antiwar stance. Feminist peace activism fell in membership, finances, and visibility from its 1920s heyday, as aggression abroad led many women to repudiate pacifism while depression at home shifted energies to other issues. Few women had the prominence in public debate that Jane Addams had during World War I. An exception was Anne Morrow Lindbergh, who wrote of her fear that fascism was "the wave of the future." Her book of that title, published in 1940, seemed anti-interventionist in spirit, although she chafed at her husband's isolationist and anti-Semitic sentiments. The language of national security was ill suited to leading women, whose feminism at this stage stressed women's role as humanitarians and idealists. Concerns dominant in World War I—democratic ideals and relief for war-torn populations—had invited women to play a leading role, but in 1940 those concerns yielded to the hard, masculine categories of technology, security, and national interest that both FDR and his opponents used. In none of those areas was women's competence presumed; in none did women have more than a toehold organizationally. "The frequency with which the word 'mother'" appeared in the names of women's groups indicates that they "often expressed very traditional attitudes toward the role of women. . . . Simple aversion to war was often the thrust of their message."[51] But "simple aversion" seemed inadequate to address the issues of the day or to unite women themselves.

FDR's policies did, of course, face formidable opposition. Anti-interventionists often stridently championed the necessity and practicality of insulating the United States from the European crisis (their views on the Far East were more complicated). Yet in some ways their conception of national security resembled Roosevelt's. Many saw no less malign a world system, though differing over the source of its evil (communism, many thought, rather than fascism) and its threat to America (let Europe's barbarians destroy each other, some argued). Likewise, many emphasized technological change as much as FDR, only taking its logic in different directions; thus they focused not on how enemy bombers might threaten the United States, but on how American air power could keep enemies far from the hemisphere. Even on specific policies, their differences with Roosevelt, while bitterly argued, were limited. With aviator Charles Lindbergh as a chief spokesman, they were even more attracted to air power than FDR. To them, armies and battleships, not bombers, symbolized militarism and adventurism. Thus they generally supported rearmament even though they fought Roosevelt over the particulars.

In these ways, his opponents also engaged in the construction of national security. If anything, the most striking quality of debate before Pearl Harbor was how few persuasive alternatives to FDR's outlook were articulated. Not that none was imaginable. A worldview free of technological determinism would have been a start, and critics like Beard did emphasize America's economic entanglements abroad and its economic needs at home. But in a culture geared to seeing technology as decisive in global affairs, critics like Beard seemed to ignore national security rather than offer a different view of it, while others like Lindbergh embraced the technological determinism that FDR articulated.

In any event, the issue raised by Roosevelt's new conception of national security was never fully joined in the years before Pearl Harbor. The immediate crisis of war abroad, not long-term views of national security, understandably dominated the "Great Debate" of 1939–1941. Certain facets of that debate further limited its depth, though not its bitterness. Long focused on parallels between 1917 and 1940, much of it looked backward rather than forward. Roosevelt's gift for finding common ground in the debate—hemisphere defense, air power, and industrial production—shifted attention from the more contested elements in his conception of national security. Even the apparent laggardness of American preparedness—stories filled the press of soldiers marching without guns, production foul-ups, foot-dragging businessmen, and disruptive labor strikes—colored debate, for it created the impression that the time was distant indeed when the nation could be a global military power. Partisan politics clarified little, since Willkie shared much of FDR's worldview during the 1940 presidential contest. Finally, the very shrillness of the debate became as much an issue as the positions taken, especially by 1941, when a long record of rich invective and bitter name calling had accumulated. All these facets of the debate, typical of American politics when great passions are generated, meant that it was often as superficial as it was ugly.

Meanwhile, American culture reflected Roosevelt's outlook in ways that transcended the particulars of debate. Cartographers, for example, urged Americans to rethink their relationships in time and space to the world. Sometimes interventionists, sometimes attracted to the trendy "geopolitics" fashionable among Nazis, mapmakers also had a professional need to change their output, once geared to land and sea travel, to the age of aviation. New maps and globes urged Americans to see Japan and the United States as far closer to each other than once thought; to realize that Buenos Aires was farther from the American heartland than all European capitals save Moscow; to think of the United States and Europe as joint members of an Atlantic community; to understand American proximity to potential aggressors using polar routes of attack; and to ask, "Can America Be Bombed?" as a science museum headlined one exhibition. No ivory tower exercise, cartography influenced renderings of the world crisis offered by the media, like the powerful *Time-Life-Fortune* chain. By dramatic use of red lines, menacing arrows, and concentric rings, the press offered images of America's "encirclement" in a "closed-space" world system. Cartographers' work paralleled that of aviation promoters pushing programs of global "airmindedness" to educate American youth in harsh realities and train them in aviation technology. Wittingly or not, such efforts buttressed the construction of national security underway.[52]

The new media abetted that construction, in part because of their bias toward the interventionist position. Radio newscasters were "uninhibited by any tradition of independent political advocacy or of diligent news-gathering," as one historian puts it. According to another, they were virtual "tools of the administration," not least because radio (and to a degree Hollywood) depended on the federal government for various kinds of licensing and oversight. Such bias put a premium on magnifying the threat to America of war abroad, and on obliterating a sense of psychic distance between Americans and their putative allies under siege abroad. With good reason, Archibald MacLeish celebrated Edward R. Murrow's famous radio reports on the Luftwaffe's blitz against Britain: "You burned the city of London in our homes and we felt the flames that burned it. . . . You destroyed the superstition of distance and time." Or, as one historian put it, Murrow "made Americans think of the Battle of Britain as a prelude to the bombing of New York or Washington."[53]

But the media's role in shaping views of national security went beyond immediate (and hardly uniform) sympathies. Whereas newspapers retained a local identity and audience, network newscasting had no evident local affinities. It could only plausibly cover national and international events for a national audience. Radio as well as newsreel thus had a powerful commercial incentive to treat distant events as immediate and threatening to Americans and to orient their attention outward, even if only superficially. Only by doing so could radio command an audience and advertising revenues, and thereby challenge the print media as Americans' primary source of news, which it did with striking speed between 1938 and 1941. The use of radio by FDR and New Deal agencies prepared the way, but the Munich crisis ushered in modern newscasting; one CBS commentator delivered 102 broadcasts in eighteen days, and the networks learned the commercial viability of news. "For the first time history has been made in the hearing of its pawns," the *Nation* claimed after Munich, and observers soon noticed that even in remote places "shoe drummers, gas station attendants, truck drivers, county farm agents—everybody was listening."[54] Thus radio newscasters deliberately conjured up a picture of a seamless world, while radio itself did so as a medium regardless of newscasters' intentions, simply through the speed and immediacy of its live coverage of events abroad.

The newer media's role in the construction of national security was also contingent on circumstances, not simply on the media's inherent qualities. In isolation from other influences, images of a seamless, war-mad world might have deepened the determination of many Americans to withdraw into isolation. But in concert with the efforts of politicians and intellectuals, the media strengthened the mood and arguments underlying the new conception of national security. That was all the more so because their portrayals of war abroad were vivid enough to be alarming but not gory enough to be disillusioning, as they carefully balanced their need to exploit events abroad against conventions of reticence and the dangers of antagonizing audiences and advertisers.

Specific depictions of war's outbreak further buttressed the conception of national security. "WAR! BOMB WARSAW," screamed a *Chicago Tribune* head-line about Germany's invasion of Poland in 1939; the *Chicago Daily News* simply said, "WAR!" It was war in an almost generic sense that seized attention more than any one nation's specific threat. The immediate message in such coverage, paralleling the antiwar mood of the 1930s, was "not that the 1939 conflict was the wrong war; it was that war itself was ruinously wrong," one historian has suggested. But to see the evil as abstract and generalized also gave it a lasting quality, suggesting that the danger to America lay not only in what Germans or Japanese might do but in the insidious and inescapable nature of modern war itself. That message, if momentarily of use to the anti-interventionist forces—who, after all, wanted to enter such folly?—reinforced the prevailing sense of peril.[55]

Other currents in media treatment of the war flowed into the new conception. For one thing, the media highlighted the most technologically advanced forms of war. Germany's dramatic conquest of Western Europe and its aerial bombardment of England were the arenas of war for which American journalists had a ringside seat. Emphasis on "lightning" warfare meshed nicely with a popular culture that primed Americans to focus on technological wizardry and apocalyptic dangers in warfare. In contrast, the grindingly important war in the Atlantic and the Nazi invasion of the Soviet Union, both less evidently on the cutting edge of technology, were sprawling and inaccessible to newsmen, less subject to vivid presentation. For some of the same reasons, Japan's war in China and its advances on Southeast Asia also lay at the margins of news coverage.

Indeed, media coverage of the Far East revealed one way in which the construction of national security was incomplete. Despite images of a closed world system, the new view was heavily attuned to Europe and the Western Hemisphere. That focus reflected the cultural affinities of most Americans and the administration's strategic priorities, as well as FDR's fears about volatile American attitudes toward Japan; the country seemed "ready to pull the trigger if the Japs do anything," he once remarked.[56] But it also reflected the preoccupation with technology at the heart of the new conception: the Japanese were widely regarded as racial and technological inferiors; only Pearl Harbor would pull the Far East onto Americans' mental grid of a closed world system.

In many ways, however, the new conception of national security had taken remarkable hold before Pearl Harbor. Of course, that hold is easier to measure among elites and their institutions than at the grass roots. Opinion polls showed overwhelming approval of rearmament, substantial satisfaction with how the administration handled it, determination to stay out of war, and gradual resignation to the likelihood of entry. But polls were geared to crises, not to broad changes in sensibility and apprehension. Americans did display an enormous appetite for news and commentary about the world crisis, but crude evidence of their orientation to far-away events reveals little about its content.

There is also teasing evidence in language of "how widely the war had pene-trated the consciousness of Americans," as terms like *blitz*—the common label for Germany's swift methods of attack in 1940 and 1941—became popular. In Chicago, a candidate for an Elks office "saw his 'blitz' fizzle," citizens "orga-nized a 'blitz' on rats," the Woman's Christian Temperance Union planned a "*Blitzkrieg* on Booze," and a League of Women Voters official urged members not to be "blitzkrieged out of their convictions." (Roosevelt once condemned the "blitzkrieg of verbal incendiary bombs" hurled at him in the 1940 cam-paign.) Whether such language revealed a subliminal incorporation of technol-ogy's impact on warfare—or just the endless appeal of war metaphors—is im-possible to say.[57]

Popular culture provides another clue to mass opinion. The credibility some Americans found in the "War of the Worlds" broadcast, which deliberately mimicked newscasts about the Munich crisis, owed to "the penetration of apoc-alyptic expectations," according to one historian. As pollster Hadley Cantril wrote, "A mysterious invasion fitted with the mysterious events of the de-cade," and the "psychological disequilibrium" created by the Depression strengthened readiness to believe that the worst might befall America in war. That readiness was also shown by Americans' robust appetite for a pulp litera-ture of technological and ecological apocalypse—horror films depicting sci-ence run amok, space-age fiction, and novels like L. Ron Hubbard's *Final Black-out* (1940), which depicted global decimation unleashed by atomic and biological weapons. High-brow artists found a popular outlet for apocalyptic themes as well. James Thurber's bitter fable *The Last Flower* appeared in *Life* magazine (November 1939) and concluded about a future war: "This time the destruction was so complete, that nothing at all was left in the world, except for one man, and one woman, and one flower." Such literature was hardly con-sumed only by the masses; magazines such as *Astounding Science Fiction*, like "a probe sunk into the back brain of American technology," influenced some of the scientists who conceived the atomic bomb. Most of all, such literature re-vealed widely felt anxieties about American vulnerability and longings for technological mastery that both influenced and were tapped by the architects of national security.[58]

Institutional change more obviously marked the construction of national se-curity and drove it home to Americans. Between Munich and Pearl Harbor, federal officials and their counterparts in other institutions built a national se-curity bureaucracy. To be sure, the process was haphazard, overseen by FDR in his usual confusing and casual way, and often backward-looking, based partly on the improvisations of 1917 and 1933. Likewise, chaos and conflict often dis-rupted the new machinery of mobilization, especially when it faced two di-lemmas: how to balance competing demands on resources, and how to weigh immediate military strength against its long-term growth. Should veteran mili-tary men be sent abroad to protect American outposts, or be kept home to train still larger forces? Should aircraft factories rush to produce an existing proto-type soon to be obsolete, or wait for new designs that might take years to enter production? To men weighing such decisions, they possessed an unprece-dented complexity and gravity. The crucial decisions were made, however, with a tolerable degree of error and with remarkable control by Roosevelt over them.

The confusion and conflict in mobilization obscured its novel elements, in-cluding its scale and complexity and its creation while the nation was techni-cally still at peace. A bewildering string of agencies—among them the War Resources Board, the National Defense Advisory Commission, the Office of Production Management—oversaw the mobilization of industry and labor, linked them to the armed services, financed new facilities, and gingerly allo-cated resources. Linkages between government and science were more stable, agencies like the National Defense Research Committee (1940) and the Office of Scientific Research and Development (1941) staying intact for the whole war. While the army and navy remained constitutionally and functionally separate, their ties with each other and with the White House grew. Much in that arena still got transacted at a personal level—George Marshall for the armed forces and Harry Hopkins for the White House were key figures—but the stodgy Joint Board soon became the wartime Joint Chiefs of Staff. Meanwhile, new agencies took charge of the first peacetime draft, propaganda efforts at home and abroad, military intelligence and internal security, civil defense and eco-nomic warfare, and other activities of the vigilant state.

Complex and ambitious, this apparatus was also notable for its sophistica-tion in planning over the long term and on a global scale. Strategists weighed competing threats in Europe and the Far East, assigned decisive priority to the former, and sketched with some accuracy the huge requirements of waging global war should the United States plunge into it. Planners adjudicated com-peting demands on resources from the armed forces, allies like Britain, wary industrialists, and consumers eager to enjoy a returning prosperity. Many looked further into the future, to the political settlements that might come out of the war, the weapons the nation might then want, the economic clout it might then wield.

The institutional machinery of national security was novel in one other way: some of its creators were determined that it outlast the current crisis—that they construct something permanent. The scale and specifics of that machinery would, they knew, change after the war, and their opportunities to peer into the future were limited. But for generals like Marshall, exasperated at the nation's apparent lack of preparedness in the 1930s; or for scientists, frightened about the weapons other nations might develop and attracted to the benefits of gov-ernment sponsorship; or for corporate leaders, getting accustomed to defense contracts and eager to protect American economic interests abroad—for such people, some enlarged, permanent machinery of mobilization seemed necessary for self-interest and national safety. To James Conant, the Harvard University president deeply involved in scientific mobilization, it seemed in 1940 time "for a majority of the thinking people to became convinced that we must be a world power, and the price of being a world power is willingness and a capacity to fight when necessary." A State Department official confided to his diary that year that "the only possible effect of this war would be that the United States would emerge with an imperial power greater than the world had ever seen." Another observer discussed publicly "the maintenance of a powerful military force as part of the normal structure of our society."[59] Not all federal and private leaders shared such views, and their ability to impose them on other Americans remained uncertain. To some degree, the permanence of their creation was suggested only by implication: the dearth of pledges by Roosevelt and others of a war to end all wars implied that there would be no end to the perils the nation now faced.

With different emphases, however, the outlook of many elite figures echoed that of Roosevelt. By the time of Pearl Harbor, the construction of national security, though not complete, was well advanced. It would prevail to a substantial degree for the next half-century of American history.

The Shadow of War

"The situation today is utterly different from that of 1917," Gen. George Marshall told the nation on September 16, 1940. "*Then* we were at war—but we foresaw small possibility of military danger to this country. *Today*, though at peace, such a possibility trembles on the verge of becoming a probability." Marshall aptly characterized the nation's uncertain situation and nervous mood. Never before had war's shadow hung so ominously and yet so elusively over the nation. War raged far away in Europe and China, but apparently with unprecedented potential to reach the Western Hemisphere. Americans were preparing for it yet had no idea if or when they might enter it. The nation was slipping into a twilight world of neither-war-nor-peace, at once a noncombat belligerent and nonbelligerent in combat. Yet there was also welcome change—a prosperity long denied and a mission long apparently missing during the previous two "decades of divided purposes," as one commentator called them.[60]

The period before Pearl Harbor was also a training ground for the new age of national security, an unwitting rehearsal for the Cold War. On the eve of Pearl Harbor, just as in the dawn of the Cold War, preparedness seemed an open-ended challenge, enemies lurked at home and abroad, the proper means to stop them were unclear, and government assumed new powers in the attempt to do so. As the line between war and peace disappeared, a war mentality flourished even with no fighting war to wage, temporary mobilization shaded off into permanent militarization in ways hard to recognize, and the challenge yielded attractive but seemingly unintended changes. Mobilization was regarded as a necessity forced on Americans, prosperity and purpose its unintended consequences. Metaphors echoed that outlook. At the outbreak of war in Europe, FDR wished he could "offer the hope that the shadow over the world might swiftly pass. . . . The disaster is not of our making; no act of ours engendered the forces which assault the foundations of civilization."[61]

The Roosevelt administration's grand strategy both caused and reflected this mood of uncertainty about whether the nation was at war. Neither privately nor publicly did FDR rule in or (with election-year exceptions) rule out a plunge into full-scale war. The linchpin of his strategy was galvanizing the "arsenal of democracy," as he proclaimed the United States to be on December 29, 1940. America's war production would succor its fighting allies (primarily the British and Soviets), prepare an American war machine, deter enemies, and just possibly keep the nation out of war. There was duplicity in his vagueness about whether Americans might fight, but the resulting "credibility gap was not simply a Presidential exercise, it was a national project. Everyone helped out."[62] Americans focused more readily on production itself, with the prosperity it induced and the symbols of power it yielded, than on the war making it might make possible.

Despite his vagueness, Roosevelt did signal certain preferences. His dramatic call in May 1940 for the nation to make fifty thousand planes a year, his promotion of Lend-Lease, his efforts to tighten the economic noose around Japan, and his deployment of American naval power in both oceans all conveyed his wish to use the nation's economic and technological resources, rather than its ground forces, in the world struggle. They also conveyed, for all FDR's talk of a shrunken world, the lingering hope to remain at arm's length from it—to have allies bear the brunt of any fighting on land, as seemed more likely after the Soviet Union entered the war in June 1941. Other authorities supported those preferences. When Congress barely renewed conscription in August 1941, Walter Lippmann argued that a large ground army was "the cancer which obstructs national unity"; any American war effort should consist "basically of Navy, Air, and manufacturing." Opinion polls reflected similar preferences.[63]

So did Roosevelt in private. In June 1940, he told military planners how he imagined the United States at war, "but with naval and air forces only," along with aid to its allies. A year later, Harry Hopkins found him still "a believer in bombing as the only means of gaining a victory." "There must be some kind of factory in every [German] town," FDR argued, and bombing every town "is the only way to break the German morale." FDR, Averell Harriman once observed, "had a horror of American troops landing again on the continent" and entering "trench warfare with all its appalling losses." In effect, Roosevelt was waging a cold war against the Axis powers, hoping that at most it would become a limited hot war for the United States. Marshall, for one, knew how hard it was for

Americans to mobilize without a declaration of war, and urged resisting the easy way out: "But *must* we *declare war* in order to facilitate training and morale? *Must* you *burn down* the building in order to justify the Fire Department?" Americans' sense of being in a twilight of neither-war-nor-peace reflected national policy.[64]

The mobilization of resources was FDR's top priority. In line with national strategy, mobilization favored sophisticated, capital-intensive weapons—fifty thousand planes; battleships, aircraft carriers, submarines, and other craft for a two-ocean navy; and new devices pursued in secret (and often in concert with the British, who retained a technological edge in many areas), such as radar and the atomic bomb. For a variety of reasons, production accelerated fitfully, but FDR undoubtedly regarded his production goals as galvanizing objectives more than realistic quotas.

The resulting economic boom was unevenly distributed. It favored regions where capital-intensive industries thrived: coastal cities, the far West with its aircraft companies, and the industrial heartland when automobile companies began shifting to the production of tanks and planes. In addition, the boom favored and inundated the nerve center of it all, Washington, D.C. In the long run, it also rewarded large companies wielding ample capital and expertise, although it momentarily staved off oblivion for marginal competitors, like Packard and Studebaker in the auto industry, that jumped more readily onto war contracts than the lumbering giants. In general, too, the boom came later to blue-collar workers and last to marginal groups like black Americans. In turn, such unevenness fostered intense labor-management conflict in 1940–1941, to the point that "the industrial war" often succeeded in "crowding the battle against Hitler off the headlines."[65]

In some ways, however, the "industrial war" masked the substantial harmony evident during mobilization. Conflict erupted spectacularly in two sectors dominated by two willful leaders, the auto industry's Henry Ford and the coal union's John L. Lewis, both violently anti-Roosevelt and both symbols of an older, personal style of leadership. Elsewhere, business and union leaders were growing accustomed to the intricate compromises in government-industry-labor relations that the New Deal promoted. Corporate leaders dominated those relations as well as government's apparatus of mobilization, but less firmly than in the previous war or in the postwar era. Because businessmen lacked expertise or vision in critical areas, and for political reasons as well, FDR included holdover New Dealers and labor leaders in the apparatus; one in particular, the United Auto Workers' Walter Reuther, played a critical role in converting the auto industry to war production.

Despite its technological emphasis, mobilization produced wide national prosperity by 1941, partly because the United States was pioneering mass production by low-skilled labor even of complex items like ships and aircraft. Mundane items from foodstuffs to tents were also in heavy demand by allies and the American armed forces, and, because of their simplicity, were often more readily rushed into production. Thus farm income, critical when almost half the population still lived in rural areas or small towns, increased sharply in 1941, though it also helped finance mechanization that worsened the plight of tenants and laborers. With few controls yet on consumption and with pent-up demand from the Depression for civilian goods, that sector also grew briskly, while overall GNP for 1941 ran 25 percent higher than in 1940. Unemployment finally slipped below 10 percent late in 1941, while those already working often found their hours and wages increasing. For one magic year at least, both guns and butter seemed abundant.

There is no doubt what drove the burgeoning economy. In 1941, federal spending was four times its mid-1930s figures, and its 20 percent of GNP was double Depression-era levels, six times its share in the 1920s. Defense spending caused all the increase, seizing 13.1 percent of GNP in 1941, up from less than 1.5 percent for most of the 1930s. The mighty effects of what came to be called military Keynesianism were evident, and welcome indeed to Americans starved of the symbols of affluence and often the substance of a tolerable life.

The proximity of war-borne affluence to recent economic calamity was critical. Had the boom followed on the heels of general prosperity, its benefits would have seemed minor and its dislocations painful. As it was, the newfound prosperity, by emerging in the wake of a terrible depression, forged a powerful connection between affluence and militarization, one that "would be impossible to forget," notes one historian. Some noticed it at the time. "The New Deal fought an uphill battle in its efforts to restore prosperity. Now we accept with little question governmental intervention in industry on behalf of a great defense program."[66] But for the moment there seemed little need to dwell on that shift: the new prosperity appeared driven by the need to mobilize against distant enemies, not by designs to revive a stagnant economy.

As for the concentration of power in Washington that resulted, it elicited barbs as it had in the 1930s, but surprisingly little sustained opposition. FDR's foes still suspected his lust for power, but they also harped on his failure to curb strikes, control resources, and concentrate executive authority—that is, they "agreed that timidity was the most persistent shortcoming of the Roosevelt Administration." FDR's liberal supporters gave similar views more positive expression: "Only through the chief executive can we find the concentration of power that is necessary."[67]

If prosperity seemed the unintended by-product of rearmament, some recognized a different relationship, one evident in FDR's defense of the New Deal and at the core of militarization. For many liberals, prosperity was a precondition, even a tool, of rearmament, not just its consequence. "To be worth dying for, a political system must make possible a society that is worth living in," the National Resources Planning Board maintained: democracy had to outperform totalitarianism to win the struggle against it. In that light, social welfare programs were not "sentimental humanitarianism" but the "first line of national defense."[68]

Such comments suggested the many ways, beyond mere affluence, in which mobilization was welcomed, just as it had been in 1917. Words and emphases had changed. In the colder language of 1941, Americans extolled various changes—the solidification of the New Deal that liberals wanted, for example, or the dismantlement of it that many conservatives sought—less as lofty goals in themselves than as instrumental tasks subordinate to national defense. Memories of World War I were too acute for a sense of plastic possibilities to be expressed as lavishly as in 1917. But in tempered form it reappeared, though now often denuded of overt "political ideology," which one contemporary saw as useful only "to the extent that it helps or hinders . . . the purpose of the state."[69]

The United States had to mobilize human as well as economic resources. The army grew eightfold in two years, to nearly 1.5 million men by the summer of 1941. This task might have seemed easy, given the large pool of unemployed, but national leaders recognized that while sheer numbers were no problem, their distribution among many claimants (of which the armed forces were only one) was. For good reason, the draft law was called (as in 1917) the Selective Service Act. Its many exemptions included critical occupations, and 12 million of the 17 million men registered received deferments (almost 50 percent of the 1 million first called for induction were rejected as physically unfit).

The most charged aspect of conscription was its novelty as the nation's first peacetime draft, prompting fears of a coercive state and of American boys dying in Europe. Conscription "will slit the throat of the last great democracy," thundered Montana senator Burton K. Wheeler, one of FDR's harshest foes.[70] Yet the surprise about conscription was the ease with which Americans accepted it. Some 86 percent of those polled in August 1940 approved draft legislation, and while millions avoided service legally—the rush of young men to marry was almost a national embarrassment—only a few hundred openly violated the 1940 act.

Acceptance of the draft owed to several factors: its removal as an issue from presidential politics (both Willkie and FDR supported it), good timing (the measure reached Congress in the wake of France's fall), and a nod to anti-interventionists (a ban by Congress on use of draftees outside the Western Hemisphere or American bases). Then too, the draft's shrillest opponents gave up much ground, usually granting the need for larger armed forces and objecting only to the method. Most tellingly, their alarms about dictatorial government fell mostly on deaf ears.

Felt necessities were only one reason for acceptance, however. The New Deal had accustomed many Americans to an activist state. Just as the Civilian Conservation Corps had taught the social and economic benefits of army life, backers of conscription now noted such advantages. Stating an old rationale,

Marshall touted the opening afforded by military service to bridge social divisions and enhance "respect for constituted authority." Writing shortly after Pearl Harbor, John Steinbeck celebrated how military service gave men an escape from "directionless depression" and an "antidote for the poisons of this idleness and indirection." The inductee will become a better man, proclaimed one contemporary: "He will eat simple foods at regular hours . . . straighten his posture," and, "whether he likes it or not, communicate with nature in all her moods." Although its advent was "not a matter of choice," ran a more abstract 1941 commentary, "the day of the positive state is upon us." Mobilization offered "vast and largely unexplored" chances for the military to help attain "desirable social and economic ends," ends which meant that military officers could no longer remain "apart from the main current of American life," just as "an ineffective army" was no longer "a sign of grace."[71]

In that spirit, politicians joined experts on health and social welfare to study the draft's evidence of appalling physical and educational conditions among many young men, and to use the national emergency to remedy those conditions. Reformers and experts took up specific challenges—improving literacy or dental care, curbing venereal disease and prostitution (to critics, each military camp attracted a "veritable carnival of vice"). Eleanor Roosevelt hoped that the conditions revealed by the draft would spur a national health program, and Franklin took up the cause, once again fusing social welfare and national defense. "It isn't at this time a matter so much of aiding immediate national defense for this year, or the next year, as of getting a stronger race of Americans in the days to come." Half-jokingly he suggested a "periodic [medical] checkup on everybody" and the government's "right to say to that fellow, 'Now, look, don't die.' . . . Constitutionally, he has the right to do it [die]. But the Government ought to know what his attitude is." His humor nicely captured prevailing attitudes: national defense and social welfare, rather than clashing objectives, required each other.[72]

The mobilization of human resources also offered opportunities for specific groups—at least men in them, since the task was understood in gendered terms. Although not designed to change inequities of class and race, mobilization nonetheless made some change possible, especially for African-Americans. Blacks often felt indifferent to the struggle in Europe and suspicious of the racial dynamics in the developing Asian conflict, but more vexing was the patent discrimination they faced in war plants and the armed forces. Usually poor and residing in a South where Jim Crow still ruled, black men were attracted to military service, with its promise of income and a measure of status, only to find their entrance often blocked when they volunteered or got drafted. Even if allowed in, they faced discrimination and segregation; though an important legal step, a ban on racial discrimination in the 1940 Selective Service Act changed little in practice. Writer Langston Hughes caught the irony: "We are elevator boys, janitors, red caps, maids—a race in uniform," but not in the nation's uniform.[73] Perhaps most of all, there was the infuriating prospect of joining a war for freedom without having it at home, added to bitter memories of dashed expectations in the last war.

In the spring of 1941, black leaders wrung what leverage they could from this situation, threatening a march on Washington unless FDR acted. Fearing political turmoil, Roosevelt grudgingly offered just enough to get the march called off: an executive order, with a weak enforcement mechanism, barring discrimination by employers and labor unions engaged in defense business, plus token changes in the armed forces. His rationale was clear: national defense, not social justice. A nation facing "totalitarianism" needed all its workers and needed to strengthen its "unity and morale by refuting at home the very theories which we are fighting abroad."[74]

The episode was a turning point in race relations. A new black militancy coincided with the state's growing need for resources and for ideological consistency, yielding the mass-action tactics, rationales, and—in men like A. Philip Randolph—much of the leadership that would shape race relations for decades to come. For blacks, the opportunity opened was a mixed blessing; offering them new leverage, it also subordinated racial justice to national security; tactically empowering them, it also ideologically circumscribed them. Still, FDR's action acknowledged that national security could open the way for social justice inadmissible to most white Americans as a goal in its own right. The needs of national security were challenging fears of activist government in the arena of race, just as they did in the field of social welfare.

As a lever for social change, national security largely stopped at the nation's borders. It could not override ingrained prejudices against outsiders trying to get in or against others, such as Hispanics and Japanese-Americans, still seen as aliens. The issue emerged forcefully regarding Jewish refugees from Europe. By and large, Congress and the administration barred the door, with support from most Americans, whose anti-Semitic prejudices were probably peaking at this time. The administration lacked the will and the political need to challenge those prejudices, and some Jewish leaders feared that any challenge by them would only inflame anti-Semitism. Powerful memories of distorted propaganda about German atrocities in World War I diminished the credibility of charges against the Nazis. About 150,000 Jews did enter the United States by mid-1942—not a bad record compared to that of other nations, but a mere fraction of those endangered. That many prominent Jewish refugees got in showed how celebrity, class, or ability to serve national defense (as refugee Jewish scientists did in the atomic bomb project) created loopholes. That Christian refugees also faced some obstacles to admission, while the plight of Asian refugees was barely even an issue, suggests that anti-Semitism also shaded off into diffuse nativism and racism, and into antiradicalism, given the equation some made between Jews and leftist conspiracies.

Indeed, the refugee issue arose just when a mobilization of fear was advancing alongside the mobilization of economic and human resources. Although challenged by African-Americans, among others, racism and nativism flowed in other directions opened up by the fear that impending war bred. National government offered leadership in this form of mobilization as in others, and while racial and ethnic groups were rarely the intended or only target, the fear of alien influences had permeable boundaries. Since World War I, Walter Millis later noted, "a quasi-religious nationalism had been sedulously cultivated in the United States," so that patriotic rituals and symbols only lately invented now seemed timeless (and required) for Americans. With their help, a once unimaginable "degree of regimentation and centralization . . . had by 1941 become no more than a normal and patently necessary order of affairs."[75] Evident in many spheres of American life, that spirit of regimentation shaped the mobilization of fear in particular.

Roosevelt himself sounded the alarm about subversion. It flowed logically from his conception of national security, after all, that subversion could leap the oceans just as weapons might, and that "total defense" required vigilance against enemies at home. "We know of new methods of attack," he announced in May 1940. "The Trojan Horse. The Fifth Column that betrays a nation unprepared for treachery. Spies, saboteurs and traitors are the actors in this new strategy." So too might be those with no ties to an enemy: apostles of "group hatred or class trouble" were among the forces of "undiluted poison."[76] Even those who simply opposed his policies, he suggested, might be enemies of the nation.

Before Russia's entry into the war, FDR sometimes warned of communist subversion, as had lurid congressional investigations (often aimed at his administration) in the late 1930s. More often, he set his sights on Nazi saboteurs, homegrown (often German-American) sympathizers, and right-wing extremists. The far right was a motley bunch—usually racists and anti-Semites, heirs to various Catholic and Protestant anxieties, generally rabid foes of communism. It included the Reverend Gerald L. K. Smith (Huey Long's former ally), William Dudley Pelley (of the Silver Legion), Elizabeth Dilling (author of *The Red Network*), and Father Charles Coughlin (the famous "radio priest").

Against such people, Roosevelt and other politicians helped to foment a "Brown Scare" before and after Pearl Harbor.[77] Although directed at different targets and practiced on a lesser scale, it resembled the Red Scares at the close of World War I and after World War II in its sloppy regard for civil liberties, affinity for conspiracy theories, manipulation of concerns for national security, and institutional machinery. Indeed, the Brown Scare was another act in the rehearsal for the Cold War, going far to generate the mentality and the apparatus mobilized against the left after World War II.

Lending specific content to the Brown Scare were the concerns and tactics of antifascist forces. Already in 1935, Stuart Chase had complained that he could "hardly go out to dinner, open a newspaper [or] turn on the radio without encountering the term 'fascist.'" That term was flung in many directions—at times at the New Deal itself—as if many Americans were more interested in some homegrown fascism than in its German and Italian prototypes. Liberals and leftists most often wielded the term, their charges echoing the countersubversive themes (less often the viciousness) of the radicals on the right whom they attacked. Behind them lay a legacy of countersubversive crusades, as well as fears set loose by World War I of how cunning practitioners of propaganda could dupe the gullible masses. Popular culture fanned such fears with pseudodocumentary exposes, novels such as Sinclair Lewis's *It Can't Happen Here* (1935), films like *Black Legion* (1936), and radio commentary (Walter Winchell repeatedly urging the arrest of foes on the right). Such literature ignored the right's genuine American roots and exaggerated its ties to enemies abroad— "Is Lindbergh a Nazi?" one interventionist pamphlet asked in 1941—just as few antifascists recognized that "there was no necessary connection between conservative theology and far right activism . . . a majority of devout fundamentalists, because they were poor, southern, or both, voted for Roosevelt."[78]

Liberals thereby conjured up images of a closed world of insidious ideology and subversion. In their view, right-wingers at home were importing or mimicking the ideas and tactics of fascist forces abroad—and had to be stopped. Roger Baldwin at the American Civil Liberties Union accurately detected among liberals and radicals a drift toward "'Liberty for Our Side' only." Even those who warned against "mass hysteria" also believed that "tolerance for the intolerance of alien systems" could not be accepted by true democrats. In that spirit came Lewis Mumford's proposal to outlaw as treason the espousal of fascism, and Max Lerner's desire for a Truth in Opinion Act, whose commissioners would root out "poisonous" propaganda.[79] Congress and FDR would not go that far, but many liberals supported renewal of the House Committee on Un-American Activities in 1938 and passage of the Alien Registration Act (the Smith Act) in 1940.

At the same time, Roosevelt, removing earlier prohibitions on political surveillance, pressed the Federal Bureau of Investigation into a wide-ranging probe of "subversive" groups on the far right, as well as mainstream anti-interventionist organizations like America First and public figures like Joseph Kennedy, Burton Wheeler, and Charles Lindbergh. Despite his animus toward the left, FBI director J. Edgar Hoover, a master empire builder, complied with a zeal exceeding FDR's intentions, offering a flood of reports about right-wingers to a keenly interested Roosevelt and making plans to detain alleged enemies of the state. Legal prosecution generally awaited formal entry into the war, when it revealed "scant links between Berlin and even the most vicious anti-Semites."[80]

Promoted by different forces, the fears mobilized on the eve of war did not fully cohere. Anti-Semitism stood beside fear of fascism, suspicions of Italian-Americans jostled with surprising tolerance toward German-Americans, racist sentiments toward Japanese coexisted with sympathy for beleaguered Chinese, a general nativism counterbalanced a sense of solidarity with allies abroad. Most widespread, however, was fear of the fascist forces, shading off into general anxiety about the nation's security.

Mobilization induced another fear as well—of the very machinery that produced it. Liberal critics likened the FBI to both the Gestapo and the Soviet secret police when it intruded on the politics and privacy of their political compatriots. A few on the left, like the redoubtable Socialist Norman Thomas, questioned FBI actions against the fringe right, just as some conservatives rose to defend civil liberties for their political foes.

In a more reflective fashion, intellectuals ruminated on changes that might outlast the war. In 1941, political sociologist Harold Lasswell announced the emergence of the "garrison state." Though warning of the coming "supremacy of the soldier," he in fact depicted a subtler development, the emergence of "specialists on violence" versed in modern technology and merging the skills of the soldier, the manager, and the "promoter of large-scale civilian enterprise." Such men might manipulate "universal fear" and exploit "the bottom layers of the population."[81] Lasswell's audience and intentions were largely scholarly, however, and most intellectuals were preoccupied by the immediate crisis, to which fear of a "garrison state" took second place. Similarly, suspicions about state power voiced by conservatives like Herbert Hoover, whatever their lasting validity, were for the moment driven by animus toward FDR and his interventionist policy.

In general, then, criticism of the emerging national security state displayed occasional insight but limited clout. Although flowing from some of the same antistatist currents, it lacked the sting and ideological coherence of earlier attacks on the New Deal. Like attacks on conscription or economic mobilization, it also fell victim to the intense factionalism among Roosevelt's opponents and to alarm about the nation's safety.

Just as the state mobilized, so too did culture itself, although, given its decentralized nature, it did so in a less speedy and systematic way. Hollywood, for example, was notoriously slow to identify with the interventionist cause or to treat the world crisis. Whatever the sympathies of its many Jewish leaders, they were long offset by fears of alienating key segments of the global market and by the vigilance of Hollywood's chief censor, who suspected that Jews in Hollywood "were trying to use the Nazis' treatment of Jews to make propaganda pictures." *Confessions of a Nazi Spy* (1939) breached the dam, while deeper forces eroded it. Nazi conquest of Europe ended concern about making films palatable for audiences there, and Britain's survival made it a boom market for anti-Nazi films. The state's heavy hand—the administration's threat of antitrust action—also played a role in moving Hollywood toward an interventionist stance. So too did informal cooperation among administration figures, interventionist groups, and Hollywood executives, writers, and artists. In the end,

Hollywood presented the interventionist view with far less nuance and balance than other media. Meanwhile, the anti-interventionist cause did not lend itself to the dramatic uses Hollywood made of rearmament, which was easily glamorized in newsreels and films about spectacular war games and dare-devil pilots. No wonder FDR publicly thanked the industry for its "splendid cooperation."[82]

Cooperation reached its zenith in September 1941 with the release of *Sergeant York*, the most sophisticated and influential interventionist film. FDR greeted World War I hero Alvin York at the White House for a special screening, the army used the occasion to recruit, and luminaries attended the lavish New York premiere: Eleanor Roosevelt, Gen. John J. Pershing, Wendell Willkie, and Time-Life's Henry Luce. Supporting interventionism itself, key films also drove home broader messages. *Confessions of a Nazi Spy,* for example, disputed old notions of war as something formally declared, as Edward G. Robinson asserted that Germany was already at war with the United States: "It's a new kind of war but it's still war."[83] *Sergeant York* did not directly address the issues of 1941, but as a moral drama of York's passage from Christian pacifism to militant realism during World War I, it suggested the futility of pacifism in 1917, 1941, and an indefinable future.

More important than such overt messages, however, was Hollywood's promotion of a war mentality—a sense of the inevitability of war and the pervasiveness of its needs—that transcended partisan positions on foreign policy. In achieving that effect, other media also played a role. "The war was everywhere—the movies, the songs, even the terminology of sports. One saw it in a summary of the match between [Joe] Louis and [Billy] Conn: 'A speedy light cruiser of the ring failed to withstand the heavy firing of the greatest dreadnought of modern boxing." Radio continued its role, as did cartoonists, novelists, and journalists, who showed themselves or their hardboiled heroes undergoing a conversion experience in which they shed the cynicism of the interwar years to make their weary but determined commitment to democracy. Making war "an instrument of merchandising," advertisers worked defense into their messages—"Anyone buying a new Plymouth today," ran one ad, "has the satisfaction of not only obtaining the finest car in Plymouth history, but of knowing he has also given support to the defense production structure."[84]

The state's role in shaping culture became more sophisticated as war approached. While many federal officials favored draconian censorship and heavy-handed propaganda, others, including FDR himself at times, recognized that a softer sell and indirect pressures on the media gained their objectives at less political cost. They eschewed most of the strong-arm methods of 1918—or of 1941 in places like Germany—in favor of an informal public-private cooperation that would largely prevail for decades after the war.

One minor incident provided another foretaste of the Cold War. Exasperated by the drift of media preferences, anti-interventionist congressmen launched an investigation into Hollywood in the fall of 1941, just when *Sergeant York* appeared. The effort was led by Sen. Gerald Nye, who "reassembled the cast of conspirators he flayed so effectively in his 'merchants of death' hearings of 1934–36," now finding them in Hollywood and its Jewish leadership. Though deaf to the subtler methods of cultural control, Nye grasped the insidious sanitization of war endemic to modern culture: Films showed no men "crouching in the mud . . . boys disemboweled, blown to bits. You see them merely marching in their bright uniforms, firing the beautiful guns at distant targets." Hollywood's defense, mounted by Wendell Willkie, was slippery in ways that invited the industry's later capitulation to different purposes. While admitting that "we make no pretense of friendliness to Nazi Germany," Willkie denied pressure from the White House. "Frankly, the motion-picture industry would be ashamed if it were not doing voluntarily what it is now doing in this patriotic cause." Though ignoring the state's armtwisting, that statement pointed to both the larger achievement and the larger problem: that the shapers of culture willingly served the state's purposes.[85]

Nye's sally against Hollywood was another incident in the "Great Debate" over foreign policy. The fall of France in June 1940 helped the interventionist cause by shattering analogies between 1917, when France had stayed the course, and the new crisis. In the following year came the fiercest debate, from which the administration wrested public support for rearmament and Lend-Lease, but only after the accusations got nasty. Assailing the Lend-Lease law, Sen. Robert Taft declared that "the very title of the bill is a fraud. Lending war materiel is much like lending chewing gum," and "certainly we do not want the same gum back."[86] While administration spokesmen implied that Lindbergh and his kind were Nazis, the aviator responded in a famous speech charging that Jews, New Dealers, and the British were dragging the country into war. The final months before Pearl Harbor saw the exhaustion of debate—not of its bitterness, but of its capacity to generate new arguments and real dialogue.

The debate exposed few clear divisions among Americans beyond those about interventionism itself, although ethnicity was a factor. In opposing Roosevelt, "Pacifists enlisted along with former military men, social reformers marched beside ex–Liberty Leaguers, labor activists showed unaccustomed solidarity with businessmen, and communists [before June 1941] joined ranks with Christian fundamentalists." Despite accusations that it harbored German sympathizers, America First resembled interventionist groups more than the German-American Bund in its ideology and class composition. Although diversity meant that "noninterventionists could never achieve real unity," it also dogged interventionists, except that the White House was on their side and worsening world crisis strengthened their hands.[87]

More important than the course and contentions of the debate, however, were its tone and terms. Marking the advent of a "realist" paradigm for foreign policy, debate to a remarkable degree focused on American self-interest rather than on American ideals or the plight of peoples abroad. Other rationales never disappeared. Interventionists urged a "Fight for Freedom," as the most determined lobby of liberals was called, and expressed shame and disgust that the United States had turned its back on the "golden opportunity" for world leadership "handed to us on the proverbial silver platter" in 1919, as Henry Luce put it in *Life*. For their part, FDR's opponents warned that entry into war would undermine American democracy and lead to other dangers: to the tune of "God Save America," proposed one Irish-American Congressman, sing, "God save America, from British rule." But such ideals and fears were often hazily articulated, seen as inadequate for coping with brutal times, or dismissed as artful propaganda glossing over real interests. They took second place in debate behind various calculations of national security.[88]

Often regarded as a sign of maturity for the nation, the "realistic" temper of debate also had drawbacks. It tended to undercut more passionate arguments and to encourage reliance on cool-headed elites for decision making, consequences that extended beyond World War II, contributing to the illusion of an "end to ideology" in postwar America. It foreshadowed the muted, vague sense of purpose most Americans had during the war. And it contributed to the framework in which Americans understood the war's acts of inhumanity. The brutalities of Nazis and others would be regarded as tragic, but even more as emblematic of the generic horrors of war from which the United States had to shield itself—to prevent or stop such acts lay beyond the nation's goal of self-protection, except insofar as victory itself ended them. The realist paradigm, if not alone responsible for such consequences, made it difficult to apply any standard higher than national security to the country's actions in war.

The temper of debate contributed to one other consequence, the tendency to regard the emerging dominance of national security as imposed upon Americans by external forces. Because debate focused on America's safety, most Americans avoided pondering whether their nation or its leaders also sought power for reasons other than defense. In the realist paradigm, "defense" was the word constantly deployed and insistently shouted—and accurately reflecting the sensibility of most Americans.

The exhausting, enervating quality of the Great Debate had much the same effect, making America's slide toward war seem irresistible and beyond its control. In 1940, two observers noted, Americans "seemed to be watching the enactment of a drama in which their role had already been fixed." "In a fundamental sense, there was no foreign policy debate after lend-lease," argues a student of Chicago's newspapers, which by late 1941 "had ceased trying to influence policy or arouse opinion. They settled back uneasily to await events." By that time, argues another scholar, a "propaganda din so pervasive and so diverse in its sources" was telling. "Its effect, much to the disappointment of militants, was not to shock or enrage, but to numb the resistance to war." Though hardly universal, a palpable sense of helplessness—in the face not only of global events but also of an ugly and stalemated public debate—had set in, a mood both confirmed and amplified by public opinion polls. Some still argued otherwise, but foreign nations and forces, it seemed, not American choices, dictated the nation's course. "Blindly, unintentionally, accidentally and really in spite of ourselves, we are already a world power in all the trivial ways," argued Henry Luce in his famous "American Century" editorial urging the nation to exercise the power he thought it had no choice but to wield. By the time the Great Debate ended, it seemed less an episode in national decision making than another phase in the process by which Americans accommodated themselves to a militarized course.[89]

Smoothing the path to war, that process also foreshadowed the Cold War. To be sure, the rehearsal differed from the production to follow. War's worst horrors, genocide and nuclear warfare, were barely imaginable in 1941. The dread sense in 1941 of sliding into a war *already going on* differed from the later fear of a war *that might happen*. What was novel in 1940, like a peacetime draft, was less startling when repeated during the Cold War. The rehearsal was brief and intense, the Cold War protracted and inconclusive.

But like the Cold War, the eve of World War II exhibited both the urgency and the partiality with which militarization came into American life. Affluence alongside anxiety, mobilization without war, a powerful state but persistent antistatism, acute danger amid lingering safety, felt innocence and a formidable drive for power—such dualisms would also mark the Cold War era. War remained elusive, Roosevelt publicly worried in July 1941. "People in this country unfortunately haven't got enough idea of what modern war means," he complained.[90] Soon they would learn more.

The Chip on the Shoulder

The events of 1941, and the manner in which Americans shaped and saw them, sealed their sense of an inadvertent, unwilling plunge into the age of national security. Writing shortly after Pearl Harbor, anthropologist Margaret Mead probed that psychology of inadvertence. "Aggression in the American character is seen as response rather than as primary behavior," she observed. "The chip on the shoulder . . . is the folk expression of this set of attitudes. In many parts of America small boys deliberately put chips on their shoulders and walk about daring anyone to knock the chips off." For Mead, that boyish folkway exemplified "a special American form of aggressiveness," one "so unsure of itself that it has to be proved." With Pearl Harbor, "Japan came along and pushed the chip off our shoulder and left us free to fight."[91] She was right: in the Atlantic as well as the Pacific, the United States indeed put the chip on its shoulder.

To be sure, as Mead's analysis suggested, any American intention to provoke war was murky at best, and hardly comparable to the vaulting ambitions of the

Axis powers. Japan, Germany, and Italy, though less in concert strategically or ideologically than most Americans thought, were reaching the zenith of those ambitions in 1941. After a skillful campaign of deception, Hitler sprung his armies on the Soviet Union in June 1941 and thereby forged the unlikely Anglo-American-Soviet alliance against him. He also escalated his submarine war in the Atlantic just as Lend-Lease and British desperation were accelerating the flow of American supplies. Among the contending Japanese elites, the conviction hardened over the summer that Japan, at war in China since 1937, would have to strike before the Anglo-Dutch-American economic noose and American rearmament irrevocably turned the odds against it. With the Soviet Union in a death struggle with Germany, with all European imperial powers except Britain conquered in their homelands, and with the British and Americans scrambling to counter Germany, a rare chance opened up for Japan to overrun Southeast Asia, the Dutch East Indies, and more. There seemed no way to pursue that course without also striking at American forces.

The American government perceived Japan's intentions imperfectly, in part because many officials still clung to a model of limited war: in the spring of 1941, some thought German preparations to attack the Soviet Union were another Hitlerian bluff, and in the fall some doubted Japan's capacity to mount several offensives at once, hoping the one they did unleash would come against Russia. Inevitably in a large and loose bureaucratic system, American officials disagreed about enemy intentions and American priorities. Moreover, Anglo-American intelligence, thanks to new means for decoding Japanese messages, was inundated with a flood of information it could not readily sift, while Japan's diplomacy was even more confused than America's and charged racial images distorted perceptions in both Tokyo and Washington.

In this confusing situation, Roosevelt had the advantage of a unified administration. There were no dissenters left in it, only those like Henry L. Stimson, the seventy-three-year-old secretary of war, who chafed at FDR's disingenuousness and championed more overt entry into the war against Germany. Stimson, Undersecretary of State Sumner Welles, and Harry Hopkins were Roosevelt's closest confidants, while the navy, the hair-trigger in confronting Germany and Japan, was the armed service he most closely monitored. An informal War Council—Stimson and Secretary of the Navy Frank Knox, Adm. Harold Stark and General Marshall as military chiefs, and Hopkins and Secretary of State Cordell Hull—also met with Roosevelt to provide some system to offset his highly personal style of command. In late summer 1941, at FDR's direction, the armed services formulated a "Victory Program," a coherent if unavoidably contingent statement of strategy and logistics.

By then, American global strategy was reasonably clear and consistent in design. Roosevelt still sought to wage limited, undeclared war against the Axis. If he occasionally hinted at doing more, it was probably to placate anxious allies or impatient subordinates, and if he held back from doing more, his calculations of national interest, as much as congressional and public opinion, were probably the reason. He certainly knew his course could lead to all-out war, an eventuality he accepted and with some candor publicly acknowledged in 1941. But undeclared belligerence retained powerful advantages as long as it might last and its tensions could be endured: more time to mobilize American resources, broad public support, and avoidance of the burdens of fighting— especially a war with Japan, for which the United States was ill prepared. "In particular," one historian adds, Roosevelt feared that formal entry into the war might cause a "disastrous cutback in supplies to the Allies as Americans demanded total concentration on U.S. rearmament, and that war with Germany would inevitably mean war with Germany's ally, Japan."[92]

Within that general framework, Roosevelt still regarded Germany as the greater threat, placed top priority on extending the Atlantic lifeline to Britain and later the Soviet Union, and hoped that military deterrence and Hull's gift for foot-dragging diplomacy would keep Japan at bay. For several reasons, however, Japan now weighed more in his calculations. Its expansion threatened American interests, Britain's ability to hang on, and his own credibility. Having denounced appeasement in Europe, he could not practice it in the Far East, especially before an audience of Americans, including some in his own administration, both indignant and sneering about Japan's pretensions to power.

Executing grand strategy was another matter at a time when combat-ready American forces were few and widely scattered, when the global situation seemed to change weekly, and when the pressures on Roosevelt, particularly from Winston Churchill, were intense and conflicting. Moving gradually—out of fear of public opinion but also to allow the navy to become battle-ready— Roosevelt increased the American presence in the Atlantic in stages during 1941. The fleet first patrolled the western Atlantic, then convoyed merchant vessels, and finally assisted British warships directly and gained authorization to fire on German subs, while a divided Congress approved the arming of American merchant ships. Against Japan, the administration employed a volatile mix of diplomacy and deterrence, with the one sometimes at crosspurposes with the other and the combination strong enough to be provocative but too weak to be intimidating. By late summer, after further Japanese expansion in Southeast Asia, these measures included a virtual embargo on the flow of oil to Japan from the United States, its allies, and pliant Latin American nations. But the administration's hope rested above all on air power: belated efforts began in August to base long-range bombers in the Philippines, where they might deter or disrupt further Japanese expansion. It was FDR's last, desperate attempt to turn the intimidating tactics of Munich against the Axis powers.

Although these measures addressed multiple purposes, they in effect placed the chip on America's shoulders before its enemies. "I am not willing to fire the first shot," Roosevelt once told confidants; as a Cabinet member added, "it seems that he is still waiting for the Germans to create an 'incident.'" (At an emotional level, perhaps that incident had already occurred, for in May FDR dreamt of retreating to a bomb-proof cave while German bombers passed over New York City.)[93] Enemy responses did not precisely parallel American challenges—it was in the Atlantic where American ships first fired on (and were fired on by) the enemy—but it was Japan that knocked the chip off the American shoulder on December 7. And in the larger balance of things, the Axis powers offered the ultimate provocation, through military conquest. American policy nonetheless had its provocative qualities.

The importance of this series of mutual provocations and responses lay not in leading the parties to war (deeper forces presumably accounted for that result) nor in tarnishing the rightness of the Allied cause, but in sustaining the American posture of aggressive innocence that Mead explained. In turn, it was the apparent hypocrisy of that innocence that Roosevelt's opponents attacked. Already in November 1940, Charles Beard, fearing war with Japan, had observed that "wars are no longer declared. Situations exist or are created. Actions are taken by authorities in a position to act. The people wait for their portion."[94] Anti-interventionists had long argued that FDR was leading the nation to war, while the administration defended its course as the best way to keep the United States out of war, or at least full belligerency. Now opponents attacked the administration for specific provocations to the enemy in the Atlantic— American moves against Japan were both more secret and less worrisome to most opponents—and added that with Germany battling the Soviet Union (whose defeat fervent anticommunists eagerly awaited), Hitler's credible threat to the United States had diminished.

Wrong about many particulars, more convinced than Roosevelt himself that he wanted all-out war, shrill in their attacks, sometimes dismissive of Axis power and sometimes exaggerating it, FDR's opponents nonetheless made a valuable contribution to debate. Above all, they kept alive the view that the United States shared responsibility for its plunge into world war and an age of national security. Since the late 1930s, Roosevelt and his supporters had presented their policies as reactive to external threats and forces—if the nation had a choice to make, it involved only how to react. Anti-interventionists insisted that the nation had choices and that reaction itself was a choice, one triggered not by (or only by) the dictates of national safety but by conniving allies, imperial ambitions, a misplaced democratic idealism, the New Deal's failure to bring recovery, or a devious President. Among their many failures, anti-interventionists could rarely agree on which of those factors was governing the drift into war. Their larger virtue lay in challenging the posture of helplessness that most Americans, and their leaders, had assumed.

They made another contribution as well by criticizing the extraordinary powers assumed by the President without a declaration of war and warning of the perils to democratic process and ideals in a militarized America. "Foreign policy," Charles and Mary Beard had worried in 1939, "could easily be made the instrument to stifle domestic wrongs under a blanket of militarist chauvinism, perhaps disguised by the high-sounding title of world peace." Charles Beard, among others, though supporting the objectives of Lend-Lease, condemned the specific legislation as "a bill for waging an undeclared war," decrying the wide discretion it gave Roosevelt and foreseeing its futility unless the United States protected its convoys of treasure from German submarines.[95] The outbreak of undeclared war that autumn prompted more criticism of executive authority. Bitterly offered, it was well founded, even if administration behavior did not fulfill the doomsday predictions some critics made. FDR's exercise of power had its legal, constitutional, and historical precedents, but he stretched them far and established a precedent for successors to go even further. That was so not only in his handling of military force but in his use of the FBI and other agencies against his opponents.

Seeking to maintain a posture of American innocence, Roosevelt also stretched the meaning of particular events. On September 4, the destroyer *Greer*, operating near Iceland, trailed a German submarine which, against standing German orders but on the belief it was under assault, initiated an unsuccessful attack on the American ship. In public comments, FDR reported only the German attack—"piracy legally and morally"—not the pursuit carried out by the *Greer*, and announced orders for warships to shoot on sight when engaging German subs. On October 27, after a German sub torpedoed the destroyer *Kearny*—without sinking it, but with the death of eleven Americans—he announced that "history has recorded who fired the first shot." On occasion FDR's metaphors suggested something else, as if he sought to knock the chip off Germany's shoulders. Following the *Greer* incident, he proclaimed that "we have sought no shooting war" (the phrase itself, implying a "nonshooting" war, was awkward). "But when you see a rattlesnake poised to strike, you do not wait until he has struck before you crush him."[96] But most public comments by Roosevelt and other officials juxtaposed general exhortations to beat Hitler against professions of American innocence in specific circumstances.

Meanwhile, the autumn crisis in Japanese-American relations caught FDR's foes, and to a degree his own administration, off-guard. It had been overshadowed by the threat of war in the Atlantic, by the complicated ballet of Japanese-American diplomacy, and, within official circles, by growing confidence in American deterrence. Stimson, for one, was buoyant in October, after the first B-17 bombers arrived in the Philippines. "Far from being impotent to influence events in that area," he wrote Roosevelt, "we suddenly find ourselves vested with the possibility of great power." The bombers, he mused on another occasion, might even help "to shake the Japanese out of the Axis." Administration leaders still hoped to deter war with Japan, or keep it limited and undeclared. "There is war in China and there is war in the Atlantic at the present time, but in neither case it is declared war," Marshall reminded his staff. Going further, FDR polled his Cabinet about "whether the people would back us up in case we struck at Japan down there," hinting that the United States might strike first, perhaps after an incident offered a pretext to do so. On November 15, Marshall, taking journalists into confidence, expressed his hope that deterrence would work—once the Japanese learned of the B-17s, he suggested, they would conclude, "We'd better go slow"—but if deterrence failed, he would "set the paper cities of Japan on fire" without "any hesitation about bombing civilians."[97]

The administration's plan for its new bombers was unclear, since they lacked the range to strike Japan effectively, although some officials vainly hoped to arrange for them to refuel at Soviet Siberian bases close to Japan. Whatever the plan, it ended literally in ashes. Japan caught American forces by surprise not only at Pearl Harbor but in the Philippines, where the B-17 force, not scheduled to reach full strength until February, disintegrated. There followed rapidly the American declaration of war on Japan, and then Germany's declaration on the United States—a relief to many in the administration, for the readiness of Americans openly to enter war against Germany remained in doubt.

The deployment of the B-17s and the hopes vested in them revealed American attitudes on the brink of war and during it: a chronic underestimation, rooted in part in racial stereotypes, of Japanese military abilities and a persistent overestimation of American technology. In turn, so opinion polls showed, most Americans seemed to view war with Japan—though not with Germany—eagerly, almost cavalierly. "U.S. Cheerfully Faces War with Japan," *Life* claimed on the eve of Pearl Harbor. Americans felt, "rightly or wrongly, that the Japs were pushovers," a schoolboy's word congruent with Mead's metaphor of a nation placing a chip on its shoulder.[98] The hope of unleashing its bombers against Japan, perhaps in a surprise attack, also accounted for much of the indignation felt about Japan's act of "infamy" (as FDR called it) on December 7. What galled American leaders was not simply Japan's treachery but their frustration at having it occur before the United States could mount its own surprise.

Most Americans accepted the rendition of Japanese treachery offered by FDR and other leaders, bringing to a conclusion the process Mead later described. Even the virulently anti-Roosevelt *Chicago Tribune* concluded that war had come "through no volition of any American." One journalist, an ardent interventionist, did protest "our pose of injured innocence" and the belief "that we were innocently minding our own business when the door opened and there was the Axis with a knife."[99] But only Roosevelt-haters, right-wing fanatics, and lonely historians like Beard continued to challenge the "pose of injured innocence," often doing so with unsustainable charges of a Roosevelt conspiracy to promote the Pearl Harbor attack; even those charges simply shifted "injured innocence" from the nation as a whole to everybody outside the administration. Left intact was a sense of America's helplessness, in a closed world dominated by malign forces, to resist its entry into war and the militarization that went with it.

There were redeeming virtues in the performance of the nation's political culture. More than before the previous war or the ones to follow, Americans did address the great issues of war and peace in a sustained fashion and with wide public participation. It may even be that the "Great Debate" gave them a sense of participation in national decision making that enhanced acceptance of its outcome. The numbness, futility, and bitterness of debate by the autumn of 1941 cut the other way, however. By then, waiting anxiously, most Americans must have felt scarcely more control over their own government's course than they did over the global crisis into which fate seemed to have sucked them.

TRIUMPH, 1941–1945

In Pearl Harbor's Wake

On the night of December 8–9, 1941, Gen. John DeWitt, head of the Western Defense Command, berated a crowd at the San Francisco mayor's office. "Japanese planes were over this community last night," he insisted, condemning city officials and residents for "shameful" and "criminal" conduct. "I cannot promise you to prevent any bombing of San Francisco, but don't be jittery. Learn to take it. You've got to take it, and if you can't take it, get the hell out of San Francisco before it comes."[1] Across the country, Librarian of Congress Archibald MacLeish prepared to evacuate the capital's cultural treasures. Japan's attack on Pearl Harbor not only brought the United States officially into the war but seemed to confirm Americans' gathering fears of a dangerous world and imminent attack. It thereby shaped initial American actions in the war and underwrote militarization in the long run, providing the most enduring symbol of its apparent necessity.

In December 1941, it is true, Pearl Harbor was not yet the touchstone of alarm, anger, and veneration that it would become. The full measure of catastrophe there—eighteen ships and nearly two hundred planes destroyed or crippled, some twenty-four hundred Americans dead—was kept secret from Americans on the grounds of security, although Japan measured American losses with some accuracy. In headlines, Pearl Harbor competed with Japan's striking advances against American forces in the Philippines, caught off-guard despite word of the earlier Pearl Harbor attack, and against other American, British, and Dutch positions. Moreover, the official start of German-American war captured attention, while Japan's culpability was often obscured by hints that it had done Germany's bidding (the Pearl Harbor attack was "the method of Hitler himself," FDR said). Not yet did Pearl Harbor crowd out other events of that cacophonous winter.[2]

Nor were first reactions to Pearl Harbor uniform. Rage was widespread but not universal. "No one showed much indignation," one journalist noticed at the Navy Department. Hostile acts toward Japanese-Americans were few. Panic about Japan's military prowess did not immediately take hold: in Manila, Washington, and London, officials for a few days still hoped to carry out the immediate "burning of Japanese cities by incendiary bombs," as Winston Churchill put it. National unity was loudly proclaimed but did not go much beyond a vague determination to win the war.[3]

Political constructions as much as visceral reactions, the emotions attributed retroactively to December 1941 took time and further American defeats to be shaped. Perhaps the most common first responses, from the President's inner circle to ordinary street corners, were simple relief that the agonizing tension of recent months had ended, fatalistic resignation to the awful task ahead, and an upbeat embrace of the purposefulness that war might bring. Few mourned the end of an ugly era marked by a cynical business culture, the "betrayal of the peace," grinding depression, and a bitter debate about foreign policy.[4] Though with little of the war fever of 1917, Americans had reasons to accept war's onset.

Still, the Pearl Harbor attack soon served as a powerful symbol of American innocence, Japanese perfidy, and lasting peril to the United States. Its symbolic power derived not simply from the event but from the way Americans fit it into their new conception of national security. Pearl Harbor served to confirm that conception, as Roosevelt told the nation on December 9: The "terrible lesson" learned in the "past few years" and the "past three days" was that "there is no such thing as impregnable defense against powerful aggressors who sneak up in the dark and strike without warning. . . . We cannot measure our safety in terms of miles on any map any more." Playing schoolmaster to a radio audience on February 23, he asked Americans to spread their world maps in front of them while he expounded on the military geography of American vulnerability and strategy.[5] "Isolationists" presumably blind to that vulnerability were dealt a death blow by Pearl Harbor, it was widely assumed. Although shocking, Japan's attack was assimilated into existing perceptions of a closed world.

Consequently, too, panic mounted after December 7 about attack on the United States—panic unfounded in retrospect but the logical outcome of years of talk about technological wizardry, blitzkrieg war, and American vulnerability. FDR warned on the ninth that "the attack at Pearl Harbor can be repeated at any one of many points, points in both oceans and along both our coast lines and against all the rest of the hemisphere." Ordinary citizens abetted the alarm with claims of spotting Japanese aircraft and with countless rumors (Japanese-American farmers, it was said, cut their cane fields into vectors to guide attacking enemy planes). If anything, high officials felt the panic more, at one point fearing a German attack on the Sault Ste. Marie locks through which most of the nation's iron ore passed. Few officials were as excitable as DeWitt, but Army Chief of Staff George Marshall ordered precious men and materiel diverted to home defense. A few incidents gave the alarm credibility. Japanese and German submarines sank ships near American coasts, and in February, days after FDR's warning that it was "perfectly possible" for New York City or

Detroit to be bombed, a Japanese sub lobbed shells into a Santa Barbara petroleum complex. As late as June 1942, with Japanese forces on the move in Alaska's Aleutian Islands, the War Department feared air raids on the West Coast. A vast apparatus of civil defense—blackouts, block wardens, air raid drills—now sprung into action that both drew on local anxieties and carried the national alarm down to the local level. Even a small inland city could "act as if it were immediately behind the battlefronts. More than one pair of eyes had looked into the heavens expecting to see a fleet of German bombers," and "the great trial blackout of August 1942" encouraged "everyone in the midcontinent homes of Jonesville to think of the enemy as a threat to their own security." Children caught up in air raid drills, or given I.D. tags and fingerprinted on the chance they would be killed or evacuated, faced fears and rituals commonly associated with the atomic age. In Wausau, Wisconsin, as one adult later recalled a childhood scene, "howling sirens screamed a cruel warning. The whole scene filled my imagination of a real attack." The lessons of American vulnerability were imprinted with special force on youngsters.[6]

Panic did more than reveal fears of national peril. It marked a wild lurch—from dismissal to exaggeration—in views of enemy capabilities, and a lingering inflation of what the bomber could do. Most of all, it served to mobilize the nation in the absence of the immediate peril most combatants faced: in a war fought "on imagination alone" by most Americans, the imagination searched for some real-world confirmation of danger. The panic thereby also confirmed Americans' understanding of the war's stakes. Insofar as Pearl Harbor presaged attack on the United States, national survival against predatory enemies seeking "the conquest of the United States" (as FDR put it) seemed at stake more than ideological or moral meanings to the war. Many Americans still saw such meanings, but those were subsumed under a more diffuse fear of dangerous enemies.[7]

Particularly the Japanese enemy, whose threat and evil seemed to most Americans confirmed by Pearl Harbor. The administration remained at pains to designate Germany as the greater enemy but rightly worried that many Americans, attuned to the war's racial dimensions, had different preferences. Like other responses to Pearl Harbor, racist sentiment did not emerge fullblown on December 7. The movement to put 120,000 Japanese-Americans on the West Coast into concentration camps, for example, crested only in the spring of 1942. It responded to no real threat, federal agents having already detained those seen as dangerous, but officials and journalists regarded the absence of sabotage as a sign of the clever deviousness of Japanese-Americans. (In Hawaii the threat was more plausible, but their numbers and economic value precluded systematic incarceration.) Incarceration also drew on continuing American humiliation in the Pacific (the last outpost in the Philippines fell in May), on a desire to wreak vengeance on the only available version of the enemy, on greedy schemes to seize Japanese-American farms and businesses, and on efforts by officials to placate those emotions and act on their own prejudices. Beyond those specific impulses were the fears of subversion already rising before Pearl Harbor and a "more generalized xenophobia" spreading after it.[8] Thousands of German- and Italian-Americans were also locked up, some of whom were patently dangerous, but far more numerous, politically strong, and economically vital than Japanese-Americans, they met far less severe treatment.

Animosity toward the Japanese also shaped American operations abroad in 1942. United States forces stopped Japan's navy at the Battle of Midway in June and took the offensive by invading Guadalcanal in August. In the European war, the grim task of getting aid to Britain and Russia in the teeth of German submarines was vital, but only the invasion of North Africa in November marked a major offensive effort. Operations like April's Doolittle bombing raid on Tokyo, which lacked much tangible military purpose, responded to popular fervor for action first against Japan and played to the "exterminationist sentiment" among Americans, shown in June when a patriotic parade in New York displayed "a big American eagle leading a flight of bombers down on a herd of yellow rats."[9]

Fears of American strategic vulnerability and Japanese racial evil dominated initial American perceptions of the war but hardly defined all the reactions of a diverse people. For some, war with Japan raised troublesome racial issues (one black sharecropper reportedly told his boss after Pearl Harbor, "By the way, Captain, I hear the Japanese done declared war on you white folks"). Conservatives saw a golden chance to scuttle the New Deal, while liberals like Vice President Henry Wallace sought to cement loyalties to the war effort by sketching expanded social programs or by asserting liberal truths about "one world," the title of heretic Republican Wendell Willkie's bestseller. For most Americans the war meant more specific things: the annoyance of rationing or the pleasure of rising wages, a draft call to heed or a son to mourn, a small business to fold up because merchandise was scarce or a defense plant job to take in a distant city. But the mood of Americans in 1942 was mercurial and hard to identify. They seemed to display confidence that their cause was just but perplexity about why it was, and "a kind of puzzled boredom about the war in general" that shifted into "talk of the war being over in six months."[10]

Even less clear was the long-range significance they saw in Pearl Harbor's apparent lessons, for in 1942 Americans said little about their postwar military power. Exceptions to the reticence did little to challenge it: the book *Victory through Air Power* (1942), a notorious appeal (later rendered in animated form by Walt Disney) to incinerate Japanese cities, portrayed postwar American hegemony effortlessly achieved through the bomber. Reticence owed little to immersion in the task at hand, for speculation about war's aftermath in other ways was rife, or to confidence that this war would be the last one, which few Americans had.

Instead, it owed to other limits on the wartime imagination. Many liberals feared that mention of the military's role in the nation's future would sap the current will to fight. "Proposals in Congress for a great standing army after the war are confessions of defeat," Margaret Mead argued, and "weaken us as a people." "Men fight better when they know for what they are fighting," Stuart Chase wrote, but the possible need for "a larger military machine" after the war was hardly bracing; economic justice and security would better galvanize Americans. More generally, Chase and Mead, like many others, had a cyclical view of history in which a recurrence of the Great Depression was the nightmare. "We can't go back," Chase declared, but he obviously feared that "we" could. Focusing on culture, Philip Wylie feared much the same—the return of a botched civilization (unless the war made Americans realize that "hundreds of thousands of American flowers of womanhood are whores. And that millions of noble American men get in bed with them"). For a future imagined as a reversion to the ugly past, there was little need to extend the vectors of wartime change into the future. Commentators instead imagined a bell curve of historical change rising during the war and then receding to prewar normality; they foresaw war's ripple effects but no lasting militarization. Even Wylie, who decried America's prewar military weakness, envisioned a pacific American hegemony after the war: "Conversion for world reconstruction would open up the one everlasting frontier. We can win the war and re-establish man."[11]

Thus few Americans in 1942 extrapolated their new lessons about national security into the future. They were surrounded by evidence of their military might, but it was obviously geared to this war's exigencies. Militarization was regarded as something different—the evil which the enemy practiced—and thus lacked explicit sanction, remaining contingent on a war yet to be won and on issues yet to be faced, even as the implicit sanction offered by Pearl Harbor grew in symbol and memory.

Pearl Harbor had made its mark, but how deeply was not immediately apparent. It became an all-purpose metaphor for disaster; Americans might "suffer another Pearl Harbor," ran one gloomy prediction of postwar economic depression. It sparked images of a world shrunk by aviation; newsreels and morale-boosting films made Midway "not a speck in the Pacific but 'our front yard'"; "What's Chungking doing in Nevada?," asked a Consolidated Vultee Aircraft ad (see fig. 3). Yet for Americans imagining new peril but still safe from attack, Pearl Harbor was also an elusive symbol, as an English visitor realized while flying over Nebraska. The "stewardess deposited my lunch tray. . . . As I reached avidly to attack my butter pat there, neatly inscribed on it, was the injunction REMEMBER PEARL HARBOR. It needed the butter to remind one of the guns." Madison Avenue techniques should not be equated with wartime moods, but the need to use them was revealing.[12]

The Business of War

At the height of the American war effort, the British observer D. W. Brogan summed up "the American way of war," which he thought "bound to be like the American way of life." It was "mechanized like the American farm and kitchen (the farms and kitchens of a lazy people who want washing machines and bulldozers to do the job for them"). It was practiced by "a nation of colossal business enterprises, often wastefully run in detail, but winning by their mere scale." To Americans, Brogan concluded, "war is a business, not an art; they are not interested in moral victories, but in victory. No great corporation ever successfully excused itself on moral grounds to its stockholders for being in the red; the United States is a great, a very great, corporation whose stockholders expect . . . that it will be in the black.[13] Indeed the great corporation did run "in the black," promoting victory abroad, affluence at home, and militarization in the long run.

However dusty, the measures of American productive triumph remain dazzling. Manufacturing output doubled between 1940 and 1943. Armaments production increased eightfold between 1941 and 1943, to a level nearly that of Britain, the Soviet Union, and Germany combined. Output of ships, often by remarkable assembly-line methods, was staggering. Most telling was success in technically advanced fields: aircraft production zoomed from 5,856 in 1939 to 96,318 in 1944—more than double what any ally or enemy produced, even though the United States made bigger planes. Under Lend-Lease, it also supplied its allies: 400,000 motor vehicles and 2,000 locomotives to the Soviets, and over a fourth of Britain's military equipment by 1944. Friends and foes performed just as impressively, given the burden of combat and destruction under which they labored: the Soviet Union outproduced America in tanks by 1944, for example, and Germany and Japan reached peak production that year despite Allied bombing and blockade. By the same token, America's insulation from attack and enormous resources—half the world's manufacturing took place in the United States by 1945—partly accounted for its superiority. But American triumph was not a simple one of "mere scale," as Brogan put it. In aviation (despite German breakthroughs in jet aircraft and rockets), in electronics, and in atomic weapons, American inventive supremacy (with Allied and refugee assistance) was unrivaled. Making the American triumph doubly gratifying, the production of nonwar goods also increased—a luxury no other major combatant enjoyed—despite the cessation of some products (automobiles) and the rationing of others (gasoline, for example).

Roosevelt facilitated this productive triumph. He did so through key decisions—to push aircraft production, for example, and to authorize the Manhattan Project to build atomic bombs. He also did so through public oratory, driving home the centrality of production in modern war with mundane but telling illustrations: "Every Flying Fortress that bombed harbor installations at

Naples," he reminded Americans in July 1943, "required 1,110 gallons of gasoline for each single mission," or "the equal of about 375 'A' ration tickets—enough gas to drive your car five times across this continent."[14] Such oratory served several purposes: it reinforced the new conception of national security, linked demands abroad to sacrifices at home, and shifted attention away from war's grimmer dimensions. Roosevelt appreciated the fundamentals of this war—what it took to win, to minimize American sacrifice, and to maximize American output.

His translation of that appreciation into organized action, on the other hand, seemed wanting, or so many contemporaries judged it. No one agency or individual except FDR himself ever controlled the vast apparatus of economic mobilization. The War Production Board (WPB) came closest but delegated much of its authority to the armed services and large corporations. Its coercive role was confined largely to issuing orders limiting production of finished products and use of raw materials, each order functioning "like the turning of a valve or a the throwing of a switch," sending "materials coursing through the machine, so that they emerged as helmets or pup tents rather than as breadboxes and hammocks."[15] Moreover, much in the mobilization effort lay beyond the WPB's purview—in the hands of agencies like the Office of Scientific Research and Development, the Office of Price Administration, and the Reconstruction Finance Corporation (a New Deal holdover). A superagency established in 1943, the Office of War Mobilization, added little coherence to the system, but it did exploit the talents of the master political fixer who headed it, James Byrnes, former South Carolina senator and Supreme Court justice.

Not surprisingly, given the plethora of competing authorities, the gears of the machine sometimes jammed. Especially in 1942, critics excoriated waste, sluggishness, and corporate profiteering. Mobilization was "bitched, botched and buggered from start to finish," charged Bruce Catton, writing from his vantage point on the WPB staff. Costly mistakes were made, like Ford Motor Company's troubled effort to mass-produce bombers, the air force's tardy support for the P-51 fighter needed to accompany its bombers, and the rush to make an ill-designed B-26 bomber (to flyers, the "Flying Prostitute—no visible means of support"). Given the "polycratic chaos" of Nazi mobilization (disguised at the time by its totalitarian image), why did apparent American chaos yield victory?[16]

Besides favorable circumstances of geography and resources, superior prescience was critical. By late 1941, American, British, and Soviet leaders grasped the likely length and demands of the war and geared mobilization accordingly, whereas Hitler and the Nazis, overconfident after initial success with blitzkrieg tactics, delayed full mobilization until 1942–1943, even then hesitating in important ways. Fidelity to their ideological goals—as in keeping women at home rather than employing on the scale the Allies did, or slaughtering Jews and others rather than exploiting their labor more fully—also hamstrung the Nazis, while the Allies' ideological caution allowed all energies to flow into the pursuit of victory, the only goal commanding universal support.

The peculiar "chaos" in American mobilization was just as important, for chaos also meant flexibility. Whatever the formal bureaucratic boundaries, key groups and individuals could press possibilities blocked in one channel through another and sustain elaborate webs of communication. Thus the atomic bomb project was pushed by scientists despite the military's initial cool response, and resistance by some aviation firms to assembly-line production was likewise overcome (it was not in Germany). Fluidity across overlapping realms of authority did trigger bitter turf wars, but they were by-products of a healthy process. Even in Germany, skillful improvisation outside formal structures accounted for much of its belated success at production, but individual fiefdoms within the Nazi economic kingdom were jealously guarded and Hitler intervened in their workings capriciously. In contrast, Roosevelt gave wide latitude to experts in their fields, while the permeable boundaries of American elites and state organizations promoted movement among them by individuals and initiatives. Indeed, one source of America's success in the production war was the intricate meshing of military and civilian elites, in contrast to the rigid subordination to Nazi power faced by such elites in Germany.

In turn, that success set in motion vital changes in the American political economy, including the regional redistribution of power and wealth. The war transformed the American West, where federal defense dollars flowed because of its proximity to the Pacific war, its presumably favorable climate, and its sparsely inhabited lands suitable for testing new technologies like jet aircraft and the atomic bomb. The big winner was the West Coast, especially California, which received 12 percent of all war orders and saw its aircraft and shipbuilding facilities reaching from San Diego to Los Angeles become "the nation's largest urban military-industrial complex." The inland West was less favored by the boom in manufacturing (although Denver, oddly enough, churned out submarine-chasing ships), but it prospered through the growth of military bases and the expansion of agricultural and extractive industries. The war effort "transformed a colonial economy" into a "diversified" economic powerhouse paced by advanced technologies and elements of what came to be called a "post-industrial" system. Despite the West's lingering dependence on federal monies, its subordination to the North and the East rapidly faded. In the wake of that grand change came others: a new image, as companies like Hughes Aircraft and Douglas Aviation emerged as heroic enterprises of technological victory; national preeminence for institutions like the University of California and the Caltech Jet Propulsion Laboratory, where prominent American and émigré scientists flocked; a hastened, though hardly complete or effortless, entry into the mainstream of American life for Hispanic Americans; and a massive population shift into parts of the West. "It was if someone had tilted the country: people, money, and soldiers all spilled west."[17]

The West's gains were not necessarily other regions' losses. The South's coastal areas saw a "staggering" transformation, initiating the "Sunbelt" prosperity noticed in the 1970s and 1980s; and for southerners "the war challenged their provincialism," drawing them more fully into an American identity and bringing federal power more forcefully to their region. Those sectors suffering economic or population loss belonged to no single region but instead were scattered among rural areas and small towns (interior northern New England, for example). Wartime prosperity in other sectors, however, sometimes masked long-term shifts aggravated by the war. Farm output and income soared, but the farm population continued to shrink. In older industrial states like Michigan (only New York exceeded its share of prime defense contracts), "the shape, if not the size, of [the] economy emerged from the war relatively unchanged." Those states prospered for the moment but lacked the new industries that would fuel continued prosperity.[18]

The war accelerated regional shifts of a grander sort as well, those on an international scale. Large American corporations emerged from the war flush with capital and expertise, eager to exploit markets abandoned by weakened European competitors, more maneuverable as a result of newly decentralized structures, and backed by the world's most powerful government. Once more concerned with domestic markets, those corporations became multinational firms and reached the zenith of their international power in the two decades after 1945. Although that development was largely on hold until the war was over, it was assisted by changes during the war. America's economic leverage allowed it to arm-twist allies dependent on American assistance into accepting tariff and monetary agreements that pried open much of the world, especially Europe's colonial empires, to American trade and investment. Soviet power, revolution and chaos in much of the decolonizing Third World, and other factors would limit the American achievement. And it was dubious indeed to claim, as Secretary of State Cordell Hull once did, that American principles of free trade and democracy were "beneficial and appealing to the sense of justice, of right and of the well-being of free peoples everywhere."[19] But Hull and others did much to realize an old vision of an open economic world dominated by American capitalism.

Most telling, however, were changes internal to the American political economy. The war effected a partnership between big government and big business, after decades of erratic and sometimes strained relations, which largely held for the half-century to follow. Both conscious policy and inadvertent consequence forged the partnership, which "successively mobilized big business, aggrandized it, and linked it to the military establishment." National leaders decided that only generous cooperation with corporate giants could win the war—in the oft-quoted comment of Secretary of War Stimson, when a capitalist country goes to war, "you have to let business make money out of the process or business won't work."[20] Since men like Stimson dominated mobilization—

three-fourths of the WPB executive staff were "dollar-a-year" men who remained on their company payrolls—their views prevailed.

As a result, mobilization enhanced both the immediate profits and the lasting power of larger corporations. Procurement flowed to them; by 1943, one
hundred companies held contracts for 70 percent of defense production. Wartime policy guaranteed them profits, freedom from competition and antitrust
action in most cases, and government capital or other incentives for plant expansion. Newer industries like aviation, synthetic rubber, and atomic energy
were almost wholly financed by government capital. For many companies, the
bonanza went far beyond wartime profits: they gained by "squeezing out marginal competitors, forging permanent links with the national government,
gaining the inside track on research into new technologies, and absorbing state-
financed capital expansion at highly favorable rates after the war."[21] Among
companies not doing essential war work, smaller firms often folded, but larger
ones with clout in Washington and money to advertise often succeeded in identifying with the cause: Coca-Cola accompanied the troops overseas and a stick
of Wrigley's gum went into each soldier's K-ration package. Tough proposals
to cap or tax individual salaries and corporate profits were beaten back or watered down, while federal policies on reconversion to a peacetime economy
were also beneficial to the interests of big business.

To be sure, the triumph of institutional bigness was uneven: some upstart
companies blossomed magnificently, and an old runt like the Packard Motor
Company saw employment zoom from seven hundred to thirty-nine thousand
workers. Nor was that triumph confined to business, evident as it also was
among educational institutions, labor unions, agricultural interests, and government itself. But other institutions lacked the power, the will, the unity—or
all three—to challenge corporate dominance of the political economy. By the
same token, many a lesser company like Packard floundered again after the
war.

The corporate-government partnership was palatable to most Americans because it seemed to be a temporary expedient and was accompanied by broad
prosperity, even by a small but notable downward redistribution of income.
(The rich got richer, but at a slightly slower rate than other Americans, and nonwhite male workers' share of income rose sharply.) When military spending
produced abundance, few Americans were inclined to quarrel over the relationships of power that resulted.

Indeed, popular animosities during the war, stoked by FDR's enemies but
shared by many in the administration, ran far more against workers and unions
than against corporate giants. When union leader John L. Lewis broke labor's
wartime no-strike pledge in 1943—coal workers faced stagnant wages and an
appalling casualty rate ("approaching that of combat") of five hundred miners
killed or hurt weekly—he became perhaps the most hated American, seen as
an enemy who sabotaged the lives of servicemen, since coal was vital to the

entire war economy. FDR handled the devilish issues of labor, wages, and inflation adroitly and "saved the union movement without compromising productivity." But on occasion he threatened to draft striking workers or seize struck industries, and he supported a national service law (never passed) to "prevent strikes" and "to make available for war production or for any other essential services every able-bodied adult in this Nation."[22]

Meanwhile, friction involving government and business did not cease, but it usually involved the play of competing interests, including rivalries within the armed forces, rather than a coherent "government" pitted against a cohesive business community. It could hardly be otherwise when businessmen were running much of the government. Accordingly, resentment against the governmental discipline that war entailed was limited. Experience with a more powerful state during the last war and the Depression, the adroit mixture of voluntarism and coercion with which government mobilized the economy, and the felt gravity of danger to national security all kept the lid on adverse reactions, if not on grumbling about Washington's follies, corporations' greed, or labor's selfishness.

Tentative terms for a lasting business-government partnership were set by the war. Government (especially the executive branch) and business (especially large corporations) would be the senior partners in the firm. Congress would help set policy and broker disputes but would function more as an arena for conflict than as a decisive force itself. Junior partners would be organized labor, agricultural interests, and small business, all of which gained a measure of security—union membership soaring to nearly fifteen million by 1945—at the price of abandoning ambitions for a dominant role. Even their status as junior partners was often in doubt. The aircraft industry, for example, remained notoriously antilabor, thanks to the illegal anti-union tactics of some of its leaders, to southern California's antilabor culture, and to the abundance of "celery pickers" and "country boys" who, at least as long as the Depression's effects lingered, felt "nigger rich" on eighteen dollars a week and proved difficult to unionize.[23]

Occupying a middle position in this hierarchy were military and scientific institutions and their leadership. They lacked the capital or the insider power of corporate and political leaders, but the war did enhance their importance and status, and their skills and values were merging with those of political and corporate leaders in the complex effort at technological warfare. With generals like George Marshall assuming weighty diplomatic and administrative responsibilities, with corporate executives deeply immersed in waging war, with scientists reaching beyond mere invention to guide military and even diplomatic policy, once-clear distinctions among these groups were fading. Their roles increasingly overlapped (one scientist, for example, served simultaneously as a vice president of American Telephone and Telegraph, member of the National Defense Research Committee, and president of the National Academy of Sciences). The merging of roles was evident not only among top leaders but among ordinary servicemen with prized technical skills, such as air force pilots and technicians, who looked forward to attractive jobs in civilian business after the war. At the institutional level, government sponsorship of science and technology forged linkages among the armed services, private corporations, and educational institutions like the Massachusetts Institute of Technology.

What resulted was a triumph for neither "civilian" nor "military" values but instead, as Harold Lasswell had anticipated, their substantial fusion. A "civilian militarism" emerged in which "civilians not only had anticipated war more eagerly than the professionals, but played a principal part in making combat, when it came, more absolute, more terrible than was the current military wont or habit."[24] The fusion was reflected in wartime culture, the heroes of which extended beyond old-fashioned captains of industry and blood-and-guts generals to include corporate wizards like shipbuilder Henry Kaiser, master "organizers of victory" like Marshall and Gen. Dwight Eisenhower, and elite warriors whose skills lay as much in technology as in combat.

Partnership involved policy as well as relations of power. In this regard too, war delineated possibilities without fixing them firmly, above all suggesting how to reconcile conflicting visions of the role of government and business in securing the nation's future prosperity and power. Among champions of activist government, the war marked a retreat from designs for government coercion of economic enterprise in favor of federal fiscal policy: the spigot of government spending rather than the hammer of the state's regulation would guide economic energies. The astounding prosperity produced by wartime spending, corporate capture of the governmental apparatus of regulation and mobilization, and the baleful example of totalitarian coercion all promoted this shift among liberals, who also began to abandon Depression-era assumptions of chronic economic stagnation. They could readily see the war as a triumph of John Maynard Keynes's principles of government investment and deficit financing: only about half of the wartime federal budget (which rose from 9 billion dollars in 1939 to 100 billion in 1945) came from taxes, the rest from war bonds and other borrowing. As Robert Lekachman archly put it in the 1960s, "The war pointed a sharp Keynesian moral. As a public works project, all wars (before the nuclear era) are ideal. Since all war production is sheer economic waste, there is never a danger of producing too much."[25] At the same time, corporate leaders also increasingly set aside their reflexive suspicions of federal authority—some had done so long before the 1940s—to accept a major role for fiscal policy in promoting prosperity. The common ground of fiscal policy defined the means by which government could stimulate the economy without coercing its private institutions.

To be sure, that common ground remained ill defined and contested—just how much government spending, focused on what activities, backed by what tax and monetary policies? Looking beyond the war, some liberals favored a "social Keynesianism" emphasizing social welfare and public projects; corporate leaders tended to prefer a "business Keynesianism" harnessing private enterprise by lowering its taxes or buying its goods; economic conservatives, still powerful in business and both political parties, found either approach offensive, even immoral. Less clearly articulated was the "military Keynesianism" that would partly prevail, in which defense spending would be a major lever of stability and growth.

Still, the war experience, combined with fear of renewed depression, did chart a broad area of agreement, as well as specific possibilities alluring to many groups. Federal sponsorship of science and technology, for example, promised rich benefits: for corporations seeking skilled personnel and new products; for scientists and universities overcoming old inhibitions against government patronage; for military leaders embracing technological warfare; and for those liberals eager to see Americans enjoy technological abundance.

Forging links among government, business, science, and other partners, the war effort demonstrated the temporary attractions of militarization—prosperity, power, victory—and hinted at more permanent ones. But Americans could hardly be faulted for failing to debate those attractions fully during the war. They were, after all, on a course only partly of their choosing. Europe had been "the center of the process of militarization," setting in motion "a militarization of the world" in which Europe itself became the "first and main casualty."[26] Americans were relative newcomers to this historical process. Their future course was neither easily foreseen nor fully set, contingent as it was on decisions yet to be made and on a sustaining ideology yet to be completed.

Most Americans did see some connection between war spending and the return of prosperity. It was driven home to them in their daily lives, trumpeted in the media, and analyzed by economists. The necessity of government action to avert a postwar depression was a staple of wartime commentary, while advertising and political rhetoric instructed Americans to regard prosperity and affluence as not only a reward for victory but as the core of that "American way of life" for which they were fighting. Wartime affluence also raised expectations by improving living standards: even with rationing, per capita food consumption increased (annual meat consumption rose from 134 pounds to 162 pounds).

Despite the war-induced prosperity, the urgency to extend it after the war, and the widespread assumption that government would be responsible for it, Americans rarely addressed the future relationship between national security and national prosperity. Instead, debate stalled largely at the point reached in 1942, stuck on the danger of a return to the 1930s and the alternatives posed by New Dealers and their opponents. The U.S. Chamber of Commerce simply noted in 1944 that a postwar depression "would be rooted ultimately in the cessation of governmental demand for armaments." Its stance was typical during and after the war, according to two historians: "Missing from the political discourse of this period was sustained discussion of the long-run implications for business of these momentous changes [wrought during the war] in the federal government's role in the economy." Even among heads of the largest corporations, who had gone farthest "toward accommodation with the newly enlarged national state," such discussion was slight, just as expectations of a postwar military market were generally low.[27]

Discussion was scarcely more brisk among liberals. They sometimes railed against corporate capture of the machinery of war mobilization; Roosevelt, though now wary of antibusiness rhetoric, assailed the "pests who swarm through the lobbies of the Congress and the cocktail bars of Washington" and "the whining demands of selfish pressure groups who seek to feather their nests while young Americans are dying." But liberals rarely foresaw that national defense would shape the American economy in some lasting fashion. Thus Stuart Chase, writing at the war's end, extolled the "five-year miracle" of production triggered by wartime spending, but added that "the conclusion here is not that chronic warfare is the cure for chronic depression." Thus Roosevelt, in January 1945, argued that private "purchasing power" must become "sufficiently high to replace wartime Government demands."[28]

Silence on the economics of postwar national security was not total. On certain specifics, attention could be intense. Generous aid to veterans, for example, received enormous discussion and approval, its potential for mitigating a postwar depression being one of its appeals. The contributions of government-sponsored science and technology to prosperity and military power were also widely recognized. Given the interest-group focus of American politics, however, debate about future military spending dwelt on specific sectors and the competing interests at work in them rather than on macroeconomic effects, and it addressed programs tangential to or outside the core budgets of the armed forces.

It is true that by 1944, ambitious plans for postwar defense had been sketched by the armed forces and their allies among scientists, scholars, and businessmen. In 1944, for example, Secretary of the Navy James Forrestal, a former Wall Street executive, determined that "American business [would] remain close to the Services," founded the National Security Industrial Association, while General Electric's Charles Wilson preached "full preparedness" after the war based on a partnership of government, industry, and science.[29] But these views, confined to a minority of businessmen anyway, were not the stuff of wartime headlines, and their proponents paid little attention to the macroeconomic effect of the postwar military programs they sought.

In short, those worried about the postwar economy paid little attention to spending on national security (except to assume its virtual cessation), while those worried about national security rarely probed the economics involved (except to worry about what monies they could get). Two streams of wartime imagination thus ran parallel to but largely separate from each other, one striving for postwar abundance and economic security, the other for postwar power and military security.

Efforts to foresee the future were complicated by a wartime celebration of "free enterprise" and "free science" that obscured the linkages forming among the armed forces, business, and science. In reality, given government's massive spending and its guarantees of corporate profits, "free enterprise" triumphed only insofar as the organizing talents of businessmen were substantial. Wendell Willkie, for one, condemned "propaganda on the part of powerful groups who have not practiced real enterprise in a generation." More pervasive, however, was praise for "individual initiative and free enterprise," as one company put it, or claims that Americans were fighting against "being pushed around by some bright young bureaucrat," as Republic Steel maintained. " 'If Free Enterprise had not flourished here,' *The Saturday Evening Post* informed an imaginary housewife in Hamburg, 'the cause of world freedom might now be lost for centuries.' "[30] Like praise for "free science," such claims were advanced to inflate the reputations of the interests involved, to fight government restrictions on the largesse they received, and to reflect real but exaggerated differences between the United States and its enemies in how they mobilized for war. Whatever the motives, wartime advertising and rhetoric sustained an older and increasingly irrelevant paradigm of conflict between national government and private interests and masked the thick web of connections between them.

During the war, and among many historians after it, the most significant struggle seemed to have been over the fate of New Deal efforts at social welfare and economic regulation. That contest was indeed important, sharply fought, and substantially won by the New Deal's opponents, whose bitterness toward FDR scarcely abated during the war. Republicans were emboldened by big gains in the 1942 congressional elections, led by the intelligent conservative senator Robert Taft, and often joined by Southern Democrats upset by the urban priorities and racial liberalism of many New Dealers—those "social gainers, do-gooders, bleeding-hearts and long-hairs," as southern conservatives regarded them.[31] Together, these forces scuttled or scaled back New Deal relief agencies, although insurance programs like Social Security remained intact. Roosevelt put up little fight, regarding some programs as temporary or made unnecessary by the war, viewing victory in war as more urgent than domestic legislation, and envisioning new initiatives once the war ended. Liberals, disillusioned as in 1918 that war failed to promote social reform, took some hope from those initiatives and from FDR's 1944 election victory over Thomas Dewey, who promised to keep the welfare state but run it better.

But the wartime campaign against the New Deal threw a smokescreen of symbolic antistatism over deepening government responsibility for social welfare and economic prosperity. Along with other forces, that campaign did not so much diminish such responsibility as redirect it into new channels carved out by the preeminent concern with national security. The failure to secure national health insurance, and the contrasting success of the GI Bill for veterans' assistance—certainly a welfare program, and an expensive one at that—illustrated the shift.

So too did Roosevelt, as he continued to link an older liberalism with national security. Urging an "economic bill of rights" for Americans, he suggested that wartime morale and efficiency required new federal guarantees of economic security: "Our fighting men abroad—and their families at home—expect such a program and have the right to insist upon it." He also implied that such guarantees would serve America in the future, "for unless there is security here at home there cannot be lasting peace in the world." Indeed, his use of "security"—a resonant word for Americans in the wake of depression and in the midst of war—linked its various meanings. "The one supreme objective for the future," he announced, is "Security. And that means not only physical security . . . from attacks by aggressors. It means also economic security, social security, moral security—in a family of Nations." He followed a similar line on specific measures like federal aid to impoverished school districts: "Nothing can provide a stronger bulwark [against war] in the years to come than an educated and enlightened and tolerant citizenry, equipped with the armed force necessary to stop aggression and warfare in this world." Similarly, he supported compulsory service for young men after the war as simultaneously serving defense, social welfare, and reform, goals linked in his 1944 campaign rhetoric, in which FDR compared the war effort to the New Deal just as he had earlier compared the New Deal to mobilization in World War I. Just as Americans had "joined in a common war against economic breakdown and depression," they now "joined in a common war against the Fascist ruthlessness," FDR proclaimed. New Deal programs were "fortifications . . . built to protect the people." The "coming battle for America and for civilization" resembled earlier "battles against tyranny [the fascists] and reaction [the New Deal's foes]." FDR's rhetoric hardly gained him all the legislation he wanted, and it soared above the possibility of military-business linkages to sustain power and prosperity, but it showed how liberalism was directed into the new channels of national security.[32]

In such ways, the politics and economics of wartime mobilization strengthened the forces of militarization without yet guaranteeing them victory. War taught Americans to associate defense spending with prosperity, even if they did not think much about how the connection might be sustained, and it taught them to regard their industrial and technological muscle as the key to prosperity at home and power abroad, even if they could not anticipate how much they would flex it. It enhanced the power of large corporations, accommodated them to national government, and encouraged them to pioneer advanced technologies for military markets, even if few businessmen foresaw how the wartime bonanza might be sustained after the war. It redirected liberals, and key intellectual elites like scientists, toward the needs and opportunities of national security, even if they did not abandon older visions. It coopted alternative power bases like organized labor, even as wartime prosperity seemed to make the bargain acceptable. And amid all those changes, the drama of older issues—the danger of a return to the Depression, the venerable struggles among capital and labor and government, and the demands of war itself—obscured the possibility that temporary changes might become permanent fixtures. Up for election again in 1944, Roosevelt "realized that there was no more effective way for him to run than again to make the race against the memory of Herbert Hoover."[33] Such pardonable political expediency hardly directed attention to the critical changes underway during the war.

Strategies for World Power

Just as D. W. Brogan saw the American way of war as "mechanized like the American farm and kitchen," American military officers believed that "American policy is to expend machines rather than men." The United States, they argued, "may well have altered the dictum to 'get there fustest with the mostest men' to a more sensible and more economic—'get there last with the most machines.' Machines are cheap in America; men are not."[34] American strategy, they knew, derived from the nation's economic and technological abundance. That abundance substantially allowed it to substitute machines for men or to pay others to fight—one reason that Britain's losses of life were heavier proportional to its population than America's (250,000 and nearly 300,000 combat deaths, respectively), and the Soviet Union's far heavier (at least 7 million in combat).

Reliance on American abundance made sense for several reasons. It was precisely that abundance that allies, often skeptical about the combat abilities of Americans, most wanted the United States to provide. Nations at war usually draw on their strengths and minimize their weaknesses, and economic abundance was America's greatest asset—bombers, battleships, infantry-support weapons, radar and code-breaking machines, plus the ingenuity and industry to produce them. It also possessed a tradition of drawing on that abundance—as well as on its immunity from attack and allies generously endowed with manpower—to prevail in warfare. A preference for machines over men likewise responded to memories of the costs of ground warfare during World War I and to fears among leaders of how well Americans would tolerate such costs on the vaster scale of World War II. It also reflected Americans' deep-rooted antistatism—it took considerable governmental coercion to tap American abundance and conscript millions of men, but far less than if the American ground army had borne a heavier burden of fighting.

Reliance on American abundance also flowed from the peculiar currents of American militarization, dominated as it was by civilian elites and their values. Those elites—businessmen, scientists, lawyers, economists, among others—naturally prized the technical, organizational, and economic skills they possessed, and they allied most easily with technically sophisticated branches of the military, especially the Army Air Forces (AAF). Like most Americans, they associated combat zeal with the crudities of militarism, either the atavistic kind supposedly displayed by suicidal Japanese soldiers or the regimented, totalitarian version demonstrated by the German armed forces. To American elites, the nation's technological virtuosity in warfare did not seem like militarism at all: it derived from the values and expertise of civilians more than of military men; it minimized the sacrifice of American lives; and it seemed to free Americans from the brutality and bellicosity which its enemies practiced. As General Electric's Charles Wilson argued, "We can possess the mightiest and deadliest armament in the world without becoming aggressors in our hearts, because we do not have the intoxicating lust for blood which periodically transforms the German military caste."[35] Americans were to wage war coolly, their passion confined to the grim determination to prevail at minimum cost.

But war without passion was impossible. American war making displayed a "technological fanaticism"—a zeal to inflict technological destruction on its enemies—that contrasted with the apparent human fanaticism of genocidal Nazis and crazed Japanese. By virtue of their economic and technological superiority, Americans could act out war's destructive impulses while seeing themselves as different from their enemies. Rarely witnessing the human costs to the enemy, scientists could press new technologies on the armed forces, air force crews could incinerate enemy cities, and battleships could pummel Japanese-held islands from miles offshore. The intricate technology of war provided physical and psychic distance from the enemy. An aircrew felt nothing about what its bombs did, Charles Lindbergh concluded from firsthand experience in the Pacific: "It is like listening to a radio account of a battle on the other side of the earth. It is too far away, too separated to hold reality." The euphemistic language of technological war increased the distance. The destruction of Japanese cities was only "pin-point, incendiary bombing," their civilians simply "dehoused" and the atomic bomb dropped not on a city but on "a military base," according to President Harry Truman. The nature of air power aggravated both its destructiveness and indifference to it. While the gains made by armies and navies were easily measurable (territory conquered, ships sunk), the results of bombing were so hard to calculate that the AAF routinely judged the effort made—the number of sorties run or bombs dropped, or what its own historians called the "numbers racket"—rather than the effect achieved.[36]

Technological warfare, then, did not so much limit American fury as provide a new conduit for it, particularly for the racial passions that erupted in the Pacific war. It also allowed the growth of American military power to proceed with Americans distinguishing themselves from their militarist enemies and disguising their own visceral attractions to destruction. And for Americans alone, the attractions of technological warfare were not challenged by being on the receiving end of it.

Certainly, too much can be made of these distinctions. The war was a highly technological struggle for all combatants, whether the Germans who fired rockets at London or the Soviets who shelled much of Berlin into rubble, just as it was brutal for all those who had to fight, including Americans. Homefront knowledge of war's horrors hardly prevented Russians, British, Germans, and others from meting them out to enemies. Euphemisms were sometimes recognized as such; they could not always protect the scientist with moral qualms or the general facing a difficult decision, much less the aircrew shot up by the enemy or the infantryman in combat.

Moreover, economic and technological prowess simply made victory possible; only strategy and combat could make it happen. Abundance provided options; leaders still had to sift and implement them. Between 1940 and 1943, American strategists decided how to do so. They placed first priority on defeating Germany as the more formidable foe. In line with a generation's faith in strategic bombing, they emphasized its use against enemy factories, cities, and lines of supply, in concert with economic strangulation by Anglo-American naval power. Hedging their bets, however, they also prepared a large army, itself formidably equipped for technological war, to invade the enemies' homelands.

In setting and following this course, American strategists and soldiers were largely equal to the task—victory over Japan without invasion capped their success—but not before meeting formidable obstacles. The first of those arose when Americans had to fight before they had fully mobilized—less a problem in the war against Germany and Italy, where allies could shoulder the burden until American forces were ready, than in the Pacific, so much an American war. Imposing geographic and strategic barriers also delayed the effort to bring American technological superiority to bear: far-away enemies could not be blockaded until their naval forces were subdued, nor bombed until bases near them were secured.

Here, too, the Pacific war, with its vast distances and its island outposts tenaciously defended by the Japanese, often presented the greater challenge, one poorly anticipated because Americans had underrated Japan's military prowess. American forces approached Japan along two lines: one campaign, dominated by the American army (with Australian help) and Gen. Douglas MacArthur, pushed northward from the Solomons and climaxed with the invasion of the Philippines in 1944; the other, more a naval operation commanded by Adm. Chester Nimitz, proceeded westward across the central Pacific through Tarawa, the Marshalls, and the Marianas Islands, from which American B-29 bombers could strike Japan itself (an effort to bomb Japan from Chinese bases proved a logistical nightmare). Even though some Japanese-held islands were bypassed (critics argued that more could have been), the fighting on those invaded was perhaps the most brutal of the war for American soldiers. In contrast, from the start Great Britain provided air bases (as well as its own huge Bomber Command) for the bombing of continental Europe, as soon did reconquered North Africa and southern Italy, although German forces caused horrible losses among Allied bomber crews (British Bomber Command lost nearly 50,000 men), which gained superiority and decisive results only in 1944.

Conflicts among the Allies also shaped strategy. All wanted to harness American abundance, but they differed over how to tap it and how much to count on it. Stalin belittled the Anglo-American bombing of Germany and invasions of North Africa and Italy as poor substitutes for a real second front—an invasion of France and Germany—that would lower the Soviet Union's horrible burdens in fighting the bulk of German forces. British leaders like Churchill abhorred the costs of such an invasion, preferring action in the Mediterranean, where British interests were large. Generals Eisenhower and Marshall appreciated Stalin's needs, doubted that bombing alone could defeat Germany, and disputed the value of invading North Africa and Italy (where, despite Italy's surrender and Mussolini's overthrow, a costly and largely pointless Allied campaign dragged on until 1945 thanks to tough German resistance). But they hesitated to invade France until American forces were fully mobilized and combat-tested. That came only in June 1944, carried out under Eisenhower's command by British, American, Canadian, Free French, and other forces. The war against Japan provoked less inter-Allied conflict, if only because it was such an American effort.

Conflict within the American armed forces, however, was endemic regarding both theaters. At stake were differing strategic visions, the control of wartime resources, bragging rights to victory, and in turn claims on postwar budgets and status. FDR provided some guidance, particularly in goading American commanders to bomb Japan, but the principal mechanism for resolving intramilitary conflict, the new Joint Chiefs of Staff, was committed to working by consensus and only cautiously resolved its differences. The AAF resented still being subordinate to the army and called on to support ground and naval campaigns, deeply believing its bombers could win the war if given the chance. The navy just as adamantly maintained the virtues of sea power. In the Pacific, MacArthur—"the most pompous, grandiose, and mendacious American commander in World War II," and a threat to FDR as a possible candidate for the presidency—pursued the army's vision (at least his version of it) of victory. For good reason, contemporaries and historians have described the war among the American armed services as often more fierce than the war against the enemy. Marshall, the armed forces' preeminent strategist and politician, helped to compromise such conflicts. So, too, did sheer American abundance by 1944, which allowed a redundant strategy whereby each service could pursue its favored course. Wasteful in many ways—necessitating two routes to Japan instead of one and compelling bombers to blast factories that blockade had already crippled—such redundancy, in line with an American tradition of "strategies of annihilation," did have the strategic merit of bringing all forces to bear on the enemy.[37]

Political objectives also presented obstacles to strategy—or more accurately shaped it, since no strategy made sense that did not meet such objectives. One objective was uncontroversial among most Americans—the "unconditional surrender" of Germany and Japan. Others were more problematic. It was one thing, for example, to have the Soviets bear the brunt of the war against Germany, quite another to let them move too far into Central Europe in the process. That prospect added another reason for the invasion of France and Germany by the Western Allies and provoked bickering among Anglo-American leaders about whether to conquer Berlin before the Soviets did (the costs of such an operation, among other things, dissuaded Eisenhower from the attempt). Political objectives also led the United States into a hapless effort to assist China in the war against Japan and allowed MacArthur to prevail in his determination to liberate the Philippines even though many strategists doubted their importance in the war. Perhaps most important, strategy was shaped by preferences evident in political culture. Americans' indignation over Pearl Harbor and racial fury toward the Japanese eroded the Europe-first strategy and helped sanction the final onslaught on Japan, the firebombing and atomic bombing of its cities in 1945. Although not uncomfortable with such preferences, Roosevelt and his military leaders sometimes felt hemmed in by them.

Finally, grand strategy was complicated by operational obstacles which American leaders, trusting their nation's technological prowess, often underrated. They misjudged how well strategic bombing forces could assess, locate, and hit critical targets ("We made a major assault on German agriculture" was the wry comment of one bomber crew), and they discounted the enemy's ability to withstand such attack. They overrated the ability of bombers to strike enemy forces close to Allied lines in France—two disastrous attacks in July 1944 killed or wounded hundreds of Americans—and the capacity of naval firepower to pulverize Japanese forces in their island outposts ("Maybe we'll walk ashore," one colonel mused before the invasion of Tarawa).[38]

Such misjudgments paled in comparison to those made by the enemy, however, and by 1943, Allied forces were on the offensive in both theaters. By the end of 1944, Eisenhower's forces were nearing Germany's western borders as Soviet forces swept eastward, and other American forces were bombing Japan's cities and crippling its economy through a remarkable submarine campaign. By then, too, American scientists were nearly sure that atomic bombs would be ready within several months. Allied unity seemed to peak just when the war effort did, as conferences of Churchill, FDR, and Stalin at Tehran (November 1943) and Yalta (February 1945) attested.

By 1944, too, American planning for the postwar era was in full swing. For decades after 1945, many historians, Cold Warriors, and Roosevelt-haters argued that the administration, fixated on victory and oblivious to American interests and Soviet intentions, failed in such planning. But their charges were essentially wrong, inspired by frustration that America's preeminent power had failed to secure all its ambitions after World War II. Granted, wartime plan-

"Come on in, I'll treat you right. I used to know your Daddy."

Fig. 1. At the start of their age of militarization, most Americans understood war as an external force bearing down on them. This 1937 Pulitzer Prize–winning cartoon by C. D. Batchelor indicated their anxiety that another European war might erupt and draw them in. Showing war as a diseased whore luring men to their death, it also revealed the strikingly—sometimes maliciously—gendered ways in which war was often portrayed in modern American culture. (Reprinted by permission of Tribune Media Services)

WHEN THE SHADOWS ARE GONE...

As spring follows winter, so peace will return, allowing the world to resume its progress to better ways of doing things. Far-sighted men are thinking of the future, keeping tomorrow in mind while doing today's urgent task.

Today we of Keasbey & Mattison willingly give precedence to orders from defense industries, as you would have us do. Our plants are running day and night, we are enlarging our working force and adding to our machine capacity. Even so we are finding it difficult at the present time to deliver some products to many of our customers.

But, like you, we are keeping one eye on the future. When normal times return ... when we are able to ship you everything you want, when you want it ... we expect to have found ways of doing things better, offering you asbestos products that will last longer, prove more economical and serve your purposes better.

To that end, we need your help now. Can you, who use asbestos materials, give us some ideas for tomorrow? Have you encountered some specific problem that could be overcome by a new application of asbestos? We will give thorough consideration to any suggestion, in the hope that it will prove to be practical from a manufacturing standpoint. We'd greatly appreciate a letter from you.

* * *

Nature made asbestos;
Keasbey & Mattison has made it serve mankind ... since 1873.

KEASBEY & MATTISON
COMPANY, AMBLER, PENNSYLVANIA

Fig. 2. Appearing in the Dec. 8, 1941, issue of *Newsweek*—one day after the Pearl Harbor attack—this corporate advertisement offered a simple visual statement of war as an external force that Americans were loathe to engage, rendering it as a set of menacing shadows hovering over a scene of domestic tranquility.

What's Chungking doing in Nevada?

THIS, YOU WILL SAY, is a strange-looking map of the United States.

There's Chungking, China, about where you'd expect to find Elco, Nevada.

We put it there to remind you that you can fly from Chicago to Chungking in 39 hours elapsed time — about the same time it takes to travel from Chicago to Elco, Nevada, by train.

And that's why we put Moscow, Russia, where San Antonio, Texas, ought to be — and Singapore up near Seattle, Washington.

The number of hours shown over each of these foreign cities represents the elapsed time by air from Chicago to that foreign city. Its location on the map shows the approximate distance you could travel in the U.S. by train in the same time.

For example, if you were to leave Chicago by plane for London just as a friend of yours left by train for Atlanta, Georgia, both of you would reach your destinations at about the same time.

Perhaps you hadn't thought of the world as being so small. But it is. Today, because of the long-range plane, *no spot on earth is more than*

60 hours' flying time from your local airport.

No longer, in a world shrunk so small, can there be such a thing as a hermit nation. Not when the Atlantic can be spanned in 372 minutes, and the broad Pacific in only 35 hours!

As a nation, we didn't fully understand this, at first. But when we *did* become aware of it, we quickly recognized the need for speeding the production of vast numbers of military aircraft, and training the personnel to fly, fight, and maintain them.

This has been done — is still being done. And mastery of the air — which was not ours

CONSOLIDATED VULTEE AIRCRAFT

Fig. 3. Wartime culture was rife with images of "a world shrunk so small" by technology, as this corporate advertisement in *Life* (Sept. 6, 1943) put it, that there "can be no such thing as a hermit nation." Also common was the promise, as the ad continues, that wartime technology would yield postwar peace and bounty, with aviation "welding the peoples of the earth together in friendly trade and intercourse and mutual understanding." (Reprinted by permission; all rights reserved)

Fig. 4. Wartime culture—corporate advertising in particular—promised that military inventions would yield postwar technological plenty, a promise that persisted largely unchallenged into the 1960s and reemerged in the 1980s. (*Life*, May 14, 1944.; PHILCO is a registered trademark of Philips Electronics North America Corporation)

Fig. 5. War suspended or altered existing restrictions on erotic images. Although perhaps not a conscious depiction of same-sex eroticism, this advertisement (*Life*, Aug. 16, 1943) celebrated the joys and demands of an all-male military environment. While Cannon noted that *Life*'s readers "might not enjoy the bathing facilities of our boys in the service," the boys depicted seemed to be doing so. (By permission of Cannon Towels, a division of Fieldcrest Cannon, Inc.)

Fig. 6. This typical government poster caught several themes in wartime culture: the assurance of technological triumph through American air power, the sense of the enemy's bestial nature, and the belief that subhuman enemies deserved vindictive destruction. (Courtesy National Archives, Still Picture Branch, 44-PA-978)

Fig. 7. World War II widened the opportunities for favorable depictions of African-Americans, as in this U.S. government poster of boxer Joe Louis in uniform, in a notably manly and aggressive pose. But the poster's caption also implied that blacks were to subordinate their interests to the grander cause of national safety and moral righteousness, and wartime culture rarely depicted blacks and whites serving together on an equal basis. (Courtesy George Roeder and National Archives, Still Picture Branch, 44-PA-87)

Fig. 8. One of the most enduring images of World War II—and adapted to count-less political purposes after it—Joe Rosenthal's photograph of this semistaged scene on Iwo Jima in February 1945 was also a reassuring image, meshing indi-vidual effort with collective will, excluding war's grislier aspects, reaffirming classical poses of heroism, and celebrating American victory. (Courtesy George Roeder and National Archives, Still Picture Branch, (W&C, no. 1221)

Fig. 9. As illustrated for *Life* (Aug. 20, 1945), the destruction wrought on Hiro-shima by the atomic attack was invisible beneath the explosion's giant cloud—a depiction that celebrated Americans' military might while obscuring its conse-quences. At the war's end, as at its start, war for most Americans remained quite literally a shadowy phenomenon, its substance hard to grasp. (Rendering by A. Leydenfrost for *Life* magazine)

ning for the postwar was chaotic, deprived of FDR's close attention, and unevenly articulated to the American people, but it hardly lacked content and
purposefulness.

It was shaped in part by the view of recent history now prevailing among
American leaders. In that view, the calamities of economic depression and
world war had been avoidable, caused by the abdication of leadership by the
United States and by the failures of the world's democracies. The victorious
powers of World War I, in this reading, imposed a punitive peace that poisoned
German politics, disrupted the global economy, and helped to usher in a global
depression, which in turn bred the conditions that dictators exploited. They
squandered the chance to use the League of Nations to control economic chaos
and military aggression, in part because the United States had refused to join it.
Instead, the Western democracies tried policies of appeasement, disarmament,
and isolationism that emboldened the aggressors—"an invitation to Mussolini,
Hitler and the Japanese war lords to run the world," according to Navy Secretary Forrestal in 1944.[39] And they failed to grasp the dangers posed by new
technologies and ideologies operating in a closed world system. For many
Americans, the Versailles Treaty ending World War I symbolized the start of
these follies, Munich their apogee, Pearl Harbor their consequences for Americans, and German V-2 rockets the future that such foolishness could bring.
Soon Hiroshima and the Holocaust would join the litany of symbols. It was a
strikingly dark and self-castigating view of the past for a triumphant nation to
adopt.

It was a past that must not and need not be repeated, Americans were told.
Now loomed a "second chance" for them to lead the world. This emphasis on a
second chance obscured any American drive for power. Americans were, it
seemed, looking backward more than forward, atoning for sins of the past
more than seeking domination of the future. Just as they saw war as forced
upon them in 1941 by aggressors (emboldened by the democracies' weakness),
so they now saw postwar power and responsibility as simple necessities. If a
measure of American domination ensued, it involved no lust for power and
would be welcomed by all nations seeking liberation from the traumas of depression and war. "No one charges us with wanting anything of anybody
else's," Marshall asserted, and "no one is fearful of our misuse" of military
power.[40]

Several versions of second-chance thinking emerged among elites, including
plans for a new world organization to promote economic recovery and collective security, and unilateral efforts to promote global capitalism under American auspices. Among these versions, however, the ideology of national preparedness was especially influential. Brogan noticed that "Americans have
long been accustomed to jest at [their] repeated state of military nakedness.
'God looks after children, drunkards, and the United States.'" Those days now
seemed gone. As Walter Lippmann put it, Americans "have come to the end of

our effortless security" (and of "limitless opportunities," he added). Advocates of preparedness stressed the political and technological imperatives for replacing indifference to military power with a new "state of mind, so firmly imbedded in our souls as to become an invincible philosophy," as one scientist said. Future aggressors would only be deterred by military force. As one admiral put the commonplace argument, if the United States had shown its military might *"before, and not after,* a series of Munich conferences, . . . the personal following of any future Hitler would be limited to a few would-be suicides." Preparation to deter or wage war could not again await the onset of a crisis, not for "a nation grown so large in a world that has shrunk so small," not for an age when an enemy could strike with "a sudden devastation beyond any 'Pearl Harbor' experience or our present power of imagination to conceive." For those aware of the atomic bomb project, peril loomed even larger: "Every center of the population in the world in the future is at the mercy of the enemy that strikes first," advised the scientist Vannevar Bush. Advancing such arguments, advocates of preparedness codified and projected forward the new conception of national security outlined on the eve of World War II.[41]

The various strands of second-chance thinking could be harmonized in some ways. Advocates of preparedness argued that American forces might serve in a United Nations "International Police Force," and some proponents of an "open-door" world economy appreciated the military foundations on which it might rest. There were nonetheless important tensions among these schemes— would powerful American armed forces, critics asked, alarm other countries and undercut the new United Nations?

There were also tensions among those preaching preparedness. Each military service predictably favored its own kind of military power. Fueling the tensions was the services' bitter struggle over whether they should be joined in a single department of defense, a goal underlined for many Americans by Pearl Harbor, and their unseemly scramble to lay claim to postwar budgets. The quarreling services compromised some differences—the army's Marshall agreed that "Air Power will be the quick remedy" for future aggression, all gave lip service to universal military training, and all sought a much larger peacetime establishment and tighter linkages among its military and civilian components. The air force, however, gained the upper hand in this struggle. It exaggerated its role in victory, promised maximum power at minimum cost, and tapped deep currents of technological anxiety and optimism. Aerial technology loomed as the ultimate source of both danger and deliverance for the United States. In the wrong hands, it would leave the nation naked to total destruction. In American hands, it might make possible a Pax Aeronautica for the world. "The people are sold on peace through air power," *Fortune* concluded in June 1945.[42]

For his part, Roosevelt seemed to gloss over the tensions, his vagueness calculated to satisfy conflicting interests at home and to hedge his bets in an uncertain world. Thus he gave sturdy support to the new United Nations but shrank from egalitarian designs for it, happy to see it dominated by the "Four Policemen"—Britain, the Soviet Union, China, and a United States retaining military supremacy. Though inattentive to the intricacies of postwar military planning, he supported its essentials, including cooperation among military, industrial, and scientific institutions and retention of overseas bases from which American air forces could operate globally. Above all, his atomic policy, however devious and inconsistent, showed his determination to maintain American power without ruling out loftier possibilities. He indicated his willingness to use atomic bombs against Japan and his interest in working with the Soviets and other powers to control the new weapon, but he also decided to maintain an Anglo-American monopoly on atomic weapons (and American dominance of that partnership). He understood both the commercial potential of atomic energy and its diplomatic potential as a counterweight to Soviet power or other threats. He, too, had drawn the familiar lesson "that if we do not pull the fangs of the predatory animals of this world, they will multiply and grow in strength—and they will be at our throats once more in a short generation."[43]

Numerous sources of friction and uncertainty complicated any effort to act on that lesson. Anglo-American relations during the war were often fractious, for example, with some Americans both alarmed at the decline of British power and angry at the British for exercising what remained of it. British decline was at least roughly calculable. Far harder to predict were the fortunes of that vast "Third World" (as it came to be called), where powerful movements sought to overthrow imperial rule by European overseers or by Japan, or to challenge less formal Western domination, including that by the United States. Regarding that vast, unsettled arena, American leaders displayed a certain sympathy for the forces of decolonization, a decided reluctance to give the matter high priority, and a distinct ambivalence about whether decolonization would really work to American interests.

Such problems could not be divorced from the tangle of questions about Soviet intentions. British leaders, for example, had sometimes been willing during the war to accommodate Soviet power in Eastern Europe, to the consternation of American diplomats. Soviet leaders had long showered rhetorical support, if less practical assistance, on revolutionary forces in the colonial world. The war had done little to abate American distrust of Moscow, even though political rhetoric and popular culture celebrated the Soviet Union as an ally in the antifascist struggle. Wartime sympathy for the Soviets barely obscured the friction between Soviet and American leaders over strategy, over Stalin's policy as his armies swept through Eastern Europe, over Soviet espionage (in America's Manhattan Project, for example), and over the daily grind of diplomatic contact, which led diplomats like George Kennan to deplore the Soviets' duplicitous ways.

Yet as the war drew to a close, uncertainty about Soviet intentions governed American planning more than a fixed conviction of their danger. That conviction gripped some factions in the State Department and other conservatives long horrified by communist ideology and Soviet ambitions, but it had less of a hold on the armed forces' uniformed and civilian leaders (excepting Navy Secretary Forrestal). Many military leaders had found their Soviet counterparts more cooperative than American diplomats had; many appreciated how the savage war would leave the Soviet Union preoccupied with its internal reconstruction; some had confidence in American power to prevail anyway; few anticipated a protracted American military presence, except perhaps through air power, in Europe after the war. In the ranks as well, similar attitudes may have prevailed: writing in 1944, Dixon Wecter was aware of Soviet-American tensions and of the potential for "some kind of Red Scare" after the war, but found the American GI "more likely to look toward our present enemies for the next war."[44]

Certainty about a Soviet threat was not necessary, however, to make the case for postwar preparedness, for that case rested on propositions far broader than any threat from one power. The world revolution in technology and politics and the permanent danger it offered to American security seemed sufficient alone to compel preparedness. Later proof (as Americans saw it) of Moscow's hegemonic designs served only to confirm that argument.

Put differently: a "cold war" mentality, constructed out of the experience of depression and world war, preceded the Cold War itself with the Soviet Union, and to a degree it defined how Americans came to understand the Soviet threat. That mentality extrapolated the recent past into the future: another Hitler leading another totalitarian nation might threaten a newly vulnerable America and cause another world war (no other kind seemed imaginable), and to stop that threat required possession of the military power that could have deterred Hitler and did finally defeat him. That outlook also extrapolated currently predominant forms of technological power, especially aviation, into the future.

As with other dimensions of wartime experience, the effort to script a future based on recent experience was still contingent at the war's close and clouded by old labels and issues. Just as Roosevelt ran against Hoover in the 1944 campaign, politicians still debated the evils of "isolationism," the design for the United Nations to replace the old League of Nations, or the terms for unifying the armed forces. Militarization proceeded, obscured by that bell-curve model of history in which a return to past evils seemed more likely than entry into a decisively new age.

Perceptions of War

As Dixon Wecter said in 1944, "The consequences of any big war spread in circles to infinity."[45] Soon, ignoring that truism, most Americans remembered the war as involving an almost universal experience of unity and common purpose. Later, critics assailed that memory, arguing that beneath the surface of public culture, with its omnipresent talk of victory and freedom, lay sharply varied experiences shaped by gender, race, ethnicity, religion, region, age, and other factors. Somewhere between those two views of wartime experience lies the rough if variable truth.

Neither empty nor uniform, public culture provided one way for Americans to divine meaning in their experiences. Moreover, almost all had *some* experience of the war, and an awareness that "theirs was a world suddenly grown small and complicated." This was "total war"—in perception at least, one well evoked by Margaret Mead: "The simplest mountain farmer may live on a remote spot where a parachutist drops . . . . Just as any tree or bush, any village or suburb, is as possible a target for a bomb as a forest or a city, so total war stretches out the human beings who form a nation into a great straggling chain, as strong as their ability to join hands rapidly again if one drops out." More than at any other time in their history, a consciousness of shared experience gave Americans an intangible but powerful unity.[46]

For the most part, they shared something else: belief in the American cause and vagueness about what made it virtuous. Polls attested to that vagueness, just as leaders feared that it might undermine morale. Abundant commentary exposed a vapid, even banal sense of purpose. "By and large," Wecter noticed, "the symbols of this war have not caught on. The V-for-Victory is quickly debased to a monogram on handbags; a truss manufacturer in California lately advertised, 'To the Four Freedoms Add a Fifth: Freedom from Rupture.'" Such trivialization reflected reality, Wecter realized: "Lacking a Nanking, or a Coventry, or the abattoirs of Kharkov, we Americans have not felt the same passionate defense of our soil and skies that our Allies know."[47] Abstractions— liberty, peace, power—might have defined purposes, but they suffered a reputation for having duped Americans in World War I. Indeed, many saw maturity in how Americans waged war without the idealistic fervor of 1917.

True, an elaborate public-private machinery functioned to censor the press and enlist the nation in the cause. The sometimes tense relationship between Hollywood and Washington yielded a flood of fictional, didactic, and news films, and skillful propaganda like the *Why We Fight* series made for the army by director Frank Capra. Together these films powerfully shaped public culture, helping to make it perhaps more uniform than at any point in the nation's history and to create a real dimension of wartime unity.

A hodgepodge of federal agencies competed in shaping that culture, however. Nominally in charge, Office of War Information chief Elmer Davis "felt like a man who had married a wartime widow and was trying to raise her children by all her previous husbands." Hemmed in by Roosevelt-haters, secrecy-minded military officials, and profit-hungry businessmen, agencies like OWI often capitulated to the prevailing vagueness, preferring that war's purposes emerge indirectly through entertainment or the "use of sacred and sentimental symbols."[48]

As a result, the war was ubiquitous in culture—the flag was everywhere, and even Tarzan "enlisted for the Allies"—but its purposes were hazily articulated. Few Americans knew much about the Atlantic Charter signed by FDR and Churchill in 1941. Polls claimed that the people were more interested in domestic than in international affairs. And the messages they got from government, corporate, and media depictions of the war's purposes—painter Norman Rockwell's renderings of FDR's "four freedoms," for example—generally invited them "to join the war effort in order to defend *private* interests and discharge *private* moral obligations," above all those involving their families. Like most peoples, D. W. Brogan noted, Americans viewed war parochially: "We know that the Chinese were fighting the Japanese long before we were, but we don't *feel* it. We could remember, if we tried, that the Poles were fighting the Germans" before anyone else, "but we don't feel any urgency to recall it." For good reason, then, Treasury Secretary Henry Morgenthau decided that war bond drives would have to instill rather than reflect national purpose—he would "use *bonds* to sell the *war*, rather than *vice versa*." Using Madison Avenue methods to sell the war, however, only compounded the trivialization those methods were supposed to counter.[49]

For sure, even shallow slogans and images had content. They spoke to real concerns of Americans battered by depression and bewildered by war in portraying them as fighting cunning Nazis and cross-eyed Japanese in defense of Mom, apple pie, the flag, and a suburban home. Expressed in the slogans and symbols of an advertising culture, however, those concerns did not easily congeal into articulate purposes. The satirical poster fashioned by one disillusioned propagandist "displayed a Coca-Cola bottle, wrapped in the American flag, with a legend below: 'Step right up and get your four delicious freedoms. It's a refreshing war.'"[50]

The outlook of most GIs seemed to typify broader attitudes. They knew little more than "that power in the hands of the United States and our Allies is power used less cruelly and bullyingly than in Axis hands." For them, America's enemies "were dragons to be slain, after which the hero could return to his fair lady in her fair land." Even that simple outlook faded for men in combat, whose "microcosmic" world extended only a few yards. Many also regarded America's allies (Russians excepted) "with tolerant contempt." "England? My God! You never saw so many perverts in your life," one soldier reported. "And France, I'd say, is a country without morals." Some observers saw in such attitudes a healthy realism "far less likely to go sour than the heady wine turned to vinegar of a Lost Generation" of World War I soldiers. Still, it was worrisome that the average veteran "saw the war as a vague conspiracy conceived by men of whom he knew nothing and motivated by forces of which he had no comprehension." Soldiers "knew what the war was against," concluded one sociologist, "but few . . . had any idea of its purpose." Brogan, too, thought that the American soldier knows "what he is fighting *against*," but much less "what he is fighting *for*; the American way of life does not seem to him to be in much danger," although Brogan did not see that vagueness as a peculiarly American failing. The soldier's sense even of what he fought *against* was belatedly instilled. After seeing a Nazi death camp at the close of the war, Eisenhower commented, "We are told that the American soldier does not know what he is fighting for. Now, at least, he will know what he is fighting *against*." Now, in this case, was the spring of 1945.[51]

Sometimes purposes later attributed to the American war effort failed even to reach obvious audiences. As Leslie Epstein recalled his Jewish childhood, "In California, in sunshine, the conflict was far more a matter of the Japanese than of the Germans and the Jews . . . . The Germans in movies were simply too adult, . . . witty, cunning, prone to understatement and reserve" to elicit the fear or hatred that the Japanese did. By the same token, sensitivity to the war's purposes may not have coincided with the advantages of social class often assumed. Wecter found "that enlisted men attach greater importance than do officers to the aims of the war," and "the ideology-conscious classes of our big cities [presumably working-class and ethnic-identified Americans] probably come nearer than any other group to feeling this war a crusade."[52]

Then, too, it said something that the shallowness of American purpose was itself repeatedly criticized during the war. It was common to lament that "fascism is still an unreal thing" to the American soldier, who "cannot really hate it."[53] Liberals like Vice President Henry Wallace, and black leaders with a sharp eye for hypocritical claims of a fight for freedom, tried to hammer out more pointed war aims. Others, more pessimistic, feared malign rather than uncertain purpose, seeing in American wartime corporate and military power the sort of fascism that Norman Mailer claimed to expose in *The Naked and the Dead* (1948). If exponents of sharper war aims did not much succeed, it was in part because Roosevelt calculated that Americans' urgency to achieve victory was sufficient and because he feared that sharper debate about war aims, or about inequalities among Americans, would erode the unity needed to achieve it (one reason that FDR dumped Wallace as running mate, replacing him with Sen. Harry Truman in his 1944 reelection bid). In the process, however, some liberals exposed an unsettling diversity of opinion underneath the freedom-and-apple-pie rhetoric.

There was little such diversity regarding the Japanese, however. Beyond a broad sense of American virtue, what united most Americans was racial hatred. It was shared by white allies fighting Japan and mirrored by Japan itself, so that mutual hatreds played off each other. Japanese racism was different, however, less vicious in its words and images, though not necessarily in action, as atrocities against whites and other Asians showed. Japan's racism sprang in part from Asia's historic subordination to the Western powers. It mingled contempt for the West with awe of its power, whereas American hatred displayed a far more uniform disgust. Thus, while Japanese propaganda portrayed Western leaders as superhuman devils, demons, and ogres, American propaganda showed the Japanese as subhuman—apes, insects, rats, reptiles, or octopuses—although it also betrayed a lurking fear of Japan's power.

Almost no one doubted that Americans despised Japanese far more than Germans. "The slogan was conspicuously *Remember Pearl Harbor*," Paul Fussell notes. "No one ever shouted or sang *Remember Poland*." Few also doubted that Japan was the more fanatical foe, even though only Germany practiced systematic genocide and persisted in the war until invaded. Racial hatred found ugly expression in wartime propaganda, treatment of Japanese-Americans, and military action, and more subtly among political and intellectual elites. "Exterminationist" impulses erupted among Americans, as in the March 1945 Marines *Leatherneck* magazine, which pictured a loathsome, bucktoothed Japanese insect and looked forward to "the gigantic task of extermination." Images also shaped action, in such atrocities as killing surrendering Japanese soldiers (or German soldiers, too, but not in racial fury).[54]

More than timeless racial animosity was involved, however, for the war's course and official policy kept altering it. That animosity was stoked by the viciousness of fighting on Pacific islands where no retreat was possible, by revelations carefully timed by the American government about Japanese atrocities against American POWs, and by new technologies facilitating vengeance against the Japanese. By the same token, hatred of the Japanese was not universal; some Americans challenged it and surprisingly, troops fighting the Germans expressed that hatred more than those fighting the Japanese. That hatred also began breaking down late in the war, especially as revelations about Nazi genocide helped discredit racist attitudes among Americans. That shift was too little and too late, however, to arrest the destruction of Japanese cities or to alter a unity based on loathing of the Pacific enemy.

Assumptions about American virtue and Japanese evil united most Americans broadly but not enough to bridge a chasm, perhaps the war's deepest, between civilians and fighting men and women. Though hardly oblivious to the soldiers' plight, civilians were perhaps less sensitive to it simply because of their own improved chances to live longer: due to better economic and medical conditions, life expectancy rose during the war despite over 400,000 military deaths. Not surprisingly, soldiers and their spokesmen condemned the casual affluence and the indifference to war's brutality among Americans safe at home. Marshall and Stimson worried that civilians would not stay the course and accept the sacrifices needed for victory. Down the ranks, more visceral resentments arose. Reporter Robert Sherrod spoke for many at Tarawa when he condemned how the war was sanitized in the media and how Americans at home were "wallowing in unprecedented prosperity." Wecter found returning veterans resentful of "paunchy vacationers and fat wives pushed around in bath chairs. . . . Rumors of chiseling, profiteering, indifference to the war . . . set the returning soldier's teeth on edge." So too did media coverage that made the war "a kind of Rose Bowl game, with us always marching down the field." "Civilians were different, more like 'foreigners,' indeed rather like the enemy," Paul Fussell later recalled. Troops hated "the complacent, unimaginative innocence of their home fronts and rear echelons" about the disease, deprivation, and dehumanization they experienced.[55]

Yet, as the mention of "rear echelons" suggests, more was involved than a simple chasm between soldiers and civilians. Bitterness also arose among combat forces toward troops behind the lines, and among enlisted men toward officers. Moreover, danger did not always wear a uniform: thousands of civilians died in war-related work, while many military personnel never left the United States or faced danger abroad. In technological warfare, the burden of combat fell on a few—perhaps 20 percent of the huge force assembled—in contrast to those servicemen "for whom the war was merely foreign travel tempered by excessive regimentation."[56]

Even those facing combat differed depending on when and where they served, their rank and branch of service, and other factors. Troops in Europe endured long, drawn-out slugging matches, but those assaulting Pacific islands often saw action telescoped into a few horrible days or weeks, then long periods of excruciating boredom and exposure to disease. Even when combat came very close, men could keep their distance. Watching a kamikaze raid on a nearby American aircraft carrier, Marine aviator Samuel Hynes "didn't know what was happening to human lives while we watched, but even if we had, I wonder if it would have mattered . . . perhaps a mile is too far to project the imagination to another man's death." Most Americans were well trained, but as manpower and patience ran short near the war's end, some were rushed into combat with just six weeks' training (many quickly paid the price). Higher class or educational status offered little protection from service or death in it, but it did raise the odds of gaining officer rank and service in the navy or air force, and therefore of securing status and amenities that enlisted army men could only envy, especially given the contempt they faced. (Army soldiers "were called Doggies," Hynes recalled, "which was short for Dog-faces, and Marines despised them, along with their commanders.")[57]

To add to the complexities, combat was hardly the only danger faced by men at war. Although this was the first American war in which battle deaths (291,557) outnumbered others, 113,842 still died out of combat (including some 36,000 airmen, compared to 52,000 in combat), as disease and accidents took a heavy toll. Even in combat, death often was not due to enemy guns: thousands died in accidents of assault as gliders crashed, landing craft struck reefs, and ships foundered at sea. The enemy accounted only for one-fifth of the B-29s downed in bombing Japan, the rest falling to navigational errors, fuel exhaustion, and equipment failure over the trackless ocean, so that B-29 crews "began to fear their own aircraft and our field orders more than the devices of the enemy."[58] For these men, the enemy, and hatred of him, seemed a secondary, even irrelevant matter.

Gender and minority status shaped experience as well. It often limited exposure to combat—almost entirely for women and often for blacks, long deemed incapable of fighting. But being female, black, gay, or ethnic left many vulnerable to informal abuse and official discrimination within the military, and off-base as well. The armed forces also thrived on inculcating a hatred of the enemy that often was displaced onto fellow Americans, just as hatred of the "nigger," "pansy," "bitch," or "kike" was sometimes exploited by officers as a kind of warm-up for the dehumanization of the enemy which combat presumably required.

Given that war jumbles peacetime categories even as it reinforces them, however, many outsiders also found unexpected opportunities. World War II jarred open the door to professional careers in the military for some blacks and women. Native Americans, profiting from white stereotypes of them as warriors, faced little segregation in military service, became valued for special skills (the Navajo language was an unbreakable military code), found praise for their heroism, and enjoyed an unprecedented "chance to interact simply as individuals on the battlefields and in the factories." Japanese-Americans culled from incarceration camps compiled a splendid combat record that challenged racial stereotypes. For gay men with a taste for drag, the armed forces sanctioned troupes of female impersonators to entertain soldiers where women were barred. Desperate for manpower, doctors and draft boards whisked other gays into service despite prohibitions against them. Indeed, with 16 million Americans from almost all social categories serving, it was not always clear who was an insider and who was not. And for all groups, the solvent of war might suspend normal prejudices. Arriving at a Pacific island, Sam Hynes was bemused to see the notice of a court martial: someone "had been found guilty of sodomy. How, I wondered, could there be only one sodomist? And which one was he?"[59]

Also blurring the categories of wartime experience was the changing relationship between civilian and military values. Old-fashioned military brutality and "chickenshit" persisted. Yet they had limits. Swamped with millions of men, professional officers and NCOs—those "prone to look upon the soldier as a bundle of conditioned reflexes, a belly, genitalia, and a pair of feet"—could not train a fraction of them, and the task fell heavily to officers fresh from civilian life. Leaders like Marshall—sympathetic to the men in service, worried about the military's public image, aware that men cost more than machines—sought to curb mindless practices and bestow the best medical care, training, and entertainment, especially on expensive men, such as aircrews. While the military's task was to transform civilians, in the process civilians "were transforming the Army." Moreover, the technical skills needed by the armed forces often resembled those valued in civilian life. There seemed "little to distinguish the functions and problems of many of the soldiers and civilians," observed one sociologist. Indeed, many tasks were simply performed by civilians; the air force alone employed a half-million, including many women. Strengthening the civilizing forces was the contractual relationship between soldier and country: elite warriors like airmen often served a specified number of missions rather than "for the duration," and all servicemen exchanged the risks of service for the promise of benefits afterward.[60]

In the face of such complexities, the notion dissolves of a "real" war experienced only by soldiers or men in combat—the war was "real" to all, soldier and civilian alike. The sharp line often drawn between those went to war and those who did not illuminated one truth about the war but disguised another. In a war where civilian and military roles often overlapped and where all Americans were presumably asked to serve in some fashion, that distinction often faded. For other countries at war, it often collapsed altogether—under a barrage of enemy bombs, many civilians rightly felt that they too were on the front lines. While American civilians could only imagine such dangers, they too often felt they were—or might soon be—on the front lines.

Still, all the infusion of civilian values and efforts to humanize military service could not mitigate the depersonalization and terror many service personnel faced. "The ex-soldier never forgets his serial number," Fussell writes. "Nor, if he had no middle name, the way one was supplied, in the army NMI (No Middle Initial), in the Marine Corps NONE, so that he ended as John NMI Jones or Frederick NONE Smith, in name as little different as possible from other people." Brutal training seemed designed to make men long for combat. Soldiers expressed their bewilderment and resentment, in wild gossip, for example; a rumor that Eleanor Roosevelt wanted "all venereal cases [to] be quarantined on some offshore island" proved so believable that "she felt obliged to issue a denial," according to Fussell, who sees rumor as preferable to a terrifying "absence of narrative." Or soldiers responded with literary frankness and foul language, yielding American culture (to mention the mildest example) acronyms like SNAFU (Situation Normal, All Fucked Up). "Indispensable both to those administering chickenshit and to those receiving it, *fucking* helped express the resentment of both sides."[61]

It is, to be sure, impossible to calculate how much the soldier's perception of World War II, much less the reality of it, differed from that in earlier wars. Certainly, despite expectations of a rapid war of movement, much action in both theaters of World War II resembled conditions on the Western Front in World War I—an engineer's war over highly fortified lines and positions. Okinawa was a "latter-day Verdun," with "a stinking compost pile" of dead Marines and Japanese, where "fat maggots tumbled out. . . . We didn't talk about such things. They were too horrible and obscene even for hardened veterans," Eugene Sledge, a Marine, recalled. Even so lofty a figure as Eisenhower noticed that in France it "was literally possible to walk for hundreds of yards at a time, stepping on nothing but dead and decaying flesh." Not new, either, was the excruciating tension of waiting for combat, the humiliation of soiling oneself (the phrase "scared shitless" possessed a "literal truth"), the pain at seeing a buddy dismembered, and the experience of it all by the very young (conscription reached eighteen-year-old Americans, and younger boys could enlist).[62]

Nonetheless, Americans who wrote about combat in World War II expressed a keener sense of the mindless, anonymous nature of war than had the soldiers of World War I. Where the latter gave their characters a "persisting individuality as they buck against the forces opposed to their uniqueness," the soldiers of the Second World War were rendered "devoid of personal identity"—"the ball turret gunner," "a pilot from the carrier"—and bereft of hope for preserving their individuality. "You are something there are millions of," poet Randall Jarrell addressed a convalescent soldier.[63] The shift in tone and substance was due in part to familiarity with the literary themes of World War I, which many writers sought to extend rather than simply replicate, and to an emphasis in American culture during the interwar years on machine-age dehumanization and cosmic purposelessness.

To an indefinable degree, it also owed to new technologies, which created new terrors. Crews on airplanes and submarines, trapped for hours or weeks in fragile devices, were vulnerable to emotional breakdown, all the more so because there was no rational way to explain why some survived and stayed sane and others did not: veterans were as vulnerable to death as novices and the "neurotic" might resist breakdown better than the "normal." Even more than infantry soldiers, such men also depended for survival on a handful of fellow crewmen, whose loss could be devastating: "the 'survivor's guilt' haunts the individual; he is 'ghosted,' as one man put it, by his dead friends, who will not leave him alone." Problems arose due to the apparent meaninglessness and grinding impersonality of bombing unseen targets. "The sense of aimlessness of the war ever quite left me," Hynes wrote of his experience dropping bombs on Okinawa. "Occasionally we dropped on the wrong troops. . . . But our own soldiers were not much more real to us than the enemy." Given such experiences, the war moved the technologies of destruction and the questions they raised closer to the center of cultural anxiety, and it widened the gap between an official culture more blandly comforting and manipulative than ever and the lived experience of many ordinary Americans at war.[64]

Not surprisingly, the fighting man's traumas were unknown to most civilians, although not just because they were inherently inaccessible. The veterans' inability to speak of those traumas, the homefront's safety, and the nature of technological war were also reasons. Strategic bombing was notoriously difficult for journalists to cover, for example; rarely could they ride the bombers, much less depict the hell unfolding on the ground. In a visual culture, the war was in some ways a movie for many Americans, one in which much of the war never appeared.

Inaccessibility was also constructed by political and cultural authorities who chose how to render combat, and the war's manifold other aspects, to Americans at home. They forbade publication of photographs of dead American soldiers until the fall of 1943, when homefront complacency, mounting casualties, and demands from ordinary Americans for greater frankness prompted them to change policy, even then making sure that only intact bodies of isolated individuals were shown. They endorsed Hollywood's escapist, heroic, and sanitized films. They censored the visual record of war's horrors abroad and its images of unsettling changes among Americans themselves—photos of black soldiers dancing with white women, or American GIs fighting with Allied soldiers, were taboo. They presented the bombing of cities as a process of surgical destruction administered by cool-headed Americans. "They censored above all the war's complexity," concludes one historian.[65]

Several considerations governed such decisions, which were common among all combatants though varied in substance: a vague sense of what Americans would tolerate; a careful calculation not to upset families and taxpayers; and a broad concern to avoid questions about the methods and costs of American war making. Those considerations expressed a utilitarian concern for victory and power. A less sanitized approach might have made little difference, and the one taken did dampen celebration of martial virtues and bloodthirsty actions. It nonetheless made worse the impoverishment of civilian sensibilities about this war and modern warfare.

The conventions and techniques of American culture also governed representations of the war. Fighting men were rendered as "just like us," thrust into extreme circumstances but unchanged by them. Corporate advertising portrayed warriors in highly stylized ways reflecting dominant class and ethnic prejudices; most men appeared as "good-looking Aryans, blond and tall, beloved by slim blonde women and surrounded by much-desired consumer goods," as if "all young men are in the Air Corps, where they are officers almost by definition."[66] Of course the purpose of such ads was to sell products or sustain a company's image until it resumed civilian production, not to portray combat, but their ubiquity made them an important lens for Americans on soldiers' experiences.

Similar circumstances and conventions limited understanding of war's impact on other peoples. The Nazi Holocaust was the most famous example. Dimensions of the American response evident earlier—the timidity or indifference of politicians, the fear of some Jewish leaders of inflaming American anti-Semitism, the skepticism about claims of German atrocities—persisted. Until the war's last months, words and pictures were unobtainable, sanitized, censored, or shunted off into inconspicuous places. Language and categories inherited from World War I also limited comprehension: "atrocities," the dominant term, implied specific acts of cruelty and murder, not systematic "genocide," as it was later called. And while the fate of Jews in Europe received little mention, that of others—gays and Gypsies in Nazi camps, Japanese civilians in torched cities, Chinese murdered or starved in countless numbers—almost never crossed the screen of wartime imagination. It could hardly be otherwise, since even their own soldiers' suffering was beyond the reach of most Americans.

All these factors rendered the experience of war benign for most Americans at home, except when the loss of loved ones intruded. Affluence, promises of more of it after the war, and a measure of upward social mobility enhanced many Americans' satisfaction. Just as important was their sense of being caught up in the excitement and purpose (however vague) of a grand event. Many— the ordinary war worker, the housewife salvaging scrap, the scientist seeking a new weapon—felt what one woman later recalled: "Do you know, it was more lively during the war! It seemed like there was life, and it was a mixture of the emotional thing about fighting and the boys were gone." "In simple terms," argued one student of wartime moods, most Americans "had more fun in the second World War, just as they did in the first, than they have had at any other period of their lives." To their everyday satisfactions was added a general sense of social harmony. War inflamed many passions, but it also allowed "internal antagonisms" to be "drained out of the group onto the common enemy."[67]

Enhancing acceptance of the war was the nature of governmental authority and a growing accommodation to it. Although more centralized than in World War I, this war effort still proceeded through a labyrinth of local and private authorities—draft boards and civil defense teams, corporations and charities—that preserved an ethos of voluntary service to the cause and local identification with it. During World War I, a combustible mix of voluntarism and state authority exploded in repression and vigilantism. In its own way, World War II was just as repressive, insofar as such comparisons can even be made, but few Americans experienced it that way, in part because the repression was focused more tightly by the state onto fewer and more marginal groups—"fascists," real and alleged German saboteurs, Jehovah's Witnesses and other conscientious objectors to military service, and above all Japanese-Americans. Especially in the months after Pearl Harbor, some liberals and conservatives wanted the net cast wider, to include "defeatists" or "divisionists" or communists or Jew-baiters or anti-interventionists like Charles Lindbergh, but they rarely got their way. The FBI and military intelligence exercised far broader surveillance than in the previous war, and the courts only belatedly resisted the engines of internal security, but sharp memories of the ugly repression of World War I helped curb its random release in World War II.

Then, too, Americans entered World War II more accustomed to Washington's authority, which was in turn more practiced and sure-footed. The sheer length of World War II also made a difference. Mobilization, the machinery of state, and ideological consensus were far more in place by December 1941 than in April 1917, and then had nearly four years, not nineteen months, to be fine-tuned. Finally, the magnitude of World War II provided more extensive outlets for the energies and fervor of Americans—in military service for some 16 million, in scrap and war bond campaigns, on rationing boards and civil defense teams, in war jobs or charities.

In these and other ways, the war was a study in contrasts for most Americans. Bombarded by talk of danger to the nation's very survival and of imminent attack on its soil, they survived at home without the danger ever becoming real. Anxious or devastated about the fate of loved ones far away, they could barely imagine that fate. Conscious of a world ripped up by war, they had little to help them comprehend how other nations experienced the tragedy. The 1941 ad showing a bomber's ominous shadow over a modest suburban home had it about right: the shadow was indeed ominous, but the substance of tranquility and abundance remained. Americans had made their entrance into a new world of war and perpetual danger, but for most, the entrance was only partial, providing a terrifying glimpse that did not offset the satisfactions of war.

Neither that aspect of wartime experience nor most others directly hastened the course of militarization. Certainly most Americans did not become fond of war: Wecter was right that "the intoxicant of war *per se* is no longer so compelling."[68] Their experiences nonetheless contributed indirectly to militarization. The relative ease and emotional satisfaction of wartime for most Americans muted debate about the war itself and about subsequent militarization. No one said that war and military power were desirable, but policy on both unfolded against a backdrop of substantial silence or equanimity about their burdens. A sharper confrontation with war might not have altered the outcome—nations that suffered more, like Britain and the Soviet Union, still strove after the war to maintain their military power, and American combat veterans usually supported their nation's postwar military might. But American experiences did shape how the outcome would be understood.

In this broad realm of experience and mood, as in other arenas of the war, the presumption of history's cyclical nature also masked the potential for militarization. American morale, "formed around a goal of expedient necessity, implies the suspension of previous aims and values rather than their transformation," one scholar commented in 1943. "The common expression 'for the duration' is more than a convenient circumlocution. . . . It signifies the thought and expectation of roughly resuming from the point of interruption occasioned by the war." There would occur, Wecter wrote in 1944, an "X-Day for eleven million American men now in uniform," almost a magical day when uniforms were shelved and the nation jerked back, however awkwardly, to normality. The enormous focus during the war's last years on veterans' readjustment to civilian life—in many speeches and books, that seemed the only issue worth discussing—exposed that expectation. It suggested that only men in uniform (female veterans were rarely mentioned) had been changed by war and that their readjustment would complete history's cycle. It disguised how the war had facilitated a "transformation" rather than a mere "suspension" of American aims and values. Even the acerbic Wecter closed his account with assurance about the veteran, and hence the nation: "As he went forth, so he will return: friendly, generous, easy-going, brave, the citizen-soldier of America."[69]

In this deep structure of mood and expectation, World War II retained a warm glow of purposefulness, satisfaction, and vividness that operated powerfully for decades. Though few celebrated war itself, World War II became a baseline against which to judge individuals and the nation, and a model for what they could achieve at their best. Americans remembered, or were told to recall, that they had been happiest in the "good war," when their nation's purpose (so it seemed) and power (without a doubt) reached their zenith. If much in later decades failed the test of comparison to World War II, the comparison itself did much to define politics and culture, as did the urge to recreate the lost moment.

Decades later, one veteran nicely captured how the war operated in memory: "When I recall these difficult times, I am always startled to realize how vivid they still seem, how much more alive we were. . . . By comparison, my childhood seems like a painted landscape in a museum, but my dates as a soldier are carved in granite, a few incidents, some of them irrelevant, still standing in bold relief after the erosion of forty years."[70] That the veteran was Ralph David Abernathy, the prominent civil right leader of the 1960s who had served in a segregated army, suggests how broadly spread was the glow of World War II, even for those with reason to detest it.

The Militarization of Social Change

In December 1944, the surprise German counterattack that prompted the famous Battle of the Bulge also prompted change in American race relations. Facing unforeseen casualties among white troops, one of Eisenhower's commanders urged giving black soldiers in rear echelons "the privilege of joining our veteran units at the front" by volunteering for combat (which some had already seen in Italy and the Pacific).[71] They got that privilege, in segregated units that fought well alongside white soldiers.

The incident revealed the ambiguities of social change rooted in a necessitarian logic of war. Few white men had the luxury of volunteering for combat, but "privilege" reeked of the demeaning circumstances of black soldiers brought into battle. War's exigencies carried them partway into the egalitarian host of armed Americans, but the blurriest line separated an implicit statement of their equality from a momentary exploitation of their lives.

During the war, black activists and white allies uneasily walked that line, mixing demands for justice with utilitarian arguments. While FDR sometimes argued that racial change would jeopardize victory by unleashing social conflict, civil rights leaders countered that the status quo jeopardized it even more by denying the nation the full contribution of blacks to victory, the ideological difference from racist enemies it needed, and the image abroad it wanted to cultivate. "Our failures" in race relations, Walter White warned, "are being watched by other colored peoples, who constitute a majority of the peoples of the earth." "Are you for Hitler's Way or the American Way?" asked a group protesting segregation in Washington, D.C.. Black newspapers and organizations equated "Deutschland and Dixieland." The War Department's own film *The Negro Soldier* (1944) pointedly showed a preacher reading "the racist invective of *Mein Kampf*." Assisting such stances was a scholarly assault on racism that filtered into the popular press. Fascism, Ashley Montagu argued, showed "where we end up if we think that the shape of the nose or the color of the skin has anything to do with human values and culture."[72]

African-Americans had fought before, however, only to resume inferior status in the military or be forced out of it altogether. The import of December's initiative was even less clear set against the larger, troubled record of wartime race relations. Though energetic, the Fair Employment Practice Committee (FEPC) "by no means reflected the sentiments of the Roosevelt administration, which opposed its creation, gave it lip service instead of support, used it callously to defuse black protest, and blocked it when political expediency so dictated." White and black workers sometimes allied, but violence against blacks (especially by rural whites new to industrial labor) often erupted in the workplace and corporate leaders branded the FEPC the "Devil's Workshop." Labor's response to blacks' aspirations varied, but especially in the South, no white unionist dared "to be called a nigger lover" and white labor leaders "faced the contradiction between a narrow democracy that privileged the interests of the white majority and a more inclusive vision that sought equal rights for white and black alike." Blacks still endured legal and informal segregation, ugly racial violence, and painful humiliations: they watched German prisoners-of-war dine where black soldiers were forbidden, saw champions of racial change labelled "communist," and found sympathizers like Eleanor Roosevelt subjected to vicious rumors. "Before victory in Europe and Japan, blacks knew that they had lost the battle for victory at home."[73]

Yet this war was different. Like other wars, it produced immense temporary change with ripple effects long after, but more than that it also forged a lasting interaction between national security and social change that was hard to foresee in 1944. As important as the gains and losses for particular groups in this new era was a basic change in the rules of the game: the language and perceptions of national security increasingly set those rules. Even if only giving them lip service, FDR enunciated the new rules: "In some communities employers dislike to hire women. In others they are reluctant to hire Negroes. We can no longer afford to indulge such prejudice." Or as one black woman said, speaking to both race and gender, "Hitler was the one that got us out of the white folks' kitchen."[74] Appeals for equality grounded in the necessities of global power and image only gained force when world war gave way to cold war. This war's aftermath would be different.

Even temporary social changes were massive in race relations and other spheres. Renewing an old migration, blacks flooded out of the rural South into its cities or to those in the North and West, where labor shortages gave them some leverage in gaining jobs. They joined whites in a migration to wartime jobs that often bred sharp conflicts, intense even when race was not an issue, between a town's new and older inhabitants. Detroit's 1943 race riots, in which blacks suffered the worst, were the most infamous result. Even in a southern city like Birmingham, however, blacks' "daily, unorganized, evasive, seemingly spontaneous actions" against petty or violent indignities from white bus drivers and passengers showed how the war began to undermine Jim Crow and how resistance to it went beyond middle-class black organizations. Black ambition, white racism, and wartime need sometimes curiously worked together. Military leaders desperate for manpower looked to ill-educated blacks previously excluded from service, just when black resentment at exclusion mounted and Mississippi senator Theodore Bilbo vented white fury at how the draft was "taking all the whites to meet the quota and leaving the great majority of the Negroes at home." As a result, "the army committed itself to a major effort to upgrade the education of black recruits," as well as poorer whites and non-English-speaking members of minorities.[75]

The entry of women into the work force, promoted by government and business as another requirement for victory, was equally visible. The paid female work force grew over 50 percent between 1940 and 1945; three-fourths of new female workers were married, though only a minority of mothers worked. By 1945, women comprised 36.1 percent of the civilian labor force. More striking was the movement of a few hundred thousand into military service, where they now gained formal military status rather than serving, as women had previously, as mere adjuncts to the armed forces. Most women in and out of the military still held sex-stereotyped jobs in nursing, clerical work, light assembly, and the like, but others worked in heavy industry, served as military doctors, or (for about one thousand women) tested and ferried warplanes.

Real or alleged convulsions in family life were another dimension of wartime social change, attributable in part to accelerated geographic mobility, the absence of fathers, and the entry of mothers into the work force. Alarm mounted about the breakup of extended families, juvenile delinquency, wifely infidelities, and the threat to social stability and family integrity that these changes presumably posed.

The war also diminished ethnic and religious cleavages, in part because they were subordinated, at least in theory, to "the idea that what united Americans was a great deal more important than what divided them." Wartime culture and military service worked powerfully to assimilate European ethnics, especially the men among them, and to forge their American identity. That cinematic staple, the multi-ethnic and interdenominational army platoon or bomber crew, only crudely reflected reality but also reshaped it, and Hollywood made sure that "foreigners were no longer funny folk with ridiculous accents and incongruous customs," with exceptions for Germans and Japanese. Some groups also gained from political initiatives. Movies changed in part under pressure from federal officials who feared alienating allies abroad or ethnics at home. Eyeing the ballot box, FDR minimized restrictions on German and Italian aliens. Jewish and Hispanic-Americans also made gains, despite persisting hostility toward both groups (and violence by servicemen against Mexican-American "zoot-suiters" in Los Angeles). Other factors diminished social divisions: wartime migration loosened ties to ethnic neighborhoods; immigration's virtual end shrunk the proportion of noncitizens in the population. Such easing of ethnic friction worked hand in hand with the muting of class lines that wartime affluence encouraged, although there were limits: "Where ethnic distinctions were muted and class lines blurred, racial differences were exacerbated."[76]

Italian-Americans illustrated how "the war was the fuel of the melting pot." They began the war in an awkward position—a widely disdained minority, one earlier inclined to regard Benito Mussolini favorably, their homeland officially at war with the United States until 1943. Despite those disadvantages, they made notable gains after Pearl Harbor. It helped that they expressed passionately American loyalties in ways that "flattered the nation's ego," and yet felt little need to forgo "traditional Italian patriotism" since Mussolini was now viewed as its betrayer, not its exemplar. It helped also that the press now treated Mussolini as a joke rather than a menace (the "Sawdust Caesar" full of "balcony braggadocio"), thereby dismissing the ugliness of his fascist rule and the fact that many Americans, WASP as well as hyphenated, once admired him. Contempt, like fear, had a price—FDR thought Italians were "a lot of opera singers," while Germans were "dangerous"—but it let Italian-Americans off the hook to a degree. Baseball's DiMaggio brothers, music's Arturo Toscanini, Hollywood's Frank Capra, and New York's Mayor Fiorello LaGuardia became icons of loyalty and achievement, and Italian-American men found military service, during and after World War II, a vehicle of assimilation, upward mobility, and in some cases political electability. So did other European ethnics, especially Catholics: John Kennedy's wartime heroics on the PT 109 were vital for him at the ballot box in the late 1940s. For these ethnic Americans, the war was a major reason for their attachment to patriotic culture in the Cold War and for their fury at those who attacked it during the Vietnam War.[77]

If European ethnics benefited, Filipinos in America met more complex crosscurrents in war's melting pot. Eleanor Roosevelt caught the idealist wave, praising Filipinos who fought beside Americans at Bataan as "an excellent example of what happens when two different races respect each other." Change came, but at times in ironic ways: Filipinos were urged to buy the land of interned Japanese-Americans, whom many Filipinos scorned, showing how war redirected social hostilities as much as it ameliorated them. For Asian-Americans generally, as for blacks and even more so for European ethnics, leverage was wrung from wartime need for their service and the spirit of unity against racist foes. As one Asian Indian argued, given Hitler's claim for "the right of the mythically superior Nordic" race to conquer "so-called inferior peoples," the United States could "ill afford to practice racial discrimination" toward "Asiatic countries" or their kin in America. Barriers to immigration and military service were lowered, to "silence the distorted Japanese propaganda," as FDR put it. It made all the difference if a group identified with a country (like China and the Philippines) ravaged by the enemy or resisting its advance (as with India, though under British rule). Wartime leverage had limits, however. Dominant views could still be hostile, lumping all Asians with the Japanese enemy, or casually condescending: the war was "a personal grudge" for "these pint-sized soldiers," the *American Legion Magazine* said of Filipinos in American uniform.[78]

For other social groups, wartime change was less apparent or lasting. Disabled Americans saw their needs and contributions highlighted, as they provided a draft-proof pool of workers for labor-hungry businesses or returned home injured from war duty, but they remained marginal to mainstream America. Even more ambiguous were the changes for gay and lesbian Americans, who were barely acknowledged. Rare indeed was a public prediction like Philip Wylie's, that wartime conditions "will inaugurate a new spread of homosexuality," much less his admonition that "to treat it as a fiendish manifestation, like ax-murdering, is silly."[79]

Still, perceived wartime needs did make for change. Military officials often only winked at the ban on homosexuals, and their preference for the young and the unmarried—a pregnant woman was the last thing they wanted—tilted recruitment and conscription toward gay men and women. War jobs and military service took gay people away from family and small-town culture into cities with gay bars and other elements of a new subculture. Military life blurred boundaries between homosexuality and heterosexuality; sharing a buddy's bunk or shoulder was so common that you "could get away with it in that atmosphere," as one officer put it.[80] For many lesbians and gay men, the war experience made it easier to realize and act on their identities. Elements of their experience even surfaced to popular attention, though no one put a label on them. *This Is the Army*, replete with outrageous drag routines by soldiers, toured the nation as stage show and movie. For gay Americans, the war marked a transition to a more cohesive sense of community and a new public profile.

For them, however, as for women generally, with whom their fortunes often were linked, the war cut in two sharply opposed ways, yielding both heightened progress and heightened peril. Growing visibility was part of the problem—a woman in a nonstereotyped job as welder or doctor, or a gay soldier whose sexual identity was revealed, was also exposed to discrimination and ridicule. There were subtler problems as well, including changes in public policy and culture, the full effects of which only emerged after the war. The military, for example, urged on by psychiatrists and other experts, formalized a pathological concept of homosexuality and applied it punitively to gays and lesbians, especially after the war. The war thus placed liberating and repressive forces on a collision course with each other, leading "to a redefinition of homosexuality as a political issue."[81]

A similar collision awaited many women. From the start, the call for them to serve the cause was halfhearted and contested. It was never as strong as in Britain, which used conscription to channel women workers. It was resisted by male-dominated unions and companies. And it was sharply limited regarding military service; with female soldiers often branded as sluts (or lesbians), recruitment fell far short of General Marshall's goals. Moreover, propaganda and political rhetoric insisted that women return to traditional roles as wives and mothers after victory—the apron was nearby in many wartime advertisements picturing women at work—or indeed that they had never departed from those roles. The ubiquitous term "homefront," where most women presumably served, implied that they never really left the home but only extended its reach. Even in uniform, their female commanders maintained, they were "only performing the duties that women would ordinarily do in civilian life" and were "as likely as other women to make marriage their profession" after the war. The pressure on working women to return home was all the greater given the blame they got for family turmoil and child neglect: the "latchkey child was one of the most pitied homefront figures of the Second World War, and his or her working mother was not only criticized but even reviled." Too, women were assigned responsibility for smoothing male veterans' readjustment to civilian life. Federal law gave force to such attitudes; returning veterans (who were mostly men) had a claim on jobs that civilians, in many cases women, had taken during the war. As a result, "the breakdown of the sex-segregated labor market necessitated by World War II did not survive." The war did promote lasting changes—draining women away from agriculture and domestic service, leading married women to work—but not in the status and sex-segregated nature of most women's work.[82]

Often sharing prevailing attitudes, many women found them reinforced by practical circumstances: loneliness and disruption of family life, wartime scarcities, and the absence of men made paid work a burden for many, especially given a rising birthrate (the vaunted postwar "baby boom" began during the war). Hence some women worked reluctantly or briefly, eager to go home when the war was over. They had reason to embrace "the ideology of 'family togetherness'" usually associated with the postwar years but swelling during the war.[83] As always, many women—widowed, divorced, poor, black—had no such luxury, and wartime surveys showed that most working women wanted to keep their jobs, but prevailing attitudes and law, while not arresting women's long-term movement into paid labor, constricted the terms on which they would work after the war. It could hardly be otherwise, given that women's role was grounded in calculations of national expediency more than social justice.

Those calculations also limited women's role in politics. Shortages of men in government and party organizations opened some doors for women—their share of government jobs doubled between 1940 and 1944—and the visibility of a few women like Eleanor Roosevelt and Frances Perkins was striking. Still, political women during the war and early Cold War years "emphasized women's responsibilities as citizens rather than women's rights."[84] Thus, while war raised women's importance to the nation, it also subordinated their interests to a presumed collective urgency. Moreover, war swelled institutions of power that men dominated, while subordinating or shrinking the social welfare bureaucracies in which professional women earlier had gained numbers and power.

Wartime cultural conservatism also limited changes in gender and women's roles. Especially early in the war, the forces of sexual restraint and censorship were on the march. The Post Office launched a new crusade to eliminate obscene material from the mails, and the movie industry reiterated its ban on "illicit sex without adequate compensating moral values, offensive sex suggestiveness, nudity . . . sex perversion," and the like.[85] While such measures curbed images degrading to women, they also rested on the notion that women were responsible for maintaining sexual virtue, all the more so since they presumably stayed behind to maintain the home. Men in service, too, were urged to practice sexual restraint, but as a matter of military necessity rather than moral duty. Wartime anxieties about sexual license, like those about family instability, bore down far more on women.

Women's roles and duties were at least matters of open if not edifying debate. Less apparent was an undercurrent of charged images of women that swelled in Anglo-American culture during and after the war. At one level, these images were positive, or so it might seem in the wartime idealization of "Mom" as a symbolic repository of the security for which soldiers presumably fought, or in the fad of the far-away soldier's pin-up girl, seen by Wecter as "not only a symptom of sex but a symbol of home."[86]

At another level, however, these images exposed dark emotions, like the ugly insistence that women sacrifice sexually to men (even as they were also to uphold sexual virtue). "Jokes about women going 'all-out' for the war effort were legion," one historian notes, while the Treasury Department once sold war bonds with a "detachment of thirteen New York chorines who boarded the Washington-Richmond train wearing the scantiest of bathing suits, the rest of their bodies covered with ten-cent defense stamps. . . . Inviting passengers to purchase stamps and peel them off, the chorines brought in five hundred dollars to the U.S. Treasury in the space of nine minutes." Urged to serve men sexually, women also endured male resentments over the sacrifices men made or the emasculation, literal or figurative, men faced. John Hersey portrayed the "war lover" as "a sadistic woman-hater, who in bed "makes hate—attacks, rapes, milks his gland; and thinks that makes him a man."[87]

Other images betrayed resentment of the authority and comfort women gained at home. "The fat wife comfortably sleeping / Sighs and licks her lips and smiles," one poem began. Soldiers' letters found some of them "beginning to wonder about their henpecked status after the war, in returning to the masterful women whose pictures they see driving rivets and loading trucks." With poetic license, women could even be held responsible for men's awful fate in war:

O war is a casual mistress
And the world is her double bed.
She has few charms in her mechanized arms
But you wake up and find yourself dead.

Movies soon reflected male anxieties: portrayals of female competence gave way to images of "treachery or helplessness" (or "downright stupidity"). Women's manipulative evil was powerfully conveyed by Barbara Stanwyck in *Double Indemnity* (1944), as she seduced Fred MacMurray into killing her husband.[88]

There was also fear that a feminized America would be unequal to the task of war and world power. Even before Pearl Harbor, maternal overprotection—or deprivation—was seen as undermining the nation's moral fitness or masculine fiber. "What has become of the manhood of America, that we have to call on our women to do what has ever been the duty of men?" ran a complaint against allowing women into the armed forces. Jonathan Daniels put the argument for masculine virtue more positively: "In an America grown magnificently male again we have the chance to fight for a homeland. . . . [Now] a man can be what an American means, can fight for what America has always meant." Painter Thomas Hart Benton, in phallic imagery, hoped that "when this war is over, a new and better America whipped into shape by sacrifice and hardened by a rebirth of male will is going to rise. If this does not occur there will be no America."[89]

No wonder, Susan Gubar concludes, that women's literature about World War II documented "women's sense that the war was a blitz on them," or that one historian offered the ambiguous title *Women at War with America.* In turn, men's alienation from women sanctioned their intense bonds among each other—though not sexual ones, "for homosexuals are typically presented in World War II literature as guilt-ridden, pathologically violent, and suicidal." Other images—propaganda portraying women infecting soldiers with venereal disease and novels portraying Nazis as depraved homosexuals—linked women and gays with the enemy.[90]

Of course, cultural images were hardly uniform and hardly reflected the diverse experiences of real men and women. And it may be that any protracted war tends to inspire such images, given the premium it traditionally places on masculine virtue, male sacrifice, and women's support of those values. In many countries besides the United States, nationalism and war have promoted degrading images of women and homosexuals, the repression of sexual license unleashed by war's dislocations, and "pro-natalist" ideologies and policies enshrining the family and women's role in servicing men and breeding children.[91] But World War II exacerbated those tendencies. Men entered it with little of the protective idealism felt in World War I, and sensed greater emasculation and dehumanization at the hands of advancing technology. And women felt less of the cohesion and optimism provided by feminism at its high tide in 1917, and a keener sense—in anticipation though not experience for Americans—that modern technology made the homefront, and therefore women, vulnerable to destruction.

Just as war offered both heightened promise and heightened peril for women and homosexuals, it did so for all marginal social groups to some degree. Prejudices overlapped in complex or seemingly bizarre ways: Jews were sometimes lumped with Germans as initiators of Europe's war; rumors in the South of "Eleanor Clubs" fused notions of gender and race in visions of "colored cooks and maids who have vowed to abandon domestic service as degrading."[92] Still, promise and peril were not confronted equally by all groups. Some enjoyed striking but transient gains: the incomes of American Indians and their contacts with white society soared during the war, but the gains often did not outlast the war and assimilation disrupted their individual and collective identities.

Groups had different experiences in part because they had varied access to the ideological leverage the war provided. Even superficial acquaintance by most Americans with Nazism tended to discredit racial and ethnic prejudice. No comparable leverage existed for women and gays, although Eleanor Roosevelt did denounce rumors of immorality and lesbianism among servicewomen as " 'Nazi inspired,' evidence of Hitler's desire to 'get all women back into the home and out of the war effort.' " And leverage came belatedly at best to Japanese-Americans, or to Indians, whose contribution was often valued only in white terms ("A red man will risk his life for a white as dauntlessly as his ancestor lifted a paleface's scalp," ran one journalist's praise).[93]

Whatever the balance sheet of gains and losses for these disparate groups, however, they had in common the linkage of their fortunes to the institutions, rationales, and culture of war. Members of each group tried to wrest what they could from that linkage—in turn only tightening it. That was evident in the way some women's groups used the war to revitalize support for an Equal Rights Amendment, now halfheartedly endorsed by both major political parties, and to give women permanent, regular status in the military. It was evident in race relations—in the very assumption that the federal government had in defense contracts the sanction it presumably otherwise lacked to ban discrimination, and in the decision of black leaders to make integration of the armed forces their premier goal. Even the most marginal groups evinced the pattern: gay veterans indignant over the denial of benefits or military careers formed the first, fledgling gay rights groups.

The attachment of social change to war and national security in turn made the federal government more than ever the key force in social relations. While the war weakened New Deal liberalism and conservatives seized on it to get government out of "social engineering," in fact the war deepened government's immersion in social welfare and social change. It also shifted the action, however, from New Deal social service agencies to institutions of war, above all the armed forces, which reluctantly or resentfully pioneered new roles for women and blacks. While that shift was anomalous, assigning reform to an authoritarian institution, it also made it hard to categorize the military as a conservative institution. Even hidebound officers had to accept social change.

The GI Bill, passed by Congress in 1944, was the crowning example of government's new role in social change. Garnering enormous attention, it embodied the war's competing forces of change and stasis. Some of those were parochial: the American Legion weighed in heavily, as did the housing industry and higher education, both hopeful that GI benefits would help them recover from the war, when college attendance and home construction shrank. Grander designs for national power and prosperity also shaped the bill. Speaking to wartime exigencies, FDR saw it as giving "emphatic notice to the men and women in the armed forces that the American people do not intend to let them down." As one official bluntly put it, "The need to uphold the morale of the servicemen compelled the Administration to act." Retraining veterans in new specialties like aviation and electronics also would strengthen America's future military and economic power, just as rewarding this generation's soldiers was vital for recruiting the next. Over such specific calculations hung a general sense of obligation to veterans, made stronger because most were drafted.[94]

The result was a sharp departure from past programs for veterans, which had been narrow, miserly, and often corrupt. For 16 million veterans, the Servicemen's Readjustment Act of 1944 offered unemployment benefits for up to a year, aid and preference in getting jobs, tuition and living allowances to pursue education, low-interest mortgages (some 3.75 million veterans bought homes under the law, often with a token one-dollar down payment), loans to purchase businesses or farms, medical care through the Veterans Administration (VA), subsidies and rehabilitation for the disabled, and special access to surplus war property. There were limits to the generosity. Southern whites fearful of losing subservient black labor trimmed the law's educational provisions. Denied coverage were veterans dishonorably discharged (which included many gay men

and lesbians), convicted of criminal acts, or engaged in quasimilitary duty—
Merchant Marines, despite their severe casualty rate, and Women's Airforce
Service Pilots.

The measure narrowed and rechanneled the impulse toward expanded social welfare that many liberals championed. Shortly before passage, Wecter
predicted that aid to veterans would be folded into "broader ideas of social responsibility" arising out of the New Deal, with national health and accident
insurance "on the cards." But as one historian notes, "New Deal attempts to
link indissolubly veterans' benefits with general needs of the population failed:
the GI Bill of Rights emerged as a veterans' measure." That failure split the nation's welfare system into "one for the general population, one for the veteran
population," creating "a special welfare state" for those "deemed especially deserving." Outlays on veterans' services and benefits, averaging $7 billion in fis-
cal years 1947–1950, were more than triple all other spending on social welfare,
health, housing, and education, and half as large as the defense budget, cush-
ioning its sharp decline in these years. By the same token, the GI Bill showed
how war sanctioned initiatives in social welfare ordinarily unacceptable to
many Americans, a sanction that would endure long after the war. National
power, never absent even in the 1930s as a rationale, justified action more than
social justice and economic stability.[95]

The GI Bill also mirrored dominant social and cultural values, above all regarding gender. Female veterans did use the GI Bill, but there were few of them,
so that benefits flowed overwhelmingly to men. The results were stunning in
higher education. Veterans flooding campuses made up almost half of the 2.3
million college students by 1947. Schools happy to admit women during war's
lean years now scrambled to find places for subsidized male veterans. More
women did graduate (104,000 in 1950 against 77,000 in 1940), but although they
comprised 40 percent of all graduates in 1940, they were just 25 percent in 1950.
Similar declines for women were evident in medical and graduate programs
and in the ranks of college faculties. Wives did benefit indirectly when husbands raised their educational status, got a low-interest mortgage, and climbed
the socio-economic ladder. And the GI Bill was not solely responsible for such
shifts—cultural images discouraged women from pursuing education and
careers—but its importance was immense.

And protracted. It took years for all veterans to take advantage of the law,
and the Korean War created a new cohort granted similar benefits. The stick of
federal power reinforced the carrot of veterans' benefits: postwar law usually
deferred men from the draft while attending college, a powerful inducement
for them to do so. Even in 1959, women comprised just one-third of all college
graduates—not yet back to their share in 1940. And federal policy had subtler
effects. Men's huge numbers on campuses, along with high federal spending
on technology and science, strengthened technical fields to which men were

attracted and often partially trained as a result of wartime service, and tilted the educational system away from women's interests. In turn, the GI Bill helped build a system that trained people to staff the corporations, laboratories, and bureaucracies of a militarized America.

Other provisions of the GI Bill reinforced its effects on gender. The financing of veterans' mortgages sped suburbanization, which, like the return of men to colleges, also flowed from pent-up wartime demand. The ideal of suburban life paralleled the ideal of higher education in prescribing domestic roles for women: marginalized in colleges, they were to find their niche as wives and mothers in the suburban home. Certainly that niche was hard to find in the federal Civil Service. While the GI Bill extended preference to female veterans, wives of disabled veterans and widows of deceased ones, one-half of all federal civilian employees were veterans—usually male—by 1954.

As with gender, the GI Bill reinforced dominant values of class and race. Like much New Deal legislation, it served a broad constituency of middle-class and upper working-class Americans. College stipends were of little use to veterans, disproportionately poor and black, who had not completed high school, although the bill also made provisions for vocational education. Even under the bill's generous terms, home buying was out of reach for many poorer veterans, and the bill offered little to those who needed to rent. Some of the bill's discriminatory effects were inadvertent, but also intractable: banks could hardly write VA mortgages for Indians in tribal communities lacking individual land deeds. Other such effects were more deliberate: federal agencies like the VA favored the purchase of new homes in suburban developments with legal or de facto racial barriers few blacks could challenge, and they often "red-lined" poorer, inner-city districts, contributing to their long-run deterioration. Explicit racial discrimination in allocating GI benefits compounded these effects.

Government's wartime role in social welfare extended beyond the GI Bill. While national health insurance was anathema to most doctors, Washington underwrote medical care and research to an unprecedented degree. The antibiotic penicillin was a dramatic breakthrough, while new programs raised health care for mothers and children, especially in military families (with the morale of servicemen again a concern), and enhanced the status of emerging medical specialties, especially psychiatry. Some wartime policies challenged dominant interests and values, but thereby also lacked widespread or at least lasting support. Hoping to bring mothers into the work force, the federal government funded thousands of day-care centers, only to have women stay away in droves until late in the war. Likewise, it embarked on a home-building program for war workers flocking to places like Hanford, Washington, and Hartford, Connecticut, but home building, like child and health care, largely returned to private authorities after the war.

Such patterns of social change and policy in wartime America contrasted sharply to those in some other nations. In Britain, for example, the war sparked the ascendancy of the Labor Party and a broad consensus to have the welfare state provide nearly universal coverage. On the other hand, few nations matched the United States in its expansion, however grudging, of opportunities for women and minorities, and of course Germany only made repression more total.

Many Americans grasped the specifics of wartime social change. Far more elusive was the long-term process whereby social change became harnessed to national security, in part because the process was dependent on still unsettled decisions about postwar policies. In addition, the interest-group focus of American politics zoomed in on the fate of particular groups, not the broader linkage of social change to national security. In turn, that linkage was itself complex. Both liberals and conservatives became invested in manipulating the war experience to achieve social goals, often forging alliances (as with the GI Bill) hardly reducible to familiar political categories. Moreover, governmental action was highly varied, ranging from near silence regarding gays to the visible but ambivalent messages about women to the slow but growing effort on behalf of civil rights for racial minorities. Given such variations, the pattern itself was hard to discern.

The presumption of a return to the status quo also shaped speculation about social change. Indeed, one purpose of the GI Bill was to return veterans, and hence the nation, to the status quo (an idealized version of it, course, not its Depression-era form). Some authorities did predict change, but often erroneously: the early postwar years failed to yield a "further rise in the status of women." Racial change was widely anticipated, but also hard to predict. Blacks had reason to despair that it would come; southern politicians, hardly bowing to the inevitable, were only emboldened to fight it; and the aftermath of World War I augured badly for that of World War II. And indeed the racial change to come built less on the war's meager legal achievements than on the lasting expectations it fostered and financed: many blacks, especially southern veterans, ended the war more willing to migrate, better trained to achieve success, more adequately paid in their jobs, and more determined to break racial bonds, just as military service launched the careers of many black leaders. But such deeply structured sources of change were not easily gleaned in 1945.[96]

In any event, most Americans were primed by the war to focus on the danger of new economic disaster and the lure of postwar affluence, not on social relations. The militarization of social change during the war had been intense and profound—unique among the nation's modern wars because of the sheer numbers mobilized in the war effort and the political and ideological stakes involved in the global struggle. But as with other facets of American life, its continuation into the postwar era remained both obscure and contingent on decisions yet to be made.

The Crossroads of Victory

Victory took many forms in the spring of 1945: the Allies' triumph over Germany, their success against Japan, and their effort at lasting peace when the new United Nations met at San Francisco. These victories offered Americans real satisfactions but only limited joy and little clarity about the future. The Pacific war was more costly than ever. Rifts among the Allies widened. And the sweetness of victory was diminished by a stunning encounter with war's horrors. Reactions to the war's final triumphs and tragedies abetted America's militarization, but that result was neither readily evident nor coherently pursued in 1945—it could not be, given the flux at home and in a world torn asunder by war.

A bewildering display of death and destruction unfolded in 1945. The destruction of enemy cities mounted, in a torrent of Russian shells on Berlin, in the last Anglo-American bombing of Germany, and most notably in Japan. In March, one American B-29 raid alone killed at least 85,000 people in Tokyo, leaving behind "a drab and monotonous panorama of hopelessness,"[97] and the ensuing firebombing torched all of Japan's major cities except those saved as targets for the atomic bomb. Such bombing contravened every standard of warfare that American leaders had professed in the 1930s, but with few exceptions (private doubts by Secretary of War Stimson, for example) it aroused little controversy. The long erosion of moral scruples during the war, the visible impatience of most Americans to get the war done (vacationing, inflation, job absenteeism, and the like were mounting), the promise of victory that bombing seemed to offer, and the desires for vengeance it satisfied all forestalled controversy. So too did new evidence of the enemy's fanaticism: the sight of emaciated American POWs freed during the liberation of the Philippines; the scale of Japanese kamikaze attacks during the American invasion of Okinawa.

In part because Americans regarded the Japanese as the more bestial enemy, however, the most shocking revelations came when Allied armies overran Nazi death camps before and after Germany's surrender on May 8. Stunned American commanders like Eisenhower ordered their troops, and Germans as well, to view these horrors; battle-hardened soldiers, visiting congressmen, and journalists were left nauseous or numb by what they saw. Words, pictures, and newsreels swept back to the United States—"Lest We Forget," as an exhibition mounted by publisher Joseph Pulitzer was titled.

A few critics at the time, and more later, faulted Americans for indifference to the fate of European Jews and to the nature of genocide. Yet by and large, Americans were not insensitive. Rather, the categories and concerns of 1945 shaped meanings different from those that emerged later. The terminology of "atrocities" still governed—"genocide" and "Holocaust," evoking systematic extermination, came later. Inheriting an idiom of speechlessness about war's horrors, reporters and officials announced that "they had no words to describe the camps . . . even as they did so at great length and in sometimes grisly detail," and insisted that at best only pictures, as in the Pulitzer exhibition, could convey the camps' meaning.[98]

That is, they emphasized their own horror more than the evil done, but they did so as their way of grasping that evil. Concerned with German wickedness, they also rightly regarded it as emblematic of the general scourge of modern war evident that spring in other ways, such as the physical destruction in Europe and the spectacle of some 30 million displaced persons there. Not surprisingly at the end of a brutal war, they deployed the story of genocide not just to warn of what Germany could do or Jews could suffer, but to signify what war itself entails and to insist that it never again occur—the messages of Pulitzer's "Lest We Forget." As *Time* put it in somewhat different terms: the causes of Nazi genocide were "deeper than any tendency to scientific brutality on the part of the German people. They lay in the political philosophy of totalitarianism, *which is not the exclusive property of any people.*"[99] Hence Americans' focus on their own horror, which expressed the fear that they too could become the victims of war and had narrowly escaped being so in this war. Parochial in some ways, cosmopolitan in others, those reactions were nonetheless powerful.

Meanwhile, in secret, American leaders carried on a ragged discussion about the atomic bomb. Objections to its use against Japanese cities were offered by leading military figures (Marshall, Eisenhower, Adm. William Leahy) and scientists like Leo Szilard, but the former were diffident in their opposition and the latter outside of—and outmaneuvered by—the inner circle of decision-makers. As a new president inheriting Roosevelt's decisions, Harry Truman was disinclined to entertain doubts or resist the long-developing bureaucratic momentum to unleash the new weapon. Several arguments supported use of the bomb on a Japanese city. It would speed victory for impatient Americans and for leaders fearing the costs of invading Japan (although their expectations of American losses were far below the figures of one million and the like later attributed to them). The bomb's use might instill caution in the Soviet leadership and shock the world into controlling this awful new technology. But none of those arguments was very cogently or consistently advanced. More decisive was the sense that restraint in American bombing had already disappeared, and that the Japanese deserved nothing less and would submit to nothing else.

Just as critics faulted American responses to the Holocaust, some decried the insensitivity of American leaders to the radical novelty and evil of atomic weapons. No clear moral line, however, separated the firebombing of Japanese cities from their atomic incineration; the death toll at Hiroshima was not much larger than at Tokyo on March 9. And some who appreciated the bomb's threat to humankind, like physicist Robert Oppenheimer, also endorsed its use against Japan as a way to dramatize that threat to the world. On August 6, the

American air force destroyed most of Hiroshima with one atomic bomb, and on August 9 much of Nagasaki with another (even many defenders of the bomb's use questioned the need so soon of this second attack). Between those dates, the Soviet Union, fulfilling an earlier pledge, entered the war against Japan, playing a role in Japan's surrender that most Americans, transfixed by the bomb's apparent decisiveness, soon overlooked.

A cacophony of reactions to the bomb's advent arose swiftly among Americans. Some stressed pride in American achievement and satisfaction in gaining vengeance against the Japanese. Truman announced that the Japanese "have been repaid many-fold" for Pearl Harbor; a minority of Americans wished the war had gone on longer so more atomic bombs could have been used against Japan. Others—especially soldiers who assumed that an invasion of Japan was the only alternative to the bomb's use—welcomed the peace that the bomb had speeded, and the bomb itself as a tool for enforcing continued peace. Overlapping those reactions was another: as in responding to the Holocaust, many Americans saw the bomb as evidence of the scourge of modern war—in the face of which the wisdom of American use seemed a minor matter. "[One] forgets the effect on Japan," according to the *New York Herald Tribune*, "as one senses the foundations of one's own universe trembling."[100]

Despite professing their sudden entry into a new world, however, Americans had to employ an existing idiom to grasp the novel, just as in confronting the Holocaust. So they compared the bomb's effects to "conventional" B-29 attacks, and they drew on a tradition of apocalyptic prediction about war in order to see the atomic future in stark terms, as a choice between doomsday and deliverance. *One World or None* was the title of a 1946 bestseller by the Federation of American Scientists. "Peace in the world, or the world in pieces" was the final line of the country music song "Old Man Atom." Journalists, scientists, and preachers drove home this Manichean outlook: they were "haunted by fears of an even greater catastrophe," worried that nations were "doomed to fall into the ditch," or afraid that humanity stood "on a tiny ledge above the abyss of annihilation." How much other Americans shared such fears is less clear, but they were given dire warnings of what atomic war would mean, including ecological extinction ("a world of troglodytes," "the mammalian world's death warrant"), and graphic depictions of what an atomic bomb could do to New York or Chicago. "Sole possessors and users" of the new weapon, Paul Boyer has written, "Americans envisioned themselves not as a potential threat to other peoples, but as potential victims." As with the Holocaust, so with the bomb: understandably, Americans worried about the implications for their own safety and sanity, so narrowly preserved in the war just ended.[101]

Those fears about the future of war contrasted with another mood in 1945—pride, exuberance, even arrogance about American power. Few Americans could avoid some awareness of their nation's singular position in possessing the world's most powerful economic system, formidable military might, advanced science and technology, and adaptable (if quarrelsome) political system. Few also dwelled on the temporary nature of many of those advantages, which owed in part to the demolition or exhaustion of other nations in war.

Ambition was both the parent and offspring of American power. Not for the first time, but more boldly in 1945, leading Americans sketched grand goals for the nation. It would rebuild a war-torn world. It would construct a world economy based on free trade and free enterprise that would benefit the United States but also foster abundance, and therefore peace, for other nations. And it would enforce that peace with its own military force or, so it seemed possible in 1945, through the benign instrumentality of the United Nations. Britain's global role in the nineteenth century was one model for American hegemony, a model that some Americans (and British and others) explicitly urged the nation to follow.

The American vision in 1945 involved more than hegemony, however. It drew also on the fear of vulnerability drummed home since the late 1930s and dramatized by genocide and atomic warfare. Military power seemed vital less to score new triumphs of global dominance than to prevent new disasters of depression and war. And sometimes it held no clear purpose at all, but was cherished in its own right and as a symbol of American achievement—as Truman put it, the atomic bomb was "the greatest thing in history."[102]

Ambition, arrogance, and fear justified, at least for many Americans, their nation's continued possession of great military power. But how much power, and of what sort? No consensus existed in 1945, in part because arrogance also undercut the urgency to answer such questions. So great was American power that its continued triumph seemed inevitable to many Americans; to some, the atomic bomb alone guaranteed it. Leaders did foresee dangers—Soviet power, an uncontrollable nuclear arms race, a fractured world economy, and (though it drew less scrutiny) revolution in China and Europe's colonial empires. Confident of their ability to master such challenges, however, Americans tolerated considerable uncertainty about how their vaulting ambitions were to be met.

Uncertainty was mirrored in and exacerbated by political instabilities. FDR had left behind a complex, ambiguous legacy of policies toward the postwar world—and no one quite knew what it was, given his gift for secrecy and indirection. Truman's leadership was more uncertain than complex, more erratic than ambiguous. Far from quickly becoming a Cold Warrior, "he wavered for almost two years, in fact."[103] His atomic policy was no firmer, buffeted by clashing displays of arrogance and doubt regarding the bomb's use against Japan and its potential leverage in the postwar world. (Told he had "an atomic bomb up [his] sleeves," Truman replied, "I am not sure it can ever be used.")[104] The political flux extended beyond Truman, however. Whether by his choice or their own, the top wartime leaders nearly all retired: gone by the fall were Stimson, Morgenthau, Marshall (until Truman called him back for a mission to China), and a host of others. The armed forces were locked in bitter struggle over the lessons of Pearl Harbor and the terms of a unified defense department, while Congress, as it usually does after a war, sought to reassert its power. The institutional flux was even greater in the global arena. The Roosevelt administration had constructed the apparatus of international cooperation it favored, but few Americans knew how organizations like the United Nations would function.

Nor did they agree on how such organizations should function. Despite an end-of-war embrace of "internationalism," nationalistic moods were evident. A minority railed against the United Nations ("a monstrous crime against American liberties") and against alleged giveaways of American money and interests to the Soviets (and the British). Liberals also sounded nationalist themes insofar as they sought to project "our way of living, the only way worthy of a free man" (as Sen. J. William Fulbright put it) onto the rest of the world, just as nationalism was evident in the contrasting visions of the "American Century" and the "century of the common man" earlier proclaimed by Henry Luce and Henry Wallace. The "brittle" internationalism of Americans in 1945, Geoffrey Perrett has argued, was "really little more than the old-fashioned boosterism on a global scale." Many Americans, notes Robert Dallek, believing that technology and mass communications had knit together their own nation, "assumed that the same state of affairs could take hold abroad; one America could now become one world." Heartfelt but vague, such assumptions were hard to translate into concrete policies and left Americans ill prepared for the power politics that the Soviet Union—and the United States and its allies—practiced at the war's close.[105]

Partisan politics displayed and coarsened these unstable moods. The war had accelerated a long decline in the party system: geographic mobility weakened old loyalties, interest groups often mobilized voters more effectively than party structures, racial politics cut across party lines, and the Republican–southern Democrat coalition continued to gain power in Congress. American political parties rarely represent strong class or ideological coalitions, but they did so even less in the 1944 elections, which took a toll on the pronounced liberals and conservatives of both parties. Yet there was no evident alternative to the party system for shaping a national consensus, and Republicans and Democrats competed more rancorously than ever as the fiction of wartime unity dissipated. Red-baiting in particular intensified, as when Dewey asserted in 1944 that the Democratic Party "is subject to capture, and the forces of Communism are, in fact, now capturing it," and it extended beyond party politics, aimed at the civil rights movement, organized labor, and liberals generally. In July 1945, *Life* asserted that "the fellow-traveler [of communism] is everywhere: in Hollywood, on college faculties, in government bureaus, . . . even on the editorial staffs of eminently capitalist journals." Hollywood stars rallying for FDR responded in kind: "The old red herring, the old red herring, it looks like Hitler and it smells like Goering." Such charges indicated how powerful but amorphous concerns about national security were shaping politics.[106]

Discontent boiled up from below as well, among interest groups and masses of Americans eager to enjoy peace. Open challenges to Truman's foreign policy were few, but his plans to curb inflation, convert the economy to peacetime status, and maintain labor peace were soon in shambles, dismantled by the administration itself or destroyed by fears, real and manipulated, of an enlarged federal government. Pent-up consumer demand averted the long-feared postwar depression, but not nervousness and conflict over the economy's future. More disturbing to Americans leaders was a furor over the slow pace of military demobilization (careful plans were ruined by the Pacific war's unexpectedly abrupt end). "Bring Back Daddy" clubs sprung up, baby shoes tagged "bring daddy home" flooded Congress, one representative wailed that "a generation of fatherless children would make our country a second rate power," and riots erupted among GIs abroad demanding a boat home. Navy Secretary James Forrestal thought he saw the influence of left-wingers and communists, but the clamor drew from many sources: conservatives extolling the needs of families disrupted by the war; resentments of federal power, military authority, and the burdens of occupying defeated enemies; and Republican bashing of Truman. The clamor also exposed the nervousness of leaders even at this moment of their nation's supreme power. Rapid demobilization, Truman feared, was costing America the power to prevail abroad, without which "we are heading directly for a third world war."[107]

In truth, most Americans were not going to forfeit that power, but the uproar over demobilization did reinforce wartime perceptions of the terms on which they would accept its global use: they wanted to rely on the nation's economic and technological muscle rather than on a mass army. Reactions to the atomic bomb strengthened that formula, and the collapse of support for universal military training—not even the enormous esteem of Marshall and Eisenhower salvaged the army's proposal—confirmed its political wisdom. It was not an ideal formula in the eyes of military and political leaders, since they had only the sketchiest idea of how to use the atomic bomb in future crises and worried about the signal sent to potential aggressors by the nation's reluctance to keep masses of men under arms. But it was a tolerable formula. It still provided far larger forces (including the army) than before World War II. It drew on American economic and technological strengths assumed to be enduring. Particularly for advocates of a globe-circling air force, it promised to extend American power abroad while preserving at least an illusion of American isolation and easy security. Militarization would proceed, but in a partial fashion acceptable to most Americans.

As that formula for American power emerged in the fall of 1945, the meanings of the Holocaust and Hiroshima coalesced, to take their place alongside the war's other great symbol, Pearl Harbor. Those events dictated no single course for Americans: pacifists, advocates of world government, isolationists, champions of preparedness, and others could deploy them to their respective purposes. As interpreted, they sometimes carried conflicting meanings—for some at least, Pearl Harbor had justified racial vengeance, while the Holocaust demonstrated its ultimate horrors. They could also be trivialized: "By 1947, the Manhattan telephone directory listed forty-give businesses that appropriated the magic word, including the Atomic Undergarment Company."[108] Nonetheless, they all surged to national attention at the close of the war, when Pearl Harbor became the object of a widely noticed congressional investigation.

As many Americans interpreted these events, they had much in common. All three were read as signs of the radical discontinuity of this war from the past. Precedents for them, processes leading to them, the historical background of them—earlier surprise attacks, earlier episodes of genocide, the long escalation of aerial bombing—were largely forgotten. History, it seemed, had been sundered, humankind had begun a new era. The sense of rupture was most emphatic in reactions to the atomic bomb. As "a blinding, shattering force," its advent ranked only "with the discovery of fire, and the discovery of agriculture," according to Stuart Chase. The "Atomic Age" had begun, announced *Life*. "The final crisis in human history had come," wrote one minister.[109] Pearl Harbor and Nazi genocide elicited a similar if less pointed sense of rupture.

Shock was heightened by contemporary focus on technological novelty: on the stunning distance traveled and surprise achieved by Japanese aircraft, on the mechanized efficiency of Nazi death camps, on the otherworldly power of the bomb and its radiation. Understandable, that focus nonetheless slighted the political, moral, and institutional forces behind these acts—both *their* novelty and their historical roots.

Americans also continued to render these events in a highly abstract or generalized fashion, seeing them as indicative of the evil of war in almost a generic sense, one transcending a particular nation's agency or a particular people's fate. Even as he took pride in American achievement, Truman downplayed the bomb as an American invention: "Providence" had denied it to the Germans; "having found the bomb [as if almost by accident] we have used it."[110] Hence, too, disparate events would become linked in language: "holocaust," a term quickly applied by some to Hiroshima, later also became a term for Nazi genocide, suggesting that these different horrors had something fundamental in common. Technology, too, seemed to cut across national and ideological boundaries, even to lie behind human control. What stretched ahead was "science, the endless frontier" (as Vannevar Bush titled an important 1945 report), as if the disembodied force of science was moving nations to the abyss of extinction (or to peaks of fulfillment).

This abstract formulation of meanings was in some ways naive or expedient: it obscured Nazi anti-Semitism, facilitated American embrace of West Germany in the Cold War, and lent inevitability to American development and use of the bomb. But it also emphasized just what FDR and others had earlier asserted about national security—that the peril to American safety was fundamental and permanent, rooted in inescapable changes in technology and warfare to which the United States was compelled to respond, not just in the transient threats of particular nations.

The resulting fear and insecurity were evident in how Americans imagined the future of war. Few could see war taking any form but total, global conflict: the next war would be a repeat, if far more cataclysmic, of World War II, as if the evolution of war had reached a conclusion. Imagining any other war, anything between world peace and world destruction, became difficult. This outlook was evident in the military's postwar plans to reassemble a mass World War II–style army, wage epic naval campaigns once again, girdle the globe with bombers carrying atomic weapons, and launch a nuclear assault on Soviet cities in the event that Moscow "initiated aggression" or indicated that it was "imminent."[111]

Of course, armed forces routinely model the future on their current experience. More surprising, their opponents often did likewise. The new *Bulletin of the Atomic Scientists,* published by scientists and intellectuals critical of the nation's postwar nuclear policy, introduced its famous "doomsday" clock with its hand set a few minutes before the midnight of nuclear destruction, a symbol (one critic later wrote) that validated "the premise of the threat—of nuclear holocaust, of World War III." (Other voices also employed the metaphor: one fundamentalist periodical saw "the hands of the clock of Bible prophecy . . . moving onward and upward to the time when it must strike—the midnight hour.") The anxiety about another world war was hardly misplaced, but it overrode awareness of warfare's possible changes and divergent forms. Nor did later experience much alter expectations. Colonial wars in Asia and civil war in China late in the 1940s, the Korean War in 1950, the busy record of communist subversion: most Americans, policymakers in particular, tended to regarded them all as steps along, or minor diversions from, the path to total war.[112]

Notions of total war and images of its most shocking events had something else in common: even as they emphasized the nation's new vulnerability to attack, they also evoked its lingering remoteness from war. Pearl Harbor, Hiroshima, and the Holocaust all happened far from continental America. They were known to most Americans only through verbal and visual images of what happened there (those of atomic destruction heavily censored for decades by the American government), or of what *might* happen to the United States. Such images implied what the nation had escaped, the unique condition that Americans feared to lose and longed to retain. Stuart Chase wanted American and world leaders to witness first-hand an atomic blast, and all others to see films and photographs of Hiroshima and Nagasaki: "We must constantly be *shocked* into awareness—as when lightning strikes close by." John Hersey's famous written account, *Hiroshima* (1946), was celebrated for providing "the means to *see* what even pictures could not reveal," as one historian explains its impact.[113] Texts like Hersey's and symbols like the mushroom cloud substituted for realities which Americans could only understand second-hand. They operated both to challenge and to reinforce a sense that the nation still was insulated from the devastation of modern war.

Images of past and future mass destruction did underwrite militarization, but given their abstract or vicarious quality, they gave it little specific shape, only adding to the flux and uncertainty in politics and institutions. With militarization geared to grand historical changes, to charged but weightless symbols, to drastic alternatives of doomsday or deliverance, it was at once urgent and directionless. The resulting confusion did not prevent continued militarization but did help make it partial, erratic, sometimes secret, and hard to grasp. Thus, while American leaders placed a premium on their atomic clout and scientists worked to enhance it, manufacture of atomic bombs almost halted and the air force did little to prepare for delivering them. While universal military training failed in Congress, conscription was temporarily (so it seemed) renewed. While the American government helped to prosecute Nazi war criminals, the American armed forces secretly scrambled to capture Nazi scientists and technology. The list could go on—of secret and public initiatives taken, of others left to languish. There was not much coherence to it. Insofar as these untidy initiatives helped to make America a global policeman, that was not clear in 1945 and 1946, especially since leaders cried out that demobilization was turning the American giant into a pygmy.

It may well be that Americans prefer their great changes in war and foreign policy to emerge piecemeal, with the grand labels that give them coherence only coming later. Roosevelt announced a "New Deal" even before he knew its contents, but no such label attended the militarization developing during and after World War II, either from defenders or detractors. Even a coherent statement of national policy came only in 1950, its contents partly secret long after that year. In the late 1940s, only the term "Cold War" imparted some coherence to the changes underway, and "containment" to the specific policies undertaken, and those terms hardly captured the full breadth of the changes.

The reluctance to spell out the course the United States took after victory seems utterly understandable, given the flux at home and abroad and the shock felt in response to the war's final events. At the same time, that hesitation, like much else during the 1940s, allowed militarization to proceed—poorly understood, raggedly debated, inadequately acknowledged. As John Gillis describes America's militarization: if "the old militarism glorified war but often failed to prepare for it, the emerging militarization process intensified the preparation while concealing its purposes and obscuring its consequences."[114]

By the same token, however, the terms justifying militarization left space for challenging it. Because it was cast as a response to external threats and global changes in technology and politics, the possibility remained to reverse its course. Eager militarists would have grasped military power for its own sake or for the conquests it made possible. Reluctant warriors—which was how most Americans saw themselves—presumably wished to shelve their arms if threats could be subdued, technology controlled, international relations stabilized. If there was hypocrisy in that view—a denial of attractions to military power and hegemony—it also left open a different course. The legitimacy granted America's militarization was both powerful and tenuous: Americans felt they *had* to accept it, but they presumably wished to abandon its burdens as soon as possible. For decades after 1945, American leaders rarely thought that moment was imminent, but other Americans had sanction to search for it.

CONSOLIDATION, 1945–1953

Transition

With the war over, "its backwash smears over us," wrote journalist John Gunther in 1946, as the nation succumbed "to greed, fear, ineptitude, fumbling." Popular, prolific, and rarely profound, Gunther nonetheless caught Americans' quarrelsome, anxious mood and asked biting questions about its meaning. Do the nation's strife and lack of vision "show that, to become efficient, this country needs the stimulus of war? Does it mean that 295,000 Americans have to be killed in order to give us true effectiveness as a nation? Were the dead no more than bait?" The nation's self-image as the last bastion of freedom would mean little, Gunther worried, "until the country [learned] better to manage its own peacetime affairs."[1]

National leaders gave him cause to worry. When strikes gripped steel, automotive plants, coal mining, and railroads, wartime reflexes jerked into action. Within one year, Truman had the government seize coal mines, railroads, meat-packing plants, oil refineries, even the Great Lakes Towing Company. When railroad workers defied a government order in May 1946, he threatened to draft them into the army and penned a bellicose speech to Congress. Wartime strikes had been "worse than bullets in the back to our soldiers"—by implication, so were the postwar strikes—and Truman wanted his "comrades in arms" who had "fought the battles to save the nation just as I did twenty-five years ago" to join him in defeating "Communist" labor leaders "and the Russian senators and representatives." It was time to "hang a few traitors . . . , tell Russia where to get off and make the United Nations work."[2]

Notorious for letting off steam in letters never mailed and speeches never uttered, Truman by no means always turned his invective into policy. With the railroad strike settled just as he began speaking, his inflammatory comments were never delivered and the bill to draft workers never passed Congress (among other things, conservatives feared that it would also allow corporation executives to be drafted). Still, the impulse to apply wartime reflexes to postwar problems was widespread. Clark Clifford, Truman's key aide, worried that a

President without the power to subdue labor could hardly square off against Stalin and "deal with the darkening world situation." Truman's enemies could play a similar game. The American Medical Association branded his plan for national health insurance "the kind of regimentation that led to totalitarianism in Germany." Worried about such talk, Eleanor Roosevelt gently chided Truman about the danger of slipping, "because of the difficulties of our peace-time situation, into a military way of thinking." She might have cautioned many other Americans as well.[3]

Some of the pinched and bitter mood of 1946 soon dissipated, as the great strikes were settled (or crushed), as restless veterans and war workers found new niches, and as unexpected prosperity blessed the nation. Gunther's questions nonetheless remained appropriate, hinting at one reason why militarization would become consolidated in the coming years. In the wake of the vapid materialism of the 1920s and the economic desperation of the 1930s, World War II *had* brought Americans prosperity, purpose, and vigorous national government. At the same time, however, it had left unresolved the problem that Roosevelt had artfully finessed: how government could achieve the legitimacy to foster prosperity and purpose in peacetime. First as model and metaphor under the New Deal, and then as arena of action, war had provided temporary solutions. In 1946, alternative solutions were unclear and contested. The solutions finally chosen made permanent many of the militarized features of American life and politics improvised during the 1930s and World War II. War—as deed or state of mind or model, as horror to be contemplated, deterred, or waged—moved to the center of American political culture in a more lasting way.

Several forces drove this process: a chaotic international system that invited the rise of Soviet and American power and the clash between the two; the sense of American vulnerability to the perils of modern war; the chronic inability of national government to act "save in war or its surrogate"; and the legacy of World War II, in which the nation had found its greatest triumph and a model for its future. The Cold War, and the decisions by American leaders to wage it, catalyzed these forces and drew them together into a powerful ideological configuration. National leaders set the pace by offering a rhetoric of peril, by consolidating the wartime apparatus of national security, by plunging ahead in the arms race, and by confronting communism and Soviet power. Their leading role was underlined by their persistence in the face of evident reluctance or disinterest among war-weary Americans.

The Cold War did not alone *cause* these developments. Because it so consumed national energies and went on so long, however, it obscured the process of militarization, making the latter seem a response to the Cold War rather than its antecedent (and therefore destined to wither away should the Cold War end). To be sure, the pace and scale of that process were often keyed to the Cold War's dynamics: American armed forces shrank drastically after 1945, and only in 1950, in response to a perceived escalation in Soviet power and pressure, did force levels, defense budgets, and the apparatus of national security take on their full Cold War dimensions. From another vantage point, however, that gradual course marked the inevitable growing pains of militarization as much as the Cold War's dynamics. (Much the same notion of fitful and reactive advances can, after all, also be applied to Soviet behavior: Stalinization of Eastern Europe did not emerge full-blown in 1945, when Soviet armies first provided the opportunity, but in stages over the next four years linked closely to the consolidation of American power in Europe, in a classic action/reaction syndrome.) Of course, militarization required time to overcome resistance, crystallize objectives, and identify threats. But five years to consolidate the process—or a decade, if one dates its start from 1940 or so—was a remarkably brief time for a great nation to complete such a historic change.

Moreover, much that emerged by 1950 had been planned, desired, or foreseen by 1945, before the Soviet Union became the galvanizing focus of American leaders. Already by then those leaders sought to disseminate an ideology of preparedness, to forge a permanent military-industrial-scientific establishment, to reorganize the armed forces, to institute a permanent system of universal training, to acquire far-flung military bases, to occupy defeated enemies with American forces, to retain a monopoly of atomic weapons, and to create a high-tech American Pax Aeronautica. That they did not know quite how or when they would achieve these objectives, that they did not achieve them all, that they quarreled about how to do so and about the merits of other forms of power—all that seems unsurprising regarding the fulfillment of grand but necessarily inchoate designs.

American military power also helped to underwrite an American imperium, but, understandably, empire was as hard to recognize as militarization. After all, America's postwar empire rested little on territorial acquisition, plunder, or brute force, although more than most Americans cared to admit. Instead, it was maintained through consensual arrangements with allies and clients that often prodded the United States to exercise more power or sometimes defied that power. Above all, measured against crude Soviet aggression, American policy seemed reactive and American ideals lofty. In short, it hardly seemed like empire, at least not of the sort that European powers once amassed. Perhaps, say historians fine-tuning the language, it was only "consensual hegemony" or "empire by consent," at least in Western Europe: "the American 'Empire' in Germany was less imperial than federal" and West Germany was "more like a state such as California or Illinois than . . . a colony or protectorate." The "preponderance of power" Americans sought, argues another historian, "did not mean domination," only the creation of "a world environment hospitable to U.S. interests and values."[4]

Even put that way, however, the ambition was grand, and the results of it resembled other empires in striking ways. "Of course, every empire defines its

role as defensive," Charles Maier has noted.[5] In that way, in the riches generated for the imperial center, in the universalist claims for American ideals, in
the racial or gendered language used to describe nonwhite peoples, in the resentments it aroused, and above all in the reach of its military power, the
United States after World War II achieved much of the reality and many of the
trappings of empire. Precisely how much seems a matter only for quibbling.

In the late 1940s, Americans could only dimly grasp the militarization and
empire building at work. For good reason, they still often looked to the past,
worrying about renewed economic woes and refighting old battles over the
New Deal, labor, and capital. Their dominant codewords suggested modest,
not messianic, aspirations. "Security," economic and national, was the word
most often enshrined in official pronouncements, its neutral tone and defensive
connotation making it a proven "consensus-builder" and belying the ambitious thrust of American policies.[6] National leaders did also speak of grave
challenge and permanent change, but the daily mood was one of crisis and improvisation. That mood was not only how most Americans experienced the period but what helped them to endure and tolerate the changes they were experiencing. Given a script, they might well have rejected it.

The Militarization of American Policy

On February 9, 1946, Joseph Stalin delivered a speech which set Washington
abuzz. He praised the wartime antifascist alliance but also stressed development of heavy industry to support Soviet reconstruction and armed strength.
Given its mixed messages, Stalin's speech drew a surprisingly alarmed response from American pundits and officials. It was "the declaration of World
War III," Justice William Douglas told Navy Secretary James Forrestal, a
zealous Cold Warrior who thoroughly agreed. Walter Lippmann believed that
since Stalin had decided "to make military power his first objective, we are
forced to make a corresponding decision." Only Commerce Secretary Henry
Wallace noted that, given the near global reach of American military bases, "we
were challenging him and his speech was taking up the challenge."[7]

The dramatic month after Stalin's speech exposed nearly every codeword,
reflex, concept, and personality that would dominate the American outlook
early in the Cold War. Days later, the story broke of Soviet espionage agents
seeking American atomic secrets. Truman condemned "appeasement" of the
Soviet Union, while GOP leaders condemned him for allowing it (as Sen. Arthur Vandenberg put it privately, Secretary of State Jimmy Byrnes had been
"loitering around Munich"). From Moscow, George Kennan sent his influential
"long telegram" outlining a rationale and strategy for containment of the Soviet
Union. On March 5, Churchill issued his famous warning of an "iron curtain"
descending on Europe, asking the English-speaking peoples to reverse the situation by relying on the bomb that "God has willed" them. Soviet pressure on

Turkey to share control of the Black Sea straits led Forrestal to propose sending the battleship *Missouri* and a naval task force there.[8]

Perhaps the Cold War had not yet begun (historians disagree about the key date, as if a complex and incremental struggle could be traced to one moment). There was as yet no formal American Cold War "policy," no naval task force reached Turkey for another six months, and Truman still waxed hot and cold on the Soviets.

But the essentials of American leaders' outlook were becoming evident. The new struggle was largely the old one against totalitarians in new guise—the notion of Stalinism as "red fascism" tightened the imaginative linkage. "The Soviet Union's assault upon the West," argued one State Department official in 1947, "is at about the stage of Hitler's maneuvering into Czechoslovakia." And since it was, the mistakes of the 1930s had to be averted and the lessons of World War II acted upon. American leaders soon repeated many of the words and actions that preceded Pearl Harbor—what was novel in 1940 was precedent by 1946—albeit without benefit of FDR's masterful rhetoric, and with the fervent hope to avert the final cataclysm. Although all instruments of power had to be deployed, military force seemed critical, less because Stalin was about to unleash his armies (privately, few Washington insiders thought so) than because he allegedly (like Hitler) understood no other form of power. "Unless Russia is faced with an iron fist and strong language," Truman thought, "another war is in the making." If an armed America resulted, it hardly seemed by American choice; as Lippmann said, "we are forced to make a corresponding decision."[9]

To be sure, that outlook was hardly the sole cause of the Cold War. Drastic changes in the structure and modes of power within the international system probably made Soviet-American conflict in some form inevitable. So much had the war damaged other major powers that the resulting "vacuum" of power (as contemporaries often called it) invited Soviet and American power to flow outward. Both had enormous power—although on balance the advantage lay with the United States—as well as global aspirations. Both also possessed the recent historical experience, and the plausibly threatening enemy, to cast those aspirations sincerely in defensive terms, as Stalin did in his brutal subjugation of Eastern Europe and Truman did in America's more subtle deployment of power.

Nor did American leaders focus only on the Soviet threat. They knew that diverse American interests hardly all fit within the Cold War framework. Their supreme achievement under Truman, the Marshall Plan to aid Western Europe, was shaped in part by humanitarian motives, cultural affinities, and economic anxieties—a prostrate Europe dragged down the American economy as well as inviting Soviet aggrandizement. Likewise, their intricate policy of "dual containment" in Europe was "designed to keep both the Soviet Union and Germany from dominating the Continent." Distrust of both those powers led American leaders to push for Germany's division and the Federal Republic's incorporation into the Western alliance, while anticommunism led them "to a deplorable series of compromises with the legacies of Nazism," including repatriation to the United States of German scientists associated with the Nazi regime. But again the motives were complex: those scientists were snatched in order to benefit American scientific and corporate interests as well as American military power, to deny Germany the capacity to rearm, to beat out friends who seemed to be getting the jump on the United States (as one official complained, "We have caught the French red-handed again stealing scientists out of our zone."), and only gradually to wage the Cold War on another front. Even within the Cold War framework, American leaders recognized differences of interest among communist nations more than their public images of a monolithic enemy acknowledged.[10]

Still, the American outlook did much to turn an inevitable rivalry into a bitter Cold War and to strengthen the forces of militarization. For all the complexity with which American leaders privately calculated American interests and enemy threats, they chose to "scare hell out of the American people" in presenting the Truman Doctrine in 1947, to highlight the communist menace in defending the Marshall Plan, to deploy a language of Manichean struggle ("Nearly every nation must choose between alternative ways of life," announced Truman), and to pour out a stream of analogies to World War II and dire warnings about impending military cataclysm.[11] That is, they subsumed diverse interests and diverse modes of power under the grand themes of Cold War, containment, and World War III—especially in public, but in private as well.

Meanwhile, the militarization of American policy and the escalation of the Cold War proceeded in confusing fits and starts. The panic shown in the late winter of 1946 soon abated, though Soviet-American negotiations on Eastern Europe and control of atomic weapons kept the pot boiling. Panic returned a year later, when British withdrawal from Greece and Turkey prompted the Truman Doctrine, with its open-ended promise "to support free peoples who are resisting attempted subjugation."[12] Over the following year, the Marshall Plan took shape, signed by Truman on April 3, 1948, and providing $12.4 billion to Western Europe over the next four years. By then, the drumbeat of crises and initiatives was relentless. In February 1948, a Communist coup in Czechoslovakia furthered the Stalinization of Eastern Europe. An ensuing war scare in March, complete with loose talk of a Soviet invasion of Western Europe, was in part manufactured by Washington officials in order to force Congress to approve the Marshall Plan, reinstate conscription, and step up defense spending. But the coup did touch a raw American nerve, validating fears of totalitarian aggression and Western weakness embodied in powerful images of Munich and appeasement: had not Hitler's triumph over the Czechs ten years before led to world war? A few months later, as West Germany's revival proceeded under American auspices, the Soviets launched a blockade of West Berlin, the Anglo-French-American zone deep within Communist East Germany. A new war scare gave way to the mighty spectacle of the American airlift that nurtured West Berlin until the Soviets lifted the blockade in May 1949. By then, the North Atlantic Treaty Organization, designed to provide military and political security to Western Europe, was being finalized. Months later two more blows struck: the Soviets exploded an atomic bomb and Chinese communists completed their rout of Chiang Kai-shek's Nationalists.

The Cold War in Europe offered Americans a clear and apparently familiar story line: once again, as in the 1930s, their cultural cousins were in desperate straits facing a totalitarian enemy. The Cold War in Asia offered few such satisfactions. The American vision of Japan's place in that struggle did become clear: it was to be an anticommunist bastion, demilitarized (except for American forces based there) but anchoring its own prosperity and that of East Asia through mutual trade and American assistance. Nothing else in Asia seemed as obvious. Many Americans sympathized with the anticolonial revolts sweeping Asia—in British India, the Dutch East Indies, French Indochina, and elsewhere—but since they were carried out against America's Western European allies, they raised tough questions. Should the United States help its allies cling to their empires and thereby alienate the subject peoples whose allegiance in the Cold War it also sought? Or should it oppose its allies' efforts and thereby risking alienating *them*? With regard to Indochina, Washington found no satisfactory answer to those questions. China confounded and divided Americans even more. When Truman and Secretary of State Marshall prudently limited American aid to the Chinese Nationalists fighting communists for control of the nation, they also diluted the moral force of American anticommunism. Did it apply only where victory was relatively easy, as in Europe? Did their China policy, Republicans charged, constitute appeasement or something worse, traceable to treasonous "giveaways" by Roosevelt at Yalta?

No arena of policy made the administration more vulnerable, and none was more vexing, than that involving Asia. Several factors added to the rancor and confusion. The line between "communist" and "noncommunist" forces—fairly sharp in Europe, from which most Americans drew their understanding of the Cold War—was blurry at best in Asia's struggles, where nationalism and anticolonialism loomed so large. Alliances between Moscow and Asian communists were easily exaggerated; they were shaky even to the communists involved. Few Americans were of Asian background, and Americans' affinity to and experience of Asia were shallow, so that they readily reduced diverse peoples to a monolithic, devious horde. Nor had its military and political actions in World War II given the United States the intimate knowledge and powerful positions acquired in Europe: in the Pacific war, the apt name for it from an American vantage point, the country's major operations had been confined largely to the perimeter of Asia.

The Truman administration responded to developments there and to Soviet power in Europe with policies that hardly seemed the stuff of militarization to most observers. Congress reinstituted military conscription, but on a yearly basis and without the system of universal training many leaders wanted. The National Security Act of 1947 elaborated and consolidated the institutional apparatus of militarization, but it was accompanied by bitter conflict that even seemed to devour its primary architect (James Forrestal, the first secretary of defense, committed suicide). What often grabbed headlines was not the scale of this new apparatus but instead the spectacle of armed forces fighting over budgets, forces, and missions. The climax came in a "revolt of the admirals," furious when Defense Secretary Louis Johnson canceled a supercarrier in favor of funding the air force's B-36, a huge hauler of atomic bombs powered by six-piston motors (with jets soon added). To journalists covering these squabbles and politicians weighing in on them, little of this looked like the forward march of militarization, certainly not the impulse of military men to cling to familiar bureaucratic turf, older forms of weaponry, and past wars as models. Instead, it just looked like a mess.

Compounding the image of military debilitation was the swift shrinkage of American forces after V-J Day and the dubious methods used to measure their strength. American leaders decried an apparent collapse of usable power as the 12 million personnel in uniform at the war's end shrank to fewer than 1.6 million by 1947. With most of those tied down in occupation, logistical, and training duties, combat-ready forces were few. To insiders privy to secret information, even America's ultimate weapon seemed frail: only nine atomic bombs were available as of June 1946 and fifty-three two years later, the air force was poorly equipped and trained to carry them, and no clear strategy governed their use, much less the full spectrum of American military power. Fiscal watchdogs, who included Truman himself and Republicans fretting about American impotence, kept defense budgets low, at least in the eyes of military officials.

Amid all this, the broader course of militarization was hard to fathom (or easy to ignore). Rarely did politicians or pundits compare American demobilization to the Soviet Union's, which was only somewhat less drastic. Their baseline was the mammoth wartime force, not prewar peacetime standards, as if history were irrelevant unless it yielded dire warnings about the future. Even a force of 1.6 million personnel was five times larger than its prewar counterpart of the mid-1930s. Defense spending, earlier about 15 percent of the federal budget and 1.5 percent of GNP, now seized one-third of the former and 5 percent of GNP—excluding swollen costs of debt service, veterans' programs, aid to allies, and the like. Likewise, the defense system could do far more after World War II than before: assume occupation duties of unprecedented scale and geographic range, maintain far-flung bases, produce nuclear weapons, churn out new bombers and jet fighters, and develop more advanced weapons. Despite a shortage of combat-ready forces, it could swing into action with striking speed and force, as it did in the Berlin airlift in 1948 and Korea in 1950.

It also had unprecedented legal and political underpinnings. With the brief exception of 1940, the United States now had its first peacetime draft. NATO marked an extraordinary departure from American traditions: informal alliances had proceeded American entry into both world wars, but this alliance involved a legally binding treaty ratified by the Senate. The Central Intelligence Agency, created in 1947, was granted constitutionally dubious powers of secrecy and action, and soon exceeded those powers. Most important, here was a system that American leaders were willing to use and increasingly preferred over diplomacy. The United States hardly disarmed after 1945. The growth of its military power simply lagged behind an even more striking escalation in the missions its leaders called on it to fill.

Containment and militarization also met resistance, as the clamor for rapid demobilization had made clear. In October 1945, only 7 percent of Americans regarded foreign problems as the "most vital" ones facing the country (Forrestal that month thought the country was "going back to bed at a frightening rate" and thereby opening the way for "the coming of World War III"). Public opinion toward the Soviets, and toward the Truman administration for being too "soft" on them, soon turned negative, yet in 1947 the State Department still found that 67 percent of Americans thought the UN "the best chance for peace" and only 28 percent approved of "trying to stay ahead of the Russians by building atomic bombs." One State Department official compared the situation to that before Pearl Harbor: "powerlessness on the part of the government to act because of Congressional or public unawareness of the danger or cost of inaction." By 1948, polls found most Americans worried about the Soviets, but also 63 percent "wanting a meeting with Stalin or some other bold stroke to reduce the danger of war."[13] Americans were no uniform mass; race, religion, and other factors sorted them out. Catholics, for example, especially those of Eastern European background, were keen on an anti-Soviet policy. Still, that mysterious entity, "public opinion," rallied slowly to the cause. Many Americans distrusted the Soviet Union and wanted to see it knocked around but were unwilling to pay a great price to do so.

Administration officials, casting themselves as cosmopolitan realists who grasped the enemy's threat to America, interpreted indifference to their Cold War policies as signs of a parochial, uneducated public opinion. Accordingly, they sought to manipulate it—viewing the Truman Doctrine, for example, as "the opening gun in a campaign to bring people up to [the] realization that the war isn't over by any means," in Clark Clifford's words. Ironically, they felt they could instruct Americans in global realities only by distorting them, although they also sought to bank the fires of anticommunism they stoked, lest "the hysterical sort of anti-Communism" get out of control, as George Kennan worried. Their elitist approach to public opinion gained credence from writers and scholars who reacted to Hitler's manipulation of the German masses by emphasizing the gullibility and ignorance of ordinary people. As Richard Barnet has summed up their outlook, "To encourage hope based on the capacity of the average citizen to govern was to promote dangerous illusions, for Hitler and Stalin demonstrated how easily populist yearnings turn into nightmares."[14]

The notion of level-headed elites pitted against volatile masses was misleading, however, for leaders too were prey to visceral instincts and abrupt changes of mood. They could panic and talk of initiating atomic war, or (as with Forrestal) become paranoid about Jews, communists, or other alleged enemies. Having set one course, they could repudiate it: Kennan spent much of his remaining career disputing implications in his containment policy that others thought self-evident. Then too, some, like Kennan, were bundles of ethnic and class prejudice who loathed much of the society they presumably defended. On occasion, they also descended to crude repression and red-baiting. Intelligent, capable men, they nonetheless succeeded in shaping public opinion because of their power more than their superior rationality.

Indeed, the very claim of that rationality rested on notions of class, race, and gender dominant among policymakers at this juncture. These leaders tended to regard ordinary Americans much as they perceived women and nonwhite peoples—as "emotional, irrational, irresponsible, unbusinesslike, unstable, and childlike," or, in the case of Hindu men, as passive, "effete," or homosexual. Secretary of State John Foster Dulles, for example, believed that India's leaders had "an almost feminine hypersensitiveness with respect to the prestige of their country" (whereas Western observers often thought "Indian women were heartless, domineering, and emasculating"). Whether foreign or American, such people, American leaders assumed, needed the tutelage of their patriarchal authority, though less so if they were staunchly anticommunist—Asian leaders in that mold were assigned a more virile, masculine, aggressive image.[15]

That outlook in turn rationalized the leaders' authority over precisely those groups generating much of the opposition to American policy: feminist peace organizations, African-Americans like Paul Robeson, neutral leaders like Indian prime minister Jawaharlal Nehru, and rebellious colonized populations abroad challenging America's alliance with Europe's imperial powers. The celebration in 1940s American culture of male authority, family order, and "traditional" women's roles reinforced the policy elite's role as a wise, fatherly overseer to dependent, unruly, and uninformed peoples at home and abroad. To be sure, their patriarchal view was hardly held by them alone, since the global experience of war in the 1940s reinforced male authority in many settings; among Americans, peace activism and opposition to policymaking elites were perhaps more male-dominated early in the Cold War than at any time in the century, and no more male and masculinist elite could be found than the Soviet Union's. Still, policymakers' sense of class, racial, and gender hierarchies helped to forge their posture of superior wisdom and authority.

Power and manipulation did not, however, alone throttle resistance to national policies, for the resistance itself was diffuse and divided. As during 1940–41, it was sustained by two broad political forces that shared little but their resistance. The conservative wing, dominated by Republicans like Sen. Robert Taft, was nationalist, unilateralist, and "isolationist" in the view of the foreign policy establishment. The other source of resistance consisted of leftists and disaffected liberal Democrats, led by Henry Wallace after Truman fired him from the Cabinet in 1946 and through his quixotic Progressive Party campaign for the presidency in 1948.

Not only could the opposition camps cooperate little with each other, but each was compromised on its own terms. Taft strenuously criticized the over-extension and militarization of American policy, the growth of entangling alliances, the President's usurpation of power in war and foreign policy, and, on occasion, how all those trends worsened Soviet-American conflict. Mindful of plans "to maintain a force so preponderant that none shall dare attack us," Taft warned that "potential power over other nations, however benevolent its purposes, leads inevitably to imperialism." Only reluctantly did he vote for NATO after promises (soon repudiated) from Secretary of State Dean Acheson that West Germany would remain disarmed and that no "substantial" American force would go to Europe. But anticommunism and political opportunism also tempted conservatives to beat up on the Truman administration for failing to defend America and stop communism in Asia—as noted pacifist A. J. Muste remarked, "For isolationists these Americans do certainly get around." And as in 1940, conservatives also embraced the central component of American power—a formidable air force, now carrying atomic weapons—since it appealed to their vision of American power unfettered by alliances and the coercive apparatus of mass armies. For the Truman administration, conservatives were a mighty nuisance but not a serious obstacle.[16]

Among leftists, who offered many of the same arguments made by conservatives, the main problem was the ease with which Cold Warriors could link them ideologically to communism and the Soviet Union (the presence of real Communists in the Progressive party did not help). Their position now resembled that of FDR's right-wing foes before Pearl Harbor, who had been compromised by their alleged affinities to fascism. Subject to vicious red-baiting, leftists and pacifists quarreled among themselves and mustered little effective opposition to administration policies after 1948.

Opposition weakness also testified to the power of the national security paradigm and the memory of World War II. Concepts of "totalitarianism" and "red fascism" conflated the emerging struggle with the one just won, as did the drumbeat of comparisons between Stalin and Hitler, between "appeasement" in 1938 and "weakness" in 1948, and between Pearl Harbors past and prospective. With defeat only narrowly averted in the last war, with new weapons only worsening the nation's vulnerability, with the next war sure to allow no time to mobilize, with a new enemy only more insidious than the last one, what Americans could resist the rush to arm their nation and confront the enemy? They could, as some did eloquently, question the means and consequences of doing so. Far fewer could challenge the reigning paradigm and its analogies to World War II, especially since those analogies hinted at a silver lining in the dark clouds of global struggle: if a display of force could have stopped Hitler before World War II, then a display of will might now bring victory and avert war. Success required not a rash plunge into war but a steady capacity and willingness to risk war—or even just the appearance thereof.

All these currents of mood and policy surfaced in most hyperbolic form in debate over nuclear weapons. The sheer scale and depth of that debate testified to the seriousness with which Americans took the issue (a stunning 98 percent of them knew of the atomic bomb after Hiroshima). Just as strikingly, however, they thought of the bomb as an instrument of their own potential destruction. For all their pride in American achievement, for all their nation's lead in this new technology, they imagined their imminent doom. Memories of World War II, stories of communist espionage, graphic presentations of what nuclear attack would do to American cities, and then news that Stalin had his own atomic weapon all reinforced the imagined peril and the paradigm of national security.

Of course, that sense of peril also drove Americans to consider alternatives to an arms race. Proposals emerged from crusading world federalists like Norman Cousins, thoughtful intellectuals like Stuart Chase, agonized scientists like Robert Oppenheimer, hard-headed statesmen like Henry L. Stimson, and from the administration, whose plan for international control of atomic energy was both bold and self-interested. Still, atomic peril was also paralyzing. Those who warned darkly of it wanted to provoke political activism, but their binary depiction of alternatives—"world state or world doom," as journalist Max Lerner put it—did not chart an apparent practical course between utopian and unthinkable outcomes. It fostered a fatalistic belief in technological determinism, as if the bomb rather than people determined the world's course, and a deep fear whose focus could be transferred from the bomb to the Soviets—with the bomb so horrific, how terrible was the prospect if Moscow perfected it? With "fear of the Russians" replacing "fear of the bomb," the "dread destroyer of 1945 had become the shield of the Republic by 1950."[17]

The bomb was already emerging as such a shield in national strategy before 1950. Military leaders envisioned the nuclear obliteration of the Soviet Union at the start of the next war. A full statement of strategy was slow to emerge, prey to the conflicts among the armed forces, and strategy went beyond the bomb, embracing, as in World War II, a capacity to mobilize quickly for general war and to assist allies in bearing the burden of war as much as possible.

But the bomb was the heart of the matter, and with it intractable dilemmas about how to base grand strategy on it, as the nation's nuclear omnipotence constantly seemed to yield its nuclear impotence. American and Western European leaders recognized that actual use of nuclear weapons might destroy much that was to be defended. As a French premier memorably put it, although the United States might once again liberate Europe, "the next time you probably would be liberating a corpse." "One use of it [the nuclear sanction] will be fatally too many," the strategist Bernard Brodie later noted.[18] Hence, although use of the atomic weapon and even a "preventive" nuclear attack against the Soviet Union tempted some leaders, their stress was on deterrence. The bomb, like America's whole system of arms and alliances, was meant to dissuade enemies from unleashing war and convince them of America's will to respond. Deterrence hardly resolved much, however, especially once the Kremlin acquired nuclear weapons: was it credible to threaten it with nuclear retaliation if the ensuing war might destroy the United States or its allies? Yet if the threat was not credible, what use did America's atomic weapons have, and what risk did the country run of committing the fatal error of "appeasement"?

Haunted by such questions, American leaders kept looking to the atomic weapon to make a political or psychological impression on the enemy, since its practical use in war was so doubtful. During the Berlin crisis, for example, the Truman administration leaked word that sixty B-29s were being sent to England, hinting that they could wage nuclear war. Though they carried no atomic weapons, the bluff went forward in order to intimidate Moscow and set a precedent for a permanent American nuclear force in Europe. In such ways, nuclear policy kept slipping deeper into the murky, unmeasurable realm of morale and impressions.

That realm governed the Truman administration's decision, finalized in January 1950, to make a hydrogen bomb. It recognized the danger of further escalating the arms race and the absence of any compelling military reason for plunging ahead, since defense officials doubted that H-bombs could do much not already possible with atomic weapons. Less tangible criteria overruled such reasons for caution. Given that the Soviets might develop the new weapon, Joint Chiefs Chairman Gen. Omar Bradley argued that "possession of a thermonuclear weapon by the USSR without such possession by the United States would be intolerable"—"profoundly demoralizing" to Americans and a "tremendous psychological boost" for the Soviet Union.[19] Thus the administration took the next step in the arms race in order to reassure Americans and allies and to avoid appearing to appease the Soviets by letting them catch up.

The rationale was as important as the decision itself. Policies based on specific capabilities and situations—the power an enemy could amass here, the army to be deployed there—might have yielded large, costly forces, yet ones of measurably specific duties. Impressing enemies and reassuring friends, on the other hand, was an open-ended task devoid of measurable criteria for judging its fulfillment: would it take fifty or five thousand nuclear weapons to complete the job? To be sure, as Cold War policymakers pointed out, morale and credibility were themselves realities of the global struggle, ones the state could hardly banish from its calculations. Yet to base decisions primarily on them risked an endless escalation in the arms race, the formation of alliances, and the spending of money. It made sense only in a world shaped by Munich and the tragedy of the 1930s, when precisely the anti-Fascists' failure to display their will seemed to have led them into war.

These dynamics of militarization reached fuller expression in the wake of the H-bomb decision, in April 1950, when the National Security Council at last offered a full statement, known as NSC-68, of national strategy. NSC-68 justified "America's assuming the role of world policeman and came close to saying that all change was directed by the Communists and should therefore be resisted." Its brief for militarization was startling—it proposed a virtual trebling of the American defense budget to $35 billion a year. Equally significant, while its authors hardly ruled out world war, they emphasized the intangibles of will, patience, and coercion. American security now seemed "to depend as much on *perceptions* of the balance of power as on what that balance actually was," leading policymakers "vastly to increase the number and variety of interests." That outlook, so expansive and so ungrounded in the calculable, gave powerful impetus to militarization.[20]

Truman ordered NSC-68 kept secret, but deliberations over it within the administration gave one more clue to the sources of militarization. Attuned to Keynesian economics, impressed by the economic lessons of World War II, the authors of NSC-68 were optimistic that rearmament was not only affordable but would foster economic growth and "a higher standard of living."[21] No more than FDR in 1940 did these men justify rearmament as a way for government to promote economic growth. National security was the rationale. But even more than Roosevelt, they were aware of the reciprocal relationship that seemed to exist between prosperity and armaments.

Like most Americans, they preferred that the bargain whereby defense stimulated growth remain tacit. To acknowledge it was to admit to one of the deepest motives for militarization. Some critics and journalists knew better. *Business Week* recognized the potent "combination of concern over tense Russian relations, and a growing fear of a rising level of unemployment here at home." *U.S. News and World Report* wrote sharply that "government planners figure that they have found the magic formula for almost endless good times . . . [the] Cold War is an automatic pump primer."[22] Such forthright characterization was rare in 1950, however. Rearmament was supposed to meet a growing peril. Prosperity seemed only the inadvertent, though welcome, by-product.

The Political Economy of Militarization

"Mr. Prima Donna, Brass Hat, Five Star MacArthur," Truman wrote in his diary on June 17, 1945. Gen. Douglas MacArthur seemed "worse than the Cabots and the Lodges—they at least talked with one another before they told God what to do. Mac tells God right off." It was one of many fulminations by Truman against MacArthur that revealed not only his feisty temper but his way of accommodating himself to the militarization of institutions—by asserting civilian control over the armed forces. Having kept the generals and admirals in check, Truman, like most Americans, did not recognize how much militarization itself proceeded. After all, he was, in James Forrestal's view, "the most rocklike example of civilian control the world has ever witnessed."[23]

The first struggle over civilian control involved nuclear weapons and energy. The War Department proposed that a commission dominated by military men hold responsibility, but scientists fearing restrictions on their work, congressmen wary of military aggrandizement, and Truman himself swung behind legislation passed in 1946 setting up a civilian Atomic Energy Commission. It was not much of a victory for civilian control, however, because it still provided for a powerful Military Liaison Committee and a web of security regulations, and even more because civilian leaders and experts served military purposes. Tensions were abundant in this "loosely federated government-industrial-military complex,"[24] a sprawling network of government laboratories, universities, and production plants run by private corporations, and the military's interest in bombs often clashed with scientists' pursuit of research and corporations' interest in nuclear energy. Still, by the 1950s massive budgets permitted all parties to pursue their goals. The AEC became a powerhouse developer of nuclear weapons operating in deep secrecy, banishing dissenters (Robert Oppenheimer in 1954), and brushing aside problems of environment and health in the testing and production of nuclear devices. The struggle over civilian control obscured how civilian elites matched the zeal of military officers in pursuing national security.

A similar outcome emerged on a larger scale from the National Security Act of 1947. Unification of the armed forces and civilian control over them prompted a protracted political battle, often focused on whether a single military chief of staff would preside over the system. Truman feared "that a chief of staff might arrogate too much power to himself and become a 'man on horseback,' an opinion widely held in Congress."[25] Therefore the new law required that the Joint Chiefs of Staff simply serve as "principal military advisers to the President and the Secretary of Defense." Only in 1949 did Congress even authorize a chairman for the JCS, which indeed remained effectively under civilian control.

Having disarmed any future "man on horseback," Congress and the administration were free to establish a wide-ranging apparatus of national security. At its core were the three armed services (the air force now independent of the army) and the Joint Chiefs, presided over by the secretary of defense. It was an ungainly structure resulting from political compromise. The much-heralded unification of the services in fact left each much autonomy. Although later reforms gave the secretary of defense more authority and staff, the services' rivalries with each other and independence from the secretary's (or Joint Chiefs') control remained endemic, to the consternation of Truman and later Presidents.

In many ways, the new law's most significant provisions involved less-noticed agencies outside the Defense Department: the National Security Resources Board, to link the services with corporations and universities; the National Security Council, to advise the President; and the Central Intelligence Agency, to "coordinate" intelligence activities. Other key agencies were already long in place (the FBI, the National Advisory Committee on Aeronautics) or separately authorized (the AEC). And beyond the governmental apparatus lay institutions closely linked to it: university and corporate laboratories; think tanks like the RAND corporation; trade and professional associations; and businesses providing products and services, from weapons to wiretapping.

However complex and evolving, the system developed by 1949 would remain largely intact for several decades. Its significance lay less in specifics than in its scale and rationale. It embodied the conviction that in an age of instant and total warfare, the vigilant nation must be constantly prepared by harnessing all its resources and linking its civilian and military institutions—indeed, obliterating the boundary between those institutions, just as the line between war and peace seemed to be disappearing. So powerful was this conviction that it drew little challenge in the late 1940s, even as countless particulars aroused strong debate.

The place of national security in the federal government swelled accordingly. Federal employment grew more than fourfold from 1932 to 1952, when it reached 2.6 million civilians (plus 3.6 million in uniform), of whom 1.3 million worked for the Defense Department and thousands more for other war-related agencies. Size alone does not always command power (the Post Office remained a huge bureaucracy, for example), but the swelling apparatus of national security slowly made a difference. For a while, with strong secretaries of state pitted against weak or short-term defense secretaries, the State Department held its own, abetted by Truman's trust in secretaries of state Marshall and Acheson. In the long run, State's place receded; even when its leaders were strong, militarized policies demanded military expertise. The defense secretaries assumed growing power and, especially in the 1950s, so did agencies like the CIA and AEC. And precisely because those agencies were too huge and labyrinthine for the White House to oversee, the compact National Security Council emerged as the President's major instrument of advice and policymaking. Nor could Congress often call the shots over this vast system. After fierce budget battles in the late 1940s, primary initiative rested with the White House and the defense agencies, while most of the time Congress (or its key committees) could only exact leverage by brokering turf wars, service rivalries, and regional conflicts, not by assessing and setting the overall budget. And despite constitutional provisions for public accountability, Congress was often in the dark, especially about the finances and activities of the AEC, the CIA, and other intelligence agencies.

Just as empire did not look imperial to most Americans, the militarized state did not look militaristic. Here was no monolith in which orders came down from a Hitler or a Politburo. Instead, the American system was complex and cumbersome, its parts often battling each other, its President and other key players sometimes baffled, its initiatives often flowing upward or sideways rather than down from the top. It operated not by sheer command alone (though taxes, conscription, repression, and secrecy did proceed) but by consensus and brokering, by contracts and laws, and in some measure by the consent of the governed. At times, as in the armed forces' backstabbing rivalries, it hardly seemed to operate at all. In many areas of their lives, it touched Americans lightly, and constitutional and political traditions, however frayed, allowed them to challenge it, as on occasion some did. Its burdens were also kept light by the nation's overwhelming abundance, which sustained unprecedented growth in both defense spending and the civilian economy. As in World War II, this potent combination of political pluralism, institutional complexity, and economic abundance proved more efficient than crude command systems.

What gave the system much of its cohesion and success was its leaders' shared outlooks, overlapping roles, and class affinities, which overrode old distinctions between "civilian" and "military" in political culture. At the center was a cohort of policymakers in departments and agencies like State, Defense, the CIA, and the AEC. They had a common background in elite eastern schools, law firms, corporations, and government. They were sometimes wealthy men (Nelson Rockefeller, Averell Harriman), often heirs to Henry L. Stimson's tradition of patrician leadership (Robert Lovett, John J. McCloy), usually veterans of FDR's administration, and only rarely products of elective politics. Cosmopolitan by virtue of business or government service, they were "a new transnational political elite," men "whose relationships and perspectives cut across national lines," though American interests came first. Pragmatic, adept at building consensus within American government and with allies, they were often deaf to their own ideological impulses. Sometimes, as with Acheson, their elitist style elicited "populist envy and rage." And yet, though Truman could snort at such men himself, they worked smoothly with him.[26]

Outside the inner circle, others lesser in rank shared much of the elite's background and outlook—diplomats like George Kennan, strategists like Bernard Brodie, and science and academic officials like James Conant and Vannevar Bush. Of these junior partners, scientists were the most prone to doubts. Fears about compromising their professional autonomy and participating in the arms race emerged from elder statesman Albert Einstein, young physicist Philip Morrison, computer genius Norbert Wiener, and (ambiguously) from Robert Oppenheimer. The doubts were valid: they "would be mobilized to support the existing order only to the extent that scientists did not themselves question that order." Most scientists, however, saw "no reason for refusing" government's help "in doing the scientific work that one would have tried to accomplish even without such help," as Louis N. Ridenour, a University of Illinois dean and air force chief scientist, put it. After all, government patronage could not be judged against an earlier standard of purity. Research universities already relied on philanthropies and corporations, the latter "at best a fickle and demanding partner," whereas the federal patron served the public weal rather than private greed, and proved less fickle and more generous. Most academic scientists and officials accepted the paramount role that government, mainly its defense agencies, now played in funding and shaping science. That role arose, it has been argued, "chiefly due to the indispensability of science-driven technologies like atomic energy and radar," but scientists did much to define indispensability in the first place and benefited enormously from its effects. In turn, they changed. The military-university-corporate alliance "defined the critical problems" for them, indeed "virtually redefined what it meant to be a scientist or an engineer"—a commitment to big science and to technique.[27]

Civilian leaders shared outlooks and duties with military leaders. Few officers were more alarmed about the Soviets and the nation's security than Forrestal; few matched physicist Edward Teller's zeal for nuclear weapons; few championed air power better than Secretary of the Air Force Stuart Symington. The rush of wartime officers into civilian government, corporate, and research posts (Gen. Walter Bedell Smith as head of the CIA, Gen. Omar Bradley as board chairman of Bulova Research Laboratories, Gen. Leslie Groves as vice president for research at Remington Rand) also eroded civil-military barriers of outlook, status, and experience. In "business circles," *Business Week* noted in 1952, "the word has gone out: Get yourself a general."[28]

As that comment indicated, the interests they defined gave ballast to the ideology of national security shared by policy elites, military officers, corporate leaders, and scientists. As they saw those interests, they ranged from the broad goal of preserving the nation's safety, abundance, and power to narrowly calculated matters—a professional's career, a university's funding, an agency's prestige, a company's profits. To most, national interests shaded off into institutional and individual ones without clear distinctions, triggering few qualms. The most famous, if often misconstrued, statement of their outlook came when Charles Wilson, former head of General Motors and defense secretary designate, said that "what was good for the country was good for General Motors and vice versa."[29] For most such men, any clash of interests involved less an individual's vertical relationship to the system than horizontal conflicts among institutions and companies fighting for power, resources, and status.

To be sure, within each group calculations varied, as business illustrated. Many companies, still wedded to free enterprise and government retrenchment, took little interest in how defense monies might sustain them or the economy, but they also did not oppose the drift in national policy as long as it avoided New Deal–type initiatives. It helped that "increased expenditures for defense, highways, and space did not displace existing private investment," though less noticed was how "defense industries absorbed large amounts of capital and large numbers of highly trained technicians at the expense of such basic industries as steel, automobiles, and oil." The way was open for firms in newer fields like electronics, aviation, and nuclear energy to forge tight links with Washington. For companies like Boeing, Du Pont, Bell Labs, and General Electric, the benefits included profits—in industries like electronics, "indirect and direct military demand accounted for as much as 70% of the total output" by the mid-1960s—plus development at government expense of new technologies adaptable to civilian markets, of inventive laboratories, and of a proficient work force. Government's role in promoting television, computers, and jet aircraft for defense purposes unlocked huge civilian markets, especially since the funds involved "exceeded by far the capacities of industry, of universities, and of private foundations." Nor were benefits confined to leading firms; new technologies spawned new firms and assisted others with few ties to defense. "We are living under a curious kind of military Keynesianism," argued historian Richard Hofstadter, "in which Mars has rushed in to fill the gap left by the decline of the market economy."[30]

Whether the result was a "power elite" running a "permanent war economy" that C. Wright Mills excoriated in 1956 is debatable. Mills himself gave the term *power elite* elasticity, seeing the tensions and gradations of status within it, and the "permanent war economy" was hardly a total war economy. Even at its postwar peak of over 10 percent of GNP during the 1950s, defense spending provided a technological cutting edge and a supplement to lagging private investment, but hardly the economic system's sole support. Later historians differ little from Mills, however, arguing that defense spending "had far-reaching impacts on the level of aggregate business activity and the patterns of investment," even though "other types of spending might have produced greater benefits for society or a greater multiplier effect in the economy." Defense spending also provided national government a key tool of economic control. And since most people saw it "as an absolute necessity in a dangerous age," it did all this while igniting little "political controversy." Indeed, Charles Maier has argued, just as "the commitment to mobilization helped overcome deep conflicts between the New Deal and its opposition" on the eve of Pearl Harbor, so too did a similar commitment a decade later: "Disputes that were shelved in 1940 were to be shelved again before Korea." This was indeed a "permanent war economy," if only partially so.[31]

What spawned this "permanent war economy"—or "military Keynesianism," "military-industrial complex," "gunbelt," or "metropolitan-military complex"—has confounded critics and historians, their many terms reflecting their disagreements. Its roots went back to the early twentieth century and

World War II accelerated its development, but the post-1945 mobilization of so much of a nominally peacetime economy was new in scale and nature.

Economic interests provide a partial explanation. Some corporate behemoths certainly benefited, but their catalytic role was minimal—fledgling entrepreneurs like Donald Douglas and newer companies like Boeing were often bigger beneficiaries, although of course they became giants in the process, while many big industries (steel, railroads, autos) sought to find their profits in a robust civilian market after 1945. Scientists and universities played key ideological and technical roles in the process but lacked the power and cohesion to set it in motion. Congress had the formal power to do so, but its role was limited, aimed more at defending established turf than at expanding it. Moreover, any "theory" of Congress's decisive role "would suggest broad dispersion of defense contracts across the states" rather than the remarkable regional concentration that developed, often at the expense of still-populous states with clout in Congress.[32]

Greater influence seemed to lie with alliances between defense bureaucracies and local "boosters"—politicians, publishers, developers, and others. They were especially aggressive in West Coast cities, which harbored civic dreams of imperial glory, had long relied on federal monies and military bases, faced a sharp downturn after 1945 as wartime spending ceased, and recruited defense bases, industries, and laboratories in lieu of the industrial base older regions possessed. Boosters were also important in older regions facing economic stagnation, such as New England and much of the South. Indeed, so powerful were local and private interests that a tail-wags-dog story can easily be told in which the "center"—national leadership—fades before the power of a "periphery" of dispersed but aggressive interests.

All of these interests were important, but no one was decisive. Indeed, there was no stable "system" or "complex," insofar as such terms imply coherent and centralized intention and direction, only an accretion of interests, forces, and objectives that later looked like a system—"a polycentric configuration that change[d] consistently over time."[33]

The very multiplicity of forces and interests involved in the peacetime war economy shielded it from analysis and attack. Opponents naturally homed in on specifics—evil generals, greedy capitalists, congressional experts in pork—but since no one element bore primary responsibility, attack on it produced no persuasive explanation or decisive change. Those who tried to see it whole—figures as diverse as C. Wright Mills and Dwight Eisenhower by the 1950s—revealed a system so complex that opponents might despair about where to begin dismantling it, giving the impression of a system beyond control. And insofar as impressions governed realities, it *was* beyond control. Besides, it was ideological forces that undergirded the peacetime war economy—the ideology of national preparedness, and the state's dependence on war and defense for its role in national life. Only an assault on these ideological underpinnings could arrest militarization. No assault, at least of a broadly appealing sort, arose in the late 1940s and 1950s.

Why did Americans put up with this? The victory of "civilian" control, the sense of "absolute necessity," the incremental growth of militarization, and the dispersed character of the interests involved were reasons. Just as important, the war economy was also made to appear and to a degree function as congruent with dominant aspirations for prosperity and technological abundance. "Who could seriously complain about the results achieved by U.S. businesses between 1945 and the late 1960s?" two historians have asked.[34] Beyond sheer prosperity, there was the promise, first offered in wartime advertising, that war-born ingenuity would yield wondrous civilian devices. Television, airliners, and other marvels emerged from military research ("spin-off," as it was later dubbed). Americans were told of the connection in advertising, government pronouncements, paeans to science, magazines, and science fiction. No youngster reading *Popular Mechanics* could miss it, and it suffused material culture—in cars with rocketlike grills and space-age fins or bicycles resembling jet fighters in miniature. Far from an obstacle to affluence, national security seemed the path to it, even incidental in the face of its benefits.

These promises flowed most lavishly regarding nuclear energy. One newspaper foresaw an "earthly paradise"; another's cartoon depicted "a beneficent goddess opening the locked chest of 'ATOMIC ENERGY' "; one tract, *Almighty Atom*, predicted cost-free power, and atomic airplanes and cars. Given dread about the bomb and skepticism about nuclear energy, it required a skillful government and private campaign to sustain these "fantasies of a techno-atomic utopia"—one waged in part to put a benign face on the atom's military development. Despite silly talk of "atomic-energy vitamin tablets" and the like, the promises were hardly confined to a lunatic fringe. University of Chicago president Robert Hutchins believed that atomic energy could "usher in a new day of peace and plenty" and develop "the most backward places of the earth." The left-liberal daily *PM* imagined "the Utopia that men have dreamed of through centuries of war, depression, famine, and disease." A *Nation* writer wanted atomic bombs used "to dig canals, to break open mountain chains, to melt ice barriers, and generally to tidy up the awkward parts of the world."[35]

Tellingly, the promised utopia was often presented not as an alternative to the bomb's development but as its product. "Through medical advances alone," *Atlantic* claimed in 1946, "atomic energy has already saved more lives than were snuffed out at Hiroshima and Nagasaki." "Out of the ashes of Hiroshima and Nagasaki," wrote one doctor, "a beneficent atomic energy . . . will rise phoenix-like to benefit the health and welfare of our nation." In an especially tasteless example of such linkage, one article on radioactive isotopes depicted "a pajama-clad man, obviously a recently recovered invalid, standing erect and smiling in the midst of a mushroom-shaped cloud, his empty wheelchair in the background." The "splitting atom," argued an AEC commissioner in 1953, "has been our main shield against the Barbarians—now, in addition, it is to become a God-given instrument to do the constructive work of mankind." Given its promise, "atomic energy is *only incidentally* a military weapon," Philip Wylie argued in 1945. Were weapons the end and civilian wonders only the by-product—or the reverse? Perhaps few Americans could have said in the late 1940s.[36]

Some of these promises were thankfully never realized: no atomic cars zoomed forth; no polar icecaps melted. Others reached belated fruition, and together they formed the dense mass of messages telling Americans not only to tolerate the militarized state but to embrace it as the source of wonders in their daily lives, focusing only "incidentally" on its military dimensions. The swords, if not beaten into plowshares, would at least generate them.

If that seemed to many an acceptable bargain, it still was a contingent one. It rested on the proposition, disputed at the time by some, that war (or preparations for it) stimulated economic progress. "The role of war in promoting industrial progress had been small compared with the role of industrial progress in bringing on war," argued John Nef acidly in 1950. "Warfare is less a cause for industrialism than its shadow and its nemesis."[37] It also rested on sustaining prosperity at home and economic power abroad, without which the bargain might unravel. Even early on, some Americans, including Truman fitfully and Eisenhower forcefully, worried that defense spending might undercut prosperity and power. In more troubled economic times, the doubts deepened.

Social Relations in a Militarizing Nation

Isaac Woodward, a black war veteran still in uniform, met the South at its ugliest when he took the bus home in 1946. Angry that Woodward took so long in a "colored" rest room, his driver summoned local law officers, who arrested, beat, and blinded Woodward with a nightstick jammed into his eyes. The incident drew enormous attention, thanks in part to the National Association for the Advancement of Colored People, and Truman expressed shock. "I had no idea it was as terrible as that. We've got to do something."[38] The affair showed how social relations worked out in the shadow of war. It made all the difference that Woodward was a veteran.

Though gradual, the militarization of policy and institutions was to some degree calculable; wars, weapons, and bureaucracies provided some measure. The militarization of social relations was more subtle. The reforms that flowed from it could entice leftists suspicious of anti-Soviet policies and infuriate reactionaries wedded to the Cold War, but it could also endanger the former and isolate the latter. It involved not only conscription of social resources but the recasting of social relations in light of national security, and a complex deployment of the language, models, and modes of warfare. While it often advanced a centrist, liberal, assimilationist agenda—no mean feat in the social climate of the 1940s—its significance went much further.

The most celebrated example of this process was Truman's 1948 order desegregating the armed forces. Racial segregation, discrimination, and disenfranchisement still ruled legally in the Jim Crow South and in some national institutions like the military, and informally in the North. If anything, the situation for black servicemen and -women worsened in 1946. Their few wartime gains seemed to slip away; most military leaders staunchly defended the old ways; crude violence against them erupted.

But a return to the prewar status quo was impossible. Unlike the aftermath of World War I, the forces producing change during this war outlasted it because national security persisted as a high priority. Military leaders worried about recruiting African-Americans and feared that Congress might balk at renewing selective service if segregation and discrimination persisted. Concern was greatest in the air force, the service least bound by tradition and a caste of Southern white officers and best connected to the civilian world, where wartime policy and personnel needs already had prompted some desegregation. Lt. Gen. James Doolittle, a Shell Oil executive before and after the war, warned air force colleagues that desegregation was "being forced on industry . . . and it is going to be forced on the military. You are merely postponing the inevitable and you might as well take it gracefully."[39]

Left alone, few in the military would have acted, but they were hardly left alone, especially by those mindful of the war's racial crimes. White liberals like Eleanor Roosevelt and labor leader Walter Reuther pushed for change, while the GOP flatly declared its opposition to military segregation. More decisive was pressure from black Americans. Already mobilized by the war, they defied military segregation from within the armed forces and protested it through their national organizations. In 1947, A. Philip Randolph revived the strategy of his 1941 March on Washington Movement. He demanded legislation to end military discrimination and segregated facilities for troops crossing state lines, to provide federal penalties for attacks on servicemen, and to exempt enlisted men from the notorious poll tax in federal elections. When Congress took no action, he demanded an executive order from Truman and called on black and white youth to defy the draft in order to resist "permanent military slavery."[40]

Truman had already appointed a Commission on Civil Rights, which recommended a stunning range of racial reforms. On July 26, 1948, he acted. Responding to the various pressures (the Berlin crisis that summer added to them), shocked by what he had learned about racial prejudice, aware that Congress would not act and happy to embarrass it, he was also desperate for votes in the upcoming election. He ordered "equality of treatment and opportunity for all persons in the armed services without regard to race, color, religion, or national origin."[41] His order hardly swept all before it. Only the political pressures and personnel needs prompted by the Korean War made the armed forces implement the order fully, few blacks gained senior rank or admission to the service academies (legally long open to them), and neither Truman nor Congress did much else to achieve racial reform. Nonetheless, his order was a bold step—and a bold gamble that paid off. Southern Democrats bolted the party, ran South Carolina's Strom Thurmond for the presidency, seized thirty-nine electoral votes, and won as many votes as Wallace and the Progressives (over a million each), but Truman gained the loyalties of northern blacks and most liberals and won his famous triumph over Thomas Dewey.

Whatever the diverse motives and pressures behind Truman's action, national security was the dominant and least contestable rationale for racial change. That was evident in how he drew on his constitutional power as commander in chief and acted in the military sphere rather than some other. It was just as evident in the language justifying change, which emphasized the need for an efficient military force and the nation's image and alliances in the Cold War. As Eleanor Roosevelt put it, civil rights "isn't any longer a domestic question—it's an international question," one that "may decide whether democracy or communism wins out in the world." Undersecretary of State Acheson had warned in 1946 that "discrimination against minority groups in this country has an adverse effect on our relations with other countries." Similarly, Truman's Civil Rights Commission declared: "An American diplomat cannot argue for free elections in foreign lands without meeting the challenge that in sections of America qualified voters do not have access to the polls." Truman labeled racial discrimination "an invitation to communism" and warned that "the support of desperate populations of battle-ravaged countries" was at stake. "We must have them as allies" and "can no longer afford the luxury of a leisurely attack upon prejudice and discrimination." As he told the black press in 1947: "We are learning what loud echoes both our success and our failures have in every corner of the world. That is one of the pressing reasons why we cannot afford failures. When we fail to live together in peace, the failure touches not us, as Americans alone, but the cause of democracy itself in the whole world." Or as he once put it more crudely, "The top dog in a world which is 90 percent colored ought to clean his own house."[42]

Black leaders also employed this rationale. Randolph argued that segregation "is the greatest single propaganda and political weapon in the hands of Russia and international communism today," and indeed the State Department estimated that half of all Soviet propaganda against the United States focused on racial issues. Paul Robeson, the radical black actor, singer, and activist, also worked this rationale, in his own way: American policy toward Africans "is similar to that of Hitler and Goebbels," he allegedly declared, and American blacks would never "go to war on behalf of those who have oppressed us for generations" against the USSR, which "has raised our people to . . . full human dignity."[43]

The demands of war and national power shaped the struggle for racial change far beyond Truman's order, in both time and the issues addressed. When Jackie Robinson broke the racial barrier in major-league baseball in 1949, the House Un-American Activities Committee wanted him to "give the lie to statements by Paul Robeson that American Negroes would not fight in case of a war against Russia," a request Robinson fulfilled. When civil rights leaders sought a new Fair Employment Practices Committee after the outbreak of the Korean War, they joined considerations of efficiency and morale: "Our country can no longer enjoy the luxury of wasted industrial manpower" and "our men in Korea need to know in their hearts and minds that they are not fighting in vain." When the Truman administration filed a brief in behalf of school deseg-regation, in cases leading up to the epochal *Brown v. Board of Education* decision of 1954, it cited Acheson's warning that discrimination was "a source of con-stant embarrassment to this government" and its "moral leadership" in the free world. No one summed up these claims better than Dwight Eisenhower during his 1952 campaign: "In a time when America needs all the brains, all the skills, all the spiritual strength and dedicated services of its 157 million people, dis-crimination is criminally stupid."[44]

Eisenhower's statement caught the changing nature, force, and limits of the national security rationale. During World War II, leaders like FDR had often invoked wartime need to resist racial change, claiming it might trigger reaction and violence impeding national morale and efficiency. Now the argument more and more cut the other way. Viewed by leaders in Washington pressing the nation's mobilization and containing communism, racial segregation seemed a foolish waste of national resources, an outdated practice fouling the machinery of national power. However reluctantly, the armed forces now would have to help pioneer racial change.

This reworked necessitarian rationale had sharp limits, however. "Crimi-nally stupid" was not the same as morally unjust. Civil rights leaders, and Tru-man himself on occasion, did also invoke morality and justice, but national se-curity was the dominant rationale, and the most persistent, even into the 1960s, when racial equality was advanced more as a goal than as a means to a different end. In the meantime, it both forced and circumscribed racial reform. Racial changes grounded in concerns about justice generated less enthusiasm, at least among whites. The dominant thrust was assimilationist: African-Americans would be prized for their ability to fade into national institutions like the army and to subordinate their interests to the grander national cause; and the armed forces' conservative officer corps would carry out the grand experiment in inte-gration. Moreover, the gnawing worry of national elites about America's image at home and overseas meant that much action taken was little more than win-dow dressing designed to polish that image: the Fair Employment Practices Committee during the Korean War canceled not a single defense contract, and well into the 1950s desegregation of the armed forces proceed as if "staged for the benefit of foreign and domestic observers rather than benefiting the black serviceman himself."[45] Preoccupation with national security, then, made the reform impulse both urgent and limited. To be sure, that impulse continued to surge in initiatives by state and local governments, courts, unions, colleges, civil rights groups, and minority citizens themselves. Still, executive action was the cutting edge, and national security the dominant framework.

The limits of that framework were doubly evident when opponents of racial change exploited its most charged element, hysterical anticommunism. Southern Democrats were the most vicious at this game. When the Supreme Court invalidated restrictive housing covenants, one congressman told the House: "Mr. Speaker, there must have been a celebration in Moscow last night." Communists had "won their greatest victory." Strom Thurmond declared that "the radicals, the subversives, and the reds" had captured the Democratic Party; the civil rights agenda was designed "to create the chaos and confusion which leads to communism."[46] Foes of civil rights, whether southern bigots or officials of the FBI, pointed out that communists championed racial equality, which allowed many Americans to regard it as an evil idea imported from abroad. Moderate groups like the NAACP were said to be led or manipulated by communists; in response they purged their ranks, exchanged dossiers on alleged subversives, and trimmed their ideological sails. The tenuous wartime alliance of white and black workers in Congress of Industrial Organizations unions wilted when the Red Scare decimated those unions. Scholars disagree on how much anticommunism curbed racial reform—most likely it pushed reform into narrower but faster-running channels—but national security certainly cut both ways.

The most vulnerable were radicals like Paul Robeson. Except for sports stars (and Robeson had been a star college athlete), he entered the Cold War the most admired and influential black American. During World War II, his militant antifascism had been useful to American leaders, and his close ties with (though not membership in or subservience to) the Communist Party had been tolerated. But his support of Henry Wallace in 1948, his defense of the Soviet Union, and his denunciations at home and abroad of American racism destroyed his political and artistic careers. The FBI hounded him; the entertainment industry, along with local officials and mobs, strangled his career; the State Department (arguing that race relations were a "family affair" not to be aired abroad) lifted his passport, a fatal blow to his activities; Eleanor Roosevelt disavowed him; a witness before Congress branded him "the black Stalin among Negroes." Many African-Americans still defended Robeson, but their leaders became wary of association with him; even the militant Bayard Rustin argued, "We have to prove that we're patriotic." Robeson made his enemies' task easier. Implacable in condemning American racism and imperialism, myopic about Stalin's brutalities, he was incapable of the skillful maneuver that might leave him intact to continue the fight, even excoriating other prominent blacks for their "craven, fawning, despicable leadership." That his struggle to regain his passport lasted until the late 1950s (he was a broken man by then) indicated how persistent the ugly mood was, especially when a black man was involved—or a black woman, as with entertainer Josephine Baker, also hounded by agents of the state for her views on race.[47]

That mood also encouraged a general celebration of American perfection. What, after all, was the point of waging the global struggle if not to defend a superior system, and how could that system win if it were not superior? As Richard Polenberg argues, "It was only a short step from insisting that communists did not want to improve conditions to denying that conditions needed much betterment. The Cold War produced a constant tension between a desire to affirm the fundamental soundness of American institutions and a recognition that those institutions . . . were in many respects defective." Social commentary by scholars and the media reflected the changed mood. Although the war's modest tendency to narrow income gaps soon ended and the concentration of corporate wealth continued, scholarly work backed away from its prewar emphasis on class differences, stressing instead the "fluidity, diversity, and freedom" of American society and the absence of sharp conflicts within it. In this "Cold War atmosphere . . . a thoroughgoing critique of social institutions was fast going out of style."[48]

Not that a critical stance altogether disappeared. Some critics and scholars found the racial divide in America inescapable and troubling, and many more assailed the bland conformity of mass culture, suburbia, and corporate life. Their categories of analysis were more often psychological than social, however, and their lament was more for the boring sameness of Americans than for the divisions among them. Along with more politicized forms of anticommunism, social commentary had an impact that leaders could not miss. As one Truman aide put it in April 1949, "The consuming fear of communism has led many sincere persons into the belief that . . . change (be it civil rights or a compulsory national health program) is subversive and those who urge it are either communists or fellow travellers."[49] Militarization did not alone cause this mood, which also drew on conservative reaction against New Deal liberalism and racial change, and on the triumphal outlook that victory in war promoted, but together these forces helped to keep the reform impulse intense but narrowly channeled.

Nonetheless, black Americans, measured by their prewar status, benefited from the country's pursuit of national security. Did other social groups gain accordingly? Much depended on their political clout, place in the Cold War, and prior mobilization and group consciousness. Blacks had several advantages, despite enormous obstacles: their importance in the armed forces, their position in the contest over the loyalties of nonwhites in the decolonizing world, and their rapid movement into northern cities, where they could vote and have it count. Other groups sometimes lacked such leverage and found their fortunes worsening.

That was so for many women. The Women's Armed Services Integration Act of 1948, passed just days before Truman's order on racial integration, did seem to subject women to the same militarizing forces that were reshaping the black experience, by giving them permanent, regular status in the armed forces. Rep. Margaret Chase Smith, who led the cause, did invoke justice, but national security was again the dominant argument for change. Army Chief of Staff Dwight Eisenhower saw "plain efficiency" at stake, especially since a "push-button war" would draw in all Americans. Shortages of female personnel, above all nurses, underlined the case. The cause of national security embraced gender equality less easily than racial equality, however. The new law barred women from combat, limited their numbers, rank, and authority over men, and left gender ideology intact: most female enlistees, Ike promised, would serve briefly and then "ordinarily—and thank God—they will get married." Given how few women were allowed to serve, "integration" also lacked the quantitative effect on women that it had on black men, who enlisted or were drafted in large numbers.[50]

Indeed, militarization constricted more than it enlarged women's rights and opportunities. Wartime legislation on veterans' benefits and job preference limited women's employment. The federal bureaucracy's tilt toward national security curtailed job openings in social services, where women had had greatest success. Notably, the few women to gain high-level posts came from or entered into the newly powerful agencies of national security: Anna Rosenberg as assistant secretary of defense under Truman; Oveta Culp Hobby, wartime head of the WACs, as the first secretary of health, education, and welfare under Eisenhower; and Eleanor Dulles (sister to John Foster and Allen), head of the State Department's Berlin desk in the 1950s. Women who pursued political careers, in official positions or private lobbies, often faced red-baiting if their politics were liberal, lesbian-baiting if their status were single, or more complex charges—when Richard Nixon called Helen Gahagan Douglas a "Pink Lady . . . right down to her underwear" during their 1950 Senate contest, he linked "liberated women, unchained sexuality, and the Communist menace." Truman laughed away women's issues: "It has been my experience that there is no equality—men are just slaves and I suppose they will always continue to be."[51]

Beyond gender politics lay ideological shifts prompted partly by anxieties about war and national security. Cultural images often presented women as war's helpless victims, or alternatively as its cause, linking women's sexuality to war's destructive forces (as in the bikini swimsuit and "Atomic Bomb [burlesque] Dancers"). Hollywood mirrored the bifurcation, giving viewers little choice between helpless or horrendous female characters. Enjoined to avoid those extremes, women were to play supportive, domestic roles in the atomic age, especially since Soviet women were demonized as mannish and aggressive. They were expected to maintain the bomb shelter, or "Grandma's Pantry" as it was sometimes called; "Aren't they just perfect naturals for our mass feeding groups?" asked a female civil defense official. They were "to rear children who would avoid juvenile delinquency, stay in school, and become future scientists and experts to defeat the Russians in the cold war." In the postwar "ideology of male responsibility" for the international and domestic order, women were to show "patriotism by conforming to a domestic ideology of female subordination." Fear that wartime service had emasculated men, masculinized women, and alienated the two from each other strengthened this ideology; sharply rising marriage and birth rates reflected it; politicians of many stripes articulated it. As Adlai Stevenson argued in 1955, the college graduate's job was to keep her husband "truly purposeful" and help "defeat totalitarian, authoritarian ideas." With the nation's very survival apparently at stake, women's claims to equality seemed laughable, irrelevant, or even subversive.[52]

These dynamics, many evident in the 1930s, did not owe only to militarization. Nor did "domestic ideology" always serve to justify a militarized course: before and after World War II, "isolationists," often Christian fundamentalists, invoked a version of it to fight conscription and universal service, arguing that military life would corrupt draftees' morals and deprive them of their mothers' nurturance. Militarization dictated no single gender regime, and no single such regime promoted it. Circumstances—how militarized agendas intersected autonomous anxieties about gender and sexuality—mattered. Still, in the postwar years an ideology of strong men and supportive women was bent to serve those agendas, while its role in countering them diminished. Even more telling as a marker of militarization, *any* ideology of sex and gender, like any of race and ethnicity, now had to address its alleged effect on national power. Never neatly determinative, that sphere was nonetheless inescapable.

To be sure, black Americans wrung advantage from this crisis atmosphere despite facing an ideology at least as imprisoning as that facing women, but that suggests how ideology and politics differed in content and effects among various groups. Women also met a different fate because they lacked a common set of goals, leverage at the polls, and a perceived place in the global contest of loyalties. How could the Nazi record underline their cause in the way that it illustrated the evils of racism? Where were the masses of women waiting elsewhere, as nonwhites (presumptively male) apparently were, to choose between communism and the free world? With the evils of fascism and communism seen in racial and religious terms, with their ideals and practices about gender largely ignored (perhaps because they were too similar to what governed in the United States), with women's autonomous power hard to see in a militarized world, few could argue that America's global image hinged on its treatment of women. Instead, the Cold War's outcome seemed to hinge on women's loyal service.

The fate of gay men and lesbians also illustrated the pernicious effects of militarization. Again their fate was entwined with that of women, as one congressman's warning made clear: "The cycle of these individuals' homosexual desires follows the cycle closely patterned to the menstrual period of women," so that a few days each month "the homosexual's instincts break down and drive the individual into abnormal fields of sexual practice," ones that presumably made homosexuals who served the nation's defense unreliable or vulnerable to blackmail.[53]

A recasting of stereotypes also jeopardized gay men and women. In an older gender system categorizing people along male-female rather than gay-straight lines, notions of "sissy" men and "mannish" women had rendered them reassuringly identifiable, if sometimes laughable, and allowed others given to normative gender roles to engage them sexually without the stigma of homosexuality. During World War II, however, homosexuals served in large numbers, in uniforms and with duties that erased visible distinctions between them and other Americans. As a result, new stereotypes stressed their ordinary appearance and lurking invisibility. "The Sapphic lover," warned two pulp journalists, "is seldom obvious," and "unsophisticates who think of queers as prancing nances with rouged lips and bleached hair" must realize that "pansies in the State Department do not wear skirts over their striped pants," and that "fairies" include "tough young kids, college football players, truck-drivers and weather-bitten servicemen." By the same token, even straight-appearing men and women no longer easily escaped suspicion of being gay. And as the warning about State Department "pansies" indicated, new notions of invisible gays were linked to fears about national safety, including those about debilitating, effete privilege in the upper reaches of essential institutions.[54]

Trying to locate in imagination what now seemed invisible in appearance, politicians, journalists, filmmakers, and doctors linked homosexuals with communism and fascism. As a congressional report claimed, they lack the "outward characteristics or physical traits . . . of sex perversion," rendering them an insidious threat akin to, and drawn to, the invisible communist. A new sex panic linked gay men to abuse of children, and prescriptive literature viewed them as immature men who failed to maintain the families and careers needed to win the Cold War ("They cannot compete. They always surrender in the face of impending combat"). They were thus regarded as a menace to the homefront and the war front as well. Straying from Freudian tradition, psychoanalysts, often refugees from Nazi Europe, frequently ascribed the ugliest pathology to homosexuals (they were murderers, trapped in "the holocaust of illness" and "trying to extinguish the race") and linked them to Nazism. The few experts who suggested otherwise were condemned for producing claims that "will be politically and propagandistically used against the United States abroad, stigmatizing the nation as a whole in a whisper campaign," as Edmund Bergler, the era's leading analytic theorist in this arena, assailed Alfred Kinsey's reports on human sexuality.[55]

Gays reaped many of the burdens and few of the benefits of militarization. "Sex perverts" were publicly vilified by executive agencies and congressional committees, purged from government and military service, and pursued and exposed by local police in vice raids. The modern apparatus of antigay ideology and repression now emerged, derived less from timeless animus than from historically specific anxieties. Militarization redefined antigay hostility and the danger gays presumably posed—to national as well as moral safety, the two inextricably joined. Truman showed how early and easily the linkage emerged when he justified his decision to fire Commerce Secretary Henry Wallace ("a pacifist 100%") for seeking friendlier Soviet-American relations. "All the 'Artists' with a capital A, the parlor pinks and the soprano voiced men are banded together," he complained privately in 1946. "I am afraid they are a sabotage front for Uncle Joe Stalin."[56]

Formal resistance to homophobia was nearly impossible. One attempt, the Mattachine Society, found its initial leaders (ex-Communists ironically purged from the party for their preferences) driven out by their fearful followers. No mainstream group, nor the American Civil Liberties Union, would defend them, prejudice was rampant among leftists (inclined to see homosexuality as a form of capitalist decadence) as well as conservatives, and homosexuals in power like the FBI's Hoover and Joe McCarthy sidekick Roy Cohn were worse than useless (and themselves sometimes gay-baited). Unlike other groups, gay people could not gain leverage by touting their wartime contributions, since doing so risked condemnation or jail. The fate of gays under the Holocaust was unknown, while no restive mass of homosexuals overseas seeking to choose between communism and democracy was evident.

Even vicious attention offered long-run advantages to gay people. The lurid magazine article or publicized vice raid provided the novice a guide to the bars, codewords, and folkways of the gay underworld. In 1957, when San Francisco police seized copies of poet Allen Ginsberg's *Howl*—which celebrated men who get "fucked in the ass by saintly motorcyclists" and savaged Cold Warriors who prayed before "Moloch"—they sent sales of *Howl* and knowledge of that city's gay community soaring. Indeed, the mounting antigay campaign helped forge a new gay identity that slowly made resistance possible, just as resistance, as in Ginsberg's case, often would include challenges to militarization itself. Few could foresee that course of events in 1950, however.

If blacks made gains and homosexuals fared worst under militarized social relations, European ethnics probably benefited the most. Unlike the case after World War I, "the anti-communist impulse . . . did not flow primarily along nativist channels"; indeed, Eastern European immigrants "would come to be identified with the far right rather than with the far left."[57] American Jews could identify with the victims of Nazism, and often of communism. East European ethnics, and the Catholic church with which they were usually associated, were seen as patriotic Cold Warriors, easing their task of assimilation. German-Americans, rarely the brunt of hostility anyway during the war, saw West Germany enlisted in the anticommunist cause. The Cold War hardly dissolved all distinctions: anticommunism recast ethnic identities more than it obliterated them, as Americans of Polish, Ukrainian, or other backgrounds asserted their ties to oppressed brethren behind the Iron Curtain. Divisions along religious lines remained even sharper, as Catholics, Protestants, and Jews usually maintained their social and cultural distance. Still, the machinery of national security—most obviously compulsory military service, less directly corporations, bureaucracies, and universities—did mingle diverse groups. By the same token, the outlook reshaping race relations worked even more readily on ethnic and religious divisions: barriers against Jews, Catholics, or ethnic groups might persist informally but seemed out of place in a nation seeking to tap all of its resources at home and to polish its image abroad. Fear that Americans would appear divided in facing the enemy discouraged, though hardly ended, intense ethnic and religious assertiveness, and American leaders emphasized the nation's homogeneity. Rarely in American history did the melting pot seem to bubble so fiercely. At least for ethnics of an assimilationist bent—probably a great many after World War II—the ideal of homogeneity served a useful purpose.

Other groups fared less well. Mexican-Americans were frequently deported as national security risks or for other reasons. Opponents of Native American tribal community and land ownership labeled those practices as communistic, and the federal government moved toward "the complete merger of all Indian groups into the general body of our population," as Truman put it. Chinese-Americans divided among themselves when communism triumphed in their ancestral nation, and they came under more suspicion, acted on by the federal government through a notorious "Confession Program," when Communist Chinese forces entered the Korean War.[58] For non-Europeans, the obstacles included both longstanding prejudice and temporary circumstance: the Cold War was too murky and embryonic in much of Asia and Latin America for these groups to trade easily on their position in the global contest for loyalties. The Cold War's growing intensity in those areas after 1950 did make for change, however: immigration quotas, once wildly tilted to Europeans, were suspended, relaxed, and finally abandoned in 1965.

All this suggests that militarization imposed no one pattern on all social groups, but in one sense it did. What mattered as much as the fate of particular groups—a balance sheet of losses and gains for each—was the manner in which all found their status judged by their perceived position in hot and cold war. Older impulses still operated—that bundle of prejudices, aspirations, and advantages that defines American society—just as national security was often invoked to legitimize impulses that lay entirely outside its arena. But that is also the point. That arena was inescapable, and as many could attest—the black officer who gained authority, the woman hesitant to choose a career, the lesbian WAC dishonorably discharged—its dynamics were powerful. Those dynamics privileged a utilitarian case for social change and circumscribed claims based on justice. The distinction was not absolute, since justice often seemed in the interests of national power, but it was persistent.

Compounding this militarization of social relations was the partially militarized economy, which reshaped social relations in ways largely beyond the reach of formal argument and consciousness. Of these effects, the regional "remapping" of the United States, creating a new "gunbelt," was the most obvious.[59] World War II, requiring mass production of highly standardized products, had showered its economic benefits widely, since established industries like auto and steel in the Northeast and Midwest were adept at mass production. The reduced scale and mounting technological focus of postwar military procurement, on the other hand, prized mass production far less. Instead of millions of rifles or thousands of bombers frozen in design for long production runs, the Pentagon sought handfuls of aircraft carriers and hundreds of new jet fighters and bombers—all so complex and fast-changing technically that designs could not be fixed for high-volume production, and skilled design teams and workers were valued more than masses of blue-collar laborers.

To be sure, this shift was not total—small-batch production had long characterized naval armaments and the Korean War brought new demands for high-volume output—but it nonetheless accelerated regional redistribution. Older mass-production industries were neither well suited to meet the new demands nor keenly interested in them as long as civilian markets were robust. Thus weapons development and production gravitated south and west—to bulging nodes in the nuclear weapons complex like DuPont's vast Savannah River plant in South Carolina; to aircraft companies in Los Angeles and in Seattle; and later to rocket and space-exploration complexes in Georgia, Florida, Texas, and the West. As late as 1952, New York was still the top recipient of military contracts, and midwestern states took a handsome share of them. Just six years later, California had far outdistanced New York, Texas and Washington had moved into the top ranks, "the Midwest's share fell catastrophically, never again to recover," and the top ten military contractors were now all in electronics and aviation.[60] Tanks from Detroit were out, jets from California were in. Pockets of defense work remained in the old heartland, but the shift was rapid. To its beneficiaries, it owed to their climate, open land, strategic location, and entrepreneurial spirit. Those attributes, however, were probably not the decisive factors. Instead, complacency among corporate and political leaders in the old heartland, the high-tech emphasis of defense procurement, and aggressive promotion by boosters figured heavily in the shift.

These regional shifts, vital in redistributing capital, expertise, and population, also reshaped patterns of race, class, and ideology. Resources flowed to corporations that had less need for blue-collar workers and to areas where unions were usually weaker, undercutting organized labor and the benefits for black workers of their success in northern cities at gaining industrial jobs and integrating industrial unions. Like other Americans, blacks could follow the economic tide to California, Connecticut, or back south, but doing so meant still another disruption, and sometimes relocation to areas where African-American institutions had shallow roots and white Americans were exceptionally hostile. Similar results, though less dramatic and harder to ascertain, may have unfolded for women, who, like most black Americans, lacked the training needed for many technical jobs in defense industries, although they might join the low-paid secretarial support force also required in large numbers. For gay people, the maze of security clearances and requirements in the private and public sectors of defense work presented a special barrier.

In turn, the partial war economy weakened the New Deal coalition, liberal reform, and racial progress. Undercutting organized labor and job openings for black Americans, it swelled opportunities for white-collar workers whose economic status tended to make their politics Republican and conservative. And corporate, political, and media leaders in these prospering areas sustained an extraordinary revulsion against federal power and "social engineering" even as they embraced Cold War views promoting federal power, connived for every federal dollar, and fostered a massive re-engineering of America. California's urban boosters "would curse the federal government for the mess in which the war had left them, but each would plaintively beg"—or skillfully lobby—"for more of the economic resources that came with the mess."[61]

This involved no Republican or conservative conspiracy, however, since Democratic presidents and Congresses were essential in creating the peacetime war economy, and the local coalitions that landed military contracts and bases transcended party and ideological distinctions. And regional and economic shifts had other sources beside the workings of militarization. Nor were racial reformers helpless in face of these changes—the civil rights movement reached the peak of its success in the midst of them, in part by capitalizing on other facets of militarization.

But economic militarization eroded the ground beneath them. It "contributed to the segregation of Americans by class and race" (and probably by gender), and to the growth of "large pools of an urban underclass as well as displaced blue-collar workers." In a manner similar to the effects of suburbanization, the economic and regional effects of militarization worked beneath the surface to undercut formal efforts at racial integration and social equality.[62]

Understandably, it was difficult to foresee and shape many of the consequences of militarization for social relations. As historical process, militarization was largely unrecognized or implicitly denied by the language of crisis and improvisation, and in any event of incalculable duration as of 1948 or 1952. Its effects were complex and long-term (many noted here were only incipient in the 1940s), far from uniform across all social groups, sometimes contradictory even for a single group, and useful enough for many to be welcomed in an unquestioning fashion. All that such groups had in common—but this was a great deal—was their inescapable participation in an arena of social relations profoundly shaped by militarization.

Culture in War's Shadow

Advancing American Art, an overseas State Department exhibit of modernist works, unleashed a furor in 1947. Traditional artists issued a "War Cry" against radical trends "not indigenous to our soil." The media lambasted "left-wing painters who are members of red Fascist organizations." Politicians saw "Communist caricatures . . . sent out to mislead the rest of the world as to what America is like." The matter dragged in Truman ("If that's art, I'm a Hottentot") and Congress, causing the exhibit's premature end. Into the 1950s the charge kept echoing that modern art (or literature, or music) weakened America, corrupting it at home or debasing its image abroad: Congressman George Dondero insinuated the homosexuality of modernists, saw them as part of "a sinister conspiracy conceived in the black heart of Russia," and declared modern art communist (though Stalin also condemned it) "because it does not glorify our beautiful country, our cheerful and smiling people, and our great material progress." Tellingly, defenders of modern art worked in a similar framework, hailing it as symbol of American freedom and power: "The main premises of Western art have at last migrated to the United States, along with the center of gravity of industrial production and political power."[63]

Hardly the first time that art generated political conflict, the debate over modernist art was instead novel because of the framework of controversy shared by defenders and detractors: their focus on national safety and power even in peacetime. It was a sign that in culture as in other arenas, militarization was proceeding. It did not simply mean the conscription of cultural resources to wage hot or cold war, or a culture that celebrated national power. It meant also the manifold ways in which Americans couched their cultural anxieties and ambitions in terms of national security, and in which anxieties about the nation's safety suffused culture. It meant, that is, the seeming inescapability of war in American culture, both in its formal apparatus of entertainment and the arts, and in its broader systems of language and symbols.

No one explanation persuasively embraces large-scale cultural change, however, and the best the historian can do is to acknowledge the complexities involved. To the extent that culture became militarized, the change occurred through private and decentralized initiatives and out of the moods and anxieties of ordinary people, not just through elite pressures (themselves often conflicting). Although historians still write books like *The Culture of the Cold War*,[64] much sprang from well-springs deeper than the Cold War conflict: from exposure to global war, genocide, and frightening weapons; from the nation's attempt to exercise global power; from anxieties about what America itself was becoming; and, since no culture reinvents itself overnight, from older cultural traditions that shaped reactions to all of these developments.

Disparate in sources, culture's militarization was also complex in results. The postwar years are easily remembered as an "age of anxiety." And plausibly so, since reasons for anxiety existed and since people so self-consciously employed the label, as when the British-American poet W. H. Auden published "The Age of Anxiety" in 1948 and Leonard Bernstein gave a symphony the same title a few years later. Yet the era also saw buoyant optimism and soaring ambition about America as the world's cultural capital, economic engine, religious savior, or protector and policeman. Americans could imagine their nation both in ruins and in muscular hegemony over the world. The point is not that anxiety or optimism (or some other mood) triumphed. (One scholar finds an ambivalent "culture of contingency" ascendant in the late 1940s.[65]) The point is that both moods were shaped by and focused upon the experience and threat of war and the global struggle.

Given the diverse nature of culture, the subtle means of resistance it offered, and its resistance to any sudden change, militarization in this sphere was more partial and uneven. Still, by certain gross if imprecise standards, a militarized culture was emerging in an impressive range of phenomena. The postwar suburban boom, for example, driven in part by pent-up wartime demand and generous financing for veterans, was also cast as a weapon in the Cold War. "No man who owns his own house and lot can be a communist. He has too much to do," proclaimed William Levitt, the mogul of suburban development.[66] Embodying the myth of a classless society, suburbia served as sign of American superiority and as defense against insidious ideologies. The scourge of polio was also cast within the culture of war: fundraising campaigns against it drew on techniques of wartime mobilization; March of Dimes posters echoed wartime propaganda (in 1952, "This Fight Is Yours" featured a grim soldier looming over a crippled child); polio's stealthy contagion seemed comparable to communism's insidious ways, and the unknowableness of its peril to that of nuclear attack.[67]

Film also reflected the culture of war. War movies were a conspicuous genre, one virtually invented during World War II, but other genres reflected similar concerns. Science fiction films projected war into the future or presented it in thinly veiled allegories. So too did Westerns: *High Noon* (1952) offered Gary Cooper as the retired lawman (the United States after World War II) alone facing the returned enemy (totalitarianism), his fellow citizens (America's allies) too weak-willed to fight, his women (a feminized American culture) pleading for peace until Grace Kelly (a Quaker) joins the cause. Similarly, John Ford transferred "the ideological concerns of the World War and its aftermath from the terrain of the combat film to the mythic landscape of the Western," and thereby created "the mythic basis for a new ideology" (resting "on a deliberate and consensual falsification of history") uniting Americans against "the threatening advance of Soviet Communism."[68]

Religion generally and religious revival particularly, though shaped by many forces, also reflected contemporary concerns about war, weapons, and world power. When seventy thousand people packed Chicago's Soldier Field for a Memorial Day 1945 "Youth for Christ" rally, they demonstrated how "World War II and the early stages of the cold war encouraged the reinvigoration of evangelicalism." During the war itself, "piety became more fashionable along the Potomac," religious novels soared to the top of the bestseller lists, and Americans sang "Praise the Lord and Pass the Ammunition," even though one fundamentalist complained that "passing the Lord and praising the ammunition" more aptly caught their mood. The religious revival of the postwar era involved "not so much religious belief as belief in the *value* of religion," argues one historian, above all "the conviction that religion was virtually synonymous with American nationalism."[69]

There was more going on than that, however. A bland sense of "the *value* of religion" did often emerge in the pronouncements of national authorities, the ecumenical religiosity of movies, and the images of corporate media outlets, but there was also the complex faith of theologians like Reinhold Niebuhr, the intense convictions of many Protestants, the apocalyptic predictions of an end-time centered on the atomic bomb's advent, and a more general sense of "new beginnings" prompted by the bomb that spilled across the political and denominational lines of American religion. Like many Americans, religious leaders regarded the bomb's appearance as a sign of ultimate evil or as a call to greater deeds in the world. Early in his ascent to evangelistic stardom, Billy Graham offered a potent mix of Christian anticommunism and apocalyptic prediction, presenting America variously as both called to prevail and doomed to be destroyed in the global struggle (Los Angeles was the enemy's top choice for atomic attack, since it was "known around the world because of its sin, crime, and immorality"). More generally, "Visions of *Pax Americana* . . . provoked a new global triumphalism among American evangelical leaders" who sought "greater conquests for Christ." John Foster Dulles wanted "Americans to extend their conception of morality and spirituality to the rest of the world," as his views have been summarized; President Truman wanted the nation "to bring the golden rule into the international affairs of the world"; and one senator argued that "America must move forward with the atomic bomb in one hand and the cross in the other."[70]

Religious identities and conflicts, too, were often defined in terms of the global struggle. Catholics sought legitimacy by pointing to the church's resistance to communism in Europe. "Long the subject of nativist taunts by the nation's Protestant majority, they could at last assert their Americanism—and question the patriotism of others—through the vehicle of the Anti-Communist Crusade." Francis Cardinal Spellman, unofficial "chaplain of the Cold War," led much of the church in that crusade, urging followers to embrace Sen. Joe McCarthy, attack "perverts," force public officials to ban allegedly obscene films, and challenge the "Communist floodings of our own land." Many Protestants joined that crusade. Others, reflecting old religious tensions and new ways to express them, pointed to the Pope's authority over the church and saw Catholics "as blind followers of a totalitarian system, apparently not unlike the Nazi or Soviet regimes."[71]

Pervasive anxieties about the atomic bomb were at the core of this militarized culture. A "cultural crisis" and a virtual "national town meeting" ensued after Hiroshima, sparing hardly a nook or cranny of American culture. Even when political debate about the bomb waned, cultural anxiety about it persisted—in cheap 1950s films featuring irradiated insects and monsters unleashed by nuclear explosions, creatures that "filled a vacant space where the public declined to see real weapons." Anxiety also persisted in citizens' ordinary decisions: considering relocation, one scholar pondered "the question of relative locations and the atom bomb" and another returned from Europe, where "war and the Russians were too near." When public controversy resumed in the mid-1950s, over fallout from hydrogen bombs, its themes were cultural as well as political, questioning scientific authority and pioneering a modern ecological consciousness.[72]

Political authorities played a major role in militarizing culture. They offered cues, and sometimes none-too-subtle coercion—Hollywood got the message to change its films from congressional hearings conducted in 1947. While most of the New Deal and wartime apparatus for funding and directing culture had been dismantled, new governmental mechanisms sprung up: for intellectuals, the Congress for Cultural Freedom, secretly funded by the CIA; for the masses, a "Zeal for American Democracy" program and a "Freedom Train" touring the nation in 1947, displaying the Constitution and the Declaration of Independence for visitors to view; for the anxious, "Atomic Energy Week" and a myriad of other programs from the AEC designed to offer benign cultural images of the atom. Routine features of the national security state, with no intended cultural agenda, also had profound cultural effects: a generation of young males faced conscription, leading many quickly into college, others into a military experience that disrupted ties of family and region and race, and all to face some version of a common rite of passage. State and local authorities played a vital role as well, shaping public education to reflect Cold War ideology and policy, or working with the American Legion to enact in 1950 a mock Communist coup in Mosinee, Wisconsin, an event that "garnered vast publicity—on radio, TV, newsreels, and the pages of *Life*." Many efforts worked across complex lines of authority. Throughout the 1950s, federal, state, local, and public-school authorities cooperated to mount civil defense drills—cultural "pageants in their own way," as one historian rightly notes.[73]

In turn, the militarization of culture was linked to America's imperial role in the world. Although not a new process, American intellectual currents, cultural fads, and consumer products now surged outward to an unprecedented degree, soon slipping past the Iron Curtain with surprising ease. The global spread of American culture was not always imperial in inspiration or result; red-baiting propelled some leftist American scholars to flee abroad and gain influence there. Too, official efforts to export culture, like *Advancing American Art*, misfired if they challenged political and cultural norms at home. And the culture at issue was not just the project of "Americans." From the soundtracks of films to rarefied work in science and the humanities, it also relied on refugee scholars and artists fleeing fascism or communism.

Still, imperial needs did change the cultural and intellectual work of Americans. Fostering the Third World's economic modernization led economists in new directions; exporting art and literature changed audiences and experiences for American artists; justifying American military power redirected the energies of humanists and social scientists. In broad ways, the sword was lashed to the Bible, the slide-rule, and the cinema. American armies of liberation and occupation cleared the path for, or directly employed, the missionaries, professional experts, corporate representatives, and others who followed in their wake. The CIA covertly funded or sponsored the work abroad of trade unions and cultural organizations, and it monitored the cultural and intellectual work that Americans did overseas (and sometimes at home). Defense agencies hired or contracted professionals in nearly every line of cultural and intellectual work, and shaped the lines of international intellectual influence quite sharply.

Culture, however, was too diverse and unruly for political authorities, themselves often at odds, to dictate all of its militarized forms and content. Nor is it sufficient to argue that Americans naturally responded to world war, atomic weapons, and cold war with the ambitions and anxieties they expressed: what, after all, instructed them that *those* were the proper responses? Other forces must also have been at work.

Reactions to postwar affluence may have played a role. As Warren Susman has suggested, affluence gave Americans a sense of a vision fulfilled, but also a feeling of dread that the abundant society was hollow or that affluence allowed dark forces to surface. "In Hollywood and in the America of the 1940s and early 1950s, the fulfillment of our sweetest desires leads inevitably to the brink of danger and damnation," and a "dual consciousness of an ideal, completed society and inner rebellion developed." Brooding *film noir* movies, the pessimistic writings of theologians like Reinhold Niebuhr, even the extravagant fantasies of comic books and science fiction, seemed to juxtapose economic fulfillment and spiritual damnation. The dread seemed borne out by phenomena abroad and at home: the capacity for evil revealed by world war, totalitarian governments, and new weapons, or by rebellious youth, insidious commies and queers, or unscrupulous McCarthyites. "We have everything," worried the editor of the *Cleveland Press*. "We abound with all of the things that make us comfortable." But "something is not there that should be—something we once had." Examinations of totalitarianism seemed to show where the resulting spiritual drift might lead: Erich Fromm in *Escape from Freedom* (1941) and T. W. Adorno in *The Authoritarian Personality* (1949) diagnosed pathologies in the modern, alienated personality to which Americans might fall victim, just as masses elsewhere had succumbed to Nazism and communism. Were the Americans who were drawn to communism or McCarthy not examples, social critics asked?[74]

In that fashion, anxiety about what America had become meshed with "discovery of the horrors and hypocrisy of the modern world."[75] If the nation had met its historic destiny to create the abundant society, what now was to be its mission and how was it to ward off the evil and decay that might set in? At least as fashioned by Cold Warriors in government and other institutions, the consuming focus on enemies abroad and safety imperiled met both needs. It provided a new mission, one at which Americans had already proven adept in world war, and one so grand that it ran no risk of quick fulfillment. Widespread notions of "maturity" buttressed the new outlook: the truly mature nation, like the truly mature individual, took on new responsibilities, such as those for world peace and order. At the same time, those notions revealed an underlying unease, as national elites worried whether Americans would have the maturity to follow them and shoulder new burdens.

Such an explanation of postwar culture is necessarily speculative, but it helps explain the paradoxical mix of moods evident: the brittle assertion of American superiority and the gnawing sense of American hollowness; the extraordinary focus on external threats and the deep fears of internal subversion and sloth. Of course, an unanswerable chicken-and-egg question remains: Were certain values upheld to maintain the nation's strength, or was national security simply invoked to uphold values desired for other reasons? The point is not that anxieties about national safety *caused* certain cultural prescriptions, but rather that culture was inescapably colored by those anxieties.

Writers, intellectuals, and artists helped to give shape and expression to the themes that ensued in this militarized culture. They had already worked to fashion meanings for World War II, just as many found it their duty to serve in the Cold War. As in other professions, most historians accepted "American ideological mobilization," as Peter Novick has called it. "Total war, whether it be hot or cold, enlists everyone and calls upon everyone to assume his part," announced the American Historical Association's president, Conyers Read, in his 1949 address. "The historian is no freer from this obligation than the physicist." Merle Curti found Read's speech to be "really dreadful from a president of the AHA," and many intellectuals resisted conscription when so baldly phrased. Others made their contribution, however, as when historians embraced new Western civilization courses in order to mobilize students against totalitarian dangers. When the Massachusetts Institute of Technology began government-sponsored work on political warfare (in addition to its far larger weapons programs), historian Elting Morison offered a response typical among liberal intellectuals: he worried about the secrecy involved and the power of "the garrison state" but did not oppose the project. And since that project was secret, no open debate about it emerged at MIT (or at most other schools).[76]

It was the shift in focus—to matters of war and weapons—more than ideological changes per se that revealed the militarizing process. For sure, ideological conservatism marked and facilitated that shift. Many artists and intellectuals became disillusioned by the rigid banalities of the American Communist Party, by the monstrosities of Stalin's regime, or by the perils of any avowedly ideological system. Political pressure from college trustees, government agents, or fellow intellectuals abetted the change. The result was the much noticed flight of intellectuals from Marxist or other radical politics, as they (ironically) fashioned an ideological defense of their presumably nonideological politics. The sources and impact of this flight can be exaggerated, however. It did not embrace all artists and intellectuals, and evident as it was before and during World War II, it did spring only from postwar anticommunism. A focus on the rightward drift of high culture also obscures the shift in agendas even among those who opposed national policies.

Prominent postwar writers traced this grand shift, although they hardly always celebrated it, as they explored experiences and themes in war and national security: John Hersey in nonfiction (*Hiroshima*, 1946); Norman Mailer in *The Naked and the Dead* (1948); Irwin Shaw in *The Young Lions* (1948); James Jones in *From Here to Eternity* (1951); and Arthur Miller in *The Crucible* (1953). In one sense, this outpouring of literary attention, often portraying America or its government savagely, was not surprising, certainly not to readers of post–World War I fiction, but its themes, like its sheer bulk and critical acclaim, were notable. Writers in the 1920s had looked back on a war that had come and gone, often less interested in the war itself than in what it showed about the hypocrisies of American culture or the frailties of human nature. Post–World War II writers hardly missed those themes, but for them war was an ever-present menace, not just a bygone revelatory event. They looked not only back on the last war but ahead to the next one, dreading it and the values that would produce it.

Of course, many postwar writers—southerners like Tennessee Williams and Eudora Welty, and chroniclers of middle-class life like John Cheever—largely avoided war themes and settings, stressing instead the intimate and the personal. That focus, however, may have reflected their desire to create a space beyond the reach of the state, the bomb, and the communists—to preserve individual autonomy in a war-mad world. Even in those private spaces, war could intrude: Cheever's "Country Husband," suddenly flooded with memories of wartime brutality, stared at a room of people "united in their tacit claim that there had been no past, no war—that there was no danger or trouble in the world."[77]

Arthur Schlesinger, Jr., the young historian and Democratic liberal, exposed the shift in cultural emphases in *The Vital Center* (1949). Americans, he argued, live in "an age of anxiety" and "look back to totalitarianism, to concentration camps, to mass starvation, to atomic war." They face "a permanent crisis which will test the moral, political and very possibly the military strength of each side." Schlesinger believed that "Soviet power will surely spread everywhere that it meets no firm resistance."[78]

Schlesinger demonstrated how many intellectuals, even while consumed by issues of war and national security, ignored the deeper process of militarization, their own country's role in it, and the manner in which it was changing the nation. "History has thrust a world destiny on the United States. No nation, perhaps, has become a more reluctant great power." Despite his bleak concern about totalitarian menace and atomic peril, Schlesinger located the causes of modern anxiety elsewhere, in "industrial organization and the post-industrial state, whatever the system of ownership," which "impersonalize economic relationships." He made little allowance for how the Cold War and the prospect of atomic war might instill anxiety, in part because he saw the enemy's menace as above all ideological and covert: "The special Soviet advantage—the warhead—lies in the fifth column." Consequently, Schlesinger said nothing about how militarized institutions and folkways might spring from the nation's own impulses and redefine life for Americans. To be sure, that was in part because, although anticipating a possible test of "military strength," he distrusted the impulse to intimidate the Soviet Union with a "flourish of guided missiles and atomic bombs." Yet in sidestepping the world of war and weapons and locating "anxiety" outside of it, Schlesinger created a jarring, myopic tract of his times.[79]

He made a potent brew by adding to Cold War fears a bundle of cultural anxieties about the moral decay, impersonality, and immaturity of Americans in a time of peril. Industrialism breeds anonymity and ennui, he asserted, and "drives the free individual to the wall." In response, the foolish and faint-hearted, like the "wailer," grasp at simplistic solutions: totalitarian ideologies, hysterical anticommunism, or the fraudulent radicalism of Wallace's Progressives, who serve "the purpose of those who wish free society to fail." "Conservatism in its crisis of despair turns to fascism: so progressivism in its crisis of despair turns to Communism." In strikingly phallic language, Schlesinger saw the psychic immaturity of enemies to the right and left of him as undermining the national equanimity needed for winning the Cold War and curing the woes of industrialism. Progressives are "soft, not hard," with a fatal "weakness for impotence." Totalitarianism "perverts politics into something secret, sweaty and furtive like nothing so much . . . as homosexuality in a boy's school: many practicing it, but all those caught to be caned by the headmaster." Indeed, communists resemble homosexuals, he suggested: "They can identify each other . . . on casual meeting by the use of certain phrases, the names of certain friends, by certain enthusiasms and certain silences," in a way similar to a "famous scene in Proust" (the homosexual French writer) when two characters "suddenly recognize their common corruption." Schlesinger saw real radicals (the liberals he liked) as smart and virile (and presumably male). They would oppose totalitarianism, purge subversives by "constitutional methods" (unless "a clear and present danger" emerges), and preserve the "limited state." Perhaps radical as measured against postwar conservatism, Schlesinger's blueprint was quite limited by other standards, but toughness and cool realism defined his radicals more than their programs. They had "radical nerve," embraced freedom as "a fighting faith," and knew that it would survive "only if enough people believe in it deeply enough to die for it." "The center is vital; the center must hold."[80]

Other intellectuals shared many of Schlesinger's emphases. Historian David Potter, in *People of Plenty* (1954), brilliantly explored the impact of economic abundance on the American character, but he saw little role for war and military power in making or protecting that abundance, or for abundance in shaping an American military style. In *American Life: Dream and Reality* (1953), sociologist Lloyd Warner explored the satisfactions that war had for Americans, but in an ahistorical manner: he made war's appeals seem timeless, as if World War II and the Cold War created or expressed nothing new. Writing a few years later, John Kenneth Galbraith came closer to the mark in *The Affluent Society* (1958). The problem he addressed—of private wealth and public impoverishment in a system still geared to insufficiency—was worsened, he noted, by the devotion of so many federal resources to defense. Yet Galbraith's discussion of "the illusion of national security" was so brief and compartmentalized, and his faith in the expansive capacity of the American economy so strong, that the Cold War and militarization slipped from his view. Even when intellectuals viewed America's global hegemony and military power suspiciously, they could also see those developments as signs of national maturity, since, wrote historian Richard Hofstadter, they also entailed "the final involvement of the nation in all the realities it had sought to avoid, for now it was not only mechanized and urbanized, but internationalized as well."[81]

What distinguished liberal intellectuals was less a lack of critical edge, the sin for which they have often been savaged, than the focus of their critical aptitude. They sometimes dealt insightfully with the problems of mass culture and affluence and the dangers they posed for America in the Cold War, but the transforming capacity of militarization largely escaped their attention. When they did notice it, their impulse was to caution against excesses—the hysterics of McCarthyism, the temptation to unleash atomic bombs—but not to criticize the system that underlay them. They examined how an inadequate culture undermined national security, not how national security redefined culture. Thus their critiques of American "conformity" explained it as the result of almost everything except the demands of war and national power.

To be sure, there was perhaps a subtle resistance involved in identifying other agendas, like problems of industrialism and abundance—to do so was to stake a claim that national security was not the only concern. At the same time, however, the intellectuals' mordant portrait of a vacuous consumer culture and its soft and soulless inhabitants suggested their fear that Americans would be inadequate to the demands of national security. The problem for them, Schlesinger believed, was that "the world tragedy still has the flickering unreality of a motion picture." Anxiety "is not yet part of our lives—not of enough of our lives, anyway, to inform our national decisions."[82] No wonder so many of this generation of intellectuals would soon be attracted to the muscular postures and policies of John Kennedy.

Women might have offered a distinctive voice on these matters, as they had before and would again, but in many ways this period marked the nadir of their modern political and cultural presence, including a dramatic shrinkage in their representation in many professions. Eleanor Roosevelt, perhaps the most prominent postwar female figure, advanced an assertive liberal agenda, but usually within a Cold War context. The long tradition of feminist cultural criticism largely fell silent or was denied much of an audience.

There were, of course, those who saw militarization and resisted it. They often worked outside dominant intellectual institutions or found themselves pushed to the margins. The radical journalist I. F. Stone poured out a stream of topical commentary. In 1956, the journalist and historian Walter Millis, in *Arms and Men: A Study in American Military History*, condemned the major powers' military policies for having "extinguished" freedom for much of the world and "pressing more heavily upon [Americans] than is generally realized." Although "adopted everywhere in the name of 'national security,'" Millis wrote, those policies "have spread a corroding sense of insecurity through all the more advanced peoples of the earth" and brought them "within possible distance of the extinction of civilization, if not of humanity itself." In the same year, Columbia University sociologist C. Wright Mills published *The Power Elite*, condemning a triumphant "military metaphysics—the cast of mind that defines international reality as basically military," for which he held civilian elites more responsible than military men.[83]

Perhaps the most angry and respected among these voices was Lewis Mumford. A public intellectual rather than an academic, earlier a dogmatic antifascist, he was largely invulnerable to typecasting as left-winger or fellow traveler. Already shedding his technological optimism before World War II, he responded to that war, his son's death in it, and the atomic attacks that closed it by a quest to stop the warfare state that consumed the rest of his long life (1895–1990). That this wide-ranging intellect became so consumed was itself a marker of militarization—it embraced those who resisted as well as those who followed.

Just as telling were Mumford's message and its fate. He sought the heart of the new militarized system and condemned it, not just the excesses which other intellectuals usually criticized, seeing those excesses as inherent in the system. The result was an uncompromising position: "Abandon the Atomic Bomb! Give it up! Stop it now! That is the only order of the day," he proclaimed in 1946. Above all, he sought to strip away "the warfare state's vaunted veneer of scientific rationality." To that end, he savaged reigning notions of the political neutrality and intellectual objectivity of scientists, "berating them for their alliance with the military and capitalism" and antagonizing a great many of them. Mumford found an audience, but not always a receptive one. He could not be ignored, but reviewers and opponents typed him, even in a more sympathetic political climate during the 1960s, as an anti-intellectual, angry, despairing old man, despite his effort to chart an optimistic course away from the madness he perceived.[84]

Particularly in his attack on science, Mumford ran into an intellectual outlook developed on the eve of World War II and tenacious after it. "The denigration of ideology, one of the most characteristic features of American culture in the cold war era, was directly related to the celebration of objectivity as the hallmark of thought in the Free World," argues Peter Novick. Scientists, historians, sociologists, economists, and other intellectuals disparaged the claims of ideological systems and the wisdom of ideological debate ("Democracy of the American brand is anti-ideology," argued Jacques Barzun). They saw themselves engaged in "the disinterested search for objective truth," whereas scholars and scientists in totalitarian systems practiced "gangster science" done on the state's orders. American intellectuals struck that posture even though, as Novick acidly comments, "'gangster science'—highly organized, mission-oriented research—became the dominant [American] mode of scientific organization."[85]

Whatever its epistemological validity, the presumption of intellectuals' objectivity was a revealing cultural norm. Shielding them from criticism of their role in militarization, it also showed the reach of militarization, as "older notions of an adversarial posture between intellect and power were abandoned as 'immature.'"[86] It was also shared by many policymakers, who saw themselves as realists objectively assessing enemy threats and American interests. In both cases, that norm disguised moralistic and ideological impulses while it legitimated claims to power. Moreover, the norm spread far. Americans were told, perhaps more than at any other time in their history, to trust objective experts to solve all sorts of problems, from the riddles of nuclear strategy to juvenile pathology and family conflict.

Just as the values of intellectuals limited dissent in a militarized culture, so did older patriotic values that defined the outlook of many Americans and often had the power of the state behind them. Patriotic culture was sustained by Hollywood movies about World War II, by the activities of patriotic groups, and by efforts to memorialize epic moments of the war like Pearl Harbor and Iwo Jima. At the war's close, Joe Rosenthal's famous photograph of Marines raising the flag at Iwo Jima was plastered on newspapers, stamps, war bond ads, recruiting posters, and trolley cars, so that it quickly "became the definitive, collective memory of war: its classical, sculptural calm; the absence of bloodshed; the triumphant lift of the Stars and Stripes all suited the national temper." That "classical calm" contrasted sharply with the highly disordered and anonymous images of destruction associated with death camps and bombed cities. It indicated a widespread and often state-supported effort to re-construct a belief in war's orderliness and America's purposefulness. That effort was capped at Arlington Cemetery in 1954 by the unveiling of an Iwo Jima memorial (based on Rosenthal's photo), an outsized piece of "heroic realism" (to a few critics, too much like the Stalinist version) that seemed to embody American patriotism and power.[87]

This patriotic culture was no untroubled repetition of earlier pageantry. *Sands of Iwo Jima* (1949) featured the staunchly anticommunist actor John Wayne but presented his character as "pursued by private demons," just as many war films "represented the feelings of men at war—not their heroic deeds." Herman Wouk's bestselling novel, play, and movie *The Caine Mutiny* (1951) caught the tensions, as it seemed first to endorse and then to condemn an officers' revolt against an irrational naval commander. The popularity of images like those about Iwo Jima and the ending of Wouk's drama, however, suggested the enduring appeal of a heroic view of war, a celebratory regard for American power, and deference toward military authority. Significantly, government propaganda showed how individual initiative, military rationality, and national triumph could endure even in atomic war.[88]

Despite the reach of patriotic culture, resistance did appear among ordinary Americans, not just elite figures like Mumford. It came not only in politicized ways—the work of radical unionists or the lyrics of pacifist songs, for example—but in less articulate cultural forms such as teen films and rock'n'roll. So at least some adults thought in the 1950s, when they placed rock'n'roll on a slippery slope (marked also by bad grades, delinquency, teen-age pregnancy, and suggestive movies) that might end in the abyss of communism or besmirch America's image abroad. Such concerns prompted Republican Clare Booth Luce, for example, to work with the State Department to force the withdrawal from the Venice Film Festival of *Blackboard Jungle* (1955), a Hollywood film about unruly big-city high school students. And perhaps the fears were not baseless: If politics is defined "as an abstract body of thought," argues George Lipsitz, then rock songs "were apolitical," but if defined "as the social struggle for a good life," rock "represented politics of the highest order."[89]

Even the culture of consumption offered a subtle resistance. When Americans flocked to suburbia, purchased new products, and glued themselves to television sets, they signaled that their priorities lay with the quality and prosperity of their daily lives, not with national power and grand crusades abroad. To be sure, those daily habits rarely involved conscious resistance to national priorities, which most Americans tacitly approved in opinion polls and voting booths, and may have lured many Americans into a complacency that coopted any resistance, as some foes of Cold War policy charged.

Yet cultural resistance does not always entail conscious defiance, and certainly intellectuals and politicians often worried that the habits and values of consumer culture undermined the toughness needed to prevail in the world.

True, consumer culture and its female homemakers were deployed as weapons in the Cold War, as when Vice President Nixon, in his famous 1959 "kitchen debate" with Soviet premier Nikita Khrushchev, pointed to the American kitchen as an emblem of American superiority. "Would it not be better to compete in the relative merits of washing machines than in the strength of rockets?" asked Nixon. Although "unwitting soldiers," notes one historian, "women who marched off to the nation's shopping centers to equip their new homes joined the ranks of American cold warriors." But it was one thing for Americans to take pride in their affluence, another to overindulge it, and Khrushchev's boast that Russian rockets were bigger was nerve-wracking. As historian Samuel Flagg Bemis charged in 1962, in a complaint common after the Sputnik "crisis," Americans had been "experiencing the world crisis from soft seats of comfort, debauched by [the] mass media . . . , pandering for selfish profit to the lowest level of our easy appetites, fed full of toys and gewgaws, our military preparedness held back by insidious strikes for less work and more power, our manpower softened in will and body in a climate of amusement." Affluence stirred pride, but also alarm for the nation's safety.[90]

Although political dissent was often silenced by direct repression, cultural resistance was less subject to the state's heavy hand, for its modes were too diffuse, honorably American, or uncalculated, as with the culture of consumption. In a nation waging a confusing global struggle and lacking the clarity imposed by full-scale war, it was often hard to agree on what constituted subversive, divisive, or wrongheaded values. Was modern art corrupting or a symbol of American superiority? Did consumer culture embody the American Way of Life or undermine the will of a people at war? Was angst over nuclear weapons a logical reaction to them or the entering wedge of opposition to national policies?

Given those uncertainties, one option was to contain dubious or rebellious impulses rather than crush them, much as leaders sought to contain communism itself. Political and professional authorities relied heavily on cultural containment, Elaine Tyler May suggests in *Homeward Bound*. Too sophisticated to believe in the wisdom or practicality of stamping out those impulses, they tried instead to contain sexual liberalism, juvenile defiance, women's complaints, male revolt, and escalating spending habits within the home and the "traditional" family, an ideal largely invented in the postwar era. Through early marriage and freer sexual practices, for example, young people would safely enjoy an enlightened, even indulgent sexuality. Much the same might be said about dominant responses to artistic innovation or to the cultural practices of ethnic, racial, and religious minorities.

Adding urgency to this drive to contain culture was new evidence of its plasticity. Wartime mobilization had revealed that presumably stable arrangements of class, race, gender and the like were malleable: women *could* drive rivets; gay men *could* bayonet enemies; blacks *could* fly planes. Political and professional elites responded to this plasticity by asserting the presumed timelessness of cultural norms, though less so when race was involved: the idealized family *was* traditional; women's domestic roles *were* natural; the homosexual's pathology *was* immutable. Of course, many of their actions went far beyond containment—homosexuals could be locked up, books censored, film directors blacklisted—and containment all but collapsed in the 1960s, but it usefully describes the principal achievement, if not always the conscious intent, of cultural authorities early in the Cold War.

Meanwhile, political leaders continued to shape cultural rituals. On February 7, 1954, the Reverend George Docherty warned his congregation of Washington, D.C., Presbyterians that the 1892 Pledge of Allegiance to the Flag was inadequate—"in his imagination, he could hear 'little Muscovites repeat a similar pledge to their hammer-and-sickle flag,' for the USSR also claimed to be a republic with justice and liberty." The Constitution might mandate separation of church and state, but "an atheistic American is a contradiction in terms." President Eisenhower, having heard Docherty's sermon, told a national radio audience later that day that all Americans, whatever their "personal creed," believed in a higher power. Congress passed a resolution inserting "under God" into the pledge in time for Ike's signature on Flag Day, June 14.[91] National security, it seems, demanded that God, too, enlist in the cause.

The Red Scare

In 1947, the same year that *Advancing American Art* aroused such controversy, House Un-American Activities Committee (HUAC) chairman J. Parnell Thomas asked a question endlessly repeated in the coming years: "Are you now, or have you ever been, a member of the Communist Party of the United States?" His target was screenwriter John Howard Lawson, one of the "Hollywood Ten," a group of writers and directors soon jailed for contempt of Congress after refusing to cooperate with the committee (two ended up in jail with Thomas, who was later convicted of accepting kickbacks). The HUAC inquiry fed on suspicions of Hollywood as an alien, Jewish industry that propagated the communist line and subverted cultural values. In fact, the Hollywood Ten were or had been party members; Screen Actors Guild president Ronald Reagan was not wholly off-base in testifying about communist influence. Their influence on filmmaking was another matter, however, since producers and studio heads were no more inclined to buck the political tide in 1947 than in 1941. It strained things for writer Ayn Rand to cite *Song of Russia* (1943) as communist-inspired because it showed smiling Russians (in reality they only smile "privately and accidentally," she claimed). But the Red Scare now had its audience and stars; as laconic offscreen as on, Gary Cooper testified that he disliked communism "because it isn't on the level."[92]

The Red Scare was a highly politicized form of postwar militarization, a form closely linked to its cultural dimensions. As the Hollywood Ten case suggests, the boundaries between culture and politics were blurry and victims were found in many sectors of American life. Libraries, universities, and public schools waged or suffered anticommunist witch-hunts. Members of many trades and professions (including wrestlers in Indiana), workers in many businesses, even recipients of unemployment compensation (in Ohio) were required to sign loyalty oaths, while the Cincinnati Reds were solemnly renamed the "Redlegs" for a time, lest anyone question the baseball players' patriotic credentials. Although most sensational in Washington, the Red Scare also bubbled up in the activities of state legislatures and municipal governments, creating a crazy quilt of laws and rules banning in one locality what was legal in another, and it was carried on by private organizations like the American Legion, the Catholic church, and countless smaller and now forgotten groups. Some Americans were more vulnerable than others: political liberals and radicals, especially if linked with the New Deal; homosexuals in government or military service; foreign-born citizens and aliens (though this Red Scare was notably less nativist than the first); on occasion, even real communists. So fickle were the winds of suspicion, however, that they crushed many who had no reason to suspect their vulnerability.

Although predating Republican senator Joe McCarthy's sensational career and never confined to it, "McCarthyism," as it came to be called, was at the heart of the Red Scare. Defined that way, it was short-lived compared to the broader course of militarization, lasting until the mid-1950s, but it also drew deeply from the history, institutions, and anxieties of militarization. Its precedents lay in the first Red Scare at the close of World War I and the Brown Scare of World War II; "Truman did not invent so much as codify, institutionalize, broaden, and tighten FDR's jury-rigged wartime program."[93] Its assumptions were the same ones pounded home before and after Pearl Harbor: that old distinctions between foreign and domestic policy, between war and peace, between dissent and treason, between external and internal enemies, had evaporated. It was not, then, some unfortunate or expendable excess of militarization but something near its core, just as repression and surveillance outlasted it.

Among the many paradoxes of the Red Scare was the seeming disinterest of its most infamous leaders in the fundamentals of national power and the global struggle. Men like McCarthy cared little about the intricacies of nuclear strategy, the deployment of American power abroad, or the world beyond American shores. In fact, they often showed disdain for such matters. It was domestic enemies they sought (though offstage McCarthy seemed to bare even them no ill-will). It was the Cold War at home they wanted to win—root out the traitors, appeasers, and deviants at home, and triumph abroad would naturally follow.

Indeed, in that sense they resisted the broader course of militarization. They saw no permanent crisis but instead wanted a quick victory. Temperamentally and politically, their kin were some military officers and other Americans who wanted a preventive nuclear attack on the Soviets that would end the Cold War without the fuss of large-scale mobilization, cumbersome alliances, or frustrating compromises. Provincial or reactionary figures like McCarthy hardly alone caused the Red Scare, since men of wealth and power (the Kennedy family) could support them and Truman Democrats had their own fears for internal security, but McCarthy and his kind did much to set the Red Scare's tone. Frequently, their attacks fell on the leaders and symbols of the very institutional apparatus—the State Department, the Pentagon, and the presidency itself—erected to wage cold war and protect national security.

By the same token, their appeal came partly from their attacks on big government, whose scale and anonymous power alienated many Americans grounded in individualist and antistatist traditions. After all, McCarthy and his kind leveled their most sensational charges against the men (and on occasion women) who wielded that power, especially those with a privileged social background (Truman's provincial origins made him a less easy target). McCarthy revealed that thrust in his first major address on the communist danger in February 1950: Neither minorities nor disadvantaged Americans "have been selling this nation out," he declared, "but rather those who have had all the benefits . . . —the finest homes, the finest college education, and the finest jobs in Government we can give." Alger Hiss, the former assistant secretary of state convicted (after one hung jury) in 1950 of perjury about his communist connections during the 1930s, was a favorite target. A graduate of Johns Hopkins and Harvard Law School, Hiss embodied stereotypes of eastern establishment privilege, and his defenders, so one journal called them, were "the American respectables, the socially pedigreed, the culturally acceptable." Secretary of State Acheson, with his British airs and lofty manner, was another favorite target—the "Red Dean of the State Department," according to McCarthy, with his "cane, spats, and tea-sipping little finger." If officials also seemed effete, hints of homosexuality were added to denunciations of them.[94]

Power and privilege made others vulnerable as well. "Adlai [Stevenson] the appeaser," according to Nixon, was a "Ph.D. graduate of Dean Acheson's cowardly college of Communist containment." The "China hands" in the State Department often fit the same bill. Though less a symbol of privilege, no one became the object of a more vicious attack than Gen. George Marshall, the era's supreme figure in national security. Indiana senator William Jenner called him "a living lie," "a front man for traitors," and "either an unsuspecting stooge or an actual co-conspirator with the most treasonable array of political cutthroats ever turned loose in the Executive Branch of Government." He was, said McCarthy, part of "a conspiracy so immense and an infamy so black as to dwarf any previous such venture in the history of man." McCarthy's career climaxed in 1954 with attacks on the Pentagon. However wild, those attacks displayed his consistent focus on the upper reaches of the national security state.[95]

Though less in the public eye than men like McCarthy, the institutional apparatus for policing dissent and subversion sustained the Red Scare. Truman's Loyalty Review Board, the military services and the AEC, the CIA and J. Edgar Hoover's FBI, and congressional committees variously scrutinized and harassed individuals, watched for spies, made the public case for repression, infiltrated and sabotaged suspect organizations, exchanged a wealth of information (often outrageously inaccurate), and arrested, fired, or deported alleged offenders, with little interference from a compliant court system. Their avowed target was communists—spies and dupes doing the Kremlin's bidding—and while men like McCarthy rarely proved their accusations, real enemy agents did seek America's secrets, and the Communist Party USA and allied groups did follow Moscow's heavy-handed direction (though less slavishly than most Americans thought).

To many Americans, the case of Julius and Ethel Rosenberg, executed in 1953 as "atomic spies" for the Soviet Union, gave convincing proof of a communist danger. They, at least Julius, likely did play a role in passing information about America's nuclear weapons program, but responses to their case also showed how authorities exaggerated threats during the Red Scare (and how gender and anti-Semitism could also play a role). Grossly distorting the role of the Rosenbergs and atomic espionage generally in the Soviet nuclear program, as if Soviet scientists had no talent in such matters, Judge Irving Kaufman asserted that the Rosenbergs handed Moscow the atomic secret "years before our best scientists predicted Russia would perfect the bomb," although Soviet development of the bomb matched the predictions of many of those scientists, and declared that their espionage "has already caused . . . the Communist aggression in Korea" and perhaps the lives of "millions more innocent people" in the future.[96]

Still, subversive activities or party connections were by no means the only target of the Red Scare: beliefs and behavior of a wide range could bring people under suspicion. One could be a "loyalty" risk even if not a "security" risk, or, as Robert Oppenheimer found out in 1954 when the AEC denied him a security clearance, one could be "a loyal citizen" but still a security risk. Nor were beliefs the only sign of presumed danger, as thousands of homosexuals found out (their presumed vulnerability to blackmail by the enemy was an enduring myth of the Cold War), and as McCarthy kept insinuating: he called Dean Acheson "the Red Dean of fashion" and sought to root out the "Communists and queers" and "prancing mimics of the Moscow party line in the State Department." The looseness of such standards showed how the Red Scare fed on more than fear of communism. Militarization in other forms conscripted economic, social, and cultural resources; the Red Scare embodied an attempt to conscript the most intangible resources of all: conscience and loyalty, an all-encompassing but also hopelessly vague state of mind and character.[97]

It is true that the state conscripted those resources in a chaotic and capricious fashion—the "state" was really a hodge-podge of agencies and headline-grabbing individuals often at odds with each other, not the efficient machine associated with totalitarian regimes. Hence one reason for the agony of Americans who faced inquisitors insisting that they recant a murky past, name untrustworthy associates, or otherwise enlist in the cause: the process was made even more excruciating by its vague and ever-shifting standards. Caprice and chaos indicated not the absence of militarization but its characteristic American form, however. Pluralistic, civil libertarian, and antistatist traditions, like bureaucratic rivalries, ruled out the operation of any monolithic machine. A political system that both practiced repression and denied the intent to do so allowed authority to scatter in all sorts of directions, which only encouraged its capricious use.

The Red Scare also fed on frustrations over America's apparent failure to "win" the Cold War despite its ideological, economic, and nuclear superiority. World War II had made "total victory" the American goal in facing totalitarians, yet many Americans did not see their government pursuing total victory in this new war (and probably did not want it to). What could explain America's failure to win when it possessed the means to achieve victory, if not corruption or sabotage of the will to win? Men like McCarthy had a nasty answer to that nagging question: traitors in the upper reaches of government and other institutions were denying America victory in the Cold War. Hence, too, the close correlation between apparent American defeat in the Cold War and the mounting zeal of those campaigns: they peaked in the late 1940s and early 1950s, when communist rule in Eastern Europe and China was consolidated, when the Soviet Union acquired atomic weapons, and when the Korean War reached a stalemate.

Who ruled at home drove the Red Scare as much as who conquered abroad, however, so it was also driven by partisan politics. Democrats were often ardent practitioners, whether to berate opponents in their own party, to protect themselves from Republican charges that they were "soft" on communism, or to act on their own worries about national security. In a major step, Truman initiated a new loyalty program in February 1947, providing an apparatus for discharging "disloyal" federal employees and formalizing the attorney general's listing of groups deemed "totalitarian, fascist, communist, or subversive." Democrats also issued some of the most purple rhetoric. As J. Howard McGrath, Truman's attorney general, warned, "There are today many communists in America. They are everywhere—in factories, offices, butcher stores, on street corners, in private business. And each carries in himself the death of our society." Or as Adlai Stevenson declared during his 1952 presidential campaign, "Soviet secret agents and their dupes" had "burrowed like moles" into governments everywhere, and "one by one the lamps of civilization go out and nameless horrors are perpetrated in darkness." Centrist Democrats like Truman did try to restrain free-swinging witch-hunters like McCarthy and to maintain due process in efforts to root out subversion, but they also red-baited

Wallace and the Progressives and sanctioned a widening net of federal efforts to weed out domestic foes. Meanwhile, southern Democrats attacked advocates of civil rights. "One of the most vicious movements that has yet been instituted by the crackpots, the Communists and the parlor pinks in this country is trying to browbeat the American Red Cross into taking the labels off the blood bank . . . so that it will not show whether it is Negro blood or white blood," charged Congressman John Rankin.[98]

Democrats were usually on the defensive, however. Insofar as they believed they "stole the Republican thunder" with Truman's loyalty program, they were wrong—they only further validated suspicions soon turned back against them. Republicans stood to gain the most from the Red Scare and pressed it hardest for political advantage. Long out of the White House, frustrated anew by Dewey's stunning loss to Truman in 1948, they sought to discredit the Democratic party by placing New Deal liberalism on a slippery slope that ran down to socialism and communism. The country, charged Republican Congressman Karl Mundt in a typical attack, "for eighteen years had been run by New Dealers, Fair Dealers, Misdealers and [Alger] Hiss dealers who have shuttled back and forth between Freedom and Red Fascism like a pendulum on a kukoo clock." In 1950 Richard Nixon declared that his opponent for the Senate, Helen Gahagan Douglas, "follows the Communist Party line." Despite their knowledge of the witch-hunters' dishonesty, GOP leaders like Senator Robert Taft egged on McCarthy, Jenner, and other Republicans, Taft telling McCarthy "if one case [alleging subversion in the Truman Administration] didn't work, to bring up another." The aftermath of the 1952 elections demonstrated anew the role of partisan politics in the Red Scare: when McCarthy continued his accusations even though the GOP now controlled the White House, Republican leaders moved, slowly but effectively, to drive him from power, helping to engineer the Senate's narrowly crafted censure of McCarthy in 1954. Meanwhile, a generation of younger Republicans like Nixon launched their careers by going after alleged communists and subversives.[99]

The result was a politics dominated by the rhetoric, symbols, and issues of national security. Citizens continued to vote on other issues and habits: there is little evidence that McCarthyite tactics alone swung many elections. "Everyone was against communism," Richard Fried notes, "but there were limits to the exertions the average citizen was willing to invest in that sentiment." Still, especially in the early 1950s, the politics of fear dominated many election campaigns, screamed out in the headlines, seized Congress's attention, burdened Presidents, and gutted leadership in key agencies. In that environment, there was limited room for other issues—racial and economic reform, for example—just as one thrust of the Red Scare was to keep such issues at bay. Even after the furor abated at mid-decade, many of its attitudes and practices persisted, just as the continuing use of the term *McCarthyism* into the 1990s, by then used to discredit people and beliefs across the full range of political activity, showed how the term continued to inform "our language—with a sloppiness worthy of its origins."[100]

The fate of two institutions illustrates the Red Scare's effects. Organized labor was systematically purged of communists and other radicals. The 1947 Taft-Hartley Act required union officials to swear they were not communists, management and conservative union leaders used the law as a tool for purging labor's ranks, and federal agencies like the AEC worked to discredit radical unions like the United Electrical Workers. Though labor's postwar conservatism had many sources, the Red Scare abetted a change that left unions ill equipped and disinclined to challenge Cold War policy and corporate control of the work force.

A similar though less brawling change unfolded in academia. Teachers fired or denied jobs probably numbered only in the hundreds, but, as Peter Novick notes, "the scarcity of overt instances" of repression was merely a "measure of its effectiveness." "Like the apocryphal small-town Nazis who petitioned Berlin to send them a Jewish shopkeeper so they could boycott him, there may have been the will within the university and the profession to repress dissident historians and historiography, but there wasn't much dissidence to repress." Publicly, elite schools proclaimed their defense of academic freedom and autonomy. Privately, they cooperated with the FBI and other agencies, in an effort nourished by mutual dependency between the academy and government regarding defense-related matters, and shrouded in a web of secrecy and deception. The mood was captured in 1949 by Yale's president: "There will be no witch-hunts at Yale because there will be no witches." Harvard president James Conant announced the same policy publicly, and privately with a vengeance. At its worst, it extended to seeing any opposition to dominant policies "as subversive—of nation, of family, of social order itself; it was to be hunted and uprooted." In response, some intellectuals were worried or defiant. "What is the new loyalty?" asked historian Henry Steele Commager. "It is, above all, conformity. It is the uncritical and unquestioning acceptance of America as it is." Many intellectuals, however, questioned only egregious abuses of state authority, not the basic need to exercise it against subversion and dissent. The good liberal state, they trusted, would operate by fair methods. Hence their shock when Oppenheimer was banished from the AEC: he fell victim not to raving congressmen or reactionary college trustees but to "the executive branch of the federal government—the very institution the intellectuals had fancied as their staunchest ally." Intellectuals were hardly "modern Dr. Frankensteins" now "horrified by the monster they had created," characterizations that overstate their influence, but "liberals' own militant anti-Communism" did contribute to the Red Scare.[101]

The Red Scare had mighty effects. Some were ironic over the long term: it fostered opposition to militarization from angry students, disillusioned liberals, indignant homosexuals, militant African-Americans, and others furious at its workings and its legacy. In the meantime, however, it helped to crush opposition to America's militarized course. The day-to-day dominance of its moods and issues traced the scale and depth of militarization. It is true that driving the Red Scare, alongside fears for national safety, were disparate conflicts rooted in region, ethnicity, gender, class, politics, and foreign policy. That, however, is the nature of militarization: it never arises solely out of military need, real or imagined. Its force derived from the manner in which all sorts of conflicts become subsumed under or attached to dominant anxieties about national security.

The Elusive War in Korea

"The average GI," commented Eric Goldman a few years after the Korean War, "had not the slightest idea why he was battling on these far-off hills. 'I'll fight for my country,' Corporal Stephen Zeg of Chicago put it, 'but I'll be damned if I see why I'm fighting to save this hell hole.'"[102] Probably most Americans felt like Zeg, their reflexive patriotism offsetting their considerable bewilderment. While they fretted, the war's consequences—in many ways the completion of America's militarization—settled in.

The war broke out in circumstances few Americans understood, although many were chronic features of the Cold War. Like many other Asian nations, Korea had been under imperial rule, although Japan, not a Western nation, had been its brutal overseer until Japan's defeat in 1945. As with Germany and Austria, Korea's military occupation had been divided, supposedly temporarily; Soviet forces assumed the task in the north, American in the south. The United States government, in order to contain both communism and South Korea's internal disorder, threw its support—reluctantly, at the instigation of American authorities in Seoul, but decisively—behind conservative political and social forces led by Syngman Rhee, a Princeton Ph.D., Korean nationalist, foe of Japanese rule, and head of a repressive and sometimes murderous government. In the north, a communist regime under Kim Il Sung took power through force, Soviet aid, and substantial popular support. The situation was unstable: each side was armed by a patron of uncertain reliability and each laid claim to the whole nation, prompting a civil war between them in the late 1940s.

American military leaders, pressed by commitments elsewhere, minimized Korea's strategic significance. Like Gen. Douglas MacArthur, commander of the occupation in Japan, the Joint Chiefs believed that "any commitment to United States use of military force in Korea would be ill-advised and impracticable."[103] They got American forces withdrawn in 1949, but the State Department resisted full disengagement, stressing South Korea's symbolic importance and the psychological repercussions of its fall to communism. Secretary of State Acheson walked the fine line in a famous January 1950 address, later blamed for encouraging North Korea's attack, in which he placed South Korea beyond the American defense perimeter but affirmed the hope it could be supported without military force. That hope seemed reasonable, since American officials anticipated no full-scale attack from the north.

Then, on June 25, 1950, the long civil war suddenly escalated when the North Korean army rolled across the 38th parallel, overwhelmed Rhee's forces, and swept through his capital of Seoul and beyond. Given five years of superpower jockeying for position, this war was probably doomed to become a Cold War battlefield, but American reactions helped seal that outcome. Reflexes conditioned by years of global crisis now snapped into place. To be sure, evidence that Stalin directed the North Korean attack was scant: the absence from the United Nations of his ambassador, who might have vetoed American-sponsored action, suggested that at least the timing of Kim Il Sung's offensive took the Kremlin by surprise. The press of American commitments elsewhere and the suspicious logic of Cold Warriors also might have stayed the administration's hand: it could have assumed that "cunning Kremlin strategists . . . were trying to entrap the United States" into a diversionary conflict or a killing ground.104 That this was a civil war between repressive regimes also argued for caution. On the other hand, Stalin likely played some role, giving the attack a green light if not instigating it, and in any event it was hard to know what his role was (even the Cold War's end yielded only teasing evidence that it was paramount). Conversely, the fact that Moscow distanced itself politically and militarily from North Korea at the war's start allowed Washington to entertain intervention without great fear of confronting Soviet forces.

Whatever those complexities, American leaders interpreted North Korea's offensive as part of Stalin's master plan for world conquest and placed it on the familiar grid of recent history. The American ambassador in Moscow labeled the North Korean attack a "clear-cut Soviet challenge" and State Department experts were certain that North Korea's government was "absolutely under Kremlin control." As Truman later recalled, he flew back to Washington meditating on "earlier instances" of aggression: "Manchuria, Ethiopia, Austria. I remembered how each time that the democracies failed to act it had encouraged the aggressors to keep going ahead. Communism was acting in Korea just as Hitler, Mussolini, and the Japanese had acted ten, fifteen, and twenty years earlier." At a key Washington conference, the view was unanimous that "refusal to repel the aggression would be nothing but 'appeasement.' And appeasement, as history has shown, would ultimately lead to war." By that reasoning, "we had to make a stand some time, or else let all of Asia go by the board," Truman argued. "If we were to let Asia go, the Near East would collapse and no telling what would happen in Europe." Press and politicians sometimes echoed that view: "Talk about parallels!" declared one Democrat in referring to "the actions which led to the Second World War." The 1930s did not offer the only analogy, but others (to Greece and Czechoslovakia in the late 1940s) offered the same lesson. Truman quickly decided to send American forces to Korea despite the reluctance, often shown during the Cold War, of many military officials.105

Tied to this sense of history were considerations of politics and policy. Few politicians or pundits in the days after June 25 called for the dispatch of American forces to Korea, but for an administration already taking blame for the loss of China and Eastern Europe to communism, embarking on new commitments in Asia and Europe, and weighing the rearmament plan laid out in NSC-68, the outbreak of war seemed both trap and opportunity. American intervention in Korea would open the fiscal spigots for rearmament, while inaction risked new abuse from opponents and a fatal blow to rearmament, which would be hard to justify if Truman seemed unwilling to use it. And, so policymakers also worried, if communists triumphed in Korea, a wider war in Asia might ensue under worse circumstances, diverting even more resources from Europe and jeopardizing Japan's pivotal role in the anticommunist alliance and its economic well-being. "Truman had to have a crisis to sell the NSC 68 program."[106] His reasoning resembled FDR's in 1941: action was necessary in the Far East in order to uphold a Europe-first priority, even as it risked undermining that priority. How could he proclaim a global struggle against communism and then elect to wage it only in Europe?

As in 1941, a President's expansive view of his prerogatives also encouraged intervention. Taft and other Republicans wanted Truman to consult Congress or seek a declaration of war, but Truman and Acheson maintained both the right and necessity of quick executive action. As Truman commented when he ordered in the first ground troops on June 30, "I just had to act as Commander-in-Chief, and I did."[107] That conception of his constitutional powers conflated his authority to command forces *in* war with his right to commit them *to* war (Article II made him commander in chief of American forces "when called into the actual service of the United States"), making him the nation's commander in chief, not just the military's.[108] Truman had precedent on his side but went beyond FDR's notable example in the Atlantic in 1941: Korea would be the largest war yet waged on presidential authority. Recourse to the United Nations Security Council, which sanctioned "police action" against North Korea's invasion, assisted the end run around Congress's power to declare war. Ironically, it seemed easier to get the UN than Congress to take action.

The parallels with 1941 ran beyond hard policy to intangible matters of mood. As they had after Pearl Harbor, some observers noticed how Americans welcomed the clarity of war after years of tension and confusion. "Never before," noted Joseph Harsch about his twenty years in Washington, "have I felt such a sense of relief and unity pass through the city."[109] In that spirit, some Washington insiders seemed to welcome possible Soviet or Chinese intervention in Korea as the pretext needed to launch a decisive nuclear attack on the Soviet Union. As in 1941, cultural and racial arrogance also made recourse to war easier. The administration initially committed only air and naval forces, because it sought to contain American involvement but also because it underestimated the enemy's military power and political appeal to South Koreans. The unlucky American ground forces rushed into battle in July—from Japan, where they had suffered the ills of lax training, alcohol, and venereal disease endemic to an occupation force—shared that optimism but met a superior force and humiliating defeat.

With their defeat, Truman's only choices seemed to be full-scale war or total retreat. He opted for the former, and a see-saw year of war sent Americans oscillating between exuberance and despair. After American and South Korean forces were driven into a small enclave in Korea's southeastern corner, General MacArthur launched a daring counterattack: on September 15, his forces carried out an amphibious, World War II–style landing at Inchon, on the western shore far behind North Korean lines, and then quickly recaptured Seoul and swept north beyond the 38th parallel. In a fateful decision shared by MacArthur, the Joint Chiefs, the White House, and the UN General Assembly, allied forces then struck north toward the border with China in order to reunite Korea. They also discounted warnings of possible Chinese intervention. That came in full force at the end of November, overwhelming MacArthur's overextended forces and sending them reeling back across the 38th parallel, along which the front stabilized by March 1951.

At that point MacArthur triggered a sensational crisis that laid bare the frustrations of containment. Amid back-biting over responsibility for November's disaster and talk of diplomatic efforts to end the war, he sent his forces across the 38th parallel again, called for Nationalist China (Formosa) to attack China, threatened to bomb China, and insisted that Asia, not Europe, was the decisive Cold War arena. Much of this differed little from the outlook of Washington policymakers a few months earlier: reunification had been their goal; Truman himself had publicly suggested possible use of atomic bombs in Korea; various officials had even discussed "the atomic bombardment of Soviet Russia itself" or similar schemes if Peking or Moscow continued to support North Korea. But MacArthur had gone public, after years of rancorous relationships with two Presidents, and an infuriated Truman fired him. Much hoopla ensued, as Truman's standing in opinion polls plunged and MacArthur returned to the United States "to receive a welcome that would have made Caesar envious," basking in ticker-tape parades and addressing Congress. One exasperated Truman advisor scripted a mock version of MacArthur's welcome in Washington: "12:30, Wades ashore from Snorkel submarine . . . 1:50, Burning of the Constitution; 1:55, Lynching of Secretary Acheson; 3:00, 21–atomic bomb salute; 3:30; 300 nude D.A.R.'s leap from Washington Monument . . . ." Tedious congressional hearings soon took the wind out of the drama and produced Gen. Omar Bradley's famous repudiation of MacArthur's strategy as one that "would involve us in the wrong war at the wrong place at the wrong time and with the wrong enemy."[110]

Truman and many others, then and later, construed his firing of MacArthur as a triumph of civilian over military authority, but it was never primarily that, as the Joint Chiefs' firm support of his decision made clear. Instead, MacArthur had tapped frustration over the ambiguities of containment, as the administration proclaimed a global struggle, played on memories of total victory in World War II, briefly sought such victory in Korea—and then, after China entered the war, settled for much less and for an endless Cold War. By showing "unrelenting hostility toward China and Russia, without ever doing anything to destroy the Communist nations," the administration seemed to "be accepting permanent tension, permanent risk, and a permanent postponement of the social and economic promises of the New Deal."[111]

Certainly the conduct of the Korean War during the rest of Truman's presidency promised no better outcome. The war became a contest among entrenched forces on a scarred and cold landscape, with the enemy making futile charges and allied forces unable to gain a decision. It was even uglier for World War II veterans called back to combat while younger Americans escaped it (until conscription pulled them into the pipeline), and by its end fifty-five thousand Americans had died in this "meat grinder of American manhood," as Congressman Albert Gore called it. Far more Koreans and Chinese succumbed—perhaps a million, even two million civilians alone in one estimate. By 1951, most Americans, as judged by opinion polls, wanted out of Korea and disliked Truman's handling of the war, but it dragged on, with armistice talks deadlocked in disagreements over prisoners of war.[112]

Truman did succeed in containing both communism and the impulse to wage world war. Still, it was a near miss. Korea was a limited war only in that it did not see atomic weapons used and did not spill beyond Korea's borders. Within those borders, it was as ferocious as any modern war, exposing anew the nature of American warmaking. In particular, the use of American air power reprised many of the motives, methods, and results seen in the war with Japan (with Japan now providing the air bases). Mindful of homefront repugnance at spilling American blood, frustrated in the ground war, and entranced by the promise of air power, American leaders unleashed the bombers again. B-29s spilled their incendiaries on Pyongyang, North Korea's capital, in January 1951, and the firebombing continued until nearly every North Korean city had been substantially destroyed and thousands of civilians killed. Fighter-bombers used similar tactics against smaller towns and villages close to the ground combat, showering their inhabitants with napalm; reports on the raids, I. F. Stone thought, had "a kind of gay moral imbecility . . . as if the fliers were playing in a bowling alley, with villages for pins." The air force sought to terrorize the populace into surrender; as Defense Secretary Robert Lovett put it in 1952, "If we keep on tearing the place apart, we can make it a most unpopular affair for the North Koreans."[113]

Strategic bombing could not, however, force surrender against an enemy with limited industry that drew much of its supplies from China and Russia. The bombers' other main goal, interdicting enemy supply lines running down to the front, met more success, but the communists' abundant manpower compensated for lost trucks and trains, while the celebrated American bombing of bridges across the Yalu River made less difference in winter, when the river froze anyway. The most effective use of American air power was in close support of ground forces. Meanwhile, the bombing effort was costly to the United States. Chinese fighters took a heavy toll of American aircraft and the firebombing provided communists an opportunity to protest alleged war crimes (committed also by communist forces, and by South Korea's on a scale either greater in reality or more easily documented).

The desire to do more bombing, though ridiculed when MacArthur displayed it, kept surfacing among Truman and other officials. Their public threats to attack China or the Soviet Union could be seen as attempts to intimidate the enemy rather than actually unleash atomic weapons, except that in private, too, they frequently and seriously considered employing such weapons. As late as January 27, 1952, even though (or precisely because) the war had settled into a stalemate, Truman mused in his diary about issuing the Soviet Union an ultimatum whose rejection would mean nuclear war. "It means that Moscow, St. Petersburg, Mukden, Vladivostock, Peking, Shanghai, Port Arthur, Dairen, Odessa, Stalingrad and every manufacturing plant in China and the Soviet Union will be eliminated."[114] Public opinion hardly seemed to restrain him: polls and political commentary showed consistent support for use of nuclear weapons. Truman knew, however, that American allies opposed such a drastic step and that the Soviet Union had atomic bombs and the capacity to deliver them on those allies, though not yet on the United States. His fantasy probably measured his frustration as much as his intention.

The atomic bombs did not fall, but the Korean War activated, enlarged, or redirected many facets of America's militarization, and in general completed it. That was most evident in the sheer scale and ambition of national security policies after June 1950, as the grand plans of NSC-68 sprung to life. The war instigated or crystallized commitments to aid the French in their war against insurgents in Indochina; to assist the Filipino government against the Huk insurgency; to protect and arm the Nationalist Chinese government on Formosa; and to repudiate previous consideration of diplomatic recognition of China's new communist government. It tightened a new Japanese-American alliance, as American spending in Japan for the war effort accelerated Japan's economic recovery, while a peace treaty granted the United States extensive military bases in Japan and Japan the opportunity for limited rearmament and enormous industrial expansion. The war brought to NATO the membership of Greece and Turkey, American support for West German rearmament, and more American forces to the Continent. The United States also acquired new bases in North Africa and the Middle East, substantially completing its aerial encirclement of the communist bloc. And it increased several-fold its military aid to allies, if only to assuage a fear among American leaders that inaction would weaken "foreign resolve and American reliability," a rationale that would virtually forbid any future cutbacks.[115]

A vast increase in defense budgets was the foundation of the administration's policy. Expenditures on national security (excluding veterans) more than tripled, reaching fifty billion dollars in 1953 (two-thirds of the federal government's budget), and their share of GNP shot up from 4.6 to 13.8 percent. The size of the armed forces more than doubled, peaking at 3.635 million personnel in uniform in 1952. Much manpower and money went to Korea, but much also to Europe, to new bases elsewhere, and to sharply expanded weapons programs. A new generation of jet fighters and bombers entered the pipeline, including nearly two thousand B-47 bombers and the longer-range B-52, along with jet tankers, supercarriers, and new tactical weapons, and work accelerated on long-range rockets and missiles and on an expanded nuclear arsenal. In October 1952, the United States tested its first hydrogen bomb—in a supreme irony, its fallout may have given Soviet scientists critical clues for designing hydrogen bombs, as Oppenheimer apparently feared in opposing a test.[116] Just as telling was work on tactical nuclear weapons small enough in weight and explosive power that tanks and artillery could shoot them. The goal, said the AEC's chairman, was "atomic weapons in almost as complete a variety as conventional ones, and a situation where we can use them in the same way."[117]

Swelling resources also underwrote new strategies for all-out war. Most experts in the late 1940s had counted on nuclear weapons to deter the Soviet Union's initiation of general war, but they also had regarded such a Soviet action as unlikely. In the 1950s, such a war seemed more imaginable and the American resources to fight it more abundant, and strategists contemplated waging it by nuclear assault on the Soviet Union and with nuclear and conventional forces in Western Europe. True, any imagined scenario for war still presented formidable difficulties. Experts could not figure out a sure-fire defense against nuclear attack on the United States, or give plausible assurances to European allies about how they could endure nuclear war, or discover how to win limited wars with acceptable American losses. Consequently, fierce debates erupted in the 1950s over which strategies to pursue and which forces to emphasize. Two factors diminished the significance of these debates. Even warfighting strategies fit into deterrence—rearmament of NATO allies, dispatch to Europe of more American forces and weapons—and the very talk about these matters was designed to deter Soviet action. These strategies presumably reinforced America's credibility, the paralyzing concern of its policymakers and one so capacious that it sanctioned all manner of weapons and forces. And the enormous expansion of resources made all options, to a degree at least, feasible. As in World War II, the tendency was to cover all bases, pursue all strategies, favor all military services, even at great cost. It was part of an outlook that gave the Truman administration "very much a sense of direction without destination," bereft of ways to limit and coordinate the means and ends of American policy.[118]

A telling measure of the militarization of American policy came from a leading figure who sought to restrain it. By 1950, George Kennan was entertaining

withdrawal of American power from Central Europe, Germany's neutralization, and American restraint in the nuclear arms race. "We are not yet ready to
lead the world to salvation. We have to save ourselves first," he had written
darkly. Yet he supported American intervention in the Korean War and mused
at its outbreak on the possibility that "we could . . . even bomb in Manchuria" if
China entered the war. Although warning against the attempt to reunify Korea
and willing to consider Japan's neutralization as part of a settlement of the Korean War, this man suspicious of a militarized foreign policy felt compelled to
endorse it in Korea.[119]

Truman's exercise of executive authority also displayed evidence of militarization. In 1948, he authorized the CIA to engage in a wide range of covert activities (one of its first was to fund anticommunists in an Italian election), which
would expand under Eisenhower. Indeed, in its "political and illegal uses of
intelligence and investigative agencies," its actions abroad "based on claims of
inherent powers and executive privilege," and its resistance to "congressional
oversight of executive branch activities," Truman's administration foreshadowed the abuses of power associated with later presidencies.[120]

For several reasons, Truman discounted the arrogation of executive power
and the broader militarization taking place on his watch. He viewed himself
modestly, after all—not for him the trappings of what came to be called the
"imperial presidency." He had reined in MacArthur. He saw containment, rearmament, and limited war not as a militarized policy but as a safeguard against
"a much higher level of mobilization" that would be required if the nation withdrew from the world and then faced a totalitarian onslaught, as he warned late
in his presidency. Withdrawal "would require us to become a garrison state,
and to impose upon ourselves a system of centralized regimentation unlike
anything we have ever known. . . . Its adoption would be a mandate for national suicide."[121] By his reasoning, war and rearmament were ways to avoid
becoming "a garrison state," not steps toward its creation.

He was hardly alone responsible for the celebration of presidential power.
Liberals defending FDR's legacy and Cold Warriors fearful of congressional
parochialism championed the cause. The prospect of "push-button" war, and
the sense that only experts could understand the dilemmas of nuclear strategy,
seemed to make congressional declarations of war impossible, although Truman brushed aside Congress even when time to deliberate was available, as at
the outbreak of the Korean War. The opposing view of presidential power came
primarily from McCarthyites demanding the secrets of executive bureaucracies
and conservatives fearing congressional impotence and presidential usurpation. The limits of opposition were revealed in *Life*'s response to Taft's insistence that Truman get congressional approval before committing American
forces to NATO. *Life* could criticize Truman savagely, but the fundamental matter "is the duty and power of the President to act for the United States in foreign
affairs. His hands are America's hands," it declared in a sweeping conflation of

person and nation. "They must not be tied." As conservative philosopher Clinton Rossiter maintained in 1960, "the President is not a Gulliver, immobilized by ten thousand tiny cords," but instead "a kind of magnificent lion who can roam freely and do great deeds so long as he does not try to break loose from his broad reservation."[122]

Roam he or his deputies did, especially in agencies like the AEC and the CIA. Once, Truman was corraled. When he seized steel mills facing a strike in 1952, invoking his power as commander in chief, the Supreme Court ruled that he had exceeded his authority. Intrusion on corporate interests marked one limit, but one outweighed by his ability to wage a long war, and do much else, on the strength of his power as commander in chief.

At the same time that the Korean War allowed American leaders to complete their militarized policies, however, it also set limits on their ambitions. When MacArthur's forces moved north toward the Yalu River in the fall of 1950, centrist and conservative Cold Warriors, long at odds with each other, had joined in a vision of rolling back communism—of overthrowing, not merely containing, a communist regime, Kim Il Sung's. China's intervention, raising the costs of rollback to apocalyptic levels, shattered their alliance, so that "the rollback strategy and its historic constituency then drifted toward the oblivion of crackpot surrealism . . . and containment became the modal choice of foreign policy elites." In some policy circles, even more in election-time political rhetoric, armed liberation of the enemy's lands still appealed, but Truman's Republican successors had little stomach for it in practice. As Treasury Secretary George Humphrey told the National Security Council in 1954, "an aggressive course of action to roll back Communism" was "not worth the risk it entails."[123]

The Korean War's effects extended into other arenas of American life as well, those beyond matters of grand strategy and presidential policy. The frustrations of the war fed the Red Scare. Although some liberals and leftists criticized the administration for not pursuing diplomatic options to end the war, the great weight of criticism came from the right. McCarthy was quick to pounce, already declaring in July 1950 that "highly placed Red Counselors" in the State Department were "far more deadly than Red machine gunners in Korea."[124] The infamous charges against Defense Secretary Marshall followed. So too did new legislation, the Internal Security Act (the McCarran Act), passed over Truman's veto with the widespread if grudging support of liberal senators like Minnesota's Hubert Humphrey and Illinois's Paul Douglas.

In culture, too, the war's effects were substantial, although that story remains largely unwritten by historians. For young boys encountering an ongoing war for the first time, Korea may have made an indelible impression, as they played with widely marketed models of American Saber jets and Soviet MIG fighters, perused a wealth of comic books on the war, and watched fiction films and triumphal television documentaries—both released in volume during the Korean War—on World War II. The Korean War helped to reconfigure racial images in culture, without doing much to abate their ferocity: South Koreans, and at greater distance Japanese, were now America's allies, but images of fanatical hordes of Asian foes once attached to the Japanese now got applied to North Koreans and Chinese.

Explanations for the nation's record in war also emerged as a major cultural theme. American soldiers' supposedly questionable performance—and even loyalty, since a few dozen American POWs refused repatriation back to the United States after the war—were sometimes blamed on their alleged homosexuality, on the stifling mothers who presumably induced it, and on a more general lack of manly fiber among American boys. The turncoats' "appalling girl-lessness" before going off to war seemed a telling factor in their treason. By making the turncoats into cultural outsiders, such explanations did offer hope about the virtue of most Americans, but they also revealed how failure to achieve victory in Korea nourished doubts about American potency and prowess, doubts persistent in time and voiced by diverse social commentators. In *The Feminine Mystique* (1963), Betty Friedan endorsed the view that the turncoats' disloyalty indicated "'a new softness'" among young men and the emergence of "the apathetic, dependent, infantile, purposeless being." She implicitly linked that development to male homosexuality, seen by her as "spreading like a murky smog over the American scene" because of "the feminine mystique," which "has glorified and perpetuated in the name of femininity a passive, childlike immaturity which is passed on from mothers to sons, as well as to daughters."[125]

Yet in other ways the Korean War revealed the curious partiality of militarization. It had only limited impact on the daily lives and consciousness of many Americans. With important exceptions—those drafted or called back into military service, those scrutinized for disloyalty—they rarely felt the heavy hand of a government at war, or of war itself. The economy's mighty capacity for expansion kept inflation in check, wage-price controls at a minimum, tax revenues growing, and consumer goods overflowing. Anyone who perused *Life* saw considerable coverage of the war, but mainly on the stateside politics of how to win it, and almost none of the war advertising ubiquitous during World War II, or of photographic coverage of the war's gruesome aspects. In the popular press, other matters often bulked larger, ones that invested public culture with a sour mood: the recriminations prompted by the Red Scare and a drumbeat of scandal in the Truman administration, in college basketball and West Point football, and involving organized crime. Wild rumors about the communist menace at home, panic about being on the brink of World War III, and strident calls to unleash America's nuclear arsenal were all juxtaposed to the repose and affluence of everyday life. Little bridged the chasm between the two. War remained shadowy, its issues agonizing but its presence elusive.

In part because it seemed so elusive, the Korean War did little to disturb the prevailing model of total war. In some ways, it even seemed to fit that model: it was seen as a possible prelude to another world war, just as one reason given for waging it was to stop a course of events leading to such a war. Meanwhile, many of the generals, weapons, strategies, and attitudes came right out of World War II, just as once again there were allies—Brits, Turks, and others—although Americans and South Koreans bore the brunt of the effort. Otherwise, Korea seemed an anomaly—outside the main channels of war's historical course, lacking analogs in America's past or in contemporary experience (such as France's simultaneous war in Indochina). What most Americans still feared and most experts still contemplated was another, more cataclysmic world war. The very frustration set loose by the Korean War seemed to rule out another "limited" war like it in the future. Although army strategists could not so cavalierly dismiss the war, since theirs was the service that would most have to fight any similar future war, strategic thinking remained focused on nuclear war, or on a general war in Europe that might lead to it.

The tendency to regard Korea as an anomalous war reflected the dominance of World War II in the American imagination. Korea apparently fit no script left behind by that war. Dwight Eisenhower, the general who had declared the invasion of France "the great crusade" and written *Crusade in Europe*, capitalized on that dominance in his 1952 election campaign. As President, he would have to come to terms with it.

THE UNEASY BALANCE, 1953–1961

Politics in a Militarized Age

Mickey Spillane's *One Lonely Night* was a bestseller in 1951, with its hero Mike Hammer: "I killed more people tonight than I have fingers on my hands. I shot them in cold blood and enjoyed every minute of it. . . . They were Commies. . . . They were red sons-of-bitches who should have died long ago." As Eric Goldman noted, "It was a day for Mike Hammerism, in books or in politics."[1]

So it often was in the 1952 presidential contest. True, early on Ike seemed to say little, and that rather badly ("'Now he's crossing the 38th platitude again,' reporters would sigh.").[2] Nor was hot-blooded rhetoric his forte, since he cast himself as above the political fray. He also had loftier themes, concerning the need to match the means and ends of American foreign policy to each other and to the nation's limited resources. The GOP campaign, however, relied heavily on crude formulas—"K_1C_2," (Korea, communism, and corruption), evils which Republicans accused Democrats of abetting or even welcoming. That Eisenhower, as army chief of staff and NATO supreme commander, had helped to shape Truman's containment policy did not much bother him (or Truman when he attacked Ike), in part because he usually left the dirty work of making these charges to others, such as his young running mate, Richard Nixon. Still, Ike did not always rise above the nastiness, and campaigning in Sen. Joseph McCarthy's home state of Wisconsin, he acceded to advisors insistent that he not defend George Marshall against McCarthy's notorious charges.

Driven in part by desperation, his opponent, Adlai Stevenson, sometimes turned nasty too. The one-term Illinois governor was not well known; he had a quick wit and mind but lacked the common touch; Korea and the Truman administration were heavy crosses to bear. On racial matters, his party shelved its 1948 commitment to civil rights, while his running mate was John Sparkman of Alabama, where all-white politics still ruled—choices, one historian suggests, matching Ike's "great shame of embracing Joseph McCarthy on the campaign trail." Democrats also worked the vein of anticommunism mined by the GOP—albeit more defensively, and with denunciations of McCarthyism by Stevenson. Truman presented Stevenson as "one of the first to warn that the Russians were becoming a threat to peace" and claimed that Ike's statements at the close of World War II about Soviet-American friendship "did a great deal of harm." Stevenson traced blame further back: communists "had begun to make headway in the U.S. only after the Republican regimes of the 1920s had bungled the national economy into collapse," his charges have been summarized.[3]

As usual in presidential elections, articulate differences between the candidates mattered less than their abilities to exploit the moods and language of the time. In working the memory of World War II, the frustrations of Korea, and the fear of a final cataclysm, Eisenhower's campaign was masterful, for all his obvious advantages. He was *General* Eisenhower—in campaign literature, in press coverage, in detractors' damnations—with all that this label summed up about his heroic status ("Ike" served the same purpose). His opponent was *Governor* Stevenson—the imbalance was obvious. References to war suffused Ike's rhetoric. "I have enlisted," he announced before the GOP convention. "I'm going to Chicago—as a soldier in the ranks," although as West Point graduate and senior officer, he was hardly a common soldier. Having won nomination, he was again a commander, telling Americans to "realize that today you are the combat troops" needed to win the election and presumably to defeat tyranny. Democrats might fire "red hot salvos," but that did not bother him: "I've been shot at by real artillerists." Soldiers, he claimed, knew war best and hated it most. He capped it off with a pledge to go to Korea if elected.[4]

This exploitation of his career testified to no crude man-on-horseback militarism. Although military service became a prerequisite for the presidency for nearly a half-century after 1945, just as it had after the Civil War, no other officer came close to Ike's feat, not even those like MacArthur who wanted the chance. There was no broad yearning to see generals and admirals in politics, but Eisenhower's triumph did reflect the primacy of World War II in political imagination and the deeply felt wish to wrest the virtues of war from war itself—to secure peace and prosperity after civilians seemingly had floundered in the attempt. Unlike MacArthur, Ike exuded little trace of the *warrior* spirit, perhaps because he possessed little of it. Like Marshall, he had been a great "organizer of victory" in war. Now he would organize victory for peace and prosperity.

In 1952, peace was the big issue, and the one Eisenhower more readily addressed. Largely insulated by his career from social issues, he articulated hopes for domestic tranquility and prosperity in a general way but with little feel for the problems of ordinary Americans. As President he would be bothered more by the carping demands and ugly parochialism of his own party's conservatives than by the aspirations of black or poor Americans, to which he was deaf. The one social group with which he felt an affinity was businessmen, to whom he granted many high-level appointments; even that affinity often seemed shallow.

But Ike was superbly positioned to address national security and to act on his convictions about it—to control the spiraling costs of national defense and to restore balance (as he saw it) between its claims and the nation's need for a healthy economy and unfettered polity. He was, that is, determined to limit, though not reverse, the course of militarization. In the late 1940s, he had urged "strengthening the economic and social dikes against Soviet communism rather than . . . preparing for a possibly eventual, but not yet inevitable war," an approach he feared would overburden the American economy. He had repudiated World War II as a model for future war and the fantasy of victory in another world war. "After the world-wide devastation that grows daily more possible, none may be able to distinguish between the victor and the vanquished of a future conflict," he declared in 1950. All nations were "in the same boat," which would be "swamped in a series of atomic blasts." And he had linked the problem of war to the character of modern civilization, placing both within a moral and ecological context. The "specter as sinister as the atomic bomb," the "creeping terror" faced by "all peoples," was "the wastage of the world's natural resources and . . . the criminal exploitation of the soil. What will it profit us to achieve the H-bomb and survive that tragedy or triumph, if the generations that succeed us must starve in a world . . . grown barren as the mountains of the moon?"[5]

Eisenhower had formidable resources for acting on these convictions. His heroic status already fixed in the nation's eyes and his own, he felt little need to reinforce that status through dramatic use of American power. A military and in many ways conservative man, he was usually invulnerable to charges of being weak on national defense or communism; later, conservatives in the notorious John Birch Society and at the *National Review* advanced such charges, but to little effect. Likewise, he commanded the authority to challenge claims for more men, money, and weapons, just as he had a lifetime's memory of and exasperation with the military's parochial and free-spending ways. As he once told congressmen, "I've served with those people who know all the answers— they just won't get down and face the dirty facts of life."[6] Conventional in his views of the communist menace, he still retained from the war a respect for the Soviet armed forces, for some of its leaders, and for the legacy of Soviet-American cooperation. He also had the vague but powerful mandate that comes from a landslide election victory. If his popularity rarely translated into success for his party, that failure hampered him little, since conservative Republicans gave him fits anyway. Even luck seemed on his side: Stalin's death in 1953 appeared to open prospects for easing the Cold War.

His formidable political resources for grappling with militarization were matched by substantial personal ones. Eisenhower entered office conversant and comfortable with many of the world's leaders, a position most Presidents

work years to achieve. He possessed abundant self-confidence and keen ana-
lytical powers, if not a wide-ranging intellect. The image that later emerged of
him—as a well-intentioned but bumbling leader who let others run the show—
reflected not the man but the celebratory view of the presidency then popular,
which assumed that any *strong* President could get what he wanted. Like all
Presidents, he had problems moving the huge federal government in desired
directions; often he decided not even to try. But his temper could be explosive,
his judgments harsh, his treatment of subordinates forceful—as Nixon found
out—and his mind quick. Of his party's Senate majority leader, William
Knowland, he fumed in his diary that "there seems to be no final answer to the
question 'How stupid can you get?'" George Kennan, who had high standards
in these matters, thought Eisenhower "showed his intellectual ascendancy
over every man in the room" at one important meeting. The large role he accorded subordinates like Secretary of State John Foster Dulles reflected Ike's
respect for expert authority, but also his shrewd decision to let others bear the
political heat. "All right," he later told one advisor, "I know what they say
about Foster—dull, duller, Dulles—and all that. But the Democrats love to hit
him rather than me." "I would get hell," his press secretary protested when told
to take public responsibility for a mistake. "My boy, better you than me," Ike
replied. Even his notorious mangling of the English language in press conferences was misleading. Extemporaneous speaking was not his forte, but he was
an exacting writer and not above using his reputation for verbal clumsiness to
duck difficult issues: "Don't worry," he once told his press secretary. "If that
question comes up, I'll just confuse them."[7]

He was, in one scholar's phrase, the "hidden-hand" president. Or, as Murray
Kempton put in 1967, "he was the tortoise upon whose back the world sat for
eight years. We laughed at him; we talked wistfully about moving; and all the
while we never knew the cunning beneath the shell." Such praise concealed
real weaknesses. Eisenhower's cunning was erratically and sometimes foolishly deployed. He could confuse sincere distaste for public bombast with
simple cowardice about taking strong stances. He could equate good intentions
with concrete progress. It was his "pattern of action, if not the purpose of the
man, to husband and to guard" his immense personal resources "like savings
earned by the sweat of a lifetime," noted Emmet John Hughes, his advisor and
speechwriter. He saved them well to protect his personal popularity but left
many unspent in behalf of the causes he embraced. Still, he was in control of his
administration, at least as much as any modern President.[8]

His inaugural address barely hinted at his fears of militarization. He did
make his "first task" not to win the Cold War but to "deter the forces of aggression and promote the conditions of peace," even by negotiating with adversaries, a step anathema to Truman's administration in its later stages. Otherwise, he offered stock Cold War rhetoric. "Freedom is pitted against slavery;
lightness against the dark," ran the familiar refrain. "The faith we hold belongs

not to us alone but to the free of all the world," ran the echo of campaign promises to liberate the communist world. Faith in freedom "confers a common dignity upon the French soldier who dies in Indochina, the British soldier killed in Malaya, the American life given in Korea," ran the linkage of the American crusade with British and French imperialism. He also drafted the entire nation to the task of "winning" the peace: "We must be ready to dare all for our country. . . . No person, no home, no community can be beyond the reach of this call." In 1962, Emmet John Hughes compared those words to Kennedy's more famous inaugural—"in phrases more felicitous but in substance no different"—and wondered if anything had changed.[9]

Something had, although perhaps for the worse. Avoiding war, containing militarization—just recognizing their perils—were Ike's major achievements. They also, however, made possible a further accommodation to militarization, if only by lessening its burdens a bit. And to those who saw growing peril in the 1950s, they only weakened the nation further.

The Contending Forces

Eisenhower faced sharply different options for national security. Truman's ambitious policy, laid out in NSC-68 and implemented during the Korean War, presumed protracted struggle with communism, posited abundant American resources to wage it, and prized American ability to respond symmetrically to any aggression. Nuclear intimidation or attack, conventional war and covert action, economic and political pressure—each would be met by similar forms of American power. An alternative, advanced mostly by conservative Republicans who recoiled at the costs and compromises of protracted struggle, prized asymmetry: the United States should not meet the enemy gun for gun but instead rely on those forms of power, above all atomic and aerial, at which it excelled and which might provide quick victory.[10]

As in many areas of policy, Ike chose a "middle way" between conflicting options, grafting his limited view of resources to the Truman administration's assumptions about global struggle. For him, too, the Cold War was a protracted conflict promising no quick victory (campaign rhetoric aside), but precisely for that reason the United States had to hoard its resources, limit its efforts, and spread its burdens, or else exhaust itself over the long haul. "To amass military power without regard to our economic capacity would be to defend ourselves against one kind of disaster by inviting another," his 1953 State of the Union message declared. "We can't afford to let the negative actions of the Communists force us into world-wide deployment," he argued in 1954. "We need to be free to decide where we can strike most effectively."[11]

The result was the much-touted "New Look," an effort to limit defense spending by relying on enhanced nuclear forces, as well as alliances and covert action, rather than on costly conventional forces to counter enemy initiatives.

Confrontation with the enemy was to be selective, focused on conflicts in which American power was superior and available at limited cost. At times Eisenhower still echoed the previous administration's expansive view: "As there is no weapon too small, no arena too remote, to be ignored, there is no free nation too humble to be forgotten." But the emphasis was on American freedom "to respond vigorously at places and with means of its own choosing," in Dulles's famous phrasing, or in the National Security Council's words, it was "on the capability of inflicting massive retaliatory damage by offensive striking power." Truman's programs to mass-produce nuclear weapons and bombers created the means for this strategy—so abundantly "that the margin of American superiority seemed if anything greater than it had been in the days of the American atomic monopoly."[12]

Why did Eisenhower take this approach? Critics once singled out his fear of deficit spending and bloated government, but many considerations were at play, their weight varying among members of the administration. For Ike, those considerations all reflected his anxiety about militarization, which defined his outlook as much as the Cold War itself. He was perilously alone in that anxiety. Dulles talked of Cold War and diplomacy; Treasury Secretary George Humphrey of budgets and fiscal prudence; Defense Secretary Charles Wilson of preparedness and efficiency. Eisenhower too spoke in those terms, but also transcended them. No unbending aversion to war guided him—he had waged war and never ruled out doing so again—but a complex aversion to militarization did sustain him.

It indeed derived partly from his economic conservatism. He worried that the taxes, capital, and expertise needed for an expensive defense program, and the inflation and government debt that might flow from it, would stifle economic entrepreneurship and growth, in turn weakening the economic base needed to sustain national security. Rejecting dire Joint Chiefs of Staff warnings of national peril if cuts in the defense budget were maintained, Ike angrily proposed that the National Security Council "should have a report as to whether national bankruptcy or national destruction would get us first." The same outlook informed his denunciations of "paternalistic government" and Truman's Fair Deal, and his neo-Hooverian view of government's role as coordinator and catalyst of national energies, not regulator or financier. Because Ike's worry about militarization was shaped in part by orthodox Republican conservatism and linked to its view on domestic policies, liberals derided it as narrow-minded penny-pinching oblivious to the expansive possibilities outlined in Keynesian economics.[13]

But not only would many Americans later find Eisenhower's economic reasoning more persuasive, his worries went far beyond economic effects. Truman's proposed defense budget, he argued, would lead to "a permanent state of mobilization" destroying "our whole democratic way of life." "If we let defense spending run wild," he told a confidant, "you get inflation . . . then controls . . . then a garrison state . . . and *then* we've lost the very values we were trying to defend." "Should we have to resort to anything resembling a garrison state," he declared on another occasion, "then all that we are striving to defend would be weakened." His repeated warnings of a "garrison state" indicated concerns far broader than rock-ribbed Republican fears for free enterprise.[14]

Those concerns also derived from his cautious grand strategy, which he feared that bellicose national impulses could disrupt. Like other leaders, Eisenhower worried about the impatience and immaturity of ordinary Americans, but he feared more the lunge for the quick fix and the propensity to panic he saw among hawkish Republicans, money-hungry generals, and other well-placed people. Facing claims that 1953 was the "year of maximum danger" for the nation, he insisted privately that "we're not in a moment of danger, we're in an age of danger," and publicly that "anybody who bases his defense on his ability to predict the day and the hour of the attack is crazy." Facing a GOP effort to legislate United States withdrawal from the UN if it seated Red China, he issued a typical warning against shortsightedness, reminding congressmen that in 1945 "Germany was our deadly enemy; who could then have foreseen it would become a friendly associate?" Having employed against the Germans a patient strategy, he saw patience as a foundation now for successful strategy. For him, the "long haul" precluded the impetuous act or the budget-busting program.[15]

Eisenhower feared strategic disaster less through communist victory, about which his warnings were few, than through nuclear war. No President worried more about the dangers of initiating or stumbling into nuclear conflict. His concern drew in part on his doubts as an army man about air power. Already "damn tired of Air Force sales programs" in his first months in office, he lectured congressmen: "We pulverized Germany . . . but their actual rate of production was as big at the end as at the beginning." Even if—especially if—bombers could destroy the Soviet Union, he could see no real victory, as he told senior officers: "Gain such a victory, and what do you do with it? Here would be a great area from the Elbe to Vladivostok and down through Southeast Asia torn up and destroyed without government, without its communications, just an area of starvation and disaster. I ask you what would the civilized world do about it? I repeat there is no victory in any war except through our imaginations, through our dedication and through our work to avoid it." As he lectured South Korean leader Syngman Rhee, "If the Kremlin and Washington ever lock up in a war, the results are too horrible to contemplate." Ridiculing the "notion that 'the bomb' is a cheap way to solve things," he told his Cabinet that "it is cold comfort for any citizen of Western Europe to be assured that—after his country is overrun and he is pushing up daisies—someone still alive will drop a bomb on the Kremlin." Warning the United Nations in 1953 about "two atomic colossi" facing off "across a trembling world," he pleaded for taking the bomb from the soldiers and putting it into "the hand of those who will know how to strip its military casing and adapt it to the arts of peace."[16]

Administration leaders also said and did many things that contradicted these eloquent appeals. Simply threatening "massive retaliation" to deter communist advances seemed to do so, and Ike saw "no reason" why atomic weapons "shouldn't be used just exactly as you would use a bullet or anything else" if employed "on strictly military targets and for strictly military purposes." How did such statements square with his eloquent appeals? In part they reflected an effort to intimidate the enemy—"The ability to get to the verge without getting into the war is the necessary art," Dulles told *Life* in 1956—although Eisenhower well knew that intimidation meant nothing without a willingness, at least in the enemy's perception, to pull the trigger. It is also true that the administration confined specific threats of nuclear retaliation largely to the Asian theater, where the risks of all-out war were arguably less, and that despite talk of the tactical utility of nuclear weapons, Eisenhower never claimed that a general nuclear war was winnable or tolerable. Not for him the fantasy of nuclear triumph that Truman had privately indulged, or the gaze into the nuclear abyss that Kennedy took in the Cuban missile crisis. He never flatly renounced use of nuclear weapons, but his intolerance of apocalyptic possibilities exceeded that of many in his own administration, expert circles, and political life generally.[17]

Ike's resistance to militarization probably drew most on his fear of its consequences even if war were avoided. He was reasonably confident that war would be avoided, at least on his watch—his view of himself in such matters was not modest. He was less confident of resisting a broader political process that nurtured anxiety, swollen budgets, economic stagnation, and constraints on freedom—the evils of the "garrison state." His resounding statement of those dangers came in an April 16, 1953, address. Though blaming communists for the Cold War, he warned that even if atomic war were averted, the arms race offered "a life of perpetual fear and tension; a burden of arms draining the wealth and labor of all peoples . . . . Every gun that is made, every warship launched, every rocket fired, signifies, in the final sense, a theft from those who hunger and are not fed, those who are cold and not clothed. This world in arms is not spending money alone. It is spending the sweat of its laborers, the genius of its scientists, the hopes of its children." As he eloquently concluded: "This is not a way of life at all, in any true sense. Under the cloud of threatening war, it is humanity hanging from a cross of iron." Proposing what a post–Cold War generation would call a "peace dividend," he promised to devote "a substantial percentage of the savings achieved by disarmament to a fund for world aid and reconstruction." The savings would be used for "a new kind of war . . . a declared total war, not upon any human enemy but upon the brute forces of poverty and need."[18]

Critics often applauded these broad sentiments but attacked the strategy that flowed from them, above all its reliance on threats of massive retaliation. They decried the creation of a technologically muscle-bound America so dependent on nuclear weapons that it had no choice between capitulation and catastrophe in the face of communist aggression—a strategy at once helpless and horrifying. As the 1950s wore on, the New Look seemed a feeble bulwark against the limited wars and subversive efforts waged by communist and leftist forces in the Third World. Ike himself acknowledged the force of this criticism even before becoming President. "What should we do if Soviet *political* aggression, as in Czechoslovakia, successively chips away exposed positions in the free world?" he wrote Dulles in 1952. "To my mind this is the case where the theory of 'retaliation' falls down."[19] He never devised a satisfactory solution to the problem.

Still, critics of the New Look also tended to caricature it—it hardly denied the administration a non-nuclear capability. Between 1954 and 1958, the army fell from 1,404,598 to 898,925 personnel, but remained 50 percent larger than at its low point in the late 1940s. Other "conventional" forces, the navy and marines, shrank only by 10 percent, as did the air force. The 2.6 million personnel of 1958 marked a 30 percent decline from the Korean War peak, but the military reserves had grown and the nation was no longer at war. This force was far more capable of limited war than any previous peacetime force. It was backed up by the CIA's enhanced capacity for paramilitary and covert action, and by military resources given allies and clients (Ike insisted on foreign military and economic aid in the face of conservatives furious about fiscal imprudence and liberals suspicious of aiding despots).

If Eisenhower never plunged conventional forces into major combat after Korea, that was by choice more than because he denied himself the means. There was virtue in self-denial—he could plead incapacity to wage another Korean War—but the self-denial was more apparent than real. Most important, critics assumed that there *was* some way to challenge communist aggression militarily at little cost—a successful strategy avoiding both the agony of Korea and the insanity of nuclear war. Hanging over the arcane debates of the 1950s was a possibility few acknowledged—that military power in any form might be of little use to America, or any great power. Eisenhower came as close as any national figure to acknowledging that dilemma, although he never fully addressed the strategic and political consequences that flowed from it.

In addition to force levels, budgets measured Eisenhower's approach to national security. Defense spending fell 20 percent between fiscal 1953 and 1955 and, though rising later in the 1950s, continued to move within a narrow range. It also declined as a fraction of the national budget (from two-thirds to one-half by 1960) and as percentage of GNP (from 13.8 to 9.1 percent). Taft wanted sharper cuts, but Eisenhower did not listen, "partly because the clamor from the other side—demanding more spending on the military—was so much louder."[20] Indeed, Ike sustained his defense budgets in the face of heated protests from the armed forces and, after 1957, widespread pressure to spend more.

His budgets would have been unsustainable if he had failed to contain or liquidate a series of crises and temptations to action that peppered his first term. The most agonizing was the war in Korea. Dragging on since 1951, armistice talks had foundered ostensibly over the communists' insistence that all their POWs in allied hands be repatriated (as precedent and international law required), forcibly if necessary, while the allies postured about the POWs' right to freedom and choice. In fact, however, Taiwanese and South Korean forces sometimes intimidated communist prisoners, as did the communists theirs. Both sides used POWs as pawns in an elaborate game.

On the South Korean and American side, the yearning for total victory remained strong. In December 1952, MacArthur had advised threatening to use nuclear weapons. Ike thought the threat might be useful, but at best to achieve a compromise, not total victory, worrying that "if we're going to extend the war we have to make sure we're not offending the whole world." Through the spring and early summer of 1953, Syngman Rhee, Dulles, Republican conservatives, and some Democrats made dark noises about going for broke, and members of the GOP old guard were "heard to mutter that if Truman had signed the conditions Eisenhower was willing to accept, they would have moved to impeach him." Rhee tried to torpedo a final agreement by releasing Chinese and Korean POWs without repatriation, provoking new hostilities costly to American forces, Cabinet discussion of assassinating him, and strong-arm efforts to pull him back into line.[21]

An armistice was finally achieved in July. In a perception with profound consequences for later American policy, Ike's success was often attributed to a threat to use nuclear weapons sent by Dulles indirectly to the Chinese. But while such threat was made, it was neither needed nor determinative of the outcome—the real threat was "Eisenhower's reputation" from World War II "backed by America's atomic arsenal," and the essential compromises were already in place before Dulles's warning. One act rarely ends wars, and this war's end owed to many factors: exhaustion on both sides, new leadership in Moscow and Washington, and the major powers' grudging willingness to make concessions. Still, Eisenhower's role was critical, for he "realized that unlimited war in the nuclear age was unimaginable, and limited war unwinnable. This was the most basic of his strategic insights."[22]

In settling for something far less total victory, Ike implicitly challenged the stranglehold of World War II on the American imagination, an ironic achievement for that war's hero. True to his nature, he failed to make the challenge publicly explicit, though it was evident in the tenor of his public remarks, as he avoided triumphal or self-congratulatory comments. In other ways, too, he may have implied the Second World War's irrelevance to the 1950s. Begged in 1954 to speak at a glittering ceremony dedicating the massive monument to the 1945 flag raising at Iwo Jima, Eisenhower all but ducked the occasion without uttering a word—either disturbed by the mythic falsehoods about the original incident or uncomfortable with the romanticization of war and victory implicit in the whole affair. Likewise, once elected, he did little to exploit the memories and symbols of World War II (although, the cynic might argue, his reputation made it unnecessary to do so).[23]

Eisenhower could settle Korea on unsatisfying terms because it began on Truman's watch and because of his personal reputation. Other situations belonged more squarely to his administration. By 1953, the French were deeply mired in an unwinnable war to reclaim Indochina, while the United States government funded the French effort, supplied military personnel to assist it, and searched halfheartedly among depressing options. The French cause seemed doomed, but French withdrawal would doom Vietnam to communist takeover. The tricky middle ground only sucked the Truman and Eisenhower administrations in deeper. They knew how offensive France's imperial cause was to the Indochinese, but attempts to coerce France into granting independence to its colonies only triggered French threats to withdraw altogether, and an effort to develop a Vietnamese "third force" both anti-imperialist and anticommunist foundered on its inherent contradictions, producing hapless figureheads like Emperor Bao Dai. The possibility that the leftist Vietminh forces fighting France might be sufficiently nationalist to resist the sway of Peking and Moscow was rarely considered. Embodying all the lessons of appeasement and the 1930s, the "falling dominoes" principle, as Eisenhower publicly formulated it, assumed the unity of all communist forces and prescribed that once they "knock over" the first noncommunist country, "the last one" certainly would "go over very quickly."[24]

Intellectually, Eisenhower did not assume a monolithic communist enemy, making gestures to Tito's Yugoslavia and toying with overtures to Mao's China. Little real feel for Third World nationalism backed up his abstract perception of diversity, however, and little room existed in American politics to act on it. The administration's strategic suppleness was unmatched by a similar flexibility about politics and ideology.

Despite this confining framework, Eisenhower moved to limit American involvement in Indochina during France's final crisis in the spring of 1954. As Vietminh forces encircled the French bastion at Dien Bien Phu, a plea for American military intervention came from the French government, backed by conservative American politicians and administration leaders like Nixon, while talk of atomic bombs spread. Ike blocked the demands to go war "by putting conditions on American involvement," ones "deliberately created to be impossible of fulfillment."[25] They included Congress's assent, united support from American allies, and a host of conditions on the French, including full independence for their colonies.

Forestalling military intervention was a collective—and ambiguous—achievement. Certainly others, like Army Chief of Staff General Matthew Ridgway, also doubted that American technology could prevail. Certainly Ike's complex policy still yielded—and was designed to yield—a deeper American commitment to the area that produced the Southeast Asia Treaty Organization, lavish aid to Ngo Dinh Diem's new South Vietnamese regime, and sanction for Diem's refusal to hold elections to reunify Vietnam. Behind that effort lay typical American aspirations to be a muscular "city on a hill" to the world, exporting democracy and capitalism and making South Vietnam "the cornerstone of the Free World in Southeast Asia, the keystone in the arch, the finger in the dike," as Sen. John Kennedy put it in 1956. These aspirations, bitingly exposed in Graham Greene's 1955 novel *The Quiet American*, influenced Ike. Still, he condemned use of ground forces—"This war in Indochina would absorb our troops by divisions!"—and saw that the nation's "tradition of anticolonialism" formed "an asset of incalculable value to the Free World." Talk of using atomic bombs enraged him: "You boys must be crazy. We can't use those awful things against Asians for the second time in less than ten years. My God."[26]

As other situations showed, no refusal to use power guided Eisenhower, only a shrewd determination to act when the odds were favorable and the costs low—unless misjudged. In the nail-biting crises of 1955 and 1958 over Quemoy and Matsu—small islands near China's coast held by Taiwan's Nationalist government—the administration threatened a nuclear response if Mao's government attacked, while Dulles equated Mao's "aggressive fanaticism" with that of Hitler. Ike gained apparent victory for brinkmanship, but also "thoroughly discredited it in the eyes of the American public and allies overseas by revealing how little it would take to push the administration into a war with China," by showing the administration's "bland self-confidence that it could use nuclear weapons without setting off an all-out nuclear war," and by doing so in a crisis over real estate of purely symbolic value (although Dulles later boasted that "his most brilliant" achievement had been "to save Quemoy and Matsu.")[27]

Moreover, the outcome seemed to rest on one man whose judgment, however assessed, would have to falter on occasion. The Formosa crises showed the administration's penchant for recklessness in small matters as against restraint in larger ones. Only when the 1955 crisis threatened to explode did Ike show caution. After the Soviet foreign minister said that nuclear war would not threaten "world civilization" but only "that rotten social system with its imperialist basis soaked in blood," Eisenhower publicly reminisced about his 1945 friendship with Marshal (now Defense Minister) Zhukov, who had given him an "enormous bear hug" on his birthday. "It is necessary," comments Paul Carter, "to think and feel one's way back into the mood of the fifties to realize how remarkable a statement this was."[28]

Just as dangerous were the administration's barely covert interventions in Iran and Guatemala. Wary of plunging American forces into war, Eisenhower turned to the CIA as one alternative, sharing Gen. James Doolittle's views: facing "an implacable enemy" seeking "world domination" in a game with "no rules," the United States must "learn to subvert, sabotage, and destroy our enemies by more clever, more sophisticated, and more effective methods than those used against us." When Premier Mohammed Mossadegh nationalized Iran's oil fields and seemed to threaten Western interests, Allen Dulles's CIA helped organize his overthrow and the shah's return to the throne in 1953. When a similar drama unfolded the next year in Guatemala—its government cooperated with the Communist Party, carried out land reform, and expropriated holdings of the American United Fruit Company (to which the Dulles brothers had close ties) that it left fallow—the CIA subverted the reformist regime and replaced it with a reactionary clique. The CIA had scored two victories, at least for corporate interests, at minimal cost. The dominoes would not fall ("My God," Ike said regarding Guatemala, "just think what it would mean to us if Mexico went Communist!"). But by destroying reformist regimes, these victories also forced both areas into painful choices between reactionary and revolutionary alternatives: Guatemala experienced recurrent civil war into the 1990s; the shah succumbed to an Islamic uprising in 1979. Perhaps long-term outcomes ought not to be pinned to Eisenhower: "Sufficient unto the day are the crises thereof," notes Carter, and Ike liquidated his crises without American blood. Still, his use of the CIA may only have postponed the reckoning, and it set a telling precedent for his successors. Certainly his impulses—to avoid war, restrain militarization, but sustain American hegemony—coexisted in unstable balance.[29]

It was all the more unstable because enemies, allies, and others could upset it. That became clear in the fall of 1956. A complex crisis in the Mideast developed when the administration misjudged Egyptian nationalism and Anglo-French foolishness: Egypt's Nasser seized the Suez Canal from Britain, Egyptian-Israeli tensions swelled, and Britain, France, and Israel moved to invade Egypt, without informing Eisenhower. Just as that crisis worsened in October, Hungarians rebelled against Soviet rule, and just as they seemed about to prevail, the Red Army crushed the revolt. Given GOP talk of liberating enslaved peoples and American propaganda urging "captive nations" to throw off their shackles, Ike's refusal to aid the rebels in Hungary was embarrassing. In the Middle East, his outrage forced France, Britain, and Israel to cease their invasion of Egypt and earned the gratitude of many smaller nations, but NATO and American Mideast interests seemed imperiled.

Relief at the avoidance of war helped Eisenhower gain an election landslide in November, but avoidance seemed to hinge perilously on one man, a perception already underscored by Ike's heart attack in 1955. In the Suez crisis Eisenhower showed "a kind of good sense we can now wish had been shown by more recent presidents who were considered more worldly-wise than Ike"[30]—or had been shown at the time by Adlai Stevenson, who favored Israel and the imperial powers in Egypt rather than the UN resolution ordering a cease-fire. Still, militarization was contained and war avoided by a balance of forces—between the "free world" and its enemies, between Eisenhower and his critics, between the administration's own conflicting tendencies—that was indeed uneasy.

It was also unsteady when Eisenhower dealt with another facet of militarization, the Red Scare's legacy. At the least, his inflammatory statements on the matter were few, and perhaps both his stature and his public skepticism about militarization calmed the mood a bit. Insofar as repression waned in the 1950s, however—and civil rights leaders, among others, had reason to doubt that it did—court decisions and other changes were more responsible than Eisenhower's administration. Corraling McCarthy did not silence others in Congress who badgered the White House to ferret out communists, homosexuals, and other alleged subversives. Even when the storm in Congress abated, the executive branch's more routine and invisible machinery of repression groaned on—in some ways enlarged under Eisenhower, though neither more efficient nor more fair. Typically, he vacillated and complained, about the political pressures involved, among other things. "Why the hell should we take credit for any of these firings [of federal employees]?" he fumed; it would only mean "taking credit for what was plainly our duty."[31] His complaint made clear both his distaste for the process and his commitment to it.

The uneasy balance was also evident in the administration's dealings with Congress. The 1950s were not the golden age of bipartisanship often remembered later by Cold Warriors lamenting subsequent political divisions. Sharp differences arose between Republicans and Democrats, conservatives and liberals, Congress and the White House. In the end, "opposition forces failed to alter the substance of national security policy and foreign policy . . . , or even to increase congressional influence in the formation of those policies," argues one historian, but it was "not for want of effort."[32] At most, bipartisanship occurred by default, not design.

Conflict between the White House and Congress erupted especially over a constitutional amendment offered by Ohio Republican senator John Bricker (who had been Dewey's running mate in 1944). Bricker wanted to ban executive agreements with other nations, leaving the President only the option of making treaties, which require the Senate's consent. Behind him lay a long tradition of popular and congressional distrust of presidential power in war and foreign policy, but that tradition had become ideologically constricted. Some Democrats and liberals assailed presidential arrogance, but the animus behind Bricker's move was righteous Republican indignation over those "outrageous Yalta accords" (as one senator termed them) and other executive agreements that presumably had given communists effortless victories in the 1940s.[33]

Behind it, too, were fears that starkly demonstrated the inseparability of foreign policy and domestic politics. The Bricker amendment sought to ban treaties abridging any individual right or freedom under the Constitution or affecting "any other matters essentially within the domestic jurisdiction of the

United States." Bricker's nightmare was the United Nations, especially the draft International Covenant on Human Rights written by "global dreamers" and "international do-gooders" like Eleanor Roosevelt. He feared that the covenant might become the law of land, and with it liberalism, welfarism, even socialism. Sharing his alarm about the covenant, white supremacists feared for racial segregation and "states' rights," doctors foresaw "socialized medicine," and the U.S. Chamber of Commerce prophesied the end of "free enterprise."[34]

By a long and adroit effort, Eisenhower warded off Bricker's threat to his prerogatives. His record—better than that of most postwar Presidents—of consulting Congress helped. So did cooperative Democrats; bipartisanship did sometimes operate. But from Ike's point of view, it was a near miss and an exhausting nuisance. More than most Presidents, he avoided name calling and burned no bridges with anyone in Congress, but privately he noted: "If it's true that when you die the things that bothered you most are engraved on your skull, I'm sure I'll have there the mud and dirt of France during invasion and the name of Senator Bricker."[35]

Eisenhower also maintained, as public reactions confirmed, that the United States now valued diplomacy with the enemy, though diplomacy rarely yielded concrete results. A 1955 treaty made Austria a permanent neutral and required withdrawal of occupying Soviet and Western forces, a significant precedent not followed for solving the weightier problem of divided Germany. The United States did not even sign the 1954 Geneva Accords on Indochina. Eisenhower offered a much-touted "Atoms for Peace" program and later an imaginative "Open Skies" proposal—foreshadowing the spirit of later mutual surveillance—whereby the superpowers would give each other "a complete blueprint of our military establishments" and allow each to photograph the other from the air.[36] Every such proposal led to a nasty round of public posturing, Soviet and American leaders blaming each other for the arms race. Even more ballyhoo, but no agreements, accompanied the 1955 Geneva "Big Four" meeting of Ike and the Soviet, French, and British leaders. Eisenhower, and sometimes his counterparts elsewhere, were duly criticized for performing empty rituals that masked growing perils.

There was something to be said for ritual, however. Reminiscent of FDR's summit diplomacy, Eisenhower's version, undertaken in the face of shrill prophecies of "appeasement," established expectations and processes for superpower consultation that no later President could ignore. The lavish media attention given the Geneva summit reflected the substantive shallowness of the event, but also the hopes it aroused. As Eisenhower aide Emmet John Hughes said, Geneva "was widely understood to signalize, without articulating, the acceptance by the major powers of the common necessity to shun recourse to nuclear war." A similar signal arose from lofty and now-forgotten aspirations, earnestly supported by Eisenhower among others, that the United Nations become an effective instrument of world peace and prosperity.[37]

Nonetheless, beneath the surface of international crisis and consultation ran currents that undermined Eisenhower's hopes to contain militarization. In the sprawling national security apparatus, pressure kept mounting to develop new weapons and to subvert arms control. Through the budget process, Ike exercised general control over defense policy but not over its qualitative shift toward new, expensive weapons. By bringing scientists into the White House, he gained access to experts skeptical about new programs, but also subjected himself to more direct pressure from scientists championing an aggressive course. The administration, complained Treasury Secretary Humphrey in 1957, had been "led astray by scientists and by vested interests." By denunciations of nuclear overkill or sheer explosions of temper, Eisenhower could interrupt the momentum. He could not or would not stop it. Nuclear warheads swelled in numbers and power, their megatonnage (destructive power) soaring from 150 in 1953 to 19,000 in 1960, the historic peak. By mid-decade the United States was plunging into the next stage of the arms race, intercontinental rockets for delivering nuclear weapons. A nuclear arms race whose logic had "no connection to experience or reality" was taking over. Eisenhower and the American people insisted on "clear American superiority. How they would use that lead—except to insure deterrence, which could be assured with one hundred bombs anyway—they did not know."[38]

Historians have faulted "the inadequacy of [Eisenhower's] leadership, combined with the intractable problems he faced" and his administration's "overblown rhetoric," for creating "an atmosphere in which consideration of defense issues became nearly impossible."[39] Beyond that was a dilemma that Eisenhower barely grasped. The New Look involved a resort to technology to contain militarization—new weapons were to cut costs by minimizing force levels and averting limited wars. Drawing on an American tradition of seeking technological solutions to problems created in part by technology, it aggravated the very militarization that Ike hoped to arrest. Militarization was a qualitative phenomenon, not just a quantitative one measurable by the size of budgets or armies. The New Look accelerated it at its most technically exquisite, and exquisitely dangerous, nuclear core. Any other President might have done worse in that regard, but the higher standard of success Eisenhower set for himself makes the judgment on him more severe—as he soon felt.

Since his successors rarely did better in these matters, however, he alone was obviously not the problem. Beyond him lay a political culture hardly his to control. Humphrey's private complaint about "scientists" and "vested interests" suggested one facet of the problem. Ike could claim greater wisdom than generals and admirals, but for him to complain publicly about the pressures of scientists and other experts was virtually impossible—it would have smacked of the anti-intellectualism and cramped vision already imputed to Eisenhower and his associates too often for their political comfort. To challenge Gen. Maxwell Taylor was one thing; to dispute Edward Teller was another at a time when so much wisdom and objectivity were attributed to scientists.

One controversy over nuclear weapons did give Ike a chance to challenge the scientists' authority. A test in the Pacific of an American hydrogen bomb in 1954 stirred alarm about its sheer explosive power, but even more about the fallout that contaminated Americans, area natives, and nearby Japanese fishermen (their fate ominously resonant with August 1945). Eisenhower publicly doubted scientists' infallibility, announcing that "this time something must have happened that we have never experienced before, and must have surprised and astonished the scientists." Privately, he said that after the current American tests he would be "willing to have a moratorium on all further experimentation" with nuclear weapons.[40]

Instead he vacillated, then drifted with the tide of experts seeking more tests, more bombs, and more vehicles to carry them. His New Look strategy was one reason, but also his desire for elite control, which public debate now threatened to erode. Dissident scientists and grass-roots activists formed new organizations. Books—Nevil Shute's *On the Beach* (1957), Walter Miller's *A Canticle for Leibowitz* (1959), Mordecai Roshwald's *Level 7* (1959)—widened debate. The Soviets grandstanded with new proposals to end the arms race. Neutrals like India, hardly wishing to bathe in the fallout of Soviet and American tests, enlivened a global debate. Charged cultural symbols were at play—Strontium-90 was entering the food chain, poisoning the milk mothers fed babies.

Eisenhower was not immune to the anxieties expressed in this widening debate. Had a strong challenge to nuclear policy emerged within his policy apparatus, he might have acted forcefully: in that arena, similar to the one he knew as a commander, he could be confident and courageous. But insiders critical of the arms race were few—Eisenhower as much as anyone, and he discouraged the criticism he also sought by his choice of scientific advisors and by his willingness to see Oppenheimer forced out. A lifetime's habits made him distrust the unpredictable anxieties of outsiders. Repeatedly he considered blunt efforts to inform Americans of the nuclear danger. Repeatedly he backed away, sensing that public alarm was as likely to undermine efforts at disarmament as to strengthen them. Already in 1953, when the scientist Vannevar Bush had taken up "the case for scaring the people into a big tax program to build bomb defenses," Ike had seen "the dangers in telling too much of the truth."[41] His distrust of public candor was not unfounded, but his chosen course served him no better.

There were alternatives to Eisenhower's leadership in such matters, but as usual in American politics, they were muddled. Adlai Stevenson, in 1956 again the Democrats' nominee, proposed cutting back the draft and ending nuclear weapons tests, but also assailed the administration for not building more missiles faster. For his part, "Eisenhower thought that testing was far too complex and dangerous a subject to be discussed in a political campaign,"[42] though he skewered Stevenson on the issue when it seemed necessary. So ended his first term, four years of precarious balance in which so much seemed to hinge on him alone, and he not anticipating how "complex and dangerous" subjects might resist elite control.

His best allies on defense policy had been businessmen and conservatives, not liberals. A few months after the election, I. F. Stone aptly described the contending positions. Noting a warning by General Electric's president that "defense expenditures drain away national resources," Stone thought it "strange when only a big businessman talks as liberals used to." Stone summarized another dissenter's claim that "the Russian military menace had been built up here beyond all reasonable proportions" and that "defense had become a gravy train." "Whose name was signed to this moving appeal?" Stone asked. "Not Walter Reuther or Upton Sinclair or . . . Reinhold Niebuhr or . . . Arthur M. Schlesinger, Jr.," but "a Democratic congressman from benighted Mississippi." Liberals' "silence," Stone complained, "reflects the vast and inhibiting shadow cast across American life by the sheer size of the military budget," with labor and capital and the academy now living "off the search for ever more ingenious weapons." Eisenhower, of course, had not been silent—Stone's words mirrored his sentiments—but too often he had been timid and inconsistent.[43]

Reform in the Paradigm of War

In March 1953, the issue of generators for the Chief Joseph Dam came before an "unsuspecting Cabinet." It seemed a minor matter of domestic policy, except that foreign policy was also at stake: the White House had professed its commitment to free trade and opened bidding to British firms, but Westinghouse wanted (and eventually got) the contract despite its higher bid. For weeks the "unpleasant sound of whirring generators" filled the Cabinet room, Emmet John Hughes complained.[44] The episode showed more than the administration's capacity to get sidetracked from major issues. It also showed that few issues belonged wholly any longer to "domestic policy." Government's role in the nation's life and the agenda of reform was more than ever lodged in the paradigm of war.

The terrain suited Eisenhower in some ways, although, as Hughes later noted, reigning stereotypes about the two major political parties—"the Democrats as 'the Party of War,' the Republicans as 'the Party of Depression'"—made it hard to assess Ike's record, then and for long after his presidency. His biographer came close to the mark. Eisenhower's liberalism regarding domestic affairs was real but "usually connected with national security," and without such a connection, it "faded." Indeed, liberalism generally, not just Ike's version, was connected to national security, just as its distinction from conservatism was blurry.[45]

On occasion, Eisenhower reached beyond a mere programmatic linkage between reform and national security, as when he urged applying resources freed by disarmament "to a new kind of war . . . upon the brute forces of poverty and need."[46] That language, foreshadowing Lyndon Johnson's War on Poverty, reflected both entrapment in and discomfort with the paradigm of war: Eisenhower wanted to reach outside it but could not escape it.

His difficulty reflected a larger weakness in his campaign against militarization: he offered no compelling mission for America beyond national security. The evils of militarization he conveyed precisely and eloquently; the alternatives to it he articulated earnestly but vaguely. The war paradigm did lead him to act on a considerable reform agenda, but by the late 1950s reformers were increasingly couching that agenda in the language of justice. Eisenhower—ill at ease with that language and the groups espousing it, but wary also of claims made in behalf of national security—then often lost his grip on reform.

Was he behind the times or ahead of them? Now recalled, his words seem to belie the fatuous optimism often later attributed to the 1950s and his own leadership. At a time when Americans consumed natural resources with abandon, he worried about a world "grown barren as the mountains of the moon," anticipating later ecological concerns. In an era of faith in material progress, he warned of its inseparability from martial destruction: "Labor sweats to create, and turns out devices to level not only mountains but also cities."[47] When material values appeared triumphant, he intoned higher ideals. As faith in the power of law suffused the civil rights movement, he insisted that only hearts and heads could effect racial change. Of course, what defined 1950s optimism was less a belittlement of problems than confidence that the nation could solve them. Ike often shared that confidence, but his outlook had a darker strain as well.

He was also less in control of issues of reform than those of national strategy and foreign policy. The latter engaged his greatest expertise and sharpest convictions, whereas his ability to shape domestic policy seemed limited—one reason that modern Presidents have attended more to national security, where the constitutional and political constraints on them seemed fewer. As interest groups proliferated, political parties weakened, and media politics supplanted them, presidential power in domestic matters appeared to shrink. Master brokers like FDR or Lyndon Johnson could overcome the obstacles on occasion, as could evident majority demands. And Eisenhower had successes: he generally got what he wanted in the weighty matter of federal budgets and monetary policy; he gained a modest expansion of welfare programs (increased Social Security benefits, expanded unemployment compensation, a higher minimum wage); and he secured major programs of internal development. But the administration's grip on other matters was shaky, especially when it faced grassroots movements that circumvented party structures and elite control. Such movements had little room, except as presumed beneficiaries, in his vision of a "corporate commonwealth" advanced by partnership between government and "corporate liberals," though even businessmen often exasperated him ("They make crooks out of themselves," he once complained).[48]

Meanwhile, Eisenhower's favorite among his achievements went forward. The huge Interstate and Defense Highway System, approved by Congress in 1956 at his initiative, demonstrated the intricate meshing of national security with domestic policy. In a few decades travelers would pay little heed to the "Defense" in the official title, but in the 1950s motorists could not miss (as Ike later put it) seeing the signs "sprout up alongside the pavement: 'In the event of an enemy attack . . . .' " For Eisenhower, defense was a major reason for the new system of roads (and for the Saint Lawrence Seaway). He worried about how to evacuate cities in a nuclear war—the present system, he warned in 1955, "would be the breeder of a deadly congestion within hours of an attack"—and he rejected the option civil defense experts favored, a vast system of fallout shelters. Worried also about military transportation, he vividly recalled joining an army convoy's agonizing, sixty-two-day cross-country trip in 1919 and returning home in 1945, after seeing Germany's *Autobahnen*, to American roads in "shocking condition." Stretching behind him was the military's long role, especially that of the Army Corps of Engineers, in the nation's internal development. His choice to head a committee studying the issue brought together all these facets, plus the highway lobby: it was Lucius Clay, engineer, army general, former head of the military occupation of Germany, and member of General Motors' board of directors.[49]

Eisenhower's initiative on highways also reflected a moderate progressivism that prized a limited federal role in promoting economic stability and abundance. He saw public works programs as a fiscal tool for smoothing out the business cycle while avoiding the evils of outright welfarism. He shared the prevailing faith that grandly scaled technological development would bring "greater convenience, . . . greater happiness, and greater standards of living." In words to make a later generation shudder, he soon boasted that his highway program used enough concrete to make "six sidewalks to the moon" and moved enough rock and dirt "to bury all of Connecticut two feet deep."[50]

Eisenhower's outlook may seem odd to a later generation that sees the demands of defense and prosperity as competing against each other, a competition which worried Ike himself, but at the time those demands seemed to be mutually supportive rather than clashing—new roads, like other programs, would address both needs. It was telling that the highway program received little criticism, although Lewis Mumford condemned it, and that what did ensue rarely addressed its defense component but instead its capacity to hasten the deterioration of inner cities and interstate rail transport (Eisenhower had seen the new system operating only between cities, fearing the mammoth costs of urban construction). Revealingly, admiring views of the new highway system used war to measure the triumph: it was to be "the greatest man-made physical enterprise of all time with the exception of war."[51]

Race relations, a more charged issue than highways, fit less comfortably into the framework of war and national security, but not for want of connections to it. If anything, those connections were so many and so volatile that instead of offering coherence to debate, they helped make it spin out of control. The connections were evident in how the civil rights impulse still drew on the leadership, tactics, and arguments set during the 1940s. They were evident in the armed forces' visible, pace-setting role in racial integration. They appeared in Hollywood films: movies about World War II were among the first to eschew demeaning stereotypes of blacks, while *Bad Day at Black Rock* (1954) explored a small town's murderous racism after Pearl Harbor against Japanese-Americans, with a one-armed white war veteran (Spencer Tracy) as the hero. Since segregation and racism were still seen largely as southern problems, the Civil War, whose hundredth anniversary loomed, provided another framework of understanding. Use of federal troops to restore order and enforce integration in the South evoked Reconstruction, for example, while one senator complained early in the 1960s that "in this battle on the Senate floor the roles of Grant and Lee at Appomattox have been reversed." Indeed, the sense of racial war customarily imputed to the 1960s was already evident, only with the metaphors differently cast.[52]

The Cold War offered a closely related context. Liberals reiterated their calls to protect national power by improving race relations. "With the Communists reaching out to the uncommitted people of the Middle East and Africa and Southeast Asia," Sen. Paul Douglas reminded his colleagues, "each housing riot in Illinois, each school riot in Kentucky, and each bombing of a pastor's home or intimidation of a would-be Negro voter in Alabama or Mississippi becomes not only an affront to human dignity here in this country, but a defeat for freedom in its tough world struggle for survival." Vice President Nixon, though illiberal in outlook and equivocal on specifics, argued in 1960, "In the world-wide struggle in which we are engaged, racial and religious prejudice is a gun we point at ourselves."[53] And foes of civil rights legislation still argued that it embodied the heavy-handed manner of communist governments, and that the civil rights movement was inspired or led by communists, as the FBI told the White House.

The international scene framed the struggle over civil rights in subtler ways as well. Connections real or alleged between sex and politics, a staple of Cold War culture, dogged the civil rights movement: the sexual liaisons of Martin Luther King, Jr., were woven into the FBI's tapestry alleging his communism; the homosexuality of Bayard Rustin, another prominent black leader, endangered him with other blacks as well as the FBI. The struggle over race relations also played out on an international stage. King, failing to gain an audience with Nixon, finally met him in Ghana, where both were attending celebrations of that nation's independence, and their subsequent meeting in Washington was dubbed, "in the popular parlance of the new nuclear age, the first 'summit conference'" between the two.[54] King's meetings with Third World leaders were suspect at a time when "neutralism" in the Cold War was hardly acceptable to national leaders, much less to many other Americans; his talk of global nonviolence and disarmament posed a similar risk. On the other hand, the rush to independence of African nations, presumably ripe for wooing by the communists, shored up familiar claims about the dangers of American racism.

King was attuned to all these elements. He knew how his appeal derived from and played out on a global stage, and he sought to mobilize world as well as national opinion. The "brutality" southern white officials vented on black demonstrators, he later wrote, "was caught—as a fugitive from a penitentiary is often caught—in gigantic circling spotlights . . . a luminous glare revealing the naked truth to the whole world." He drew inspiration and tactics from the revolt of nonwhites against imperial rule, especially Gandhi's nonviolent campaign for Indian independence. His movement was also suffused with military imagery. His "nonviolent army" wielded "the sword that heals," and at the 1960 sit-in of the Greensboro, North Carolina, Woolworth's, demonstrators worked, it has been written, from a "'command center'" and operated "with crisp, military efficiency—briefing new protesters on nonviolence, quashing rumors, despatching fresh troops as needed." King continued into the early 1960s to press familiar arguments about the Cold War and the meaning of World War II, pointing to the shame of discrimination against black Americans in uniform, to the fate of Jews under Hitler, to the perversion of law in communist countries, and to American ideals in the Cold War: "Throughout the upheavals of cold-war politics, Negroes had seen their government go to the brink of nuclear conflict more than once. The justification for risking the annihilation of the human race was always expressed in terms of America's willingness to go to any lengths to preserve freedom. To the Negro . . . there is a certain bitter irony in the pictures of his country championing freedom in foreign lands and failing to ensure that freedom to twenty million of its own."[55]

Yet King also pressed this familiar argument beyond the standard line of national expediency. For him, the Cold War highlighted the moral issue of racism, not the other way around. The moral implications of hypocrisy, not the expedient dangers of inconsistency, were his concern. Indeed, King, though not alone and not without powerful precedents, recast the movement in the framework of justice and morality rather than of national power.

Eisenhower and most men around him were uneasy about the appeal to justice, or at least about acting on it. Though acknowledging the immorality of racism, Ike consistently voiced his doubt that "prejudices, even palpably unjustified prejudices, will succumb to compulsion." Shaped by Earl Warren, Ike's nominee for chief justice of the Supreme Court, the 1954 *Brown v. Board of Education* decision banning school segregation (still legal in twenty-one states and Washington, D.C.) elicited similar reactions from Eisenhower. Though affirming his obligation to enforce the decision, he pointedly refused to endorse it. "We can't demand *perfection* in these moral questions," he told his staff. "And the fellow who tries to tell me that you can do these things by *force* is just plain *nuts*." He often made these views public, seeming to denigrate the spirit and substance of the civil rights movement. Even when asserting black Americans' right to "first-class citizenship," he insisted that they "be patient."[56]

In many ways his stance was unsurprising. It was in tune with the at best gradualist approach to racial progress espoused by many white Americans. It did him no harm at the polls: in 1956 he improved his take of both black and southern white votes, and King himself claimed to have voted Republican. Nor was his stance attributable to his age. His young successor was scarcely more sensitive to racial issues until changing times forced his hand, just as in his memoirs Eisenhower later hinted that he regretted his earlier timidity: Although as President he had not endorsed the *Brown v. Board of Education* decision, "there can be no question that the judgment of the Court was right." And most Americans did as badly as Ike in foreseeing how the ideological fervor over civil rights would empower other movements. When one reporter asked why he was not "as active in trying to wipe out discrimination based on sex" as on race, the surprised President joked (as Truman had) about how hard it was "for a mere man to believe that woman doesn't have equal rights." He did endorse an equal rights amendment, and (within the comfortable confines of national security) he struck down a policy restricting promotion of army nurses that "assumes that every woman of fifty-five is decrepit," but women's rights galvanized him no more than most leaders.[57]

For the style and substance of the civil rights movement, Eisenhower had little affinity by virtue of his profession, culture, or politics. His hands-off approach clearly sprang from more than just racism, however, since his resistance to mounting demands on the federal government arose in other areas of policy as well. By the same token, the "policy of delay and obfuscation" which failed him in civil rights was, his biographer points out, the same one "he had used so successfully in various foreign crises." Moreover, there *were* real limits to what formal antidiscrimination efforts could achieve: suburbanization in the 1950s "was strengthening the de facto basis for racial segregation even as judicial rulings, militant protest, congressional action, and executive intervention were weakening its de jure basis."[58]

More surprising was Eisenhower's failure to advance the issue forcefully as a matter of national security—to speak to the dangers abroad of American racism or to the war record of black Americans in order to justify federal power in behalf of civil rights. That context offered a comfortable way to seize the initiative and preempt broader rationales for racial justice. It lay on a path well charted by the mid-1950s, one he followed on highways and other issues and, on occasion, regarding racial discrimination. Instead of following that path consistently, however, he groped at the emerging language of justice, but so tentatively that he lacked force or evident conviction. If nothing else, his reluctance to take even the comfortable path is a reminder of the elasticity of national security as rationale for reform—of how little national security was a matter of objective need, how much it was a coin of the realm to be employed or discarded depending on other purposes.

Eisenhower's fulminations against "compulsion" in racial matters were especially specious. True, he did sometimes oppose use of federal power to impose morality in other ways: regarding a proposed ban on radio and television advertising for liquor and cigarettes, he asked, "What are we going to turn out to be—a police state?" But that stance was strange from someone out of a military organization notable for coercing morality in all sorts of ways and showing a good deal of progress precisely in the realm of race. Moreover, he did impose morality where he deemed federal authority legitimate. He worked hard to end discrimination in Washington, D.C.'s federal facilities and to persuade local businesses there to do likewise. He supported desegregation of the armed forces (though it proceeded slowly). He proclaimed the need for equal opportunity in federal hiring (if doing little in practice), and he backed a moderate civil rights bill (watered down in Congress before passage in 1957) empowering the federal government to enforce voting rights. Those actions left unclear whether his outlook was really shaped by his sense of the federal government's incapacity to legislate morality, or just by his doubt that anything was deeply wrong in race relations. Nor did Ike's blithe repudiation of compulsion address the argument King and others made, that law and force could at least guarantee rights and change behavior. "A law may not make a man love me," as King put it, "but it can stop him from lynching me." And of course, many whites feared precisely that morality *could* be legislated—that federal power *would* make a difference.[59]

Much of this Eisenhower had to acknowledge, grudgingly and implicitly, in the Little Rock crisis of 1957. By then, the South's resistance to school integration was only stiffening, as white citizens' councils mobilized and local officials used quasilegal or illegal ways to circumvent the Supreme Court's decision. Eisenhower had publicly stated that he could not "imagine" using federal troops to enforce the decision because the "common sense of America will never require it." In September, Arkansas governor Orval Faubus activated the National Guard in order to prevent the entry of black students into Little Rock's Central High School, but after negotiations with Eisenhower, he simply withdrew the guard, opening the way for mob violence against black students. Feeling betrayed by Faubus, Eisenhower acted swiftly, as if "his own sense of the military code had been breached: a lieutenant (the governor) had been guilty of subordination." He sent elements of the army's 101st Airborne Division to restore order.[60]

The drama eerily resembled Cold War crises abroad: troops deployed, the media mobilized, a failed summit (between Eisenhower and Faubus), a President's test of nerves, and the language of war. Ike mused on his crises as a general and cast his actions at Little Rock in military terms: "Well, if we have to do this," he told his attorney general, "then let's apply the best military principles to it and see that the force we send there is strong enough that it will not be challenged, and will not result in any clash." Accustomed to Ike's temporizing (or, as Emmet John Hughes put it, his "definite and explicit resolve to . . . leave things undone"), white Southerners were surprised and furious. Faubus called Arkansas "occupied territory"; Sen. Richard Russell "compared the intervention at Little Rock to Hitler's use of storm troopers"; Louisiana political boss Leander Perez talked secession; others pointed out "that this time around the Feds had atomic weapons."[61]

Eisenhower himself now invoked national security, telling the nation that Little Rock's disorder denigrated its image abroad and played into communist propaganda: "Our enemies are gloating over this incident and using it everywhere to misrepresent our whole nation. . . . We are portrayed as a violator of those standards of conduct which the peoples of the world united to proclaim in the Charter of the United Nations." Hughes later gave a forceful summary of the Cold War liberalism Eisenhower expressed on this occasion. The Little Rock story "carried faster than drum signals across black Africa. It summoned cold gleams of recognition to the eyes of Asians . . . of the racial enmities that had helped to make colonialism . . . so odious to them. More than a few West Europeans—long since weary of the moralistic exhortations or pious injunctions of American policy—could smirk complacently at the crude practice of racism in the self-styled sanctuary of freedom: the preacher now was being taunted and ridiculed by his own congregation. And to tell peoples of all lands, the trained and instructed voice of Soviet propaganda could relay, in almost affectionately fastidious detail, the news of Little Rock—breathing scorn as it spoke."[62]

But Hughes was also criticizing Eisenhower, who did not sustain the argument he offered during the Little Rock crisis or the actions that went with it. Those actions, he made clear, set no precedent for him. They were taken only to preserve order, not to press integration, which Faubus soon circumvented simply by closing public schools. Eisenhower supported another modest legislative effort, the Civil Rights Act of 1960, expanding federal power to enforce voting rights and investigate violence involving the interstate transportation of explosives. On occasion he restated both the major rationales for action: "This primary work on civil rights must go on," he noted in his final State of the Union Address. "Not only because discrimination is morally wrong, but also because its impact is more than national—it is world-wide."[63] But his presidency ended with school desegregation barely started in the South, white leaders there intransigent, black militancy rising, and the perception of administration failure widespread. He had tapped fully neither the wellsprings of concern about national security nor the anger about injustice of the civil rights movement. Racism and complacency were part of the failure, but also his incomprehension about mass-based movements—that of white resistance, and even more that of black militancy.

Eisenhower's views were firmer about conservation of America's basic resources, a concern he tied loosely but forcefully to national security. His conviction that "some day the world was going to be out of exhaustible resources," as he put it in 1955, overrode his conservative views of federal authority. He was eager for the government to purchase marginal land subject to erosion and depletion, and Congress approved a much-touted Soil Bank in 1956. Government, he argued, was obligated to "protect the soil of America just as we want to protect our freedom of speech, right to worship, etc." His concern, as in his defense policy, was national power in the distant future. Eyeing the Soviet Union's apparent economic power, he urged seizing "the opportunity to plan . . . *over the long term.*" Seeking new federal health programs, he warned that without them "we as a people are guilty not only of neglect of human suffering but also of wasting our national strength."[64]

In a similar fashion, he saw educational resources as vital to long-term security and prosperity. Typically, he wanted a modest federal role, proposing federal grants for school construction in the neediest districts and poorest states. Public schools enjoyed a long tradition of local control still defended by segregationists and conservatives, but by the 1950s that tradition was colliding with efforts to increase federal aid to education, efforts grounded in the baby boom's financial impact on local budgets and by demands that schools help America win the Cold War. Conflict over whether federal aid should flow to parochial schools also arose. Caught in the crossfire—especially contentious was a move to deny grants to states defying the *Brown* decision—Eisenhower's proposal repeatedly failed to clear Congress.

Beyond his proposal loomed a debate about education which involved questions of national power and persisted in one guise or another for the rest of the century. In the 1950s, it included allegations that progressive educators interested in a "life-adjustment" curriculum were debasing the intellectual rigor, moral fiber, or practical skills of American youth. Vice Admiral Hyman Rickover showed how these issues related to national security. Rickover had ruthlessly driven the navy into the nuclear age, overseeing construction of nuclear-powered and missile-firing submarines. By 1956 he was a national scold regarding the state of American education. A bit like Eisenhower, he "had the engineer's distaste for inefficiency and waste wherever they were found—the waste of good farmland, forests, oil, clean rivers and lakes, and bright minds, 'our most valuable national asset.'" Unless American youth confronted "the terrific requirements of this rapidly spiraling scientific and industrial civilization, we are bound to go down." The Soviets, Rickover warned, had learned that lesson. "There can be no second place in a contest with Russia and there will be no second chance if we lose." Other authorities also linked educational reform to national security. For James Conant—a key science official in World War II, former high commissioner to West Germany, adviser to several Presidents, and president of Harvard University—at stake in educational reform "was the cultural and military conflict with the Soviet Union."[65]

For millions of Americans, that conflict seemed even starker after October 1957. In educational policy and other areas, the web of connections to national security only tightened as the decade wore on, even as the rationale for reform was moving beyond it. And Eisenhower found his goal of achieving moderation, balance, and focus on "the long term" more elusive than ever.

Sputnik and the Eroding Balance

Sputnik appeared to knock the nation off-balance. As G. Mennen Williams, Michigan's Democratic governor, put it:

> Oh Little Sputnik, flying high
> With made-in Moscow beep,
> You tell the world it's a Commie sky,
> And Uncle Sam's asleep.[66]

Earth's first artificial satellite went into orbit on October 4, 1957, on a Soviet rocket. Weighing less than two hundred pounds, it had no practical utility, although larger Soviet satellites and canine cosmonauts soon followed, but its symbolic import seemed incalculable, as Soviet premier Nikita Khrushchev appreciated, so eager was he to change the perception of Soviet backwardness.

If Sputnik was bait in a propaganda war, leading Americans swallowed it whole, naively or for calculated purposes. A cascade of dire warnings, expressions of humiliation, and calls for action flowed. Sen. Henry Jackson called for a "national week of shame and danger." Congressman Daniel Flood, rejecting fiscal limits on national action, cried, "I would rather have red ink in the books than red blood on the streets of America." Senate Majority Leader Lyndon Johnson proclaimed that "control of space means control of the world," with its possessor able to impose "tyranny" or "freedom." Foreseeing the miraculous developments Americans often have expected of technological change, Johnson argued that the winners in space would be "masters of infinity" able to "control the earth's water, to cause drouth and flood, to change the tides and raise the levels of the sea, to divert the gulf stream and change the climates to frigid." Three years later, the strategist Henry Kissinger, seeing Soviet advances in space as one sign of a "decade and a half" of American decline, worried that its continuance "would find us reduced to Fortress America in a world in which we had become largely irrelevant." The sense of ruptured history—at the core of this panic as in those over Pearl Harbor and the atomic bomb—was acute. "Listen now for the sound which forevermore separates the old from the new," urged an NBC announcer directing his audience to Sputnik's bleeps.[67]

As usual, Americans portraying an ominous future invoked war's dark but familiar past. Physicist Edward Teller told a television audience that the nation "had lost a battle more important and greater than Pearl Harbor," one of many references to that event and the war that followed it. Journalists Joseph and Stewart Alsop hauled out perennial analogies to Munich and the 1930s, accusing the administration of the same appeasement that led to World War II. News stories about the armed forces' rival rocket programs transported readers back to Pearl Harbor, when similar rivalries presumably had crippled America (though now German scientists like Wernher Von Braun led America's effort). These comparisons scored points against Eisenhower, heightened the panic, bolstered the call for national mobilization—and hinted at a happy outcome: if the terrors of 1941 were back, so too might be the triumphs of 1945. It likewise made sense to cite, as both Ike and the press did, the greatest triumph of World War II, the Manhattan Project, as a model for action. Such comparisons placed a diffuse and indeterminate crisis of confidence on the familiar imaginative terrain of war.[68]

Hard issues of power and survival were ostensibly at stake. If Soviet rockets were powerful enough to launch satellites, it was reasoned, they could strike the United States: massive retaliation seemed hollow, Khrushchev's boasts about his rockets irrefutable, Eisenhower's defense policy bankrupt. Given that dire situation, some members of the Eisenhower-appointed Gaither committee saw as the only recourse an attack on the Soviet Union before its lead in rocketry became insurmountable. Less trigger-happy Cold Warriors rejected that option, only to see a different danger. The Soviets, John Kennedy warned, now had a "shield" of bombs and rockets "behind which they will slowly, but surely, advance—through Sputnik diplomacy, limited brush-fire wars, indirect non-overt aggression, intimidation and subversion, internal revolution, increased prestige or influence, and the vicious blackmail of our allies. The periphery of the Free World will slowly be nibbled away. The balance of power will gradually shift against us."[69] The United States, argued politicians like Kennedy, could only return to the principles of NSC-68, building up both strategic forces and conventional ones capable of "flexible response."

Few doubted that the stakes in space involved prestige as well as raw power. Just as wavering Third World peoples presumably watched America's sorry record in race relations, they scanned the skies for signs of America's triumph or failure, for evidence that it could live up to its promise to be more creative and productive than its totalitarian competitor. That promise was also in doubt among Americans. "Gaps" between Americans and Soviets in education and science, in discipline and imagination, seemed more alarming than the missile gap itself because they threatened the possibility that the Soviets' military lead could not be overcome, and even that Americans did not deserve to overcome it.

That fear seemed borne out in December 1957, when the American answer to Sputnik was to take to the skies from Cape Canaveral in Florida. As television sets across the land tuned in and millions of children crowded school auditoriums to watch, a navy rocket with a tiny satellite lifted a few feet from its pad, then sank back and exploded, prompting jokes about "Stayputnik," "Flopnik," and "Kaputnik" that vented national humiliation. Meanwhile, Eisenhower was briefly reduced by a stroke to uttering literal gibberish.

In a few weeks, the balance between contending forces—Soviets and Americans, Republicans and Democrats, Eisenhower and the groaning engines of militarization—seemed destroyed. In truth, it long had been precarious, so dependent on Ike's personal authority, or else one Soviet ball in space could not have upended it, exposing the fragility of Eisenhower's compromises and of Americans' sense of superiority. He rightly pleaded that American military and scientific superiority remained intact. His pleas fell on deaf ears—because he would not reveal his evidence for them, but even more because most Americans did not want to believe.

Much about the Sputnik panic was in fact familiar. The alarm over a missile and space "gap" had been preceded by a lesser one over a "bomber gap" and earlier by reactions in 1949 to news of the Soviet atomic bomb. The Sputnik panic was also a technological analog to the Red Scare, shifting its spirit of recrimination and suspicions of national flaccidity to the arena of science and to the Eisenhower administration itself. The Sputnik scare also gained energy from the crisis in race relations, climaxing in September at Little Rock, that had already challenged American pretenses of superiority and mobilized grassroots movements beyond elite control. Amplifying growing doubts, Sputnik also diverted them from the racial arena onto a technological battleground whose script of national peril and renewal was both frightening and familiar. Democrats consciously exploited the chance to shift attention from racial issues, which were dividing their party.

Old worries that the United States was becoming an empty, hedonistic nation also surfaced again, yielding calls to recapture the frontier spirit and jeremiads against complacency and materialism that Puritan divines might have admired. Once emblems of its superiority, the nation's cars and television sets now seemed tokens of its rot. "If America ever crashes, it will be in a two-tone convertible," the venerable financier-politician Bernard Baruch predicted; the United States had to worry less about the "height of the tail fin in the new car and be more prepared to shed blood, sweat, and tears if this country and the free world are to survive," argued one senator.[70] Although the space program was later sold as a fountainhead of technological abundance, unease about that abundance deepened the Sputnik panic.

Like most panics, this one was not a reaction to a single event but a state of mind built over time. That was evident in an array of proposed crash programs for fallout shelters, new weapons, and new strategies. Scientists aggravated and exploited the panic, as when one group approached Eisenhower with a plan to reach the moon by using "elegant little [nuclear] bombs to drive an elegant little spaceship around the solar system," as one scientist later put it. Reworking fears of a closed society and world-system that had haunted Americans for decades, scientists promoting new ventures in space thought it "essential to the growth of any new and high civilization that small groups of people can escape from their neighbors and from their governments, to go and live as they please in the wilderness." Panic also sanctioned lavish military schemes, as I. F. Stone discovered in the congressional testimony of an air force general who proposed that warheads "could be catapulted from shafts sunk deep into the moon's surface" and argued that if a lunar balance of terror then developed between the superpowers, stations could be built "on planets far more distant, from which control over the moon might then be exercised." Such schemes hardly enjoyed unanimous military support, but Stone could be excused for concluding: "Thus, as the Pentagon maps it, peace by mutual terror would spread outward toward the far stars." The Sputnik panic seemed to have no boundaries.[71]

Eisenhower tried mightily to reestablish them. The psychology of the panic should not have shocked him, insofar as his strategy of massive retaliation already had rested on the psychological mysteries of deterrence and the symbolic import of new technology. Nonetheless, he was baffled by the Sputnik scare, partly because of his attachment to elite control and his reluctance to admit its erosion. His inability to articulate a visionary alternative to Cold War and militarization compounded his problems. For all its banality and hysteria, reactions to Sputnik did reveal a broad yearning for something more daring than he could provide. For good reasons, he would not embrace a race to the moon, agreeing with his first National Aeronautics and Space Administration director that if the nation's prestige rested on " 'When do we get a man on the moon?' " then "all sense of perspective has gone out the window." But Ike offered no substitute. Washington doggerel in 1957 indicated the problem:

> Sputnik, Sputnik in the sky
> Emitting beeps as you go by,
> Have you room in your little bullnik
> For Ike and Dick and Foster Dullnik?

Four years later, Ike was still uncomprehending, contemptuous of JFK's decision to stake national prestige on a race to the moon.[72]

Uncomprehending he may have been, uncertain he was not. His effort to dampen hysteria and restrain militarization dominated the rest of his presidency. His primary asset was the enormous authority in military matters he still commanded. A general abandoned by most of his lieutenants (though not by Dulles and the CIA), he still gained a tactical victory in a losing campaign against the forces of militarization. "It was one of his finest hours," writes Stephen Ambrose. "The demands for shelters, for more bombers, for more bombs, for more research and development of missiles and satellites, [were] nearly irresistible," but Eisenhower rejected them. "He thereby saved his country untold billions of dollars and no one knows how many war scares."[73]

A cold calculation of strategic realities guided him. Khrushchev might threaten the United States with extinction, but Ike knew it was a bluff. Secret flights by American U-2 aircraft—the evidence Ike would not make public, lest it infuriate the Soviets or terminate the reconnaissance—revealed that the Soviets were deploying few long-range rockets and could not match America's formidable heavy bombers. Knowing that, Eisenhower decided to leapfrog large-scale production of costly and combustible first-generation rockets in favor of advanced solid-fuel rockets (land-based Minuteman and sub-based Polaris missiles). Tied to that decision was a broader acceptance shared by Dulles of rough strategic parity with the Soviets, a heresy that helped prompt the strident charges of appeasement. Hardly neglecting America's military might, he was keen to maintain its qualitative lead, but numbers alone, nuclear "overkill" as it was now called, counted for little with him as he questioned, "How many times do we have to destroy Russia?" The armed forces were getting "into an incredible position—of having enough to destroy every conceivable target all over the world, plus a three-fold reserve," he complained. Even if the United States escaped direct attack and won a nuclear war, "there just might be nothing left of the Northern Hemisphere" because of fallout (atmospheric tests alone, he worried, might produce that result). Informed in 1960 that America was building four hundred Minuteman missiles a year, Ike responded indignantly (if disingenuously, for he had approved the program), "Why don't we go completely crazy and plan on a force of 10,000?" As for those peddling fear of a missile gap, Ike allegedly called them "sanctimonious, hypocritical bastards."[74]

Again and again, he exploded about the pressures on him. Those from his generals and admirals were "damn near treason." Protecting national security was vital, he told his advisors, but that did not mean the nation should try to be best at everything—precisely what many Americans felt they should do. Responding to the Gaither committee, he fumed: "I'm not going to dance at the end of the string of . . . people who try to give me . . . scare stories." When the committee recommended crash programs for fallout shelters and new armaments to wage nuclear war, Eisenhower told them, "You can't have this kind of war . . . . There just aren't enough bulldozers to scrape the bodies off the streets." He scornfully dismissed the project for nuclear rockets, sparing the universe "a filthy creature" leaving "its radioactive mess behind it wherever it goes," as one scientist later put it.[75]

His public utterances had the same substance. He upheld distinctions fast disappearing amid the panic: "There is much more to science than its function in strengthening our defense, and much more to our defense than the part played by science." Science's "peaceful contributions" and the nation's "spiritual powers" were "the most important stones in any defense structure." "We face," Ike wrote one concerned group, "not a temporary emergency . . . but a long-term responsibility," and he deplored hasty actions done "under the impetus of sudden fear." Elitist condescension could also flare up in public. At the start of the Sputnik panic, Ike spoke sneeringly to a hostile press of the Soviets' "one small ball in the air." During the 1958 election campaign, in "the most harsh and graceless partisan speeches of his political life," as Emmet John Hughes termed them, Eisenhower insisted that there would be "no appeasing Communist aggression," that "the so-called missile gap is being rapidly filled" (unwittingly suggesting it was real), and that "political radicals" and "self-styled liberals" had an "irresistible impulse . . . to squander money—your money."[76]

His flashes of anger revealed his calculated commitment to maintaining a long view of the Cold War, hoarding national resources, and restraining militarization. He expanded his familiar injunctions against the garrison state. Disarmament was necessary because "no country can advance intellectually and in terms of culture and well-being if it has to devote everything to military buildup." Once again "awfully sick of the lobbies by the munitions," he looked over advertisements by Boeing and Douglas, glimpsing the garrison state's cultural and economic underpinnings. Nor did he share the widely held view that prosperity hinged on defense spending and disarmament would mean depression. "We are now scratching around to get money for such things as school construction" and "road building" and "all sorts of things," he told reporters in 1960. "I see no reason why the sums which now are going into these sterile, negative mechanisms that we call war munitions shouldn't go into something positive."[77]

Sometimes grudgingly, Eisenhower did agree to changes: a new National Aeronautics and Space Administration (NASA); a presidential science advisor (James Killian and then George Kistiakowsky, who helped offset science hawks like Teller); modest increases in weapons and space programs; reorganization of the Department of Defense. But, as he commented on one supplemental budget he accepted, two-thirds of it went "more to stabilize public opinion than to meet any real need."[78] As before Sputnik, he supported space programs meeting scientific curiosity and military needs—the reconnaissance capacities of satellites were especially alluring—but scorned the prestige-driven race in space.

Despite his effort to restrain militarization—and because of the exceptions he allowed in order to placate public opinion and meet his own test of vigilant defense—his success was only rearguard and temporary. By one standard it was considerable: defense budgets rose only modestly in Ike's last years. Pressure kept building for more money, programs, and forceful action, however, its power emerging more sharply under his successors.

Defense-related spending on science and technology measured those forces. Such spending remained hard to calculate because much of it was buried in nondefense budgets, went to technologies with both civilian and military uses, or had little military payoff. Moreover, the share of federal research and development spending devoted to defense was declining (the National Institutes of Health budget increased tenfold over the decade). But since total R&D budgets increased dramatically (to 15.6 percent of the budget by 1965), defense-related spending still swelled: the Defense Department's R&D budget nearly doubled between 1958 and 1961, while NASA's multiplied tenfold.

The character of this spending was as important as its size. Although championed by many scientists, basic research gained a tiny portion of the federal budget. The money flowed instead to vast engineering programs like NASA's effort to get Americans into space and then to the moon. These were public works projects on an imperial scale. Only their real or imagined links to defense and their white-collar constituency and appeal isolated them from the charges of socialism and welfarism that had dogged the New Deal's far punier programs. Moreover, despite dominant images of science marching inexorably into the future—progress could not be stopped, ran the popular incantation—this was a forced march directed by the state in accordance with political pressures and perceived national need, one reason many scientists disliked NASA's programs. Hence physics and engineering grabbed the lion's share, although the frontiers of scientific inquiry often lay in other fields. As one scientist complained in 1958 (romanticizing his profession's past), "What has happened to the old ivory tower! . . . the wise men, once quietly guided by the star of Bethlehem, now frantically count time by the star of Moscow." By the same token, while scientists and universities were important, corporate contractors and government agencies were the dominant players. And long-term, capital-intensive projects presupposed still larger outlays in the future, unless huge start-up costs were to be written off in ceasing work on half-built rockets or submarines. The pattern was not new—whether Sputnik ushered in "an age of technocracy" is debatable—but the scale and sophistication of Sputnik-era projects greatly aggravated it.[79]

As his policy on nuclear weapons showed, Ike had difficulty grappling with these forces. One of his first reactions to Sputnik had been to renew his interest in suspension of nuclear tests and in disarmament generally. His motives were a familiar mix: to lock in America's advantage in nuclear weapons, cut defense costs, counter the panicky mood, and score propaganda points to offset the Soviets' success in space. Familiar forces stalled his effort. Scientists like Teller nominally subscribed to disarmament but offered a host of objections to any moratorium on testing: the Soviets would cheat, steal "our secrets," and "surpass us"; progress would stop on "clean" (radiation-free) nuclear weapons that would benefit humankind; atomic scientists themselves "would lose tone, impetus, and personnel" during a moratorium.[80] Then, just when new technology made seismic monitoring of a moratorium easier, science hawks countered with new nightmares: the Russians would resort to "decoupling"—conducting nuclear tests within mammoth underground caves in order to reduce their seismic shock—or even to testing bombs on the back side of the moon.

Some progress in Soviet-American negotiations was made, but it was bedeviled by many obstacles. Britain and France, eager to develop their own nuclear weapons (and, in the French case, to aid Israel's development as well), threw up roadblocks. Leaders vacillated: Eisenhower worried that a unilateral suspension of American tests would prompt Democrats to say, "This is our Munich"; Khrushchev worried that on-site inspections would expose Soviet weakness and bluster. Progress was also slowed by deep rifts in the American government—an obstacle to arms control often greater than the superpowers' differences—and by the poisonous atmosphere of Soviet-American relations. As one historian later complained, "Every Russian initiative was held to be a trap: if Moscow proposed a joint declaration in favor of motherhood, this would have called forth position papers from the State Department's Policy Planning Council . . . and eventually a declaration that while the United States welcomed this recognition of the sanctity of family life . . . , it would require clear indication that the USSR did not mean to derogate the status of father-hood." Such obstacles and Ike's conflicting aspirations—to push disarmament but also to retain American superiority—crippled efforts to end the decade's orgy of tests and scale back militarization. Debate on testing had another effect that few anticipated: bitter conflicts among scientists eroded their image as neutral experts to whom national policy could be entrusted, laying one basis for the revolt against expert authority and the ecological activism of the 1960s.[81]

The forces swirling about in the nuclear arena came together at an unlikely point at the decade's close—Alaska. Teller and the AEC, acting on the Sputnik-era fetish for bigness, proposed Project Chariot, a scheme to use nuclear explosives to create a new harbor on Alaska's north coast. It was to inaugurate the AEC's broader Project Plowshare, with its biblical imagery of turning nuclear swords into tools of peaceful engineering. Chariot would help in planning the nuclear excavation of a new Panama Canal operating without locks at sea level—and offer a chance to test weapons technology under the guise of peaceful progress. Journeying to Alaska to sell the program, Teller "mixed flattery with frontier bravado," promising to unlock the wealth of Alaska's coalfields and "to reshape the earth to your pleasure." Queried about other projects the AEC might attempt, Teller joked, "If your mountain is not in the right place, just drop us a card." But the project was laughable in economic terms, dangerous in ecological ones, and destructive in human terms. Alarmed Eskimos—some of whom had participated in Nagasaki's cleanup and knew about the disastrous 1954 Bikini nuclear test—joined with skeptical businessmen, local scientists, and Barry Commoner, a scientist leading the budding antinuclear and environmental movements. After an ugly struggle in which the AEC brushed aside the data of dissenting scientists and maneuvered to blacklist them, the commission gave up in 1962. It "was possibly the first government project challenged on ecological grounds," notes its historian.[82]

Given the escalating arms race, the opposition to Chariot, like the campaign to ban nuclear tests, was nonetheless wide of the mark, some historians argue. Such efforts involved a "displacement" whereby people shifted their fears away from the gravest danger, that of nuclear war. The test ban served as a "magic talisman, a way that the nation could confront a real and present danger without coming to grips with the true reality of the 1950s—the possibility of total destruction."[83] That possibility was hardly ignored in the late 1950s, however: Hollywood films, the warnings of Eisenhower and others, and a mounting controversy over civil defense all made it visible. A less psychologized explanation of nuclear politics would not neatly distinguish one "true reality" from others, would recognize that politics often begins with immediate and local dangers, and would point to the large obstacles against any direct challenge to nuclear weapons.

For despite the breach in political culture on nuclear issues, the clamor for more weapons only increased. Strategic doctrine mirrored and exacerbated the pressures involved, as theorists, officers, and policymakers scrambled to impart rationality and equilibrium to a system spinning out of control. From one vantage point, stability seemed foreseeable. Prevailing American doctrine assumed a balance of terror in which each superpower deterred the other's initiation of nuclear war with its threat of a devastating response. Refined as "mutual assured destruction" (MAD), this doctrine implied that once the superpowers gained rough parity, they would have powerful incentives to stabilize the competition—money would be saved, worried constituencies reassured, and the dangers of surprise minimized. Superiority might even be dangerous if it led the weaker power, fearful it could never survive a first strike, to launch such a strike itself.

Despite that finely spun argument, stability was unattainable: external pressures disrupted it, logical inconsistencies arose within it, and logic never fully governed strategy anyway. Given the Soviet rocket capability supposedly revealed by Sputnik, American strategists argued for a "second-strike" force able to survive an enemy first strike and still respond devastatingly. Building such a force, however, required missiles on submarines and in hardened silos, cost billions, drove the Soviets to reply in kind, and further ratcheted up the arms race. Costs went still higher as strategy shifted from "city-busting" to destroying enemy military forces. It seemed more humane and effective to target those forces, but since they were far more numerous, scattered, and protected than cities, "counterforce" strategy required far more missiles with far more sophisticated guidance systems.

The new strategies and weapons made the dilemmas of deterrence more vexing. If, some mused, the Soviets struck first by hitting America's military forces instead of its cities, the President would face an excruciating choice—a counterattack on Soviet rocket forces would find many of their silos empty, yet an attack on Soviet cities would only ensure an enemy response incinerating America's metropolises. Any claim that the United States would engage in global incineration seemed mad, yet any hint of restraint would undermine its credibility. As Bernard Brodie noticed, "The rub comes from the fact that what looks like the most rational *deterrence* policy involves commitment to a strategy of response which, if we ever had to execute it, might then look very foolish." The problems were so intractable and the reasoning so circular that one theorist wondered if war might come through "successive cycles of 'He thinks we think he thinks we think . . . he thinks we think he'll attack; so he thinks we shall; so he will; so we must.' "[84]

In other ways, too, measures to enhance the nation's safety threatened to undermine it further. It seemed sensible to protect cities with anti-ballistic missiles (ABMs) that could intercept Soviet bombers and rockets, but ABMs triggered an ugly debate. To exponents of deterrence, a nation able to defend its cities would be tempted to initiate nuclear war, trusting that it could brush off its enemy's retaliatory attack. The whole effort to solve the dilemmas created by one technology with another was dangerous. As retired general Omar Bradley warned in 1957, "Missiles will bring anti-missiles, and anti-missiles will bring anti-anti-missiles. But inevitably this whole electronic course of cards will a reach point where it can be constructed no higher."[85]

Precarious indeed seemed "The Delicate Balance of Terror," as Albert Wohlstetter, a civilian theorist at the RAND Corporation, entitled a notable 1959 article. Like him, other strategists feared that even a "moderate" technical advantage for one side might tempt it into a preemptive strike or into exploiting "new possibilities of threats, ultimatums, blackmail." Later work by Roberta Wohlstetter (also at RAND) on the Pearl Harbor disaster underlined that danger by stressing the extreme difficulty of anticipating surprise attack. The perception of perilous instability such strategists offered was driven by an "exaggerated appreciation of both the evolving technology and its impact on the strategic balance." Yesterday's weapon appeared certain to be tomorrow's junk, made obsolete by the latest creation of maniacal genius or command technology. "Every country lives with the nightmare," wrote Kissinger, that even "its best efforts" at survival "may be jeopardized by a technological breakthrough on the part of its opponent." George Kennan, more alarmed about the arms race, asked, "Are we to flee like haunted creatures from one defensive device to another, each more costly and humiliating than the one before, cowering underground one day, breaking up our cities the next, attempting to surround ourselves with elaborate shields on the third . . . ?" The acute sense of technological flux masked real sources of stability: the subsequent turnover of weaponry often was slow (three decades later, B-52s remained in the American arsenal), strategy changed only gradually, and some new technologies, like spy satellites, proved stabilizing to the international system. Stability was not, however, readily apparent in the 1950s.[86]

Other strategists saw a path out of the cul-de-sac in doctrines of limited war. Alarmed by the Soviet Union's apparent strategic superiority, appalled by the dangers of a general nuclear war, convinced that "massive retaliation" did not deter aggression, they advanced a "realist" critique of the American tradition of seeing "no goal save total victory, and no mode of war except all-out war," as

Kissinger put it. Given an impossible choice between American paralysis and global holocaust, they argued that "the only rational course is to develop a strategy capable of limiting warfare and fighting limited wars successfully." With varying emphases, civilians like Kissinger and army generals like Maxwell Taylor and Matthew Ridgway touted the utility of conventional forces and tactical nuclear weapons for enhancing deterrence and waging limited war. Still, their strategy was hardly stable or convincing. Korea was a dispiriting example, just as America's war in Vietnam, for which they laid one intellectual basis, was the tragic outcome. And as Brodie argued, no one could promise that nuclear war would stay limited, given "that war always deeply involves the emotions" and often "the collapse of inhibitions."[87]

In any event, it was never clear how much these exquisite and conflicting calculations of strategy determined policy. Civilian strategists looked to the techniques and language of economics, physics, and mathematics (including game theory). Their models of nuclear warfare were intellectually impressive but also stripped (as Brodie, and in his own way Eisenhower, realized) of those emotional components of war not reducible to quantification and computer analysis. "It was," runs one historian's mordant comment, "as if police officers were being taught the art of homicide detection in terms of opportunity and murder weapon, but never motive." There could be no rehearsal for Armageddon, only war-gaming and frayed nerves. The theorists' apparent confidence in their predictions and their ability to manage war contrasted to the gripping unpredictability of war that many Americans sensed. Moreover, tucked away at RAND and other institutes flourishing on government support, theorists were isolated from the broad currents of American life. Their forbidding language, chilling scenarios, and pose of objectivity alienated many Americans, who could learn of their work through novels and films that often presented them savagely. Reaction to *On Thermonuclear War* (1960) by RAND's Herman Kahn, with its "grim jocularity" about surviving and winning nuclear war, exposed the alienation, even if it caricatured Kahn's ambiguous purposes. Civilian strategists enjoyed a closer relationship with military officers, but they often resented or scorned the civilian expertise on which they also depended.[88]

Not surprisingly, then, broader impulses drove policy as much as strategic theory. Like the dreadnoughts of pre–World War I superpowers, bombers and rockets were valued more as emblems of national power than as servants of doctrine or as practical instruments of war. Great powers amassed them to show they were great powers and to signal their resolve to worried allies and rash enemies. They served symbolic functions that no rational calculations could express and no specific numbers fulfill.

For different reasons, many of the men in charge were also skeptical of elaborate doctrines of deterrence. "If I see that the Russians are amassing their planes to attack," Air Force General Curtis LeMay reportedly said, "I'm going to knock the shit out of them before they take off the ground." Given to exaggeration, LeMay nonetheless had, as head of the Strategic Air Command and then as the Air Force chief of staff, wide latitude under the American system of command and control, one much looser than the Soviet Union's. And his attitude persisted after his retirement in 1965. "If there is a nuclear war, the United States will be the one to start it," said one Air Force strategist years later. The influence of civilian strategists was substantial, but the disjunction between their artful theories and the coarser outlook of commanders was another source of instability.[89]

Still, the balance of terror held, and perhaps underwrote what John Gaddis has called the "long peace" of the Cold War. The symbolic value of nuclear weapons certainly implied a kind of functional restraint: they were there for show, not for use, it often seemed. Did peace endure because of the balance of terror or despite it? The answer may be both: the terror that stayed the nuclear powers from plunging into the abyss also drove them to its edge. It also encouraged them to tolerate, promote, or enter non-nuclear wars that scarred many other nations; this was a "long peace" only by the essential but singular standard of avoiding nuclear war. And what restrained the superpowers was less some *balance* of terror than mutual terror at the prospect of nuclear war, regardless of whether one side had an edge in it. They were, that is, deterred as much by their own weapons as by the enemy's, not because Americans were restrained while Soviets were reckless, or because American superiority forced a truculent enemy to back away from war. A psychological more than a military construct, the balance of terror rested less on forces than on attitudes, ones shared by superpower elites who proclaimed hatred of each other.

And it barely did hold, never more precarious than in the late 1950s and early 1960s. No episode demonstrated its fragility more than the Berlin crisis of the winter of 1958–1959. Berlin itself still stood oddly close to 1945: even in West Berlin the rubble of wartime bombing remained evident; no border guards stopped traffic between the east and west sectors; and both sectors still seemed "the pets of the occupation powers." But the dazzle of the West's Kurfurstendamm mocked the drabness of Communist East Berlin, however prosperous it was by East European standards. Khrushchev, for various possible reasons— frustration and embarrassment over the drain of population and talent out of East Berlin into the West, or fear that West Germany might soon gain control of NATO nuclear weapons—precipitated the crisis, issuing a stream of menacing metaphors: "West Berlin has become a sort of malignant tumor" and "we have decided to do some surgery"; Berlin was "a bone in my throat" and "the testicles of the West. Every time I give them a yank, they holler." Many did holler when he demanded an agreement to end the Allied occupation of Berlin, make West Berlin a demilitarized free city, and establish East Berlin as East Germany's capital—and when he hinted at another Berlin blockade if he did not get his way.[90]

Eisenhower's response was measured in the face of formidable pressures. Most NATO allies supported his cautious response, but not so many Americans. A dying Dulles spoke bitterly of spending billions on defense only to have "appeasement and partial surrender" threaten "to be our attitude." The armed forces pressed Ike to plan a military effort to break any blockade. Congressional leaders renewed their calls to increase the defense budget. Journalists asked about using NATO forces or nuclear weapons in the event of blockade. In all cases, Eisenhower rejected the pressures outright or sharply scaled back the plans urged on him. Keen to ease "pressures at home for precipitous action," he responded to questions about liberating Berlin with nuclear weapons in his typically flat style: "Well, I don't know how you could free anything with nuclear weapons." If Congress forced fifty thousand more troops on him, "Where will I put them?" he snidely asked reporters. "Well, just some place where it's nice to keep them out of the way, because I don't know what else to do with them." Moreover, he "spared no effort to assure Khrushchev a retreat with honor." Publicly he held fast to Allied rights and privately he weighed the nuclear option, but Khrushchev's ultimatum passed without incident in May. Essentially, Eisenhower talked his way out of the crisis—indeed, refused to treat it as a crisis—but not before many Americans thought a nuclear war might begin. Stability, and peace itself, again seemed to pivot on him.[91]

Berlin was only one tilt in the see-saw of events that sent hopes for detente alternately soaring and sinking. Nixon's visit to Moscow in July 1959 yielded the Kitchen Debate and a stream of vulgarities: Khrushchev likened one recent congressional action to "fresh horse shit, and nothing smells worse than that!"; Nixon retorted that "the Chairman is mistaken. There is something that smells worse than horse shit—and that is pig shit." A visit by Khrushchev to the United States produced the celebrated "spirit of Camp David," plus fury on the American right (William F. Buckley, Jr., condemned having a visitor who "profanes the nation").[92] Eisenhower embarked on globe-trotting diplomacy to round up allies for detente, but just as hopes for a breakthrough peaked in the spring of 1960, the Soviets shot down an American U-2 spy plane. When Khrushchev and Eisenhower bungled into a loud exchange of lies, accusations, and threats about the incident, the fragile process of summit diplomacy shattered.

Failure owed to more than the deeds of leaders, however—it was the product of a larger process accelerating during the Sputnik years. The Cold War and other great-power rivalries had long been waged as total struggles embracing all forms of power, but now that embrace seemed bigger than ever—*everything* counted in the global struggle, as Eisenhower indicated in his 1958 State of the Union Address. Americans "could make no more tragic mistake than merely to concentrate on military strength," he warned. For "what makes the Soviet threat unique in history is its all-inconclusiveness. Every human activity is pressed into service as a weapon of expansion. Trade, economic development, military power, arts, science, education, the whole world of ideas—all are harnessed to this same chariot of expansion."[93] At the same time, symbols of prestige—the shiny kitchen, the beeping Sputnik, the man in orbit—became detached from weapons, free-floating and indeterminate. If few criteria established what constituted "enough" weaponry, even fewer determined what made for enough science, education, cultural prestige, or moral virtue. How many Americans in space flying how high for how long would constitute catching up with the Soviets? It was gratifying to have the American pianist Van Cliburn win the 1958 Tchaikovsky Competition in Moscow—victory brought him wild acclaim in the United States—but did it suffice to show that American artists were better than their Soviet counterparts? The late 1950s involved not just the familiar perception that national security was all-embracing but a shift in emphasis: intangible components of power seemed more important more than ever in the Cold War.

The most sensational and often vulgar expression of that outlook was the race to get men in space, evoked well by Tom Wolfe. America the underdog needed its heroes, their very foolhardiness one measure of their virtue. The Mercury astronauts "had volunteered to sit on top of the rockets—which *always blew up!* They were kamikazes going forth to vie with the Russians!" They embodied American virtue, at least its white male forms, however contrived the public relations effort to represent that virtue and associate it with leaders like Kennedy (Eisenhower kept his distance from the astronauts). They were to inspire the nation's youth, rally the nation's spirit, and show, much like Lindbergh in the 1920s, that new-found technological sophistication and old-fashioned individual heroism were still congruent, at least among Americans. Familiar gendered notions of wartime virtue reappeared, with women conscripted into subordinate roles: "SEVEN BRAVE WOMEN BEHIND THE ASTRONAUTS," ran a 1959 *Life* headline about the warriors' wives. Above all, the astronauts were to beat the Soviets. In the process, as Wolfe suggests, the Cold War changed. The space race shifted a measure of superpower conflict from the deadly arena of real weapons onto the safer terrain of symbolic combat. However wasteful, the space race involved no shooting, no hurling of nuclear bombs. Widening the Cold War, intensifying its symbolic dimensions, the space race also gave it a cathartic outlet and made it more diffuse.[94]

A more diffuse struggle also reworked the links between national security and reform, as educational policy showed. Sputnik gave critics of education enormous visibility—*Life* devoted a five-part series to education in 1958—and spawned invidious comparisons between Soviet and American schools. Earlier proposals for school reform and federal aid to education now found their moment when Eisenhower signed the National Defense Education Act (NDEA). According to its enabling language, "The present emergency" and "the present educational emergency"—neither much defined, as if self-evident—required action; "The defense of this Nation depends upon the mastery of modern techniques developed from complex scientific principles."[95] The act aimed to strengthen education in science, mathematics, and foreign languages (and later other fields), providing loans to undergraduates and fellowships to graduate students (if they signed loyalty oaths). Smaller funds went to strengthen guidance and testing services in secondary schools, while separate National Science

Foundation monies went into an overhaul of secondary science and mathematics education.

The NDEA, and education generally, enjoyed a ballyhoo that obscured important continuities, especially with the earlier GI Bill. Federal aid to education had long foundered in the face of divisions over aid to private and religious schools, racial integration, and the value of local control. Like the GI Bill, the NDEA did not so much overcome those obstacles as circumvent them—national security allowed a suspension of objections to federal aid without their overthrow. That rationale also gave the legislation an elitist thrust, one stronger than the GI Bill had. Though public anxiety focused on primary and secondary schools, most money went to colleges and universities. The tension between democratizing impulses and elitist concerns was evident in contemporary debate. One Nobel Prize–winning physicist contrasted the intellectual objectivity of Soviet education with the democratic milieu that presumably crippled the American school superintendent, who decides what to teach by finding out "how many voters in this town think that the world is round and how many think that it is square." *Life* bemoaned how America's "stupid children get far better care than the bright. The geniuses of the next decade are even now being allowed to slip back into mediocrity."[96]

The tension emerged in the act's wording. It urged "that no student of ability will be denied an opportunity for higher education because of financial need"—liberals had changed Ike's original proposal for undergraduate scholarships based on merit to loans based on need—but it also rewarded students with "superior" academic backgrounds or abilities, usually students from advantaged backgrounds and schools in prosperous districts. Most likely, given the fields of study targeted, they also would be male; in terms of gender, too, the NDEA resembled the GI Bill.

The NDEA was designed to strengthen education and national defense. Along with swelling Sputnik-era technological programs, it tightened the link between the federal government and education and deepened the latter's dependence on the former. It elicited little criticism for doing so. Eisenhower himself missed an opportunity in that regard. Worried as ever about the "garrison state," he designed NDEA legislation "that served his rearguard view against the pretensions of technocracy," but he couched the danger of federal aid to education in terms of "socialism."[97]

The wide-ranging definitions of national security that prompted the NDEA did not, however, forge greater national unity, despite rhetorical appeals invoking Pearl Harbor and the like presumably designed to achieve it. Instead, the fissures in political culture only widened as the decade closed. Eisenhower himself repudiated the need for unity, in that he denied there was a national emergency. The sheer length of time, approaching two decades, of real or presumed national emergency also undercut efforts to achieve unity, for each new proclamation of crisis came to Americans inclined by now to regard such declarations as almost routine. While Americans might on occasion postpone other goals, as they presumably had in 1942, perpetual deferral was less obtainable, especially in 1958 and 1959, when racial issues and a sharp recession generated much conflict and attention. So while experts dwelled on gaps between the United States and the Soviet Union, gaps among Americans themselves also widened. They appeared on many fronts by the decade's end—in a continuing battle over rock music and in handwringing about American youth, for example, and most baldly in debates on race relations and nuclear policy.

In turn, those issues helped reenergize conservatism—not Eisenhower's cautious brand but a strident version demanding dismantling of the welfare state and victory in the Cold War. William F. Buckley's *National Review* made its debut in 1955, while *The Conscience of a Conservative* by Arizona senator Barry Goldwater hit the bookstores in 1960. Goldwater exploited the discrepancy between strident professions of irreconcilable Soviet-American conflict and the more cautious practice of American foreign policy. With World War II his model for the Cold War, he cried that it would have made no sense, "midway in the Second World War, to promote a Nazi-American exchange program or to invite Hitler to make a state visit to the United States." He condemned the "craven fear of death" that was "entering the American consciousness," to the point (referring to Khrushchev's recent visit) "that many recently felt that honoring the chief despot himself was the price we had to pay to avoid nuclear destruction." Goldwater shared with liberals a fear that America was losing the Cold War because its leadership, even its people, were flaccid. And his rhetoric resembled what the New Left would soon say: government had become "a Leviathan, a vast national authority out of touch with the people, and out of their control." Where liberals wanted to energize the state through programs like the NDEA, however, Goldwater wanted to disband it, except for its hard core of armed force and internal security.[98]

Criticism also continued among liberal intellectuals. True, no wholesale change was evident. When scholars examined "power and democracy in America" in 1961, for example, only the idiosyncratic Peter Drucker focused on military institutions. Others still offered critiques of mass culture, stressing how the nation needed to change to wage global struggle, in a spirit similar to that of D. W. Brogan, the British observer. Brogan was glad that Sputnik woke "the American public from its undogmatic slumbers (in most cases it was plain slumber)," thought that it ranked "with the shots at Lexington or Fort Sumter," and maintained that "everything in the interior life of the United States that reinforces the interior or exterior caricature of the American way of life—from rigged quiz programs upward—is dangerous in this world."[99]

Paul Goodman, in *Growing up Absurd* (1960), offered a different thrust. He lamented how society gave youth no sense of work, purpose, and community, and he celebrated Beats, hipsters, and delinquents for exposing the hollowness of American culture. Although later hailed for charting a course toward the radical 1960s, Goodman also "reflected the distaste for ideological language common to the 1950s." He took swipes at Cold War culture but gave no sustained analysis of militarization and its role in youth's ills. His criticism of Eisenhower was utterly conventional—"He has invited no real writer, no artist, no philosopher to the White House," and having Fred Waring's band play at the White House was "disgraceful"—and of the sort that Kennedy could easily disarm. Reflecting 1950s norms in another way, he ignored women: "A girl does not *have* to, she is not expected to, 'make something' of herself. . . . She will have children, which is absolutely self-justifying, like any other natural or creative act."[100]

Still, Goodman's edgy tone and much of his content anticipated broader criticism of militarized America. Writing when Goodman's book appeared, anthropologist Jules Henry portrayed a "culture against man," one sick to its core. Henry saw the Cold War not as a reluctant burden, but as a crusade fatally congruent with America's culture and economic system. "The anxiety latent in our insecure and competitive life has been rationalized—made real and specific—by the emergence of the Soviet Union as the contemporary Incarnation of fear." Worse, the affluence accompanying militarization disarmed opposition to it, since war and war preparations were seen as promoting prosperity. "The fact that war-*fear* is partly narcotized by consumption-*euphoria* habituates us to living with The Great Fear." Defense spending driven by that fear had other baleful effects, Henry claimed: it diminished investment in the nation's commercial prowess, causing America's "growing vulnerability to imports," and it reshaped "the ecological pattern of industrial development," shifting it above all to California. When economists explain that defense spending maintained national prosperity, wrote Henry, "we must believe . . . Death has won pecuniary sanctification. It is long overdue. Saint Death, I salute you! Here in the United States *death sustains life.*" Henry's treatment of militarization was not fully integrated into his analysis of American culture, and his anger made for sloppy analysis. That anger, however, also marked a break from the pallid social criticism prevalent, with notable exceptions, during the 1950s.[101]

A similar break arose in other scholarly disciplines. Among historians, the 1950s "mood of affirmation and consensus" began dissolving. William Appleman Williams's *The Tragedy of American Diplomacy* appeared in 1959, and "the new, left historiography and the student New Left," which had "common roots," were emerging by 1960. Few historians made a clean break from their earlier outlooks, but it was telling that John Lukacs, a conservative Catholic with "undivided" loyalties in the Cold War, emphasized in *The History of the Cold War* (1961) that "the struggles of men and of nations do not always clearly incarnate the divisions of Good and Evil." Lukacs criticized "a new kind of not always conscious American imperial expansion" and the notion of irreconcilable Soviet-American conflict: "Our danger" comes from those "telling themselves that an Atomic War is unavoidable."[102]

Regarding militarization, the immediate import of the work of these intellectuals—or of others like Edmund Wilson—was limited. In tone and content, their criticism did not differ greatly from what Lewis Mumford and C. Wright Mills had said at mid-decade. In the academy, it was a minority view. In impact, it perhaps did not match that of the poet Allen Ginsberg, the filmmaker Stanley Kubrick, or the middle-class critic Betty Friedan, or even rock'n'roll singers. In audience, it paled in comparison to the one Eisenhower had for expressing his doubts. Of course, he usually expressed his public doubts in circumspect ways: the anger voiced by critics at the decade's end was as important as the content of their doubts. Influence is hard to measure, but those doubts were, in volume, tone, and content, significant at least as markers of a changing mood.

Popular culture also revealed a more complicated mood by 1960. As before, depictions of the celebrated 1945 flag raising at Iwo Jima provided one measure of that culture. In 1954, Ira Hayes, the Pima Indian marine in the famous photo of that moment, died a drunk, crushed in part by the heroic status fixed on him, though given "the most lavish military burial since the internment of the Unknown Soldier." In 1960, NBC Television's *The American* offered "an expose of deliberate fraud on the part of the [Marine] Corps, a scheme to dupe the American public into believing that a brave and noble deed had transpired atop Mount Suribachi. . . . The Rosenthal picture was a 'phoney.' There were no Iwo Jima heroes, only fakes and humbugs. . . . Hayes, in his reincarnation on NBC, was driven to an early grave by the shame of telling lies at the behest of his military superiors."

The ensuing controversy was complicated by NBC's own effort, just exposed, to rig its quiz shows, and *The American* did not directly attack national policies, yet a show questioning the symbols of those policies and linking their presumed fraudulence to racism at home would have been unlikely a few years earlier. A more searing (and confused) version of the Hayes story followed. Hollywood's *The Outsider* (1962) resorted to a classic formula of American fiction—the homoerotic bond between a dark-skinned man (Hayes) and a blond, blue-eyed all-American—in order to underline the film's "least ambiguous theme: the sharp division between white and 'colored' in American society." A critique of racism was not new to Hollywood, but linking it to an unsettling portrait of a mythic moment in American military prowess was more novel. It suggested a connection between the corruption of American power abroad and the flaws of American society at home.[103]

The Outsider bombed at the box office, but it was an offbeat representative of a cluster of films (and the novels preceding them) that walked a fine line between extolling familiar values and questioning dominant policies. *On the Beach* (1959) presented the world's thermonuclear death: if to some it also "made world extinction a romantic condition," to others it was frightening.[104] Other films soon appeared exposing the frailties of nuclear command technology and deterrence logic. Often these films sought easy targets—military officers or scientists, rather than the civilian leaders who set basic policies. Moreover, it was hard to tell whether their messages were complex or merely confused: *The Manchurian Candidate* (1962), based on a 1959 novel, demonstrated that "while Communism is fiendish and still dangerous, the far right is hypocritical and foolish." In movie form, *The Manchurian Candidate*, by presenting a menacing homosexual assassin (Lawrence Harvey) programmed by his Soviet-agent mother (Angela Lansbury), either reworked or pilloried—it was hard to tell which—the 1950s conflation of "Mommies, Commies, and Queers."[105] Only Stanley Kubrick, whose *Paths of Glory* (1957) had offered a powerful antiwar message in the safer context of World War I, discarded careful balancing in an all-out assault on the warfare state, *Doctor Strangelove* (1964), with a bizarre amalgam of Wernher von Braun, Henry Kissinger, Herman Kahn, and perhaps others as its title character. In a similar vein was *Catch-22* (1961), a novel by Joseph Heller, who set the action in World War II but directed his savage wit against the Cold War's absurdities.

For all the punches pulled in such films, they were troubling, enough so in the case of *On the Beach* that "Eisenhower's cabinet discussed confidential actions they might take to undermine the movie."[106] Even if they often accepted Cold War dogmas—that a centrist liberalism stood sturdily against political extremes, that experts and leaders must be trusted—they also pushed those dogmas to the surface, exposing them to a critical gaze less available a decade earlier. Like much else at the decade's end, popular culture showed that promoters of the Sputnik panic, for all they succeeded in beefing up American power in the short term, also aggravated Americans' felt vulnerability to nuclear obliteration in ways that would eventually work against their efforts. Earlier, alarm at the bomb had shifted to alarm at the Soviets; by 1960 the process was running in reverse for some Americans.

That was hardly evident in the 1960 presidential campaign, however. Instead, Nixon and Kennedy competed in proclaiming their zeal and expertise for waging the Cold War more aggressively. Democrats stressed the fecklessness and fatigue of an old man's presidency, offering the "missile gap" and "space gap" as evidence of GOP failure. Nixon walked an awkward line between defending Ike and promising his own fresher approach, just as Ike faced his own conflicting impulses—dislike of Nixon, fear of overshadowing him, and desire to campaign for him. Kennedy's razor-thin victory measured no decisive shift on issues of war and foreign policy. No one much noticed Eisenhower's hope, offered ironically at the dedication of the Marshall Space Flight Center, that American achievements be "the outgrowth not of a soulless, barren technology, nor of a grasping state imperialism," but rather of a "probing for the betterment of humanity."[107]

Later, most Americans sensed that the breakdown of national consensus took place in the mid-1960s, in response in good part to the Vietnam War. In many ways, they were right, yet even in the 1950s the balance of contending moods and forces had been uneasy. The transition to a new presidency, and what Eisenhower said during it, only further revealed the instability and the growing doubts about militarization.

"An Insidious Penetration of Our Own Minds"

With his inauguration, John Kennedy said, the torch "passed to a new generation of Americans," those "tempered by war" and "disciplined by a hard and bitter peace."[108] But the generational change JFK proclaimed was unclear. His youth was striking, but he also drew for advice on elders like John McCloy and Dean Acheson. Both generations had experienced World War II, but older men like Eisenhower had held high rank in it and were familiar with prewar suspicions of militarism, while men like Kennedy knew little of those suspicions, waged war from lesser positions, and had their outlook more decisively shaped by the war. Proud of their ability to break from their elders, they were nonetheless more the prisoners of World War II than Eisenhower's generation.

Moreover, the very notion of a torch passed also presumed continuity: the newcomers stood in Eisenhower's shadow and sought his blessing. When Eisenhower and Kennedy discussed Southeast Asia on January 19, complex political and generational relationships were at play. Kennedy insiders later recalled that Eisenhower's insistence on Laos as "the most important problem facing the United States" had done "a disservice to the incoming Administration," in Clark Clifford's summary. "You might have to go in there and fight it out," perhaps "'unilaterally,'" Ike warned, according to Ted Sorensen and Arthur Schlesinger, Jr. But other accounts show that Eisenhower used such phrases to more ambiguous effect. Unilateral intervention, while not ruled out, "would be very bad for our relations" in Asia, he said, at best "a last desperate effort" in a region where communists had many advantages. Worried about Southeast Asia, Eisenhower was stepping up American aid and covert intervention there. But Kennedy and some of his aides exaggerated the force of his advice because of their unfamiliarity with his style of laying out all contingencies, their desire for his sanction to policies they were considering, and later their eagerness to have him share responsibility for their deepening involvement in the Vietnam War. Despite their impressions, Ike was reluctant to push them into war—and also, he soon showed, to pull them away from it. Early in the 1960s, drafting a section of his memoirs on the Dien Bien Phu crisis, he argued pointedly that the presence of large American forces in Vietnam "would have probably aggravated . . . the resentments held by Asiatics." Even had they occupied "all of Indochina . . . , their eventual removal would have resulted only in a reversion to the situation which had existed before." Lest he embarrass his successors, however, who had taken just that course, he deleted the passage, just as he supported vigorous use of American forces once Johnson committed them.[109]

Whatever the thrust of Eisenhower's advice on the 19th, his televised farewell address to the nation two days earlier had a different focus. Ike told Americans they were in a global conflict that "absorbs our very beings" and—again urging the long view—"promises to be of indefinite duration." As a result, the United States had been "compelled to create a permanent armaments industry of vast proportions," along with huge, costly armed forces. "The total influence" of this new system—"economic, political, even spiritual—is felt in every city, every State house, every office of the Federal government." He enjoined Americans to "guard against the acquisition of unwarranted influence, whether sought or unsought, by the military-industrial complex. The potential for the disastrous rise of misplaced power exists and will persist." Alarming also was "the prospect of domination of the nation's scholars by Federal employment, project allocations, and the power of money" and "the equal and opposite danger that public policy could itself become the captive of a scientific-technological elite." And as he had before, he linked these dangers to ecological perils, warning against "the impulse to live only for today, plundering, for our own ease and convenience, the precious resources of tomorrow."[110]

What did he mean? In one way, his comments were shrewdly exculpatory. Militarization had been forced on America by dangerous enemies and technologies—it was not *his* nation's fault. What happened on his watch was "compelled," while avoidable dangers (the "*potential* for the disastrous *rise* of misplaced power") lay ahead. *He* had held the line; lesser men might not.

Yet his farewell address also held a darker view of militarization and his own role in it. By describing its influence as "economic, political, even spiritual," he suggested that whatever its origins, militarization was taking on a life of its own apart from the world scene, becoming woven into the fabric of American life. Moreover, "the conjunction of an immense military establishment and a large arms industry" had already occurred, while *he* was President, whatever abuses lay in the future. And regarding disarmament, acknowledged Eisenhower, "I confess that I lay down my official responsibilities in this field with a definite sense of disappointment." Just as striking were the omissions in the address—no summons to greater vigilance against the enemy, no recitation of trouble spots in the world, and little talk of the enemy's evil. The address was remarkably inward-looking, calling for Americans to be vigilant not against enemies but themselves. Just as the Cold War was reaching a new intensity, he directed attention away from it.

Eisenhower had left behind a memorable characterization of militarization. He added to it the next day at his final press conference, when asked how to counter "the danger that public policy could become the captive of a scientific technological elite." His first response seemed lame—he named no specific steps, only urging "an alert and informed citizenry"—yet it was appropriate given his large view of the problem, for "this misuse of influence and power could come about unwittingly . . . just by the nature of the thing," against which any single step would be puny. "When you see almost every one of your magazines, no matter what they are advertising, has a picture of the Titan missile or the Atlas [missile] or solid fuel or other things, there is becoming a great influence, almost an insidious penetration of our own minds that the only thing this country is engaged in is weaponry and missiles." The syntax was garbled but the insight penetrating, and more subtle than his earlier tirades against militarism ("We are not going to be in uniforms going around yelling 'Heil' anything," he said in 1953). The problem, Ike realized, was not simply one of public policy but of culture and the nation's sense of purpose—its loss of a way to define itself except by military power. No other national leader defined the problem so broadly.[111]

Yet unwittingly Eisenhower had also aggravated that problem. By skillfully balancing conflicting needs and by keeping cold war from erupting into hot war, he had made the pursuit of national security congruent with dominant aspirations for peace and prosperity. His successors could turn his success against him: if power abroad and prosperity at home were compatible, how much more could be—had to be—achieved regarding both if greater efforts were made? The Kennedy administration was just as keen to balance "the defense effort against the other demands of the economy," wrote Schlesinger in 1965, but like many liberals who saw national resources as expansive, "it believed—correctly—that the balance could be achieved at a much higher level."[112] Ike's message about limited resources and balancing goals ("balance" appeared seven times in one sentence of his farewell) was undercut by his own success in juggling peace, prosperity, and power.

Not surprisingly, even as Eisenhower's farewell got a rousing reception, its message often got lost. Liberals dismissed it as belated, ignoring its consistency with a decade's warnings by him. "For eight years, Mr. Eisenhower has depressed his fellow Americans by a seeming inability to grasp the major problems of his era," according to the *Nation,* but now "he spoke like the statesman and democratic leader we had so long hungered for him to become." T. R. B. in the *New Republic* thought it "a strange final warning. . . . We couldn't have agreed more and yet (comically enough) a man's agreement rarely irritated us so much. He had eight years to give this warning; why wait till a minute before midnight?" Entranced by JFK's promise of activism, liberals ignored the general's message by belittling the messenger. The Kennedy men asked neither Eisenhower nor themselves any questions about it—it gave them no message at all. Five years later, Schlesinger still expressed their sneering attitude: "After eight years in the White House, even Eisenhower came to feel that something was wrong and issued his unexpected warning": *even* Eisenhower, as if he were the last person to have such fears. Besides, Schlesinger added, "the military-industrial complex was more a consequence than a cause of the problem," which "lay in the feebleness of civilian control of the military establishment"—an outdated conception of the problem, as Ike had just pointed out in his farewell. For its part, the GOP's right wing, though fearing big government, did not share Ike's alarm about the bloated apparatus of national defense. He never had many allies in his campaign against the garrison state. He left office with applause but even fewer allies.[113]

Still husbanding his personal resources, he made little effort later to sustain the message of his farewell. Even at his final press conference, he had identified "the greatest problem" facing Kennedy as "the intransigent, unreasonable attitude of the Communist bloc . . . .—this terrible problem that is none of our making." The themes of his farewell did appear in his memoirs, but blandly expressed. Perhaps his diffidence made little difference, since he soon "became a cultural anachronism," his popularity enormous but his values seemingly "quaint, curious, or—the ultimate put-down of the decade—irrelevant." His famous phrase, the "military-industrial complex," was later recovered by the antiwar movement, but largely because it was convenient, not because it seemed to capture a consistent stance on Ike's part, one soon hard to see anyway given his public calls for escalating the American war in Vietnam and his scorn for "kooks" and "hippies."[114]

Ignoring the Eisenhower of the farewell address, Kennedy's inaugural address instead echoed Ike's inaugural eight years earlier. Kennedy dealt solely with war and foreign policy, ignoring "domestic" issues like race relations. (Compared to "foreign affairs," he allegedly told Nixon a few months later, "who gives a shit if the minimum wage is $1.15 or $1.25 . . . ?") More elegantly than Eisenhower, Kennedy balanced conflicting impulses ("Let us never negotiate out of fear. But let us never fear to negotiate.") No more elegantly than Ike, he referred to "that uncertain balance of terror that stays the hand of mankind's final war." If anything, Kennedy outbid his predecessor's inaugural in calling for national sacrifice, urging Americans to "pay any price, bear any burden, meet any hardship, support any friend, oppose any foe to assure the survival and the success of liberty." And by proclaiming an "hour of maximum danger," he signaled a crisis mentality that Eisenhower always repudiated. "Crises there will continue to be," Ike admitted in his farewell address, but he admonished against "a recurring temptation to feel that some spectacular or costly action could become the miraculous solution to all current difficulties." No one could predict the "year of maximum danger," much less the hour, Ike had insisted in 1953, for "we're not in a moment of danger, we're in an age of danger." In public at least, Kennedy argued that the moment had arrived.[115]

THE CRISIS OF MILITARIZATION, 1961–1966

"Impressive to Mankind"

"I have been guided by the standard John Winthrop set . . . 331 years ago," John Kennedy explained before his inauguration: "'We shall be a city upon a hill—the eyes of all people are upon us.'" Famous for tough rhetoric, JFK gained less notice when he intoned familiar ideals, but, as I. F. Stone realized, he "seems to be a rather cautious perhaps even conventional man."[1] Winthrop's words had long been used to justify (and sometimes to contest) the expansion of American power. Kennedy was announcing that he would continue that tradition. In doing so, he also broadened the scope of America's militarization and the fissures it was producing.

He did so in his own way, however, one that often masked the nature and consequences of early-1960s militarization. More than his predecessors, JFK linked the hard imperatives of militarization to the intangible needs of image—his, his administration's, his nation's—calculating not only the raw power accrued through rockets, satellites, or Green Berets but their image in "the eyes of all people." He hardly invented the concern for image: both the lessons of appeasement and the calculations of nuclear deterrence prized the appearance of power as much as the reality. But he carried that concern literally and figuratively to new heights.

His policy on space exploration revealed these tendencies. Many scholars say little about that policy, as if it were a superficial aspect of his presidency, or one that owed more to Lyndon Johnson, who seized on it after Sputnik and advanced it as Vice President and President. Kennedy entered the White House caring and knowing little about space policy, but personal investment poorly measures the importance of presidential action (otherwise historians would say little about JFK's civil rights record). Measured by media attention, fiscal scale, role in world conflict, and place in militarization, his space policy was vital.

It was born in part of humiliation and desperation. Kennedy proceeded cautiously at first, in part because many scientists, in arguments they repeated throughout the decade, opposed a crash program to put Americans in space or on the moon, lest it disrupt military, commercial, and scientific initiatives. When Ham became the first American "astrochimp" in February 1961, *Life* proclaimed him a "real hero"—a sure if silly sign that Sputnik-era panic continued among some Americans.[2] Kennedy did not yet feel it.

By April, he did. When a Soviet rocket lifted Yuri Gagarin into space, it seemed like Sputnik all over again, as politicians and pundits bewailed the new evidence of Soviet superiority in rocketry, prestige, and sheer gall. At the same time, Soviet-American tension over Berlin and Southeast Asia was increasing. Then the April 15 landing of Cuban exiles at the Bay in Pigs in Cuba, where Fidel Castro was tightening his rule and courting Soviet support, ended disastrously and exposed its American sponsorship. Kennedy had fulfilled his promise to replace Ike's caution with activism but had worse than nothing to show for it.

"Is there any place we can catch them?" Kennedy asked his advisors on April 14, with a *Life* reporter present to convey his words to the nation. The question referred nominally to the arena of space—"What can we do? Can we go around the moon before them? Can we put a man on the moon before them?"—but implicitly to the whole arena of Soviet-American competition. "If somebody can just tell me how to catch up. . . . There's nothing more important." Kennedy defined importance above all in terms of the nation's image and a global "battle for minds and souls as well as lives and territories," as he told Congress on May 25, when he called for an American moon landing among a battery of programs to meet "urgent national needs." "No single project in this period will be more impressive to mankind," he announced, "or more important for the long-range exploration of space," and "so difficult or expensive to accomplish." "Difficult" deeds projected an image to the world, for the "very risk enhances our stature when we are successful." "We choose to go to the moon in this decade, and do the other things," he added in 1962, "not because they are easy, but because they are hard."[3]

Anxiety about image drove Kennedy's decision to "go to the moon," but this was "that most vexing of historical problems, the 'overdetermined event,'" since so many forces came into play and so little resistance emerged. There was the challenge of Khrushchev's space spectaculars (although as Ike's NASA director had speculated to Khrushchev in January, the Soviet leader might continue "until he had the U.S. committed to a costly program" and then "withdraw from the 'race'").[4] In that regard, Kennedy's sense of what was "impressive to mankind" was keen, for his space program *did* capture attention (carefully cultivated) abroad and a sense of daring and adventure among many

Americans (if more often men than women), and did so throughout the 1960s, even as the image of the nation abroad and of leaders at home suffered in many other ways.

Kennedy's own background and temperament were also important. He was inclined to personal and geopolitical risk taking, perhaps to defy his physical frailty, and certainly to gain the heroic credentials that Ike enjoyed. And he embraced the purported lessons of World War II about the dangers of national flaccidity and the virtues of big science.

Many of his key advisors had similar backgrounds and outlooks. They believed in "a far greater role for government in planning and executing social change," but less to solve the problems that vexed social-welfare liberals.[5] They were instead technocratic liberals captivated by problems of national security, although they also hoped that social, economic, and technological benefits would flow from the nation's mobilization, as they believed had occurred over the previous two decades. They saw themselves as tough pragmatists—the ideologues were woolly-headed right-wingers or starry-eyed leftists. And in space and defense programs, they had a way to mobilize the activist state that few conservatives could challenge.

Thus, unlike efforts to tackle racism or poverty, these programs met the test of securing consensus. They also marked an attempt to shore it up, however, in the face of an erosion already evident by the end of the 1950s. A grand initiative in space allowed Kennedy, elected by a razor-thin margin, to rise above the simmering divisions. As such, his space program came to indicate the bankruptcy of liberalism, critics thought—its preference for gimmicks and global muscle flexing over efforts to foster equality and prosperity at home. Since many liberals made that criticism, however, it marked their divisions as much as their bankruptcy. Nor did only liberals criticize. True to his earlier views, and having the gall to send them to an astronaut, Eisenhower wrote Frank Borman that Kennedy "drastically revised and expanded" the moon effort "just after the Bay of Pigs fiasco" and "gave the highest priority—unfortunate in my opinion—to a race, in other words, a stunt."[6]

In many ways, the giant Apollo program hardly seemed a militarized affair. It was entrusted to NASA, a civilian agency; its goal of men on the moon held no likely military payoff; its task of producing a few spectacular feats meshed poorly with the military's interest in volume production of satellites and other space vehicles (many officers disliked Apollo). And much of its appeal lay precisely in its capacity to lift Soviet-American conflict out of the military sphere into peaceful competition, with astronauts fighting a symbolic battle, an alternative to nuclear war. In the "single combat" of space, "the mightiest soldier of one army would fight the mightiest soldier of the other army as a substitute for a pitched battle between the entire forces."[7]

From another perspective, however, Kennedy's space program expressed a subtle militarization that Eisenhower had resisted. NASA found its organizational model and inspiration in the wartime Manhattan Project. It "recruited people as if it were building an army for a war."[8] It drew heavily on the armed forces' work in rocketry and space technology. It developed technologies vital to the military but off their budget. As Defense Secretary Robert McNamara knew, it expanded an aerospace industry essential to the armed forces and influential in its own right. And its astronauts were military men, a facet of their background celebrated in the 1960s.

Only NASA's carefully crafted image belied its militarized nature: in order "to differentiate U.S. efforts in space from those of the Soviets," the space program had to "portray American use of technology as benign, elegant, beyond the earthbound concerns of military and diplomatic strategy," and "project an image directly contradicting its origins." As "the greatest open-ended peacetime commitment by Congress in history" (a $20 billion program in 1961 estimates), the manned space program dwarfed any other nondefense program of Kennedy's liberal state, showing again how hard it was to justify state activism except through "war or its surrogate."[9] Blurring further any distinction between "military" and "civilian" spheres of action, it conveyed the message that the global struggle more than ever embraced both, and thus raised the very anxieties it sought to steer into safer channels. Finally, it provided a shield for the nation's biggest peacetime military buildup to date. That buildup hardly went unnoticed, but the media's gaze ran up into space, and JFK's administration presented itself through the space program as visionary in its deepest aspirations, implying that only its predecessor's failure and its enemy's ruthlessness forced its reluctant quest for more bombs and rockets.

At levels largely beyond the conscious grasp of policymakers, the space program also exuded values of race, class, and gender soon challenged by many Americans. The astronauts (like the nonflying experts and officials involved) were strikingly white, male, and middle-class in identity and values, with their wives cast (in ways sometimes embarrassing to them) as self-sacrificing women who tended to home, indeed to the homefront. The astronauts' machismo as military pilots and racecar drivers was tempered, in line with current values, by mention of their roles as fathers and companions (*Life* showed John Glenn wearing his wife's apron and flipping burgers).[10] But little in the lavish attention given them suggested an egalitarian sense of who might serve the nation in peril. Other defense programs like conscription projected a more inclusive sense of service. The space program, like other technological efforts, did not.

The meanings and images ascribed to the space program also exacerbated the difficulties Americans had in grasping the elusive nature of war. Did the space program develop military technology? Perhaps, but it also tapped fantasies of consumer abundance, just as the auto industry mimicked its appeals: "A [space] capsule is bit like an automobile," observed astronaut Alan Shepard, who "sort of wanted to kick the tires" when he saw the Redstone rocket being readied for his flight.[11] Was the space race a Soviet-American war? Yes, but the combat was symbolic and the battlefield far from American soil. Might war come to that soil? At no other time in the Cold War did Americans worry more about that possibility, yet perhaps never was it so difficult to comprehend.

Militarization at High Tide

The new administration sought to break from Eisenhower's apparent all-or-nothing strategy: "We intend to have a wider choice," Kennedy announced in July 1961, "than humiliation or all-out nuclear action." Accordingly, he promoted the army's Green Berets, backed new programs of civil defense against nuclear attack, and reversed Eisenhower's cuts in conventional forces. Billions also went into strategic forces (missiles, not the bombers coveted by flying generals): by 1967, 1000 ICBMs compared to 200 inherited from Eisenhower, 41 missile-carrying Polaris submarines, and 32,500 nuclear warheads (the all-time high for them). It was true that, more than they admitted, the new leaders "shared a world view similar to the one they ridiculed. The New Frontiersmen were only connecting the dots Ike left them." Connecting the dots was expensive, however: defense outlays stayed stable as a share of GNP (about 9 percent) because of rapid economic growth but increased 13 percent under JFK, and far more once American forces plunged into the Vietnam War and new weapons became fully funded. By many measures, the 1960s marked the apogee of America's post-1945 militarization.[12]

As Democrats saw it, the apogee came then because they faced greater peril at home and abroad than Eisenhower had confronted, or at least admitted. They worried about the thinness of Kennedy's election victory, the beating Truman had taken for alleged weakness against communism, their promises to replace Republican weakness with Democratic vigor, the spread of global struggle to new arenas like space and the Third World, and the danger that Soviet leaders would be emboldened by gaining nuclear parity with the West.

Yet those dangers did not account for America's course in the 1960s, for it persisted despite countervailing considerations and changing circumstances. For all his bluster, Khrushchev appeared less tyrannical and rigid, though more resourceful, than Stalin. The "missile gap" on which Kennedy had campaigned was quickly declared an illusion by Defense Secretary McNamara, and a stable balance of terror was now foreseeable. Soviet superiority in space and technology was questionable even in 1961, more so by mid-decade. Deep fissures emerged in the communist bloc, above all between Beijing and Moscow, while the economic, political, and military vitality of America's European allies outstripped the fondest hopes Western leaders earlier had. Communist advances in the Third World were limited: Southeast Asia was a mess by Washington's standards, but had been for fifteen years; few populous or resource-rich countries were about to "fall" to communism; only Cuba was a clear-cut (and humiliating) communist victory. At home, JFK's margin of victory had been tiny, but LBJ's in 1964 was thunderous. The worst McCarthy-era excesses had passed, militarization received renewed criticism, and domestic priorities gained support.

In the face of these changes, the Kennedy and Johnson administrations generally stayed on the same course. Arguments about the communist menace were simply retailored to fit conditions of the moment: Moscow was seen as menacing whether having fallen behind, caught up, or gotten ahead, while the split between it and Beijing was regarded as sharpening the competition between them to act aggressively. In the end, enemy threats scarcely shaped policy under Kennedy and Johnson, who most feared "not communism, which was too fragmented, or the Soviet Union, which was too committed to detente, or even China, which was too impotent, but rather the threat of embarrassment, of humiliation, of appearing to be weak."[13]

Beyond that threat, the Kennedy administration's view of alleged extremists at home also lured it onto a militarized course. It saw its pragmatic policy challenged by radicals on the far right and far left who viewed national security in apocalyptic terms. Liberals worried most—wrongly, it turned out—about a resurgent "radical right." Analyzing the John Birch Society and military officers "dispossessed" by the rise of civilian expertise, sociologist Daniel Bell thought that perhaps only "right-wing Republicans have an ideology" in 1960s America. Being "ill-equipped to grasp modern conceptions of politics," they fought "'modernity,'" that is, "the belief in rational assessment, rather than established custom." Prone to "paranoid views," right-wingers saw grand conspiracies denying victory to America and ignored the Cold War's realities in their belief that "a preventive war or a first strike" could defeat communism. Hollywood soon popularized these liberals' perceptions of the far Right in three 1964 doomsday films (one aided by the JFK White House) about crazed or power-hungry military officers who scheme to blow up the world (*Fail-Safe* and *Doctor Strangelove*) or overthrow the government (*Seven Days in May*). John Stormer's right-wing tract *None Dare Call It Treason* (1964) confirmed Bell's analysis. Deemphasizing military power, Stormer instead saw the nation's moral and ideological purity as decisive, indeed all it would take to win, but so undermined by naive or subversive liberals that perhaps it was already "too late" in "the communist timetable for world domination" to stop it.[14]

Centrists paid less attention to the Left in the early 1960s, in part because it was smaller and less conspicuous than the far Right, but it too had an apocalyptic outlook. According to the young radicals who penned the Port Huron Statement in 1962, "the Bomb" made them aware that they "might die at any time" and "may be the last generation in the experiment with living." For them, too, the enemy was largely internal, indeed much the same liberal establishment excoriated by Stormer—guilty not of selling out to communism but of promoting "the general militarization of American society," in part to promote a fraudulent prosperity. A similar apprehension of imminent peril was rising among antinuclear and environmental activists.[15]

Centrists accurately saw apocalyptic strains among their ideological enemies but failed to see them among their own kind. Bell's assumption that centrists prized "rational assessment" over "established custom" was polemically useful but deceptive. Kennedy identified the early 1960s as "the hour of maximum danger," while Johnson argued in 1961 that "we must decide whether to help these countries" in Southeast Asia "or throw in the towel in the area and pull back our defenses to San Francisco." Politicians offered such rhetoric not only in public, to mobilize support, but in their secret deliberations. In 1961, "Kennedy officials and American strategic intellectuals were publicly sketching scenarios in which the United States would strike first," notes Stephen Ambrose; JFK and LBJ privately weighed plans to destroy, perhaps in concert with Moscow, the embryonic nuclear force of Communist China, whose leaders were presumed not to fear nuclear war or value human life. Such schemes showed an apocalyptic outlook at the highest level. Centrists also were alarmist about enemies within. The far Right might "quickly wear itself out," Bell sensed, but if the "international situation" worsened, it might "begin to rally support around a drive for 'immediate action,' for a declaration of war in these areas, for a pre-emptive strike." Groups like the Birchers were, after all, "willing to tear apart the fabric of American society," just as war-mad generals were willing to tear apart world society.[16]

With that threat in mind, the Kennedy administration asserted "civilian" control over the uniformed armed forces—to the fury of many officers—through the new managerial techniques of Defense Secretary McNamara. Much like Truman and his advisors (some of whom served Kennedy as well), however, the Kennedy team thought that subduing the officers subdued militarization itself, making their approach to national security rational, safe, and effective. "Under these circumstances," one contemporary noted, "the task of the new administration became the paradoxical one of trying to curb the very power whose growth it was fostering."[17]

Their approach, they hoped, might gain the Cold War victory that had eluded Eisenhower. That aspiration above all drove militarization forward. Awareness that some international circumstances strengthened the American hand inspired their hopes to deescalate the Cold War but also their ambitions to win it—or a dual track seeking both goals. True, most Democrats regarded talk of victory as the province of crazed generals and reactionary zealots, but in disdaining such talk they did not reject the goal. Seeing a global contest of will and prestige, relegating combat to a limited if critical role in Third World contests, proud of keeping their generals on a short leash, they saw triumph ensuing not from the barrel of a gun or the belly of a bomber but from the display of superior American nerve and resolve.

That outlook might entail the very brinkmanship Democrats had excoriated when Dulles employed it; but *their* brinkmanship, they assumed, would be rationally exercised and counterbalanced by diplomatic flexibility, displays of American vitality in space and technology, and aid to struggling nations. Nor did they doubt that the nation had the resources to pursue victory. Keynesians who scorned Eisenhower's penny-pinching, they foresaw (correctly, in the short run) increased defense spending as triggering an economic expansion, which would in turn fund more ambitious federal initiatives at home and abroad. Theirs would be a victory not of apocalyptic nuclear fury or the enemy's formal surrender but of a changed correlation of forces that would impress wavering nations and place the momentum of victory on their side.

The hope for victory was implicit in Kennedy's language and metaphors, which reflected his belief that the "long twilight struggle" was nearing its end. He was "convinced," he said after the Bay of Pigs, "that history will record the fact that this bitter struggle reached its climax in the late 1950s and the early 1960s," though it might end "without the firing of a single missile or the crossing of a single border," since the losers would be "the self-indulgent, the soft societies," whether or not they had the bigger guns. The logic of a "climax" to history was that it would yield winners and losers. Kennedy did eloquently allow for a different outcome in which the superpowers both would recognize the folly of their conflict, and Johnson sketched a similar outcome. Yet since American leaders regarded the Soviet Union as the major cause of conflict in the first place, even that outcome would meet their test of American victory. In any event, it was an abstract view that Kennedy did not apply to specific crises—those, he felt, had to produce a winner, after which fruitful negotiations might ensue. His frequent World War II analogies (which Eisenhower had avoided) also indicated how much victory was his goal, and indicated as well his timetable for victory: in 1958, his references were to "Pearl Harbor, "Dunkirk," "Calais," battles at the start of World War II that had galvanized the antifascist powers. By 1961, in the midst of the Berlin crisis, they were to "Bastogne" and "Stalingrad," battles that had decided the outcome of World War II.[18]

Militarization was a broad historical process JFK inherited, but also one sustained only insofar as leaders gave it new life. Kennedy was not its prime mover, but his pursuit of victory in the Cold War, a goal Eisenhower all but rejected, accelerated its pace, as did his emphasis on intangible definitions of power—will, resolve, and their perception—which offered few criteria for judging what constituted sufficient power.

A bolder (or more desperate) Soviet leadership, focused like American leaders on symbols and prestige, provided pretext for America's further militarization. First, Soviet leaders provoked another crisis over Berlin. Khrushchev—assessing Kennedy as weak and naive, fearing Kennedy's defense program, or detesting the humiliating hemorrhage of East Germans into West Berlin—demanded that the Western allies terminate their rights of access to Berlin, which he threatened to turn over to the Communist East German government. In similar circumstances Eisenhower had refused to allow Khrushchev or the media to define a "crisis" and talked the situation through to an inconclusive end. Kennedy rejected such a cautious course and talked of crisis in dire terms. He worried, he told one reporter, "that Khrushchev might interpret his reluctance to wage nuclear war as a symptom of an American loss of nerve. Some day, he said, the time might come when he would have to run the supreme risk to convince Khrushchev that conciliation did not mean humiliation." He and the Soviet Premier had already traded thinly veiled threats of war at their summit conference in Vienna. Now, Kennedy may have concluded, "the U.S. could no longer afford to be bound by the traditional policy of excluding a preemptive first strike." His public stance was also tough. He took to the airwaves in July to invoke the dangers of appeasement and memories of World War II, and to announce a tripling of draft calls, a call-up of 150,000 reservists, and an expanded civil defense program with future measures "to let every citizen know what steps he can take without delay to protect his family in case of attack." A bitter turn of events on August 13—communist authorities began erecting the Berlin Wall to staunch the flow of refugees from the east—ended the crisis, but JFK went ahead with sending 1,500 American soldiers down the autobahn, a provocative if "empty gesture" (as Nixon denounced it) that did not insulate him from criticism for being weak in allowing the wall to stand.[19]

The contest over Berlin became the paradigmatic Cold War crisis, perhaps bringing the United States and the Soviet Union as close to war as their later, more celebrated collision over Cuba. These crises were judged largely in terms of who "won" or "lost" them and how they shaped the immediate ebb and flow of the Cold War. But leaders and crises disappear fast—Kennedy and Khrushchev were gone in a few years, and Berlin never again became such a hot spot. A more important meaning of these crises was their role in reinforcing Americans' sense of war's elusiveness.

The Berlin crisis had created a surreal atmosphere in which war appeared both agonizingly proximate and puzzlingly remote. The stakes involved seemed at once monumental (Germany, Europe, humankind), intangible (the prestige and credibility of leaders and nations), and trivial (whether East Germans or Russians would check credentials at Berlin checkpoints). No one could distinguish the shadow-boxing by leaders from their willingness actually to plunge into war. No one seemed to know, or at least make clear, what a war over Berlin would be like: certainly World War II was an outdated historical model, even though Kennedy sometimes offered it. A media blitz on the virtues of fallout shelters sent contradictory messages. On the dubious premise of a nuclear war limited to "military" targets, *Life* assured Americans that if ready, "you and your family could have 97 chances out of 100 to survive." ("Where did *Life* get that 97 percent?" wondered I. F. Stone. "Was it a copywriter's bright flash? Just as Ivory Soap is sold as 99 percent pure, is thermonuclear war to be sold as 97 percent safe?") But *Life* also noted that in polls "40% of Americans still rate their survival chances as 'poor' in an all-out nuclear attack." The gulf was now huge between the formal repudiation by leaders of war as an instrument of policy and the reality of measures taken by them that could lead to war. The insanity of war was now universally proclaimed, yet the ability of nations to enter war seemed greater than ever.[20]

Because its possible outcome was not only appalling but imponderable, the Berlin crisis helped spawn a new round of doomsday fiction which made the unimaginable real and offered bleak reassurance. In *Fail-Safe* (book, 1962; film, 1964), Americans could learn about systems for nuclear war in remarkable detail, see their failure unleash an unauthorized American attack on Moscow, and watch a steely President (Henry Fonda in the movie) avert global holocaust by nuking New York City in compensation for Moscow's obliteration. In many ways, *Fail-Safe* provided a fuller sense of nuclear perils than anything American leaders offered. At the same time, it reasserted the mysterious nature of those perils, showing leaders who "had lost all contact with reality, were free floating in some exotic world of their own."[21]

The Cuban missile crisis unfolded against the apocalyptic fears stoked by the Berlin crisis. Once again, Khrushchev prompted confrontation, although the Bay of Pigs invasion and subsequent American efforts to assassinate Castro and sabotage his regime gave the communist leaders reason to see themselves as the endangered parties. Khrushchev's decision to install medium-range missiles in Cuba was also a desperate bid to deliver on his own blustery promises of nuclear parity with the West—he did not have it, and American officials had recklessly boasted that he did not, but missiles in Cuba might at least give the appearance of it. (Khrushchev's renewal of nuclear tests in 1961—one a fifty-eight-megaton monster thousands of times more destructive than the Hiroshima weapon—probably served the same purpose.)

By early October 1962, Kennedy, realizing that the missile buildup was underway, faced severe political pressure to take action, and in his view possible impeachment if he did not. He weighed many options, including invasion of Cuba and a nuclear or conventional air strike against the missiles, but first he tried a naval blockade of Cuba to force the missiles' removal, publicly warning that the world stood near "the abyss of destruction." Soviet-American negotiations ensued, with Attorney General Robert Kennedy warning the Soviet ambassador on October 27 that unless the missiles were removed by the next day, "we would remove them."[22]

Few Kennedy insiders regarded the missiles in Cuba as a major strategic threat to the United States. They could only hit cities already within range of other Soviet rockets, though with less warning and added "throw-weight." "What difference," Kennedy asked on the 16th, "does it make? They've got enough to blow us up anyway." Publicly he did warn of "a nuclear strike capability against the Western Hemisphere," but he emphasized less tangible considerations: Khrushchev's secrecy, deceit, and betrayal of his earlier promises, and the "clear lesson" about appeasement taught by the 1930s. Privately administration officials dwelt on the psychological upper hand the missiles would give Khrushchev: he might soon move against Berlin; the West generally and Kennedy personally would be humiliated; and the global balance of power would tilt in Moscow's favor. While the missiles "did not substantially alter the strategic balance *in fact,*" one advisor soon wrote, "that balance would have been substantially altered *in appearance;* and in matters of national will and world leadership . . . such appearances contribute to reality."[23] That reasoning was hardly baseless: symbols *did* matter, or else Khrushchev would not have sent missiles to Cuba. But they mattered in part because leaders said they did, and their stance during the Cuban missile crisis left unclear why *this* symbol—not the Berlin Wall or Soviet satellites—warranted American reactions risking nuclear war.

Soviet missiles in Cuba mattered so much more because their proximity violated Americans' lingering sense of invulnerability and made palpable their free-floating fears of destruction. As Undersecretary of State George Ball later noted: "After all, America had fought two world wars without damage to its own territory. The American people had grown accustomed to thinking that the moat of two oceans was an effective barrier to external aggression. . . . If the American people had painfully adjusted to the thought of ICBMs capable of reaching our cities, it was largely because those missiles were still thousands of miles away and the danger seemed unreal. The prospect of Soviet missiles ninety miles off our borders was something altogether different; it would be an affront to our history." Americans' reactions to those missiles suggested war's persisting remoteness to them. Rockets in Siberia and crises in Berlin remained distant and unreal despite decades of talk of a seamless world. It took a nearby threat to stir the ultimate alarm. At the same time, those reactions revealed a denial of changed strategic conditions, as if the ocean barriers would remain sturdy once the missiles nearby were removed. Indeed, whether Americans had "painfully adjusted" to Soviet missiles located elsewhere was doubtful. Insistence on their removal from Cuba suggested an impulse to banish the threat rather than adjust to it.[24]

Of course, the Cuban missile crisis had no single meaning for all Americans. Still, many responses to the crisis suggested it gave substance to the shadow of war long hovering over the country. CIA Director John McCone characterized the Cuban missiles as "pointed at our heart," as if other Soviet missiles were not. Speaking to the nation on October 22, Kennedy listed the cities in the Western Hemisphere within range of the new missiles in Cuba, even though acknowledging that those places were already "on the bull's eye of Soviet missiles located inside the U.S.S.R. or in submarines." *Life* found "that nearly every city from Lima, Peru, to Hudson Bay in Canada would lie within push-button range of thermonuclear bombs in Cuba." *U.S. News and World Report* drew red concentric rings of destruction radiating from Cuba on its map of the Western Hemisphere; its columnist David Lawrence asserted that "the American people cannot live in peace as long as loaded missiles are pointed at them from a field 90 miles away." While hardly new, air-raid drills conveyed a sense of special menace, since now they took place not as a routine exercise but in preparation for possible outbreak of war. The far Right saw the outcome of the crisis as a sell-out to communism and ridiculed claims that the missiles were removed, but that ridicule, too, imputed special meaning to missiles in Cuba, as opposed to elsewhere.[25]

The notion that the crisis showed Americans their vulnerability to attack was shared and shaped overseas as well. After viewing the CIA's photographs of the missiles sites, British prime minister Harold MacMillan declared, "Now the Americans will realize what we here in England have lived through for this past many years." Khrushchev himself used the crisis to remind Kennedy that "with the advent of modern types of armament, the U.S.A. has fully lost its invulnerability."[26]

In the end, Kennedy and Khrushchev compromised: Moscow would remove the missiles; in return, Washington promised not to invade Cuba and to remove American missiles from Turkey and Italy, whose proximity to Soviet soil made them seem analogous to rockets in Cuba. Even so, Air Force Chief of Staff Gen. Curtis LeMay told a dumbfounded Kennedy, "*We should invade* [Cuba] *today.*"[27]

Then and later, many saw the outcome as a triumph for Kennedy, who presumably stared Khrushchev down and got what he wanted without war because of his determination, his tight control of the armed forces, and his nation's strategic superiority. But Moscow did not retreat before American power so much as both sides shrank at the prospect of a nuclear war in which either's superiority would have been meaningless. And Kennedy's control of the situation was more precarious than Americans, even the Kennedy men themselves, realized at the time.

The missile crisis increased the urgency of many Americans to control the arms race, an urgency conveyed by groups like the Women's Strike for Peace and SANE (National Committee for a Sane Nuclear Policy) and their public protests. On June 10, 1963, Kennedy eloquently appealed to that end, now using World War II to different purposes by citing Russia's devastating losses in it. With surprising speed, the Limited Test Ban Treaty, long in negotiation, was finalized and signed in August (though not by China or France), abolishing atmospheric but not underground tests.

Hailed initially as a first step toward halting the arms race, the treaty instead ushered in the "Big Sleep" in attention to the nuclear issue. "After 1963," writes Paul Boyer, "the mushroom-shaped cloud, the corporate logo of the nuclear age, became a tired visual cliche."[28] With testing now underground, the nuclear threat became less visible than ever and the challenge to it seemed to exhaust itself, as if out of sight meant out of mind. The antinuclear movement and the superpowers were later faulted for stopping at a symbolic victory over the nuclear dragon, since the engines producing weapons groaned more furiously in the 1960s, especially as Soviet leaders redoubled their efforts to gain parity with the United States. In 1963, as in later arms limitation talks, Soviet-American negotiations seemed designed—perhaps in tacit but cynical collusion between the superpowers themselves—to regulate (and, in terms of technical refinement, even hasten) rather than curtail weapons development, to exclude lesser powers from the nuclear arena, and to deflect the opposition of mass movements to the great powers' arms building.

Such criticism was accurate but narrow. It downplayed the obstacles to greater achievements—the technical complexities, the distrust between governments, the divisions within each, and the demands of other issues on politicians, activists, and populations. Kennedy had taken a political risk just by pushing for a modest step. And the symbolic achievement had value: the 1963 treaty did help establish that superpower conflicts were negotiable, that the arms race was abhorrent, that nuclear warfare was intolerable. Even lip service to these principles kept them alive at a time when they were widely disbelieved or disdained.

The Cuban missile crisis left Kennedy a more cautious leader, skillful in his public case for more nuanced views of the Cold War and Khrushchev's behavior, and determined that the superpowers avoid nuclear conflict. A quarter-century later, two key advisors reflected that the lesson of the crisis "is not to have a crisis, because there's no telling what will happen once you're in one," and that "'managing' crises is the wrong term. You don't 'manage' them because you can't 'manage' them."[29] Khrushchev communicated a similar message to Kennedy at the time, and the administration backed away from a "counterforce" strategy, with its fantasy that "spasm" nuclear war could be avoided through shrewd management.

But while the missile crisis moderated Kennedy's approach to superpower confrontation, it did not alter the basic policies that had brought on crisis in the first place. Asked in December about Eisenhower's warning "of the dangers of a possible military-industrial complex" and whether he "felt this threat," Kennedy did warn of redundant weapons programs and nuclear overkill but largely ducked the chance to echo his predecessor. Regarding demands from Congress or arms builders for new weapons, "I must say as of today I don't feel that the pressure on us is excessive." Accordingly, America's nuclear arsenal continued to swell (in the "strangest and least defensible buildup," its warheads in Europe multiplied from 2,500 to 7,200 between 1961 and 1966), while JFK's anxiety about China grew, as if fears calmed in one arena moved into another. Moreover, the fear of nuclear war induced by the crisis mingled uneasily with the heady sense that Kennedy and America had triumphed, and might do so again. Though wary of public gloating about victory, which might look hollow given the compromise that ended the crisis, privately Kennedy boasted that "I cut his balls off" (referring to Khrushchev), while key advisors cited the crisis as showing the "determination and staying power" that would bring victory in Vietnam. The American stance "brought about Khrushchev's backdown," *Life* opined. "It indicated a disposition on the part of the Americans to *win* the Cold War." *Life* did not mention avoidance of nuclear war as a meaning of the crisis.[30]

And that meaning did not apply to troublesome situations, like the one in Southeast Asia, that evolved incrementally and required no nail-biting moment of decision. In that regard Vietnam offered insidious temptation: it seemed to be an arena where the United States could take the initiative without risking nuclear bloodbath. As one New Frontiersman mockingly recalled, "We were not going to be in the awful business of creating Hiroshimas and Nagasakis in support of our foreign policy objectives," but would instead "send one of our Green Berets . . . to do battle with one of their crack guerilla fighters and they would have a clean fight, and the best man would win and they both get together and start curing all the villagers of smallpox."[31] The Cuban crisis did not so much ease the Cold War as direct it into different channels, ones less likely to produce nuclear conflict.

So America's involvement in the Vietnam War indicated. There, Viet Cong* in the South and Communist North Vietnam, miscalculating the speed and scale of forthcoming American intervention, were accelerating their effort to reunite the nation and overthrow the Saigon regime of Ngo Dinh Diem before Americans came in greater force. A Catholic in a largely Buddhist land, Diem was more than ever repressive and mercurial, at once demanding greater American aid and fulminating against America's imperial role. His regime "took on more and more of the properties of a sponge. Money, plans, and programs poured into it and nothing came out the other end."[32]

The Kennedy administration avoided the apparent extremes—dramatic military intervention or abandonment of the cause—settling on gradual escalation of American aid, advice, and combat support. American military personnel and advisors increased from one thousand to sixteen thousand under Kennedy, another hapless program was launched to regain control of the countryside, and American officials colluded in and helped instigate Diem's overthrow and murder in 1963, although succeeding regimes proved scarcely more reliable. Johnson agonized about intervention—arguably he made a better case privately against it than Kennedy had—but agreed to it. In August 1964, his administration both misunderstood and misrepresented incidents between American and North Vietnamese naval vessels in the Tonkin Gulf in order to take actions already decided on: bombing raids against North Vietnam and

*This is the derogatory term for the National Liberation Front invented by Diem and commonly used by American officials, soldiers, and reporters; because it is the term familiar to many American readers, its use is retained here.

passage by Congress of an open-ended resolution authorizing further action. "I didn't just screw Ho Chi Minh," LBJ allegedly boasted, "I cut his pecker off."[33]

After the 1964 election campaign, in which LBJ successfully portrayed Barry Goldwater as trigger-happy, his administration awaited the enemy incidents that would justify sustained bombing of the North, begun by American B-52 bombers and other aircraft in the spring. In turn, American air power, fiercely used by now in the South as well as against the North, required American ground troops to protect air bases, just as the troops needed more air cover—so went the circular reasoning, which reflected valid tactical concerns but also rationalized deeper impulses to enter the ground war in the South. By the summer of 1965, the pattern of escalation was set.

Another "overdetermined" act of the Cold War, escalation in Vietnam had many, even contradictory sources. The administration's acquisition of enhanced means to wage such a war encouraged it to wade in and exposed it to criticism should it hesitate. What were the Green Berets, CIA agents, nation-building experts, and helicopter gunships for, after all, if not to help win the Cold War? "In Knute Rockne's old phrase, we are not saving them for the junior prom," Walt Whitman Rostow told Kennedy in 1961.[34] The reaction of military chiefs to initial counterinsurgency tactics gave further impetus to escalation: they resented the deployment of low-tech forces outside their control, doubted their efficacy, and pushed for a conventional, full-scale military effort.

The "arrogance of American power" (as Sen. J. William Fulbright later put it) was also a factor, though in no simple way. It is hardly surprising, given the power of the United States at this juncture, that American leaders were overconfident that they could shape the world in their image, insensitive to local realities abroad, and overbearing in their "guidance of these young and unsophisticated nations," as LBJ once characterized the old societies of Southeast Asia. As Rostow wrote in 1964, the American chance for victory in Vietnam "flows from the simple fact that at this stage in history we are the greatest power in the world—if we behave like it." But decisionmakers did not naively stumble into the "quagmire" of Vietnam oblivious to the dangers there. Repeatedly, even tiresomely, they issued or received reminders of France's failure in Vietnam, the frailties of the South Vietnam regime, the appeal of the Viet Cong, and the perils of escalation. Warnings came from liberals at the fringes of power like Chester Bowles, John Kenneth Galbraith, and Vice President Hubert Humphrey, but also from respected insiders like Undersecretary of State George Ball and Sen. Mike Mansfield. Kennedy himself worried that each escalatory step would be "like taking a drink. . . . The effect wears off, and you have to take another." "The 30% chance is that we would wind up like the French in 1954," worried William Bundy in the Defense Department; "white men can't win this kind of fight." Gen. Maxwell Taylor gave a typical warning in 1964: "Not only do the Viet-Cong units have the recuperative powers of the phoenix, but they have an amazing ability to maintain morale." Though not always seriously regarded, such warnings were legion.[35]

What defined the arrogance of leaders was not blindness to such difficulties but confidence that they could overcome them and conviction that the very difficulties would magnify their triumph. They were both desperate and arrogant—but not about the same things: fearful about South Vietnam, but sure about American power. Indeed, a desperate cause was seductive: only if the United States fought tough battles, not just easy ones, could it show that it would prevail over communism. Win where the odds were bad and it would prove it could win anywhere, just as it tried to go to the moon, Kennedy had said, because it was so hard to do.

Meanwhile, the tendency of leaders to view the stakes in Vietnam as political and psychological—the loss of American credibility, the prospect of falling dominoes—left them in a shadowy world of perceptions where gains and losses defied measurement. The lessons of appeasement were repeated more reflexively than ever, although the analogy to 1938 was deeply flawed: then the great powers' resolve, not Czechoslovakia's, was in doubt and aggression across a clear international border was at issue, but in 1964 Saigon's resolve seemed hopeless and a civil war was raging. "Surrender anywhere threatens defeat everywhere," LBJ said in 1964, although the CIA doubted that the dominoes would fall if South Vietnam was lost. As the Joint Chiefs maintained (if not wholeheartedly) in 1964, "The war must certainly be fought and won primarily in the minds of the Vietnamese people." In that vein, Secretary of State Dean Rusk supported use of ground forces and the bombing of North Vietnam in 1965 as "a signal to Hanoi and Peiping that they themselves cannot hope to succeed without a substantial escalation on their part, with all the risks they would have to face." For "muscular realists," these men paid remarkably little attention to tangible matters of resources, trade, and military power. Their foolish belief that enemies and allies would see "signals" like bombing as signs of American strength, rather than of the desperation that prompted them, made escalation more tempting.[36]

Nor did liberals monopolize such thinking. Conservatives shared the preoccupation with perceptions, differing only about the means needed to shape them. Democrats' "failures," thundered Barry Goldwater in accepting the GOP's 1964 nomination, "proclaim lost leadership, obscure purpose, weakening wills and the risk of inciting our sworn enemies to new aggressions." Though later they scoffed at civilians' focus on perceptions and the course of gradual escalation that went with it, military leaders shared that focus, haggling primarily over the details and pace of escalation. Gen. William Westmoreland, for example, simply issued piecemeal pleas to add a battalion here and a brigade there, and accepted as "our strategy," as he later put it, one designed "to put pressure on the enemy which would transmit a message to the leadership in Hanoi." The Joint Chiefs supported deployment of American troops to Vietnam in 1961 in order to "indicate the firmness of our intent to all Asian nations." Brig. Gen. Edward Lansdale saw such forces as "the symbol of our national power. If an enemy engages one of our combat units, he is fully aware that he automatically has engaged the entire power of the U.S." Even that most sharp-beaked hawk, General LeMay, strayed into this land of perceptions: The United States should tell the North Vietnamese "frankly that they've got to draw in their horns . . . or we're going to bomb them back into the Stone Age." It must "convince them that if they continue their aggression, they will have to pay an economic penalty which they cannot afford."[37]

Prompted by such vague and dubious considerations, America's escalating effort in turn was obscure and puzzling to Americans. For a while, it was hardly even noticeable (David Halberstam found himself "the only full-time staff correspondent of an American daily newspaper" in Vietnam in the early 1960s). And rarely had war making seemed so civilian and so unwarlike. In 1941 and 1950, military leaders had visibly led the charge and the line between war and peace had become sharply drawn. The American effort in Vietnam, however, seemed initially so much a civilian affair—designed, controlled, sometimes even fought by civilians—that it hardly constituted war. Even the most visible military figure in Vietnam policy hardly ran to type. Gen. Maxwell Taylor— JFK's personal military advisor, then chairman of the Joint Chiefs, then ambassador to South Vietnam—was "the Kennedy-type general . . . cool, correct, handsome and athletic," a studious critic of Ike's sabre rattling, a former president of the Lincoln Center for the Performing Arts ("the *cultured* war hero"), hardly a general at all when he cut a striking figure in civilian clothes. With such men in charge, war did not seem imminent.[38]

War also appeared unlikely because means and ends were calculated in such intangible terms—less enemies killed and territory captured than signals of resolve sent and pressure on Hanoi raised. As long as the show rather than the substance of American power was regarded as the key to victory, combat seemed avoidable, or at least secondary: the United States did not actually have to defeat its enemy, only show that it could. Even when the carnage swelled, the Johnson and Nixon administrations remained geared to the shadowy realm of perceptions, rarely seeking or exposed to the blunt accounting of the death toll that General Marshall exchanged with President Roosevelt in World War II.

Initially, those appearances were not baseless: few Americans *did* die in Vietnam before 1965, civilian leaders *were* at pains to exercise control, and entry into full-scale combat *was* still avoidable. Nor were these appearances shaped only by Americans. They were rooted also in the politics of South Vietnam, where the manipulation of appearances, and of American officials, was a well-developed art. Diem's regime was "beset by an extraordinary dreamworld mentality," evident in "the parade Diem staged to commemorate the anniversary of his ascent to power—a parade that wound its way through the empty streets of downtown Saigon because no spectators were allowed to watch it." McNamara's faith in numbers led one Vietnamese general to comment, "*Ah, les statistiques!* Your Secretary of Defense loves statistics. We Vietnamese can give him all he wants. If you want them to go up, they will go up. If you want them to go down, they will go down."[39]

Appearances, however, were misleading. Civilians like Kennedy, McNamara, and Johnson, by seeing militarization as driven by red-faced generals and greedy arms builders, confused restraint of those men with self-restraint. As LBJ supposedly boasted regarding his air commanders, "They can't even bomb an outhouse without my approval." Or as he made the point publicly in 1966, "We have used our power not willingly and recklessly ever, but reluctantly and with restraint. . . . We have not been driven by blind militarism down courses of devastating aggression."[40] National leaders assumed that keeping the generals on a short leash also kept the dogs of war in check. Instead, their control made them, rather than the generals, the primary war makers.

Appropriately, once Americans plunged fully into combat in 1965, the fault finding focused on civilian more than military leaders. The effort to use military means to send political messages to the enemy aggravated the fault finding, for (as is always a danger in such efforts) it also sent messages to Americans, who understandably expected that bombs and bullets would kill enemies and yield military progress. Escalation raised hopes of military victory—many Americans felt betrayed when it was not forthcoming or did not even seem to be the purpose.

The crises of Kennedy's presidency and the moods they engendered left Americans ill prepared to worry about war in Vietnam. Anxieties had focused on a cataclysmic nuclear war, or an accidental nuclear conflict, or a warfare state lurching toward war, or the surrender of a soft nation to communism. Vietnam could not be placed on this grid of apocalyptic scenarios. It seemed to sneak up on Americans, leaders and citizens alike. A remarkable amnesia about the Korean War abetted the deception. So did initial success in hiding American involvement in Southeast Asia, as if Washington "had more faith in the ability of the North Vietnamese to behave wisely (by succumbing, however grudgingly) than it had in the American public to support its actions."[41] Nothing about the Vietnam War—its location far from the notable hot spots of the Cold War, the slow pace of American escalation, the murky nature of revolutionary war—resonated with dominant anxieties. Thus even when genuinely feared, disaster there paled in comparison to the scenarios of doom so widely shared.

Reform as War

By the 1960s, the civil rights movement was changing: gaining a wider base that included white clergy, scholars, and students; more openly defying white law and custom in the South and drawing a violent response from white authorities there; and pressing its claims as a matter of justice. Still, the familiar argument persisted that America's security and global prestige required racial progress.

It was strengthened by the liberation of more African nations from European rule and by the caution about racial issues of John Kennedy, who invoked national security more readily than justice. National security was also applied to other efforts: when JFK forced "Big Steel" companies to roll back price increases, he contrasted their greed to the sacrifices of soldiers in Berlin and Vietnam and argued that national safety was threatened.

So it remained persuasive for the NAACP's Roy Wilkins to argue in 1961 that "the continuing mistreatment of Negro citizens *is* hurting our country" and has "embarrassed" the President "in his exchanges with Chairman Khrushchev, for how can Mr. Kennedy plead for democracy in Laos when at the very moment, Khrushchev is reading about discrimination, segregation and mob action in Alabama." It remained appropriate for Martin Luther King, Jr., to note two years later that while government's resolve to defend freedom abroad took it "to the brink of nuclear conflict," it "disappeared or became tragically weak when the threat . . . was concerned with the Negro's liberty." Similarly, Kennedy, using federal troops when Gov. George Wallace barred the doors to blacks at the University of Alabama, told Americans in June 1963 that they were "committed to a world-wide struggle to promote and protect the rights of all who wish to be free. And when Americans are sent to Vietnam or West Berlin we do not ask for Whites only."[42]

Such appeals to the nation's interests and global image were not the only reason that politicians acted on civil rights—their fear of embarrassment at home and the pressure on them from civil rights activists were more decisive—but those appeals did express the paramount framework that leaders found acceptable for themselves and persuasive to many white Americans. As a result, a major antidiscrimination measure, the Civil Rights Act of 1964, was enacted, then further strengthened—after marches at Selma, Alabama, and elsewhere exposed white intransigence anew—by a 1965 law expanding federal protection of voting rights. Legalized discrimination, segregation, and disenfranchisement were now dead.

War had long given black Americans leverage to capitalize on their service to the nation and to contrast ideals proclaimed abroad to realities sustained at home. And it still did during the Vietnam era, though the terms were changing. Many now contrasted inequalities at home to the egalitarian military force abroad, rather than assailing racial inequalities in the army. As Whitney Young noted in 1967, "In this war there is a degree of integration among black and white Americans far exceeding that of any other war in our history as well as any other time or place in our domestic life." If anything, racial integration of the armed forces now victimized African-Americans: once deemed unfit to fight, blacks bore an undue share of combat and death in Vietnam until, pressed by civil rights groups, the Defense Department changed personnel policies in the late 1960s (overall, African-Americans died in Vietnam in numbers that closely matched their share of the male draft-age population and slightly exceeded their share of the overall population). "The Negro," noted *Ebony,* "has found in his nation's most totalitarian society—the military—the greatest degree of functional democracy that this nation has granted to black people." Such comments indicated divided sentiments: both pride in and resentment of the role blacks now played in war.[43]

However changed, those terms still tied racial issues to war. Many black leaders continued to wrest leverage from African-Americans' service in the armed forces, and condemned black and white antiwar leaders who threatened "this ideological weapon" by opposing the war itself. New chances to use the weapon also arose: in 1967, when President Johnson sent observers to Vietnam to insure that its elections were "free and democratic," civil rights leaders told him "it would mean much more" to send observers to Mississippi "to make certain Negroes and Negro candidates are assured justice and fair play in all elections." As LBJ, proposing new civil rights measures, told Congress in 1967, "The bullets at the battlefront do not discriminate—but the landlords at home do. The pack of the Negro soldier is as heavy as the white soldier's—but the burden his family at home bears is far heavier."[44]

Other groups also sought leverage in the Cold War, though as yet lacking mass-action tactics and a recognized place in the global struggle. Franklin Kameny, a Harvard Ph.D. in astronomy, went to work for the U.S. Army Map Service in 1957, only to be discharged for homosexuality even though the Sputnik crisis put a premium on his services. Finding himself "in the peculiarly ironic position of being in excessively great demand . . . and yet totally unable to get a job because of security problems," he challenged federal policies in the courts and led picketing by gay men and lesbians of the White House and other government agencies in 1965.[45]

Soviet-American competition provided surer leverage for women. The National Manpower Council's 1957 study *Womanpower* had deplored "the nation's failure to utilize women's talents fully" and urged their training "in subjects long stereotyped as masculine, especially math and science," even if only to release men from school-teaching to enter high-powered research. Educator Mary Bunting "taunted her colleagues" by noting how the Soviet Union "took women's abilities more seriously than America did." In that vein, the federal Women's Bureau "argued that just as the country was preparing to stockpile weapons, so, too, should it stockpile expertise in the form of bright women." Kennedy's summons for all Americans to "bear any burden" added force to this argument, helping to produce the Equal Pay Act of 1963 and the Title VII provision of the 1964 Civil Rights Act that included sex with race and ethnicity in barring discrimination in employment.[46]

Yet even as more groups invoked national security, that framework for reform was losing its primacy. Efforts to advance women's legal equality focused more on women's rights and family needs than on Cold War imperatives, just as the new feminism at mid-decade was sparked by the contempt shown by federal and corporate officials toward the legislation of 1963–1964. Cold War imperatives entirely disappeared in Martin Luther King's famous address "I Have a Dream" in August 1963. More surprising, President Johnson pitched his repeated calls for civil rights legislation far more to the demands of justice and domestic peace than to the Cold War or the Vietnam War. By mid-decade, others like King took a further step, arguing that national security was not only an insufficient rationale for racial reform but antagonistic to it, draining the energies, money, and spirit needed for change at home. America's record in war and global struggle was still cited—in 1963 the Urban League called for a Marshall Plan for American cities—but more as a model than as a reason for reform. Exponents of black power like Stokely Carmichael went further, suggesting that a real war within the United States had to be waged like the revolutionary wars by Third World peoples against imperial rule, for the black ghettoes of America were "colonies" that "must be liberated." Others resorted to a more diffuse language of war unrelated to national security—"the Battle of Birmingham" was how Bayard Rustin dubbed racial struggle there in 1963, with "total victory" the desired outcome.[47]

The older framework was eroding in part because it succumbed to growing black impatience. It had made civil rights urgent but subordinate to national needs, and prized action in arenas such as military service that were exposed to the world and controlled by the presidency. It did less to address zeal for moral reform, inequalities beyond the reach of presidential action, and anger among black Americans when legal change failed to end their powerlessness. Many had tolerated the old rationale only as an expedient basis for their cause. Most blacks, James Baldwin wrote in 1963, doubted that even the past decade's limited changes "would ever have been made if it had not been for the competition of the Cold War, and the fact that Africa was clearly liberating herself and therefore had . . . to be wooed by the descendants of her former masters."[48] In the early 1960s, few black leaders explicitly challenged the old framework—hence it lingered with some force. More often, they just moved it to the margins of their cause.

Oddly, it was moving to the margins just when militarization was intensifying. Perhaps "the easing of Cold War hostilities" now "cleared a path for reform,"[49] but it is doubtful that such hostilities really eased at mid-decade. There likely was no simple relationship between the change in the reform impulse and the course of the Cold War. Instead, a subtler process took place: competition between reform initiatives and Cold War imperatives intensified under the strain of the Vietnam War, national security became a less persuasive basis for reform for African-Americans impatient about their cause, and a more charged, amorphous language of war replaced it. By 1966 so many groups had redeployed that language to more radical purposes, and it resonated so disturbingly with the war in Vietnam, that a coherent framework for reform all but disappeared. Militarization and reform remained tied to each other, but in more volatile, confusing ways.

Prominent reform tracts of the early 1960s foreshadowed those shifts by advancing new agendas even when they did not explicitly repudiate older ones. Michael Harrington's *The Other America* (1962) urged that "the welfare provisions of American society that now help the upper two-thirds . . . be extended to the poor," implicitly undercutting militarized priorities by demanding attention to social inequalities.[50]

A year later, in *The Feminine Mystique*, Betty Friedan seemed to leave those priorities intact. As she noted irritably: "Concerned over the Soviet Union's lead in the space race, scientists noted that America's greatest source of unused brainpower was women. But girls would not study physics; it was 'unfeminine.'" She accepted the ugly argument that stifled mothers turned sons into sissies who failed the nation in Korea. Yet more than she realized, Friedan undercut Cold War priorities. Women's service to a mobilized America was only a minor theme in her call for liberation from the "housewife's trap." Women's own needs, their "search for identity," hardly fit the framework of national security at all. Other claims were also implicitly subversive. Friedan identified the 1940s as the moment when the feminine mystique, prompted by "the loneliness of the war and the unspeakableness of the bomb," took hold— she did not remember that decade as America's finest hour, at least not for women. And her disturbing comparison of the suburban home—"the comfortable concentration camp"—to Nazi death camps undercut complacent distinctions usually made between Americans and their enemies.[51]

Among academic intellectuals, too, challenges to militarized priorities were usually implicit. Most intellectuals remained cautious, inclined to analyze *how* the nation should meet its priorities more than *whether* those priorities were correct. Nuclear weapons strategy, "nation building" in the Third World, racial problems in the United States—such matters were the object of immense, technically proficient (and often boring) scholarship that left fundamental assumptions involving militarization intact.

Academic historians reflected these patterns. Despite the faultline opening among them in the early 1960s, many remained comfortable with the consensus view of history formulated in the 1950s and with an "austere posture of detachment" from immediate issues. As one historian told students worried that the Cuban missile crisis would blow them up, "There is also merit in keeping the light of scholarship burning as long as possible." Although the "antiseptic character" of that posture grated on some historians, even those with a more radical outlook as yet rarely focused on militarization and war making, instead examining diplomacy and ideology, while military history largely remained in the drum-and-trumpets mold. Casting a wider net, C. Vann Woodward wrote in 1960, "The end of the era of free security has overtaken Americans so suddenly and swiftly that they have not brought themselves to face its practical implications, much less its bearing upon their history." Pointedly deemphasizing the Cold War, he sketched the broader ramifications of militarization and urged historians to study them. His call went unheeded for the moment. Woodward himself, like many others, focused more readily on social and political history, of race relations above all. (Gender was not a focus in part because "the percentage of women in the profession fell precipitously" after World War II.) Collectively, historians' work undercut militarization only indirectly, by offering alternative agendas. Most were too enamored of Kennedy-era activism and too confident in abundant resources to see militarization as a barrier to their agendas.[52]

Critiques of the militarized state remained unusual outside the academy as in it. The Port Huron Statement of the Students for a Democratic Society was an obscure document at the time. Doomsday fiction had a wider audience but rarely addressed the underpinnings of militarization. Fred J. Cook's *The Warfare State* (1962) came closer to the mark. Working in the tradition of pre–World War II exposés of militarism, journalistic in style, drawing on voices as diverse as C. Wright Mills and Dwight Eisenhower, Cook identified "the twin theme of the Warfare State" as "more guns and bombers, yes; better education, medical care, disarmament, decidedly no." The state sustained an economy "hitched to war production" and disdained "all that welfare state nonsense like aid to education and medical care for the aged." (As I. F. Stone complained, Democrats were "committed to the arms race . . . as a grandiose WPA for perpetual prosperity until the bombs go off.") What Cook lacked in sophistication he made up for in pointedness, but writing just when Kennedy and Johnson managed briefly to fund both "more guns" and more "welfare state," he posed alternatives that to many others seemed reconcilable.[53]

Lyndon Johnson moved to center stage at this moment of flux, when old agendas and rationales were beginning to lose force but new ones were barely articulated. He played a pivotal role in reshaping the relationship between war and reform. Passionate about reform and his place in history regarding it, Johnson largely discarded the Cold War rationale for it. Although he did urge reform to help unify the nation in waging the Cold War, it was justice, equality, and the perfectibility of America that primarily drove his vision of the Great Society. But steeped in Roosevelt's achievements, LBJ made war his chief model and metaphor for the process that would realize his vision, carrying FDR's heritage further than his mentor ever dared. Reform, presented in the previous two decades as a way to strengthen a nation at war, now reemerged as itself a kind of "war." In a few breathless years, Johnson declared "war" on countless problems at home and abroad.

His most famous use of the war metaphor came in his first State of the Union message in January 1964: "This administration today, here and now, declares unconditional war on poverty in America." On March 16, urging Congress to enact the Economic Opportunity Act, he again declared "a national war on poverty. Our objective: total victory." No incidental metaphor, it received the full-dress treatment LBJ gave anything he deeply cared about: "If we can now move forward against this enemy—if we can bring to the challenge of peace the same determination and strength which has brought us victory in war—then this day and Congress will have won a secure and honorable place in the history of the nation." "This war on poverty will enlist many recruits," including "men and women of both parties," the "underprivileged" themselves, and "every American community." Women should be "the first to enlist in this war for the benefit of their children," he added. "We won the first American revolution because we were a people in arms," he proclaimed. "The battle will not be spectacular," consisting of "thousands of small efforts that add up to a vast national effort," and victory would not come "in a few months or a few years." But it seemed within grasp.[54]

Others joined the rhetorical battle, helping to make "war on poverty" one of the decade's best-known phrases. Labor leader Walter Reuther assured Johnson that "we enlist with him in the war against poverty for the duration." The mayor of St. Louis spoke of "weapons" and "ammunition" and "a coordinated, concerted, multifront offensive" in which mayors would enlist. Backers of LBJ's antipoverty programs used the war metaphor to define not only the spirit but the substance of the antipoverty effort. "If you are going to declare war," argued Health, Education, and Welfare Secretary Anthony Celebrezze, "you have to have one general of the Army. You cannot have six generals." One congressman suggested that "in recognizing this as D-day, we are just setting up a general just like we set up General Eisenhower" in World War II. Foes also used war rhetoric, albeit to different purposes, often teasing out its hidden, troublesome implications. Fearing Washington's power, Sen. John Tower called local control and representative government "the first casualty of the war on poverty." By 1966, as LBJ's programs faced mounting opposition, one critic thought that "the war on cities" might "all work out, if humane weapons are used and we evacuate the wounded. But I suspect that in the confusion the real enemies—poverty, ignorance, despair—may slip away, to live and strike again."[55]

A cascade of legislation to achieve victory issued forth. The Economic Opportunity Act of 1964 established the Office of Economic Opportunity (OEO), first headed by Sargent Shriver, who moved over from the Peace Corps. OEO presided over a new Job Corps (heir to the old Civilian Conservation Corps) and the Community Action Program, which in turn funded legal services for the poor, Project Head Start for underprivileged preschoolers, Upward Bound to advance poor children to college, and Neighborhood Health Centers. Since the loose rhetoric of a "war on poverty" easily merged with LBJ's broader vision of a Great Society, it often seemed to embrace other, generally more expensive programs instituted at mid-decade: the Appalachian Development Act, lavish new federal aid to public schools, Medicaid for the poor and Medicare for the elderly, and the Food Stamps program. In intent, result, or just mistaken public image, many of these programs aimed especially at urban black youth, all the more so once the urban riots of mid-decade made politicians desperate to find a way to calm the storm.

Why did the war metaphor seem compelling in justifying these programs? It served much the same purpose it had for FDR in 1933. It prized federal action and presidential leadership, since war was a supremely national enterprise. "It isolated the opposition and made opponents seem almost treasonous," notes one historian, or, as Johnson later put it, "the War on Poverty was not a partisan effort. It was a moral obligation and its success rested on every one of us." It obscured divisions of race and class, since war was presumed to unify the nation, even though this war was designed precisely to address such divisions. It presumed that reform was largely men's work, since that was how war was usually understood. And even more than for FDR, it revealed, as historian William Leuchtenburg wrote at this time regarding Roosevelt, that Americans still could find no way "to organize collective action save in war or its surrogate." Just as New Dealers invoked World War I, liberals now invoked World War II.[56]

If anything, dependence on war as model and metaphor was greater for LBJ in 1964 than for FDR in 1933. Far from facing an economic crisis, Johnson took the initiative on reform amid broad prosperity (accelerated by tax cuts he promoted), with no aggrieved middle class demanding federal programs, the poor as yet hardly mobilized, and no mandate at the ballot box until the fall of 1964. Whereas FDR took on a widely shared economic depression, LBJ took on problems of race and class that divided Americans, and did so at a time when liberalism was deeply invested in the Cold War and cautious in its approach to domestic problems. And more so than for FDR in 1933, national government's remembered record of achievement lay largely in national security: two major wars, stunning accomplishments in weapons, and myriad efforts to promote health, education, science, engineering, and transport in the name of national defense. It made sense to base new efforts on the kind of achievements already so well executed. "We were a generation of people who had been in World War II," Shriver recalled years later. "So when a war against poverty was launched, it was typical of all of us at that time to think of this war, the war against poverty, in terms just like the war against Hitler." Of course, using that war as a model set up total victory as the payoff.[57]

Doing so, however, soon backfired. Promises of total victory raised expectations that could not be satisfied, especially since the core OEO program was only modestly funded (at less than 1 percent of the federal budget, it "was only a pale reminder of the nearly $5 billion relief bill of 1935"), and hopes to enlarge it fell victim to budgetary restraints Johnson and Congress imposed because of the Vietnam War. Far more funding went into broad entitlement and reform programs which served middle-class and working-class constituencies as much as the poor, but since these programs were often perceived as aimed at the poor, whose lot seemed to improve so little (though more than critics admitted), the war on poverty was readily deemed a failure. Even if it did help, the poor seemed ungrateful once inner cities went up in flames. And since civil rights programs were also conflated with the war on poverty (Shriver said they "are all part of the same battle") while black Americans became angrier than ever, white critics could regard the war as having failed blacks (or vice versa). The gulf between promise and result in the war on poverty emboldened long-time opponents and disheartened once-loyal liberals.[58]

Process in that war accorded with rhetoric no better than results. Shriver became no "general of the army" and Washington hardly took exclusive command—it was not even supposed to, insofar as many reformers prized local autonomy and participation by poor people themselves in the cause. OEO programs overlapped others at the national level and challenged local political machines, which either fought them or took them under control, subverting original purposes. The resulting confusion of authority made sense in one regard: American war making had always mixed centralized direction and dispersed authority, regimentation and voluntarism. But images of Eisenhower at D-Day hardly prepared Americans for that outcome. Indeed, the entire conception of reform as war rested on the faulty premise that government and the nation become more disciplined and efficient in war, when in reality their efforts in war are often chaotic.

Subtler problems arose, ones inherent in the war metaphor but aggravated by LBJ's particular use of it. Wars require enemies, but the "poverty" that Johnson defined was abstract. As he noted in 1967 (admitting now that the war "will not be won in a generation"), there were "too many enemies: lack of jobs, bad housing, poor schools, lack of skills, discrimination." He might have named greedy capitalists, hide-bound conservatives, corrupt politicians, or others as the culprits, but, seeking consensus and avoiding "class rhetoric like the plague," he stuck to abstractions that prevented spelling out such things. Given urban riots and black resentment, it became easy for some to see the enemy as poor and black people themselves (the two often conflated). As one congressman argued, "We ought to draft our Nation's punks and hoods instead of coddling and paying them in the Job Corps." "Yeah, I helped the War on Poverty," ran a contemporary joke: "I threw a hand grenade at a bum." As a critic of Berkeley's efforts to demolish a poor neighborhood sensed, "We are conducting a *War on Poverty* with one hand and a *War on the Poor* with another." The rhetoric of reform as war, offered to transcend divisions of race and class, soon opened them wider.[59]

Again, the premise was faulty: war may unify a nation in some ways, but it also stirs passions and hatreds. Labor Secretary Willard Wirtz unwittingly exposed the tensions: "This war on poverty is not going to be fought in the tradition of emotional crusades" but through "a carefully worked out battle plan based less on praising the Lord than on passing the ammunition."[60] The whole notion of an unemotional war was contradictory, though expressive of liberal faith, on trial in Vietnam at the same time, that the rational technique of war could be disassociated from its passions.

The war on poverty foundered on internal contradictions of rhetoric and politics, but also on its intersection with the war in Vietnam. LBJ expounded the war metaphor before he made his decisions to expand military intervention in Vietnam, but he kept hammering away at that metaphor long after escalation in Vietnam, offering a dizzying collage of wars at home and abroad. Though with declining frequency, he talked of his "war on poverty" for the rest of his presidency. In 1966 he described Peace Corps volunteers (oddly, given their official designation) as "really waging the only war that we in America want to wage— the war against the inhumanity of man to his neighbor and the injustice of nature to her children." By 1966 he was also waging a "war against crime," complete with a "three-stage national strategy" and "the front-line soldier," though he condemned "treating drug addicts, once apprehended, as criminals."[61]

By then Johnson had also launched a war on disease. War had long provided images used in imagining disease, but the Cold War provided new opportunities in that regard. Comparing Soviet science to American in 1959, LBJ presented the United States as facing a "medical Sputnik." For years Mary Lasker, a prominent businesswoman and lobbyist on health issues, had employed war imagery in her campaigns; in 1964, she contrasted the "$51.2 billion [spent] to defend ourselves against possible enemy attack" to the "$911.4 million [spent] to defend ourselves against *disease enemies within our own bodies*." That year Johnson heralded his forthcoming war on disease: "This nation and the whole world cries [sic] out for this victory." Conquest would come "not in a millennium, not in a century, but in the next few onrushing decades." "LBJ DECLARES WAR ON 3 KILLER DISEASES," one newspaper headline announced. In 1965, Johnson announced "a worldwide war on disease," declared by him on the "quiet battleground" of the National Institutes of Health, with promises that Americans would "successfully conclude that war you [scientists] have declared on those ancient diseases." Appropriately, the National Cancer Institute's director in 1967 declared that "we should probably emulate the Manhattan Project." When the Vietnam War competed for money and victory proved elusive on the medical front, Johnson simply announced "a review of the targets and the timetable . . . set for winning victories in the war."[62]

Indeed, war-related imagery was probably as widespread involving disease in the 1960s as it was regarding poverty, though less controversial because it did not seem to touch on divisive matters of race and class. Less controversial, it in turn was more lasting: Nixon would declare a "war on cancer," and the "wars" of the 1980s on AIDS, smoking, and drugs followed in that tradition.

The "worldwide war on disease" also foreshadowed LBJ's effort to go global in another humanitarian effort. *"I propose that the United States lead the world in a war against hunger,"* he announced in 1966, asking Congress for new legislation. In his last years in office, he gave no "war" more attention in rhetoric than this one, save the war in Vietnam, which he repeatedly juxtaposed to the one on hunger. Like his other favored wars, the war on hunger, he maintained, was the one he wanted to wage—"the only war that we really seek to escalate"— whereas his hand was forced in Vietnam. "There can only be victors in this war," he said, contrasting it to his alleged willingness to compromise in Vietnam.[63]

Such claims showed the strains in his rhetoric: wars usually leave behind defeated as well as victorious parties. His linguistic terrain was also easily invaded by others: critics on the right derided LBJ for seeking total victory against poverty and hunger but not communism; antiwar activists suspected that the unconditional surrender he really wanted was North Vietnam's.

Johnson's awkward rhetoric suggested how difficult it was by 1966 to sort out his many wars. The consummate politician who wanted to satisfy everyone, "Big Daddy from the Pedernales" also had a war for everyone. Certainly those wars were cognitively distinguishable. Yet the lines among them blurred as all received a similar rhetorical treatment, as Johnson waged one war to placate opponents of another, as he insistently if vaguely presented each as related to the others in his quest for a perfect America and a perfect world, and each as capable of being won even as victory remained elusive. The confusion was heightened by how the struggle in Vietnam itself emerged as many different wars—guerrilla and conventional, political and military—with many different objectives: to save South Vietnam or American credibility, to stop Hanoi, or Beijing, or Moscow. When war also seemed to erupt on American streets and campuses, it took still another form. Heir to a venerable tradition, Johnson tried hard to wrest the virtues of war—its energy, unity, purposefulness—from war itself. The effort, perilous in any circumstances, was doomed when enmeshed with a real war. Where did one war end and another begin? Did LBJ himself even know? What, indeed, did "war" any longer mean?

His wars spilled into each other not only rhetorically but substantively, since reformers used the military as another weapon in the war on poverty. Assistant Labor Secretary Daniel Patrick Moynihan argued in 1964 that the armed forces should lower their entrance requirements and provide special training for poor, especially black males: because of their "disorganized and matrifocal family life," black youth "desperately needed . . . a world away from women, a world run by strong men and unquestioned authority." Surging draft calls for the Vietnam War, growing resistance to the draft from affluent youth, and urban rebellion among black youth soon made Moynihan's recommendation mesh with wartime expediency, since it provided a way both to funnel men into the army and to curb urban unrest. Under Project 100,000, Defense Secretary McNamara promised to admit men who failed the military's qualifying exam so that "they can be given an opportunity to return to civilian life with skills and aptitudes which . . . will reverse the downward spiral of decay." In reality, those men (40 percent of whom were black) received little additional training; assigned at a high rate to combat duties in Vietnam for which they were ill prepared, they in turn experienced a high rate of casualties and courts-martial and, if they survived, left the army without the skills promised to them under the program. Despite its failures, however, Project 100,000 certainly "was conceived . . . as a significant component of the administration's 'war on poverty.'"[64]

"Johnson talked about a perfect America," a biographer notes.[65] But there was something jarring about achieving perfection through a series of wars at home and abroad, especially when the enemies defined were so abstract—hunger, poverty, faltering American credibility—that victory was unmeasurable and seemed obtainable only through perpetual war. It was no less confusing given how each war was presented as both a moral crusade and a passionless exercise in technique, miraculously possessing all the fervor and yet none of the hatred usually associated with war. It all made sense only if the model of war was World War II, the one war that came nearest to perfection, at least in American memory.

Johnson and other Americans saw reform as war in part because they remembered war as process of reform. World War II, Korea, and the Cold War provided a basis for that memory: at their best, they had promoted racial change, better health, technological advances, more accessible higher education, a robust economy, briefly a modest downward redistribution of income, and in general a more resourceful federal government. The Vietnam War, however, seemed to depart from that pattern: initially promoting economic growth, it soon disrupted the economy; fought mostly with technologies in hand, it produced few new wonders; waged by racially integrated forces, it unleashed racial turmoil at home and among Americans in Vietnam. Whatever good flowed from the federal government in the 1960s came largely in programs apart from the war rather than attendant upon it. It was LBJ's misfortune to draw on war as a model for reform just when the model itself turned sour. Perhaps that was because Vietnam was a losing war; victory might have enhanced its salutary effects. But such effects were scarcely evident even in 1965, when victory still seemed possible to many.

Of course, the failure (much exaggerated since the 1960s) of Johnson's programs had many sources besides the rhetoric of war used to justify them. Support for them was often weak from the start—the Economic Opportunity Act was approved by the House 226–185, an ominously narrow margin for a declaration of war. For many programs—in education, health care, urban renewal, consumer protection, the arts, and the environment—LBJ offered little war rhetoric, fondly talking instead about the Great Society. Many also became fixtures of federal policy, surviving the Vietnam era or even prospering amid it.

Nor was Johnson peculiarly arrogant in believing that America could wage all the wars it wanted. "We are a rich nation and can afford to make progress at home while meeting obligations abroad," he announced in 1966, but that belief was widely shared. In Moynihan's formulation, "the immediate *supply* of resources available for social purposes might actually outrun the immediate *demand* of established programs."[66] And it was not unfounded—the issue was less what the United States could "afford" than who would pay for it. A decent student of economics, Johnson saw a need for tax increases but faced division among his advisors and resistance from Democratic leaders in Congress.

Still, while the gap between promise and result in Johnson's programs had many sources, his war metaphor and the Vietnam War widened it, as did his tendency to see enemies, not just opponents, when he ran into trouble. Johnson, who "had little sense of irony," could not grasp the unintended results of his rhetorical style or the motives of his opponents. As early as June 1965, he saw opposition to the Vietnam War as directed from foes abroad: "I will see a line from Peking, Hanoi, and Moscow . . . about a month ahead of the time I see it here," he told the Cabinet. Out of paranoia or a life-long habit of overdramatizing his plight, he came to see "enemies" among Kennedy loyalists, Ivy League intellectuals, resentful blacks, unruly war protesters, obnoxious journalists, and disloyal senators (all of whom on occasion returned the favor).[67] That cast of mind, though the product of many forces, emerged naturally out of his habit of waging wars. At least his successor showed it was hardly unique to Johnson.

Johnson's notion of reform as war marked a historical half-way station between a previous reform rationale tied to national security and a new one free of it—as if, though national security no longer compelled reform, its legacy still provided the language and models. For Johnson, ever seeking consensus (at least as he saw it), it made sense to seek out this middle ground. Briefly, he succeeded. Already by 1966, success was in doubt. His effort foundered on many things, among them the contradictions in his war rhetoric, the unfulfillable hopes it stirred, and the cognitive dissonance it set up with the Vietnam War. Nonetheless, it left behind a language for explaining governmental crusades used later by others who often had quite different politics. Because of that legacy, militarization persisted in political culture even when it receded in battles, budgets, and armaments.

Vietnam as War

Late in 1966, American forces in South Vietnam began planning Operation Cedar Falls, whose goal was to deny to the Viet Cong the "Iron Triangle" near Saigon, a region rich in agriculture and manpower. Lest they leak word to the enemy, no South Vietnamese officials were told of the operation in advance. It was now an American-run war, with many Americans contemptuous of ARVN (Army of the Republic of Vietnam) forces. "It's the Asian mind," an American officer commented. "Look—they're a thousand years behind us in this place, and we're trying to educate them up to our level." So Americans tightened their grip on a war and a country they officially sought to relinquish, practicing "a strange, crippled sort of imperialism," one "in which the colony is supposed, in a manner of speaking, to colonize itself."[68]

Cedar Falls showed one face of this imperialism. First, American forces shelled and bombed the Iron Triangle—B-52 bombers designed to attack the Soviet Union now devastated an ally's countryside—and blocked the perimeter of the area, hoping to trap the enemy within it. Later, giant Chinook helicopters flew in bulldozers to cut huge swathes through the jungle, so that future troop movements by the Viet Cong could be detected. "If the U.S. has its way," *Time* commented, "even a crow flying across the Triangle will have to carry lunch from now on." On January 8, 1967, American forces moved on the principal village of Ben Suc. As choppers brought in American soldiers, their loudspeakers warned townspeople not to flee. "The metallic voice, floating down over the fields, huts, and trees, was as calm as if it were announcing a flight departure at an air terminal," observed Jonathan Schell, catching Americans' fondness for cool technique in war. Since few Americans spoke Vietnamese, ARVN forces now entered the scene to sort friend from foe—a thankless task open to brutalities by all parties, given the many gradations of collaboration and apathy among South Vietnamese. American commanders saw their job as the "military" war while the Saigon government waged the "other war," the one for the "hearts and minds of the people," although American troops offered villagers "a lunch of hot dogs, Spam, and crackers, served with a fruit-flavored beverage called Keen."[69]

Then American trucks carried the villagers to a resettlement camp, an instant town safe from the Viet Cong. "WELCOME TO THE RECEPTION CENTER FOR REFUGEES FLEEING COMMUNISM," read one sign greeting them, though they hardly had fled willingly. They had lived, explained an American officer, "a life of fear . . . fear of the Vietcong, fear of the bombs. That wasn't a natural life at all." But neither was life in the new camp. Cut off from the resources and traditions that had sustained them, the relocated peasants "began a life of sitting and waiting," failing to appreciate that they had been liberated. Though some tried, they could not return to Ben Suc. American forces had set fire to it, uprooted it with bulldozers, then bombed it—"as though, having once decided to destroy it, we were now bent on annihilating every possible indication that the village of Ben Suc had ever existed," as Schell ended his account.[70]

It was another step in a process by which United States forces destroyed and depopulated much of South Vietnam in order to deny the Viet Cong use of it and to create free-fire zones to bomb and shell without scruples about killing peasants. Bulldozers and high-explosives ripped the land, bombers fired it with napalm, and forces of Operation Ranch Hand ("Only You Can Prevent Forests," ran their sardonic motto) defoliated it. Between 1964 and 1969, perhaps 20 percent of South Vietnamese became permanent refugees (millions more were temporarily displaced) because of American, ARVN, and less often Viet Cong tactics. The result was the demoralization and devastation of much of a land presumably under American protection, as the "hearts-and-minds" approach to the war met sharp limits: in the gallows humor of American soldiers, "Just grab the gooks by the balls and their hearts and minds will follow."

The warring parties differed, of course, not in innate capacity for cruelty and destruction but in their means to act on it and their stakes in the war. Increasingly supplied by China and the Soviet Union, the forces of Communist North Vietnam and the Viet Cong were hardly the primitive peasant army Americans sometimes imagined; they were molded by decades of war for control of their land and driven by ideological and nationalist zeal. Possessing awesome economic and technological resources, American forces could carry out destruction with a kind of cool abandon. Culturally remote from the Vietnamese, uninterested in seizing land and resources for their own sake, often physically and emotionally distant from the destruction as they lobbed shells and dropped bombs, they were preoccupied with technique—with the process rather than the results of delivering destruction. That outlook heightened insensitivity not only to the destruction but to the many forms of its futility (from the duds among the tons of American ordnance strewn over the land the enemy salvaged materiel for its own booby traps, mines, and other explosives).

Search-and-destroy operations, the centerpiece of the American ground war, also proved futile. They were designed to find the enemy's main forces and provoke battle with them, in which case Americans usually prevailed, but the enemy would rarely engage in battle except on terms favorable to itself. The Wagnerian crescendo of roaring helicopters and exploding bombs telegraphed to the enemy the impending arrival of American or ARVN forces, so that, as one journalist observed, each operation "was like a sledgehammer on a floating cork." Such operations also damaged the morale and discipline of American ground forces because they rarely yielded decisive battle. Men sent on too many meaningless missions, in which mines and ambush (or climate and disease) posed bigger threats than any massed enemy, sometimes vented their frustration on whatever village they stumbled upon, under a confused and hypocritical "military policy that made the killing and wounding of civilians routine." For ground troops being used as "bait" to attract enemy forces—the latter then presumably to be crushed by American firepower—the sense of powerlessness was especially acute. Such conditions, reflecting the murky ideological and military rationale for the American effort, led American soldiers in Vietnam to doubt the war's purpose far more than had their World War II counterparts.[71]

Indeed, the cruelty and futility of their methods were hardly invisible to Americans who employed them. Their humor indicated their cynicism about such methods, and ground troops, unlike bomber pilots or artillerymen, were hardly remote from the destruction. But the rapid rotation of combat personnel in and out of Vietnam, their notorious isolation from commanders, and Washington's control over the war discouraged grass-roots efforts to alter American military methods. Some retired generals also criticized those methods but, no longer in the system, they had little impact on it.

America's course in Vietnam was shaped by its previous experience in war, above all World War II. More than he usually got credit for, it is true, LBJ did try to go beyond conventional views of the Cold War. He "gladly built upon the thaw in Soviet-American relations that followed the Cuban missile crisis,"[72] abandoning his strident rhetoric and pursuing major negotiations with Moscow and (less fruitfully and out of public view) with China. Nixon would pursue detente more forcefully. What was striking was their persistence in Vietnam even as the underlying Cold War rationale weakened—at least insofar as it pertained to superpower conflict—finally to be destroyed by Nixon. These men could overcome their conventional views of the Cold War, but not their World War II–born sense of what war itself must entail—of the way to fight it and the victory it must yield.

Johnson, according to Paul Conkin, "was far less bellicose and adventurous than Roosevelt and Truman, let alone Kennedy," and he "wanted, above all else, to contain the Vietnam conflict, to prevent it from turning into the opening phases of World War III."[73] In that regard he succeeded, and measured against what he knew best—World War II and the threat of nuclear war—his success was profoundly important. That standard of measurement was also profoundly misleading, however. In Vietnam, danger lay not in horrors already experienced or feared but in new ones marginal to America's remembered history. The closest analogies were to the Korean War and the French Indochina war, neither fully scrutinized by LBJ or most other leaders. They could never examine the Vietnam War on its own terms, outside their preconceived frameworks.

Although they labored to prevent the Vietnam War from becoming World War II or World War III, they also saw it as a small-scale prototype of both. LBJ's tireless analogies to 1930s appeasement put Vietnam in the familiar framework, as did his reference as Vice President to Diem as "the Winston Churchill of the Orient." So too did resort to the weaponry, tactics, and systems developed to wage world war—the mass army, big-unit tactics, and bombing. Since most leaders derived their sense of war from World War II, their focus on technology and technique came easily. After all, the JCS chairman explained, "No one ever won a battle sitting on his ass." As Gen. William Westmoreland, commander of American forces in the South, described his strategy in 1967, "We'll just go on bleeding them until Hanoi wakes up to the fact that they have bled their country to the point of national disaster for generations." The strained analogies of Westmoreland's memoirs indicated his debt to World War II: he described the Tet Offensive of 1968 remarkably as both "a Pearl Harbor" for

South Vietnam (although the war was years old by 1968) and a defeat for the enemy (which Pearl Harbor hardly had been), who "could have been induced to engage in serious and meaningful negotiations" (Pearl Harbor bore no such result). Tet was also somehow comparable, he thought in 1968, to the Battle of the Bulge, the final German counterattack of World War II; he claimed that after Tet the enemy was on its last legs.[74]

The bombing of North Vietnam (even more tonnage fell on the South, Laos, and later Cambodia) revealed the entrapment of leaders in the paradigm of World War II. Walt Rostow, a major proponent of bombing, drew on his experience as an Eighth Air Force targeting officer during that war. The air commanders' effort to strike the North's oil, steel, and electric power industries inaccurately presupposed an economy akin to Germany's or Japan's in 1944, just as the hope to break Hanoi's will presumed political conditions akin to 1945. Such hopes were disputed by some insiders and hedged by others given to cautious rhetoric, but they persisted. As in World War II, once frustration mounted, so too did pressure to erase distinctions between civilian and military objectives: claiming that civilians had left Hanoi and Haiphong (hardly all had), the Joint Chiefs argued in 1968 that "air strikes in and around these cities endanger personnel primarily engaged directly or indirectly in support of the war effort."[75]

Using systems and strategies designed for total war, leaders and strategists thought "that their bombing doctrine suited the nature of the war. In fact, air commanders had molded the war to suit their doctrine." Insofar as World War II was an insufficient model, Cold War crises were an alternative. "The President's advisers," notes one historian, "looked to the example of the Cuban missile crisis, in which they had coerced an enemy far more powerful than North Vietnam into backing down." The comparison was not apt: Cuba was hardly as important to Moscow as South Vietnam was to Hanoi, since both were parts of the same country, and how much Moscow had "backed down" in 1962 was disputable.[76]

Much as in World War II, air power, imbued with magical strength and advanced by powerful bureaucracies, was simply redirected to new targets when old ones proved unyielding. Initial failure to intimidate the North led policymakers to focus on the North's economy or the supply lines over which allies supported it and Hanoi nourished its forces in the South. As in World War II, the American armed forces "aimed to wreck the enemy economy to produce a prostrate foe," but far from limiting the North's imports, "the air campaign fostered their growth. Hanoi's leaders pointed to the bombing to extract greater support from the Chinese and Soviets." As in Korea, aerial interdiction of supply routes imposed high costs on the North but did not stop the flow southward. As the bombing became routinized and components of the navy and air force competed for its spoils, it sometimes became bizarrely counterproductive. On occasion, commanders sent more sorties than necessary because "if you do not fly them, you can make a case that you did not really need that many anyway." As one air force colonel acknowledged, "Bombs or no bombs, you've got to have more Air Force over the target than Navy." That mentality also sent the bombers to the infiltration routes on such a routine schedule that the enemy's trucks would move off the road, sit out the attacks, and then resume their travels unharmed. While old propeller aircraft were often more effective for missions in the South, the air force insisted on using, and thereby justifying, its big B-52s and jet fighters.[77]

Critics later saw the bombing as crippled by Johnson's meticulous oversight of it and his fear that unleashing it risked war with China or the Soviet Union. In substance if not degree, however, oversight was hardly new. Even in World War II, with all wraps presumably off, civilian leaders ruled places like Rome and Kyoto out of bounds for the bombers. Defeat in Vietnam simply made restrictions controversial that had seemed uneventful in a victorious war, just as many of this war's follies were not unique to it, only uniquely exposed by it. In any event, White House restraints soon relaxed—"The penchant of niggling officials in Washington for quibbling over B-52 bomb targets had passed," Westmoreland later admitted, and Johnson and McNamara "afforded me marked independence in how I ran the war within the borders of South Vietnam," the limits of his authority. The "air chiefs' conviction that they would have gained victory had Johnson given them a free hand," one historian sympathetic to their cause bluntly concluded, "lacked substance." American bombing did escalate in a gradual fashion that diluted its shock value, but so had bombing in victorious American wars, and there is no evidence that sharper escalation would have made Hanoi a submissive negotiator.[78]

More likely, bombing the North was destined to have limited utility, and its monumental scale was a bigger problem than any restraint. The bombing antagonized world opinion while achieving limited effect, and did so at great cost in American planes, money, and lives; in 1967 alone, over 300 aircraft were lost in operations against the North, and Hanoi seized hundreds of American POWs whose fate enticed the Nixon administration into prolonging the war. Nor was a crippling restraint evident to the North: the American-estimated death toll of 52,000 civilians among 18 million North Vietnamese during the 1965–1968 bombing proportionately was little less than civilian losses in Germany and Japan during World War II. Those deaths were not evidence of genocide, insofar as they failed the test of intentionality usually accorded that term (perversely, America's destruction of its nominal ally, South Vietnam, more plausibly met that test). Nor, however, were they evidence of severe scruples in the White House. But scruples measured by what standards? Like much else, the hawks' critique of limits on the bombing indicated their dependence on World War II as the standard of measurement, one that dictated total aerial war, including use of nuclear weapons—the weapon of choice in 1945—as was advocated increasingly after 1965 (by Westmoreland, among others).

More than any other facet of the war effort, the bombing also divided Americans, prompting both stern opposition and sharp pressure to escalate it. When Operation Rolling Thunder began in 1965, mail to the White House ran against it, senators criticized it, and campus teach-ins sprung up to protest it. There was as yet none of the violence and little of the turmoil over the war that were to come. In May, Secretary of State Dean Rusk could speak to the Soviet ambassador dismissively of the "very small domestic pressure" against administration policy, in part because he wanted to trivialize that pressure.[79] Still, the portents were ominous.

Why the bombing triggered more controversy in 1965 than the dispatch of ground forces may seem puzzling; the air war, waged by volunteers, carried few obvious risks of entangling conscripts in battle. But escalation of the ground war was less sudden, and it was shrouded in obfuscation impossible in handling the air war—that was too noisy an affair to keep quiet, and since its purpose was to send signals, it had to be trumpeted loudly. In turn, its advent alerted many Americans, especially those skeptical of its efficacy, that a major ground war might follow. It also tapped deep fears about war. However grisly, a ground war had too little technological dazzle to trigger doomsday nightmares, but air war did, especially since it featured bombers originally designed to wage nuclear war.

Moreover, the air war in 1965 clashed with Johnson's reassuring words about it. While stressing the "great stakes in the balance" and his willingness to do "everything necessary" to protect South Vietnam, Johnson denied that the bombing involved any "change of purpose," hoped only "to slow down the aggression" and "convince" Hanoi of American resolve, admitted that "air attacks alone will not accomplish all of these purposes," and reiterated his desire for peace. His cautious words seemed out of step with a choice of weaponry associated with Armageddon.[80]

LBJ was of course trying to dampen the passions war arouses. As he commented in 1967, "If history indicts us for Vietnam, I think it will be for fighting a war without trying to stir up patriotism." It was a disingenuous posture, overlooking his administration's efforts (often covert or illegal) to shape opinion on the war, and implying manly self-restraint when, as Johnson sensed, he was unable to "stir up patriotism" even if he tried. In any event, war stirred passion whatever his wishes, and LBJ himself oozed passion from every pore. All he could do was plead immoderately for moderation, passionately declaiming the virtues of dispassion. No wonder Americans were confused.[81]

Their confusion was evident in the jumbled alignments of public opinion at mid-decade. It was not just that Americans divided, but that they did so in ways that defied categorization. Experts and ordinary citizens tried to impose clarity on those divisions—binary classifications of hawk versus dove, Right versus Left, conservative versus radical, and old versus young were common-

place by the late 1960s—and to find a trajectory in them, above all swelling opposition to the war.

While not without merit, those efforts failed to capture how familiar lines
dividing public opinion had become badly scrambled. Both opposition to *and*
support for the war grew in 1966 and 1967. Moreover, opposition embraced
disparate outlooks—a hard core opposing the war on any terms, others of a
fish-or-cut-bait mentality ("Win or get out," one congressman advised Johnson
in early 1966), and elite skeptics on the war like diplomats George Ball and
George Kennan who had only contempt for angry young leftists, "those per-
verted and willful and stony-hearted youth," as Kennan called them. Despite
stereotypes, "youth" took no unitary turn against the war, but like other Americans divided along complex lines of region, race, religion, and class. Ideological
divisions were also confusing. In Berkeley in 1966, opposition to the draft
"drew support from the Right" as well as the Left, both accommodating "each
other to make bitter and angry attacks against the liberal, anti-communist government they believed oppressed them." In rhetoric, too, the war produced
strange affinities: while some Americans were willing to destroy Vietnam in
order to save it, some radicals at Berkeley were proclaiming, "We've got to start
over and wreck everything before we can save it."[82]

There were, of course, patterns in this maelstrom—the challenge from many
directions to liberal anticommunism—but those patterns were not always
clear, conclusive, or the most important. Liberal anticommunism bore the
brunt of attack because its exponents were in power, but other bastions of ideology were also challenged. Goldwater conservatism remained shattered by the
1964 election, while new forms of conservatism (with which Goldwater was
not always sympathetic) took shape. The attack on accepted norms of sex, gender, and culture—most associated with an emerging "counterculture" but
hardly confined to it—had no single target, riling liberal anticommunists as
well as conservative defenders of family and patriarchal authority. Contagious
as it was, the challenge to authority racked the challengers themselves. Leftist
radicals trained their sights on "the establishment"—the entrenched machinery of racism, imperialism, militarism, and corporate capitalism—but also met
rebellion in their own ranks. So confusing were these patterns that by the late
1960s American society seemed "to be unraveling," notes historian William
Rorabaugh, but in fact "it was only centralized authority that was in decline. At
the local level, those on the bottom saw less a disintegration of society than a
rebirth of community spirit and individual liberty in opposition to a corrupt,
bureaucratic social order."[83] Though most associated with leftist radicalism,
that sense of rebirth swayed movements on the right as well.

Why did the war unleash such diverse reactions? Although often emphasized, failure to win the war was only one catalyst to the convulsions. Certainly
defeat in war was shattering to many Americans—it seemed to defy their his-

tory, to mock decades of mighty expenditures in behalf of military power, and to be doubly galling coming at the hands of a nonwhite, technologically inferior opponent. Defeat was not the only factor, however, since Americans' divisions emerged before defeat seemed certain and in some ways were declining by 1975, when defeat became final.

Americans divided over the Vietnam War for many reasons. Most obviously, national leaders never persuasively defined the American interests or ideals at stake in the Vietnam War, meeting problems evident on a lesser scale in the Korean War. At the time, their inability often seemed due to particular problems, like LBJ's famous "credibility gap." The failure to explain the war continued under three Presidents from two political parties and despite sharp changes in military strategy, however, which suggests that the war defied any convincing rationale, as many leading Cold Warriors indeed concluded by 1968.

The convulsions set loose by the war were also responses to a quarter-century's militarization, and to aspirations and anxieties long suppressed by it. As Godfrey Hodgson later argued, "The war became the organizing principle around which all the doubts and disillusionments of the years of crisis since 1963, and all the deeper discontents hidden under the glossy surface of the confident years, coalesced into great rebellion."[84] The war was hardly the sole cause of those discontents—the troubled state of race relations, for example, preceded Johnson's escalation—but to many of its opponents the war revealed how the same evil system lurked behind disparate ills in American life.

Most of all, America's war in Vietnam violated the tacit bargain which supported the nation's militarization after 1945. Militarization had been tolerated as long as it had seemed congruent with affluence and progress at home, and on the promise that the possession and display of American power, not its actual use, would largely suffice. The Korean War had both sealed that bargain and nearly upset it. Vietnam destroyed it by weakening the American economy, by jeopardizing reform at home, and by showing that the mere display of power would not suffice.

Militarization shaped not only the nature of reactions to the Vietnam War but the language used to express them. Any war produces superheated rhetoric, but political rhetoric had long been militarized for Americans in their age of perpetual crisis, all the more so as Johnson escalated his wars on various social and economic ills. With war now an indefinably broad phenomenon and its language now used to diverse purposes, it was perhaps inevitable that the divisions aggravated by the war—over race and poverty, gender and culture, and the war itself—would be expressed in war's rhetoric. Hence Johnson saw traitors and enemies, black militants foresaw revolutionary war, radical opponents of the war saw a fascist "Amerika," and many Americans felt they were plunging into a war at home. "For ten years," explains one historian, "Americans waged over Vietnam a war by metaphor for the sake of symbols of meaning to themselves."[85] That "war by metaphor" did not cause divisions among Americans, but it made them more unbridgeable, the stakes in them more absolute.

Although the "war by metaphor" raged in dispersed and localized forms, by 1966 its eruptions were evident in national politics. The Senate Foreign Relations Committee's televised hearings on the war were one sign. Oddly enough for the man in charge of foreign policy, Secretary of State Dean Rusk saw the United States as losing control of its destiny: it was in a war "where the initiative is not ours, where we did not start it, and where we didn't want it to begin with"—and where defeat meant the rollback of American power everywhere. In contrast, Senator Fulbright expressed confidence in American power. He doubted that "if we should make a compromise, then all the world will collapse because we have been defeated. This country is much too strong . . . that it would suffer any great setback." Others attacked the official claim that Hanoi was waging war across an international boundary. Vietnam was a civil and revolutionary war, maintained Sen. Frank Church, who could not "remember many revolutions that have been fought in splendid isolation. There were as many Frenchmen at Yorktown when Cornwallis surrendered as there were American Continentals." Two widely admired retired generals, James Gavin and Matthew Ridgway, criticized escalation in the American effort, though not its purposes. Former Marine Corps Commandant David Shoup soon went further. Steeped in a pre–World War II tradition of antimilitarism and anti-imperialism (the latter sometimes couched in racist terms), Shoup urged American withdrawal and excoriated the armed forces and the nation for embracing "our militaristic culture." As publication of Fulbright's *The Arrogance of Power* indicated, 1966 was the year when the solidarity of political elites on the war began to dissolve.[86]

The political agenda of black Americans also crossed the threshold that year. King, a pacifist long opposed to the Vietnam War, now sharpened his critique. On April 4, 1967, he lamented how the struggle against racism and poverty had been "broken and eviscerated as if it were some idle plaything of a society gone mad on war." "We were," he recounted his thoughts, "taking the black young men who had been crippled by our society and sending them 8,000 miles away to guarantee liberties in Southeast Asia which they had not found in Southwestern Georgia and East Harlem." He feared that war abroad sanctioned war at home by armed black men who "asked if our own nation wasn't using massive doses of violence to solve its problems." By then too, King and others, like leaders of the Student Nonviolent Coordinating Committee, were supporting resistance to the draft—a major challenge, given the military's dependence on recruiting and conscripting black men. On occasion King still wrested leverage from Cold War hypocrisies: "Nothing provides the Communists with a better climate for expansion and infiltration," he warned, "than the continued alliance of our nation with racism and exploitation throughout the world." Anything African-Americans might gain from such leverage, however, paled for him in comparison to the war's costs for Americans and Vietnamese. "Somehow this madness must cease." Though often regarded as "black" rather than "antiwar" leaders, figures like King were a key element in a growing, chaotic resistance which also included pacifists, many in the old Left, and radical students.[87]

The faultlines among Americans also extended beyond issues of the war itself. The establishment in 1966 of the National Organization of Women and a more militant gay rights movement indicated widening divisions over gender and sexual preference. These groups sometimes drew on the contagious example set by the antiwar and civil rights movements, but they also showed more complex relationships to the war's politics. Just as one woman complained in 1964 that a female in the Student Nonviolent Coordinating Committee "is often in the same position as that token Negro hired in a corporation," women in the antiwar movement found their political and sexual subservience to male leadership galling. Though women had long had a major role in antiwar organizing, mounting male resistance to the Vietnam War tended to squeeze them out; by 1965, one man later observed, "women made peanut butter, waited on tables, cleaned up, got laid. That was their role." By 1967, gender issues split the antiwar movement, though not always along simple male-female lines. "Caught up in outrage about the war and empathizing with their male friends," many women, like most men in the movement, "perceived 'women's issues' as secondary, selfish, divisive, and threatening."[88]

An emerging critique of scientific expertise gave intellectual ballast to various challenges to authority, linking them to older doubts about militarization. *Science and Survival* (1966), by Washington University botanist Barry Commoner, moved him from his earlier antinuclear activism into a larger environmental crusade. Citing the sensational electric power blackout of the Northeast in November 1965, he asked, "Is science getting out of hand?" The affirmative answer emerged in his discussion of the "greenhouse effect" and the consequences of a nuclear war. Commoner implied that what endangered national security was no longer America's enemies but the very means used to uphold it. The warning was all the more telling for its somber caution. No sensational diatribe, it came from a scientist who saw "the enormous benefits" bestowed by science as well as "its frightful threats," the knowledge of which was generating "political crisis." "Science can reveal the depth of this crisis, but only social action can resolve it."[89]

More famous intellectuals were already calling for such action. The poet Robert Lowell led them by his public refusal to attend the White House Festival of the Arts in June 1965, where John Hersey protested the bombing by reading excerpts from *Hiroshima*. Over the next few years, writers like Norman Mailer, Susan Sontag, Dwight Macdonald, Hannah Arendt, and linguist Noam Chomsky argued, as their views have been summarized, that "America appeared to be in the hands of a technological elite that was debauching the

American landscape and lusting after world dominion." Some even endorsed armed resistance to the elite: "Morality, like politics, starts at the barrel of a gun," ran Andrew Kopkind's controversial observation in 1967. To many leftist critics, even questions about why the United States was losing the war were infuriating, insofar as they implied validity to the American cause or an American destiny to win wars.[90]

A sustained assault on militarization by intellectuals was slower to emerge. Moral outrage, focused on evil leaders and immediate dangers, precluded systematic analysis among most intellectuals, who often still gave militarization short shrift. The "military-industrial complex is not one but many complexes," wrote Grant McConnell, seeming to diminish its power, just as he dismissively characterized "preoccupation with war" as "one of the unpleasant realities of government." Historian Christopher Lasch, a leading radical critic, also said little about militarization, focusing instead on flaws in the American intellectual tradition; preoccupation with their own sins was one reason intellectuals were slow to engage militarization. Scholars of a Marxist bent were readier to tackle it head on. American militarization, they argued, flowed from the need to absorb surplus capital and the American oligarchy's "implacable hatred of socialism," and it enjoyed "majestic unity" in Congress despite Eisenhower's "poignant Farewell Address." But Marxists' explanations were not always supple, certainly not the assertion that "a socialist society contains no class or group which, like the big capitalists of the imperialist countries, stands to gain from a policy of subjugating other nations and peoples." And their claims were not widely persuasive among younger leftists. Meanwhile, most liberal intellectuals were wary of seeing systemic failure at work in the war. They either reluctantly embraced the war or saw it as a tragic mistake born of outdated assumptions about a monolithic communist enemy, though Fulbright, a bellwether of the emerging liberal critique, saw a more fundamental imperial arrogance at work. On the whole, intellectuals' examinations of militarization were more the product of Vietnam-era crisis than its catalyst.[91]

Still, diverse forms of ferment were strikingly evident by 1966. At the same time, the structural underpinnings of American militarization were eroding, although such erosion was slow and less evident at the time. The bipolar international system, once dominated by Washington and Moscow, further splintered. Not only was Sino-Soviet rivalry now unmistakable, the Western bloc was also fraying. DeGaulle withdrew French military forces from NATO and the Vietnam War taxed the Western alliance: European leaders resented American demands for their support of a losing venture (as they saw it) and the fact that the war distracted Washington from attending to Europe's needs.

Those frictions, their importance often exaggerated at the time by American leaders, were survivable. More troublesome were economic changes. Prosperity, revved up further by war spending, still flowed, although inflation and other effects of the war hit some sectors like the housing industry. Long-term trends were more ominous. Most Western industrial nations passed the United States in the 1960s in growth rates for personal incomes—as did a few, by some standards, in absolute income levels—and the United States was sliding toward its first negative trade balance in a century. Motor vehicle production in the United States peaked at mid-decade, then abruptly slid, just when sales in the United States of the Volkswagen Beetle soared and Japanese auto production rose exponentially (exceeding America's by the mid-1970s).

Such shifts, barely evident in 1966 and hardly traceable only to militarization, had little immediate political effect. They nonetheless jeopardized the tacit bargain by which Americans accepted militarization in return for the affluence it presumably engendered. The regional foundation of that bargain was also sagging. Defense dollars had long flowed heavily to the "gunbelt" (coastal New England and the South, and the Far West). "Vietnam, unlike Korea, did not reverse this shift in the center of gravity," and mammoth spending on the space race aggravated it.[92] World War II and Korea had showered their economic benefits widely. Because the Vietnam War did not, it aggravated regional rivalries over the wisdom and distribution of defense spending—it was not entirely coincidental that many leading antiwar congressmen came from states which sent their sons off to war and got few dollars back.

There was, of course, no guarantee that the war's baleful effects would foster a broad challenge to militarization itself. Those effects led some to redouble the effort to win the war: victory would erase the pain. Others saw the war as the warped product of a fundamentally healthy system, which might be restored once the wound of the war was cauterized. Especially for some worried military officers, rapid extrication from Vietnam was a way to preserve the militarized system, not the first step in dismantling it. Still, even those positions opened the door to deeper inquiry about America's course in a militarized age.

Was 1966, then, the watershed year of the Vietnam War and the age of militarization? It was in 1968, after all, that American forces in Vietnam neared their peak of over a half-million personnel; that reactions to the Tet Offensive forced America's slow retreat from Vietnam to begin; that Johnson shrank from running for reelection; that assassinations and police violence troubled so many Americans. Such dramatic signposts were lacking in 1966.

Perhaps the whole Vietnam era lacked such signposts. World War II had had December 7, D-Day, V-E Day, and V-J Day. No single day marked the Vietnam War; even 1968 embraced a confusing rush of events rather than a single commanding moment. Indeed, what marked the era was a seeming *loss* of the defining moment, and therefore of a well-anchored, widely shared sense of history itself. At least since Pearl Harbor, Americans plausibly had seen themselves as undergoing common, national experiences reflected in a uniform media and political culture. But after the mid-1960s, common experiences seemed to bear down on different groups on no common timetable, as the war and the struggles over it washed unevenly over the United States. Further distorting these matters was the tendency later to consign to "the sixties" all sorts of turmoil that spilled over into the 1970s or only began then.

The dissolution of a uniform sense of history was due not to some inexplicable fragmentation but to the nature of the Vietnam War and its conduct by American leaders. The war lacked the precise start and end that, at least in retrospect, marked World War II and Korea. National leaders, far from announcing a moment when the war began, minimized the importance of each step into it and declined to crank up a conspicuous machinery to mobilize opinion, lest spotlighting the war arouse passions that would trap them. Conscription brought the war home to Americans in a far more gradual and uneven fashion than it had in World War II, coming initially to middling Americans, while affluent youth mobilized first against the war and agitation against it reached high-school-age youth only in its last years. On college campuses, some schools were already racked by turmoil in 1966 (and some of those almost placid by 1972), while others only became convulsed at decade's end. A limited, gradually escalating war also lacked the abrupt economic effects evident in 1941 and 1950 and the impact made possible earlier by rationing and wage and price controls. All wars affect various groups differently, but in the Vietnam War those differential impacts were spread out over time as well.

Of course, there is no definitive way to identify a "watershed" in history, in part because one group's watershed may be another's uneventful year, but in this cluttered decade, 1966 was the dividing point as much as any other year. By then, the American war effort was near its peak, the divisions over it were evident, the structures underpinning militarization were eroding, and—though surely this is the most elusive standard to apply—an ordered, agreed-upon sense of history was already in tatters.

PART TWO

THE RESHAPING OF AMERICAN MILITARIZATION

THE WAR MENTALITY IN TRIUMPH, 1966–1974

Turning Point

"Bomb, bomb, bomb, that's all you know," LBJ reportedly exploded to the Joint Chiefs on one occasion.[1] The American bombing in Southeast Asia, like the intensifying American war effort generally, both hastened and obscured a turning point in America's militarization as important as the one on the eve of World War II.

The outcome of this one was more ambiguous, however. In its quantifiable forms—the size of budgets and armies, the geographical reach of American power—militarization did abate somewhat, albeit too little for its critics and too much for its champions. In its subtler manifestations—the hold that war had on the politics and imaginations of Americans—it continued to swell, in a fashion that few denounced, defended, or even recognized. Richard Nixon, seeing countless enemies at home to attack and many wars on them to wage, did not alone cause that inward turn, but, even more than Johnson, he abetted it, exinpressed it, even embodied it.

The American Way of War

No one operation typified the diverse war in Vietnam, but the engagements around Dak To late in 1967 illustrated the war Gen. William Westmoreland wanted. When a defector from the North Vietnamese Army (NVA) revealed plans to attack a U.S. Special Forces camp, Westmoreland seized on the information, pouring in American and ARVN forces. "Engineers dynamited the tops off a dozen mountains to build level artillery platforms, and chemical units bathed the steep slopes with herbicides to strip the foliage." Under aerial and artillery assault, "the green jungle canopy trembled, split open, and finally hung in blackened tatters." It was "the closest thing to Big War that Westmoreland could devise." The fighting killed 287 Americans, but with a count of 1,200 enemy dead, the U.S. Army proclaimed an "overwhelming success." There were skeptics on Westmoreland's staff, however, and one journalist pointed to the problem soon exposed in the Tet Offensive: "The NVA is sucking large American forces away from population centers and bogging them down in . . . mountain fighting."[2]

Westmoreland waged war this way because of the American strategic tradition he inherited and the immediate pressures he faced: Johnson's fondness for massive governmental effort and managerial liberals' faith in technique; conservatives' demands for vigorous war making and the military's distrust of counterinsurgency tactics. All these pressures encouraged reliance on awesome firepower, aerial mobility, and big-scale organization. So too did a home-front aversion to casualties that had long shaped the American way of war and was sharpened by the murky American stakes in this war. Whatever his defects, Westmoreland skillfully translated these pressures into action. While there was little consensus about how to wage the war (there rarely has been, even in America's victorious wars), he found the middle ground where various views of strategy converged—just what a general deferential to civil authority in a democracy should do.

But he was no mere cipher through which various pressures passed unmediated. Within South Vietnam's borders, he had exceptional freedom to shape the war. Neither his predecessor nor his successor fully shared his emphasis on search-and-destroy operations. A product of the Harvard Graduate Business School as well as West Point, and a veteran of World War II, Westmoreland was unusually attuned, even for the army at this point in its history, to war's logistics and management. He was not unreflective about strategy (he read the classic texts on guerrilla warfare and France's failure in Vietnam), but he treated it unimaginatively, as another aspect of war to be managed, just as he gave dissenting views in his staff his dutiful but unimaginative attention. Westmoreland put his imprint on American war making by reflecting its basic impulses so faithfully and believing in them so deeply.

Massive firepower, extraordinary mobility, and assault on the enemy's main forces were the core of his war making. For him, one reporter observed, "killing sixteen-year-old guerrillas two or three at a time on the mud paths of tiny hamlets was penny ante stuff for an Army prepared to do battle with the legions of Lenin." As one architect of his strategy put it, "The solution in Vietnam is more bombs, more shells, more napalm . . . till the other side cracks and gives up." His emphasis on organization and technology extended far beyond the battlefield. He worked hard to provide the best in medical care and recreational facilities for American forces, acres of air-conditioned space to escape the oppressive climate, and a cornucopia of fresh and frozen foods. Added to the crushing volume of munitions and other war materiel hauled into Vietnam, this constituted the most impressive logistical achievement in the annals of American war making. He also found novel uses for American technology. Old C-47 cargo planes (military versions of the DC-3) were retrofitted with murderous electric

Gatling guns. "Westmoreland even haunted the dreams of enemy soldiers with airborne tape recordings of children crying for their fathers, and the ineffably mournful songs of Vietnamese war widows."[3]

Most modern military forces covet the latest and most in firepower and logistics. France, with American help, made no mean effort in that regard fifteen years earlier, and the NVA, aided by China and the Soviet Union, deployed tanks in the South and surface-to-air missiles in the North. The difference was that Americans possessed such things in overwhelming numbers, counted on them more to bring victory, and ignored almost everything else. "If victory would be inevitably produced through technological warfare, then even learning about Vietnamese history, culture, and social structure did not seem worthwhile to the war-managers," notes James Gibson.[4]

Nor was the firepower all for naught, at least by Westmoreland's standards. Hanoi had not anticipated its huge losses, estimated (probably on the high side) by American officials at up to 220,000 by late 1967, compared to 13,000 American dead by that year (ARVN losses ran higher). That fall, Westmoreland issued his famous comment that "the end begins to come into view" and "the enemy's hopes are bankrupt" (though Johnson had rejected most of his demands to increase the American effort).[5] Westmoreland hedged his bets, however: if his plan for victory fell short, he wanted to invade the North and use nuclear weapons against it.

His strategy staved off defeat but did not bring victory, above all because there was no real South Vietnam to defend. By 1967, Johnson and Defense Secretary McNamara sensed the possibility of defeat. Out of desperation, but also to disarm his critics, Johnson continued a familiar ritual of bombing halts, professions of willingness to negotiate, and secret feelers to that end, but the diplomatic efforts were half-hearted at best, deceptive at worst. Both sides gave a little, but it made no difference because neither would forsake its basic objective—the stumbling block that liberal doves ignored in piously calling for diplomacy, and that radical foes of the war acknowledged in their willingness to see Hanoi triumph.

Johnson was not going to be the first American President to lose a war, he made clear. "Why not, he never said, nor did the American people ask," Stephen Ambrose has pointed out. "Doves and hawks alike accepted Johnson's simpleminded proposition as if the logic behind it were obvious. Never did American hubris show itself more clearly, or more destructively."[6] Perhaps more than hubris was at work. LBJ's proposition rested on a deeper, unstated logic. War provided the rationale and impetus for the modern American state and most of what it accomplished. Defeat in war jeopardized not just American interests and LBJ's fortunes but the promise of successful collective action by Americans. If they could not win a war, what else might they be unable to accomplish?

Few Americans would peer into that abyss, and many continued to press

Johnson to achieve victory. Less imaginative than the doves, the hawks were nonetheless more homogeneous, better attuned to dominant American values, and led by a formidable politician, Richard Nixon. Nixon had seemed to take himself out of politics when he told the press after his 1962 defeat for California's governorship, "You won't have Nixon to kick around anymore," but in fact he "had just made the press an issue" in ways that resonated throughout the rest of his career and the Vietnam War. Nixon criticized Kennedy for his handling of the Cuban missile crisis and by 1964 was urging war directly against North Vietnam, but at bottom his views on Vietnam differed little from Johnson's. He warned against trying to "reach an agreement with our adversaries—as Chamberlain reached an agreement with Hitler at Munich in 1938." For him too, Vietnam lay in the mystical realm of resolve and perception; it was a test of our "will to win—and the courage to use our power—*now*." But he kept a step ahead of LBJ, his criticisms uncannily anticipating what Johnson would soon do. "When Nixon said, in 1969, that he had inherited a war not of his making, he was being too modest," since he had "spurred Johnson to ever greater involvement in Vietnam" and made it clear that the GOP "would never criticize Johnson for doing more in Vietnam" (though, being Nixon, he criticized nonetheless). Meanwhile, he adroitly threaded his way through the minefield of GOP politics, supporting Goldwater in 1964, then outflanking Nelson Rockefeller and Ronald Reagan to secure the 1968 presidential nomination.[7]

Nixon's contribution to the war went beyond his pressure on Johnson to escalate. He also helped shape the ugly politics at home about the war, often publicly uttering what LBJ felt he had to keep private as President. Since American "will" was at issue, Nixon lashed out at dissenters who undermined it. The United States "is at war," he argued in 1965, and "if anyone had welcomed a Nazi victory during World War II there would have been no question what to do." Negotiating with the enemy "would be like negotiating with Hitler before the German armies had been driven from France." Fulbright and other dissenters were "appeasers" whose course would lead to World War III in "four or five years."[8]

In analogizing Vietnam to World War II, Nixon was in step with political culture generally. (Scholars opposing the war insisted that they "would not be like the silent professors in Nazi Germany who did not criticize Hitler's aggressive foreign policy," while others condemned America's "fascist state.") Both Johnson and Nixon also resisted the logic of the analogy: to declare war. World War II was their touchstone—except when it seemed politically dangerous. It was all inconsistent and dangerous, setting up hopes for total war and total victory when they did not want the former, did not expect the latter, and had no real plan for either. By 1967, LBJ had thrown into the war almost everything Nixon had demanded, but to little avail. "These results might well have prompted Nixon to think through the whole situation again, but there is no evidence that he ever did so." Both continued the analogies to World War II, which worked for them and their supporters because they were so automatic and thought-less.[9]

But what category did capture this war? The most common one was bland and generic: Vietnam was a "limited war." That label stuck even as the war continued to escalate. While the American death toll in Vietnam was far less than in World War II, it eventually exceeded fifty-eight thousand, more than in Korea and almost half the American toll in World War I. Measured by the feroc-ity of the fighting, the American bombing (which by 1967 exceeded all that American forces had let loose in World War II), the destruction to the land, and the casualties among Indochinese, there was nothing limited about the war. As the notion of "limited" war persisted while the war intensified, most Ameri-cans lacked a realistic way to categorize this war, much less grasp the issues behind it. They were not so much polarized by the war as simply perplexed by it (something harder for pollsters to measure). Never had an American war been so hard to conceptualize.

Many, LBJ and Nixon in the first rank, blamed the media for Americans' con-fusion and perplexity. War coverage indeed was remarkably uncensored and sometimes stunningly quick and vivid. Angry politicians, frustrated generals, and bewildered patriots attacked it for undermining popular commitment to the war by exaggerating its ugliness, its futility, and its unpopularity. That view swelled after the Tet Offensive and remained into the 1990s a staple in popular mythology (students still enter college believing it, much as many still wonder if FDR knew in advance about Japan's attack at Pearl Harbor). "The war was literally piped into the living room, bedroom, and kitchen of most Americans," a retired officer later argued; the "constant force of destruction, suffering, and blood brought into American living rooms horrified and dismayed the Ameri-can people." By showing "the terrible human suffering and sacrifice of war," Nixon later wrote, television caused "a serious demoralization of the home front." This war was no more brutal than others, the argument ran, but the me-dia led Americans to think otherwise.[10]

That charge reflected Americans' self-flattering penchant for making history pivot on technological change, but little in the media's ability to cover war had changed since World War II, when it presumably had mobilized Americans be-hind war. That war had been superbly and systematically photographed and filmed by all parties, in graphic color near its end. Television only made images available more quickly—although the process still often took days, since film usually had to be flown out of Vietnam for transmission and editing—and placed them in living rooms instead of movie houses, while its cumbersome technology was probably less mobile in the field than the newsreel version of 1944. There was no compelling evidence that marginal gains in the speed and privacy with which Americans viewed these images greatly changed how they perceived war.

Even the content of those images probably swayed few Americans against the war, according to the army's historian of the issue. Opinion about the war was shaped by many factors and correlated poorly with exposure to media coverage, which most Americans took as confirmation of whatever views they already had. Fewer than half of American households even tuned in regularly to network newscasts, while the most damning commentary on the war generally emerged in obscure or elite publications, as with Jonathan Schell's coverage for the *New Yorker*. Constrained by military rules, by fear of offending political officials and public tastes, and by the threat of losing audiences to their competition, network executives were loathe to show violent scenes or (as in coverage of World War II) pictures of American dead. "In fact, the action scenes from any episode of the popular television dramas 'Gunsmoke' and 'Kojak' . . . were probably more brutal than all but a few of the most explicit films from Vietnam." By contrast, despite censorship in World War II, "*Life*'s impact could be shattering," impressing "the horrors of war" especially on the young, while the decline of still-photo journalism after World War II deprived Americans of arguably more searing images. The Vietnam-era image often cited as most shocking appeared in 1968, showing South Vietnam's National Police chief executing an apparent civilian (in fact a Viet Cong who allegedly had shot one of the chief's relatives) with a pistol on the streets of Saigon. Even then, film editors cut the footage before it showed blood spurting from the victim's head.[11]

Such images were vividly received and remembered precisely because they were so atypical—they leapt out from the generally bland and careful record of the war offered Americans. And, in tune with journalistic conventions, the controversial images generally featured individual tragedies or brutalities, conveying little of the war's scale and carnage. The bombing, tool of the war's greatest destruction, probably received less visual coverage than in World War II: Hanoi was almost as off-limits to journalists as Berlin had been; the bombing of Laos under Johnson and of Cambodia under Nixon was long kept secret; and the victims' view of bombing inherently resists close visual coverage. The bombing in South Vietnam was more accessible—but then, despite the bombs unloaded by both sides on occupied allies, nothing in World War II compared to the torrent poured down on America's ally in the Vietnam War.

Journalists had their peculiarities and their product had its flaws. They were often a cynical lot, though so too were earlier war correspondents. Moreover, for them, or at least their editors and producers, "it was an American war," and they poorly presented the perspectives of Indochinese and the war's impact on them. The media did give attention to the antiwar opposition, but its images of radical, foul-mouthed, long-haired protesters did as much to alienate Americans from the antiwar movement as to make it respectable. Indeed, the war's opponents had a strong case that the media maligned *their* cause. Long reflecting the official view of the war, press coverage did become more pessimistic after the Tet Offensive, but that shift followed more than led public opinion and emerged "not because television news producers had made some arbitrary decision to promote the opposition but because the sources in government they had cued to for news had begun to switch sides." Divisions among political and business elites, not just unruly mobs in the streets, accounted for the tilt, just as elite threats and other factors led many journalists to shy away from negative assessments of the war in the Nixon years.[12]

If news coverage undermined commitment to the war at all, it did so unintentionally, through method rather than content, by numbing more often than infuriating Americans. As in other wars, routine official briefings got turned into purple prose ("Hurtling out of an overcast sky, warplanes of the United States Seventh Fleet delivered another massive air strike against the port city of Haiphong"). Reporters and editors still imparted a linear pattern to war—"a consecutive, activist, piecemeal, the next-day-the-First-Army-forged-onward-toward-Aachen approach to a war that even the journalists covering it know to be non-consecutive, non-activist," observed Michael Arlen. Such journalistic conventions had angered many soldiers, reporters, and citizens even in World War II. Coverage of the Vietnam War, Arlen speculated, gave a citizen—"after three years in which he has read 725,000 words about Vietnam—the feeling that he couldn't write three intelligible sentences about the subject on a postcard to his mother."[13] The war's grisly images and pointed critiques stood out because they disrupted the prevailing sense of *disconnection* from the war's "realities." The "living room war" did not banish war's elusiveness, but only reflected it.

That elusiveness derived from the nature of the war itself—thousands of miles away, with right and wrong hard to ascertain, with climactic battles few and front lines almost nil. It was also constructed out of the policies of dominant authorities and the moods of the American people. Leaders could not articulate the stakes and did not want the debate over a declaration of war that might have sharpened various meanings to the war. They disguised or dissembled about many aspects of the American war effort, less to deceive the enemy than to disarm the American people, until under Nixon whole theaters of combat were kept secret even from many top officials. The media rarely challenged such attitudes and practices. Most other Americans—blessed with prosperity, taught to fear nuclear cataclysm, deceived by their leaders, uninterested in distant peoples—were neither able nor inclined to grasp this war. Even the war's opposition trained its sights largely on the immorality of American leaders or the futility of their policies—an understandable focus that still tended to push the combat and politics in Indochina to the margins. By the same token, defenders of the war like Johnson and Nixon worked harder at discrediting their opposition at home than at making the war comprehensible to Americans. No wonder that the war in Vietnam and the nation's ways of waging it emerged only slowly to them.

The Tet Offensive and the reactions it generated parted the clouds of confusion, if only briefly. The communist offensive erupted at the end of January

1968, after Westmoreland's reassuring words about progress and after he pulled American forces away from populated areas in the South in his quest for decisive battle. Communists struck in Saigon—even blasting the American embassy—and all over the South. The bloodiest phases occurred at the American bastion at Khe Sanh, where the combat seemed like a throwback to trench warfare in World War I, and in Hue, the large and lovely city where communists executed thousands of local citizens. As at Hue, American and ARVN forces successfully resisted or reversed most of the enemy attacks, inflicting huge losses on NVA and Viet Cong forces, but the cost included eleven hundred American dead, twice as many ARVN forces, and much else. "What the hell is going on?" asked CBS's Walter Cronkite. "I thought we were winning the war!" One officer's comment upon recapturing one town—"We had to destroy the town to save it"—appeared to sum up America's war making all too aptly. Dismay among Americans at home, though hardly universal, mounted, as they confronted not only the difficulties in winning this war but its very nature.[14]

Almost immediately, the contest broke out to define Tet's meaning. Conventional wisdom soon became that Tet marked a military victory for the United States and South Vietnam, but a political defeat because the press and the doves exaggerated communist achievements, missing the chance Tet provided to deliver a final blow to the enemy. Westmoreland and leading hawks argued that view strenuously; later scholars often did so guardedly, agreeing that the media, having long toed the official line, now overracted against it. Even one of Tet's planners later regretted that "we did not correctly assess the concrete balance of forces between ourselves and the enemy."[15]

But the binary categories—victory or defeat, military or psychological—were inadequate to explain Tet's meaning. The efforts of all sides to impose them reflected exasperation with the war rather than the outcome in Vietnam. Like many battles in war, Tet marked no clear turn in the military struggle. Whatever their later views, the American military chiefs conveyed uncertainty at the time, at once promising that increased efforts would bring victory while hinting at defeat without them. General Earle Wheeler was closer to the mark when he acknowledged that Tet was a "very near thing."[16]

The distinction between "military" and "political" was equally suspect, as if the two categories were unrelated to each other, which they never are in war. It struck many Americans as deeply unfair that their military victory at Tet did not yield political success, as if the latter had been stolen from them by the war's opponents. Actually, Americans had experience with war's paradoxical terms—Dunkirk in 1940 and the Doolittle Raid against Japan in 1942 were military failures but psychological victories for the Allied cause. The problem in 1968 was the difficulty in seeing any final victory down the line. In any event, the war's defenders should not have been surprised that Tet was read in psychological terms, since they had long justified the American effort for its psychological impact on the enemy (and on allies): to claim now that psychological dimensions should be downplayed ran against their whole presentation of the war.

The communists won at Tet "not by winning any battle but by launching the attack in the first place," Jonathan Schell later pointed out. "The fact that it lost the battle was nothing new—it had lost all the battles of the war since the Americans had arrived," but its ability despite massive American power still to "launch an offensive on the scale of Tet *was* new. . . . It showed that by winning battles we had not been winning the war." Americans "now understood that the war in its present form would probably last indefinitely and possibly expand greatly," and they "had never accepted, or even been asked to accept, such a prospect."[17]

For all the confusion over it, Tet marked a clear if limited turning point in politics, in the war, and in the larger course of militarization. Johnson and his senior advisers—incoming Defense Secretary Clark Clifford and "Wise Men" like Dean Acheson and retired generals Omar Bradley and Matthew Ridgway—rejected Westmoreland's plan to mobilize the reserves, bring two hundred thousand more Americans to Indochina, and sweep into Laos, Cambodia, and North Vietnam. Instead, Johnson recalled Westmoreland (bumping him upstairs to be army chief of staff), questioned search-and-destroy tactics, made a start at what Nixon would call Vietnamization (increased reliance on ARVN forces), and tried another partial halt of bombing against North Vietnam in hopes of inducing negotiations, although the war in the South raged on. American losses in Vietnam, radical protest, and popular disarray at home were factors in his decisions, but critical was the "tremendous erosion of support" (as Clifford put it) among business and other elites, albeit in part because they feared the growing turmoil at home. "The establishment bastards have bailed out," Johnson reportedly fumed.[18]

Administration leaders did not give up on victory—for a time LBJ thought that Tet had strengthened his negotiating hand. But they abandoned further escalation as a means to it (without coming up with any alternative). As a result, they capped and began to reverse the long growth in America's military presence in Asia and the draft calls used to sustain the war effort.

That they had acted to reverse militarization and limit the war effort was hardly clear early in 1968, however, in part because the political landscape was hard to read. Sen. Eugene McCarthy's near defeat of Johnson in New Hampshire's February primary was a case in point. McCarthy was an intelligent if quixotic opponent of the war and the "imperial presidency" which war had nourished, ridiculing LBJ for speaking of "my country" and "my cabinet" and "my troops." The presidency "belongs not to the man who holds it but to the people of this nation."[19] But since he got votes from many hawks exasperated with both the war *and* the antiwar movement, his New Hampshire success had little clear meaning. Johnson's decision, announced on March 31, not to run again for the presidency and to order a bombing halt also did little to indicate a historic reversal of America's course.

Insofar as America began disengaging from militarization, it did so in such a halting way, so bereft of clear and convincing national leadership, amid such confusing cross-currents of public opinion, that disengagement was bound to be limited and contested, with reengagement a possibility. Just as escalation in the war had been incremental and disguised, so now were deescalation and disengagement from militarization. LBJ and his policymakers made no grand pronouncements along those lines—they were too uncertain of their course and too wary of the Joint Chiefs and its political allies to do so. Nothing like FDR's eloquence in launching militarization or Eisenhower's insight into its consequences emerged from Presidents or their chief allies in the late 1960s. Still, by edging away from a familiar path, they made the choice of a different road possible.

Tet was responsible for that uncertain reorientation. Not alone, of course—it came after years of growing inflation, civil disorder at home, casualties abroad, and fatuous promises of success. But Tet set such problems in bolder relief. Too, it was shattering because it was so evidently war in its rawest form, cutting through years of official obfuscation and numbing media coverage. Nothing ever fully dispels war's elusiveness for those not in it (or even for those in it). To many Americans, the Vietnam War soon again seemed incomprehensible or irrelevant. Tet, however, had challenged and disrupted such sensibilities.

The "Wars" at Home

The March on the Pentagon on October 21, 1967, and Norman Mailer's account of it found the antiwar movement at its most outrageous. It was a motley group: long-time pacifists, disaffected liberals like Yale chaplain William Sloane Coffin, New Left revolutionaries, freaked-out hippies. They first assembled at the Lincoln Memorial, then fifty thousand marched on the Pentagon, which a few sought to levitate and others to shut down, at least long enough to show their fury against the war and the vulnerability of its machinery. Only a minority (media and officials exaggerated their numbers) shoved or taunted the defending soldiers and marshals, but many protesters' mood was bellicose. "We're going to try to stick it up the government's ass," Mailer earlier exhorted one crowd, "right into the sphincter of the Pentagon."[20]

They chose the Pentagon—rather than the Congress that funded the war or the White House that directed it—because they saw it as the symbol and capital of "corporation land," as Mailer put it. The Pentagon "looked like a five-sided tip on the spout of a spray can to be used under the arm, yes, the Pentagon was spraying the deodorant of its presence all over the fields of Virginia." Like the rest of militarized America—its soulless corporations and universities—it "was as undifferentiated as a jellyfish or a cluster of barnacles. One could chip away at any part of the interior without locating a nervous center. . . . Every aspect of the building was anonymous, monotonous, massive, interchangeable." In that view, the enemy was corporate-military America, its victims oppressed peoples everywhere. Precisely where it came from in the past and what might replace it in the future were, Mailer suggested, unclear to many young protesters, whose "radicalism was in their hate for the authority" and whose outlook embraced "the idea of a revolution which preceded ideology." Given that diffuse outlook, they fought each other over ideology as bitterly as they fought the enemy, but in October 1967 they knew where to strike.[21]

Demonstrators did not just protest, they went to war, at least in Mailer's sometimes playful view of things. The old notion of a "march" on Washington—the Bonus Army's of 1932 or King's of 1963—always had military connotations, but Mailer, a World War II veteran, meant war itself, not just its trappings. "They were prancing past this hill, they were streaming to battle. Going to battle!" It was, he knew, a rag-tag army, especially with the hippies ("the dress ball was going into battle"). Still, as he meditated on the violence (women especially, Mailer noted, got clubbed by the defending troops), he thought that compared to Valley Forge or Normandy or Pusan, "the engagement at the Pentagon was a pale rite of passage, and yet it was probably a true one" for these "spoiled children of a dead de-animalized middle class." Mailer gave them combat ribbons for serving in "the armies of the night," as he called his account, just as Robert Lowell saw them as "like green Union recruits / for the first Bull Run."[22]

Theirs was another in a series of seeming skirmishes across America in the late 1960s and early 1970s. Racial violence—between blacks and whites, between blacks and police or the armed forces, by blacks in their own neighborhoods—had been erupting for years and reached a new climax in the spring of 1968 following Martin Luther King's assassination, yielding a palpable sense of race war. "Do what John Brown did," the black radical H. Rap Brown advised opponents of imperialism, "pick up a gun and go out and shoot our enemy."[23] More than other social conflicts, this one also overlapped the divisions over the war, since blacks (especially women) opposed or despaired of the war more than other social groups, and black leaders like Martin and Correta Scott King and boxer Muhammad Ali were conspicuous in antiwar protest.

The same year also saw more protest against the war, more violence by some protesters indulging a fantasy of guerrilla war, and (to the approval of many Americans) more violence against them. Even a violent act whose motives were obscure, as with the assassination of Robert Kennedy, seemed connected to the Vietnam War because it added to the general sense of turmoil and because Kennedy was emerging as a critic of the war, foe of LBJ, and possible Democratic nominee for the presidency. These cross-currents came to a head at the Democratic convention in Chicago, where Mayor Richard Daley's police took their clubs to protesters and ugly echoes of World War II were heard: Sen. Abraham Ribicoff denounced Daley's "Gestapo tactics" and Daley allegedly responded, "Fuck you. You Jew son of a bitch."[24]

The struggle over the war seemed to yield a war at home across much of America. Prominent supporters—the President and his key advisors, or figures like New York City's Francis Cardinal Spellman—ran the risk of verbal abuse (or worse) with any public appearance, and protest against the war took on myriad forms, some stately, some bellicose, some playful. Nixon reflected both a widespread mood and the dominant terminology when he asserted in 1967 that "the war in Asia is a limited one with limited means and limited goals. The war at home is a war for survival of a free society." In a similar vein, referring to student activism at Berkeley, radical leader Jerry Rubin wrote that "the war against Amerika" (the spelling connoting its fascist qualities), waged "by white middle-class kids," had "commenced." Like the war in Vietnam, the apparent one at home dragged on inconclusively into the 1970s.[25]

Other social and political divisions yielded less violence but still seemed to partake of war. Counterculture hippies talked of "peace" and "love," but their goal of "liberation for all Americans" had a coercive edge (even as they repudiated "missionary aggressiveness"), and the fury they provoked often got expressed in war's words. "Freudian wars of the suburbs" seemed to erupt between young cultural rebels and indignant middle-class parents, as Godfrey Hodgson put it. Compounding the antagonism was an overlap between cultural and political rebellion which "at its silliest," Hodgson noted, "led to the sad delusion that you change society by smoking marijuana and listening to amplified guitars." The counterculture soon diverged from the political revolt, degenerating seemingly "into a mere youth cult"; as rock singer Janis Joplin declared, "My music isn't supposed to make you riot. It's supposed to make you fuck." But before that happened, the cultural revolt was promoted and feared as if one phase of a revolutionary war, one that in turn triggered what the *Atlantic* called "the war against the young"—a "real" war, it asserted, though "fortunately still confined to conventional weapons, ranging from the popgun to the five-syllable howitzer."[26]

What congealed the image of rebellious youth was its role in antiwar protest and resistance to the draft, but that image belied many complexities. Young Americans (including those in college) were, as judged by polls, in fact slightly less inclined than older ones to oppose the war; older people like Benjamin Spock and the Kings did much to lead the antiwar cause; and many middle-aged and middle-class Americans joined its moderate wing. Antiwar activism was associated with elite institutions like the University of California at Berkeley and Columbia, in part because they easily caught the media's searchlight, but it also flourished at second-tier state schools like Michigan State and the State University of New York at Buffalo, which had recently boarded the federal gravy train of defense-related research, leading antiwar faculty and students to see them as critical nodes in the defense complex. And despite appearances, no uniform activism swept over campuses. On some, faculty or religious groups, not students, generated most of the activism. At others, most faculty supported or acquiesced in the war. At state schools, administrators often faced the heavy hand and tight purse-strings of conservative legislators and trustees, had close ties to defense agencies, and worked with public authorities who shared with them the countersubversive ethos of the McCarthy era. Penn State officials "routinely" warned parents of their offsprings' radical activities and fed information to the FBI, while Kent State's president sided with students who attacked campus radicals, whom he labeled "human debris" after the National Guard killed four people there in 1970.[27] Activists themselves divided along class, ideological, and ethnocultural lines. These circumstances mobilized not only antiwar legions but also prowar groups like Young Americans for Freedom. Still, because rebellious youth loomed large in the antiwar movement, the generational chasm seemed huge and unbridgeable.

Class war also seemed to threaten. Some radicals assailed working-class soldiers and cops as tools of the "establishment." Middle-class and working-class Americans—especially if they were white, conservative Catholics or Protestants, and indebted to the patriotic culture of World War II—grew resentful and sometimes violent toward privileged radical youth, and Nixon sought to enlist this "Silent Majority" against the protesters. Explicit talk of class war was rare because dominant conventions discouraged it and the divisions involved were complex, but class divisions were real.

They were driven in part by official policy on conscription. More than in America's other modern wars, most Vietnam-era forces, especially those in ground combat, came from poor, working-class, rural, or lower middle-class backgrounds. More privileged or savvy young men could usually escape service—although not all succeeded or tried to—through deferments for attending college, for certain white-collar vocations, for disabilities they could better document, or for service in the Guard or Reserves that they could more easily wangle. In doing so, however, they only exploited a system expressly designed to channel less privileged men into military service and more affluent ones into careers (as scientists, corporate managers, and the like) that presumably benefited national security in other ways. Draft reforms late in the 1960s raised the share of personnel in Vietnam who had four years of college, but only to 10.5 percent. Moreover, there was no way to impose Vietnam's burden on all young men since the armed forces did not seek most of them—only 40 percent saw service, only a fraction of them in combat. Still, the way chosen to distribute the burden placed it on less affluent and minority Americans—and on young ones: many were eighteen or nineteen when they reached Vietnam.

As a result, class tensions smoldered and many less advantaged Americans hated "the antiwar movement as an elitist attack on American troops by people who could avoid the war." Those tensions were overdramatized, oversimplified, and even to a degree inverted, especially by the Nixon administration. In truth, black, female, and poor Americans were more opposed to the war than other social groups: black veterans viewed antiwar protest more favorably than white veterans; antiwar sentiment grew among veterans late in the war; and some antiwar leaders worked hard to bridge the class chasm. Still, working-class resentment persisted. As a firefighter who lost a son in Vietnam complained, "You bet your goddam dollar I'm bitter. It's people like us who give up our sons for the country." The sons of the affluent "don't end up in the swamps over there." Common in his social group, his conclusion—"I think we ought to win that war or pull out"—was not classifiable as "pro-" or "antiwar" but conveyed a desperate desire to have the war's burdens lifted.[28]

By the late 1960s, then, the struggle over militarization was escalating and entwining with other conflicts, to which the term *war* was widely and literally applied, even by later historians. In a hydraulic model of history, these struggles now peaked because pressure to address problems at home had mounted for decades behind the dam of militarization, which then was breached by an unpopular war. That conceptually neat explanation is inadequate, however, for militarization had not blocked reform but provided a new if limited arena for its pursuit, and some of those disillusioned with the war were hardly interested in reform at home.

Most likely, the Vietnam-era struggles arose for a more specific reason, the conjunction of a failing war with a floundering reform effort. Had the war developed in isolation from domestic reform, its critics might have pointed to reform as an alternative, but a distinction between war and reform was not possible because the activist state of Kennedy and Johnson embraced both in ways that made them inseparable. Thus dismayed Americans had little choice but to assail the system that produced both war and reform, and hence to advance a thoroughgoing critique of the American system. For many conservatives, that meant scaling back the activist state and securing quick victory in the war. For many radicals, it meant the destruction of that state, its replacement by some egalitarian and decentralized system, and a quick (though failed) end to the war. For liberals, it meant growing frustration or abandonment of the liberal faith altogether and a move elsewhere—into leftist radicalism, or more often "neoconservatism."

The contestants in these struggles also drew on various traditions of protest and patriotism. The war's opponents inherited feminist peace agitation, religious pacifism, student antiwar agitation, rural distrust of corporate militarism, black protest against war and imperialism, the fury of Beat writers like Allen Ginsberg, and the mercurial but persistent antinuclear movement. They also drew on the civil rights movement and on the general spirit of social activism and opposition to authority already growing before the war became a major issue. Such diverse sources helped to account for the movement's notorious internal divisions, but they also lent it strength, for when one component waned, another surged forward. Most arguments against militarization were not new. Mailer's "corporation land," for example, fused Eisenhower's military-industrial complex, C. Wright Mills's power elite, and the vacuous corporate culture critiqued in the 1950s. But old arguments achieved new ideological force, political immediacy, and emotional intensity in light of the Vietnam War.

Older war opponents—Mailer, Lowell, Spock, Fulbright—drew on those antecedents. Youthful activists, on the other hand, had no sense of the past, or so it was often claimed at the time, their outlook attributed instead to a mysterious alchemy of rage, egocentricity, nihilism, and idealism. To a Johnson or a Rusk, antiwar youth had no idea of what appeasement and World War II meant for their times, but it was not only the war's defenders who emphasized their ignorance of history: literary critic Leslie Fiedler saw young campus radicals as "new mutants" repudiating "the very idea of the past."[29] Even to Mailer, their usually sympathetic muse, such radicals seemed ignorant of the past—he invoked a sense of history *for* them, but he never claimed *they* had that sense.

Some—hardly all—young radicals lent weight to that view in their disdain for their elders, for old Cold War nostrums, for the "Old Left," and for earlier antiwar activism. About the long history of women's peace activism, for example, most male radicals were appallingly ignorant, even though it was renewed in the 1960s by the venerable Women's International League for Peace and Freedom and the new Women's Strike for Peace. As some male protesters enticed the soldiers guarding the Pentagon: "We have pot, we have food we share, we have girls. Come over to us, and share our girls," some of whom "unbuttoned their blouses, gave a real hint of cleavage, [and] smiled in the soldier's eye."[30]

But the notion of rebels without a past took their claim of sundering history at face value, conflated political radicals with hippie drop-outs, and betrayed the trembling of all before the chasm opening in American society. Youthful radicals, many well educated, had no less historical sensibility than young people who supported or fought in the war, or indeed than most Americans adrift in a consumer culture that seemed to cut them off from the past. Powerfully but vaguely, World War II hung over all of them. They tapped it to varying purposes, but those who saw in it the lessons of genocide and the antecedents of fascist "Amerika" probably knew history as well as those who cited the lessons of Munich or wanted Hanoi to suffer Hiroshima's fate. As their keenest student saw them, many young antiwar activists, far from cut off from family and tradition, were in fact "concerned with *living out expressed but unimplemented parental values.*"[31] Of course, young rebels were often unaware of their roots, but historical traditions usually travel beneath the radar of self-consciousness: the rebels emerged from (and altered) traditions of protest, however much they knew it. Few who waved the flag knew their debt to history and to patriotic traditions any better.

Not that patriotic culture was a static entity, however. So much attention fixed on the radical battalions in the war at home that the opposing armies of patriots were taken for granted, but they were sustained by a dense web of veterans' and religious groups, newspapers and university officials, and other institutions and authorities. Michigan State's president, for example, found that "letters and telegrams from alumni, Dow Chemical executives, and American Legionnaires swamped his desk."[32] In many schoolrooms, the Pledge of Allegiance was still recited. In many towns, occasions like Memorial Day were still solemnly honored.

Yet patriotism was losing the almost uncontested hold on public culture it had enjoyed in previous decades, and the effort to reinvigorate it met little success. A small sign of trouble emerged when Florida businessmen erected a new Iwo Jima monument in the "Garden of Patriots." "Any true, red-blooded American—or so the developers earnestly believed—would be helpless to resist the pitch to buy a tract house within sight of the statue." The new monument was dedicated on June 14, 1965, with heroes of the great war in attendance and a message read from Vice President Humphrey, and Bob Hope and Roy Rogers were later honored there. But the venture was a commercial flop; by 1970 the garden was carved up for a new development and its Iwo Jima monument crumbled. By then, even the original monument was becoming "Washington's hottest homosexual pickup spot," as "strangers met for assignations under one or another of the giant bronze boots." The malleability of such symbols was evident in 1969, when sculptor Edward Kienholz took the form of the old Iwo Jima monument to create his *Portable War Memorial*, which mocked war and patriotism. "Symbols like Uncle Sam and Iwo Jima [or the flag] no longer united the country. Now they empowered one group at the expense of another," note the historians of Iwo Jima iconography. Patriots were hardly complacent in the face of the assaults—they railed against Kienholz's insult—but they could not stop them.[33]

Nor could they revitalize patriotic culture on film. John Wayne, a celebrity hawk publicly eager to "pull the trigger" on antiwar protesters,[34] starred in and directed the only effort in that regard, *The Green Berets* (1968), made with White House help. But the stock devices of old war movies were mechanically recycled in this long, dull film. It was World War II unconvincingly warmed over, just as Wayne was recycling his own career as World War II film hero, without a trace of the moral ambiguity of some of his earlier screen characters. Fat and overage for their roles, Wayne and other actors created the impression that few soldiers were young and that the American war effort in Vietnam was itself tired. Ideologically, the film was slack, offering no way to achieve victory except by continuing to fight, and little reason to fight except for its thin depiction of a cruel, sadistic enemy (rendered much as the Japanese in World War II had been shown). Though it did well at the box office, *The Green Berets* indicated that patriotic culture had lost resolve and confidence.

National leaders could do little better. Out of the public eye, the Johnson and Nixon administrations tried to stir patriotism by promoting private lobbies supporting the war, by aiding visits to the troops by celebrities, by enlisting the political support of Hollywood stars, and under Nixon by encouraging hardhat workers to beat up war protesters. Fearful of overt machinery to mobilize public opinion, however, neither Johnson nor Nixon mounted the bond drives, civil defense drills, or scrap-and-salvage campaigns that underwrote patriotic culture during World War II. Those efforts had meshed individual self-interest and self-sacrifice with the war effort. That now proved impossible. Public efforts to rally patriotism seemed abstract or hollow, like another television show. Disconnected from the everyday lives of Americans, such efforts helped to give the war its "curious detached quality," as if "merely one more artificial, manufactured product of the Corporate State." Older actors and celebrities often rallied to the cause—in 1967 Bob Hope warned of seeing communists "off the coast of Santa Monica" if Americans did not fight—but their efforts seemed formulaic. The war's complex politics also jeopardized alliances between the White House and its patriotic allies: when Nixon began his opening to China in 1971, a furious John Wayne wrote him to complain of this "real shocker," enclosing "a hate piece 'fact sheet' on 'that Jew, [National Security Advisor Henry] Kissinger.'"[35]

Moreover, patriotic culture was never wholly insulated from the anxieties about modern warfare felt in the antiwar movement. However much they yearned to heap destruction and revenge on the enemy, many patriots still hesitated the unleash the ultimate weapon, just as the war's occasional fictional hero lacked convincing confidence in the cause. Not until the war was over did fantasies of vengeance and destruction seem safe and acceptable; only then was patriotic culture reconstituted in Hollywood and Washington. Meanwhile, like many strands of American life, it seemed defensive, angry, uncertain.

That it collided with the antiwar movement was obvious, just as the era's divisions over issues long unresolved and a war long waged were hardly surprising. Why such collisions were felt to be "wars" is less obvious, however, especially because the rhetoric of war came so effortlessly that few bothered to explain their choice of it. That sense developed most easily regarding racial conflict, given the nation's record of racial strife, its Civil War over racial issues, and a level of civil strife and use of armed force in the 1960s not seen in several decades. Perhaps it measured America's relative freedom from internal strife that when it did erupt, it seemed like "war." Nothing else registered the shock felt at these eruptions, ones Americans associated with an ideologically-riven Europe or nations in the throes of decolonization, but not with the United States. Various groups and leaders added to the seeming aptness of "war" as a defining category, as Presidents talked of enemies at home and radicals of revolutionary war. That Johnson, Nixon, indeed most Americans had little experience with combat made it easier to use war's language: they could facilely invoke what they did not really understand.

Yet their talk of war was also puzzlingly broad and generic. They spoke less of "civil war," referring to the obvious precedent in their history, than simply of "war," as if their conflicts were akin to international wars between nations, religions, or alliances (to Vice President Spiro Agnew, there raged at home "a holy war" over Vietnam).[36] Nor do ideological struggle, civil violence, and war abroad inevitably combine to produce talk of war at home. Amid the Korean War, blacks met white violence, leftists faced mob action, strikes turned nasty, and officials chased alleged traitors, but no "war" among Americans was proclaimed.

The differences between the Korean and Vietnam eras were of course major. The stakes in Korea confused many Americans, but the military action abroad was clear-cut if frustrating, and the grand American achievements of World War II were recent enough to instill lingering confidence. Violence at home was less visible than in the Vietnam era and more evidently directed at out-groups rather than initiated by them. And compared to Vietnam, Korea was a short war with a minimally tolerable outcome.

In contrast, the 1960s invited linkage between war abroad and conflict at home. One connection developed out of the insistence by nearly all parties to the war, from Presidents and their foes to leaders in Saigon and Hanoi, that its outcome hinged on the will and resolve of the American people even more than on the struggle in Indochina. That belief, more pervasive and explicit than in the Korean War, all but fused the homefront and the warfront into the same war. "North Vietnam cannot defeat or humiliate the United States," Nixon said in 1969. "Only Americans can do that."[37] If the decisive struggle was at home, it made sense to see war raging there. A perceived structural similarity between conflicts at home and abroad also linked them. Insofar as the Vietnam War was seen by opponents as a racial war—and soon also as one of male aggression against women and children—it seemed to mirror conflicts within America. Another link owed to the long American tradition of ennobling almost any cause as a "war," and Johnson's rhetorical enmeshment of his wars at home and abroad.

It was a remarkable development. In most ways, the Vietnam War affected Americans far less than had World War II, yet "war" erupted among them to a degree unimaginable in the big war, as if they compensated for this war's remoteness by fighting it at home.

That the United States was losing this war also caused bitterness. Since neither Johnson nor Nixon would admit defeat, much less explain why it was such a horrid prospect, the politics of accounting for it were surreal, with debate endless but never fully engaged. Still, Americans confronted, though never satisfactorily, a need to account for defeat. The obvious scapegoats were the war's opponents, though venom was also heaped on the media and on universities. In their own way, the war's opponents were almost as tongue-tied in the face of defeat as its defenders. They could not explain defeat as the fate of nations—it had to be the product of malign forces, a scene in the most apocalyptic of scenarios. Thus both opponents and defenders of the war embraced American exceptionalism: the fate of other nations, defeat was a historical insult to the United States.

That is a generalized explanation of "war" at home, however. Divisions over gender and sexual preference suggest how each arena of conflict had its own story along with its place in the grander one. The reemergence of feminism in the 1960s and the rise of gay liberation all had links to militarization and its convulsions. Some links are well known: many feminists and gay rights advocates took inspiration from the civil rights and antiwar movements, as well as umbrage from the discrimination they faced in those movements. Otherwise, the Vietnam War is often relegated to a minor role in the history of women and gender.

Wrongly, because the war provided a charged setting for gender issues, whose reemergence amid the war was hardly coincidental. Above all, Vietnam was more a *men's* war than World War II, in part because limited war did not demand full mobilization and because the Cold War had defined women's role far more narrowly than had World War II. Though Congress had banned quotas on female military officers, women comprised only 1 percent of active-duty personnel in 1967, compared to over 2 percent in 1945 (265,000 that year, only 35,000 in 1967). Women were rarely noticed for such service or asked to volunteer for it, and never called to sacrifice at home, take war jobs, or conduct air raid drills. Leaders treated their service far more tritely than in World War II. Asked if there was a chance to do something for military women "distressed because they are not being called upon to serve in Vietnam," Johnson replied jokingly, "Well there is always a chance of anything taking place when our women are sufficiently distressed," and the assembled journalists laughed.[38] That the Viet Cong made use of women, even in combat, was taken as a sign of their peculiar beastliness or ideological perversion. No woman emerged in the war effort as prominently as Eleanor Roosevelt or Oveta Culp Hobby had in World War II. Few, besides caricatured figures like actress Jane Fonda, even did in the antiwar movement. These patterns also coincided with growing homophobia and exclusion of gays from national institutions.

Yet even as women and homosexuals were largely excluded from the nation's war effort, they were dragged back in through symbols and images. Those often were off-hand rather than consciously deliberated, and linked to no single political position (though offered far more by men than by women), but collectively they pointed to a troubling shift in relations between gender and war.

National leaders did not alone cause that shift, but they expressed it. In May 1964, Barry Goldwater reportedly wanted to "lob one into the men's room in the Kremlin." That seemed a simple statement of aggression, but it came amid a generation's equation of male homosexuality with bathroom sex and communist subversion. Weeks later a *Life* article began, "Do the homosexuals, like the Communists, intend to bury us?" In October came a stunning political scandal, the arrest of key Johnson aide Walter Jenkins for sexual activities in a YMCA men's room near the White House, followed by alarm that state secrets might have been compromised by his homosexuality and jokes about new meaning to the campaign slogan, "All the way with LBJ." LBJ's reaction to Jenkins's arrest was strikingly gendered: "I was as shocked as if someone had told me my wife had murdered her daughter." This series of statements and events carried the implication that homosexuality, mothering, and communism were loosely linked, and that all (except presumably the mother) deserved extinction—by the bomb according to Goldwater, by murder according to LBJ. Johnson later made those connections transparent in a famous attack on the war's doubters. "There will be some 'Nervous Nellies' and some who will become frustrated and bothered and break ranks under the strain," he maintained—"Nellies" being familiar slang for nervous, effeminate gay men. Privately, he likened opposition to the war to effeminacy—of one dove, he joked, "Hell, he has to squat to piss," and as for Fulbright, he was a "frustrated old woman." He also compared it to his own emasculation through homosexual assault: When CBS News offered unflattering coverage of the war, he railed at its head, Frank Stanton: "Frank, are you trying to fuck me? Frank, this is your president and yesterday your boys shat on the American flag."[39]

Other leaders worked similar themes, as did Vice President Agnew in assailing the October 1969 Vietnam Moratorium. That burst of antiwar protest had featured (to the White House's chagrin) little violence and much middle-class respectability, but Agnew assailed it in words that evoked contemporary images of gay men. He condemned protesters who indulged in "street carnival," ran a "carousel," and were "cavorting in the streets." Their "tantrums" (presumably a mark of childlike immaturity) were "insidiously destroying the fabric of American democracy," and their allies among politicians were "ideological eunuchs." His metaphors running riot, Agnew also denounced demonstrators as "snobs" and "rotten apples," but the gendered character of his attack came through: "This is what is happening in this nation. We *are* an effete society if we let it happen here." As he had worried aloud earlier, "A society which comes to fear its children is effete. A sniveling, hand-wringing power structure deserves the violent rebellion it encourages." Apparently, effeminate weakness lurked not only in the antiwar movement but within government itself.[40]

Nixon offered a more complicated case of gendered language. He often used social class rather than gender to assail the war's foes: they were "the luckiest people in the world, going to the greatest universities," unlike less privileged youth who fought the war. He also, however, let loose male fury and a string of gendered images (describing his own daughters as "front-line troops in the battle to re-establish the traditional virtues."). Pro-war congressmen were "ballsy," his foes deserved "cold steel." "Attack," "fight," "smash," "crush" filled his comments on what to do to his enemies. When his public image appeared weak, one aide suggested, to Nixon's approval, that he "stop displaying the President as if he had a stick up his ass." Despairing of public support for the war in 1972, Nixon worried that Americans "emphasize the material to the exclusion of the spiritual and the Spartan life, and it may be that we soften them up rather than harden them up for the battle." The phallic and gendered character of Nixon's language was ubiquitous.[41]

Less obvious was its intent, since homophobic and misogynist words were staples of male language often spoken thoughtlessly. Still, national leaders linked opposition to the war with homosexuality and femininity consistently enough to suggest that they regarded failure in the war as due to some triumph of the values of women and femininity. Since they offered no explanation for why those values were malign, only a vague insinuation that they made the nation weak, their attacks clearly appealed to them and their audiences for less than conscious reasons.

That appeal derived partly from Western traditions of equating pacifism with weakness and Asian peoples with effeminacy. Johnson often cast Asian communists as women, characterizing the escalating bombing of them as constituting "seduction, not rape," though, as one historian notes, "rape sometimes follows rejected seduction." Gender politics at home figured even more in the appeal of these attacks. Women had a tradition of peace activism, more women than men opposed this war, leading feminists (Betty Friedan, Gloria Steinem, Bella Abzug, Shirley Chisholm) did so in particular, and they sometimes couched *their* opposition to this war in gendered terms: "Only a male orientation would keep us in Vietnam," argued theologian Mary Daly in 1971. Since men dominated the publicly visible antiwar movement, women's peace activism may not have figured consciously in the rhetoric of national leaders, but it overlapped a more general image of male-female conflict over women's rights that was conspicuous and often expressed in war's language. "This is not a bedroom war," National Organization of Women founder Betty Friedan told a crowd in 1970, it is "a political movement," but the denial paid homage to a war rhetoric that infiltrated public and private debate (never more than in the silly "battle of the sexes" that found Billy Jean King beating fellow tennis player Bobby Riggs in 1973). Thus in assailing the feminine and effeminate character of opposition to the war, national leaders were tapping associations allowing them to link enemies at home and abroad through a common gendered imagery.[42]

The appeal of that imagery was heightened by the blockage of older outlets for wartime frustrations. Black leaders' resistance to the war privately infuriated Johnson, but he could hardly go public with his fury given the pressure to avoid aggravating racial divisions. And no American ethnic group was closely associated with the enemy, who in any event had the same ethnic identity as America's ally. Gender offered the path of least resistance.

Any such explanation for the outlook of national leaders encounters complications, however, for some of the war's opponents shared elements of that outlook. They saw signs of homosexuality among alienated youth, scorned the androgynous style of some protesters, embraced symbols of male potency, or linked victory in their cause to the rape, emasculation, or feminization of their enemies. Mailer had wanted to "stick it up the government's ass" and likened the America out of control in Vietnam to his wife ("his love for his wife while not at all equal or congruent to his love for America was damnably parallel," he added), while the final chapter of *Armies of the Night*, "The Metaphor Delivered," found him self-consciously taking over the birthing of a new America. Other expressions of this temperament were less artful. "Fuck Julie, fuck David," a crowd of Boston antiwar protesters reportedly chanted, referring to

Nixon's daughter and her husband, David Eisenhower. The popular slogan "Women Say Yes to Men Who Say No"—that is, sexually serve men who resist the draft—also linked opposition to the war to male potency. So too did the sartorial style of some antiwar protesters late in the war: when the movement's radical wing became embittered and returning veterans swelled its ranks, its demonstrations often featured men in military fatigues or pseudomilitary dress—offering a public face of "macho stridency and militarist fantasy," as Sara Evans put it.[43]

Gender, then, was the plaything of all sides (if largely their male proponents) in the war. It is in most wars, however. Was its role in this war new? The war "discredited the style of aggressive masculinity kept fervently alive by two decades of Cold War anticommunism," Barbara Ehrenreich later claimed, but in fact such masculinity was not decisively "discredited." A process of "re-masculinization," one scholar argues, went on in discourse about the war regardless of its ideology—from Nixon to avowed foes of the war—yielding "a revival of the images, abilities, and evaluations of men and masculinity in dominant U.S. culture."[44] To be sure, most wars feature such masculinizing impulses, but in this war those impulses also faced surging feminist and gay movements. Though not peculiar to this war, tensions over gender were peculiarly sharpened and structured by the combination of women's invisibility in the war, men's failure to win it, and the arrival of gender-based movements. As a result, images of gender and sexuality entered political discourse with a coarseness and volume unimaginable in World War II.

Militarization worked at another level as well, by shaping the feminist and gay movements. They made central to their politics and scholarship the proposition that "the personal is political": personal lives and gender roles are political entities, ones historically constructed (and therefore changeable) rather than rooted in the biological destiny of men and women. That outlook fostered a noisy assertion of their personal identities in the public realm that opponents found inappropriate and vulgar: Why do *they* make a political show of personal identities? They did so because it had already been done to them. They reacted to the previous politicization of personal identities that had circumscribed their roles and invested their identities with often malign meaning in a nation waging hot and cold war. (Men's lives, too, were invested with political meaning, but of a more favorable if sometimes burdensome sort.) Radicals did not invent linkages between personal identity and politics. Instead, they tried to expose and alter those linkages. Their efforts to do so, and the tumultuous politics that followed in the 1970s, owed much to the militarization of gender roles that had already taken place.

Their methods for challenging such roles also owed something to the era's militarization. There "on the cover of the convention issue of *New Left Notes* in June 1967 was a young woman with a rifle—'The New American Woman,'" noticed Sara Evans. SCUM, the Society for Cutting Up Men organized by a few radical feminists, enjoyed a brief existence that year. "Imperialism begins at home," insisted radical lesbian Rita Mae Brown a few years later. "Let's stab the monster in its heart rather than slapping its fingertips . . . . The real glory is in shitting on other men. To fight The Man we don't need to go to Hanoi, we fight him right here." Use of "liberation" in feminist and gay ideology linked their causes to revolutionary struggles abroad. This posture of armed struggle was largely reactive and transient, however. As many activists realized, their enemies had far more armed power. Since a critique of masculinity defined these movements—since masculinity "translated into possessions, force, domination, and ultimately militarism and imperialism"—any embrace of its characteristics was suspect. Instead, the values they cherished were "intimacy, support, and virtual structurelessness."[45]

The troubling "wars" over race, gender, corporate power, Vietnam—in many ways over America's meaning and destiny—marked the convulsions of militarization. So too did artists and authors. Kurt Vonnegut's *Slaughterhouse-Five* (1968) dealt with the author's experience as a POW in 1945 during the Dresden firestorm unleashed by British and American bombers, but it was just as much about the war during which he wrote. Vonnegut's hallucinogenic narrative seemed to reflect his psychedelic times, as well as his debt to Mark Twain, who eighty years earlier had wreaked havoc with time in his savage satire about mechanized war, *A Connecticut Yankee in King Arthur's Court*. No mere literary trick, Vonnegut's time warps conveyed the absurdity of history's course in a militarized age and a longing to reverse it, as Billy Pilgrim imagined might happen for Dresden: "American planes, full of holes and wounded men and corpses, took off backwards from an airfield in England. Over France, a few German fighter planes flew at them backwards, sucked bullets and shell fragments from some of the planes and crewmen." Then American bombers flying "backwards" over Dresden "shrunk the fires, gathered them into cylindrical steel containers," and returned them to the United States, "where factories were operating night and day" to dismantle them, "so they would never hurt anybody ever again."[46] Far from offering a knee-jerk assault on war, Vonnegut captured the intricate process of technological war.

Vonnegut was a literary star, his words avidly consumed by college students, his novel on Dresden turned into a movie. Bruce Catton's *Waiting for the Morning Train: An American Boyhood* (1972) hardly seized the limelight. Dean of military historians, Catton had written a sharp account of mobilization in World War II, but his popular Civil War histories had showed no fundamental distaste for his nation or its military record. Nor at first glance did his modest memoir about growing up before World War I in a small Michigan town. He said little about the divisions now wracking America, avoided bellicose or obscene language, and eschewed the confusion of fact and fiction now popular (*History as a Novel, The Novel as History,* as Mailer subtitled *Armies of the Night*). He seemed to tell an old-fashioned story in an old-fashioned way.

Yet he was indignant. He lovingly evoked the people and values of his child-hood but disdained "seeing in the irrecoverable past a charm and a comfort which it did not have," for the past of his youth had been built on the destruc-tion of Indian culture and a monstrous environmental despoliation wrought by the lumber industry. Turn-of-the century America now seemed to share with his own time the spirit leading men "to crack the force that binds the infected planet's cells together, so that the globe lies in danger of going up in one stupen-dous flaming lifeless cloud," and man's "waste products arising from all of this lie upon the planet's flesh like an intolerable scurf." What emerged—"dimly" to the young Catton, starkly to the old man—was "the one dismaying fact that governs our progress across the Sinai desert of the modern world; we have . . . entrusted ourselves entirely to our mechanical ingenuity," only to be "made helpless by our own omnipotence." The "richest fruits" of that trust came in what Catton knew best, war, whose record in his century led him to muse darkly:

> The world had simply gone awhoring after false gods. Having committed itself to them it had to go where they took, and this was bound to lead to confusion, because of all the gods man has ever worshipped the most com-pletely inscrutable are the ones that stand behind the altars in the age of applied technology. . . . What protected man in the old days was his awareness that there were things he just could not do. . . . By the unformu-lated tenets of his new religion, what he can do he must do. The one impos-sibility now is to turn back, or to go at half speed. This machine . . . oper-ates only at full speed. Unfortunately, it cannot be steered.

Catton barely mentioned Vietnam, noting only that the same world-saving im-pulse "that led us to destroy Hitler's obscenely contrived Nibelungen Reich . . . led us a few years later into southern Asia where we made obscene contriv-ances of our own." His anger transcended the follies of the moment. But it also reflected them. "War does one thing pitilessly," he noted: "it holds up, before the eyes of the society that is waging it, the essential reality on which that soci-ety based," and that reality worried him.[47]

The disillusionment with what the United States had become—with militar-ization and the uncontrollable forces to which it was linked—reached beyond the young, the radical, the obviously alienated. In fact, it had long been nourished by some older Americans, like Vonnegut and Catton. Nor would it stop with a mythical "sixties": Catton's 1972 memoir indicated how it rolled on.

By then, a determination to end the Vietnam War and a more contested inter-est in demilitarization had set in. Those impulses stood in jarring relationship to the "wars" among Americans themselves, however. Those wars left a lasting legacy, as Americans feverishly embraced "war" to characterize a host of cru-sades and conflicts over the next quarter-century. They also indicated how complicated the politics of militarization now were. Earlier, questions about it usually had been straightforward, even if the answers difficult: How much priority should be given to national security? What measures would most enhance it?

Those questions persisted after 1965, but the apparent arrival of war *among* Americans added puzzling questions less within the reach of state policy: could America demilitarize its role in the world while its own culture and politics became more deeply militarized? Could Americans indulge a war mentality in fighting each other without acting it out elsewhere? Was war to be a lasting state of mind among Americans? More than any other person, Richard Nixon now faced those questions, and offered disturbing answers to them.

Nixon's Wars

Whether Nixon would restrain America's militarization, or had any mandate to do so, was unclear when he took office. His margin of victory was slim (43.4 percent of the voters in a poor turn-out, versus 42.7 percent for Democrat Hubert Humphrey), despite earlier prospects for a landslide; not since 1848 had the winner's party failed to control either the House or Senate. Humphrey condemned Nixon for seeking "an increasing militarization [a term rarely used in politics] of American life and American foreign policy," but he and Nixon outlined few differences on war and foreign policy, those instead being defined by third-party candidate George Wallace and running mate Curtis LeMay, the general who had carried out Japan's destruction and now sought North Vietnam's. Contrary to reports, Nixon never said he had "a secret plan to end the war," but whatever plan he did have was unclear to voters and inchoate for him. (Publicly he claimed he would not undercut LBJ's diplomacy, but privately he contacted South Vietnam's President Thieu "in an effort to scuttle the peace prospects," as LBJ knew from illegal wiretaps he could hardly reveal.) Certainly most Americans wanted the war over, but perhaps only to resume the pre-war status quo, modified so that no Vietnam happened again. It was less clear that they sought to curb the broader process of militarization or its subtler manifestations in culture and politics.[48]

As if the historical situation were not awkward enough, Nixon was an awkward figure to face it: shrewd and blind, secretive and self-revealing, flexible and dogmatic, idealistic (in his own way) and mean-spirited. A Cold Warrior whose entire career had been invested in militarization and foreign policy, he seemed badly equipped to lead the nation's reorientation. His brief time in Congress, starting with his success against Alger Hiss, focused on national security. As Vice President, his job had been to crusade against communism, appease the party's right wing, and step in as commander in chief when Eisenhower was sick. His considerable effort as Vice President to improve race relations owed much to Cold War needs. His one stab at a post outside the national security arena—his 1962 campaign for California's governorship—

exposed a tin ear for local, largely "domestic" issues, which barely rated mention in his 1962 memoir *Six Crises*. Attuned to world issues, he was also more comfortable abroad, where he often found the respect and rapport with crowds that he craved at home. He traveled overseas incessantly as Vice President, in the mid-1960s when he was restoring his political credentials, and again as President, even during his last dreadful year in office. His 1968 and 1972 campaigns, tightly choreographed even by modern standards, kept him at arm's length from the rough-and-tumble of politics and journalistic scrutiny. Only his prodigious travels on the GOP's rubber-chicken circuit took him to the grassroots.

Nixon was deeply invested in war and foreign policy, but in a narrow way. Until he became President, his career mainly consisted of nonstop campaigning, with little experience in formulating policies or running organizations. He had little interest in military history, in the details of the Vietnam War, or in the generals and admirals in charge of it, many of whom in turn distrusted him. He never cared much about the sinews of American military strength or the details and implications of arms control. To the extent such matters moved him, it was often in a juvenile, self-referential fashion. Early in 1970, he may have spent more time watching the movie *Patton* than attending to the coming invasion of Cambodia—not because he wanted to understand war but because that World War II saga nourished his "heroic fantasies," ones he shared with many men, except that Nixon "was the President, and it was dangerous in the extreme, as well as inappropriate, for him to identify with Patton and the Duke [John Wayne]." Certainly he lacked Ike's grasp of the subtler dimensions of militarization or LBJ's agony about the conflict between war and reform.[49]

Though often duplicitous, he was reasonably honest about his priorities (ones Kennedy also largely had). As he told a journalist before becoming President, "I've always thought this country could run itself domestically without a President; all you need is a competent Cabinet to run the country at home. You need a President for foreign policy." His vaunted interest in welfare reform—Daniel Moynihan's bold plan for a "negative income tax" ensuring a minimum income for all Americans—seemed hollow. "What Nixon wanted most was credit for boldness and innovation" in domestic policy "without the cost," Stephen Ambrose notes. He felt unencumbered and able to make a difference in foreign policy and global affairs, but found it vexing to haggle over domestic policy with Congress and federal bureaucracies, institutions he held in contempt. He had the skills to work with Congress but did so "without enthusiasm, without conviction, without joy, and thus without success." Campaigning in 1970, he offered few achievements in reform. "Instead, he ran against pot, permissiveness, protest, pornography, and dwindling patriotism" (but Democrats held Congress and gained eleven governorships).[50]

As that campaign indicated, Nixon did denounce various evils in American life. Pornography, he announced in condemning the "morally bankrupt conclusions" of an LBJ-appointed commission, "could poison the wellsprings of American and Western culture and civilization. . . . Smut . . . should be outlawed in every State in the Union." Like Johnson, Nixon also saw war as a model for action in such matters. He did once bemoan "overblown rhetoric . . . in which the word 'war' has perhaps too often been used—the war on poverty, the war on misery, the war on disease, the war on hunger"—but then immediately found the word "appropriate" for the "fight against crime. We must declare and win the war against the criminal elements." Since LBJ had declared war on crime, Nixon's differences from him in this regard were fuzzy, except that Nixon emphasized such wars less and linked them more to his fear that internal rot would sap national energies in the global arena.[51]

He worked hard on domestic policy because he worked hard at everything, and some achievements did issue. He wanted to "start power and resources flowing back from Washington to the States and communities," a goal met by sharing federal revenues with state governments. Through a new Environmental Protection Agency, on the other hand, Washington took on major responsibility for an emerging concern, though Nixon was furious when environmentalists helped to scuttle a supersonic airliner ("the *number one Technological Tragedy* of our time," he told his staff). His boldest initiatives in economic policy were keyed to the war, however—his wage-price freeze in 1971 addressed the inflation it had generated—and he continued to find issues of domestic policy boring and his progress on them meager, so that in 1972 he "had not campaigned on [them] and thus had not created a constituency for them."[52]

Nixon's personal and political style compounded his isolation from ordinary Americans and the issues at home they faced, for all he courted the "Silent Majority." In a peripatetic life, he had few roots, few friends, and in the White House stunningly few close associates. His differences from Eisenhower were telling. Ike's wide circle of friends, instincts to mediate, attention to diverse views, and wariness about concentrated power baffled Nixon, who (like Kennedy) mistook them for weakness, disavowing all that "'togetherness' bullshit." As Nixon observed in puzzled admiration, Ike "didn't think of people who disagreed with him as being the 'enemy.' He just thought: 'They don't agree with me.'" Here lay "the biggest single difference between them . . . . Eisenhower was a man full of love, for life and for people, while Nixon . . . all too often gave in to an impulse to hate." At times contemptuous of "that senile old bastard," Nixon also lacked Ike's hopes to heal the wounds of war and curb the forces of militarization.[53]

All this boded ill for any effort to restrain those forces. However strong that effort, Nixon had no other mission for the nation, hardly even the vague sentiments of Eisenhower and Kennedy in this regard. Contradictory as the man was, he sometimes said otherwise. "If we can get this country thinking not of how to fight a war," he wrote in 1971, "but how to win a peace—. . . thinking of clean air, clean water, open spaces, of a welfare reform program that will provide a floor under the income of every family . . . then we will have the lift of a driving dream." But he added that "it takes some time to get rid of the nightmares" associated with the war. "You can't be having a driving dream when you are in the midst of a nightmare."[54] The "dream" might have helped end the "nightmare." Nixon thought otherwise.

Yet in confronting militarization Nixon had major assets, including formidable political skills and experience. Who better to challenge militarization than one who knew its workings so well and had the Cold War credentials to insulate him from charges of being "soft" on communism and defense? Those credentials indeed served him well (as they had Eisenhower) when Nixon pursued detente with the Soviet Union and China and retrenchment in defense. Democrats like Humphrey or George McGovern, he knew, would have been slaughtered (by Nixon, among others) for such initiatives.

Nixon's biggest asset was his appreciation, abstract but keen, of the need and the means to change course. The war was tearing America apart. If the 1968 election gave him no mandate about *how* to end it, it still made clear the yearning to do so (Eisenhower, with Nixon watching, had earned enormous good will by ending the Korean War). War, militarization, and hegemony were expensive at a time when needs at home were perceived as mounting. Nor to Nixon, at least in his abstract calculus, did the strenuous exertions of recent decades any longer seem so necessary. He knew that his earlier rhetoric about monolithic communism was outdated—that divisions among and strains within communist nations were growing, while a revived Europe and Japan provided counterweights to them. Those changes in turn offered leverage for ending the Vietnam War on terms acceptable to him: detente with the Soviet Union and China would induce their pressure on Hanoi to settle; playing Beijing and Moscow against each other would keep both from exploiting the contraction of American power Nixon envisioned.

Nixon also knew that the Vietnam War could not be "won" (whatever that might mean). As he told one speechwriter in March 1968, "There's no way to win the war. But we can't say that of course. In fact, we have to seem to say the opposite." Back-pedaling from what he once had argued, in 1968 he emphasized "honorable peace" rather than victory, stressed that success hinged more on South Vietnamese efforts than on American, and ceased identifying Vietnam as essential to American interests. He pledged to "win the peace," meaning that the war "must be ended honorably, consistent with America's limited aims and with the long-term requirements of peace in Asia." All this, similar to what LBJ now thought, was dangerously fuzzy. He realized the war was lost "even if he would not admit it," Ambrose argues, but public admission was the nub of the matter: without it, Nixon risked confusion and bewilderment in his administration and in the nation. Still, in his serpentine way, Nixon was shifting ground. He still sought victory of some sort, but it would be no battlefield rout of the enemy, though weapons might assist it.[55]

Hardly a "secret plan" to end the war, since it was not quite a secret in 1968 and not quite a plan, this was only a sketch of a grand design. It also hinged dangerously on, among other things, an exaggerated notion of Hanoi's dependence on its communist patrons and their leverage over it. Although Nixon said little on the campaign trail, through his writings and other means he hinted at detente, an opening to China, a new importance for Japan, and their relationship to ending the war. (Americans were stunned by the opening to China in 1971 only because Nixon was secretive about the steps that made it happen, not about the impulse behind it.)

Nor did his grand design mean full retreat from militarization and hegemony. Nixon sought to preserve the core of both by pruning them of their most dangerous, costly, or politically onerous elements. He put it clearly in September 1969: he wanted "defense forces strong enough to keep the peace" but without "wasteful expenditures" that would sap national strength, and assistance to "free nations" without "rushing in to do for them what they can and should do for themselves."[56] Thus the United States would exit Vietnam but preserve an illusion of success by using American air power and rushing aid to Saigon. Thus the defense establishment would remain largely as it was, but purged of the conscription which offended many Americans. Thus the Cold War would still be waged, but with more focus on key allies and less on peripheral areas beyond the reach of American power. Thus the weapons race would continue, but with arms agreements to make it more palatable, predictable, and amenable to American technological superiority. Thus the power would remain to uphold American economic might, but modified by rising competitors like Japan. An overextended empire would shuck off its less essential commitments and practices.

Budgets, force levels, and arms accords reflected Nixon's goal of prudent contraction. From 1969 to 1973, defense budgets declined sharply (about one-third) when adjusted for inflation and in terms of share of GNP. Military personnel dropped from over 3.5 million in 1968 to just over 2.1 million in 1975. The 1972 SALT I agreement did not restrain the nuclear arms race but seemed to steer it into safer channels: an accompanying treaty banned most antimissile weapons, which many saw as the most dangerous form of the arms race; allowance to develop multiple-warhead missiles seemed (wrongly, as some recognized at the time) to favor America's technological superiority; SALT II talks held out promise for actual cuts in nuclear arsenals. Meanwhile, nondefense spending rose under the pressure of entitlement guarantees, because Congress continued many Great Society programs which Nixon either wanted or had no stomach to fight, and because even Nixon desired some new programs. Mindful of mounting national debt, however, and for other reasons as well, Nixon resisted transfer of federal funds from defense to other arenas. "Dreams of unlimited billions" loosed by the end of the Vietnam War "are just that—dreams," he said, denouncing "illusions that what some call the 'peace and growth dividend' [a similar term emerged in the 1980s] will automatically solve our national problems."[57]

Fuller disengagement from militarization seemed too risky to the United States' interests, credibility abroad, and self-image as a superpower, and no mandate to undertake it existed. Radical protest seemed powerful, but in political institutions dovish liberals were far more numerous, and they hardly repudiated American interests abroad. They often saw the United States as stumbling honorably into a "quagmire" in Vietnam, in what Arthur Schlesinger, Jr., regarded in 1969 as "a triumph of the politics of inadvertence" and "a tragedy without villains," not a failure of basic American policies.[58] In Congress they influenced Nixon's course and drew his fury, but few sought immediate, unilateral withdrawal from Vietnam. They too wanted prudence in the exercise of American power, not its cessation, and thus broadly shared Nixon's outlook. Hawks with apocalyptic scenarios for North Vietnam, numerous in both parties, disliked the global do-goodism, entangling alliances, and elitist tone they associated with the foreign policy establishment, but hardly urged demilitarization. Nixon borrowed their favorite means of power, the bomber, to serve his goal of a prudent contraction of militarization, while undermining the Left by phasing out the draft and slowly withdrawing ground forces from Vietnam.

In any event, Nixon would not do more, no matter what the popular mandate. Even what he did do stuck in his craw. His fate was "to preside over the retreat of American power. He hated it. Every instinct in him rebelled against it. For twenty years, in every crisis, at every turning point, his advice had been to take the offensive against the communists. Attack, with more firepower, now." But now "he had to retreat." His old instinct did not go away, however: he could attack even in retreat.[59]

All these strategic, political, and personal impulses came together in Nixon's famous "Madman Theory" for ending the war, the phrase indicating how crude impulses to destroy entwined with cold calculations of how to retreat. Nixon wanted to apply Eisenhower's method of ending the Korean War to Vietnam—without a thoughtful sense of what Ike had done and how the new situation differed. As he privately explained "the Madman Theory" in 1968, "I want the North Vietnamese to believe . . . I might do *anything*. . . . We'll just slip the word to them that, 'for God's sake, you know Nixon is obsessed about Communism. We can't restrain him when he's angry—and he has his hand on the nuclear button' and Ho Chi Minh himself will be in Paris in two days begging for peace." In office Nixon tried to act on his theory. In March 1969, he began (then soon expanded) the secret bombing of Cambodia, a neutral nation through which North Vietnam funneled some of its men and munitions. That summer, as he later put it, he decided to "go for broke" and had Henry Kissinger, his national security advisor, convey to the North Vietnamese that if an acceptable compromise were not reached, he would "take measures of the greatest consequences," a euphemism for use of nuclear weapons. Air power, its use or its threat, was once again at the center of American policy.[60]

Nixon's choice ran risks almost too numerous too mention. Bombing had long infuriated the war's opponents and seemed, for all the ground troops he withdrew, like the apotheosis rather than the contraction of militarization. It made him look like a real madman. It could hardly placate air power hawks when kept secret (as it often was), and when revealed it could only infuriate doves. That was especially so since secrecy (from Americans—Cambodians knew who was bombing them) required measures within government and against Nixon's opponents that were legally dubious and possibly grounds for impeachment. Too, there was Nixon's curious indecisiveness, despite his obsessive efforts to present himself as decisive. Far from rushing to implement his Madman Theory, he waited months to do so and then tried it episodically for the next four years. "We need a plan to end the war, not only to withdraw troops," Kissinger told Nixon and the National Security Council—eight months after they entered office presumably with a plan. Nixon in the spring of 1970 "enjoyed talking tough; he enjoyed pretending that he was making a decision about equivalent to Caesar's to cross the Rubicon or William the Conqueror's to set off for England or Eisenhower's to launch D-Day; he wanted to think of himself as an all-or-nothing kind of guy. But Nixon shrank from the 'big play,' from what he sometimes called the 'Nixon Big Charge.'"[61] Indecisiveness was a virtue in the nuclear age if it meant caution and attention to conflicting views, but of those Nixon was contemptuous. His indecisiveness was characterological rather than calculated. Combined with his secretiveness, it made his efforts to end the war erratic and impulsive.

Above all, the Madman Theory, at least as Nixon practiced it, did not work. It was, after all, only a more destructive and capricious version of what Johnson had already tried. It remained no substitute for success on the ground in the south. In 1969 at least, it did not make Hanoi budge. Like other elements of Nixon's policy—increased reliance on ARVN troops, slow extrication of American ground forces, diplomacy to bring the Soviet Union and China into play— it was doomed to work slowly if at all, and depended on what others (Saigon, Hanoi, Beijing, and Moscow) would do, making Nixon's fortune hostage to them. "The phased, slow-motion defeat was the worst mistake of his Presidency," Ambrose has concluded. "Because the war went on, tension and division filled the land, and the Nixon haters went into a frenzy."[62]

Nixon, of course, had imagined it would all go swiftly (Ho "in two days begging for peace"). Any President makes mistakes, but this was a colossal one, from a man who presented himself as supremely gifted in such matters. He blamed opponents for tying his hands and for emboldening Hanoi to hold out (in 1970 the Senate nearly approved a George McGovern–Mark Hatfield measure forcing withdrawal of all American forces by the end of 1971), but Nixon's job as President was to deal with opposition, not just bewail it. If he really had had confidence in himself and his theory, he would have acted before his opponents could act. Quicker action might not have worked, but failure at least would have demolished the delusion that bombing would yet bring peace.

Instead, Nixon clung to the delusion for four years, stringing out the attempts to make it work and the war itself. A series of temporary expedients, minor successes, enemy mistakes, and sheer deceptions sustained the prospect of an acceptable end to the war. The enemy's recovery from the Tet Offensive was slow, the Saigon regime seemed minimally more efficient and less obnoxious, draft calls plunged, and American forces shied away from costly search-and-destroy operations—with important exceptions like the invasion of Cambodia in the spring of 1970. The most disastrous allied initiative was an ARVN invasion of Laos in 1971, which Nixon tried to tout as a great success. He repeatedly stepped up the air war, sending bombers to Hanoi and Haiphong on the eve of his summit trip to Moscow in the spring of 1972. Perhaps the bombing had some effect. In peace accords drafted that fall, Hanoi dropped (among other things) its insistence on immediate expulsion of the Saigon regime and on reunification of Vietnam under communist auspices. Hanoi, however, yielded no more than Nixon and Kissinger, who, in return for Hanoi's pledge to repatriate American prisoners of war, now accepted a coalition government in the South and allowed a huge chunk of the North's forces to remain there.

The stumbling block to final American withdrawal was the Saigon regime, which balked at the sell-out it saw in the fall 1972 accords. Reelected by a landslide, Nixon unleashed the bombers on the North for one final and ferocious assault. "I don't want any more of this crap about the fact you couldn't hit this target or that one," he told the JCS chairman, but in a twist on popular notions of civil-military differences, the air force sidestepped Nixon and limited attacks risking civilian casualties. In any event, Nixon's rage was not really against the North. He bombed not to budge Hanoi, whose terms changed little, but to induce Saigon to sign by giving it a down payment on his secret promise to renew bombing after American withdrawal if Hanoi violated the accords. This was "war by tantrum," argued columnist James Reston. "We bombed the North Vietnamese into accepting our concession," noted one Kissinger aide ruefully. Not only Saigon smelled a sell-out, but many Americans—suspicious hawks and embittered military commanders, and war opponents who made a good case that the final terms could have been achieved years earlier. Still, the fig leaf of peace with honor was momentarily in place.[63]

The cost of getting it in place was enormous. The staggering toll among Indochinese continued. Nixon's bombing of Cambodia undermined the slippery neutrality of Prince Sihanouk's regime, whose collapse, along with the American invasion, paved the way for precisely what he presumably was trying to prevent, the communist takeover of another country, in this case by Khmer Rouge whose genocide far exceeded the Hanoi regime's brutalities. The toll of American war deaths continued to mount, and the American armed forces' morale and efficiency plummeted, as they became racked by drug use, racial turmoil, atrocities, corrupt and inefficient commanders, and enlisted men's violence toward them.

Those problems were rooted partly in the war's ugly nature and partly in circumstances preceding Nixon's presidency. The officer corps' careerist mentality, criticized by many officers themselves, took senior officers away from field leadership. ("What's the difference between the Marine Corps and the Boy Scouts?" ran one joke. "The Boy Scouts have adult leadership."[64]) The top-heavy command and logistical structure imposed the burden of combat on a small portion of the total forces. The rapid rotation of forces in and out of Vietnam diminished the cohesion of fighting units. Nixon, however, made these problems worse, while covering them up and shifting blame for them elsewhere. He shielded the armed forces from the sting of reappraisal by releasing Lt. William Calley, the officer partly responsible for the My Lai massacre of Vietnamese civilians, from his sentence of life imprisonment and by blaming journalists and liberals for the military's troubles. Military officers themselves were sometimes disgusted by his actions. The general in charge of the My Lai inquiry accused Nixon of trying "to appease those misguided people who either viewed Calley as an innocent scapegoat or opposed the whole idea of war-crimes prosecutions of Americans." The captain in charge of Calley's prosecution complained to Nixon about "political leaders who have failed to see the moral issue."[65]

It measured the perverse nature of Nixon's investment in militarization that he weakened the armed forces as he pursued the appearance of a victory he knew to be impossible in a war which had lost any strategic importance. Exchanging toasts in Moscow and Beijing with the big enemies, as he did in his famous summit conferences, he sought destruction of their minor surrogates (as he saw them). Determined to preserve the core of American power, he gutted it by tieing American forces down in an area beyond the effective reach of their power. Refusing to admit defeat, he denied Americans the forthright confrontation with it that might have deepened reappraisal of militarization.

Even that course had its merits and supporters—in 1972 voters did give Nixon his landslide, after all, even if affection for him was slight and the mood sour. On its own, his course abroad might have helped to heal the war's wounds and secure the prudent contraction of American power Nixon did genuinely want. But it did not stand on its own. Just as Johnson's war in Vietnam could not be separated from his other wars, Nixon's war to win the peace could not be separated from the "wars" he waged at home. No President more firmly embraced the war mentality—the deeply felt and promiscuously applied sense that every struggle within the body politic could be understood and waged as if it were a war. On that score, Nixon surpassed Johnson—no mean feat—if only because Johnson's wars were sometimes inspired by generous impulses, Nixon's almost always by mean ones. Whatever his success in constraining the formal processes of militarization, he so inflamed its political and imaginative dimensions that he canceled out that success.

Nixon's wars were numerous, starting with the 1968 campaign. He "told his staff to conduct the campaign as if it were an all-out war," filled his staff with men equally "vindictive," and urged the Secret Service and local goon squads to harass hecklers on the campaign trail.[66] For those actions he had considerable precedent and provocation in the illegal spying and harassment by police and intelligence agencies under Kennedy and Johnson, and in the disruptive behavior (directed, however, more at Humphrey than at Nixon) of some war opponents; even the inaugural parade, for the first time in history, was marred in 1969 by violence.

The 1968 campaign melted into Nixon's war against the press after he took office. As he wrote, he was "prepared to have to do combat with the media," which he stupidly and self-pityingly saw as "far more powerful than the President." The tone was set at the start by appointment of the young and ill-prepared Ron Ziegler as his press secretary, practically a calculated "insult" to the press. Nothing seized more of Nixon's time and emotions than his struggle with the media until the Watergate cover-up consumed him—and that in many ways was just another phase of the struggle. Every day he reviewed what the press had done, fired off orders to punish this journalist or counteract that story, tried to promote a congratulatory view of himself, and filled his notes and conversations with words of attack. His staff shared his outlook: "How can we use the available federal machinery to screw our political enemies?" asked John Dean in a 1971 memo. "The press is the enemy," Nixon said "dozens, if not hundreds, of times."[67]

The war against the press was one path into the labyrinth of misdeeds collectively known as "Watergate." Leaks (except when he authorized them) to the media of official information or inside scuttlebutt infuriated Nixon even more than other Presidents, and he set out to wiretap, harass, or punish officials, reporters, and other enemies real or presumed. His belief that radical foes of the war were funded, inspired, or controlled by Moscow fed Nixon's wrath, but he lashed out at people of all sorts of ideological, political, and professional positions. Nor was a real leak required to prompt action: one New York Times story during the Cambodian invasion was picked up from Hanoi radio, but the White House sought wiretaps to finger those it suspected as the betrayers of the story, Defense Secretary Melvin Laird and Secretary of State William Rogers. Fearing legal jeopardy, however, police and spy agencies like J. Edgar Hoover's FBI would not always do Nixon's bidding, at least on his terms. So Nixon increasingly turned to his own devices, jerry-built operations directed from the White House: the notorious "Plumbers" unit and the "Enemies Project."

Nixon's wars kept escalating. Reaction to the spring 1970 American invasion of Cambodia, which included widespread protest and police violence, unhinged Nixon (it was then he had a famous postmidnight talk with protesters in Washington, listening to them little, pleading that he wanted peace, and rambling on about subjects from football to the Cold War). That spring, a key aide thought, saw the "beginning of his downhill slide," when Nixon gave up on using official agencies "in his battle to quell the national uproar." A public warning from Chief Justice Warren Burger (Nixon's own appointee) against suspending "basic guarantees of the individual in times of great national stress" had no effect on him. In 1971, publication of the Pentagon Papers, a cache of secret documents on the war leaked by Defense Department official Daniel Ellsberg, sent Nixon over another threshold, especially after the Supreme Court upheld the *New York Times*'s right to print them. Among other things, he went after Ellsberg and his psychiatrist.[68]

Nixon's 1972 campaign marked another stage in his effort to root out enemies. Bypassing the traditional party machinery in favor of the Committee to Re-elect the President (CREEP), lacking confidence in his own chances and convinced that anything was permissible to enhance them, Nixon allowed— though perhaps not specifically directed—his operatives to undertake break-ins at Democratic Party headquarters in the Watergate Hotel and other "dirty tricks" over which his recently resigned attorney general, John Mitchell, presided. Once the Watergate burglars were caught, Nixon became an active conspirator in wide-ranging efforts to block investigations, lest they expose the White House role in not only the burglary but a host of other dubious operations. Discussing the cover-up and the campaign that fall, a rambling Nixon insisted that his coconspirators "recognize this, this is, again, . . . war."[69]

Behind these sentiments and actions lay cold ambition, but something more as well. Ending the war and achieving detente required, in Nixon's eyes, extraordinary secrecy, lest leaks foment disabling criticism at home, upset suspicious communist leaders abroad, or permit them to exploit divisions among Americans. For a quarter-century, Republicans had run a cottage industry condemning secret diplomacy by Democrats, but this was presumably different. Nixon dipped into that bottomless well of World War II analogies to justify secrecy: "Look at the Manhattan Project that built the atom bomb. Secrecy was necessary, and the project was successful." As he saw it, ending the war also required that the North Vietnamese see him as not only ruthless toward them but also in uncontested command of his own nation, an image that leaks would destroy. As Kissinger reportedly told him, release of the Pentagon Papers "shows you're a weakling" and damages "your image," and if other governments "feel that we can't control internal leaks, they will never agree to secret negotiations." Nixon, ever fearful of appearing a "weakling," hardly needed the explanation. Dissenters and leakers had to be crushed in the grander cause of ending the war honorably. His view of the presidency—though he assailed liberals, he took their view of the magisterial presidency to new heights—made that course all the more legitimate in his eyes.[70]

As his difficulty using the FBI indicated, he also decided to take on the federal bureaucracy, on which he heaped contempt. His disdain for the State Department and Secretary Rogers was infamous: in nearly every diplomatic initiative of Nixon's presidency, they were out of the loop, while Nixon and

Kissinger resorted to "back channels" to carry on the affairs of state. Bureaucrats generally he regarded as disloyal Democrats. "If we don't get rid of those people," he told the Cabinet, "they will either sabotage us from within, or they'll just sit back on their well-paid asses and wait for the next election to bring back their old bosses." At the same time, Nixon had no interest in making bureaucracies function better. He simply wanted to bypass and undercut them, whether Republicans or Democrats were in charge. As he fumed in 1972, "the whole damn bunch" had to resign after the election, and it was time to say, " 'Look, you're out, you're out, you're finished, you're done, done, finished.' Knock them the hell out of here." As Tom Huston, the aide charged with developing a plan to root out enemies, put it, "the bureaucracy must be treated as the enemy."[71]

Why did Nixon regard these campaigns as wars? Nixon explained his terminology even less than Johnson. He did leave behind a monumental record explaining why he hated his enemies, and his dislikes were hardly surprising or indefensible. Bureaucracies *were* often stubborn or self-serving; some war protesters *were* uncouth and violent; reporters *did* often give Nixon a hard time (though he was endorsed in 1972 by 753 daily papers, McGovern by 56).[72] Those truths help explain his passions, which differed little from those of many other Presidents, but not his unbending desire to cast those passions in the language and emotions of war. No explanation seems convincing, but there are clues. One of Nixon's striking characteristics was that he never really seemed to hate communists, at least those who ruled abroad. Perhaps he hated communism in the abstract, but individual leaders rarely incurred his fury. Even more than with most politicians, his anticommunism seemed politically calculated rather than heartfelt. He rarely relished the enemy's destruction, though he often called for it. He rarely showed the personal sense of aggression that LBJ displayed when speaking of Ho Chi Minh. He rarely summoned up the moral fervor about the enemy that Roosevelt marshaled about Nazism and other Presidents about communism. For communist leaders like Soviet premier Leonid Brezhnev and China's Mao Tse-tung and Chou En-lai, he felt an admiration and rapport bordering on affection, and he often mused on the similarities of temperament, style, and stature he saw between them and himself. Nor did he gush humanitarian sympathy for his own ally in the Vietnam War.

Yet war inevitably arouses passions even—or perhaps especially—among leaders who claim they coldly calculate geopolitical realities. A frustrating war only extended and distended those passions. And much in Nixon's life—the troubled relationship with Eisenhower, the shadow of Ike's reputation, the childish identity with Gen. George Patton—led him to seek not just a successful presidency but heroic military status. But if his passions did not run against the enemy abroad, where was he to direct them? If he was to be a heroic general crushing enemies, what enemy? Historians rightly distrust hydraulic models of energies flowing in one direction after being blocked in another, yet such displacement does seem to occur. Nixon, as he had since his campaign against Alger Hiss, took the fury usually aimed at enemies overseas and directed it against foes at home. He "could forgive and even embrace his enemies abroad," Ambrose observes, but he "could not find it in himself to forgive his enemies at home."[73] During the Vietnam War, most Americans seemed to hate each other more than the enemy. In this, Nixon was not alone. As President, however, he offered a peculiarly dangerous example.

Nixon's wars overlapped eerily with the Vietnam War itself, eroding further any line between war elsewhere and "war" at home, and they poisoned American politics, bringing a war mentality to the Oval Office. True, not all of those wars did he expressly label as such, while the White House declared so many people "enemies" that the term might seem drained of significant meaning. And insofar as Nixon's wars were secret until revealed in the Watergate crisis, their venom did not poison the public mood until 1973.

But Nixon *did* often use terms like "war," and despite secrecy, his wars had their impact long before they were fully revealed. They set the tone for the administration's dealings with the public on the Vietnam War. They turned attention away from substantive issues of war to procedural conflicts over how those issues got raised, aggravating a longstanding feature of debate on the war. They sharpened the antagonism between Nixon and the media, not only in general mood but because individual journalists and media companies often got wind they were targeted. They demoralized officials and agencies and jeopardized their support for Nixon's policies, making a reality of what Nixon had feared from the start. They expanded the repressive and illegal work of federal intelligence and police agencies (and indirectly those at the state and local level, whose "red squads" and the like form another chapter in this story)—and since Nixon could not trust those agencies, his administration formed its own apparatus, undercutting the constituted bodies. A mood many felt as akin to war— among the President and Congress and the courts, in the body politic, in the White House—arose before the Watergate crisis erupted.

In the 1972 campaign, it was evident not only in CREEP's methods and Nixon's actions but in the campaign of George McGovern, the Democratic candidate. McGovern was in many ways a classic liberal and dove, although cautious on some issues, such as abortion rights. A bomber pilot in Europe during World War II, he had credentials in war that Nixon could not match. He promised "a tough, lean military" but disavowed "major revisions in American commitments, or a major scaling down in real American security interests"—an outlook broadly similar to Nixon's. Echoing Roosevelt and Eisenhower (whom he quoted liberally), he proposed to redefine national security to include "schools for our children as well as silos for our missiles, the health of our families as much as the size of our bombs, the safety of our streets and the condition of our cities and not just the engines of war." Sargent Shriver, he said of his running mate, "commanded the war on poverty; and in the next administration, that is the war America will wage and win." Thus McGovern spoke out of a long liberal tradition of people troubled by militarization but not quite repudiating it, seared by war but clinging to it as a model for new actions. Still, he was pilloried as a pacifist, isolationist, and social radical (his was "the campaign of the three A's: acid, abortion, and amnesty," claimed Republican senator Hugh Scott). His rhetoric and politics often reinforced that image.[74]

McGovern also exacerbated the sense of a war raging within America—indeed, the sense that World War II, in a twisted new version, had returned to the land. He compared Nixon's bombing in Southeast Asia "to Hitler's campaign to exterminate Jews" and suggested that the Watergate break-in "was the kind of thing you expect under a person like Hitler."[75] Other Democrats hinted that Nixon was a war criminal. Such comparisons were hardly the bulk of McGovern's case. Harsh words, not illegal acts, they were a logical response to decades of claims that anyone opposing Cold War policies was an appeaser and that the stakes in the Cold War were like those in World War II. Still, comparing Nixon to Hitler had the result, if not the intention, of further aggravating the "war" at home. After all, given how most Americans recalled World War II, the implication was that Nixon should be forcibly overthrown: was that not what the Germans should have done to Hitler?

Such rhetoric, not surprisingly, infuriated Nixon. More surprising, a triumphant reelection—over 60 percent of the popular tally—gave him no joy. "I think as the war recedes as an issue," he wrote in his diary, "some of these people are going to be lost souls. They basically are haters, they are frustrated, they are alienated—they don't know what to do with their lives." Nixon had in mind antiwar protesters, but as often his harshest observations also applied to himself. As the American war effort in Vietnam ended, he seemed lost without that war and eager to find replacements. In his mind, his enemies were now numerous and diverse, embracing people in all of the federal government, in all walks of life (blacks, Jews, intellectuals, and businessmen among them), and in both political parties. Those enemies were "asking for it," he told his advisors, "and they are going to get it." His contempt extended to Americans generally. "The average American is just like the child in the family," he told the *Washington Star.* "You give him some responsibility and he is going to amount to something," but if "you make him completely dependent and pamper him . . . , you are going to make him soft, spoiled and eventually a very weak individual." He "sounded," Ambrose notes, "like a leader rallying his people for a protracted war."[76]

Victory in the 1972 elections left him restless. Earlier he said of his enemies, "We'll stick our heels in, step on them hard and twist." Kissinger "knows what I mean," he added. "Get them on the floor and step on them, crush them, show no mercy." His hatred deepened after the election, as if, Kissinger sensed, "victory was not an occasion for reconciliation but an opportunity to settle the scores of a lifetime." Nixon's "New American Revolution" to streamline the federal government was his old war on the bureaucracy in new guise. It even applied to his own appointees, all ordered to submit resignations. They "expected to be thanked; instead they got slapped." One advisor thought the order "the most disheartening, most surprising, and most cruel [act] of all." No wonder Nixon found Christmas 1972, with the final bombing of North Vietnam going on, "the loneliest and saddest Christmas I can ever remember, much sadder and much more lonely than the one in the Pacific during the war." That striking comparison was one more sign that Nixon, though ending America's war in Vietnam, could not let go of war.[77]

An ugly aftermath to war was not unique to Vietnam, to defeat in war (or, in 1973, the widespread suspicion that the peace accords meant it was forthcoming), or to Nixon's presidency. Social strife, economic conflict, and congressional resurgence had marked the aftermath of most American wars. The Vietnam War, in which turmoil long preceded the war's end, presented special problems.

For his part, Nixon, facing both the familiar problems and the new ones, made them all worse.

The Limits of Disengagement

During Nixon's presidency, the United States had a chance to disengage from militarization. It was largely passed up. That political outsiders failed in their efforts to press it was hardly surprising, since major change in American policy rarely comes from them. More striking, insiders, those best positioned to make change, failed to alter a course that genuinely troubled them.

A case for change did now emerge from mainstream experts and politicians. Writing near the end of the Vietnam War, historian Russell Weigley concluded, "At no point on the spectrum of violence does the use of combat offer much promise for the United States today." Vietnam augured badly for non-nuclear war: limited force had failed to achieve American goals and later resort to "unlimited, annihilative aims" had been counterproductive. Except for deterrence, nuclear weapons held no more promise. Even limited nuclear war would "destroy much or most" of the superpowers and be either brief and indecisive, "if the world were very lucky, or the prelude to general war." Schemes by defense intellectuals to limit and win a nuclear war left Weigley dubious: "War creates a momentum of its own" and "cannot be nicely controlled and restrained as strategists . . . would have it." Generally, Weigley thought that "the history of usable combat may at last be reaching its end."[78]

Bernard Brodie, his generation's preeminent strategist, offered similar conclusions. He was indignant at how the United States was finishing its part in the Vietnam War. "The idea," he wrote in 1972, "that all this tragic devastation" was justified because it kept "a General Thieu in power" and because "the President of the United States 'must be respected'" bordered "on the obscene."

Shaken by the war and by nuclear strategies he had helped to shape, Brodie speculated that war, like the "personal duel," might become "old fashioned and ridiculous." Organized violence would continue, but it might not "continue indefinitely to take the specific institutional form known as war."[79]

Brodie and Weigley summarized a long-developing critique of war and militarization, one also now advanced by intellectuals, officers, activists, artists, and politicians. "Does War Have a Future?" asked a contributor to the prestigious journal *Foreign Affairs*. Not much in any organized form was the answer, though "guerrilla war" and "barbarism" would persist. War seemed useful only for revolutionary groups unencumbered by the superpowers' ponderous forces. Even for them its utility was limited; Western governments had too much power and consent to be overthrown, however hard it was for them to wage war beyond their borders.[80]

The critique of war's utility was notable in tone as well as substance. Its best exponents were somber, avoiding the naive optimism about war's end some pundits once had shown. Working in the mainstream of American thought rather than its pacifist tributaries, haunted by the century's record of war, and sensitive to war's irrational sources, they knew that war might occur even though it served no rational ends. Few favored disarmament, at least of a unilateral sort, but a contraction of the arms race, the armed forces, and military intervention—a substantial disengagement from militarization—seemed both possible and wise.

The case for contraction was bolstered by scholarly studies and popular exposés about the "military-industrial complex," a term now more in vogue than when Eisenhower used it. Sen. William Proxmire offered *Report from Wasteland: America's Military-Industrial Complex* in 1970. Engineer and Pentagon official A. Ernest Fitzgerald denounced "the high priests of waste" (1972) with the righteousness of a patriotic populist (he was just a "country boy in the aerospace business"). Seymour Melman penned subtler critiques, *Pentagon Capitalism* (1970) and *The Permanent War Economy* (1974), explaining how the Pentagon fed on the arms race and caused "the decline of the United States as an economic and industrial system." Scientists and other experts, disillusioned by the arms race they had helped to wage, argued that American arms building was driven by indigenous pressures more than Soviet threats, with weapons invented first and missions only found for them later. As Jerome Wiesner said, "We are running an arms race with ourselves."[81]

By the early 1970s, new proposals to implement disengagement also emerged. Some exponents of arms control wanted a bare-bones strategic force sufficient only to deter the Soviets; anything more was redundant, since the superpowers' missiles "do nothing but deter the use of each other by making it suicidal."[82] Complementary cuts in warheads and delivery systems were also proposed. Given the wealth of American allies, the reduction or outright withdrawal of American forces in Europe and East Asia—an expensive item in the defense budget—seemed feasible to many, and in 1971 the Senate nearly approved Mike Mansfield's plan to cut the American commitment to NATO in half. Too, sharp cuts in overall budgets and forces levels were proposed, by McGovern and the liberal Brookings Institution among others. As they had for generations, proposals issued again to end the costly duplication in missions and weapons among branches of the American forces, while reform-minded officers tried to purge the military of corrupt and inefficient practices and streamline it for harder times and leaner budgets. All such plans risked political suicide and economic harm without new roles for defense industries, think tanks, laboratories, and bureaucracies that thrived on military spending. Energy shortages suggested one possibility: defense industries might turn to mass transit (at which Boeing made an unsuccessful stab) and in other ways solve ecological and energy problems. Few of these proposals were entirely new or particularly popular, but they now commanded greater respect, play in the media, and support in contemporary scholarship.

Disengagement from militarization did not by and large ensue, however. Just as militarization originally had many sources, so did its persistence, among them the lack of effective national leadership. The Democratic Congress did not often provide that leadership. Congress usually meets long-term change by fashioning concrete legislation rather than propounding broad outlooks. Its most notable actions were short-term (cutting off funds for the air war in Indochina in 1973) or procedural (the 1973 War Powers Act), and it repeatedly trimmed White House defense budgets. But as it long had, it resisted drastic cuts in defense that might harm local districts and favored interests. And though dominating Congress, Democrats after McGovern's fiasco were deeply divided, their conservative wing ascendant. Most famous was Sen. Henry Jackson's successful effort to stall granting the Soviet Union most-favored-nation trade status until it loosened control on Jewish emigration (which in fact had been sharply rising during detente). Jackson sabotaged detente and arms control (as well as Jewish emigration, it turned out) and assisted a new demonization of the Soviet Union evident by mid-decade. Cold War Democrats now dished out to Nixon the charges of appeasement and give-away that Nixon had long hurled. "I pray every night that Henry Kissinger won't give the Russians the Washington Monument," quipped labor leader George Meany, "he's given them every goddamn thing else."[83] For its part, the antiwar movement, fractious even at its peak, was now torn apart by internal squabbles, deprived of its obvious cause by the return of American troops from Vietnam, disheartened by McGovern's defeat, and exhausted by the length of the war and the effort to stop it. It hardly disappeared, but it only regrouped at decade's end in a new antinuclear movement.

That left Nixon, who did have a vision of disengagement and world peace. "Do we want to go back to a period when the United States and the Soviet Union stood in a confrontation against each other and risk a runaway nuclear arms race," he asked in 1974, "or do we want to . . . recognize . . . that we must either live together or we will all die together?" Though poorly articulated, his embrace (echoing Ike in the late 1950s) of nuclear "sufficiency" rather than superiority provided a strategic rationale for his vision.[84]

Nixon, however, wanted that vision implemented on his own terms, retained a divided mind about it, remained secretive about how to realize it, and proved unwilling to build a coalition on its behalf, still treating the State Department and the defense agencies with contempt, then incurring their wrath when his presidency weakened. He sought to preserve his "victory" in Vietnam even as fellow Republicans abandoned the cause (when South Vietnam's President Thieu came to Washington in the spring of 1973, all but one Cabinet member "found an excuse to skip the arrival ceremony"). He balked in 1973 at more cuts in defense spending lest they weaken his hand in negotiations to cap nuclear weapons and reduce conventional forces in Europe, arguing that "any incentive for other nations to cut theirs will go right out the window."[85]

Although familiar and plausible, that reasoning also lashed American weapons policy to a diplomatic treadmill: the United States would build up its military forces only to cut them later. And given the glacial pace of negotiations (among Western allies and American interests as well as with the Soviets), the build-up might proceed so long that when a cut-back finally came, it would only return force levels back to where the whole process started. That was substantially the pattern in the 1970s, though not solely because of Nixon's policies. The arms race continued, though not in symmetrical fashion: the United States excelled in the precision of delivery systems, which encouraged it to stabilize the number of warheads (at under twenty-nine thousand in the 1970s) and reduce their megatonnage; the Soviet Union, still by and large playing catch-up, emphasized numbers of warheads and behemoth rockets to deliver them, matching the U.S. in warheads at the decade's end. By then, more was on the drawing boards. American defense spending, declining early in the decade, rose in fiscal 1974 and more sharply thereafter, though continuing to slip as a percentage of total government spending and GNP, and no major reductions in forces abroad were instituted. By those standards, disengagement was real but distinctly limited, not the "dismantling . . . of the American military machine" that a historian, like many critics in the 1970s, soon called it.[86] Whether Soviet defense spending and capabilities were swelling, as widely alleged by some experts and hotly disputed by others at mid-decade, now seems less likely; in any event, Moscow was not recovering from a costly war—its retrenchment came in the 1980s, after its costly venture in Afghanistan.

For Nixon, disengagement was to be limited to what he and other world leaders achieved. With the notable exception of questioning mindless suspicion of the communist enemy, he offered no critique of the values and institutions that had led the nation through the Cold War and into Vietnam. Far from supporting reform-minded officers, he undermined them by suggesting that the military had been stabbed in the back by liberals and the press. In 1973, embracing the returned POWs and their "rhetoric of victorious armies and heroes," he took a major step toward reconstructing patriotic culture and furthering the nation's "amnesia" about the war's disturbing conduct and meaning. At the same time, scorning amnesty for war resisters (some of whom scorned receiving it from Nixon), he made it clear that alternative views of the war had no place in public debate. (Later, Nixon was an unrepentant recipient of a presidential pardon from Gerald Ford.) His "unwillingness to consider amnesty served only to intensify the wounds of war," as Nixon again practiced the politics of division while preaching the politics of unity. "By denying the validity of reconciliation—to forgive and to forget—the administration encouraged Americans only to forget. Instead of therapeutic amnesty, Nixon invited amnesia." Not that amnesia was unpopular or wholly his doing. "Moral debate about Vietnam," notes Peter Carroll, was "an increasingly awkward subject for hawk and dove alike," and Nixon's position "shielded the public from its complicity in the unpopular war." Nor would more debate necessarily have strengthened a consensus to demilitarize. Still, Nixon's position helped keep disengagement under his control, protected from national debate about basic values and institutions.[87]

Nixon gave another reason why disengagement would be slow when he warned in 1973 that "the pages of history are strewn with the wreckage of nations which fell by the wayside at the height of their strength and wealth because their people became weak, soft, and self-indulgent and lost the character and the spirit which had led to their greatness." Those words, echoing his 1970 plea against becoming "a pitiful, helpless giant," evoked lessons about appeasement that Nixon, like many others, had long propounded: weakness would tempt aggressors, lead to war, and destroy world peace. Yet the phrasing also suggested how much Americans' self-image, not just global strategy, was at play. Nixon feared loss of American "greatness" and moral fiber. (He worried about the selfishness of youth raised after the rigors of depression and world war, though, as a biographer notes, he "was the ultimate 'me' person.") Like many Americans for generations, he defined greatness as military power and believed that decline in moral fiber would be prevented or at least offset by military strength. Humiliation in Vietnam and the moral rot at home blamed for it made that definition even more compelling for Nixon and his followers. As long as it held, demilitarization could not proceed very far.[88]

Nixon's comment illuminated how much defense policy remained in a world apart from calculations of military or diplomatic need. Worried strategists argued convincingly that far fewer nuclear weapons would suffice to deter an enemy, the only thing they could do anyway. For others, however, those weapons remained totems of national greatness and resolve. They had their strategic arguments, of course, often spun as finely as those offered by advocates of sharp reductions, but the case for the nuclear arsenal really lay in another realm, one made perversely more charged by new geopolitical challenges. In the form most obnoxious to Americans, those now came from forces outside the Cold War framework, above all from Middle Eastern countries filled with Arab nationalism, Islamic fervor, hatred of Israel, or determination to exploit their riches of oil. The reflex response of many Americans, however, was to cling to Cold War symbols of power and greatness: to build more nuclear weapons, even if they could not stop the new challenges. Suspicion that Moscow was behind those challenges was never altogether convincing—despite its troublemaking, the Kremlin also had many disasters abroad—but it gave the response an appearance of strategic logic.

Economic difficulties provided more temptation to rebuild American military power. Consent for militarization had long rested on the affluence it seemed to yield, protect, or at least permit, just as the economic strains brought on by the Vietnam War had helped to undermine that consent. In 1973 and 1974, however, economic conditions deteriorated further and took startling new forms just when the retreat of American power seemed evident. If the price of retreat was a floundering economy, few politicians could welcome it. To be sure, there were other ways to read the economic woes—as a spillover from the Vietnam War and from neglect of the nation's economic competitiveness—just as there were other solutions suggested, by Nixon on occasion among others, such as increased investment in that competitiveness. Nor was there any widespread taste or foreseeable way for using military power to achieve economic goals. Still, it damaged the fortunes of disengagement that its start coincided with economic trouble.

Social change also activated the brake on disengagement. Such change, far from diminishing as the war ended, only accelerated in the 1970s. Emboldened in part by Congress's approval of the Equal Rights Amendment in 1972 and the Supreme Court's 1973 decision in *Roe v. Wade* granting liberal access to abortion, the feminist movement was reaching its zenith of zeal and influence, even as it divided between radical and moderate factions. Gay liberation, though oriented to local communities and lacking national organization, was at its most ideologically daring stage. Such movements reflected a pattern much noticed in the 1970s: the diminishing attachment of social groups to an overarching American identity in favor of a particularistic one—class, racial, ethnic, religious, regional, or gendered. The United States had become (or reemerged as being) "a segmented society," historians claimed.[89] The shift rarely entailed a rejection of American identity, but it did permit greater emphasis on one's social group and one's historical "roots," as Alex Haley's popular 1976 book and 1977 movie tracing a black family's history was titled.

These complex social changes offered no collective challenge to militarization, though some components did. They were too ideologically diverse—ranging from born-again Christians to advocates of sexual liberation to celebrants of Native American culture or Polish-American heritage—and too focused on the various compelling agendas of the groups involved. Therein, however, lay part of the rub. One impulse to their emergence had been the collapse during the Vietnam era of a widely shared sense of national mission in the world and of Americans' willingness to submerge their particular identities in a common cause led by national elites. Even movements that did not repudiate militarization and the Cold War—and leaders of the new Christian Right clung furiously to those causes—in many ways turned away from them by their focus on their own group and its mission. Each, according to one of their chroniclers, offered a heady sense of mission, tapping the ideal of forming a "city upon a hill" felt by the first Puritan settlers and sustained among Americans ever since.[90] Now, however, that mission less often involved America's role in the world but rather the groups' various visions of changing America. Their collective impact upon Americans was also bewildering precisely because of the sheer proliferation of missions and identities. The Vietnam War had allowed a kind of coherence, around the simple poles of opposition to or support for the war, during the first stage of this proliferation. By 1973, coherence was fast fading.

An old temptation—to stop or conceal social segmentation by stressing anti-communism, patriotism, and military power—resurfaced in the 1970s. It operated with particular force insofar as some movements, especially women's and gay liberation, seemed to express the "weak, soft, and self-indulgent" side of American life, as Nixon had put it, at a time when the American effort in Vietnam had already rekindled fears of internal weakness. In line with longstanding GOP policy, Nixon supported the Equal Rights Amendment, but his discomfort with women's liberation was palpable: "Let me make one thing perfectly clear," he reportedly said, "I wouldn't want to wake up next to a lady pipe fitter."[91]

It was less any particular movement that disconcerted men like Nixon, however, than the broader panorama of discord. Such discord rarely provoked an explicit call to remilitarize. In fact, Nixon and the GOP consigned social and political divisions to the 1960s, arguing that they were now healed by his presidency. "It is so easy to forget how frightful it was" back then, read the GOP's 1972 platform, since "a new leadership with new policies and new programs has restored reason and order and hope."[92] Those divisions were not in the past, however, as Nixon's private fury about them attested. They fired anxieties about American unity and "greatness" and efforts to foster both by amassing military power.

The pivotal year in this story was 1973. At its start, it seemed that the Vietnam War, militarization, and the war mentality might all recede from their dominant place in American life; that summer, the last American war effort in Indochina ceased after Congress mandated an end to bombing there. But simultaneously Americans entered other "wars," as they were called. Nixon had begun the year by privately declaring war on his enemies in the Vietnam War: it was time for "a total attack basis. We should hit those who sabotaged and jeopardized the peace all the way," he instructed his aide Bob Haldeman. "At all costs give no quarter whatever to the doves," he repeated a few weeks later. "Hitler would have Britain and the world if they had been in Churchill's place," he soon added. "He was," claims Ambrose, "the angriest American President." Another war, one Nixon did not want, soon opened up as his Watergate cover-up and other illegalities began unraveling in the face of congressional and legal inquiries and revelations by officials unwilling to do jail time silently. By summer, the efforts of Sen. Sam Ervin's Select Committee on Watergate and the Watergate special prosecutor to get access to White House audio tapes produced what *Newsweek* dubbed "the war for the Nixon tapes."[93]

Then a crisis over Israel and Western access to Mideast oil developed. For months, tension had been building between Israel and its neighbors over the vast lands Israel had seized in the 1967 war, while the Soviet Union and the United States jockeyed for position, although Kissinger failed to exploit the stunning Cold War coup of Egypt's decision to sever its dependence on Soviet aid. On October 6 came an Egyptian-Syrian invasion of Israeli-held lands whose force and near success shocked Israel and its allies; the ensuing tank battles rivaled in scale those of World War II. The White House first tried to restrain Israel in order to avoid further antagonizing its neighbors, then reversed itself to rush war materiel to Israel lest its beleaguered forces lose. Adding to the tension was an alert to American nuclear forces foolishly issued (probably by Kissinger, but Nixon was blamed for it) in order to warn the Soviets, who were already supplying Israel's foes and now seemed ready to airlift troops to the Mideast, to stay out. All this came on the heels of the famous "Saturday Night Massacre," when Nixon fired Special Prosecutor Archibald Cox (and the attorney general and deputy attorney general for refusing to fire Cox), as apparent constitutional war raged.

Israeli forces finally prevailed and a cease-fire was imposed, but through the Organization of Petroleum Exporting Countries (OPEC), Arab nations (and non-Arab producers like Iran) imposed an embargo, lasting from October 16 until March 1974, on sales of oil that made its price quadruple and triggered the first great energy crisis. Arab countries, seen by most American officials as incapable of cooperating with each other, now had a stranglehold on the economic lifeblood of the United States and its allies.

Oil was the "Arabs' final weapon," *Time* had warned in September, and with the embargo the language of war spread. As James Burnham argued in the *National Review,* Arabs had acquired in oil an "ultimate weapon" that superseded the nuclear bomb, since the latter was unusable whereas the Arabs' "formidable new weapon" possessed "a global range." Burnham added, "This is not metaphor. Arab oil right now is literally a *weapon,*" one "considerably more ultimate than nuclear bombs: The nuclear weapon is powerless to counter the oil weapon." It was more frightful because "Moscow was backstopping" the Arabs, and in the ultimate Soviet-American "clash of wills," Americans, Burnham suspected, would not prevail.[94]

Many commentators did not see Moscow's sinister hand or portray oil as a "weapon," but Burnham's analysis suggested why Americans found the 1973 energy crisis so jarring and so akin to war. It broke out when American power was in retreat, after a war in Vietnam in which its nuclear might had proven useless (or at least unused) and when the critique of war and weapons was growing. Oil not only gave Arab states leverage in its own right, it seemed to displace military weapons in the tide of history. Nor could nuclear weapons be used to counter the Arabs' new-found might, for oil was literally and politically volatile: the United States and its allies hardly dared set fire to it in some effort to club Arab states into submission; they seemed hog-tied, unable to use the very weapons in which they were superior. To boot, once they reopened the oil spigot, oil-rich nations would rake in billions with which to buy real weapons. Metaphors of the oil "weapon" and "oil war" had other sources as well. Oil had long been the fuel for nations at war and one of the major spoils of war. Europeans sometimes employed the same metaphor. And in the Mideast, oil was deeply enmeshed with the threat and outbreak of war.

As it often does, talk of war also reflected the shock of confronting a novel problem. In 1973, the oil embargo climaxed a bad run of economic news. Though recession and inflation were thought irreconcilable—recessions presumably lower prices by cutting demand for goods and services—now they combined in "stagflation." Shortages of staple foods and other products in addition to oil, combined with a surging ecological sensibility, produced a sharp sense among many Americans that they and the world were entering a new age of limits on resources and growth, one that challenged the American genius for sidestepping conflict over the distribution of the economic pie by increasing its overall size. Economic competition from abroad added to the worry. As sales of American cars plunged while low-paying service jobs proliferated, "a nation of hamburger stands" loomed, complained the AFL-CIO in words repeated almost verbatim long after, "a country stripped of industrial capacity and meaningful work . . . of citizens busily buying and selling cheeseburgers and root beer floats."[95]

Such changes did not catch Americans entirely unawares in 1973. Their first trade deficit in eighty years appeared in 1971. Experts had warned about rising consumption and declining domestic production of oil, some shortages had already occurred, and Congress and the White House had considered action. But the embargo forced a sharper realization of these difficulties. Over the winter, as Americans were forced to turn down thermostats, drive slowly, face empty gas stations, and meet de facto gas rationing, treasured rituals of American consumer culture seemed in jeopardy. That many of these emergency measures had precedent only in World War II reinforced the felt connections among the oil crisis, soaring prices, and war, perhaps why one concerned Illinois group called itself "Women War on Prices." The mood was dismal: "THINGS WILL GET WORSE," according to one newspaper headline, "BEFORE THEY GET WORSE."[96] Talk of war reflected shock over destruction of longstanding assumptions about endless American prosperity. It also masked conflict among American economic interests and social groups: in an "oil war" with the Mideast, the enemy was far away and Americans presumably united in their misery and indignation.

Applying the language of war to these developments hardly meant Americans were ready to go to war, despite loose talk and coarse humor about "nuking" the Arabs that bounced around during the 1970s. Still, their solutions often drew on the spirit and precedents of war: addressing a national television audience, Nixon compared the oil crisis to World War II and proposed the Manhattan Project (citing the "determination," unity, and willingness to spend money it involved) as a model for "Project Independence," his energy plan.[97] It was as if Americans could not let go of war even if they had no taste for waging it. Their forces had left Indochina, but "war" continued for them—over Nixon, oil, trade, the environment. Though of a different nature, the array of "wars" seemed as dizzying under Nixon as they had been under Johnson.

Meanwhile, Nixon's capacity to define such things faded. He no longer dominated politics, though his fate did. His futile effort to withhold the White House tapes showing his guilt dragged on into 1974. In 1973 came the indignity of Vice President Agnew's resignation amid charges that he had taken bribes as Maryland's governor (Rep. Gerald Ford succeeded him). Democrats scented blood, though it was common wisdom that they were in no hurry to see Nixon resign—a wounded Nixon promised more political returns than a GOP successor with a clean slate—and, in part for tactical reasons, liberals did not spearhead the anti-Nixon cause; the most effective Democrat was Sam Ervin, a conservative southern senator.

More surprising than liberal spleen was disarray within the GOP. Nixon prided himself on running a tight ship, but the White House sprang leaks and his staff ran for cover in 1973. "It will be each man for himself, and one will not be afraid to rat on the other," he noted accurately in his diary, but in part that was because of how he treated those around him. He lied to his aides, lawyers, and family about his role in the cover-up and other matters, pitted subordinates against each other, asserted undying loyalty to them until casting them off, and, even as word leaked about earlier payoffs, dangled money before those he feared might expose him ("Is there any way you can use *cash*?" he asked John Ehrlichman and Bob Haldeman just before they resigned). His efforts produced short-term gains but also long-term exposure to anger and prosecution. Had he taken Republican potentates into his confidence, at least early on in the crisis, he might have had the votes to block impeachment in the House, and certainly conviction in the Senate. Instead he enraged GOP stalwarts. "There are only so many lies you can take," Senator Goldwater declared in August 1974 in another fulmination about Nixon. "Nixon should get his ass out of the White House— today!"[98]

Republicans, after all, had the most to lose from a discredited Nixon still in office—their party would sink with him in the 1974 and 1976 elections—and already resented how Nixon had distanced himself from the party and drained money away from its candidates to support his own presidential bid. In crude political terms, they were the ones who forced his resignation. Meanwhile, Nixon's own appointees, especially Secretary of State Kissinger and Defense Secretary James Schlesinger, sanctimoniously bypassed him or boldly defied him in crucial matters of national security—in the Mideast crisis of 1973–1974 and when Nixon sought to work out a SALT II agreement with Brezhnev in 1974.

Nixon's best defense was that his predecessors had committed similar misdeeds, but that defense was hard to press. The claim was partly accurate, since previous presidents had sanctioned illegal wiretaps, sent the Internal Revenue Service against enemies, and done much else. But if only because they had not been caught or challenged for such acts, they had not engaged in the sustained obstruction of justice that consumed Nixon, and it was Nixon's cover-up that alarmed friends as well as foes more than the original acts he tried to conceal. In any event, a defense that pointed to predecessors' crimes required Nixon to admit his own, which he would never do.

Though the Watergate crisis had many dimensions, it also had compelling links to the history of war and militarization. Nixon praised his toughness in war and foreign policy, but in handling Watergate he displayed a macabre version of the indecisiveness that also dogged him in the Vietnam War. He compared the excruciating choices now before him to his earlier wartime decisions to invade Cambodia in 1970 and to bomb Haiphong in December 1972: "It's tougher than Cambodia and December 18th put together," he said in April 1973.[99] But time and again he sidled up to choices on Watergate—to come clean or hide completely, to burn the White House tapes or release them, to cast aside a coconspirator or defend him—only to waffle. He had an abstract model of the tough wartime President, but also antennae so keenly attuned to conflicting considerations that they crippled him. That model also made acceptable and legal to him any action taken in the name of national security, but since the latter was indistinguishable for him from his own interests, he had no convincing rationale grounded in national security for his actions.

His foes often failed to do much better on this score. Some resorted to underhanded actions, as leaks (often inaccurate) sprang in torrents from the Senate Select Committee and the Special Prosecutor's Office. Those indignant about Nixon seemed bereft of words to describe him, resorting to clichés and comparisons drawn from World War II. The White House displayed a "Gestapo mentality," according to Senator Ervin; Nixon's firing of Cox was a "Brownshirt operation" employing "Gestapo tactics," argued another Democratic senator; a member of Cox's staff indicated he was "going home to read about the Reichstag fire."[100] Obeisance to World War II as America's defining moment still ruled; thirty years in the past, it still nourished the lexicon of political invective.

Less noticed in the ruckus was how much Watergate fit a pattern of crises after America's wars. Comparison of Watergate to President Andrew Johnson's impeachment after the Civil War was inescapable, but Wilson's crippled presidency after 1918 also was worth pondering: his grand vision for world peace had been shattered even more than Nixon's, and wild rumors had arisen about his mental and physical health, as they did about Nixon's by 1974. Truman faced a congressional challenge about the integrity of key associates and about his refusal to hand over executive documents to congressmen (including Richard Nixon) pursuing Alger Hiss. President Nixon, for one, tried to learn from the Hiss case—it was a confused, self-defeating effort, but at least he glimpsed something.

Still, Nixon usually found his words and analogs for Watergate in the certainties of war rather than the ambiguities of war's aftermath. "This is a battle, it's a fight, it's war," he advised his aide Charles Colson early in the Watergate crisis. A few weeks later, furious at a leak from the FBI about Watergate, he wanted the agency purged. "The whole damn place ought to be fired," he fumed. "I think you've got to do it like they did in the war, you remember in World War II the Germans, if they went through these towns and then a sniper hit one of them, they'd line up the whole goddamned town and say until you talk you're all going to be shot." His private defense of his misdeeds involved a telling comparison: "It isn't something . . . like Hiss, for example, God-damned treason."[101]

The Watergate crisis resonated with war in other ways besides the language and emotions attached to it. It worsened in the summer of 1973 as American bombers still pounded Cambodia. Nixon tried to divert attention from the crisis by wrapping himself in the flag and embracing returning Vietnam POWs, for whom he held what he called "the largest and most spectacular White House gala in history."[102] Passage over his veto of the War Powers Act, a weak effort to restrict the President's power to wage war without congressional approval, reflected Nixon's faltering grip on Congress and its growing distrust of presidential power. Nixon also faced charges about the bombing of Cambodia and the methods by which he kept it secret, although the House Judiciary Committee did not vote to impeach on those grounds. In invoking executive privilege to shield the tapes and other documents from Congress and the special prosecutor, he relied almost exclusively on national security as his defense: without confidentiality for his conversations, he claimed, any President's efforts in diplomacy and defense would be crippled. Defending to Attorney General Elliot Richardson his right to fire the special prosecutor, Nixon pled that "Brezhnev would never understand if I let Cox defy my instructions."[103] Defending his presidency, he insisted that on it hinged the chance to hold onto victory in Vietnam, keep America strong, and bring world peace.

More diffuse anxieties also arose about what was called the "imperial presidency" but might better have been named the "war presidency." The President's power in war had been an issue all through American history. The Constitution made the President "Commander in Chief" only "of the Army and Navy . . . and of the Militia of the several States, when called into the actual service of the United States." In the twentieth century, however, the phrase was construed so that the President was, as Garry Wills puts it, "widely considered to be the Commander in Chief of the American people" in peace as well as war, as if "the president has the power to commit the whole citizenry to following his lead." Presidents were introduced or offered themselves as the commander in chief to Congress, federal agencies, and all Americans. "The phrase 'commander-in-chief' ran trippingly off the tongue" of Nixon, one observer complained before Watergate surfaced. "It seemed to please him not only to use the powers and probably to stretch them but also to utter the words over and over again in public. No other President of recent memory has used the phrase anything like so often and with such obvious gratification." It also pleased others to use it: carrying out Nixon's order to fire Cox, Alexander Haig (himself a military officer) told an official, "Your Commander in Chief has given you an order. You have no alternative." Few in Congress tackled the constitutional and political questions raised by this loose use of the term, but it hovered in the background of Watergate: it had emboldened Nixon, alarmed others, and further smudged the boundaries between war and peace.[104]

More generally, Watergate was inconceivable without the Vietnam War, so intimately were the misdeeds and the reactions to them bound up with the war's politics and paranoia. Nixon was self-pitying in 1977 when he affirmed an interviewer's description of him as "the last American casualty of the Vietnam War."[105] He was right, however, to see his fate as tied to the war.

With Nixon's decline seemed to go much of the impetus to disengage from militarization and invest in the nation's needs at home. He continued to push detente and arms control, energy and mass transit programs, a new welfare system, and universal health insurance (through a mandate to employers to provide it, with government helping to insure others). But most domestic reforms languished (many to resurface in the late 1980s and early 1990s), and others initiated, like revenue sharing with state and local governments, were cut back, while the GOP moved sharply to the right. Ford and Carter continued Nixon's efforts at arms control and detente, but met rising opposition and their own doubts.

Did Watergate and Nixon's resignation destroy a historic opportunity to end the Cold War, demilitarize, and enhance the nation's domestic vitality? So Nixon's best biographer suggests, despite his stern judgments on Nixon's character and presidency. "When Nixon resigned, we lost more than we gained."[106] Yet Watergate was not a diversion from Nixon's grand design; it was an outcome of how he chose to pursue it, one that exposed how tenuous reorientation had been in the first place. Even before he became ensnared in it, Nixon had done little to develop support for his programs in government, his party, the media, or the nation generally. His contempt for all and his secrecy with each meant that his initiatives came to public attention (and that of allies abroad) as jolting surprises, as if the nation should take them on faith because Nixon proposed them, not because he argued the case for them. It is a common complaint that politicians do not set bold agendas for Americans, but some Presidents have done so. Nixon's case is so vexing because he had the intellectual strength to advance public understanding of demilitarization, yet, despite occasional eloquence, he squandered the chance. He never summoned—could not tolerate—real debate.

Once the Watergate crisis deepened, Nixon's initiatives faced widespread suspicion (liberals "accused Nixon of seeking peace in order to divert attention" from Watergate), and to pass Congress they needed the support of Democratic liberals sympathetic to them but in no mood to do Nixon favors. In foreign policy, however, Nixon was sabotaged as much by fellow Republicans. That fact suggests that tensions in his own party and administration would have impeded him even if Watergate had not spun out of control. Furious at rising opposition to arms control in the Pentagon and among conservative politicians, Kissinger complained bitterly at the 1974 Moscow summit: "What, in the name of God, is strategic superiority? What is the significance of it, politically, militarily, operationally, at these levels of numbers? What do you do with it?" Watergate emboldened but did not create that opposition. An undistracted Nixon still would have faced it, since it came from his natural political base and since he had forged no alliance with liberals on arms control. Ronald Reagan still would have offered a version of his 1976 charge that Kissinger and Ford had made America "Number Two in a world where it is dangerous—if not fatal—to be second best" and had brought about the "collapse of the American will and the retreat of American power."[107]

Moreover, Nixon only had a limited grasp of militarization in the first place, and a narrow approach to reversing it. He worked at it from the top down: his focus was on agreements among great leaders like himself, who would enhance his own stature, not on the economic, ideological, and political structures over which such men presided. Even in dealing with Moscow, the "patronizing" idea took hold in the administration "that one could 'train' the Soviet Union, like some laboratory animal, to respond in predictable ways to a succession of positive and negative stimuli."[108] That personal approach certainly had honorable precedents, but it left progress hinging on personal diplomacy when individuals inevitably depart or change their minds, and when Vietnam had further eroded faith in secret diplomacy. Nixon's failure to confront defeat in Vietnam and to recognize where militarization had led America compounded the problem. His continued leadership (only two and one-half more years anyway) would not have insured success for detente and demilitarization, especially since (like Eisenhower) he had failed to refashion his party in his image so as to continue his policies under a successor. To argue otherwise is to give Nixon too much credit, but also too great a burden.

Nixon soon underlined how frail his commitment to reorientation was. His 1980 tract *The Real War* offered "an apocalyptic, alarmist message, more suitable to the early fifties." Nixon focused less on communism's ideological threat (he still warmed to the Red Chinese) than on the Soviet regime's hegemonic ambitions. It was time to win World War III (which had been raging, he argued, since 1945). Americans faced "a choice between surrender and suicide—red or dead." "We can afford a vastly increased defense effort," and "can postpone desirable social goals in order to ensure survival," and "can carry the twilight war to the enemy—if we *decide* to."[109] Nixon being Nixon, there is no way to know if he would have taken this turn had he finished his presidency successfully. Nixon being Nixon, there is no denying the possibility. Nixon being Nixon, he was at once a boldly idealistic and a devilishly fickle instrument for the nation's reorientation.

His successor provided it even less direction. Ford rejected the critique of war's utility. It was "fashionable in some quarters," he noted, "to charge that military force is outmoded in the modern world" and that nuclear weapons "are too destructive to use" and "won't ever be used." Erroneously equating those views with pacifism and isolationism, Ford condemned them: "We cannot turn our back on the rest of the world as we foolishly sought to do in the 1930s." He did not challenge predictions of the Cold War's imminent end but, like George Bush late in the 1980s, warned that "weakness is most dangerous when the worldwide military balance threatens to deteriorate," and in fact "at any time . . . would be folly." That is, even when things got better, they also got worse, and the United States had to stay armed to the teeth. He thereby suggested that detente would change America's military needs little, a position that hardly made detente appealing.[110]

Ford's comments on the Vietnam War continued the "pervasive politics of amnesia." Briefly, he was willing to cast blame, like Nixon placing it on foes at home rather than abroad: asked about Chinese and Soviet aid to North Vietnam's final conquest of the South in the spring of 1975, he responded, "I don't think we can blame the Soviet Union and the People's Republic of China in this case." Blame lay with Congress: he was "absolutely convinced" that if it had provided the South the aid he demanded, Saigon "could stabilize the military situation in South Vietnam today." Once the North had triumphed, however, Ford wanted Americans to forget the war altogether. "The lessons of the past in Vietnam," he said in May (and many other times), "have already been learned—learned by Presidents, learned by Congress, learned by the American people—and we should have our focus on the future." Since Ford did not say what those lessons were and Americans had differed bitterly about them, only the lowest common denominator among them—that there be no more Vietnams—was left as Ford's implicit message. No more than Nixon was he alone responsible for this mood, echoed with marvelous bipartisanship. "There is no profit at any time in hashing over the might-have-beens of the past," argued Democrat Mike Mansfield, nor "any value in finger-pointing." And the mood did not go undetected, given the habit of Americans of commenting loudly on their silences. "Today it is almost as though the war never happened," columnist Joseph Harsch noted. Still, Ford helped to reduce reflection on the war to little more than "a rancid after-taste that clings to almost every mention of direct military intervention," as columnist David Broder put it.[111]

Demilitarization was arrested by broad political forces, not just Nixon-Ford politics or amnesia about the war. Support for it had been ragged even when America's war in Vietnam raged. That war's end dissolved the thin glue that had connected disparate movements on the left: many persisted or even gained strength after 1973, but they detached from each other as the common foe, the hated war in Vietnam, faded away, and their agendas were so noisy and varied that they shifted attention from the war's legacy. Therefore, no Left-liberal coalition to press for demilitarization emerged, especially once Cold Warriors like Henry Jackson gathered new strength in the Democratic party, while Nixon's efforts in its behalf, ambivalent from the start, were now in ruins.

Yet the United States, if hardly demilitarized after 1973, was entering a new phase—the "rancid after-taste" meant something. The previous three decades had seen it wage three major wars. The following two saw many military actions but no protracted war. Even Vietnam's simplest lesson—that the nation not again go to war without popular consent and clear objectives—had a constraining effect. Critics assailed its hollowness: popular consent might not make a future war more valid or winnable than Vietnam, argued some; the United States must not be hostage to a paralyzing "Vietnam mentality," argued others. The critics were right: little strategic wisdom or moral courage inhered in the petulant demand for "no more Vietnams." How, after all, was a nation to know if a war was winnable and popular until it had plunged into it? Few Americans faced the fundamental question: Was war still a useful tool of national policy, whatever popularity or clarity of objectives might attend to it? Failure to face that question left national policy on war rudderless and expensive.

Yet the shallower lesson of Vietnam had virtue. A losing war does corrode a nation, even if the corollary—that a popular, winning war will unite it—does not always hold. In the coming years, determination to avoid a repetition of Vietnam did keep leaders from war. Many Americans lamented the sour mood Vietnam left in its wake, but one of its components was a laudable desire to avoid war, or at least some of its follies.

BACK TO THE FUTURE, 1975–1981

Mayaguez and Militarism

In May 1975, only weeks after Saigon's collapse, forces of Cambodia's new Khmer Rouge regime seized a U.S. merchant ship, the *Mayaguez*. President Ford, impatient with diplomacy and with consulting Congress as the War Powers Act required, sent warplanes and marines to the rescue, an action that cost forty-one American lives. By then, the Cambodians had already released the sailors (their only wounds were from American strafing), but even if Ford had known of their release he might have sent Americans to battle, since the rescue of American pride and credibility, not sailors, was the heart of the mission anyway. Ford and Secretary of State Kissinger had already made clear their fear that America looked dangerously weak; the President, *Time* noted, "had been hoping for weeks to find a dramatic way to demonstrate to the world that the Communist victories in Indochina had not turned the U.S. into a paper tiger."[1] The *Mayaguez* offered the way, under near-perfect circumstances— against communists linked to the victorious Hanoi regime (although it soon fought the Khmer Rouge in a grim war), where quick entry and exit were possible and the stakes limited.

Renewed pride and confidence in American credibility quickly gushed forth. "It shows we've still got balls in this country," exclaimed Senator Goldwater. It was "a daring show of nerve and steel," argued *Newsweek*. It "reassured some discouraged and mistrustful allies that the U.S. intends to defend vigorously its overseas interests," added *Time*. Few allied leaders were quoted to that effect, however, and Ford made it clear that more important was the stateside audience, which showed "an electrifying reaction" to the event. Those needing reassurance about American credibility turned out to be Americans themselves.[2]

Indeed, it was hard to take the incident seriously. It had a comic-opera quality that even observers endorsing Ford's action could not ignore. As *Time*'s mostly adulatory account noted, it "had many of the gung-ho elements of a John Wayne movie," caused an embarrassing loss of American life, and grew out of an incident that began near "Horseshit Island" (as *Time* translated a

Cambodian name). Columnist Hugh Sidey walked an uneasy line between celebration and satire. "The crisis . . . was the old-fashioned variety, the kind that
men of power in Washington, most of whom are graduates of the cold war,
could understand and relish." Sidey thought it "a lovely bit of rascality. . . . The
White House . . . looked like a Hollywood set. With somber visages and firm
jaws, the actors hurried though the mellow night in their sleek limousines."
Kissinger "flashed the V sign out the window" of his office. Defense Secretary
James Schlesinger "quoted Shakespeare and wore a melancholy mask." The
crisis over, Ford looked at "where workmen had just begun to build a new
swimming pool. 'Boy,' said the President, 'I wish that pool was ready now.'"
Here was the appearance of crisis without the substance. Officials struck grave
poses too artfully to convey real seriousness. This was not Berlin in 1958 or
Cuba in 1962. This was near-farce. Men might "relish" the moment but could
not hide that they were acting.[3]

The incident was illustrative of much that followed, though too minor to be
determinative of it. It revealed nostalgia for a presumably bygone era of American muscle, reluctance to employ that power in a serious way, and bewilderment about its utility. Over the next fifteen years, Presidents repeatedly put
American forces in harm's way—largely or wholly on their own initiative, despite the War Powers Act and Vietnam's presumed lessons about obtaining national consent—but always in arenas on the periphery of great power conflict,
where nuclear confrontation or serious conventional combat was unlikely, and
where the stakes for the United States were limited, often largely symbolic.
Where the risks seemed large, Presidents either kept substantial American
forces out of action, as in Nicaragua in the 1980s, or withdrew them, as after the
marines' barracks in Beirut were bombed in 1983. Only the Gulf War in 1991
departed from that pattern, and even then only briefly.

The use of military force is only one impetus to and measure of militarization, but an important one. Patterns of use after 1974 suggested the nation's entry into a new era of militarization, one more confused in sources and result.
Already broad, the chasm widened further between the presumed purpose of
defense policy and the actual uses of force. As explained by American leaders,
that purpose remained largely unchanged: to deter nuclear war, win if it still
broke out, contain the Soviet Union and its allies, and uphold American credibility. In a corollary to the lessons of Vietnam, military force was to defend the
nation's vital interests, to which the major threat was the Soviet Union, rather
than be frittered away in behalf of minor stakes in peripheral areas.

In reality, the use of American power rarely accorded with those definitions.
The guns fired along the periphery rather than at the core—in the Gulf of Siam,
Lebanon, Libya, Grenada, the Persian Gulf. No nuclear confrontation comparable to those of the 1950s and 1960s occurred. The enemies firing or fired upon
were at best remotely plausible as agents of Soviet power—Khmer Rouge allied with Beijing, Mideast fanatics, a junta in Grenada—and all notably be-

longed to that loose category of "Third World" peoples, as if it were either easier or more necessary to do battle with non-Westerners. Against the only serious use of Soviet military force, in Afghanistan, American guns remained in their holsters. Nonetheless, alarm about Soviet power remained the touchstone of leaders' rhetoric and proclaimed policy.

There were many ways to explain the apparent gulf between the proclaimed purpose and the actual use of American power. Only because nuclear deterrence worked so well, it could be said, did it often recede from view and free up forces for other tasks. Confronting Soviet power had never been the sole purpose of American power, it might be added, only the preeminent one. Meanwhile, interests once peripheral or taken for granted, like Mideast oil, had been added to the core by the 1970s and were threatened in part by Soviet machinations. Besides, most leaders suggested, even when Moscow's hand was not visible, it would come into play unless American power was deployed, and the credibility of that power was at stake even when the tangible interests involved were minor, confused, or unrelated to the Cold War.

A less sympathetic way to explain the gulf was later offered by Jonathan Schell, who (like many others) emphasized the absence of serious reflection about the policies that had led the United States into Vietnam. With McGovern's defeat and Watergate's distraction, those policies remained in place, leaving most Americans "repelled by the tangible prospect of any more Vietnams, yet still attracted to the policies that had led the United States into Vietnam." Ford in the *Mayaguez* incident foreshadowed the pattern to come, Carter largely put it on hold, but Reagan found the formula that satisfied the conflicting impulses left behind by Vietnam: "he gave the public McGovernite decisions accompanied by Nixonian talk," as the United States "embarked on the bifurcated course of rhetorical toughness and practical restraint."[4] Reagan's decisions (and Carter's) were hardly "McGovernite"; a more plausible precedent for his course was Ike's presidency, although Reagan outstripped the general in bellicose rhetoric and lavish spending on armaments never to be used. Still, Schell correctly saw the disjunction between "rhetorical toughness and practical restraint."

In the new era of America's militarization, the purpose of American arms was more self-reflective than ever—to bolster how Americans (at least many of them) felt about themselves, rather than to shape the world. The United States would still go to battle, but in Gilbert-and-Sullivan wars. To use such phrases risks trivializing incidents in which the lives lost were real and the interests involved sometimes substantial. But such phrases capture something of the era's flavor and substance.

Militarization did not cease. The Cold War soon seemed too serious again for that to happen, and even pseudo-war depended on the perception of peril to American interests, a perception buttressed by the realities of a disorderly world and addressed by still formidable American military power. A sharp increase in American (and other nations') arms sales, usually financed in some way by the United States government, was a special characteristic of this phase. At the same time, militarization took on a quixotic, uncertain quality, as if its foundation was crumbling even as the superstructure remained intact.

America's militarization (and the Soviet Union's as well) was now entering a more advanced or (put more pejoratively) decadent stage, one similar to the stage reached by Europe's great powers on the eve of World War I. By then, those powers had proclaimed the most dire danger, refrained from war except in peripheral areas, promoted sales of armaments abroad to shore up massive defense industries at home, and conspicuously displayed weapons of dubious utility—the colossal battleships that presumably measured their might and in-timidated their enemies but had no convincing rationale and, in World War I, little utility. By the same token, the United States and the Soviet Union now scrambled to build more complex, impressive, or simply bigger rockets, bombers, and submarines, even as their utility in war, or in deterring it, became more questionable.

No historical parallel is absolute. The world of 1975 was hardly the same as Europe in 1905. The difference in destructive power alone is obvious. Still, it might be said that militarization in America was degenerating into—or coming full circle back to—simple militarism, as defined long ago by its preeminent historian. Armies, wrote Alfred Vagts, often "forget their true purpose, war, and the maintenance of the state to which they belong. Becoming narcissistic, they dream that they exist for themselves alone. An army so built that it serves military men, not war, is militaristic; so is everything in an army which is not preparation for fighting, but merely exists for diversion or to satisfy peacetime whims like the long-anachronistic cavalry. This was well expressed by the Rus-sian grand duke who admitted that he hated war 'because it spoils the armies.'"[5] The much-noted reluctance of American military leaders after 1973 to enter combat conformed to Vagts's definition. American militarism after Vietnam also departed from that definition, however. The state and its leaders were now so long and fully identified with military force that they, more than the armies themselves, were "becoming narcissistic" and sought "to satisfy peacetime whims." Such elements had long been present in America's militar-ization, but now they surged to the forefront.

Both monstrous costs and possible advantages were involved in this histori-cal turn. The costs—in dollars squandered, nerves rattled, politics embittered—are obvious. The advantage was that a country that preened on its weaponry, rattled its sabers, and played at war was less inclined actually to wage it than a nation that took such matters seriously. As the outbreak of war in 1914 showed, play-acting can turn serious—or some players turn out to have been serious all along. Likewise, however, the nation's history after 1975 gave hope that comparisons between militarization at the start and at the end of this century ought not be pressed too far.

Carter and Militarization

No President since the 1920s came to the White House with such shallow roots in militarization. Jimmy Carter had graduated from the Naval Academy at Annapolis and as a nuclear engineer had stood in awe of Adm. Hyman Rickover, the pioneer of atomic submarines, but his service included no combat, was far back in his life (he returned to Georgia in 1953 to pursue farming and business), and of uncertain influence upon him. He was the first President since Franklin Roosevelt to move from a governorship to the White House, barely familiar with national institutions, and lacking well-defined views on the Cold War and foreign policy. He was, then, both poised to deemphasize militarization and ill equipped to challenge it.

The 1976 election campaign did little to clarify what he might do in office. Issues of ethnicity, religion, and gender dominated the campaign; though they overlapped issues of war and diplomacy, the latter often seemed secondary or out of focus until they all came together in "one of the great presidential gaffes of the past century." Debating Carter on television, Ford asserted, then confusingly defended, the claim that "there is no Soviet domination of Eastern Europe." That notion had honorable roots in America's longstanding refusal to recognize Soviet domination there and in the politics of detente: the Ford administration hoped that the recent Helsinki accords guaranteeing human rights in Eastern Europe would embarrass the Soviet Union and foster autonomy for its satellites there. Ford's assent to those accords had enraged Eastern European ethnics and Republican conservatives, however, who unleashed full-throated cries of secret diplomacy and sell-out to communism once hurled at Democrats. Echoing old pleas to roll back rather than merely contain Soviet aggression, Ronald Reagan had lamented that the accords "put the American seal of approval on the Red Army's World War II conquests." Carter understood and largely shared Ford's position, but capitalized masterfully on Ford's ill-chosen words, the savage response to which showed how almost anyone could now be accused of being soft on communism. Carter's own views were less clear. He campaigned "as a fiscally conservative advocate of full employment, a defender of 'traditional' family values who nonetheless supported the Equal Rights Amendment, a foe of military intervention who would stand up to the Soviets." More generally, he promised no more Vietnams or Watergates. He was "Lon Chaney, the man of a thousand faces," charged one journalist, referring to a famous actor.[6]

Carter's views, however, were often less at issue in 1976 than Ford's alleged foibles. Ford was pilloried as beholden to Nixon for his position and to Kissinger for his foreign policy; as stupid (LBJ had joked that "Ford had played football too often without a helmet"[7]); and as accident-prone (actor Chevy Chase impersonated him to devastating effect on television's *Saturday Night Live*). Ford's image reflected a post–Vietnam-and-Watergate urge—soon aimed at

Carter as well—to cut the imperial presidency down to size. But he did have real weaknesses: a Yale Law School graduate in the top third of his class, Ford was not dumb, but he lacked imagination and verbal dexterity, he inherited a discordant team of Nixon holdovers, he carried the heavy burden of having quickly pardoned Nixon, and he faced a political landscape where the familiar rules seemed up for grabs. That he barely beat Reagan for his party's nomination gained him no luster. That he nearly overcame a huge deficit in the polls suggested that Carter's mandate was hardly clearer than Nixon's in 1968. Carter's margin was only 2 percent in the popular vote and 297–241 in the Electoral College, though Democrats kept huge majorities in Congress.

Nonetheless, in a stunningly brief inaugural address Carter signaled his determination to break from America's militarized past. Instead of asking Americans to forget Vietnam (though he said little about it as a campaigner), he told them to learn from "our recent mistakes." Instead of promising to restore past power and prestige, he argued that "we cannot dwell upon remembered glory." Instead of seeing a muscular city on a hill reshaping the world, he wanted an exemplary America seeking its own perfection: "our nation can be strong abroad only if it is strong at home," promoting "freedom in other lands" by showing "that our democratic system is worthy of emulation." Instead of using military power, he wanted to "maintain strength so sufficient that it need not be proven in combat—a quiet strength based not merely on the size of an arsenal but on the nobility of ideas." Instead of an endless arms race, he promised immediate steps "toward our ultimate goal—the elimination of all nuclear weapons from this Earth."[8]

Carter had not set aside all the heavy baggage of American history. He did not repudiate war as an instrument of American policy or the spread of American ways and ideals. Even an exemplary America would be "strong abroad," and Carter updated an old tradition of the United States as moralizing preacher to the world. If he seemed anomalous, outside the mainstream of his nation's history, it was partly because of his rhetorical style, often religious in cadence and sources. A President willing to quote the Bible, present himself as a born-again Christian, and confront issues of pride and humility seemed strange to leading politicians and commentators, accustomed to a secular style and consigning religion to the backwaters of American life. Carter was plagued by the "weirdo factor," his aide Hamilton Jordan said, but in fact his religiosity was in the mainstream of American life.[9]

Nonetheless, he differed from his predecessors, if less in goals than in his apparent fervor in pursuing them. Style was not wholly separable from substance. In 1976, "citing Jesus' teachings, Carter often declared that 'all of us are sinful' without prudently adding that Americans in the aggregate were less sinful than others." Disturbing too to some Americans, though it echoed Nixon, was his assertion in 1977 that Americans were now free of their "inordinate fear of Communism."[10] Following on the uncertain start made by Nixon and Ford,

Carter wanted to reverse the nation's, and more grandly the world's, militariz-ation, and he spoke to many of its components, especially the arms race, with its knotty problems of arms sales, weapons testing, and nuclear proliferation. Be-fore his inauguration, he even speculated to the Joint Chiefs that two hundred strategic weapons on each side might suffice to deter nuclear war. Publicly, he challenged militarization with a force unmatched since Eisenhower. Notable too, especially compared to Nixon, was his grasp of the thorny details of these matters, the noncombative manner in which he discussed them, and his wife's role in helping him assess them.

Carter also differed from his predecessors—again, especially Nixon—in lay-ing out an alternative agenda for Americans. Abroad he would focus on prob-lems of poverty and resource management—in the parlance of the decade, on North-South rather than East-West problems. His "domestic agenda" was designed "to provide more efficiently for the needs of our people, to demonstrate—against the dark faith of our times—that our Government can be both competent and humane." The energy crisis loomed largest for him in 1977, but the promotion of human rights abroad and at home was nearer to his heart. Like preceding Presidents, he linked the arenas of action at home and abroad, as he had in his inaugural in a general way, although his linkage was loose and less central to his reasoning. In March 1977, for example, citing the Soviet ambassador's complaint about women's rights in America in response to Carter's message on human rights, he told the National Women's Political Caucus that "our failure to pass the equal rights amendment hurts us as we try to set a standard of commitment to human rights throughout the world." He also invoked war as a model for action against problems at home. "We will fight our wars against poverty, ignorance, and injustice," he announced in his inau-gural. Worried about the energy crisis, he urged Americans in February 1977 to remember that "during World War II we faced a terrible crisis—but the chal-lenge of fighting Nazism drew us together." He did not give such formulations the sustained rhetorical treatment Johnson had offered, however. As in his statements on war and armaments, he set forth his vision of progress at home in a diffuse and disjointed fashion, but he made his goals clear.[11]

Not, however, his understanding of them. Carter did not explain what forces pushed nations into war, what drove the arms race, what militarization looked like, or where it came from historically and politically. He offered bare-bones, almost aphoristic statements. Perhaps, moralist that he was, he assumed that an understanding of the problems was embedded in reactions to the Vietnam War, involving dilemmas almost self-evident. Perhaps, technocrat that he also was, he hurried to work on solutions rather than lingering to define the prob-lem. Or maybe he simply did not grasp the problem—he knew the evils that militarization caused, not the evils that gave rise to it. Whatever the case, his presidency had a curious start in which an agenda was set but not much ex-plained, actions signaled but the reasons for them not often expounded. Nor, aside from his firm grasp of the Nixon-Kissinger record on detente, did he cite predecessors like Eisenhower who had questioned militarization—perhaps because he knew little about them, certainly because he was determined to break from them. Without explaining the sources of militarization, however, he did little to prepare Americans for the obstacles ahead; without invoking his predecessors, he seemed a maverick unanchored in American political traditions; without establishing the terms of debate, he left control of it substantially to others.

As always in such matters, these patterns were not only of his making: little demand on him to spell things out arose when he took office. Carter quickly embarked on an effort, so different from Nixon, to talk with Americans in question-and-answer sessions—with personnel from every Cabinet department, ordinary citizens in town meetings and on television call-in shows, and the press—in which a striking diversity of issues (if not opinions on them) came before him. Insofar as questions about war and national security arose during these first months, they dealt less with arms control or defense budgets than with his quick decision to pardon Vietnam war draft resisters. Carter disappointed the antiwar Left by refusing to pardon those who had resisted or deserted once in uniform, and infuriated the Right—"The most disgraceful thing a President has ever done," Goldwater said with typical hyperbole[12]—though Carter thoughtfully invoked his Southerner's knowledge of the Civil War to stress the importance of amnesty and healing. More often than not, the questions spoke to other matters, like the energy shortage of that bitter winter. Carter can be faulted for plunging into arenas bound to expose him to a discordant mess of complaints—his pose of patient and still-learning schoolteacher was not the best way to control a nation's agenda. That agenda was not solely his to control, however, or clearly focused on the issues of war and armaments he emphasized in his inaugural.

Fuller shape to his ideas emerged in the spring of 1977. He confronted the Vietnam War's ugly residue, making normalization of relations with Vietnam his goal and indicating satisfaction with Vietnam's efforts to account for missing American servicemen. That issue was yet to yield its full fury, but Carter put it in perspective, noting that in World War II and Korea "we still did not account for 22 percent" of the missing but in Vietnam "all except about 4 percent" were traced. He drew clear, careful distinctions about responsibility for that war. He would not pile blame solely on the United States: "the destruction was mutual. . . . I don't feel that we ought to apologize or castigate ourselves" (or pay the communists the reparations Nixon had promised). But he would have his nation share blame, unlike his predecessors (though Carter had the luxury of bearing no personal responsibility). The United States had adopted "the flawed and erroneous principles and tactics of our adversaries" and had "fought fire with fire, never thinking that fire is better quenched with water. This approach failed, with Vietnam the best example of its intellectual and moral poverty."

Those words, spoken at Notre Dame University on May 22, were strong ones for an American President, even if sometimes misleading. (Given the enormity of America's technological war in Vietnam, the destruction there was hardly "mutual.") More generally, Carter argued that the Cold War "has become less intensive" even if also "more extensive," and that its end was within grasp. He hardly repudiated "military power," but he saw international cooperation as "an excellent alternative to war."[13]

Fresh though the Notre Dame speech was, it revealed tensions within Carter's outlook that soon sharpened. In many ways he challenged longstanding distinctions between the United States and its foes, but regarding "human rights" he kept the line sharp between "free" and "totalitarian" nations. The distinction was not inaccurate, or absolute; he acknowledged "our own shortcomings and faults."[14] Still, it concerned the very matter Carter judged most important, as if in every lesser way he saw common ground with the foe, but in the most vital one he did not.

By the time of his Notre Dame speech, Carter was also showing signs that his skill in resisting militarization was as limited behind the scenes as it was in public. His position on previous SALT agreements was blunt, accurate, and sensitive to the yearnings of many Americans: They set limits "so high that they were, in effect, just ground rules for intensified competition and a continued massive arms growth in nuclear weapons."[15] But he rushed into an arms control effort that most experts judged rash and counterproductive (though cautious gradualism, Carter pointed out, had hardly yielded much). First he ordered American nuclear arms withdrawn from Korea, then he presented the Soviets with an arms control proposal far more limiting than the one Ford had been working on. In neither case did he explore his actions with the Kremlin before going public, displaying insensitivity to its plodding and suspicious ways (and to those of his Pentagon). Soviet Party Chairman Leonid Brezhnev probably sensed both gratuitous pressure and underlying weakness in Carter's actions on arms control, and in his preachments on human rights. Tensions escalated, negotiations wilted, and Carter ended up demanding "more arms for the United States, and less for the Soviets, than Kissinger and Nixon had been willing to accept."[16] In the end, it took until 1979 to hammer out a SALT II Treaty, which differed little from the agreement Ford had tentatively negotiated and was flawed in precisely the ways that Carter had identified regarding SALT I. It limited launchers but not warheads, which could be multiplied endlessly by mounting more on existing rockets, and froze old technologies while leaving new ones free for development.

Meanwhile, the pace of developing new missiles, warheads, and space technology under Carter followed that of his predecessors. He did kill two expensive programs, one for a B-1 bomber to replace the B-52, another for a neutron bomb ("mocked . . . as the 'Republican bomb'" because it featured enhanced short-term radiation to take lives and diminished blast to spare property).[17]

Both decisions drew the wrath of conservatives, while liberals offered Carter only lukewarm support for his weapons and arms control policies. His much-touted effort to reduce global arms sales also failed; American sales, like those of many nations, increased under Carter, though far less rapidly than under Nixon and Ford. Stalled too was his effort to get a treaty banning tests of nuclear weapons, though the Kremlin was not the major obstacle: new technology demolished the old claim that Soviet cheating on a ban of underground testing would go undetected, but defense hawks and weapons laboratories raised a fresh objection, arguing that only continued testing would ensure that warheads were safe and reliable.

One way to deemphasize the Cold War and militarization was to do an end-run around them rather than tackling them head-on. Highlighting other issues might shift agendas and forestall new threats, while intractable problems in the Soviet-American relationship could await a calmer moment for solution. In that regard, far more than in his head-on attack, Carter met success. He gave much more attention to America's relationship with Africa, Latin America, and the Mideast than his predecessors. His effort to hammer out the 1979 peace agreement between Egypt and Israel was as striking for its energy as for the modest diminution of Mideast tensions it afforded. To be sure, no issue seemed entirely outside the Cold War framework—administration hawks saw value in brokering agreements that might forestall Soviet adventurism in these regions. Still, a President willing to pour great chunks of time and political capital into settling intractable problems in those areas, or into the bitter struggle which saw the Senate narrowly ratify the Panama Canal Treaty, signaled a possible break from Cold War priorities.

As leverage against militarization, however, those efforts helped Carter little. They were undervalued by many Americans, resented by some precisely because they threatened the centrality of familiar issues, and compromised by Carter himself and the American government. However laudable the effort to stop Third World countries from getting nuclear weapons, for example, it cast North-South relations into an ugly struggle between have and have-not nations, one further embittered by "the continuing hypocrisy of both the White House and Congress with regard to Israel's [nuclear] programs."[18] In any event, Carter gradually shoved North-South problems back into the East-West context. By 1979, he viewed Soviet and Cuban adventurism in Africa, the death rattle of reactionary regimes in Central America, and the attractions of Chinese-American cooperation all within that context, like Nixon seeing Beijing as counterweight to Moscow.

What had gone wrong? Carter got little help from Brezhnev's regime in Moscow. It did not constitute the doomsday threat to America many conservatives now saw. Brittle, sclerotic, defensive, it offered, in the grand Russian tradition, more show than substance—new rockets of no practical utility and strategic cooperation with mostly minor and desperate Third World regimes. Long gone was the ideological appeal to struggling nations or the technological razzle-dazzle of the Khrushchev years. But the show still appeared menacing. If the regime's brittleness masked its hollowness, it also deprived Moscow of the diplomatic boldness and suppleness occasionally evident under Khrushchev. Fearful that any compromise on its part would damage its great power status, Moscow proved truculent in negotiations and public statements. Carter got little more help from his European allies, who continued an often two-faced criticism of the United States as both trigger-happy and flaccid in its willingness to defend Western Europe. Eloquent on these issues, West German chancellor Helmut Schmidt put enormous pressure on Carter to support new nuclear weapons for NATO forces.

Carter's excessive idealism and deficient political skill were more often cited, however, to explain his political failure and his return to Cold War orthodoxy. Yet Carter's idealism differed little from Eisenhower's or Reagan's, who also waxed eloquent about ending the threat of nuclear weapons and displayed a moral fervor in waging the Cold War comparable to Carter's in scale if not focus. If Carter was different, it was because he seemed to *mean* the idealistic intentions others only mouthed, to couch them initially outside the Cold War framework, to express them in a different style, and to work harder at achieving them. Moreover, Carter was faulted as much for cynically ignoring his ideals as for pursuing them, as if a deficiency rather than an excess of idealism were his problem. Nor, as he recognized, were ideals and power unrelated: his promotion of human rights in the Soviet sphere emboldened dissidents there, helping to undermine the old regime, though Reagan would reap the credit for communism's fall. "Idealism," so difficult to measure, is a troublesome criterion for evaluating Presidents.

So is ineptitude, often attributed to Carter. By taking the initiative on many issues at once, it was often noted, Carter overwhelmed Congress, confused friends and foes, scattered his energies, and lost track of his priorities. Nor did he learn to appreciate the error: he continued to proclaim so many problems as the most serious faced by the nation (much as Johnson had accorded all his wars equal importance) that his rhetoric became numbing and bewildering. On the other hand, his much-noted inability to settle between the differing policies of National Security Advisor Zbigniew Brzezinski and Secretary of State Cyrus Vance reflected institutional tensions that have plagued most postwar Presidents. "The disarray of the Carter years," John Newhouse later noted, "seems a bit tame when compared to the foreign policy babble that followed."[19] Perhaps the most notorious example of Carter's ham-handedness was his showcasing the Iran hostage crisis and then failing to resolve it, although he hardly could have sidestepped it altogether. No doubt his course was politically disastrous, but Carter's diplomatic record on the hostage issue was better than that of his successor, who differed only in having the savvy not to highlight his own weakness (even though Reagan's hostage crises often involved American soldiers and diplomats and dragged on for years).

Carter's missteps did not outrank an experienced Eisenhower's with the U-2 incident, the disastrous slide into the Vietnam War by the cool realists of the Kennedy-Johnson era, or the inability of Nixon and Kissinger, supposed masters of realpolitik, to bring a timely end to the Vietnam War. Detente was already in deep trouble under Nixon and Ford, who, had they seen SALT II to completion, might have encountered opposition as ferocious as that faced by Carter. Already by 1975, SALT's opponents were circulating "creative distortions and outright lies." By 1979, Sen. Daniel Moynihan challenged the SALT II Treaty with the claim, so blithely dismissive of America's position in the world in 1914 or 1941, that "we have never—since 1812 . . . had to live with the idea of another power, not friendly, and having a larger military capacity." That such an outrageous assertion came from such a smart Democrat suggested how much larger forces were at work undermining Carter, whose competence became almost irrelevant.[20]

Carter succeeded better than most modern Presidents at managing the affairs of state so as to keep the nation out of war. The boilerplate criticisms of him reflected the higher standards he set for himself and the times set for him. They also reflected, amid renewed Cold War fervor, a denigration of successes outside the familiar arena of superpower conflict. Of course, when Carter himself retreated into a conventional Cold War posture, he invited evaluation by conventional Cold War standards.

What went wrong for Carter had less to do with some excess of idealism or deficiency of skill than with specific tensions in his views and with the volatile politics of the 1970s. Even at his idealistic start as President, he never proposed cuts in the defense budget, thus leaving the engine of militarization running at full speed even as he tried to control its products. Regarding defense spending, Carter was a classic transitional figure, reluctant either to accept or to reject the expansive view of resources and needs long associated with liberal Democratic Cold Warriors. (Defense spending as adjusted for inflation rose slowly under Carter, more sharply in his last budget, and fluctuated around 5 percent of GNP.) By 1979 he embraced that expansive view, but by then Republicans had rejected their own party's fiscal conservatism on defense and demanded far more military spending. Not only did Carter's course look uncertain, it was whip-sawed as the two major parties traded positions on this critical matter.

He continued to do little to explain the roots of militarization. In an eloquent October 1977 speech about nuclear arms, he told the United Nations that "we have learned in Durrenmatt's chilling words that 'what has once been thought can never be un-thought.'" That observation, summarizing common wisdom about the irreversibility of scientific progress, left unexplored where the thought came from in the first place and how knowledge alone does not dictate institutions. (As one scholar later pointed out, slavery was banished even as knowledge of how to practice it remained.) Mysterious about the causes of the arms race, Carter, like most Americans interested in arms control, was left to flail at its consequences.[21]

A puzzling gap also opened between the idealism of his goals and the reasoning which sometimes guided his decisions, such as those to ax the B-1 bomber and promote the MX (mobile experimental) missile. Those decisions were framed in terms of cost-efficiency: more bombs could be better delivered (or deployed to deter the Soviets) at less cost with one weapons system than another. A sensible basis for decisions—after all, Carter noted, the Bible gave no instruction about "whether you should have a B-1 bomber or the air-launched cruise missile"—it still seemed unrelated to his visionary quest to staunch militarization. Or worse, it could seem to critics grossly at odds with that quest, as when he supported the MX—albeit to ward off hawks opposing the SALT II Treaty—although he found it "a nauseating prospect to confront."[22] Nor did he consistently follow it: rejecting the neutron bomb, he brought moral fervor back into play. A prophet's vision seemed served by an accountant's methods, and in an unpredictable fashion at that. Carter's problem was not that he was too idealistic or too practical, but rather that his two modes seemed disconnected, floating in separate worlds.

Disconnected, too, were his campaigns for human rights and disarmament. He mistakenly thought he could coerce Moscow about the former and cooperate with it about the latter. (He had more leverage on human rights over despotic allies like Ferdinand Marcos in the Philippines and the shah in Iran, but with them Carter usually valued American strategic interests higher.) He also failed to foresee how the moral fervor of a human rights campaign would play at home, stoking the very "inordinate fear of communism" he wanted to dampen. The pursuit of scarcely less than Moscow's unconditional surrender in the moral arena resonated with hopes for a similar surrender in the military arena, hopes renewed in the 1970s and indulged by insiders like Brzezinski. A Kremlin castigated for gross abuse of people was easily made to seem eager also for war and world conquest. After all, had not precisely that combination of evils characterized Nazi Germany? That Carter's drumbeat on human rights sounded amid heightened interest in the Holocaust (and the Khmer Rouge's genocide in Cambodia) strengthened the impulse to cast problems with the Soviet Union back into the realm of war and weapons. To amass the latter seemed for many the appropriate response. Soon even Carter agreed.

The undertow of World War II was evident in another arena. In April 1977 Carter said that his energy policy required an effort that "will be the 'moral equivalent of war,'" a phrase he repeated in October. Carter's purpose was to rally popular support behind sacrifices necessary to avert "national catastrophe" and against energy interests that might engage in "war profiteering." This was war, "except that we will be uniting our efforts to build and not to destroy."[23] Carter's use of William James's famous phrase was brief, but it caught attention and helped move energy issues onto the slippery terrain of war. When business interests assailed his proposals, it seemed "like it was the day after Pearl Harbor," noted Rep. Morris Udall in defense of the President, "and you interviewed the Congressman from Detroit and he said, 'The Japanese attack was outrageous, but before we rush into war, let's see how it would affect the [auto] industry." Seeking war's moral equivalent set loose talk of war and analogies to it that Carter could not control and that worsened his image of ineptitude. When his energy plans stumbled in Congress, one White House aide foresaw "the moral equivalent of the Vietnam war"; the *Boston Globe* teased Carter for offering "the moral equivalent of Sominex"; and wags noted that the acronym for "moral equivalent of war" was MEOW.[24]

Carter had wandered onto dangerous imaginative terrain. If war was a model, Vietnam was a discouraging precedent. If World War II was the touchstone, it promised more unity and action than he could deliver. And if the "moral equivalent of war" was attractive, presumably there was something attractive about war itself, in which case a mere substitute might be unsatisfying. Few Americans wanted or expected war in 1977, but in proposing an alternative to militarization that left war as a model, Carter sent ambiguous signals about war's place in American life. By 1980 his distinction between war and its moral equivalent nearly collapsed as the energy crisis became bound up with Mideast turmoil: it was necessary, he argued, to equate "energy security with our Nation's military security; there's no way to separate the two." As Gaddis Smith has commented, Carter's "moral equivalent of war had turned into something very close to preparing for war itself."[25]

Carter's failures were so glaring that his successes and the obstacles before him easily escaped contemporaries and historians. His challenge to militarization did substantially fail, but so had challenges by his predecessors, when they even made the attempt. At least his effort helped to keep the nation out of war and to nourish hopes that proved resilient during Reagan's presidency. Meanwhile, as reactions to his "moral equivalent of war" showed, he was tripped up not only by his own failings but by swirling currents in political culture substantially beyond his control.

Clashing Cultures of War

In 1976, American bombers again attacked Hiroshima—this time in simulations around the United States staged by the Confederate Air Force, a group of military aviators dedicated to restoring World War II aircraft. Paul Tibbets, the *Enola Gay*'s pilot in 1945, returned to the controls as a B-29 made its bombing run, while spectators were told that out of the ashes of Pearl Harbor had arisen "the phoenix of future victory," the atomic bomb whose use ended "some of the darkest days of America's history." Although the CAF praised the "courageous" Japanese soldier, its reenactment sparked criticism, especially in Japan, and the CAF dropped Hiroshima from later editions of its show. Still, it complained, "the Japanese seem to have forgotten who started the war" and never "apologized" for Pearl Harbor "or other atrocities," whereas America's atomic bomb had been redemptive: it delivered the nation from its own folly and made "all future wars unthinkable." By implication, a rebirth of American power, if not its actual use, was also in order in the 1970s.[26]

The CAF's activities marked another step in the reconstruction of patriotic culture. As reaction to the Hiroshima reenactment showed, reconstruction did not proceed easily: begun under Nixon and Ford, it lacked a patron when Carter came to office; it soon confronted a resurgent antiwar culture; and it emerged in the shadows of the Vietnam War, which even avowed patriots hesitated to celebrate. Notably, the 1976 Bicentennial celebrations, though patriotic in tone, were largely nonmartial in content. But reconstruction did proceed. Its proponents celebrated patriotism, the utility and nobility of America's past wars, and, implicitly, war's utility in the nation's future. They also reconnected traditional (as they saw them) ideals of patriotism, individualism, and national self-sufficiency to visions of futuristic technology. Critics argued that technology had undercut those ideals, most recently in Vietnam. Those who thought that the atomic bomb had redeemed America and the world in 1945 believed otherwise. At bottom they offered a moral proposition: on occasion American arms had been fatally neglected, frittered away, or foolishly used, but they had never been employed in an immoral way or to immoral ends.

Americans had long clashed about these matters. But despite the intense debate it generated, the Vietnam War, especially its dispirited final phase, had obscured the cultural divide over how war was to be understood: a vague distaste for war had settled in among most Americans, sapped the strength of patriotic culture, and led to fatigue with the subject itself. But with the war over, it was safe again for imaginations to run riot—now that they played out on the imagined terrain of past and future wars rather than on the scorched earth of real war.

As both place and symbol, Pearl Harbor was one focus of patriotic culture. Unlike most American war dead, the bodies of those who died on the *Arizona* were never recovered; instead, they were "protected from any form of defilement" and treated as the sacred relics of men "denied even the exhilaration of battle and the sense of duty faithfully discharged," as a National Park Service superintendent put it. In the 1970s, one of the battleship's anchors was retrieved and made the centerpiece of a USS *Arizona* Anchor Memorial in its home state's capital, where Pearl Harbor Day services became "celebrations of patriotic revitalization." Meanwhile, Americans continued to see links or differences between Pearl Harbor and Hiroshima. Some perceived a contest between America's Pearl Harbor memorial and Japan's Hiroshima memorial over the war's meaning and the two nations' virtues. Many resented the presence at

Pearl Harbor of Japanese tourists, veterans, and paraphernalia for sale. Others distinguished a dastardly Japanese carrier attack in 1941 from a redemptive American nuclear assault in 1945, the "terrible swift sword that ended a bloody war," as one citizen wrote in 1980. Long present, such emotions swelled in the 1970s as Japanese-American economic conflict intensified and Japanese authorities defended their nation's role in World War II. Those emotions also indicated that for a reconstructed patriotic culture, World War II was the cornerstone.[27]

Fittingly, symbols of American victory at Iwo Jima in 1945, neglected or bent to unconventional purposes in the Vietnam era, were also resurrected. In 1976, the Park Service cleared away the underbrush around the Marine Corps Iwo Jima Memorial in Arlington, Virginia. At the end of the decade, amid the Iran hostage crisis, "America was urged to fight back—with a popular poster showing the two Iwo Jima Marines mounting their flag in the rear end of a prostrate Ayatollah [Khomeini, Iran's Islamic leader]," crudely restating old connections between patriotism and sexual aggression. In 1980, when the United States Olympic hockey team upset the Soviet squad, one editorial cartoonist reworked the Iwo Jima imagery by showing "the victorious American team raising the flag on a hockey stick." In Florida, in an effort to renew "patriotic fervor," an Iwo Jima statue in ruins was restored and Felix de Weldon, its long-forgotten sculptor, located to help with the task. Once Reagan took office, Iwo Jima again had a presidential patron, while in 1988 Vice President Bush stood at the foot of Arlington's Marine Corps Memorial to declare his support for a constitutional amendment against desecration of the flag. As with Pearl Harbor, Iwo Jima sometimes served other purposes—as a site for rituals of Japanese-American reconciliation and as an image to mock American weakness as well as to symbolize American resolve. Nonetheless, by 1980 Iwo Jima had been restored as symbol of American power and patriotism—or goad to their renewal.[28]

Pearl Harbor, Iwo Jima, and Hiroshima elicited effusive, often hard-edged expressions of patriotic culture. Other versions were more complex, as in that of the Committee on the Present Danger (CPD), a group of neoconservatives and Cold War liberals "contemptuous of the McGovernite triumph of 1972," who clothed "the visceral anticommunism of the New Right with intellectual respectability." Its leaders included Paul Nitze, a major strategist since the 1940s, Soviet expert Richard Pipes from Harvard, and *Commentary* editor Norman Podhoretz. Closely tied to the Ford administration, the committee helped shape a key 1976 warning by the CIA (whose director was George Bush) of Soviet superiority in arms and resolve, and opposed the SALT II Treaty. Podhoretz feared America's "spiritual Finlandization," referring to Finland's nominally autonomous but supposedly submissive stance vis-à-vis its giant neighbor. Because Soviet leaders were "even more ambitious than Hitler," the CPD advocated an array of strategic weapons (like the B-1 bomber Carter had canceled) to guard against them. It stressed the danger of Soviet political blackmail with its nuclear might, but since the Kremlin "thinks it could fight and win a nuclear war," as Pipes argued, the CPD also sought weapons and strategies to preempt the Soviet Union before such a war started or to win if it broke out. Despite "rhetorical denials that Americans were at all warlike," CPD members indulged "millennialist fantasies" in which nuclear war was "potentially decisive and purifying." Americans' fears of nuclear war, thought Pipes, reflected degradation of their will and served Soviet designs. Although unwelcome, nuclear war might still be necessary, CPD members asserted, and it differed only in degree from wars already fought. Moral Majority leader Jerry Falwell put the point more emphatically than CPD members: "A political leader, as a minister of God, is a revenger to execute wrath upon those who do evil. Our government has the right to use its armaments to bring wrath upon those who would do evil."[29]

Though deep into politics, the CPD also explicitly sought a cultural revival. The Soviet Union was dangerous, but the real enemy was internal rot; weapons were important, but the will to use them even more so. Employing a secularized version of Christian and Jewish themes, the CPD issued "revivalist declarations of decline and doom as well as expressions of revitalization and restoration," seeking a "resuscitation of American patriotic will," in the words of its historian. The United States, according to the CPD, was in a "fallen state," suffering from a sense of "injured innocence" after Vietnam, where victory had been denied because America's own goodness had tied its hands. The nation had nurtured a "culture of appeasement," argued Podhoretz, a "national mood of self-doubt and self-disgust" which he compared to the one that had prevailed in the 1930s in the face of fascism. As in other expressions of patriotic culture, World War II was the touchstone for the CPD, but so too were the twenty years after it, a time as the CPD recalled it when American hegemony had been almost total and Americans willing to "pay the price in blood to fight Communism." Amid this "new nostalgia," as Cyrus Vance scornfully called it in 1980, it was easy for CPD members to forget that in those years the United States had often lurched in fear more than it swaggered from confidence. Such nostalgia made it possible to argue that the nation now faced a "long, long age of darkness" during which "American society may be swallowed up." The rebirth of America—an end to the "dark night of the soul," Jeane Kirkpatrick called it—took precedence over, though also made possible, defeat of the Soviet Union.[30]

Hollywood also played a part in reviving patriotic culture, although as usual it generally shunned explicit messages in favor of fuzzy images and themes. *Star Wars* (1977), set far ahead (ostensibly "a long time ago") in time and far away in space, mentioned no earthly conflict, but it was easy to see the "evil Galactic Empire" with its "ultimate weapon" and "imperial storm troopers" as akin to Nazi and Soviet totalitarians and Darth Vader to their tyrants, while

Princess Leia sought to "restore freedom to the galaxy." *Star Wars*, notes one scholar, offered "a war against an evil, bureaucratic empire revealed to us . . . as at once the pompous monarchy, the faceless corporation, the darkly mystical Nazi totalitarianism, the palely ruthless Soviet presidium—a Europe that conservative and liberal Americans can once again join in loathing as the true Other." Filmmaker George Lucas deftly recombined familiar elements of Western, war, and science-fiction films; old-fashioned gunfights again blazed, though now viewers could see the bullets, and the terrain on distant planets looked suspiciously like the barren tracts in old Western films. In turn, he celebrated Americans' essential innocence in war and suggested, even for a futuristic war, the virtue of frontier individualism, loyalty to clan and country, and devilish weapons when wielded by the right side. With robots the film's most endearing characters and freedom-loving pilots embodying (as Lindbergh presumably had) both pre-industrial daring and post-industrial discipline, longfelt conflicts between men and machines, and long-felt fears of what men might do with them, dissolved. Later installments in Lucas's space trilogy suggested a darker rendering of American mythology. *Star Wars* did not.[31]

A reconstructed patriotic culture faced and in some ways revitalized an oppositional culture of war's horrors—or "antiwar culture," except that the term may be too limiting—with the result that a "fierce ideological civil war in America" raged, as one historian puts it. The oppositional culture bore similarities to patriotic culture. With Carter, it had something of a patron in the White House, as patriots would with Reagan. It too had difficulty engaging the Vietnam War, also finding its touchstone in World War II, especially the nuclear and Nazi holocausts. And it too offered religious themes of sin and redemption. While patriots asked Americans to repent for the sin of abandoning national pride, prophets against war demanded repentance by Americans (and others too) for the sin of developing nuclear weapons and risking nuclear war. Few could read Jonathan Schell's *The Fate of the Earth* (1982), the acclaimed statement of antinuclear activism, and miss that demand. "Political revivalism" defined both parties to the cultural conflict, and with it portrayals of apocalyptic dangers and millennial solutions.[32]

There were differences, however, besides the obvious ones in message. Where patriots saw continuities in the nature and utility of war, prophets of war's horrors saw radical discontinuity with the advent of nuclear weapons in 1945. Where patriotic culture had to be rebuilt almost from scratch after the Vietnam War, antiwar and antinuclear activism had been sustained almost continuously for decades, albeit with sharp ups and downs. And while both movements had their experts, the forces mobilizing against the nuclear danger drew more heavily from scientific and medical authorities, whose work seemed to buttress their outlook.

Alarm about the nuclear danger shaped the culture of war's horrors. Like the CPD, the Physicians for Social Responsibility (PSR) was an older group reborn, started in 1960 and reenergized in 1978. It was sparked into action by the CPD itself, by growing official acceptance of strategies for winning nuclear war, and by the decade's surging ecological sensibility, which emphasized the limits of the earth's resources and the fragility of its ecosystem. Further galvanizing groups like the PSR was a disaster at the Three Mile Island (Pennsylvania) nuclear plant, where an overheated reactor core in 1979 threatened to bathe the area in radiation. At first, that dramatic incident seemed to tap fear of civilian nuclear energy, corporate greed, and environmental disaster, fear also raised in the film *The China Syndrome* (1979) in which a star-studded cast dealt with a fictitious but similar incident. But fear of nuclear energy had long been inseparable from fear of nuclear weapons—the two had merged again in a 1977 television movie, *Red Alert,* featuring the "simultaneous explosion of every reactor in the United States," a disaster comparable to total nuclear war.[33] In retrospect, widespread activism in the 1970s against civilian nuclear power was a warm-up for the antiweapons activism blossoming at the end of the decade.

By then, scientists and other activists, most notably the Australian physician Helen Caldicott, had portrayed the probable effects of nuclear warfare in chilling detail. What loomed was not only the destruction of the superpowers, even of civilization, but of all advanced life and the ecosphere itself, yielding, as Schell soon put it, "a republic of insects and grass." Just as alarming was the prospect of substantially that result even in a limited nuclear war, whose radiation and fallout might plunge the world into "nuclear winter." Some of these findings were less novel than they appeared, their shock value a measure more of the long period of indifference to the nuclear danger. Anyone who had watched (as Caldicott had) the poisoning of Australia and the world in the 1959 movie *On the Beach* would not have been surprised to learn in 1979 that radiation, fallout, and the destruction of economic and political systems would be as devastating as a nuclear war's initial blast and fire. It was not novel to argue, as one expert now did, that such effects were "so catastrophic that they render any notion of 'victory meaningless,'" although the claim of that result for a limited nuclear war broke newer ground.[34]

Therein, however, lay the thrust of the culture of war's horrors—not just to advance scientific knowledge but to reawaken the nation and the world to dangers long known but long neglected. Where proponents of patriotic revival saw internal rot as the key to the Soviet threat, prophets of nuclear doom saw apathy and "technological arrogance" as the root of evil. The goal was the redemption of humankind, which required the transformation of culture itself, America's and the world's. Without it, nuclear war seemed "a mathematical certainty" to Caldicott, a choice of "death" over "life" according to Schell, just as Soviet triumph seemed a foregone conclusion to others without a revival of patriotism.[35]

Alarm about the nuclear danger peaked in the early 1980s, when Reagan's rhetoric and policies and a vigorous antinuclear movement in Western Europe further fueled it. By then it had all the features of a cultural as well as political phenomenon. Religious groups played a major role. Grass-roots activism rather than top-down organizing was a major characteristic. The full spectrum of cultural phenomena—high-brow fiction and criticism, Hollywood and television, advice columnists and rock groups—reflected its themes. For television's audiences, the most compelling moment was *The Day After* (1983), in which Kansas City succumbed to nuclear destruction (as earlier, Americans were asked to imagine their own destruction, rarely that of another nation at their hands). Responding to such programs, Senator Goldwater complained that television showed only "the negative side of nuclear weapons."[36]

In tone and substance, debate had substantially circled back to earlier phases of anxiety about modern weapons. Although the apocalyptic strains seemed fresh, in fact nearly "every theme and image" in the new debate about nuclear weapons had "its counterpart in the immediate post-Hiroshima period."[37] As earlier, there was little room in either culture, or in the conflict between them, for compromise, uncertain outcomes, or muddling through: only the most dire consequences, avoidable only through the most draconian efforts, were usually imagined. As before, the sole choices seemed to be doomsday or deliverance, just as the contending voices again divided starkly over whether enemies abroad or nuclear weapons themselves presented the greater threat to humankind.

Yet the cyclical nature of these apocalyptic strains does not fully explain their renewal in the 1970s. The feverish arms race, the Soviets' apparent acquisition of parity in it, the stodgy and disappointing course of arms control talks, and Carter's sounding of the nuclear alarm were factors. But a broad cultural phenomenon had deeper sources. Apocalyptic predictions about war had usually surged in peace and diminished in war: danger loomed largest when war was imagined, not when it was waged. And since, in the new phase of militarization, it was widely assumed that America would not again wage limited war, at least not on the scale seen in Vietnam, nuclear war was the only game in town for imaginations to play, just as the imagination was the only outlet for a nation awash in war's weapons and anxieties but averse to war itself. Skepticism about political and scientific leaders, rising during the Vietnam era and deepened by the crises in energy and environment that pockmarked the 1970s, strengthened the impulse for dire speculation: fewer Americans believed leaders' reassuring words about the benefits of detente, the trustworthiness of the Russians, or the manageability of war and weapons.

Like patriotic culture, the culture of war's horrors linked its sense of the future to a view of the past. Historians and other scholars critically reexamined, in what was dubbed a "revisionist" mode, America's development and use of the atomic bomb, its role in the Cold War, and its part in the Vietnam War. Under heavy assault were old notions of American innocence and exceptionalism —of the necessity of using atomic bombs to end World War II, and the validity of elites' explanations for their policies in World War II and the Cold War. Such notions were also questioned in high-brow culture and in popular representations of the American past. *Disturbing the Universe* (1979), the acclaimed memoir of scientist Freeman Dyson, for example, offered an idiosyncratic world of war, weapons, and science in which whimsical caprice and deadening routine ruled and technology "made evil anonymous."[38] Meanwhile, Vietnam also began to yield a stream of fiction, memoir, and oral history.

Television and movies reflected the shift toward a darker view of war and America's role in it. World War II combat films, still a Hollywood staple in the late 1960s, had virtually disappeared by 1975. The few still made either seemed leaden (*Midway* in 1976, *MacArthur* in 1978) or (as with *A Bridge Too Far* in 1977) used the epic style and star-studded cast to depict "the futility of war and the wretchedness of a specific military debacle."[39] Meanwhile, an ambitious, somber British documentary series, *The World at War* (1973), reflected the work of revisionist historians, offered a grisly panorama of mass destruction in World War II, and found acclaim and a large television audience in the United States during the 1970s.

These scholarly and cultural phenomena accelerated trends evident in the 1960s. More abrupt and arresting was rediscovery of Nazi genocide. It hardly had been unknown to Americans and had long been linked to nuclear holocaust by the idiom and mentality used to understand both genocide and nuclear weapons. After the 1940s, however, its treatment in popular culture had been only occasional and the centrality of the fate of Jews in it had often been obscured. Archival film had been slow to surface or long forgotten (as was the case with footage of Hiroshima and Nagasaki due to censorship by American officials), and historians had been slow to tackle the labyrinth of archival records and the tangle of moral and political questions. Even the common phrase for Nazi genocide, "the Holocaust," was not widely used until the 1970s.

All that now changed, for complex reasons. Israel's 1967 and 1973 wars sharpened fear of its vulnerability to destruction among Israelis and many American Jews, emphasis on the Nazi Holocaust served Israel in leveraging assistance from the United States, and many Jews increasingly chafed at their difficulty in coming to terms with their fate under Nazism. Other impulses fed rediscovery of the Holocaust, including sensitivity to American atrocities in the Vietnam War and news of the Khmer Rouge's genocide in Cambodia. Developments there, occurring just when the Nazi Holocaust gained new attention, underlined both the specificity of genocide—it happens to specific groups, not to vaguely defined victims—and its diversity: no one group could claim or fear victimization.

Rediscovery of the Holocaust reflected and accentuated a larger cultural effort to imagine the danger of modern war. New scholarship about the Holocaust—and, pointedly for Americans, about their government's wartime indifference to it—offered one measure of rediscovery. Official recognition occurred in the Carter and Reagan presidencies with initial work on a United States Holocaust Memorial Museum. Rediscovery was also evident in a more diffuse phenomenon, the growing frequency with which artists, writers, and politicians referred to the Nazi Holocaust.

For most Americans, rediscovery occurred through film. As usual, the movie industry was slow to take on a controversial and ugly subject, but the television mini-series *Holocaust* (NBC, 1978) crossed a threshold. Shown on a day "unofficially proclaimed 'Holocaust Sunday,'" given massive media attention, worked into numerous school curricula, and seen by some 50 percent of all Americans (and many Western Europeans), the series plausibly marked the point when the Holocaust entered "into the consciousness of mainstream America" and became "institutionalized into American life." Summing up the ambivalence many felt about the series, one editorialist noted, "The war is over. . . . The swastika is recycled as a junk button; Auschwitz is a metaphor. And 'Holocaust' is a television series." But therein lay the point: the Holocaust could not be reexperienced, but the metaphor was abundantly clear.[40]

More than ever, genocide seemed the accomplice of modern war, while nuclear war loomed as the ultimate act of genocide. As imagined, the relationship between genocide and nuclear war was not fully symmetrical: after all, genocide did not require modern technology, as the Khmer Rouge had shown; and the dread triggered by the Nazi Holocaust involved a past event, while that induced by nuclear weapons focused on the future. Still, the two were closely linked in the culture of war's horrors—by World War II, when both Nazi genocide and atomic war occurred; by arguments that the same mentalities lay behind both forms of destruction and the same themes of sin and redemption were appropriate to both; by the simultaneity with which the film industry popularized both in the late 1970s and early 1980s; and by use of same term, *holocaust*, to refer to both.

Rediscovery of the Holocaust also showed how much patriotic and antiwar culture had in common. Their themes and their choices of historical benchmarks overlapped. Television's *Holocaust* did not clearly serve either cause: it showed war's horrors but also the necessity of war against Hitler and, as some saw it, a quick trigger finger in the face of current barbarians.

Indeed, what drove attention to the Holocaust more than worry about Israel, shock at the Khmer Rouge, or foreboding about nuclear war was a desire to reassert sharp lines between good and evil in war after the ambiguities of Vietnam. Returning to the touchstone of World War II banished those ambiguities and reinstated the validity of war, at least when grave moral issues, as in the Holocaust, seemed at stake. As a genre, combat movies, about World War II and even more about Vietnam, no longer easily made that case, but films and commentary about the Holocaust were fresh, virtually a new genre. Like most cultural projects, this one owed to no single political force, certainly not to patriotic fervor alone, but it did at times contribute to that fervor.[41]

Accordingly, proponents of patriotic renewal regularly dipped into the chambers of war's horrors to make their case. Jerry Falwell began *Listen America!* (1980) with an account of genocide in Cambodia, tying it to the communist menace as part of his call for moral and military rearmament against the Soviet Union, whose power now made it able to "demand our capitulation." Meanwhile, so great were anxieties about nuclear war that patriots sometimes gave a nod to them, as when the Confederate Air Force asserted that Hiroshima made "all future wars unthinkable." That claim updated the old "cult of the superweapon" in attributing beneficent results to horrific weapons, allowing patriots to steal the thunder of antiwar culture. Those stressing war's horrors could not so easily tap their opponents' themes, but they did suggest that true patriotism need not be abandoned but rather redefined: it now required abolition of war and a broader loyalty—to the world, the ecosphere, and future generations.[42]

To some extent, the two conflicting cultures simply renewed an old debate about whether military power would ward off war's horrors or plunge the world into them. Now, however, debate had the fatalistic, unreal quality of the awful futures each side sketched. Neither side had much confidence that it could shape national policy, and both offered views of a past and a future detached from immediate realities, saying little about Vietnam, the war Americans now knew best, and reaching instead back to World War II and forward to a dangerous future. A benchmark for both sides, Hiroshima remained what it had been for most Americans since 1945—symbol, not comprehended event. Soviet nuclear attack on the United States, American capitulation to its blackmail, world-ending nuclear war—such outcomes were fervently asserted, but no longer against the background of the nuclear crises that earlier had peppered the Cold War. It was not that such outcomes were, as often claimed, inherently unthinkable because too awful for the mind to grasp: nuclear war had already been fought in 1945 and had generated an abundant record. But for many reasons that record was rarely examined, and debate on war's nature stayed where it had long been, "above the battle."[43] If it had a weightless quality, so too did the hope for cultural transformation on which each side made the future hinge. Such transformation is by nature a long-term process, yet each emphasized dangers so immediate that their resolution could hardly await the always predicted but ever elusive redemption of American (or world) culture.

Since the cultures of patriotism and of war's horrors were not sealed off from each other, many impulses did not clearly fit either category. Aside from the Bible, the decade's bestselling nonfiction book was Hal Lindsey's *The Late Great Planet Earth* (1970), a "premillennial view," based on Lindsey's reading of Biblical prophecy, of the future "end times." Lindsey had much to say about war, weapons, and the Soviets, often placing them in the well-worn grooves of rightwing ideology. The prospect of nuclear war drove him almost to ecstasy: "Imagine, cities like London, Paris, Tokyo, New York, Los Angeles, Chicago—

obliterated!" Though Lindsey warned against ceasing to live in the earthly world, his promise that Christians would escape the final cataclysm by being lifted up in the "Rapture" made it seem almost welcome.[44]

Prophecies like Lindsey's—and many variants washed over America in the 1970s and 1980s—were another measure of anxiety about nuclear war and another impulse behind rearmament. As Paul Boyer notes, "many prophecy writers, increasingly mobilized into the ranks of the New Right, now treated God's prophetic plan and Reagan's military buildup as indistinguishable." Reagan and key officials in his administration seemed to echo Lindsey's outlook; as Nancy Reagan "groaned 'Oh, no' off camera," Reagan admitted his "'philosophical' interest in Armageddon" during the 1984 presidential debates, while Lindsey boasted of speaking to officers at the Air War College and the Pentagon. Those who embraced his outlook tended to support or acquiesce in American nuclear rearmament, seeing it as step mandated by God's plan. Critics, revealing their own apocalyptic outlook, worried "that apocalyptic belief might inspire some future president or military to try . . . 'to make the inevitable, paradoxically, even more certain.' "[45]

Yet as that paradox suggests, belief in the end-time dictated no single position on war and armaments. The inevitable, after all, required no human intervention. Some premillennialists denied that nuclear war was inevitable, or at least knowable in its timing and circumstances. Rev. Pat Robertson, having "predicted the ultimate holocaust by 1982," backed away from such assertions once 1982 passed and his political ambitions swelled. Evangelicals could dismiss Lindsey's "science fiction fantasy" and condemn him as "the Geraldo Rivera of the Christian world." Rev. Billy Graham's surprising revision of his "premillennial fatalism" marked another path: by 1982 Graham was in Moscow preaching that the arms race was "a moral and spiritual issue that must concern us all" and offering a plan to abolish nuclear, biological, and laser weapons. And it was "the logic of premillennialism" that Christian "energies" were "better spent in winning souls for Christ than in trying to shape world events." While the cause of moral reawakening often strengthened the crusade for military rearmament, it also comprised a separable, sometimes competing agenda.[46]

Films about the Vietnam War, despite the antiwar label sometimes pinned on them, also lay in the no-man's land between clashing cultures. Like much supposedly antiwar literature of the 1920s, their focus was less on war per se than on war as a lens into the corruptions of America at home. None said much about American entry into the Vietnam War, leaving it beyond viewers' comprehension. As usually portrayed, the trauma for Vietnam veterans was not that they had gone to war but that they had done so in a losing and unappreciated effort, in an alien land peopled by untrustworthy Asians, or for the wrong reasons (or good ones not sufficiently acted upon). Combat was usually secondary in these films, as in *Coming Home* (1978), or treated in its most exotic aspects, as in *Apocalypse Now* (1978). A sense of wounded nationalism also lurked in films like *The Deerhunter* (1978): the problem was not patriotic virtue but its betrayal by cynical politicians who went to war, peaceniks who opposed it, or an Asian people "so irredeemably mired in moral corruption that it hardly deserved to be saved." By the 1980s many films "portrayed the major tragedy of Vietnam as a loss of American innocence rather than the loss of both Vietnamese and American lives."[47]

Few Vietnam War films fell clearly into a "prowar" or "antiwar" category: for commercial reasons, filmmakers usually avoided categorical stances; for artistic reasons, they might seek greater complexity. While most Vietnam films were not "about combat at all, but about the destructive effect it had on American society," that effect could be seen as a powerful reason not to go to war. And while it was possible to see the war portrayed in these films as only a "metaphor for chaos," others saw the moral chaos as one of these films' "metaphors for the war." Still, as the babble of conflicting comments on Vietnam War films indicated, none offered the certain voice against war evident in *All Quiet on the Western Front* in 1930, or in occasional films after World War II. Only a handful of films about Vietnam even appeared in the 1970s. The most telling Vietnam War film, claims John Hellmann, was *Star Wars*, ostensibly not about Vietnam at all.[48]

The style and scale of these films were as telling as any overt message. While far from glamorizing war, they sometimes presented it as a Wagnerian spectacle oddly disproportionate to the minor action and technocratic routine that characterized much of the war itself. Portraying Vietnam as mysterious, most films made the war there incongruous—disconnected from traditions of American war making in Asia and offering no larger lesson about war's meaning and utility. What instruction, after all, could an atypical war offer about war generally? A few less grandly scaled films, such as *Go Tell the Spartans* (1978), focused more on combat and offered a modest statement of war's futility, but those films did not draw large audiences and lavish commentaries.

The ambiguities of Vietnam films in the 1970s seemed resolved by the 1980s, especially in *First Blood* (1982) and *Rambo: First Blood Part II* (1985), in which actor Sylvester Stallone, promoted as "this generation's John Wayne," asks, "Do we get to win this time?" President Reagan, suggesting how he might meet the threat of Libyan terrorists, "was quoted worldwide as saying 'I saw Rambo last night and now I know what to do.'" Patriotism seemed in full flower both on screen and in the White House, where an actor-politician fused the two worlds. Yet the Rambo films hardly suggested that war was useful. "The implausible circumstances and convolutions of plot used by these movies," notes one analyst, suggested the filmmakers' extreme discomfort "about America in the role of the technologically advanced invading superpower" and conveyed their longing "for our traditional posture of the underdog jungle fighter," a posture hardly suitable for waging war on a major scale. The message of the

Rambo films seemed to be that "the United States military could have won the war if the government and American public had let them." Yet Rambo himself did not really go to war, but to a kind of compensatory substitute for it as he tried to rescue American POWs left behind in Vietnam.[49]

Indeed, these films exuded such indignation at the state—it presumably covered up the presence in Southeast Asia of American POWs—that it was hardly to be trusted to lead the nation in another war, or to administer the vast system of militarization that made modern war possible. In fact, the faceless, cynical, neutered bureaucrats who presumably ruled that system were as much Rambo's enemy as the bestial communists he encountered in Vietnam. The Rambo films did celebrate war of an individualistic, atavistic, premodern sort, adding a glitzy overlay of high-tech weapons to an old mythology about noble Indian savages (or about white men fighting them: it was hard to tell). They also stirred the war-lust and patriotism of some viewers. It was difficult, however, to take them seriously, especially as a brief for remilitarization. Nor did they have an uncontested hold on Vietnam's cinematic terrain.[50]

Just as Vietnam War films rested uneasily between the two cultures, so too did the smoldering controversy and flamboyant mythology about POW/MIAs which the Rambo films exploited. As Jimmy Carter had pointed out, far fewer Americans were unaccounted for after Vietnam than after earlier wars; if any lingered in Southeast Asia, captive or otherwise, they must have been few. Politics and culture, not the numbers, drove this issue. Its origins lay in the Nixon administration. With bipartisan help and aid from figures like businessman H. Ross Perot, Nixon had highlighted the issue of American POWs in order to sustain support for his war effort and to counter doubts about the atrocities and destruction in Vietnam it sanctioned.

Still, this was an unruly beast for politicians to ride. Nixon swore in 1973 that he had achieved "the return of all our prisoners of war," but some Americans, long told of communist duplicity, thought otherwise. By the late 1970s, POW/MIA flags, bumper stickers, and bracelets proliferated, politicians mandated the display of POW/MIA flags on government buildings and other rituals, and *The Deerhunter* transformed "POWs into crucial symbols of American manhood," presenting "American white working-class men as crucified prisoners of the Vietnamese." By the 1980s, with a President apparently believing the mythology, Hollywood vigorously presenting it, and lobbies aggressively publicizing it, controversy intensified, as did the notion of "a vast government cover-up and conspiracy." Reagan himself was usually exempt from blame: the wrongdoers were the faceless bureaucrats who had long peopled the conservative imagination—and of course Reagan hated bureaucracy.[51]

For good reason, critics charged that the POW/MIA mythology was instigated by conservative forces trying to restore a patriotic culture and a hawkish foreign policy. It did have those results: it blocked diplomatic relations between the United States and Vietnam; emphasized the evil and barbarism of communists; buried questions about wartime atrocities by American and ARVN forces; reasserted Americans' essential innocence and goodness in war; kept the Vietnam War alive as an issue ("THE WAR'S NOT OVER UNTIL THE LAST MAN COMES HOME!" shouted a 1984 movie ad); and allowed politicians to strike patriotic poses.[52]

Yet its themes of bureaucratic conspiracy and elite manipulation also saturated the culture of war's horrors. Aggrieved friends and families of missing Americans had diverse politics, some distrusting conservative Republicans. The resonance of the mythology with the plight of American captives in Beirut in the 1980s also made trouble for the Reagan White House. Above all, the POW controversy looked back to old wrongs rather than forward to new deeds, and stoked distrust of what government might do in war. Its place in patriotic culture was an uneasy one—its emphasis on old sins tarnished prospects of new glories.

The POW/MIA mythology was also the perverse offshoot of a long cultural tradition regarding war's victims. Starting with the American Civil War and swelling during World War I, the work of recovering, naming, and memorializing the dead in war (and in other catastrophes, as responses to AIDS would show) became an enormous project in many nations. It often sanctioned and sanctified war making: treating bodies as sacred relics gave meaning to the loss felt by survivors and seemed necessary because modern war making rested on democratic consent (even if fabricated); it would not do to honor only the generals when all were asked to sacrifice. The Vietnam Veterans Memorial in Washington, D.C., emerged out of that tradition, but it, and even more Washington's Holocaust Memorial Museum, also "made manifest the fact of stupendous mortality" in war. The importance ascribed to such projects mounted in the 1970s and 1980s, even though the numbers of American dead or missing in Vietnam were far smaller than in the world wars (remarkably, efforts to identify American dead from World War II and Korea also continued in the 1980s). Such projects had no single or stable meaning, but Americans were memorializing their war dead more elaborately as they became more reluctant to go to war, as if memorialization took the place of war itself. To name meticulously every American who died in Vietnam, as the Vietnam Veterans Memorial did, or to demand the identification or return of every missing American there, as the POW/MIA forces did, was to insist on the preciousness of every life lost in war. Despite its partisan and bellicose purposes, the POW/MIA movement, keeping the memory of sacrifice alive, also declared such sacrifice to be extreme, warranted only in the gravest circumstances, if at all.[53]

A more diffuse cultural phenomenon, commentary on the "me" generation, had a less pointed but vital place in the clash of cultures. Writer Tom Wolfe announced, "It's the Me-Decade" in 1976, helping to start a cottage industry among popular and elite pundits who saw grave flaws in the personality of Americans—their loss of connection to the past and to each other and their pursuit of empty self-aggrandizement and self-awareness. "Hedonism," "narciss-ism," "cult of the self"—so historian Christopher Lasch summarized Ameri-cans' spiritual ills in 1976. In *Haven in a Heartless World* (1977) and *The Culture of Narcissism* (1978), Lasch further explored those ills. His goals were avowedly radical—to explain how modern bureaucracy, professional elites, and capital-ism sapped Americans' vitality and self-reliance and to challenge a cultural radicalism "so fashionable, and so pernicious in the support it unwittingly pro-vides for the status quo."[54]

Lasch's observations, if not his explanations for them, seemed borne out by many phenomena in the 1970s. Americans apparently were pursuing a preen-ing sort of self-fulfillment, judged by their attraction to jogging and other forms of fitness, to popular self-help therapies, and to magazines like *People* (where Lasch himself appeared in 1979) and *Self*. Even when they worked with others politically, they often abandoned broad agendas and constituencies in favor of single-interest lobbies attending to narrow causes or specific groups. A few ob-servers saw these phenomena as signs of grass-roots revitalization. Most, like Lasch, saw political disarray, psychological selfishness, and cultural barren-ness. The apparent aimlessness of the Carter presidency seemed both cause and product of these deeper ills. Carter himself confirmed that diagnosis in his most famous address, offered in July 1979 in the backwash of consternation about his energy policies and commentary about Lasch's book. Americans were having a "crisis of confidence." Politicians had failed the nation, he admit-ted, but he also blamed the crisis on Americans generally—they preferred "to worship self-indulgence and consumption" in a failed effort to "fill the empti-ness of lives which have no confidence or purpose." Americans seemed to have lost a sense of service to the nation or to any entity beyond their own selfish interests.[55]

Whether Americans had become more materialistic, selfish, and parochial was unprovable, but the claim was hardly new. It updated old worries stated by patricians like Teddy Roosevelt, renewed on the eve of World War II by critics fearful that Americans lacked the will to fight, and reworked in countless ways during the Cold War. As in the 1970s, such complaints had been tied to social change at home, which, it was feared, undercut America's strength and leadership in the world. In the 1970s, those complaints also coincided with the end of conscription (the most obvious measure compelling service to the na-tion), of confidence in America's military prowess, and, so it seemed possible at mid-decade, of the Cold War that long had given Americans a national mission.

Criticism of Americans' self-centeredness came from sources too ideologi-cally divergent to yield a singular political result, and Lasch hardly wanted to beat the drums of patriotism and militarism. The Left could not control this dis-course, however, especially since it was more fragmented than ever, and Lasch, in his nostalgia for patriarchal culture and scorn for the new gender politics, unwittingly linked arms with conservatives (Falwell picked up his key words, though not his historical arguments). Lesbianism attracted "women who repeatedly fail to find a union of sexuality and tenderness in their relations with men," Lasch argued, rehashing an old view of homosexuality as failed heterosexuality. "After the turmoil of the sixties," he concluded, Americans "retreated to purely personal preoccupations." His dismissal of new forms of radicalism and his distinction between 1960s "turmoil" and 1970s "narcissism" carried, like much else in the decade, "an essentially conservative message," notes Peter Carroll—about "the futility of seeking change."[56]

Therefore, despite its complex politics, the discourse on "narcissism" drifted toward reinstating the tattered values of patriotism and militarization. Lasch himself seemed to presume that the American character, once sturdy during the age of imperial expansion and military glory, had collapsed during the Vietnam era. Few Americans baldly suggested that remilitarization was desirable as a way to overcome internal disarray—instead it was needed, the familiar argument ran, to deal with a disorderly world. For Carter in 1979, it was "on the battlefield of energy [that] we can win for our Nation a new confidence," but the military metaphor was slippery, and it was possible to argue by 1980, as one general did amid crises over Iran and Afghanistan, that "crisis revives the spirit of this nation."[57] If the price of disengagement from militarization was cultural and moral disarray, on top of economic dislocation and stagnation, it indeed seemed high.

Precisely how the clash of cultures shaped politics is hard to determine. Cultural phenomena evolve gradually, at the periphery of vision for politicians. But in the late 1970s, the clash of cultures was more bitter in tone, apocalyptic in content, and engaged by politicians than at any time in the Cold War. In turn, that conflict provided a structural underpinning for the stage of militarization the nation was now entering. How were such polarized moods and stances to be satisfied by national leaders? A show of war making, military might, and patriotic zeal without their substance constituted a compromise. The weapons, words, and symbols of war satisfied those yearning for patriotic culture; inaction in practice held at bay those fearing the final cataclysm. A renewed but oddly hollow Cold War gave form to the compromise. Carter presented the compromise belatedly and awkwardly. Reagan would do it better.

The Social Dimensions of Conflict

Cultural conflict among Americans about war and military policy was tied to their social conflicts. Struggles over the social sources of national power were hardly new in the 1970s, but their context and configuration were changing. Challenges arose from groups heretofore of minor concern to military leaders, while a shrinking army was less accommodating to democratizing pressures than one hungry for personnel, although the move to an all-volunteer force complicated matters. The necessitarian rationale for an egalitarian military force—that it was essential for America's global image and its efficient use of resources—continued to diminish in cogency. Above all, the improbability of major war—except possibly a nuclear war in which the military's social make-up might matter little—altered the social conflicts and anxieties of Americans. Though the shift was subtle and only partial, more at issue now was the composition of America's society rather than its ability to exert power abroad.

Of all these struggles, those over the racial composition and chemistry of the armed forces, though hardly the least important, were the most familiar. Still, racial issues remained vexing because military leaders took them more seriously and because they followed widespread racial strife and racial nationalism among American forces in Vietnam—one 1970 poll found that over half of black enlisted men "objected to taking part in the war because they believe it is a race war pitting whites against nonwhites."[58] Moreover, at a time of shrinking federal efforts to foster racial equality, the military loomed as a lonely bastion of progress, even though inequalities persisted (blacks comprised a high share of the military's prison population and its troubled Vietnam veterans but a minuscule share of its officers).

The advent of an all-volunteer force in 1973 sharpened these issues. Many male and female African-Americans continued to look to military service for education, heightened status, and upward job mobility, while young whites, in part because the decade's economic dislocations hit them later, were less inclined to sign up. Blacks' share of the military's enlisted ranks rose to 18.4 percent by 1978, 27.5 percent of the army's (33.2 percent by 1981), even more of combat branches. In response, nervous politicians, commanders, and journalists worried about the armed forces reaching a racial "tipping point" beyond which whites would stay away in droves, as they did in urban neighborhoods when blacks moved in, though if a tipping point operated, it "served mainly to purge the service of many whites whose prejudices kept them from tolerating blacks."[59]

The content of those worries was complicated. Ostensibly they often involved not race but the low educational levels of recruits. For much of the 1970s, fewer than half of male army volunteers had high school diplomas; only recession and the military's improving status in the early 1980s prompted better-educated youth to sign up; even then retention remained a problem in combat branches. Indeed, social class was at issue, as notions of the ignorant, untrainable poor were common in debates on military sociology: "I WANT YOU FOR [THE] U.S. ARMY," ran one newspaper cartoon—"Even If You Can't Read," it added in smaller type.[60]

But issues of race mixed with those of class and educational status in ways difficult to confront openly. Hanging over the controversy, usually unspoken, was a distorted image of real racial and class tensions that impeded the armed forces during the Vietnam War's later stages: would an even poorer and blacker armed force fare even worse in a future war? Suspecting that it would, some military leaders and their civilian allies disliked the armed forces' new demographics, but they could hardly condemn them openly without alienating minority groups supplying much of the volunteer force. Reformers in and out of the armed forces saw the challenge differently—as one not of race and class per se but of retraining officers to deal with the tensions involved and to enforce rules of equal opportunity—but support from the White House for their efforts was often weak before Carter's presidency. Liberal critics condemned the unfairness of leaving combat to poor and minority Americans but detested efforts to limit their numbers, or conscription to spread the burdens more evenly.

Meanwhile, images offered by both conservatives and liberals of the military as a foreign legion for America reeked of narrow nationalism—as if poor and minority soldiers were somehow less American. It was certainly fair to ask, as one expert did, "What kind of society excuses its privileged from serving in the ranks of its Army?" But the answer, usually ignored, was that American society long had: the military, never a cross-section of society, had often been a refuge for marginal Americans, on whom it drew (because of loopholes in the draft) in about the same proportions in the draft's final years as it did after 1973 as a volunteer force. It was the racial (and gender) composition of the armed forces that shifted most in the 1970s, not the economic and educational status of recruits. Moreover, because black recruits more often held high school diplomas, they saw greater pay-off in military service and were more likely "to fulfill their voluntary obligation" by reenlisting. In turn, those patterns suggest that focus on the recruits' class and educational status was only a more acceptable way to exercise anxieties about their racial make-up.[61]

There were limits, however, on how much the military's racial make-up could still generate controversy. The great issues of law and policy had already been settled, even though the resulting rules were not always enforced. The military's social composition was driven by economic and demographic forces largely beyond anyone's control, except by drastic actions like conscription that few wanted to take. Ideological divisions broke down on these issues: although for different reasons, liberals were as squeamish as right-wingers about the military's social profile, and about the fact that the armed forces maintained a better record of racial progress than most institutions in America. The Cold War prism for viewing these issues—would the military showcase America's egalitarian ideals or its endemic failings?—had weakened. And despite the ugliness of the racial climate in the 1970s, few whites now openly argued that racial minorities were unfit to serve.

Not so, however, regarding the place in the military of women and homosexuals. Women's share of the ranks rose sharply—from less than 1 percent of the army in 1964 to 10 percent by the early 1980s, their numbers in all branches tripling in the 1970s to 150,000. More at issue was their entry into the hallowed academies at West Point, Annapolis, and Colorado Springs. In the end, the requisite legislation passed Congress by wide margins in 1975, in part for what

turned out to be an unfounded reason: proponents argued that imminent ratification of the Equal Rights Amendment would mandate such an outcome
anyway. Difficult debates and hearings preceded passage, however. Male military leaders—senior military women were not called to testify—argued that
since the academies were designed to train officers for combat, which women
were forbidden by law to enter, women had to be barred from them. That argument was disingenuous, barely disguising a belief that women simply were unfit for high rank and combat responsibility. The academies admitted male cadets they knew might never see combat, while the technical complexities of
modern war had blurred the line between combat and noncombat service—
bullets might fell nurses, technicians in air-conditioned bunkers might launch
missiles, and truck drivers might determine the fate of a mission. Still, the debate did expose what was unknowable to all parties: How would women perform in combat? That question captured a major difference between gender
and race as issues in the armed forces: a long combat record existed for racial
minorities, almost none for women.

Revealing also was the nervous attention given the first women at the academies. Their problems and progress, followed as if a version of the 1973 tennis
match between Billie Jean King and Bobby Riggs, often got snickering treatment: it was a matter of "Beauties and the Beast," a *Time* headline ran; "At West
Point there is even more concern than usual these days about certain portions of
the female body," began a *Newsweek* article. Some adjustments in physical
training and fewer in curricula proved necessary to accommodate women but,
unsurprisingly, "the greatest obstacle" for female cadets was "the attitudes of
men—faculty members and students." Women's actual entry into the academies renewed the feverish debate about whether—in reality, how much—
they might enter combat, along with wild speculation about the sexual morals
or day-to-day comfort level for men and women thrown together in close quarters. Little noticed "while the mighty Navy anguished over female sailors" was
the fact that the lowly Coast Guard put mixed crews to sea quietly and with
little incident.[62]

In 1975, just as the issue of women in the academies peaked, Air Force Technical Sergeant Leonard Matlovich, a decorated veteran of combat in Vietnam,
challenged the military's ban on homosexuals. His was not the first such challenge, but it was the first to bask in the media's glare: he graced the cover of
Time, which dubbed him a "celebrity in the armed forces." Moreover, similar
cases were bubbling up in the courts, some officers evinced a more tolerant attitude, and a gay subculture was surfacing in military culture: informal groups
provided support and circulated newsletters, gay discos bustled on aircraft carriers, and the hit song "It's Raining Men," its title alone appealing to some gay
men, rang out even at remote bases. Cases like Matlovich's also chipped away
at one old rationale for exclusion—the claim that homosexuals were vulnerable to blackmail disintegrated when they were not closeted. That Matlovich

was probably the best-known (to the straight world at least) gay man at mid-decade demonstrated again the close nexus of social conflict with military matters.[63]

Though Matlovich eventually won back-pay and an honorable discharge, military policy only became more emphatic and encompassing as Cold War fervor and moral conservatism gained in Carter's administration and triumphed in Reagan's. "Homosexuality is incompatible with military service," the Pentagon decreed in 1982.[64] As always, gay men and women continued to serve, but the pace of vicious witch-hunts, gross violations of due process, and cavalier expulsions (sometimes of straight personnel misidentified as gay) accelerated. The case for gay personnel was badly hurt by the Defense Department's vigor in suppressing internal studies that undercut its claims. Even more, their cause was not yet clearly linked with that of women and racial minorities, and thus did not locate military homophobia in a broader system of white male dominance. In fact, however, anti-gay policies were valuable to male authorities seeking to curb the expanding roles of women in uniform and to counteract women's frequent charges of sexual abuse and harassment by male personnel. For those purposes, lesbian-baiting was a favored tactic: Pentagon policy gave men a powerful tool for intimidating women. Hostility to women was an important factor behind the tightening of anti-gay policies.

The progress in military institutions made by women and sought by gays was all the more remarkable given how little support they got from the movements they seemed to symbolize. Still influenced by the radical politics of the Vietnam era, most feminist and gay groups looked askance at acceptance by an institution regarded as unchangeably racist, sexist, militarist, and imperialist. Why help *it* wage war? Entry into the oppressor's institutions was all the more suspect now that feminist and gay thought emphasized fundamental differences (whether rooted in biology, history, or culture) between men and women and between gay and straight people. The middle-class composition of most feminist and gay groups also diminished interest: they were ill attuned to poor and minority constituents who had keener aspirations for military service.

To be sure, gender-based movements were split between assimilationist and oppositional stances—should they destroy hegemonic white male society or strive to enter it on a equal basis? Gradually a middle ground was staked out: entry might be a means to transform, rather than acquiesce in, dominant society, and methods once scorned as accommodationist—the pursuit of legal equality, elective office, media coverage, respect in mainstream institutions—became more attractive. The Equal Rights Amendment had that thrust for many proponents, as politicians like Rep. Patricia Schroeder pressed for women's admission to the service academies. At the same time, gay rights groups recast homosexuality as a minority identity rather than a revolutionary sensibility; that thrust emerged in Harvey Milk's successful efforts to win election in 1977 as a San Francisco supervisor and to defeat the Briggs initiative (which would have banned homosexuals from public-school teaching in California), and in the broader effort of gay activists to meet the political challenge of the New Right. Still, military institutions remained secondary for these movements in the 1970s.

That offered no comfort to their opponents, who feared precisely what some gender activists sought—the dissolution of dominant society and of the armed strength it presumably provided. Indeed, those activists upset older, gendered notions of national strength in many ways. That was the case when thousands of gay men and lesbians silently marched through San Francisco after the assassination of Harvey Milk and Mayor George Moscone, and later fought an ugly battle with police following news that the assassin had gotten a light sentence. Like the Stonewall riots in 1969, those scenes eroded stereotypes of limp-wristed homosexuals. So too did the tough, muscled appearance popular among gay men in the late 1970s, which emerged just as popular culture urged straight men to develop a softer demeanor. "It is now in straight discos that one finds the soft-looking and long-haired males," one gay writer soon observed; "gays are too busy striking masculine poses and flexing their pectorals."[65] Masculinity and aggressiveness, once equated with heterosexual authority and embodied in military institutions, had slipped their traces, at a time, patriots alleged, when the military itself had become dangerously weak. Who now were the more soldierly Americans?

Women's peace and antinuclear activism offered a related challenge. By the end of the 1970s, women had a prominence and autonomy in peace activism unattainable during the Vietnam War. In many ways they comprised *the* dominant force in moving the culture of war's horrors into practical activism. They figured prominently in gender-integrated efforts (Helen Caldicott in activist circles, Representative Schroeder in mainstream politics), generated much of the critical scholarship and polemics, and developed their own separate campaigns. In the process, they often "contrasted women's intrinsically peace-loving, life-preserving, non-violent manner against men's violent, exploitative and plundering nature," as one historian summarizes their outlook. "Take the Toys Away from the Boys," read a placard popular in the Women's Pentagon Action, which declared that "a feminist world is a nuclear free zone." That outlook linked together male propensity to go to war, to use violence against women in rape and in pornography ("RAPE IS WAR!" declared one 1976 poster), to despoil the environment, and to exploit Third World nations.[66] It was an ideological stance most associated with (though not confined to) radical lesbians and feminist separatists, whereas many mainstream feminists feared that such a stance undercut their cause (if men were unchangeably violent, why bother to reform them?). But whatever the stance, women's prominence in the peace movement was striking, especially since few women stood out in the forces of rearmament. Antiwar sentiment, castigated by its enemies in the 1960s as vaguely feminine, now was embraced by its proponents as feminist.

No wonder, then, that the forces of moral and military rearmament saw their twin causes as inseparable—successful defense of the nation required beating back feminists, homosexuals, leftists, black leaders, and others. Often the linkage between military and moral rearmament was only implicit in thinly coded language. To columnist George Will, efforts to gain municipal ordinances protecting gays from discrimination were "weapons in a battle" and threatened "the moral disarmament of society"—but "disarmament" was a loaded word in the context of contemporary debate, connoting martial weakness as well. Jerry Falwell argued that "homosexuality reaches a pandemic level in societies in crisis or in a state of collapse," implying America's defenselessness, made worse because lesbians defied male authority ("In the Christian home the woman is to be submissive") and because homosexuals, who "must recruit" because they "cannot reproduce," eroded the ramparts of society by targeting its youth. Against such enemies, "the church should be a disciplined, charging army," argued Falwell, who issued military metaphors in profusion. "Christians, like slaves and soldiers, ask no questions."[67]

Norman Podhoretz, for one, did not leave things implicit: the "culture of appeasement" included the "kind of women who do not want to be women and . . . men who do not want to be men." He recalled the abandonment in England of "proper manhood among homosexual writers of the 1920s," who presumably paved the way for Britain to appease the Nazis. Meanwhile, Podhoretz's spouse, writer Midge Decter, attended to the homefront, excoriating gay men for being in "flight from women," putting "our very existence as women on the line," and living lives of "drugs, sado-masochism, and suicide." Decter uttered not a word about national defense, but she was billed as "executive director of the Committee for the Free World," and the portrait she sketched of gay men would have made any patriot shudder. Furious respondents to her diatribe further exposed cultural divisions on these matters by calling up the Holocaust, accusing Decter (writing in a magazine sponsored by the American Jewish Committee) of "replicating the historical patterns of modern anti-Semitism" in her attack on homosexuals.[68]

Attacks like Decter's nonetheless betrayed a shift in the faultlines over issues of gender and war. Among those who assailed homosexuality, an older derogatory language ("perverts," "faggots") diminished, at least in public forums, and psychological and sociological explanations (however fraudulent) for homosexuality now jostled alongside moral ones. The mere fact that the task of purging this contagion, once performed by public authorities, now fell to moral reformers indicated that forward positions had been abandoned and a rearguard action was taking place. So too did the reformers' coalescence behind the candidacy of Ronald Reagan—a divorced man from the fleshpots of Hollywood was not the ideal leader (he even opposed the Briggs initiative). In the 1980s, revelations that some leading moral conservatives were themselves homosexual complicated matters further. And the broad claim of moralists, that homosexuality undermined national vigor and safety, proved hard to pin down. It was left as a sinister insinuation rather than spelled out in convincing detail, and old equations between communism and homosexuality or feminism, while hardly extinct, became fuzzier in the conservative critique.

Perhaps that was because moralists cared less about homosexuality than about using it as a symbol of forces that exercised them more. While Decter moved in circles where she encountered gay men (not lesbians, by her account), for people like Falwell's followers, homosexuality seemed an abstraction, a scourge of distant cities or strange neighborhoods. Far more woven into their daily lives were changes in male-female and black-white relations, but because homosexuality was less acceptable to most Americans and more openly stigmatized, it better mobilized the troops, opened pocketbooks, and symbolized the cause.

The successful campaign against ratification of the Equal Rights Amendment, passed by Congress in 1972 and facing state legislatures for a decade after, revealed the central focus of moral conservatism, and the tensions in its effort to link moral and military rearmament. While ERA opponents warned of unisex bathrooms, flamboyant lesbianism, and gay marriage, they focused more on how the ERA would affect heterosexual behavior for the worse. For Phyllis Schlafly, the person most responsible for the ERA's defeat, the worries of some women—that the ERA would abolish laws protecting women from onerous work practices, for example—involved "minor ramifications" compared to the dangers posed for national defense. Schlafly's roots lay in hard-right conservatism of the 1960s, when she assailed communism's military and moral threat, and she claimed expertise in arcane matters of megatonnage and deterrence, excoriating Ford and Kissinger for their SALT diplomacy. Moreover, she and her allies drew on the ideals and forces of patriotic renewal—groups like the Daughters of the American Revolution and FLAG (Family, Liberty, and God).[69]

Schlafly hammered away at the ERA's impact on conscription and military service, an issue for which ERA supporters were badly prepared because the end of the draft in 1973 seemed to permit them to duck it. Schlafly, however, correctly asserted that a ratified ERA would invalidate any future legislation obligating only men to serve. She objected mightily. Women were physically weaker, she noted, and their presence in the armed forces would undermine national security. "The Soviet Army, she said ominously, is less than 1 percent female and its combat troops are exclusively male." Schlafly found the draft issue great for gaining recruits, especially among younger women: it "has lowered the average age of our movement by about 20 years," she boasted. It also furthered her ambitions to be an authority on defense issues and to mobilize women behind rearmament, as she did with considerable success. When Carter proposed compulsory draft registration in 1980, she helped make sure that women were exempted. "The phones have been ringing off the hook ever since

Jimmy Carter stabbed the women of this country in the back," she announced, taking pride in launching Dads Against Drafting Our Daughters in a shrewd effort to tap protective sentiments among men toward women. Those had been voiced in the ERA debate since the early 1970s, when Sen. Sam Ervin, an ERA opponent, begged Congress to "prevent sending the daughters of America into combat to be slaughtered or maimed by the bayonets, the bombs, the bullets, the grenades, the napalm, the poison gas, and the shells of the enemy."[70]

Such rhetoric, however, exposed tensions in the outlook of ERA opponents. If the peril to America was as great as Schlafly claimed, the case for exempting women from the task of meeting it was shaky—indeed, some patriots hinted that all Americans should accept the ultimate sacrifice of waging nuclear war should it be necessary—just as an appeal to women's selfish interests was awkward when offered by a patriot. Moreover, the focus of Schlafly and her allies on nuclear weapons and nuclear war was oddly out of synch with their anti-ERA images of women trapped in foxholes or burned by napalm—images echoing the Vietnam War, the sort of war Schlafly was determined that the nation never again fight.

Schlafly probably worried less that women would fight badly than that men, if let off the hook, would not fight at all. Female competence held no terrors for her; she embodied it in a tireless and successful political career that any liberated woman might envy. Despite impressions to the contrary, she was driven not by animus toward women but by a conviction that men were shucking their responsibilities to women and the nation, and would do so even more cavalierly if the ERA were ratified. Feminists who trust men to support women "because of love, not because of the law," were foolish, Schlafly argued; the "ERA would eliminate that obligation." "From the vantage point of the antifeminists," Barbara Ehrenreich observed, "the crime of feminism lay not in hating men, but in trusting them too well." The New Right's outlook exhibited "a profound contempt for men" and, inverting nineteenth-century gender ideology, saw men as "'passive, fragile," while women were "'active' and 'can do everything.'"[71]

Schlafly did not explicitly tap that reasoning in arguing against the ERA on national security grounds, but it was implicit in the outlook of conservatives, whose patriarchal model of the good society placed a heavy burden on men to defend family, God, and country. "In the calculus of the right, flag and family have never been independent variables: A threat to one is a threat to the other." If the ERA allowed men to flee their duties to women, they would flee their duties to the nation as well. Indeed, the whole point of defending the nation would be lost, Congressman John Schmitz suggested, for "defense of our women and girls is one of the most basic reasons why we men are prepared to fight. . . . If we are willing to see them [women] killed, mutilated, or captured because they are 'equal,' we might as well say, 'come and get them!'" Korea and Vietnam had already stirred fear of men too soft or drugged to defend America.

Fear of lost patriotic manhood also made gay men seem scary: on their own they might be harmless, but not if "part of a conspiracy to sissify the last remnants of American military manhood," as Ehrenreich summed up New Right fears, or if (in an inversion of such fears) their hypermasculinity contrasted depressingly with straight men's lassitude in defending home and family. As Falwell asked in a radio tirade against homosexuality, "Is it any wonder that we are the laughing stock of the world? Is it any wonder that nations and terrorists thumb their noses at this once proud land?"[72]

Fears of moral disarmament at home and military disarmament abroad were so entwined in the anti-ERA and allied movements that it is hard to say which loomed larger, but anxieties about moral decline were often paramount. At this stage of militarization, with scenarios of Soviet attack ever more fanciful, the drive to mobilize American military strength had a hollow quality. A serious effort to mobilize might have allowed for—in a bullying way even demanded —inclusion of women and gays in the cause, as indeed happened (on different terms) in World War II. Strenuous moralizing by many conservatives (and some liberals) about these groups suggested that they were most exercised by threats not to national defense but to the social order they cherished—to the protected position of middle-class housewives whom Schlafly courted, to the male authority she both defended and mocked, to the "traditional" family that seemed in disarray. To be sure, moral conservatives paraded their patriotic virtue—Falwell's broadcasts began with the American flag and ended with the Liberty Bell—and labored to fend off the strategic peril seen in Carter's Panama Canal and SALT II treaties. But Christian evangelicals often "divided over Vietnam, . . . race relations, national defense, social welfare, and a host of other issues," while exhibiting "virtual consensus on questions of morality," anxieties about which loomed larger and more salable.[73]

Those anxieties marked a departure from the older conservatism of men like Barry Goldwater, who had emphasized martial strength abroad more than moral consensus at home. They also offered a religious sensibility alien to cosmopolitan calculators of national advantage, who now faded from prominence—among Presidents after Ford, only Bush came fully from their tradition. For the moment, religious resurgence fostered remilitarization. In the long run, however, the agenda of moral regeneration rested uneasily aside the cause of martial revitalization, and sometimes overwhelmed it. Falwell admitted as much: "If God is on our side, no matter how militarily superior the Soviet Union is, they could never touch us." If so, moral rearmament was more urgent than military power.[74]

The New Cold War

Protesting the Soviet invasion of Afghanistan, President Carter canceled American participation in the 1980 Moscow Summer Olympics. The United States did go ahead with the Winter Olympics at Lake Placid, New York, where its defeat of the Soviet hockey team was heralded as a victory by the David of democratic amateurism over the Goliath of totalitarian athletics, indeed, a symbolic victory in the Cold War. *Time* thought it "a bit foolish, even sad, to savor the victory as an act of geopolitical symbolism," but proceeded to do so. *Newsweek* was less apologetic. "This was not just a sports story. It was a morality play on ice." Despite capitalist wealth and communist hardship, it saw the Americans as "the working-class scufflers against the lordly elitists with the full government scholarships." "We typify the American public in how we feel about the Russian situation," argued an American player. "The only difference is that we can do something about it on the ice." Even the tonier *New Yorker*, though hewing to its antinuclear line, defended "this country's delirious response to the Olympic victory," noting that sports and war are "closely related." Still, it suggested Americans' skittish mood that their leaders chose to retire from this field of battle rather than risk expected defeat in the summer games.[75]

Withdrawal from those games was not Carter's most important response to the Soviet invasion, but it was a revealing one. Its purpose was to send a "powerful signal of world outrage" over the aggression and to pressure Moscow to end it, or else lose the opportunity offered by the games to showcase itself to the world. But the hope for such weighty results from a symbolic action also indicated Carter's difficulty in finding effective measures and enlisting national sacrifice to wield them. So too did grumbling by many Americans about more substantive actions, such as a cut in American grain sales to the Soviets, involving real sacrifice on their part and real economic pressure on Soviet leaders. Even as the will to sacrifice seemed fickle, however, many Americans treated the events of 1980 as a replay of the 1930s, making the Olympics carry heavy symbolic freight. Secretary Vance, though still committed to detente, offered the familiar analogy: "I look back to the 1936 [Berlin] games, when I was in college, and I think in hindsight it was a mistake for us to attend." Vice President Walter Mondale elaborated the analogy. Olympians in 1980, though "born a full generation after the Berlin Olympics," must share in "linking that history to their duty." Hitler's course was "a chronicle of the free world's failure—of opportunities not seized, aggression not opposed, appeasement not condemned."[76]

Given that outlook, Carter's efforts to strengthen detente, deemphasize the Cold War, and restrain militarization collapsed during his last two years as President. The final blow to his efforts was the seizure in November 1979 of American hostages in Tehran by Ayatollah Khomeini's revolutionary regime, and the invasion of Afghanistan in December by Soviet forces trying to prop up a client Marxist regime. Both events had complicated antecedents, including miscalculations by the Carter administration. Though less eagerly than its predecessors, it had encouraged the shah of Iran to buy weapons (mostly from the United States) "with the abandon of an alcoholic using a credit card in a liquor store." And it had been oblivious to signs of his impending demise. Just as telling was the response to these events of many Americans, who felt keenly that American power was collapsing, that the Soviets (as one journalist told Carter) "don't believe that you or the American people will fight," and that the next world war loomed. According to defense analyst Edward Luttwak, "Afghanistan was merely the weakest" of many possible victims. "Now the others wait their turn, facing a Soviet military empire once again on the move" and brimming with "operational confidence," a quality whose "emergence now completes the matrix that will lead to war unless we are very much luckier than we deserve to be." The *Chicago Tribune,* running a lengthy series entitled "U.S. Military: Too Weak for War?" answered that question: "If the Russians want to start a war with the United States, their chances of winning it may never be better than now."[77]

Carter made the twin events in the Mideast the focal point of his remaining months in office, becoming hostage to them and embracing the new Cold War. Soviet action in Afghanistan constituted "the most serious threat to world peace since the Second World War," he announced on January 20, 1980. Despite such rhetoric, his alarm and his policies fell short of what hawks like Henry Jackson in his own party or Ronald Reagan in the GOP wanted, but they were enough to have him all but abandon his already faltering efforts to restrain militarization. Carter withdrew the SALT II Treaty from consideration by the Senate, though hoping that his reelection would allow him to revive it. He also curtailed high-technology sales to the Soviets, backed the MX missile and other costly programs (including forerunners of Reagan's Strategic Defense Initiative), sought greater increases (5 percent annually in real terms) in the defense budget than those (3 percent) already made, and strengthened his call for compulsory draft registration. Though wobbly, his reaction toward turmoil in Central America suggested a similar stance: he first opposed, then tried to help, and then turned cold on Nicaragua's revolutionary Sandinista regime; and in one of his last actions, he decided to support El Salvador's brutal military regime. Rhetorically, Carter did try to end his presidency on a different note: his farewell address warned that the "danger" of nuclear war "is becoming greater." But those words, more earnest than memorable, did not reverse the policies he had embraced.[78]

Carter's role in the Cold War's renewal was both considerable and difficult to assess. Like Truman in the late 1940s, he lacked a popular mandate, good relations with Congress, success with his "domestic" programs, and economic stability—soaring energy prices and unprecedented inflation continuing to plague Carter—and he met the temptation of redeeming his presidency through forceful foreign policy (notably, Carter consulted Clark Clifford, who had helped to shape Truman's policy). Neither man admitted to such temptation, however, and since acting on it did not redound to their lasting political benefit, they either miscalculated in listening to its siren sound or more likely made no concerted calculation at all, instead shifting ground in an incremental and muddled fashion. What is clearer is that political culture exerted enormous pressure on both men to sound the alarm about the Soviets. For Carter, that pressure took the form of demands for patriotic renewal, fears for American safety, and a diffuse anxiety that no national agenda except the Cold War gave Americans a sense of unity and purpose and that competing issues were even trickier to deal with. The Cold War returned to the forefront of politics in part because other agendas—race, gender, and energy for Carter—seemed to entail even more rancor and frustration.

The Soviet Union's responsibility for the Cold War's renewal is also unclear. It is unlikely that its leaders saw invasion of Afghanistan as a step toward global hegemony, which soon became remote anyway as their effort in Afghanistan bogged down, or that they wanted to crush detente, which they probably saw as almost dead anyway. On the other hand, the Kremlin was blind to the fury the invasion unleashed (as when it intervened in Hungary in 1956 and Czechoslovakia in 1968, it embarrassed even many communists outside the Soviet Union) and did little to calm it (the Soviet government's claim that the Afghan government had invited it in resembled the claim made by the United States when it entered Vietnam's war). And it had hardly been averse to seeking strategic and political advantage abroad, even if its recent efforts, mostly involving impoverished regimes (in Somalia and then Ethiopia, in Vietnam and Cuba, among other places), had yielded little payoff. At a deeper level, mounting peril at home to the socialist vision and the Brezhnev regime— sagging economic growth, tenacious dissidents, ethnic tensions, a troublesome urban counterculture—provided pressure to find redemption abroad or at least prevent further losses there. The United States and the Soviet Union were hardly the mirror images of each other some pundits glibly posited—their strengths and weaknesses were too different. Yet if their leaders were frustrated about quite different problems, they both responded, as great powers in trouble at home often have, by reemphasizing old visions of their transcendent role in the world.

They now entered what was sometimes dubbed the "New Cold War," but the phrase had the crudeness of all such terms. In the sullen core of Soviet-American relations, it was too much like the old Cold War, which had never quite ended anyway, to be new. Once again nuclear policy, America's exposure to destruction by the Soviets, and improbable dangers of NATO's collapse or war in Western Europe generated enormous attention, while the actual firing of guns and jockeying for position took place in the Third World (now less in Asia, more in Africa and the Mideast). Geopolitically, the most dramatic change from the early Cold War was America's tacit alliance with Communist China, but that did little to change the ideological tone of the charges that Americans and Soviets hurled at each other or the strategic anxieties they expressed. At the same time, however, agreement among Americans to confront the Soviet enemy (and probably of the latter to confront America) on fields of fire did not match what it had been earlier: there would be no Korea or Vietnam, or policies of the historical novelty that had marked NATO or the space race. The new Cold War resembled the old one so often in words that it was hard to see how it differed in deeds. It also differed because the dramas that most convulsed Americans in 1980, the twin crises over energy and hostages, were at best the Cold War's bastard offspring, so poorly did they fit its framework. To see a "New Cold War" reflected real continuity, but also comfortingly over-emphasized it, offering hope that old reflexes and formulas would fit new situations.

Those reflexes were evident in references to World War II and appeasement that were more widespread and promiscuously applied than at any time since America's entry into the Vietnam War. The SALT II Treaty was a frequent target. To sign onto it, argued Democratic senator Henry Jackson, would be "appeasement in its purest form. . . . It is all ominously reminiscent of Great Britain in the 1930s, when one government pronouncement after another was issued to assure the British public that Hitler's Germany would never achieve military equality—let alone superiority. The failure to face reality today, like the failure to do so then, that is the mark of appeasement." Less weighty policies received similar treatment. As Carter moved to formalize diplomatic relations with Communist China, backers of Taiwan, whose government Washington had earlier recognized as China's legitimate authority, saw Carter as "our American Chamberlain," as one complained to *Time;* "Only the umbrella is missing." Carter's response to aggression reminded Ronald Reagan of Chamberlain "tapping the cobblestones of Munich," while columnist George Will quoted the *Economist* about " 'appeasement' " by Carter, who "may be the most dangerous President since James Buchanan" (whose "attitude was an invitation" to the Civil War). It was as if, complained the *New Yorker,* "our history books contained accounts of but one event—the Munich agreement in 1938 . . . from which we drew but one lesson; namely, that the use of force is always the best solution to intractable difficulties in our foreign affairs." Americans seemed "to have applied the Munich lesson to every international crisis but the one it truly fitted—Munich itself." Invoking that benchmark transported Americans back past the muddled years of Vietnam and its aftermath, wiping them off the slate of historically instructive events, and reinstated the centrality of World War II in national policy and national myth. Carter, though less strident than many in invoking the 1930s, deplored "isolationism" and asserted Vietnam's receding relevance, arguing "that not every instance of the firm application of the power of the United States is a potential Vietnam."[79]

The much-noted "Carter doctrine" emerged logically from this revised view of what was relevant from the past, as well as from fears of how the situations in Afghanistan and Iran might join. "Discounting the Ayatollah's rabid hatred of Communism, Carter [like many Western leaders] tended to hear only Khomeini's vicious assault on the United States which he called 'the great Satan,'" and suspected "that Khomeini would allow a Soviet penetration of Iran," which would have threatened the West's oil sources. To prevent that, American leaders reasoned, required conveying to Moscow precisely that antitotalitarian resolution lacking in the 1930s. Carter made it "absolutely clear" that any effort by an "outside force to gain control of the Persian Gulf will be regarded as an assault on the vital interests of the United States of America," one to "be repelled by any means necessary." In diplomatic parlance, "any means" meant nuclear weapons.[80]

His threat raised a dilemma obvious as soon as Carter uttered it. To use nuclear weapons in the Mideast risked torching the very interests that the United States sought to protect, while to use those weapons against the Soviet Union itself was scarcely more credible, since a wider war would engulf the Mideast as well. The dilemmas of nuclear deterrence were hardly new, but they were starker in 1980, when fear of nuclear war was reaching a new peak. Carter's threat was thus easily likened to Dulles's in the 1950s, at once dangerous and empty, and especially cavalier if read as a Western threat to consider the nuclear destruction of non-Western peoples, in a region where no regime except Israel had nuclear weapons or an apparent role in American decisionmaking. In part because his nuclear saber rattling provoked such anxieties, more modest means were instead used to confound the Soviets—the United States through the CIA, and other countries, funneled arms to Afghan resistance forces.

Nonetheless, Carter's threat was another indication that nuclear weapons and strategy generated much of the anxiety at loose in the new Cold War. Among Americans, debate was driven above all by the widely shared and hotly disputed perception that the Soviet Union was gaining the strategic upper hand: its rockets and warheads might soon have the numbers and precision to knock out America's land-based ICBMs and bombers, and therefore to launch a preemptive strike gaining it victory with few losses, or (just as bad) simply to threaten to do so in a way that would force the West to capitulate. As Reagan, campaigning in 1980, explained the danger, America was becoming so weak that "the Russians could just take us with a phone call."[81] Many American nuclear forces would survive a Soviet first strike, but in this scenario they would be hostage to Soviet superiority—a President would hesitate to retaliate, knowing that Soviet forces could then destroy American cities. The Kremlin, it seemed, also held another trump card—a remarkable apparatus of civil defense, which would minimize its losses in a nuclear exchange.

That scenario was wildly improbable, as critics pointed out. Evidence for a vast Soviet civil defense system was sketchy at best (later knowledge of the Brezhnev regime's gross inefficiencies made it even less plausible). Even if real, such a system depended on giving Soviets days of advance warning of war, unlikely (among other reasons) because such warning would alert American and NATO intelligence to the Kremlin's designs. A Soviet preemptive strike was also improbable. The slightest miscalculation in rocket trajectories would disrupt the pinpoint attacks required, and Soviet rockets would have to traverse unpredictable atmospheric conditions and be exquisitely timed so that initial explosions did not knock out later warheads (committing what experts termed "fratricide"). Soviet leaders would also have to assume that American forces would not unleash a "spasm" response—at either the first sign of a Soviet attack or after such an attack by the surviving forces—destroying the Soviet Union even if it did the United States no good. The American command system, more on a hair-trigger than the Soviets', might not wait to see if the Soviet attack was "limited" to missile sites, or decide that it made no difference that it was, or simply misread the "limited" attack as an all-out one. As an army chief of staff had argued in condemning fantasies of limited nuclear war, "One mushroom cloud will be reported as one hundred, and that will probably be the end of the world." And should surviving American forces respond, Soviet leaders could not doubt their fury: America's vast submarine force, largely invulnerable to a preemptive strike, alone could destroy the Soviet empire many times over. Even if its presumed plan seemed workable, the Kremlin would have to ponder whether its empire could tolerate the indirect effects— radioactive fallout girdling the globe and dust cooling its climate—even of a one-sided nuclear war. Alarmists retorted that Soviet leaders were too dumb or arrogant to worry about such problems—and therefore willing to try what Secretary Harold Brown ridiculed as a "cosmic throw of the dice"—but their retort was at odds with their image of coldly calculating Soviet leaders.[82]

Baseless or not, the specter of impending defeat was captured in the notion that the United States faced a "window of vulnerability." It was a curious metaphor, in part because of the slippery way it referred to both time and space—to both a physical gap in American defenses and a period of time when vulnerability presumably would be acute. The metaphor evoked a sturdy American home with a window inadvertently left open and preyed on fears of both crime and Soviet duplicity (Democrats being "soft" on both): wily Russians would sneak into the homes of complacent citizens. The image of violated American domesticity had other resonances. It tapped old notions of a fortress America and it exposed norms about gender, since it was touted above all by patriotic conservatives: if the country was a home, it was men's job to defend it. The domestic imagery reached a logical climax in advice offered in 1981 by Deputy Undersecretary of Defense Thomas K. Jones about how Americans might close the window and resist nuclear attack: "Dig a hole, cover it up with a couple of doors and then throw three feet of dirt on top. . . . If there are enough shovels to go around, everybody's going to make it."[83]

Notions so fanciful were driven by something more than fear of Soviet attack. The window of vulnerability had precedents in the bomber and missile "gaps" of the 1950s (and the "throw-weight gap" of the mid-1970s). Like them, it served partisan ends—to discredit the party in power, Democrats now instead of Republicans—and broader purposes: to reinstate the centrality of military might in American policy and of the Cold War in American life. Nightmares of Soviet triumph also inverted dreams of American victory. Ever since Billy Mitchell in the 1920s, sketches of what the enemy might do by air against America thinly disguised what some Americans wanted to do to others. What they now wanted, or at least thought useful to pretend they did, was victory, political or military, over the Soviets. Not surprisingly, the return of the Cold War brought renewed visions of winning it.

Among other ways, those visions surfaced in the Carter administration's final strategic plans. Presidential Directive 59, in Brzezinski's words, allowed for use of nuclear weapons "at levels ranging from tactical to the strategic, selectively at a large variety of targets over protracted periods of time." In short, it offered the option of waging limited and victorious nuclear war. In particular, it stressed "decapitation"—destruction of the Soviets' command system. Since American war plans had long posited a variety of options, PD-59 involved more a shift in emphasis than a revolution in strategy, but it was a notable shift. How much Carter and his team embraced was never clear (Reagan's administration grasped it more firmly). Many strategists in and out of government doubted the likelihood of keeping nuclear war limited and the wisdom of "decapitating" the very government with which the United States would have to deal to keep such a war limited. As Secretary Brown conceded, "What might start as a supposedly controlled, limited strike . . . would very likely . . . escalate to a full-scale nuclear war." Since the administration leaked word of PD-59, one of its purposes may have been the familiar one of shoring up deterrence; as John Newhouse puts it, "If the Soviets did see limited nuclear war as an option, Brzezinski wanted them on notice that it would be a two-party game." But in war planning, the game playing went on at so many levels that intentions became impossible to unravel, especially since keeping the enemy guessing was one point of the game.[84]

Whatever the intentions, *talk* of winning a nuclear war was now back in fashion, in the Carter administration in a hesitant way, and more forcefully among other strategists and pretenders to the throne. The most notorious instance of that talk came in January 1980 at the height of crisis in the Mideast, in comments by George Bush, who sought the GOP's presidential nomination. Bush rejected the idea that "there is no such thing as a winner in a nuclear exchange," and argued that if "command and control" systems, "industrial potential," and "a percentage of your citizens" were insured "survivability," and if one side "inflicts more damage on the opposition," then "you can have a winner." Ronald Reagan echoed Bush's outlook, though he was more careful to couch it in terms of what the Soviets believed: "We have a different regard for human life than those monsters do," he argued, and they "decided some time ago that a nuclear war was possible and winnable." Though it retained its defenders, the notion of war's disutility, almost accepted wisdom early in the 1970s, was now severely challenged.[85]

Victory, whether in the game of strategic deterrence or in war, required new weapons like the MX. Carter tolerated that missile as a distasteful concession to foes of his SALT II Treaty and to the need to close the window of vulnerability—the MX would presumably be immune to a preemptive strike by the Soviets. Others saw the MX as a war-winning weapon—its many warheads would be so accurate that *they* could carry out a preemptive strike, one devastating to the Soviets because they depended more than the United States on land-based missiles, the only kind vulnerable to such a strike.

Still, debate on the MX—and no weapon ever generated more furious and foolish debate—showed how hard it was to achieve such a millennial goal, or even the modest aim of rearmament. The forces of rearmament were as strident as ever, but opponents and skeptics were better mobilized than in the 1950s and 1960s. The long MX debate had many facets, but like a vulture hovering over a dead carcass, it kept circling back to the vexing question of how to base the infernal machines—they had to be invisible to the Soviets for their safety and yet countable by the Soviets in order to verify compliance with SALT II, while having the capacity for utter precision possible only by operating from fixed silos.

When the dilemma about basing the MX arose, debate "entered its rococo period." Countless schemes emerged: one for "concealing each MX in a fifty-mile covered trench through which it would randomly travel"; another for a shell game in which two hundred missiles would be shuffled among forty-six hundred shelters whose ports could be opened for Soviet aerial inspection; and others to shuttle the missiles among opaque water pools, to mount them on trucks or railroads or dirigibles or seaplanes, and to put them in the oceans or the Great Lakes. Those proposals not technically ludicrous involved outrageous economic and ecological costs, threatening to make the MX (as the air force allegedly boasted) "man's largest project." Or they jeopardized one branch's prerogatives—the air force reaction to putting the MX on diesel submarines seemed to be: "Put some of our missiles underwater? You've got to be out of your *mind*." The various plans prompted "snickering and giggling" among experts, while popular magazines had a field day depicting them. By 1982, "densepack" was in vogue—bunching the missiles would presumably force incoming Soviet warheads to commit "fratricide" against each other. Then the Reagan administration gave up, settling for half the original number, plunking them in old Minuteman silos, and promoting a new single-warhead Midgetman.[86]

The MX was not the first weapon caught in a political crossfire, but no previous system generated such public rancor, bewildering technical debate, and despair that no alternative was any good. The spectacle of a great nation ostensibly rearming but disarmed by its internal bickering was not a pretty one. It seemed to send signals eerily like those arising in the debate on women in combat. Carter's hope that draft registration would convey "the country's unity and resolve to the Soviet Union" dissolved into "a murky altercation about the influence of women on men in trench warfare," the *New Yorker* noted, so that "a somber declaration of national purpose to the world has degenerated into a highly visible domestic quarrel." That quarrel, like the one over the MX, suggested that Americans lacked the keen sense of national peril and unity evident earlier in the Cold War. Indeed, denunciations of Americans along those lines were another ritual of the period. Even Republicans, complained conservative columnist George Will, would not oppose grain sales to the Soviet Union lest they lose the farm vote: "They usually are thrillingly fierce about Russia, but now say: Let's be tough as nails with the Russian bear but, golly, let's not stop feeding it." More lugubriously, exiled Soviet writer Alexander Solzhenitsyn moaned that "the West simply does not believe that the time for sacrifices has arrived"; its "sleek god of affluence" had replaced its "high-minded view of the world."[87]

The problem was not Americans' disunity or lack of will, however, but the implausibility of the threat they were summoned to meet and the methods by which they were asked to meet it. Debate was unresolvable on the MX and ugly on draft registration because neither was needed: massive American armies were unlikely to march, Soviet rockets were not about to overwhelm American defenses. Reagan's surrender on the MX in 1983 was telling: "America's deterrent wasn't broken and Reagan didn't fix it," John Newhouse later concluded. At most, debate on the MX showed that land-based missiles were now obsolete; it was time to cut off one leg of the nuclear triad (bombers, submarines, and land-based rockets). More baldly than most weapons, the MX served political more than strategic needs (if the two can be disentangled)—to placate politicians who claimed that SALT II would disarm America and to offer signals of American resolve, lest forgoing the MX give "an important perceptual advantage to the Soviets" and offer "a dangerously misleading signal," as Defense Secretary Brown argued.[88]

Once again, intangible criteria justified a decision. By their logic, the costlier a weapons program the greater its "perceptual" advantage: it showed that America would stop at nothing to fight its adversary. That rationale also drove draft registration—needed, Carter said, "to increase our preparedness," demonstrate "our resolve as a nation," and "deter Soviet aggression." Such reasoning had long driven defense policy, but it was now further divorced from a real world of threat and combat and more self-referential, as if it involved less what Soviets thought of Americans, or even what Americans thought they thought, than what Americans thought of themselves. Carter said as much in telling news executives "that a strong America, willing to exert its strength when necessary, is an integral part of the psyche of our country and also a legitimate role for America to play," making defense sound secondary and inadvertent. The "narcissistic" quality of militarization now swelled.[89]

Other unsettling currents swirled in strategic debate. Strategic jargon made weapons seem to be curiously human and people curiously inanimate. As the *New Yorker* noted, "When one nuclear missile is lost in the explosion of another, the experts call it 'fratricide,'" while nuclear weapons were said to "'proliferate,' and to bring forth one 'generation' after another, as though death itself had gained the power to give birth and multiply." Moreover, Soviet and American cities were left open to attack, lest the nation able to defend its cities would be tempted to start a war. "Once, military forces were deployed to protect the civilian population, but now the civilian population is deployed to protect the military forces."[90]

The excruciating focus on nuclear weapons and war was all the more remarkable because it was irrelevant to the challenges most galling to Americans in 1980, the plight of American hostages in Iran and the nation's sagging economic position in the world. Few thought that the MX would rescue the hostages or signal American resolve to Tehran: indeed, in prevailing American images, crazed Islamic fanatics were oblivious to such ordinary measures. Yet the sense persisted that America's humiliation there resulted from the flabbiness of its nuclear muscle, and that toughening it would command the respect that would prevent further indignities. That reasoning flowed from a nostalgic desire to recapture a remembered age of simple issues and undisputed glory, and to escape the baffling challenges Americans now faced. Defining power broadly, as the product of the health of all its systems, was frustrating when those systems seemed in disarray; it had not been very popular even when pressed, albeit haltingly, by a popular President Eisenhower. Defining American power in military terms offered the promise, if a rather wistful one, of sweeping aside such complexities. If old terrors returned with the new Cold War, so did an illusion of familiarity and decisive power. America was ready to plunge "back to the future," as a 1985 movie was titled, and soon elected a leader who embodied that oxymoronic aspiration.

Meanwhile, Carter's effort to free the American hostages in Tehran raised questions about the utility of more modest military forces. Complex negotiations with Iran yielded little in the opening months of 1980, and Democrats like Sen. Ted Kennedy scented blood, hoping to deny Carter renomination. Against his better instincts, Carter ordered a rescue mission in April, but American helicopters foundered in the desert, aggravating America's humiliation (although their fate might have been worse if they had reached Tehran). Secretary of State Vance opposed the mission and resigned (as Gaddis Smith later noted, "a rare act in American history") to protest it and the whole drift of Carter's policy.[91]

The failed mission was strenuously analyzed, as if it embodied all the ills of a floundering military machine. It was too minor and improbable a mission to bear such freight, but as the only field-test of American power, it had to do so, being used, as one columnist shrewdly noted, "to discredit whatever" Americans "were already of a mind to discredit." Carter was "at the top of the list," with American defenses competing for that spot. Carter was "talking loudly, with a small stick," announced *Newsweek*, which used the occasion to compare every aspect of America's combat posture unflatteringly to the Soviets'. The Iran mission was "a popgun shot heard around the world," it claimed, adding that America's allies were outraged because such actions "could drive the Iranians directly into the Soviet camp—or even plunge the superpowers into a confrontation." *Business Week*, like many observers and a growing chorus in Congress, wondered if the failure proved "that the Pentagon has come to expect too much from its complex hardware," which might be "disturbingly prone to failure." Indeed, for years critics had wanted the Pentagon to focus less on weapons, more on readiness and training—advice Carter seemed to endorse in 1979, amid much talk of developing a "Rapid Deployment Force." But that opinion was at once fashionable and largely unimplemented amid demands for more armaments.[92]

In the meantime, a withering assault on the policies guiding rearmament was mounted. Faulting the military for managerial and technological top-heaviness, army officers Richard Gabriel and Paul Savage assailed the loss of a warrior spirit in *Crisis in Command* (1978), a much-discussed and disputed critique. Far from assigning the military's troubles in Vietnam to familiar culprits like meddling civilian superiors, they found that the army "had literally destroyed itself" because its leaders had lost touch with combat and embraced the career-building values of the corporate world. The cohesion of combat forces was undermined by officers who prized career advancement over leadership in battle, by methods of training designed to "produce troops like sausages," and by a system of rotation that severed bonds among soldiers and sent them home as soon as they learned to fight. The army had become an inverted pyramid top-heavy with officers "literally tripping over each other" in Vietnam. The "successful army centers itself on the values and experiences associated with combat," pleaded Gabriel and Savage, but they doubted that the officer corps would take that view—it "should have been appalled" by the disintegration of unit cohesion in Vietnam, but "we find no evidence that it was."[93]

James Fallows worked that pessimism onto a larger canvas in *National Defense* (1981). He too sought "to restore the military spirit," but also saw a system and culture of defense deeply resistant to restoration. Pentagon officials were oblivious to the ineffable nature of warfare and obsessed with a quixotic "pursuit of the magic weapon." As a result, weapons were too few, costly, and fragile to permit ongoing use in training or battle, conferring theoretical superiority but battlefield impotence. The Pentagon, "in business to spend money," had created a technologically musclebound giant. The "baroque arsenal" (as another critic called it) also imposed such monstrous design and development costs that many corporations were fleeing the weapons business, leading to a "thinning out of the contractor base" that made it doubtful that "the United

States could quickly gear up for war production if the need arose." And weapons programs rested on perceptions of the Soviet threat and nuclear war that had little basis in reality.[94]

Fallows saw the military as a house of cards inadequate for national defense; those peering deeper into the shadowy realm of strategic weapons saw something worse. After news in 1980 that the computer systems controlling America's nuclear weapons had gotten fouled up and sent an alert of impending Soviet attack, one newspaper posed the morbid question, "Doomsday by a short-circuit?" and the *New Yorker* issued another mordant comment: "Nuclear fantasy, it seemed, restless after so many years of being cooped up in the spectral world of the computers, was seeking revenge against human reality by trying to supplant it altogether." The specter of accidental nuclear war now received more attention than at any time since the early 1960s; the communications and command systems for America's arsenal seemed more fragile and jumpy than ever. Evidence also mounted that those systems were operated so that "if the United States does not strike first in a crisis that develops into a nuclear war, it may be unable to strike back at all in any organized way." In 1985, Daniel Ford summarized evidence that had been gathering since the late 1970s. Although strategic plans were presumably designed to deter or limit war, "trying to indoctrinate the Strategic Air Command about controlling escalation is like thinking a Dutch uncle talk can keep a hot rodder from flooring it when the red light yields to green." In Ford's portrait, the system was hot-wired for Armageddon.[95]

Reflecting their times, such critiques were sometimes confused and generally more cautious than comparable ones early in the 1970s. Their stance was critical but their politics vaguely centrist—Fallows, who had "deliberately avoided military service" in Vietnam, sniped at both patriotic conservatives who demanded "'more' defense [but] never themselves wore the uniform" and "politicians of the left" who embraced "the same mechanical, technological view of warfare" as the defense hawks.[96] Critics updated old complaints about the military-industrial complex and reflected the mounting sentiment of the 1970s that the federal government could not do anything well. But they eschewed the predictions about war's end made earlier in the decade and often implied that a leaner, meaner military might have won in Southeast Asia. They assembled some of the evidence used by antinuclear activists but avoided their dogmatic stances. While they did not greatly slow or alter rearmament, their work, widely discussed and echoed by the mass media (CBS News, for example, in a major 1981 documentary) helped sustain opposition to rearmament during the Reagan years and to suggest it rested on a fragile foundation.

Their critiques also reflected the stage of militarization the United States was entering. Despite anxiety about technological change, weapons development was now cautious and incremental. Most weapons of 1980 were developed or foreseen by 1950: B-52 bombers still flew as one leg of the nuclear triad; ICBMs had their precursors in German rockets of World War II; the tank, the helicopter, the jet fighter, and the aircraft carrier dominated conventional forces in 1980 as they had in 1950. All these weapons did exist in ever newer or retrofitted versions, with stunning enhancement of their precision, power, speed, or numbers, and crammed with miniaturized computers and electronics barely glimpsed thirty years earlier. But decades of spending had generated ingenious refinements of old ideas more than revolutionary new weapons—little on the scale of change seen between 1915 and 1945. Soon the weapons of World War II themselves sprang to life again, as old battleships bristling with new gear steamed back to sea. It was an era of elaboration and ornamentation, a bit like the trills and arpeggios that eighteenth-century composers piled onto simple musical forms. No wonder observers thought that the arsenal had entered its "baroque" or "rococo" age and expressed an awed contempt for the elaborate structures created.

Centrist critics questioned whether the United States was rearming effectively, others whether it should at all. Richard Barnet, the most trenchant of these critics, summarized their arguments in *Real Security* (1981). Barnet acknowledged that "the decline of American power is real," but attributed it to forces over which the United States had little control—"decolonization" and global "financial and economic interdependence"—and to the arms race, in which American (and Soviet) leaders committed "self-inflicted wounds." Barnet disputed the alarmists' portrayal of Soviet defense policy, arguing that the high portion of Soviet GNP spent on defense reflected economic weakness and inefficiency, not greater real output. "Being 'outspent' by the Soviets ought to be seen more as a badge of their weakness than a threat." In any event, what drove the arms race was not tangible criteria of power but a foolhardy quest to enhance "perceptions" of power. "Once the purpose of military spending is to create 'perceptions,' and weapons are procured primarily as symbols, there is never enough." Moreover, the power procured was generally useless because it was grossly destructive and because military and economic power were "decoupling." Frustrated over hostage taking, energy shortages, and the "often puzzling behavior of the Soviet Union," Americans had an understandable "impulse to reach for the gun. Yet when we do reach for the gun, it does not seem to work the way it used to work." The eroding economic position of the United States most worried Barnet, who warned that rearmament was hastening that erosion, which in turn undermined the nation's military strength. Nor did he see the Soviet Union as a serious threat. Long before Mikhail Gorbachev's advent to power made it fashionable to say so, he argued that the Soviet "economy is stalled, and the very legitimacy of the system is in question." Barnet did not declare the Cold War over or war a thing of the past, but for the superpowers, "war is not a national-security option in the nuclear age." Indeed, arguing that "the arms race is the greatest threat we face," he decoupled national security and military strength.[97]

As with centrist critics, or for that matter bellicose exponents of rearmament, Barnet offered few startling arguments—Eisenhower had asserted that national security rested on economic and spiritual as much as on military strength. The lack of novelty owed less to a failure of imagination than to a kind of historical gridlock: too little had yet changed in the world system and in how Americans saw their place in it to alter greatly how they debated militarization. But while the arguments were familiar, a shift in emphases was evident. The economic dangers of militarization now were rising to the top of the agenda. In their own way, even advocates of military renewal acknowledged the dangers: the new Reagan team decided that rearmament would be funded by caps on or cuts in the growing nondefense sector of federal budgets. The assumption that military power and economic affluence worked in benign synergy with each other was not wholly in ruins, in part because its demise was painful to admit. It was, however, now questionable enough that rearmament provoked sharp debate and a widespread sense that its economic foundation was at best unstable.

Indeed it was. The nation's competitiveness, especially in fields it long had dominated (automobiles) or recently pioneered (computers and electronics), continued to slip, and a yawning deficit in merchandise trade emerged (a surplus in services got little notice). Washington's bailout of Chrysler Corporation in 1980 (a similar lifeline had been thrown to Lockheed) dramatized the problem: America's global economic supremacy was eroding. Nor was the federal government imaginative or concerted in response. It flailed away at stop-gap actions (as with Chrysler) but offered no guidance of the sort presumably given by Japan's central planning agency, both feared and admired by worried American experts. Particularly in the 1980s, federal policy offset economic sluggishness by deficit spending and by encouraging individuals and corporations to borrow, but that too was a stop-gap measure whose leverage declined as financing the debt seized more of the federal budget. Those trends also undercut federal efforts to provide economic security for Americans and to make investments in science, education, and "infrastructure" that might restore American competitiveness. Poorer women and their children bore the brunt of economic decline, but many other Americans, despite impressive job creation in the 1970s, faced stagnant or falling real incomes.

Those general trends had many causes, but also many links to militarization. Whether militarization had made for a net gain or loss in America's economic health was not easily reducible to summary judgment, however. Common wisdom was that it starved business of the capital and expertise needed to remain competitive, while rivals like West Germany and Japan, freeloading off of American defense, poured their treasure into efforts to wrest markets from the United States. But no automatic mechanism insured that cuts in defense would send dollars and scientists into other fields. Certainly the Pentagon had underwritten American supremacy in some markets—aviation, space communications, nuclear power—where the overlap between civilian and military technologies was high and the capital required so huge that few companies could survive without recourse to both civilian and military markets. Military markets, however, were also now "more narrowly specialized, with less spin-off for the decisive consumer industries."[98] The engines and airframes of American bombers in the 1940s and 1950s had been adaptable to development of commercial airliners, a vast market in which American companies triumphed. But in the "baroque" era of weaponry, warplanes were built to performance standards and crammed with electronic gear useless or too costly for the passenger jet: to take an extreme case, 1980s "stealth" technology supposedly made warplanes invisible to enemy radar, but airliners depended for their survival in crowded skies precisely on their visibility.

In short, the economic benefits of militarization were probably declining. Worse, for those worried about defense, its economic base seemed in jeopardy: a contracting industrial system might make the Pentagon dependent on foreign sources, which in turn might gain a whip-hand over American defense, especially if they also funded America's mounting debt. America would resemble Britain in 1940, still technically supreme in many fields but so dependent on others' capital, resources, and factories that its supremacy in practical ways dissolved.

Many of the complaints and fears regarding these matters were exaggerated, misplaced, or devoid of sufficient context. The United States in 1980 was only loosely comparable to Britain in 1940, just as the role of military force in deciding the fate of nations was probably not in 1980 what it had been forty years earlier. Handwringing about America's declining prospects in the military arena also slighted similar difficulties (admittedly hard to know in the Soviet Union's case) that other military powers experienced. Insofar as a "'militarization of the world economy'" was "now advancing faster than it [had] for a generation," the ills of militarization were also now widely shared.[99] And the complaint that allies let the United States bear the burden of their defense overlooked how American leaders had wanted that burden and the power that flowed from it, and exposed a reversal in notions of what made the United States virtuous: before 1940, most Americans had deplored the life-draining, economically profligate habits of militaristic states; now, many embraced those habits and regretted that Japanese and Western Europeans had abandoned them.

Just as strategic policy looked backward at this critical juncture, so too did economic policy, as "the lure of military Keynesianism" endured. In effect, or by default, national leaders decided that renewed militarization would redress or at least forestall the ills that militarization itself had bred. Such reasoning emerged baldly in the Reagan administration, as Defense Secretary Caspar Weinberger praised the "substantially beneficial effect on the economy" of its defense programs. Most members of Congress, regardless of their party, gladly joined the effort to make "the defense bill a jobs bill," as one senator put it. Once again, air and naval power remained the popular route, promising strength without mass sacrifice and rewarding powerful economic and political interests. Meanwhile, public-sector investment was not about to be upgraded, given widespread opposition to increased taxes and the illusion that Americans suffered unduly under them (compared to their economic competitors, they did not).[100]

Under Carter and then Reagan, military revitalization rested on shaky foundations. Though its noisiest advocates, many conservatives at heart prized it less than moral regeneration. Its strategic logic was flawed or frightening (or both). The geopolitical assumption underlying it—a Soviet menace immediate, titanic, and growing—was debatable at best. The nostalgic, patriotic fervor fueling it was informed by American self-doubt more than external realities. The economic strength needed for rearmament was questionable and the economic wisdom of rearmament even more so. The new Cold War, as intense on the surface as the old one, lacked the old foundations. It gained new life (as Barnet implied) as a convenient way for beleaguered superpower leaders to package, subsume, or avoid disorder in their internal polities and the world system—a familiar function but a fragile basis for remilitarization. And the hands at the rudder were unsteady—Carter, informed but reluctant; Reagan, confident but uninformed.

Most Americans did not closely follow the end-of-the-decade debates about defense policy, in part because those debates were more arcane than ever. Nonetheless, their sense of despair and powerlessness, according to one adept chronicler of their moods, resembled in more diffuse form what worried policymakers. "Running out of gas," thought Rabbit Angstrom, the John Updike character who returned in *Rabbit Is Rich* (1981). "The fucking world is running out of gas." Rabbit himself, moving agilely to sell Toyotas at Springer Motors, was getting rich, but all around him were signs of a nation running on empty and impotent in ways unimaginable for the generation, at least as it was remembered, that had defeated fascism. "In the park a World War II tank, made into a monument, points its guns at tennis courts where the nets . . . keep getting ripped away." Rabbit's outlook on the world's convulsions was volatile. He "pulls for the Rams the way he does for the Afghan rebels against the Soviet military machine." But he also felt, "Who needs Khomeini and his oil? Who needs Afghanistan? Fuck the Russkis. Fuck the Japs, for that matter. We'll go it alone, from sea to shining sea." To such sentiments, Ronald Reagan was finely attuned.[101]

THE ILLUSORY REMILITARIZATION, 1981–1988

Restoration

Ronald Reagan's good luck as President seemed to begin on his first day in office. On the morning of January 20, 1981, the word finally came through that Iran would release the American hostages it held, in return for a pledge to arbitrate the fate of the huge Iranian assets the United States had frozen, but Iran did not release the plane carrying the hostages until moments after Reagan had taken office. Reagan had nothing to do with the arrangement (unless, as some insiders later charged, his operatives had connived with Iran to postpone it until after the 1980 elections), but in public image and memory he would get credit for it, just as he long escaped much blame for his administration's failure to gain the release of hostages in Lebanon who had been taken on his watch. He would also claim credit for restoring American power: with its hostages freed and new armaments accrued, the United States itself seemed freed from the humiliations of the 1970s, from the appalling spectacle of being held hostage to grim Soviet designs, oil-rich nations' blackmail, and crazed kidnappers of Americans. As not only his backers but often his critics saw him, Reagan seemed to have restored national security as America's supreme priority, and to have renewed the military power he saw as its core.

That achievement, however, was largely an illusion, as even some administration insiders complained. The new weapons, swollen defense budgets, and martial poses were real, of course, and they had the capacity to make real changes in policy and armed action occur, as did happen at times. His greatest achievements and his political success rested largely elsewhere, however, in his "shrewd concentration on *domestic* policy," as Garry Wills wrote. "That is the meat and potatoes of our politics, the thing on which most elections hinge. Yet modern Presidents forget or suppress this basic information."[1] Reagan, usually at least, did not. In his presidency, stunning growth in weapons and budgets disguised the growing fragility of America's militarization and the continuing inward turn of its energies.

Reagan and Remilitarization

No modern President understood the substance of militarization more poorly, presented its appeals more beguilingly, and diminished its primacy more decisively than Ronald Reagan. Regarding it, his historic role was thus obviously paradoxical, like his role generally as both the dominating figure and the insubstantial presence of the 1980s. He vigorously championed renewal of the nation's military strength, yet the renewal was curiously hollow. Militarization continued, but geared less to the wider world and more to Americans' sense of their own needs, to the point that they waged "war" more within their own borders than against external enemies. That inward turn, developing since the 1960s, marked the 1980s even more. Indeed, militarization changed course more than it had at any time since the 1930s.

Reagan foreshadowed that course in his 1981 inaugural address. Despite his well-earned reputation as a Cold Warrior, he turned most of his attention to the major source of his election victory, an "economic affliction of great proportions" (regarding which "government is not the solution" but "the problem"). He did call for "sufficient [military] strength to prevail if need be," and warned that "we will act" if necessary to preserve national security, but added that having armed strength offers "the best chance of never having to use that strength." Indeed, use hardly seemed necessary given that "no weapon in the arsenals of the world is so formidable as the will and moral courage of free men and women," which comprised the "weapon our adversaries" lack and the one "we as Americans do have." Like Carter, Reagan wanted the United States to prevail abroad by force of example, not arms: "We will again be the exemplar of freedom and a beacon of hope for those who do not now have freedom." Instead of denouncing today's enemy, Reagan plunged into a misty past of long-ago American battles and their heroes. Even that past offered only hazy instruction in 1981: "The crisis we are facing today does not require of us the kind of sacrifice that . . . so many thousands of others were called upon to make" in the world wars. All that it required was "our best effort, and our willingness to believe in our selves." Faith more than works would suffice.[2]

Reagan's inaugural reflected his memories and experiences of World War II and the Cold War. Because poor eyesight barred him from combat, Reagan had served in Hollywood as an Army Air Forces officer making training films and morale-boosting movies, though he later claimed personal memory of events abroad that he could not have witnessed. For him, it was a storybook war of easy triumph over bad guys abroad (and over problems like racial segregation at home)—a war won by faith and good attitudes, not by grisly sacrifice. Earlier Presidents had summoned the spirit of heroic sacrifice and the substance of bold innovation in World War II to urge Americans to accept new demands. Reagan, never experiencing and not now recalling the sacrifice or the innovation, invoked the war as a pleasant memory. Critics found his use of World War II shallow or dishonest, as it sometimes was ("Representative government defeated statism" in World War II, he said in 1986, banishing the Soviet Union from the Allied coalition), to the point that it got him in trouble, as in his 1985 visit to a German cemetery where Nazi SS troops were buried.[3] But he was in touch with how most Americans had known or now remembered the war; like Reagan, they had spent the war at home immune from its destruction, found salvation in it from faltering fortunes, and enjoyed it in many ways. Sacrifice and death had been less common experiences.

Reagan's sense of the Cold War was not that different: a matter of proper attitude and faith, and of saying the right words in behalf of both. He had his bruising moments as president of the Screen Actors Guild from 1947 to 1952, helping to purge Hollywood of communists and other troublesome folk, but the purge had not been hard to carry out—industry moguls quickly trimmed their sails to the new winds—and Reagan's memories of it seemed soft, unencumbered by a sense of conflict or peril. His experience of the rest of the Cold War was mainly a matter of words: "The Speech" praising free enterprise and denouncing the communist menace that he offered for years, first as a spokesman for General Electric, then as an aspiring politician campaigning for Goldwater in 1964, and later on his own behalf. He came to the White House inexperienced and uninterested in the difficult calculations that national leaders made about budgets, weapons, wars, alliances, and crises. Given his conservatism and his ties in California to corporate leaders and lobbyists in its air-power wing, it is not surprising that during his 1966 campaign for California's governorship he proposed to "level Vietnam, pave it, paint stripes on it, and make a parking lot of it."[4] But such impulsive comments were the product of no coherent view about how to use military force. As governor for eight years, he learned little more about the realities of national security (or of California), but proved effective at inspirational messages and flexible in compromising his doctrinaire conservatism. His 1980 campaign hardly brought him up to speed, since the Iran hostage crisis often eclipsed larger issues about national security. In any event, it was the right words and attitudes—a benign persona that dulled the sharp edge of Republican conservatism—more than his programmatic agenda that got him elected.

The imperial style of the Reagan White House reflected its lack of seriousness about asking the nation to sacrifice in behalf of victory. Like their close associates—wealthy businessmen, over-the-hill entertainers, the designer/ doyenne Diana Vreeland—the Reagans basked in an imperial glory crudely adapted from the great monarchies and aristocracies of the past. He "preferred to reign rather than rule," noted one journalist. Other presidential couples had struck imperial poses, but none so lavishly as the Reagans, or with such desire to project an image of "opulence, privilege, and historical fantasy." Their penchant for "decorative, aristocratic femininity" drove home the message—true sacrifice would have enlisted women into the cause, but for the Reagans, no national austerity was required to gain victory. With weapons serving preening purposes, it made sense that national leaders also preened before the public. The Reagans acted as if they were already celebrating the nation's imperial victory, a posture that rendered moot real efforts to achieve it.[5]

Championing martial renewal, Reagan did wring vast funds from the national treasury in its behalf. Yet from the start, the renewal, which Carter had in fact started, seemed hollow. It was accompanied by no coherent policy for using the increased power (or for doing much else abroad), or even much interest in using it. Although Carter's administration was faulted for incoherence, the Reagan team stumbled even more in this regard, though it was more artful in public relations. As Alexander Haig, Reagan's first secretary of state, later moaned, the White House was "as mysterious as a ghost ship." One heard "the creak of the rigging and the groan of the timbers and sometimes even glimpsed the crew on deck," but who was steering it "was impossible to know." Haig wrote in anger, and the ship of state sailed more smoothly under his successor, George Shultz, while Caspar Weinberger, a wily bureaucratic player, provided continuity as secretary of defense. Still, these leaders and their agencies rarely hammered out common policies, nor did the ineptly led National Security Council. Indeed, it was "this inability to make the normal channels work" that helped pull the NSC staff into the rogue operations exposed in the Iran-Contra affair. Reagan was no help: insiders displayed remarkable agreement about his lack of interest in most aspects of policy and the rudderless course he often followed. "What Reagan actually did," Frances FitzGerald later wrote, is "impossible to discover" in these insiders' memoirs. Reagan compounded the problem by choosing key people—like William Clark as deputy secretary of state and national security advisor—who were appallingly inexperienced in foreign policy, in part because he had run *against* government so long that he knew few insiders versed in that field. Most officials rarely saw Reagan, who showed them (if he recalled who they were) a cool indifference that belied his warmth before the camera.[6]

Reagan did have his preferences: to build American military strength, pursue the Strategic Defense Initiative (SDI), condemn the evils of Soviet communism, and take an unbending line on arms control. But those preferences seemed sufficient unto themselves—what to do with the resulting power a secondary matter. In general, "the administration seemed unable to translate America's vast military power into concrete diplomatic gains," a critic later noted.[7] More likely, it rarely tried. Even at the Defense Department, Weinberger and the Joint Chiefs, though critical of a crippling "post-Vietnam" mentality among other Americans, seemed gripped by it themselves, reluctant to put American forces in harm's way except where easy victory was assured.

What counted most—if not always for Reagan or for everyone in his administration, then in the collective impression they made—was the proper posture. Military strength was amassed to bear witness to, rather than to act on, American superiority and moral resolve. Some Reagan insiders talked of winning a nuclear war against the Soviet Union, but probably regarded the talk as essential, not the act. Like many Americans in the 1980s, they "wanted to be respected as a superpower without paying the price," and they "regarded military power as something to be valued in itself, independent of any actual uses."[8] Their attitude had deep roots in American Cold War policy—in the lessons of World War II and in the logic of deterrence—and was similar to the Eisenhower administration's posture of rhetorical bluster and practical caution. But that posture had been a calculated one for Eisenhower. Under Reagan, it seemed more a matter of hazy faith, one unaccompanied by Ike's fear of militarization's costs.

It also expressed a stage of militarization in which making Americans feel good was more important than shaping the world. As Stanley Hoffmann noticed in 1984, "This mood was perfectly expressed by the summer Olympics in Los Angeles, whose somewhat mindless, rather than aggressive, chauvinism thoroughly shocked European commentators. What Americans celebrate is their regained success; the focus is on themselves, not on the outside world." It helped Americans to feel that "We're number one!" as crowds chanted amid the Olympics in a "pageant of national narcissism," and that it was "morning in America," as Reagan put it in 1984. Whether it was dawn or midnight elsewhere was of less interest.[9]

The tenor of Republican conservatism, and fissures within it, also accounted for this lack of interest. Many conservatives wanted more military power and wanted to use it, but others mistrusted sustained engagement with the outer world, regarded moral revival at home as a higher priority, and believed it the key to triumph over communism. Reagan and his speechwriters knew their mood: he asserted in 1983 that the world struggle "will never be decided by bombs or rockets, by armies or military might. The real crisis we face today is a spiritual one; at root, it is a test of moral will and faith."[10] Such words served calculated purposes—they were addressed to the National Association of Evangelicals and designed also to counter the nuclear freeze movement and fears that Reagan was trigger-happy. But the words also rang true with the course of the administration and Reagan's own beliefs.

In other ways, too, the renewal of national security rested on an insecure foundation. Even its priority was unclear: the administration initially gave more attention to its domestic agenda of tax reform, cuts in nondefense spending, and deregulation. Nor did renewal address the challenges that often vexed Reagan and other Americans in the early 1980s: it proved useless in countering the Soviet-inspired crackdown by Polish authorities against the Solidarity movement; of little utility for coping with terrorism and hostage taking; largely unneeded for two initiatives the White House did consistently pursue (arming Afghan rebels and Nicaraguan "Contras" required only a trickle of easily available armaments); and irrelevant for stopping the erosion of America's economic position and waging the "trade war" announced during the 1980s.

The common critique that emerged of Reagan's presidency was that it substituted illusion for substance, ignored the latter's troubling content, and was guilty of "sleepwalking through history," as one account put it. This critique must be viewed cautiously, however. It was not the one that opponents initially offered: they feared that the Reagan team believed its illusions and might act on them by unleashing nuclear war. The dichotomy between illusion and substance has been such a staple critique of modern presidencies that the historian hardly knows how to apply it to Reagan and may wonder if it simply misses his presidency's substance. After all, his victories in foreign policy "were in the areas that mattered most to liberals: Reagan kept the country out of war; he grudgingly accepted the inevitability of the arms-control process and negotiated . . . the first true disarmament treaty of the nuclear era; he used military force sparingly . . . and helped remove undemocratic regimes in the Philippines and Korea." It was correct to point out that such achievements were often accidental or "grudgingly accepted," but so are many achievements of any President. Reagan, John Newhouse noted, had the "good luck" of never having "to confront a foreign policy crisis," but a crisis is often what leaders choose to define as such. Reagan faced few crises because he recognized few.[11]

Yet no law of history prevented Reagan from being *more* caught in illusions than other presidents, as his subordinates often complained. Perhaps the problem was his rootlessness: "the American Midwest was his credential rather than his essence," which derived from the fantasy world of southern California and its movie industry, and he "evidenced no sense of geographical identity or family tradition." More likely, what gave him enormous appeal—his ability to embody the nation's myths—also limited him, for he believed in those myths so strongly that he saw little need to put them into action. They did the work themselves; only their repetitive intonement was usually needed; even the occasional act was designed less to make them work than simply to demonstrate their magic. As Garry Wills noted, "Reagan was always Reagan, trusting more to words than actions, to weapons bought than to weapons used. He actually believed that if one just took a tough stance, then bullies would scatter. When they failed to, he bought a bigger bomb and assumed it would work the next time."[12]

From the vantage point of an evolving militarization, the grip of those illusions on Reagan seems less his doing than the product of deeper structures. He reigned at a time when many Americans felt deeply wounded by failure in Vietnam, profoundly afraid of risks that might repeat it, yet still determined that their nation police the world's bullies. Reagan offered the nation's past greatness, extrapolated effortlessly into the future. "The power of his appeal is the great joint confession that we cannot live with our real past, that we not only prefer but need a substitute. Because of that, we *will* a belief in all his stories."[13] Offering illusions of greatness at little cost in American lives, Reagan satisfied broad and contradictory yearnings.

Doing so, however, made remilitarization rest on a foundation of fervent but fickle public moods and required keeping the illusions afloat, no easy task in the long run. In other ways, too, renewal rested on a broad but shallow base of popular, political, and expert support. Reagan's first-term defense budgets sailed through Congress, but specific programs like the MX missile and the Strategic Defense Initiative met stiff opposition. The sense of many Americans that economic needs deserved greater priority generated specific critiques of Reagan's course as well as a general, inarticulate unease about it. And since Reagan made no call for national sacrifice, he offered no framework in which Americans might weigh competing priorities.

Nor did Reagan Republicans achieve a lasting revolution in political loy-alties. Reagan's personal appeal and the party's machinery were formidable, but they yielded only modest gains for the party outside of presidential elections—in Congress, statehouses, and municipal governments, where Dem-ocrats often retained power, although the appointment by Reagan and Bush of a majority of federal judges and Supreme Court justices had a profound and lasting effect. Mere comparison of party strengths does obscure the conserva-tive drift—partly under the pressure of Republican success—of the Demo-cratic Party, and the limits set by two Republican Presidents on what Demo-crats could do once back in power. But opinion polls and votes in Congress also showed that Reagan conservatism lacked breadth and consistency of appeal. Americans responded positively to Reagan's rhetorical assault on federal activ-ism and Soviet evil, but less fervently to the programmatic substance of that assault, like cuts in environmental programs or crusades against Nicaraguan Sandinistas. Given Reagan's ballot-box and legislative success, it was easy to see him as ushering in a political sea-change, and important shifts did occur—the shift from Carter to Reagan of many white Protestants in 1980, for example, and Reagan's hearty embrace of far-right Christians. Yet GOP conservatism of some sort was already long in the tooth by the 1980s, ascendant since Nixon's election in 1968, albeit interrupted by his fall. While it was compared to the "Roosevelt Revolution," the much-touted Reagan revolution—"this phenome-nal upheaval," a reporter gushed in 1983—was more like Eisenhower's suc-cess: decisive at the top but shallow beneath it, with Bush's modest victory over a weak foe in 1988 comparable to Nixon's razor-thin loss to a strong opponent in 1960.[14]

Nor had Reagan "catalyzed a deep cultural outpouring similar to that of the New Deal era, which was integral to the transformations the New Deal wrought in American life." His presidency emboldened cultural conservatives, but they added little to the complaints already assembled in the 1970s, met sharp opposition rather than transforming America, and became uneasy about the glib attention Reagan gave them. Since under Reaganism "the artistic imagination, along with everything else, was to be privatized, a matter for the Glorious Free Market to sort out," there were limits on the administration's power to reshape cultural life. To be sure, public authorities could still condemn or bless various cultural currents. Thus Reagan embraced the muscular heroics of Hollywood's Rambo and dined with author Tom Clancy, whose thrillers demonizing the Soviet Union and celebrating American war technology were the decade's most popular fiction, while Sen. Dan Quayle, displaying Clancy's *Red Storm Rising*, told his colleagues, "Have you read this book? ASAT [Star Wars] technology is what wins this war!" Such actions mattered: if Reaganism did not initiate a "deep cultural outpouring," it did give respect and power to one already developing. Even in popular culture, however, conservatives reinforced older themes rather than cultivating fresh ones.[15]

All these considerations made the renewal of national security lavish but short-lived, energetic but empty. In the end, so too did the enemy against which renewal was directed. A bit like Reagan himself, the Soviet threat appeared by the end of the 1980s to have been both formidable and insubstantial, impressive when viewed from afar but hollow when seen close up. Militarization did not halt, because it was a historical process never driven alone by the Soviet threat in either its real or imagined forms. But its scope contracted and its thrust shifted.

The Perils of Remilitarization

If moral virtue would triumph, as Reagan argued, why bother with military might? The answer was that faith still demanded expression in works, and familiar forces pushed for action: powerful interests; real or imagined economic benefits; well-honed geopolitical and strategic doctrines; and well-rehearsed anxieties about the dangers posed by the Soviet Union and other regimes.

The dangers of appeasement and the lessons of World War II formed Reagan's major rationale for rearmament in 1981, one he offered easily when Prime Minister Margaret Thatcher was around, given their ideological and personal affinity. "Our challenge today," argued Reagan after noting Anglo-American sacrifices in World War II, "is to ensure that belligerence is not attempted again" as a result of "the false perception of weakness." The United States, having "unilaterally disarmed, you might say" during the 1970s, had fostered that perception and thereby lured Moscow onto a reckless course in Afghanistan, Poland, Central America, and elsewhere. Reagan was fond of quoting Churchill on the dangers of appeasement and of "casting aside . . . the panoply of warlike strength," though like most Americans he ignored Churchill's other thoughts on this subject ("Appeasement from strength is magnanimous and noble and might be the surest and perhaps the only path to world peace"). History's lessons dictated rearmament and cast Reagan in a Churchillian mode. For his part, Defense Secretary Weinberger "fancied himself an amateur historian and believed that America's position in 1981, in relation to the Soviet Union, was equivalent to Britain's in the 1930s in relation to the Nazis. His hero, Winston Churchill, had saved Britain through rearmament."[16]

In a sense, this was all that constituted Reagan's outlook in 1981, plus his belief that, as he argued in 1980, "the Soviet Union underlies all the unrest that is going on. If they weren't engaged in this game of dominoes, there wouldn't be any hot spots in the world."[17] Cabinet secretaries or policy experts might see a more complex world, one that Reagan soon confronted. In 1981 he did not burden himself with complexities.

Not for several more years did the Soviet Union's changing fortunes much affect Washington's basic calculations. Soviet weaknesses were not unknown: sluggish economic growth relative to that of the Western powers (and China) and an inability to match them in advanced technologies, not to mention civilian goods; a clumsy, aging, if still repressive leadership; disaffection within its borders and in its satellites; hostility from Chinese leaders, who also appeared more adept at transforming their country; the roiling forces of Islamic fundamentalism near the Soviets' own Muslim population; and military frustration and diplomatic isolation resulting from intervention in Afghanistan.

The Reagan administration variously denied, ignored, or bent to preconceived purposes these weaknesses. Particularly regarding space defenses, it offered clashing arguments—that the Soviet Union was ahead and that it could not really compete, while a high-stakes game of forcing it to do so would expose its weaknesses. More generally, the Soviets' weaknesses presumably made them desperate to triumph in the military arena, since no other realm offered the remotest chance of victory. Islamic fundamentalism was seen as Moscow's stalking horse, and perversely as a threat greater to the United States, far from its locus, than to the Soviet Union, whose borders it hugged. The broad pattern of Soviet decline was hard to address, especially since it might also raise questions about American decline, which Reagan was not about to admit. In general, the Soviet Union was seen as ever more menacing whether in decline or in ascendance—an old game among American leaders, but now more exposed as evidence of Soviet decrepitude mounted.

History's lessons and Moscow's menace did little, however, to determine how much and what kind of rearmament to strive for. Of course, it had to be more than what had Carter sought, but beyond that? Prevailing strategic doctrines filled in the blanks. Adopting the "symmetrical" view of defense once associated with Democrats, the administration decided to match Moscow gun for gun and ship for ship. Since land-based rockets were the enemy's forte, the MX missile would go forward. Since the Soviet navy had expanded, so would the American fleet. Since the United States should prepare to wage and win nuclear war, more efforts to "harden" America's strategic weapons and systems of command and control were in order. Since the Pentagon decided that the United States should be able to wage three and a half wars (whatever that might mean) around the globe (Nixon had settled for a one-and-a-half-war capability), expansion in a host of mundane areas—transport, ammunition and supplies, training and logistics—also seemed in order. Only in personnel levels were the goals modest: having pooh-poohed Carter's scheme for draft registration, Reagan could hardly add millions to the armed forces, and anyway believed, like other officials, that new technologies could replace hordes of men under arms. Reagan also made it clear that his subordinates were not to worry about costs—"Defense is not a budget item," he told them, "you spend what you need."[18]

Still, the administration could not remain publicly cavalier about the economic consequences of its defense program. So it also defended that program's macroeconomic impact, which indeed helped to end the recession of the early 1980s. Keynesian pump priming was hard for Reaganites to tout, however—it smacked of what bad Democrats presumably had done and did not address contemporary concerns focused on the economy's long-term competitiveness as much as on its momentary robustness. Therefore the administration justified programs like its "strategic computing initiative," designed to improve battlefield management and beat the Japanese in developing supercomputers, as enhancing both "national security and economic strength." Likewise, proponents of the Star Wars program promised it would secure a "renaissance for the American labor force, particularly the unemployed in the 'smokestack industries.'"[19] It made political sense to defend weapons programs as enhancing competitiveness, even if the consequent de facto "industrial" policy, which subsidized the scale and shaped the contours of America's economy, violated pious claims about liberating free enterprise from Washington's dead hand.

In turn, the defense budget reflected and rewarded the political strength of technically advanced defense industries, laboratories, and regional lobbies, primarily in the "gunbelt" that stretched from New England through the Southeast and Southwest and up the West Coast. Though hardly unitary, these interests were better positioned than ever to shape the defense budget. In the 1940s and 1950s, when defense dollars were widely scattered and fewer congressional districts lived or died on military monies alone, the benefits to a politician of securing new contracts or facilities or blocking the loss of old ones were limited. The increasing regional maldistribution of defense outlays had changed that pattern. Now a minority of districts depended painfully on those outlays, consisted heavily of skilled defense workers attuned to the ideological and economic claims of remilitarization, and elected politicians able to stake those claims. Their stake was magnified by the complex nature of defense projects: weapons with long lead times for development, lengthy production runs, and expensive facilities promised long-term economic benefits; they also imposed enormous start-up costs that made early termination difficult. Unlike monies to patch a road here or build a post office there, defense outlays were not a spigot readily turned on and off: they engaged politicians in a more permanent fashion. The consolidated regional basis of militarization thus gave a more limited set of interests a greater stake in its future.

Given how Congress and its committee system work—an aggressive minority often more decisive than a pallid majority—key politicians had great power over the scale and content of defense spending. Their clout was strengthened by the close ties that Reagan and many of his subordinates had to the corporations, culture, and political networks dominant in the gunbelt, especially California. Advocates of space defenses like the scientist Edward Teller could get past the White House gatekeepers and reach Reagan far more readily than leaders of older or less defense-oriented firms. GOP control of the Senate from 1981 to 1987 and the renewed coalition between Republicans and southern Democrats—whose "boll weevils" often represented buckles in the gunbelt— also helped. Liberal Democrats would be compliant if their districts embraced places like Hartford, Connecticut (home to Pratt and Whitney) or Long Island (home to Grumman Aircraft), which were rewarded in the logrolling that shaped appropriation bills. No more than railroads in the nineteenth century or automobiles in the mid-twentieth could these interests forever resist the forces reshaping the political economy. But in the 1980s they retained the strength to bend those forces to their purposes.

They helped to account for the content of remilitarization in the 1980s. Reagan sought a 10 percent increase over Carter's last budget, sustained more increases until Defense Department spending exceeded $300 billion in 1986, and drove the share of GNP officially devoted to defense from 5.1 in 1979 to 6.6 in 1983. More likely, defense's share of GNP was nearer 10 percent, for more than ever defense spending was tucked away, often by deception, elsewhere in Washington's dense bureaucratic jungle. Most of the Energy Department's large budget went to nuclear weapons and research on space defenses, for example. And the Federal Emergency Relief Administration, ostensibly funded to cope with natural disasters, began "a top-secret multibillion-dollar program to help the government survive a nuclear war," its funding hidden under the rubric "submitted under a separate package" and overseen by, among others, the National Security Council's Oliver North.[20] In dollar terms, the defense budget nearly doubled between 1979 and 1983; after inflation, it increased nearly one-third—a growth rate far larger than worldwide totals and those of the Soviet Union and the Warsaw Pact, whose spending had risen sharply during the 1970s. This was the fastest growth in "peacetime" defense spending since the eve of Pearl Harbor, and all the more notable because it was accompanied by no great increase in military deployment and action, which had soaked up earlier spurts in defense outlays.

The spending splurge was weighted to big-ticket weapons. The B-1 (which Carter had canceled) and B-2 (Stealth) bombers and Trident submarines went forward, as did new cruise missiles, first deployed in Western Europe in 1983 and mounted also on warplanes and surface ships. So too did MX missiles, even without a plausible scheme for basing them. The build-up in aerial weaponry and expanded research on space defenses drew the greatest attention and criticism. Just as striking, however, was Reagan's ambitious plan for a six-hundred-ship navy, including the Trident subs, new carriers, smaller surface ships, and four World War II battleships, symbols of past glory refitted at a cost of billions. While the megatonnage of American nuclear weapons continued to decline and their numbers (surpassed by Russia's on Reagan's watch) remained static, an expensive effort to make new and replacement warheads continued. Many of these weapons owed their conceptual genesis, initial research, or production start-up to the Carter, Nixon (with Trident), or even Eisenhower (with the B-1) eras. What marked the Reagan administration was the sheer scale of its spending on them and its refusal to make choices among them.

What the United States gained in military strength was hard to measure, since there was no major battle test, but it was probably little compared to the costs. The value of new strategic weapons presumably lay in shoring up deterrence and Reagan's diplomatic leverage, though some entered conventional combat, a role for them sought by military leaders more than they acknowledged. As Paul Kennedy soon noted, "The fact that the Reagan administration in its first term spent over 75 percent more on new aircraft than the Carter regime but acquired only 9 percent more planes points to *the* appalling military-procurement problem of the late twentieth century." That problem included a drive for technological exquisiteness which made each weapon so complex and expensive that few could be purchased, plus the sheer waste and fraud possible when a few manufacturers and one buyer were in collusion with each other and tolerant of whatever abuses resulted. The most glaring example of that problem was the B-1 bomber—rushed to production lest the newer Stealth bomber preempt justification for it, saddled with multiple functions that helped drive its cost to a half-billion dollars apiece, yet so deficient in its electronics that refitted old B-52s were "in some ways more advanced than the B-1s," and so vulnerable to elemental problems like "multiple bird strikes" (as one crewman called them) that most of the bombers had to be grounded for years to get them fixed.[21]

The record was mixed in other ways, too. Active-duty personnel increased only about 5 percent, and combat training, transport, and logistics, though improved, remained stepchildren in Pentagon priorities. That unmeasurable element of military capability, the morale and fitness of personnel, probably did rise, for reasons for which Reagan could claim credit, if in some cases of a perverse sort: burgeoning defense budgets and patriotic pride made military men and women feel more valued, while the Reagan recession of the early 1980s helped to channel better-educated recruits into the armed forces. But failures in the American intelligence system, often the linchpin of successful operations, sometimes rendered moot any gains in capabilities: Marines in Beirut were caught totally offguard by a car-bomb driven into their headquarters on October 23, 1983, killing 250 Americans; in the Persian Gulf, where American forces endured an ill-defined mission amid the Iran-Iraq war, the USS *Stark* was hit by a missile fired from an Iraqi plane in 1987, and the USS *Vincennes* mistakenly shot down an Iranian civilian jetliner in 1988. Even the easy invasion of the tiny Caribbean island of Grenada on October 25, 1983, produced embarrassing glitches in communications and intelligence. None of these tests was big enough to prove much, and all were accompanied by censorship that made judgment difficult, but the Reagan record was at best a mixed one.

That huge expenditures produced few operational gains mattered little to Reagan. The Beirut fiasco and the removal of American forces after Reagan's solemn promises to keep them there—a humiliating if sensible retreat for American power—were forgotten like a bad movie: his actor's instincts taught him "that one does not try to go on with a routine that is flopping; move to the next one if the first is not reaching the audience."[22] The new show, an invasion of Grenada to overthrow a band of eccentric Marxists, came days after Beirut and eclipsed its bad notices. The readiness of American forces and their use in murky contests like Lebanon's never much engaged the White House.

Instead, its attention fixed on confronting the Soviet Union, and in ways which did not involve direct combat or even Moscow's greatest misdeeds. Though assailing Soviet intervention in Afghanistan and influence in Central America, the administration showed its greatest outrage over the curious affair of August 31, 1983, when a Soviet fighter shot down Korean Air Lines civilian flight 007, which had strayed into Soviet air space en route to Seoul. The White House quickly had some evidence (more emerged later) that the Soviet action was a colossal error (as Americans later committed in shooting down an Iranian airbus), but Reagan portrayed it as a calculated act of inhumanity revealing the fundamental nature of the "evil empire," as he had labeled the Soviet Union earlier in 1983. Perhaps no other moment in his presidency saw Reagan, usually kept on a tight leash by his handlers, take to the airwaves so often. He spoke almost daily, complete with alleged tape recordings of Soviet pilots in the incident, to condemn "this barbaric act," to assail those who "flagrantly lie about such a heinous act," to threaten an end to diplomacy ("What can be the hope of legitimate and moral discourse with a state whose values permit such atrocities?"), to suggest that the Soviets would never honor any agreements they signed, and to urge more American rearmament, which the KAL incident spurred. In this outrage, "totalitarianism has shown its ghastly face once again," he maintained. "This was the Soviet Union against the world. . . . It was an act of barbarism." It was also an incident for which there could be no equivalent American response, however, and where the Soviets inflicted a more deliberate evil, in Afghanistan, Reagan confined his response to assisting rebel forces. Indeed, the pattern of his presidency was to assail Soviet evil loudly but take armed action against lesser foes. The goal of rearmament vis-à-vis the So-viets was to appear stronger, not to use the strength.[23]

If enhanced military power had a sustained, practical purpose for the admin-istration, it was in the diplomatic, not the military arena—as the lever to force caps on Soviet military power and achieve disarmament. To be sure, that for-mulation gives a coherence to Reagan's arms control policy that it rarely had. Even by the American presidency's untidy standards, this one was plagued by "remarkably shrill policy disputes between agencies," inattention or capricious direction from the top, and warring assumptions: if the Soviets could not be trusted to honor *any* agreement, it was hardly clear why they would abide by one forced on them by America's superior power.[24] Confusion was evident right from the start, when the administration grudgingly agreed to abide by the terms of Carter's SALT II Treaty, even though Reagan had roundly condemned it and still did not want it ratified.

The Joint Chiefs, more fearful than ever of an unregulated strategic environ-ment, emerged as the most consistent if cautious supporter of arms control and critic of civilian officials' outrageous statements about winning a nuclear war. JCS chairman Gen. David C. Jones was the most notable voice in this regard, especially because he was an air force officer. Retiring in June 1982, Jones warned that "it would be throwing money in a bottomless pit to try to prepare the United States for a long nuclear war with the Soviet Union."[25] By then, however, the Joint Chiefs' clout in the White House was disappearing.

Discordant voices, bellicose posturing, and top-level indirection crippled Reagan's initial efforts (insofar as there were any) at arms control, baffling allies in Western Europe and adversaries in Moscow. By most accounts, the Kremlin expected from Reagan roughly what it presumably got from Nixon: a tough but consistent leadership whose realpolitik Moscow could constructively engage. Instead, it had difficulty finding any consistent message and any discernible set of American negotiators in charge, while it faced American saber rattling that served some Soviet officials jockeying for position and programs. On occasion, a breakthrough threatened. In November 1981, Reagan astounded most diplo-mats by offering the "zero option" on mid-range missiles in Europe—the So-viets would dismantle theirs and the United States would not deploy its new ones in the works—but this one-sided deal was dead as soon as offered (no one, John Newhouse later noted, foresaw how Mikhail Gorbachev "would have the wit to take NATO up on the zero offer and then pocket the larger part of the credit for making it happen"[26]). The next summer, veteran negotiator Paul Nitze concocted a similar deal during his famous "walk in the woods" at Geneva with his Soviet counterpart, but despite JCS approval, Richard Perle and Caspar Weinberger at Defense scotched the deal. In fact, few civilian leaders wanted *any* agreement early in the 1980s, preferring to stall on negotia-tions until America's arms build-up put it in a commanding position. The few noises and proposals offered were insincere and defensive, often made to out-maneuver the nuclear freeze movement.

Indeed, that movement and related political currents influenced the culture and diplomacy of nuclear weapons far more than the administration admitted, or perhaps was even able to grasp. Proposing to cap nuclear arsenals at current levels, freeze advocates generated widespread support at the grass-roots (a 1982 demonstration in New York gathered 750,000 people by police estimates) and secured broad support in Congress—only by a narrow 204–202 vote did the House of Representatives reject an "immediate freeze." Although branded as radical by its foes, a freeze itself was a modest measure given the existing size of nuclear forces. It was instead the diverse base, evangelical fervor, and political critique of the movement that alarmed advocates of rearmament, plus its international reach. The American freeze movement owed much to a dramatic mobilization abroad in 1981. "Everywhere in Western Europe (except France), the impending arrival of the new [American] missiles had swelled the ranks of antinuclear groups," drawing in the churches and "middle-class people of all ages and political tendencies." In the United States, Catholic bishops also weighed in, condemning the superpowers' reliance on nuclear weapons as deterrents and influencing Adm. James Watkins, a Catholic and chief of naval operations, who saw the navy losing personnel if they thought their service to America's nuclear force was "incompatible" with the bishops' pastoral letter. Soon trusted allies on rearmament wavered: "I'm not one of those freeze-the-nukes nuts, but I think we have enough," explained Goldwater in announcing his opposition to the MX program, which hawkish western senators questioned on grounds of its costs and environmental damage to their region.[27]

Although Reagan and Weinberger insinuated that foreign agents had helped "instigate" the nuclear freeze movement,[28] it helped push Reagan toward his problematical breakthrough on armaments, the Strategic Defense Initiative announced on March 23, 1983. The ideas and technologies for defense against rocket attack were more familiar than Reagan's startling speech and the startled reaction to it allowed for. They derived from older efforts (effectively banned by the 1972 Antiballistic Missile Treaty) to build ground-based, nuclear-tipped interceptor rockets and from progress in the 1970s on laser and particle-beam weapons to shoot down Soviet rockets after launch or during reentry into the atmosphere. In 1978, the *New York Times* announced, "Weapon That Fights Missiles Could Alter World Defense Focus," and promised that "despite the costs and problems, beam weapons offer hope that an all-out missile attack could be infallibly thwarted."[29] Before and after Reagan took office, a group of retired defense officials, corporate leaders, and scientists—Teller first met Reagan in 1967—took their case to him and pressed it through their lobby, the High Frontier Panel, even as they squabbled over which technology should get the green light. They also circumvented and alienated most science and defense agencies, which looked askance at their plans for technical or political reasons (the air force feared an expensive project that might steal dollars from its bomber and missile programs).

SDI's proponents appealed to Reagan's heartfelt faith that America (and the world) could be delivered from the threat of nuclear destruction. When his military chiefs suggested, "Wouldn't it be better to protect the American people rather than avenge them [through nuclear retaliation]?" Reagan pounced on the words, which he worked into his March 1983 address on SDI (soon dubbed "Star Wars" after the movie of that name). Reagan was ideally suited to reflect in an unmediated fashion the cultural fantasies behind space defenses. Four decades earlier, he had starred as Brass Bancroft in the movie *Murder in the Air*, blowing up an enemy's plane with "a new super-weapon," an "inertia projector" whose rays were to "make American invincible in war" and "the greatest force for world peace ever discovered." He shared the belief of many Americans, especially those enamored of air power, that America's exposure to destruction violated a national birthright, one that new technology could restore. Their outlook, which yoked notions of an isolated Fortress America to visions of global hegemony and technological utopianism, had never disappeared during the decades when mutual assured destruction made the world's safety hostage to the threat of its obliteration. It crept nearer the surface in the 1970s in fantasies like *Star Wars* and in work on space-based weapons. Reagan brought it fully to the surface, imagining deliverance from the threat of obliteration through exotic weapons that, like the cinema's inertia projector, "could intercept and destroy strategic ballistic missiles before they reached our own soil or that of our allies," as Reagan put it. They would form "a shield that could protect us from nuclear missiles just as a roof protects a family from rain," according to Reagan, linking futuristic technology to familiar idealization of the American home.[30]

His 1983 speech unveiling that vision was a strange affair. It caught many insiders by surprise, with Secretary of State Shultz and his aides reportedly "stunned, flabbergasted." It showed Reagan's odd knack for making the utterly familiar seem like a startling revelation—he warned that the Soviets have "weapons that can strike directly at the United States," as if they had not had such weapons for decades. It offered no strategic rationale for a radical change in defense policy; indeed, Reagan noted that the existing "approach to stability through offensive threat has worked." Nor did he complain about the economic and political burdens of the arms race. Instead, his grand but vague goals were to demonstrate "our peaceful intentions," forge "a truly lasting stability," reclaim "the very strengths in technology that spawned our great industrial base," and "achieve our ultimate goal of eliminating the threat posed by strategic nuclear missiles."[31]

Reagan's SDI speech unleashed a furious debate and sparked "a chorus of instant rejection and ridicule," as the *National Review*, a supporter, accurately put it. Most experts doubted the feasibility of space defenses, less because individual weapons would not work than because only a perfect system—attainable, if at all, at intolerable cost—made any sense: one that allowed some warheads to get through would be neutralized if the Soviets multiplied their warheads or launched low-flying cruise missiles from submarines. Critics warned darkly and with some justification that SDI's backers really wanted the United States to win a nuclear war—with SDI, it might launch a first strike, confident that its space defenses could block whatever Soviet rockets survived the initial blow. (As Reagan acknowledged, "If paired with offensive systems," his proposed weapons could "be viewed as fostering an aggressive policy.") In turn, critics predicted a hostile Soviet reaction and an arms race ratcheted up, literally and figuratively, to still higher levels, a prediction validated by Reagan's admission that "probably decades" would elapse before SDI would be in place. Reagan's vision, fumed a former Defense Department scientist, was "cruel and irresponsible, like a physician offering laetrile to patients afflicted with cancer." Reagan was presented in political cartoons as a dunce: satirist Art Buchwald "portrayed Reagan's old movie friend, Bonzo the chimpanzee, instructing a gullible president in the wonders of missile defense." Offering a more nuanced judgment a few years later, Garry Wills saw Reagan's presentation of SDI as another reason to see him as "that most disarming of political apparitions, the kindly fanatic . . . the demagogue as rabble-soother."[32]

The criticisms of SDI helped erode its political appeal. Not that its immediate impact was negligible. It opened a gusher of funds for cooperating university scientists, defense laboratories, military agencies, and corporate contractors, who foresaw "the business opportunity of a generation" and pursued it in "a fish-feeding frenzy." It alarmed Soviet leaders, who "played into Reagan's hands by imparting a credibility to S.D.I. it would not otherwise have had." It further poisoned arms control talks.[33]

But SDI's impact soon diminished. Since a workable space defense was decades away, initial work on SDI had no effect on strategies of deterrence. The Pentagon still did not warm to SDI, questions about its costs and feasibility mounted, the *Challenger* space shuttle disaster and the Soviet reactor explosion at Chernobyl raised more doubts in 1986 about the reliability of big technology, and Congress trimmed Reagan's requests for funding. SDI soon became just another weapons program: costly, still alarming to critics and promising to supporters, but bereft of the transformative powers for good or ill initially ascribed to it.

The critics missed an essential point, however: the debate on SDI transformed political culture even though every specific claim Reagan made was shaky. Particularly as he presented it, "SDI sought to save technology's virtue from, as it were, violation by the nuclear monster," an observer later noted. SDI "was often criticized as a technological 'fix,' meaning a belief that technology can fix things; but in fact it was meant to *fix technology* itself," that is, to restore faith in its redemptive potential and to overcome the dread associated with it in the nuclear era. Reagan's analogies between SDI and the weapons of World War II reinforced this effort to "fix technology"; space weapons, he suggested, would be like radar in 1940, which had helped the British beat back German bombers (he did not note how radar later guided Allied bombers to their targets). Whether SDI was workable or wise mattered less than whether the ensuing debate reinvigorated Americans' technological optimism. To a degree it did, as part of a general mood in the 1980s that celebrated American technological prowess in war, capped by an exultant fascination with American arms during the Gulf War. With SDI came visions of "a restored and renewed America" and a safe "return to prenuclear security by conquering the final frontier of space."[34]

In a closely related and more personal achievement, Reagan realigned conservative and liberal opinion on the nuclear issue. Conservatives usually had regarded the Soviet Union as America's greatest threat and nuclear weapons as America's protection from it. Reagan jumped the conservative ship by portraying the threat as less Russia than nuclear arms themselves, promising to deliver the United States and the world from it, even to share SDI technology with the Soviets once it was developed. He thereby stole the thunder of disarmament's liberal advocates and embraced their utopianism, so long excoriated by conservatives, about solving the nuclear problem. SDI's foes found themselves awkwardly condemning a visionary solution to the nuclear menace. If they won the debate on SDI's practicality, Reagan nonetheless forged a "striking transformation in conservative rhetoric" about nuclear weapons, aligning it with the hostility to nuclear weapons dominant among Americans and linking the utopian goal of disarmament to old American fantasies of technological mastery. "Isn't it time to put our survival back under our own control?" asked Reagan in 1986.[35]

More than any other American in the 1980s, although perhaps no more than Gorbachev in Moscow, he shattered the assumption that the world was forever stuck with expanding arsenals of nuclear weapons. Whether Reagan intended this "striking transformation" was doubtful: after all, he really wanted the SDI weapons and could imagine them girdling the globe, and for many SDI supporters the utopian visions were probably a hypocritical gloss on a scheme designed to gain the upper hand against the Soviets. But confusion, hypocrisy, and unintended consequence are usually hallmarks of great historical change: the achievement still stood.

By instinct more than intention, Reagan had stumbled onto the terrain—that of culture, broadly construed—where the Cold War was above all waged in its waning days. Almost no other terrain, besides proxy wars, was left. Except through gross miscalculation, no nuclear or conventional war between the superpowers was plausible. Their race for supremacy in strategic weapons had long become more symbolic than substantive, and both parties faced resistance to its further acceleration. The Soviet Union and the United States had never been economic competitors, both confronted economic challenges for which the other was not responsible, and the Reagan White House was loathe to impose economic sanctions on the Soviets that would hurt key American interests (although "most of the public continued to regard Jimmy Carter as 'soft on

Communism,' Ronald Reagan as 'hard' "). Culture, long contested by the superpowers, was the remaining battleground, on which continued "the febrile competition between Washington and Moscow for the moral high ground." What was critical was the ability of each to mobilize its population behind shared cultural values, to project those values to the world, and to win the battles over those values. Hence the importance assigned to the 1980 and 1984 Olympics, to the contest over the meaning of the Korean Air Lines incident, to the struggle for the moral high ground on nuclear issues, and to the rituals of superpower diplomacy. By the same token, Reagan's greatest achievement lay not in changing the tangible correlation of forces between the Soviet Union and the West, but in mobilizing American and world opinion against Moscow.[36]

The Soviet Union was losing the cultural struggle, though for reasons that went beyond Reagan's success in it. Its parade of infirm leaders—the reins of power passed quickly in the early 1980s from Brezhnev to Yuri Andropov to Konstantin Chernenko—disheartened its own population and presented a dreary image to the world. Moreover, Western cultural values were penetrating the nation in a process that Soviet leaders, for all their heavy-handed rule— or because of it—could not stop. That process speeded up as economic stagnation, urban decay, political isolation, and dismay over the Afghan war eroded whatever visionary appeal the Soviet system once had, and as the black-market economy enhanced access to Western goods, popular music, and culture.

Generational change speeded the process. The great claim of Soviet rulers to their subjects' loyalties was victory in World War II, but younger Soviets had not experienced that war and its peril. While intellectual dissent, cheered on in the West, mounted, the appeal of American and British rock music and the parallel growth of an urban gang culture were also striking, as graffiti dotted the urban landscape. Hewing no single ideological line, urban subcultures were variously fascistic (hailing Hitler), pacifist ("GORBACHEV—MURDERER OF AFGHAN CHILDREN," in mid-1980s graffiti), outrageous (rock groups with names like Enraged Clitorises and the Menstrual Pads), and playful (deliberately confusing Beatle John Lennon with Lenin himself in a pun on the old Soviet slogan, they scribbled in 1981, "Lennon lived, Lennon lives, Lennon will live"). What the various youth cultures had in common, however, was a fascination with Western popular culture, a relish for using the English language, and a proclivity to mock official Soviet culture. Soviet authorities fought back, first by fiat, then by a subtler cultural containment in the 1970s—sponsoring a safer, official Soviet rock and visits by select Western artists (Britain's Elton John and America's B. B. King in 1979, for example). These measures at best met partial success, however. Little overt challenge to Communist rule emerged, but the regime was being hollowed out from within. As one historian concludes, the upheaval that came with Gorbachev "could not have occurred had there not been for some time a vibrant underground culture waiting to go public."[37]

This subtle process, hard to discern in the early 1980s, was not one that administration leaders grasped or directly advanced. Reagan predicted freedom's inevitable triumph over totalitarianism but hardly saw it as imminent (though in 1983 he asserted that the "last pages" of communism's "sad, bizarre chapter in human history" were "even now . . . being written"). And he did not connect it to the counterculture arising in the Soviet Union, since conservatives had long reviled cultural phenomena like rock'n'roll and asserted that America's moral and military might would usher in victory. The stage was set for the Cold War's end, and Reagan, adept at theater, had, almost unwittingly, helped to set it.[38]

The decisive moves on that stage came from Soviet actors, but the fortunes of Reagan's administration also played a role. By the start of his second term, Reagan could point to the nation's military and moral rearmament, as he saw it, but to few gains in world affairs as a result. Instead, his foreign policy was in trouble. Rearmament had not made Moscow budge much on arms control, and Reagan refused to cash in Star Wars for negotiating leverage on the Soviets. Western-supplied rebels blocked Soviet success in Afghanistan, but the stalemate there had no foreseeable end. In Central America, Reagan's support of anti-Sandinista rebels in Nicaragua (the "moral equal of our Founding Fathers," he called them[39]) and despotic right-wing regimes elsewhere gratified anticommunist conservatives but elicited little wider support, and in October 1984, Congress passed the Boland Amendment, blocking for two years military aid to Nicaraguan "freedom fighters." Some displays of American armed might—in Grenada in 1983, against Qaddafi's Libyan regime (accused of sponsoring terrorism) in 1981 and 1986—were cheering but insubstantial; others, as in the Lebanese civil war, were feckless; none altered the plight of American hostages in Beirut. Meanwhile, the appalling Iran-Iraq war, begun in 1980, threatened Western oil interests, while the struggle between Israel and its Palestinian subjects and Arab neighbors continued unresolved. Remilitarization itself was about to run its course: it was reaching the levels Reagan had earlier sought, it no longer sailed effortlessly through Congress, it contributed to an alarming federal debt, and it prompted concern from experts, allies, and financial markets about the nation's economic course. Posturing about American might and Soviet evil helped win the 1984 election but could not silence complaints that posturing was about all that constituted American foreign policy. Within the White House, desperation grew to do something historic. It would soon smooth the path toward the Cold War's end, but it first surfaced in the Iran-Contra affair.

That affair had tangled roots. Competing Muslim and Christian factions, each with outside support, had started tearing Lebanon apart in the 1970s, and the Palestine Liberation Organization had used it for operations against Israel. At first, the Reagan administration saw the mess there in Cold War terms, especially fearing intervention by Syria, presumably a Soviet client. In 1982, Secretary of State Haig gave the green light to an Israeli invasion of Lebanon, a move that only worsened Lebanon's civil war and ensnared the United States more deeply, especially when the Israelis allowed Christian militiamen to massacre Palestinians in refugee camps. Intervention by American, French, and Italian forces fared no better, yielding disaster for American marines. American forces eventually withdrew, as did the Israelis from most of the country, but Americans (and others), including the CIA station chief, became hostages in Beirut of radical Muslims apparently doing the bidding of Iran's Ayatollah Khomeini.

Reagan had excoriated Carter for softness on terrorism and publicly struck a defiant, no-deals stance, but that stance, "calm and confident, concealed a terrible inner anxiety about the fate of the hostages."[40] It was a curious obsession for a man presumably bent on defeating communism, and his manner of acting on it was wholly out of synch with his public posture, with minimal standards of orderly governance, and with the law as it applied to dealing with terrorism, to aid for the Contras, and to accountability before Congress. Nonetheless, the White House launched a new operation, with two military officers, National Security Advisor John Poindexter and his deputy, Oliver North, taking charge, with CIA director William Casey helping out—and with Reagan, Vice President Bush, and others approving to a degree difficult to pinpoint. The scheme involved selling arms (generally through the Israelis) to Iran (hungry for weapons for its war with Iraq) in return for the freeing of American hostages. It also siphoned off profits from these arms deals (to which it added funds solicited from wealthy Arab rulers and right-wing Americans) to funnel support, banned under the Boland Amendment, to the Contras.

It was an illegal operation that showed again how national leaders used the presumed needs—in this case, not very urgent ones—of national security to justify illegal acts. It was also a stupid operation. Men who flattered themselves on differing from Carter by having a clear sense of priorities and a coldly realistic view of the world risked their reputation and legal status on a vexing but minor issue, and they naively trusted Iran's strong-willed rulers, who got the better of the deal: releasing almost no hostages, they got their weapons, plus the satisfaction of seeing Satan America embarrassed when the affair publicly unraveled late in 1986. Exposure in turn left Reagan with unpleasant choices: to take responsibility for the misdeeds and assume the political and legal risks involved, or to plead forgetfulness and appear an amiable fool unable to control his subordinates. Mostly he opted for the latter course, with a measure of sheer cover-up thrown in, but it was not a pretty sight.

The Iran-Contra affair and the failure of policy that underlay it further lubricated the path away from Reagan's militarized policies. How much it did so is hard to judge; Nancy Reagan's desire to see "her husband remembered for having lowered the risk of nuclear war" reportedly dated to 1984, the year Ronald began hinting at a change of course.[41] But in tandem with other changes, including Reagan's insistence that nuclear weapons were now the great threat to Americans, Iran-Contra helped set a new course.

Meanwhile, Mikhail Gorbachev took over as Soviet party chairman in the spring of 1985. In a series of incremental but breathtaking changes, he and other officials set out to revamp the Soviet system, inspired in part by Khrushchev's aborted fling with reform and the anti-Stalinist mood he had instilled. Reagan and many of his political allies later took credit for forcing the change—an odd stance since many of them, including Bush, initially had insisted that no real change was taking place, only a cosmetic facelift that made the Soviets a more formidable menace. In any event, the Soviet revolution of the 1980s, like most great changes, was multidetermined. To the extent the Kremlin tried to match it, the Carter-Reagan arms buildup did increase the strains on the Soviet econ-omy; Gorbachev reportedly complained "that Reagan was using S.D.I. to wage economic warfare against him." It is doubtful, however, that SDI "contributed significantly to the West's triumph in the Cold War," as one historian later claimed. Rather, it was one more wave in that sea of troubles, many apparent before SDI was launched, into which Gorbachev saw the Soviet system sinking. Had Kremlin leaders been confident about their system, they would have rushed to match Reagan's rearmament, or at least to construct a convincing fa-cade of doing so, but their confidence was plummeting. They did not desire to throw out the old system—it was to be reformed in order to harness the ener-gies presumably latent in it—but Gorbachev's reforms were sufficient, along with other changes, to end the Cold War.[42]

Particularly stunning, and not always welcome in Washington, was Gor-bachev's daring diplomacy on arms control and other matters and his ability to strut the stage of a global media culture. Soviet desperation and American rear-mament gave the Reagan administration negotiating clout, especially since the Kremlin exaggerated prospects for workable American space defenses, but at mid-decade the administration was still adrift on arms control. It was Gor-bachev who seized the moment and grabbed much of the credit for the agree-ments that ensued. Those "were largely the result of aggressive Soviet diplo-macy rather than American efforts," notes one commentator, while another concluded that "Moscow, not Washington, held the initiative during most of Reagan's second term. Washington reacted, often sluggishly."[43]

It did so for several reasons. Suspicion of the Soviets, cultivated for genera-tions, was a heavy drag on the administration, both in its ranks and in its broader conservative constituency, which had little notion of a cause to replace the one that had served it so long and well. The administration's internal disar-ray continued. "The real problem is that we have no consensus in the system," complained Les Aspin, a leading Democrat on these matters—an old problem that had only grown worse under Reagan and that insiders acknowledged as much as point-scoring Democrats. If the Soviets "came to us and said, 'You write it, we'll sign it,' we still couldn't do it," lamented one State Department official in 1988. Reagan still did little to forge consensus within the system. Key players like the Joint Chiefs supported arms control, but he rarely touched base with them. His most famous moment in that regard came at the Reykjavik summit with Gorbachev late in 1986, when Reagan, without consulting his own government or American allies, seemed to agree on a scheme to eliminate in ten years all nuclear weapons and the rockets carrying them. Reagan's instinct—to bypass entrenched interests—was sound, but only if he had the resolve to follow it up with persistent efforts to rally their support. He did not. He had no idea of how to get where he wanted to go, confused grand intentions with their realization, then succumbed to the advice of his handlers. His "arms control position was inadvertent. He got to it one step at a time, with little, if any forethought about where he was headed." Gorbachev and Reagan "tried to do too much too soon. In playing at one-upmanship with the major transaction that lay before them, they overstrained the tolerances of their systems—at least, America's."[44]

Reagan "wasn't an adventurer who saw nuclear arms as usable weapons; instead, he was an abolitionist—a far more convinced disarmer than Carter," John Newhouse claimed. He was "no admirer of arms control and its works. He wanted to have the advantage in nuclear weapons, or else to rid the world of them." But that stance, not so out of step with his predecessors', was a wish, not a plan, one inexorably tied to his naive vision of SDI. "In return for a small and probably meaningless concession on Star Wars," Reagan could have gotten "a strategic arms agreement of a scale that no predecessor would have ever tried for." But he refused to bargain with SDI, probably sensing "that a dream like Star Wars, once interrupted, cannot be resumed. To the end, he ignored the substance of progress in order to keep faith with its shadow."[45]

As a result, he and Gorbachev settled for a modest achievement. Earlier the Kremlin had rejected the "zero option" and "intrusive" measures to verify arms agreements, but Gorbachev stunned Washington by agreeing to both, making American diplomats, who had long made propaganda hay out of Soviet resistance to on-site verification, "choke on our own vomit," and leaving Pentagon officials aghast at the prospect that Soviet counterparts might roam American facilities.[46] Still, the administration had to embrace the Intermediate Nuclear Force Treaty since it incorporated so much that Washington had long demanded. Signed in December 1987, it mandated elimination of missiles with a range of up to three thousand miles. Though it left arsenals of long-range rockets intact—Strategic Arms Reduction talks (START) were dragging on inconclusively—it marked the first superpower agreement to dismantle, rather than merely cap, a substantial class of weapons carrying nuclear warheads. That was sufficient, along with other steps taken between 1986 and 1988, to liquidate the Cold War.

Why had the Cold War ended, and so abruptly, when detente in the 1970s had failed? In many ways, of course, the appearance of an abrupt end was misleading. "Cold War" was always a stubbornly simplistic term for a variety of shifting conflicts, many on battlefields not the least bit "cold," and many disguising clashes of interests and ideology that had little to do with its presumed content. Many of the struggles associated with the Cold War also ended long before the late 1980s. The United States' conflict with China, at times regarded as an enemy bigger or at least more bellicose than the Soviet Union, largely ended with Nixon's opening to China. The division of Europe persisted, but fears that war was imminent there or that Western Europeans would succumb to intimidation faded gradually if unevenly after the last crisis over Berlin in 1961. New conflicts did erupt as older ones abated, especially in the "Third World" (a grossly loose term of convenience that itself owes to the Cold War), but the proxy wars in Africa and Asia were for the most part dwindling by the early 1980s, or simply no longer of great interest to American leaders. Meanwhile, conflict with leftists in Central America, and with Vietnam, North Korea, and Cuba outlasted the Cold War's nominal end, which suggested that many of their dynamics had little to do with the Cold War. The Cold War at home, too, wound down after the mid-1950s; much of its legacy and countersubversive ideology persisted, even gained new life in the 1980s, but they thrived in different contexts. Thus many facets of the Cold War had dwindled away or ended altogether before Reagan and Gorbachev shook hands. What ended then was the Soviet-American conflict—to be sure, the Cold War's most defining and dangerous feature, but hardly its sum and substance.

Like any big change, this one had many causes. From the standpoint of leaders and policies, Reagan, largely inadvertently, had prepared the way, and Gorbachev and his allies, by their diplomacy and internal reforms, translated the possibility into reality. No change in the competence or vision of American leadership had intervened, but Reagan's instinct to wage the Cold War on the battleground of culture, and Gorbachev's surprising agility on that terrain, did alter the struggle.

From the vantage point of its history, militarization had reached a stage where its burdens were so immense and its benefits so meager that leaders were forced to alter its course. Of course, in its "objective" conditions, it had reached that stage long before, in the maelstrom of two world wars. On the other hand, those wars had also catapulted the Soviet Union and the United States to superpower status, and after the worst bloodletting ended in 1945, the short-term benefits of militarization had seemed large, its immediate demands unavoidable, and its long-term burdens debatable. Those burdens sank in during the 1980s, more sharply in Moscow because it could not so readily bear them and because Washington was reluctant to admit them. Soviet and American leaders thus arrived by different routes at the conclusion that the contraction, if not the cessation, of militarization was in order.

By conventional standards of ideology, it was odd that Ronald Reagan presided over this historic change, but the irony was explicable. He was always an ideologue more in words than in action; by temperament he was flexible and easy-going, and, by long experience in corporate America, more a company

man than a bold innovator; as President, he surrounded himself with pragmatic conservatives more than true believers. Even at the height of remilitarization, he was more interested in its show than its substance and, though willing
to spend a great treasure in its behalf, uninterested in costly sacrifices and bold
initiatives to translate military power into leverage on the world scene. Pushing
remilitarization, he exposed its hollowness inadvertently. So too, more self-
consciously, did his opponents, without whose pressures Reagan might not
have taken the steps he did. And more than Reagan grasped, the foundations of
militarization were eroding in the United States, just as in the Soviet empire. By
1986, that erosion, coinciding with Gorbachev's moves, was taking its toll.

Eroding Foundations

Attention to the economic foundations of remilitarization emerged slowly in
the 1980s. Reagan's policies were controversial from the start: he was sure to
"become king of the deficit-makers and undisputed master of the national debt
mountain," complained the *New Leader* in 1982.[47] Initially, however, his popularity, the jolting "Reagan recession," and the Cold War's stridency tended to
mask long-term trends. By mid-decade, with Reagan lacking a strong agenda
for his second term and Cold War tensions easing, critics saw the trends coming
into focus.

The critics faulted Reagan's administration for neglecting disadvantaged
Americans, ignoring the "feminization of poverty," and despoiling the environment. Mounting federal spending and debt belied Reagan's promise to
shrink government (spending at all levels of government as a percentage of
GNP increased early in the 1980s after a slight decline under Carter). Instead,
Reagan only shifted its priorities, as he favored national security and neglected
social welfare, economic renewal, and an "infrastructure" allegedly so decayed
that the nation had become an "underdeveloping [country], a modern economy in reverse gear." A near collapse of the banking system raised questions
about deregulation and left an administration presumably averse to bigger
government taking on the enormous task of bailing out that system. Critics also
assailed the leaders in charge, who (like Interior Secretary James Watt) were
sometimes contemptuous of the very functions the law enjoined them to perform. Scandals in the administration heightened that suspicion, as did Reagan's disdain for public service. As Federal Reserve Chairman Paul Volcker put
it in 1987 (without mentioning Reagan), "Mediocrity in our public services
would, in time, become an invitation to mediocrity as a nation." Mediocrity
was precisely what critics saw emerging.[48]

Above all, they pointed to the nation's slide from being the world's greatest
creditor to its greatest debtor, from enjoying a trade surplus to groaning under
huge trade deficits, and from being the world's richest nation in per capita
terms to one challenged by several Western European nations and Japan. Soar-

ing federal, personal, and corporate debt seemed a major culprit. "Our fiscal policy since 1981," complained the *New Republic* in 1987, "has allowed people living today to enjoy higher consumption at the expense of those who will be living tomorrow." The Reagan boom, they charged, was transient, driven by defense spending and by debt—by writing "200 billion dollars' worth of hot checks every year," said vice presidential candidate Lloyd Bentsen in one of the 1988 campaign's few memorable lines—rather than by growth in savings and investment that would ensure long-term competitiveness. "There is nothing wrong with importing capital," the *New Republic* noted, but the United States used it "to increase our consumption and government spending, not our investment."[49] Reagan, critics charged, had fostered a "demand-side" rather than "supply-side" boom that produced a widening gap between rich and poor, and stagnant or declining income levels for most Americans (two trends widely documented in the 1980s). That gap jeopardized not only social justice and stability but economic competitiveness, which was badly served by an ill-trained, despairing work force and by corporate leaders who seemed more bent on short-term plunder than on lasting competitive zeal. The economic blight of the old manufacturing "Rustbelt" in the Midwest and Northeast underlined the failure of Reagan's policies, as did the descent of blue-collar factory workers into minimum-wage service-sector employment, while jobs in the revitalized defense sector favored white-collar (and generally white and male) workers.

The administration had its defense. Federal spending and debt were rising, they responded, because Congress and the Democrats refused to pare back give-away programs (although the budgets Reagan submitted differed little from those Congress passed). Defense spending, they pointed out, was growing no faster and sometimes slower than programs like Medicare and subsidies like farm-price supports, although social welfare spending by all levels of government declined slightly as a percentage of GNP during the 1980s. Supply-side economics had not yet fully worked because it had not yet been fully tried. The Rustbelt's travails were attributed to structural changes in the global economy, not to Reagan's policies (but Carter's were routinely blamed). Meanwhile, job creation was robust (more so than in much of Western Europe) and a dramatic drop in inflation—in turn a stimulus to the housing and other industries—was a notable achievement. Reagan's best defense was prosperity (or at least, easy money) after 1983, whatever its unevenness. Income gaps between rich and poor, white and nonwhite, men and women, or the United States and other nations were denied, treated as statistical flukes, or dismissed as opponents' propaganda.

For both critics and defenders at mid-decade, the relationship between remilitarization and economic vitality remained opaque. The charge that rearmament caused mounting federal debt was only half-valid: other spending was also plausibly responsible. More than that, it was the balance between revenue and spending, not just the latter, that was at issue. Meanwhile, though defense took a rising share of GNP and the federal budget, it still bulked less large in the economy than a few decades earlier, so that any cuts in it would now have less macroeconomic effect. In any event, few of Reagan's political challengers proposed big defense cuts.

Nonetheless, the relationship between defense and the economy seemed troubling. To sophisticated critics, the nub of the matter was the investment of huge resources into an arena of innovation and production increasingly irrelevant to global competition in civilian goods and services. While the pattern was hardly new, Americans were reminded that their toughest competitors, especially the Japanese, spent far less on defense and thus had more capital to invest in civilian enterprise. Nor was capital alone the issue. Critical was the devotion of scientific resources to defense and the decline in "spin-off" from defense to the civilian sphere. Indeed, some critics now saw "spin-off" reversing: new civilian technologies were more likely to meet military needs than the other way around. Moreover, altering priorities, even if agreement emerged to do so, seemed likely to be painful. Corporate contractors, private and public defense labs, and scientists and engineers working on defense projects enjoyed a system with little competition. It was hardly clear that they could shift from creating weapons for a guaranteed buyer to designing cars for a competitive market, or that corporations would want to do so, since profits in defense work were often higher than in the civilian market. "Our industry's record at defense conversion is unblemished by success," the head of Martin Marietta later noted.[50] In sum, even if Americans could afford rearmament in a fiscal sense—after all, higher taxes or cuts in other spending could pay the bills—their nation's economic health was in jeopardy.

At issue, besides what militarization cost in deficits accrued or products neglected, was what it purchased. If Americans had had convincing evidence that military power still enabled them to protect their economic vitality or carve out new economic frontiers, the case for remilitarization might have been irrefutable. Rearmament, however, was not convincingly deployed to those ends. Instead it was keyed to an increasingly hollow Soviet threat and touted as enhancing American pride. What it purchased in tangible terms was unclear. Once the foundation of an American economic imperium, it now seemed a wobbly superstructure astride a crumbling economic base.

Whether Reagan's investment in military power was wasted in the sense that it served little purpose was a possibility rarely highlighted in the mid-1980s. Instead, Americans usually read about more humdrum though real forms of waste—Pentagon scandals that revealed corruption in defense procurement and outrageous prices for items as mundane as hammers and as huge as bombers. "We stole it fair and square" seemed the attitude of the companies involved, according to an insider.[51] Left unclear was whether those items were useful even if fairly and parsimoniously purchased.

Nonetheless, debate had proceeded far enough by 1986 to subvert the linkage between military might and economic prosperity that had sustained militarization. The latter had long seemed a stimulus to prosperity and a way to protect it. When limited demilitarization coincided with economic woes in the 1970s, the old linkage had been reaffirmed, at least in a negative way. But remilitarization in the 1980s, though it stimulated momentary prosperity for some, no longer promised lasting economic strength. Even the administration made only a half-hearted case that it did: although it defended programs like Star Wars as staking out a new economic frontier, by and large it argued that prosperity would swell for other reasons, like the magic of supply-side economics—implicitly, *despite* remilitarization rather than because of it.

Near the end of Reagan's presidency, all these elements of economic anxiety, criticism, and prediction came together in Paul Kennedy's tome *The Rise and Fall of the Great Powers* (1987), and in the surprising reaction it generated. As Kennedy acknowledged, few of his arguments were novel: he drew on scholarship long accumulating and worries long voiced. This was a work of "haute vulgarization," one critic sniffed, "remedial reading for the ill-informed."[52] Still, Kennedy summarized diverse critiques in a single volume of daunting heft and dispassionate tone, weaving them into a storyline about the ascent and decline of imperial powers that many Americans vaguely knew from dusty textbooks about Rome, Persia, and Great Britain. His timing, with the Cold War thawing and debate about America's fortunes growing, was perfect. It helped that as a British scholar (relocated to Yale) he eschewed obvious polemics and understood imperial decline as only an Englishman presumably could. He approached Americans as an uncle who worriedly, if a tad condescendingly, reminded his younger nieces and nephews of their kin's earlier fate. The fact that the United States seemed to have inherited Britain's hegemonic role made Kennedy's avuncular meditation all the more appropriate.

Kennedy offered no rant against militarization. He grasped the role of military might in the rise of great powers and refused to attribute America's faltering economic fortunes solely to its quest for military power. Japan had excelled economically because it basked "under the American strategic umbrella, but perhaps even more because of fiscal and taxation policies which encouraged an unusually high degree of personal savings" and other statist policies "totally different from the American laissez-faire approach." Moreover, American policies had sustained "domestic prosperity," arrested "Soviet expansionism," helped to integrate Europe's former colonies into the world system, worked to restore "the economies—and the democratic traditions—of western Europe" and Japan, and "maintained the liberal international order." Unlike many critics of the American imperium, Kennedy had little quarrel with these achievements.[53]

Still, the costs incurred and the failure to face them troubled him. He granted the inevitability of relative American economic decline once nations torn up by

World War II recovered, but he summed up contemporary anxieties precisely: "The real question was not 'Did the United States have to decline relatively?' but 'Did it have to decline *so fast*?' " He did not think so. American leaders had overvalued military strength, neglected the economic sinews of power, clung to a myopic view of the Soviet threat, and plunged into a self-defeating arms race. "The difficulties experienced by contemporary societies which are militarily top-heavy merely repeat those which, in their time, affected Philip II's Spain, Nicholas II's Russia, and Hitler's Germany. A large military establishment may, like a great monument, look imposing to the impressionable observer; but if it is not resting upon a firm foundation (in this case, a productive national economy), it runs the risk of a future collapse." The American state (and, he suggested, the Kremlin) had failed to balance "the short-term security afforded by large defense forces against the longer-term security of rising production and income," precisely the balance Eisenhower vainly had sought.[54]

As a result, the United States faced the dilemma of "imperial overstretch," the tendency to take on more global obligations than it could meet and to sap its economic health in the process, while other nations seized economic leadership. "Great Powers in relative decline instinctively respond by spending more on 'security,' and thereby divert potential resources from 'investment' and compound their long-term dilemma." To make the dilemma worse, it could not be solved by a sudden retreat from power: As "*the* global superpower," the United States "requires much larger defense forces," without which its hegemonic position would crumble. Kennedy predicted no swift or total collapse of American power—the nation was too big and rich for that. Still, he ended on a note both earnestly pessimistic and pointedly sardonic: "One is tempted to paraphrase Shaw's deadly serious quip and say: 'Rome fell; Babylon fell; Scarsdale's turn will come.' "[55]

There were limits to Kennedy's analysis. Grappling as much with Britain's decline as America's, he tended to read the former into the latter. His choice of Britain as primary model—rather than Germany, France, or Japan, major powers which remained more economically vital—guaranteed a gloomy outlook and served as a *measure* of his pessimism more than evidence for it. Kennedy regretted the casual arrogance of earlier British leaders and current American elites, who blithely assumed that minor adjustments would suffice to deal with imperial overstretch, and he admired nations like Japan which pursued state programs of economic growth, but like many Westerners he tended to exaggerate Japan's mysterious harmony and statist strategizing. By the same token, to see American leaders as taking a "laissez-faire approach" to economic challenges confused ideology with practice: though arguably with less coherence and success than its competitors, the American state had done much to fashion the nation's economy. Perhaps because Kennedy viewed the American state as rudderless, he in turn offered little guidance about how it might balance military and economic goals. He vaguely enjoined Americans to manage decline more prudently but fell silent about the hard choices involved in doing so, as if they were stuck in a historical dilemma for which there were few solutions. Missing also was a clear sense of whether military supremacy was essential any longer for global hegemony (or global order).

Jeremiads about its decline were as old as America: offered by New England Puritans, by patriots fearing the early Republic's corruption, by Americans fearing racial mongrelization or the frontier's end, by others shaken by the Great Depression, and by Cold Warriors. For Americans grappling with their future, the jeremiad had been a favorite genre (one essential to advocates of martial and moral revitalization in the 1970s). Neither Kennedy nor most commentators on his work placed it within that tradition.

Nonetheless, his book helped to consolidate a consensus that America was in decline. It confirmed the gathering suspicion that militarization was eroding the nation's economic vitality. It also helped to take that suspicion a step further by arguing the reverse proposition: gradual economic decline would in turn erode military hegemony. Without factories to produce weapons and inventiveness to create them, the United States would have to depend on foreign sources or on its own subsidized defense industries. Without economic growth, it would lack the capital to plow back into military strength and, though Kennedy did not say so, a contented population willing to put up with military demands.

Surprisingly, this long and often laborious academic book generated much attention. The reviews poured out in the first half of 1988 in the mass market as well as the expert press, sales soared, and Kennedy himself attracted much media attention. "Is It Twilight for America?" asked a typical headline. Vaguely centrist in its politics, Kennedy's book had something for everyone: for defense hawks, an assumption that military strength remained essential; for skeptics about America's course, evidence that the quest for such strength had gotten out of hand. Critical responses were not always favorable, but even hostile reviewers seemed compelled to engage Kennedy's book. Others saw it as relevant to the forthcoming election campaign. "The presidential candidates have yet to directly address the issues the book raises," wrote *Newsweek*'s John Barry, but they "are not unaware of polls showing widespread public unease over economic decline at home and competition from abroad." Americans "could be ripe for a debate over America's role in the world."[56]

Little such debate had occurred in 1984 or would arise in 1988, however, for reasons that the *National Review* inadvertently illuminated. America was in decline all right, Samuel Francis agreed in reviewing Kennedy's book, even as the communist threat had worsened: he compared Eisenhower's success in crushing Guatemala's left-wing regime in 1954 to Reagan's ineffectual response to "the much more tangible threat to U.S. interests . . . represented by Cuba, Nicaragua, and the various insurgencies they support." But the failure there and earlier in Vietnam suggested "that it is not the erosion of America's 'productive base' that is the problem, but the lack of will or capacity on the part of America's elite to understand and make use of power." Kennedy failed to explain America's decline because he had "little to say about the cultural foundations of this weakness" and did not "believe them particularly important, any more than most of his elite readers" did. Francis's shrill review revealed persistent fissures among conservatives, many frustrated that cultural renewal had not yet arrived, that Reagan had not exercised American power forcefully, and that by 1988 he even seemed willing to call off the Cold War.[57]

Despite his exasperation with GOP leaders, Francis captured the basic stance of Reagan in 1984 and Bush in 1988 in beating back the doubts Kennedy voiced. Facing the charge that the material foundations of power were eroding, they shored up its "cultural foundations," denied that its "productive base" had declined, accused Democrats of lacking "the will or capacity" to use American power, and hailed patriotic culture. Some conservatives disagreed: "Reagan's the biggest deficit spender in history," the *Chicago Tribune*'s financial editor complained; "he caused most of the deficit problem today, not Congress. People love Reagan because he's a closet liberal who preaches conservatism."[58] That view did not prevail in Republican Party councils, however.

The GOP's embrace of the religious Right at its 1984 Dallas convention— where the campaign buttons read "Christians for Reagan" and "Cut Out All Non-Defense Spending Now!"—indicated how it emphasized moral revitalization, but its neatest trick was to turn criticism of its policies into criticism of America itself. As UN Ambassador Jeane Kirkpatrick put it in 1984, the Democratic nominee was "bad news Fritz [Walter] Mondale," one of the "blame America first crowd." That accusation was already common in conservative intellectual circles (which included Kirkpatrick): as Joseph Epstein complained, "the contemporary literary scene is rife with writers" who evince "a fairly crude sort of anti-Americanism." Mondale was equated with the weakness of will and penchant for handwringing about America's faults that had presumably paralyzed Carter's presidency. His running mate, Rep. Geraldine Ferraro, was labeled "untested," with all the resonance of such a notion in the nuclear age—because she was only a three-term congresswoman, or because she was only a woman. Reagan himself "promoted themes of redemption, patriotism, and family," seeing an America "where everyday is independence day, the Fourth of July," growing tearful upon visiting the Normandy battlefield of World War II, and, in another television ad, "embracing Olympic champions, while a voice proclaimed 'America is Coming Back!'" "The country is on a patriotic ego trip," John McLaughlin noted approvingly, "proud of itself and unself-consciously enjoying the nationalistic binge." The message was that American power was robust, that Democrats lacked the will to use it, and that patriotism would cement its "cultural foundations." It was a message that Mondale countered earnestly but ineffectually. His most famous line—Reagan will "raise taxes, so will I. He won't tell you, I just did"—addressed mounting economic worries, but to no avail. His attempt to "appropriate the [national] security issue" and that of liberals generally to insist "that the flag belongs to everyone" left them clinging to a pallid me-too version of Reaganism. What Reagan did confidently, in soft focus in 1984, Bush did in a more brittle fashion in 1988, asserting the cultural bases of national power in the face of fears about America's material decline.[59]

That assertion reaped political dividends, but it also shifted political debate to territory as shaky as the economic terrain, where disunity seemed to jeopardize national power and where even conservatives divided among themselves. Americans usually understood their cultural divisions in the 1980s in terms of competing conservative and liberal visions, the former (the "affirmers" one historian calls them) reaching to unite Americans behind "traditional" and patriotic values, the latter wanting Americans to join in a common celebration of their diversity.[60] The line between these visions was smudged, however, and ugly divisions disrupted each camp, ones that opened to public view at the start of the 1980s, when Sen. Barry Goldwater excoriated the religious Right.

Goldwater was happy in 1981 to celebrate Reagan's victory, to see the pendulum swing "to the conservative, moral end of the spectrum," and to embrace many values of the religious Right. But he was also stung by its opposition to the Supreme Court nomination of fellow Arizonan Sandra Day O'Connor because of her presumed views on abortion, insisting that "many fine conservatives" accept "regulated abortions," though he did not share his wife's belief in "freedom of choice." Disassociating his conservatism from "'the new right,'" he declared "that the religious issues of these groups have little or nothing to do with conservative or liberal politics." Religion has a role in politics, but "the moral majority, pro-life and other religious groups," he complained, "cajole" and "complain" and "threaten you with loss of money or votes or both." He was "sick and tired of the political preachers" and "the threats of every religious group who think it has some God-granted right to control my vote on every rollcall in the Senate." They jeopardize "our political system" and divert "us away from the vital issues"—"the serious economic and military dangers in this country today"—on which Americans should focus. "Can anyone look at the carnage of Iran, the bloodshed in Northern Ireland, or the bombs bursting in Lebanon and yet question the dangers of injecting religious issues into the affairs of state?"[61]

Goldwater's outburst got only limited play. "There is less here than meets the eye," a commentator soon claimed; "none of the nastiness betokens any major ideological split within American conservatism."[62] Goldwater now seemed a rogue figure, committed to conservatism's vision of geopolitics and political economy, not to its moralistic cultural agenda (he had endorsed Ford over Reagan in 1976). But while Reagan's benign presence kept antagonisms among conservatives from boiling over, their "ideological split" persisted in the 1980s, widening as the communist menace shrunk.

As in the Soviet-American rivalry, culture seemed the arena of contest among Americans in the 1980s, with the meaning of war's history often what they fought over. Struggles continued over patriotic sites at Pearl Harbor, at the Alamo, at Little Big Horn, and other "sacred centers." In Texas, the League of United Latin American Citizens challenged the control of the Alamo site exercised by the Daughters of the Republic of Texas, the latter's backers mounting an Alamo-like last stand against rising Latino power. Further west, Native Americans challenged dominant mythology about whites "opening" the West to progress, seeking to have the battlefield where Custer had fallen stand as a memorial to Indians who had perished there. To honor Custer in the middle of their homeland, charged Indian activist Russell Means, was like erecting a "Hitler national monument" in Jerusalem (or, as he had earlier suggested, "a Lt. Calley National Monument in Vietnam"). Means's comparison was a telling reminder of the instability of the patriotic past: World War II could be bent to different purposes, and indeed one of his opponents suggested that memorializing Indians "who killed 261 American soldiers" would be like Jews erecting "a monument to the Nazi SS." That these struggles over how to remember America's military past often ended inconclusively or surprisingly—by 1991, "Custer" had disappeared from the official designation "Little Big Horn Battlefield National Monument" and the superintendent was a Native American woman—indicated partial failure by the forces of patriotic renewal.[63]

The struggles over patriotic sites overlapped contests over American education, as those who saw a stable past with a fixed meaning contended with those who regarded conflict over that meaning as welcome in a democracy. The former view was emphasized by conservative intellectuals who "led the fight in the 1980s to reinterpret Vietnam as a noble war," by Education Secretary William Bennett and others stressing fundamentals in education, and by two surprising bestsellers of 1987, Allan Bloom's *The Closing of the American Mind* and E. D. Hirsch's *Cultural Literacy: What Every American Needs to Know* (although Hirsch identified himself as a liberal). These authorities, notes one historian, were part of a trend which saw public schools and their critics look to "the success of the parochial schools, especially their emphasis on regularity, uniformity, discipline, and control," and "move toward a much more deliberately ecclesiastical model." Behind their efforts, observed another historian, lay "the same sense of America's cultural deterioration" that had been apparent in the jeremiad popular at the close of the previous century, with a similar conviction "that culture is less something that *is* than something that *was*." As Bloom put it, "Today's select students know so much less, are so much more cut off from the tradition, are so much slacker intellectually, that they make their predecessors look like prodigies of culture."[64]

Conflict over education in the 1980s had much in common with Sputnik-era debate: a fear of declining American power, of youth becoming "slacker," and of a rival's apparent superiority in the schoolhouse. This debate, however, also marked great changes since Sputnik's alarming beep-beep. The fact that Japan, not the Soviet Union, prompted the alarm was another sign of the Cold War's imminent demise and of a shift in the focus of anxieties from military power to economic vitality ("cultural literacy" would enhance America's "economic prosperity," Hirsch emphasized).[65] Different, too, was nervousness among some Americans about the success of Asians and Asian-Americans in education's scientific and technological arena—there had been no such challenge *within* American education in the Sputnik era, only the external threat of apparent Soviet superiority. Social divisions underlying debate on education also seemed sharper in the 1980s. Many older Americans resented the demands, especially from property taxes, made by any investment in education comparable to that of the Sputnik era. As the quality of public education seemed to decline, as the proportion of poor and minority students increased, or as its curriculum offended heightened religious sensibilities, many middle-class parents deserted the public system in favor of private schools (and demanded taxpayer support of their efforts to do so).

Meanwhile, conservatives' views on education and its role in national strength were telling. Education Secretary Terrel Bell fought administration efforts to abolish his department, supported federal aid to education, warned of "a nation at risk," as his 1983 study was titled—and was dropped from the Cabinet after Reagan's reelection in 1984. Administration conservatives, as they did regarding the American economy, generally denied that Americans' technical and material capacities were in jeopardy or that federal monies to enhance them were in order. Instead they saw culture as the key to educational success—students should learn a common and glorious past and embrace the values of patriotism and self-discipline that presumably flowed from it. That conservative tracts like Bloom's demanded cultural renewal, while Kennedy's tome called for economic revitalization, showed the fault lines.

Debates on education were mirrored in the higher reaches of academe. One division was opened by some scholars' "assaults" on the assumption that truth is stable, objective, and knowable. These assaults, fierce in disciplines like literary studies, were often viewed as constituting a unitary postmodern sensibility, although in fact there was a dizzying "forest of . . . 'posts'" in postmodern intellectual life. Proponents of objectivity condemned the assaults, as if "defending the life of the mind against enemies who had infiltrated the fortress and were attacking from within." Nor did political ideology give coherence to intellectual debates as it had in the 1960s; the dissidents were ideologically diverse, and Marxists or other leftists often defended objectivity. Earlier, most intellectuals had been in rough agreement about the objectivity (and value) of their work. By the 1980s, agreement was impossible: collectively, at least, they could not define a common culture for Americans. It was not just that they disagreed—they long had—but that now their attitudes "on the objectivity question were so heterogeneous that it was impossible to identify anything resembling a dominant sensibility."[66]

Their fragmentation took other forms as well. Women, gays and lesbians, African-Americans, and other minorities continued to attack the social make-up of academic disciplines and to fight for power in them. At least as disconcerting, especially in fields like history that had long prized breadth of knowledge, was the splintering of each discipline into subfields alienated from each other. The problem in history, noted Peter Novick, was "not just that the whole was less than the sum of its parts, but that there was no whole—only parts." C. Vann Woodward had once described the profession of history as "a habitation of many mansions," but by 1982 he thought it more like "scattered suburbs, trailer camps and a deteriorating central city." This form of fragmentation also predated the 1980s, but the sense of cultural incoherence was now more acute, leaving Novick grasping at Biblical verse to characterize his profession: "In those days there was no king in Israel; every man did that which was right in his own eyes." In the academy then, too, the cultural foundation of national power seemed, if not crumbled, then badly splintered, each block well crafted but the structure itself bewildering and its architects at odds about what it should look like. A more positive view—that such struggles were what gave strength to the edifice—was one few intellectuals took.[67]

Another division widened in the 1980s under the impact of AIDS. It testified to how sexual orientation was now a fault line in culture that the disease was branded a "gay plague" early in the decade. By 1985, AIDS and the federal response to it were objects of a bitter struggle. Despite early expectations that the disease would destroy the gay movement, AIDS mobilized it further and extended its focus, once largely local, to national politics, as gay activists demanded federal efforts to cope with the disease. In 1985, the death from AIDS of actor Rock Hudson, exposing as gay a preeminent celluloid icon of heterosexual masculinity, deepened old fears of an invisible homosexual menace but also revealed such masculinity as an unstable pose. Initial images of AIDS as a gay disease and homosexuality as a pathology persisted, but also became contested as other social groups joined the ranks of recognized victims, and as gay men were occasionally celebrated for coming to grips with death and dying in ways instructive to other Americans. Beneath the ugly struggle over AIDS ran less evident themes. The triumphal view of American science, disputed since the 1960s, further eroded as it seemed unable to curb the plague and as AIDS activists challenged scientists pronouncing on the disease. AIDS, like other problems in health care, also stoked more concern about whether national security should (or even could) remain a dominant priority and whether government could adapt to other challenges.

Too, the AIDS debate highlighted differences, surprisingly sharp among conservatives, between inclusive and exclusive impulses in American culture.

Many conservatives, especially right-wing Christians and the Roman Catholic hierarchy, regarded AIDS as God's or nature's punishment of homosexuals. But after a lengthy silence, Surgeon General C. Everett Koop—in image "an ultra-conservative fundamentalist who looked like an Old Testament prophet"—infuriated many conservatives in 1986 by shunning moralistic judgment on people with AIDS, endorsing "safe sex" programs, and urging federal mobilization against the disease. The fissure among conservatives that Goldwater identified in 1981 again opened.[68]

By 1987, the cultural divisions highlighted by AIDS were no nearer resolution than those erupting over patriotic rituals, education, and intellectual life. Gays and lesbians carried out that year the biggest march on Washington since King's in 1963, new activist organizations like ACT-UP (AIDS Coalition to Unleash Power) sprang up, and politicians in national government now identified themselves as gay. Closely related was the striking cultural presence, shaped partly by the demands of the AIDS crisis, of gays and (to a lesser extent) lesbians—tennis player Martina Navratilova, or figures in the arts like writer Larry Kramer and photographer Robert Mapplethorpe. Another conservative counterattack emerged late in the decade but, like earlier efforts, this one succeeded more at preaching to the converted than at altering long-term trends— indeed, the effort to stigmatize homosexuals as a group strengthened the perception of them as an identifiable minority rather than a collection of random moral perverts. That straight Americans were becoming more "tolerant" of homosexuals was often asserted, probably unlikely, and surely unprovable. That they were compelled to acknowledge a changing reality was certain.

Concurrent struggles over gender and abortion followed a roughly similar course: a "backlash" (as Barbara Ehrenreich called it) early in the decade against the feminist agenda,[69] then a reinvigorated feminist politics, and stalemate by the end of the Reagan years. Defeat of the Equal Rights Amendment was the great antifeminist triumph, made possible in part by the GOP's embrace (unimaginable a decade earlier) of an anti-ERA and anti-abortion agenda. As in confronting gay rights, conservatives also scored judicial victories—just as the Supreme Court's *Bowers v. Hardwick* (1986) decision left states free to criminalize sodomy, *Webster v. Reproductive Health Services* (1989) allowed states to restrict abortion rights—while Congress and the Reagan administration ended federal policies supportive of abortion rights. Through much of the decade, the momentum lay with the anti-abortion movement, supported (as in the anti-gay cause) by a once-unlikely alliance among the Catholic church and conservative Christian (and Jewish) denominations. Meanwhile, the mass media often portrayed feminist aspirations as passé and professional women as doomed or dangerous. By late in the decade, countermobilization by feminists and their allies had brought the struggles to an inconclusive point.

As in other cultural battles of the decade, the familiar story of conservative resurgence masked shifts in the cultural politics of gender. Gay and feminist leaders now stressed the needs of families and stable relationships, partly because "the conservative emphasis on the family inevitably left a mark," but also because of changed priorities. AIDS was one catalyst for gay men, as a sharp rise in childrearing was for lesbians, and gay fiction, like Armistead Maupin's surprisingly popular series *Tales of the City*, often placed the family (albeit not a "traditional" one) at its center. Feminists faced several pressures. As it became evident that "men, not women, were the principal beneficiaries of [the] emancipatory trend" of the 1970s, they tried to shore up benefits and protections for women. Those were being decimated by Reagan, who argued that programs for poorer women fostered "indolence, promiscuity, casual attitudes toward marriage and divorce, and maternal indifference to child-rearing responsibilities." Meanwhile, younger women facing the multiple claims of work and family and older ones reeling from divorce faced a job market in which women's income remained stubbornly stagnant. One thrust of this drive to protect women yielded an unlikely alliance: feminist antipornographers joined conservative moralists in efforts to stop pornography that presumably encouraged male violence toward women. A new view of gender accompanied these shifts: many feminists, especially minority women, now argued that "equality did not necessarily mean the erasure of difference" between men and women.[70]

Few of these shifting impulses fell easily into "conservative" and "liberal" categories, but their net effect was to complicate conservatives' efforts to achieve cultural cohesion under their auspices. Whatever it meant, "family" had been their domain at the decade's start. By the late 1980s, "family" was contested ground to which many voices, some once improbable, now staked a claim.

Just as important, and largely unnoticed at the time, these debates moved further away from questions of national and military power. In the 1970s, moral revitalization had been persistently if loosely linked to restored American power, but by the late 1980s conservatives' moral agenda was now more obviously an end in itself: dangerous feminists, diseased homosexuals, single mothers, promiscuous teenagers, angry blacks, and various others had to be purged from the nation because they jeopardized its moral fitness more than its power. The link between the two hardly disappeared, but the tilt toward the former continued.

By the end of Reagan's presidency, conservatives, despite notable successes, had failed to regenerate the nation's cultural foundations to their satisfaction. They proclaimed what Reagan had achieved in that regard, yet saw a lengthening list of cultural ills, plus the embarrassing exposure of moral and financial turpitude by televangelists like Jim Bakker and Jimmy Swaggart. Their frustration mounted during Bush's presidency. By its end, William Bennett was devising an "index of leading cultural indicators" designed to chart "America's cultural decline"—after twelve years of GOP rule designed to reverse such decline.[71]

Whether or not a "decline" had occurred, it was clear that American society and culture were as "segmented" in the 1980s as they had been in the 1970s. The greatest divide remained racial, especially for inner-city blacks—more impoverished and, so most commentators believed, more culturally isolated from American life. America seemed a nation of enclaves at best coexisting and at worst battling with each other, divided along lines of class, race, ethnicity, religion, gender, sexuality, and other factors: hardly the "Lebanon" Goldwater had pointed to, but prone to hostility and violence on a worrisome scale. Nor did a fiction of us-against-them give coherence to the segmentation: rich against poor, minorities against white, gay versus straight—binary categories were popular but unconvincing since they repeatedly got jumbled. White and black gay communities decimated by AIDS viewed each other warily, some lesbians resented how AIDS dominated the gay agenda, tensions between blacks and Hispanics exploded, and class divisions among African-Americans deepened. The cross-cutting divisions were many, the tapestry of social and cultural division dense.

Were cultural unity and the cultural foundations of national power in fact in decline? That was far harder to measure than economic vitality, which was at least subject to quantifiable measurements (however disputed). Insofar as cultural cohesion is in the eyes of its beholders, however, it probably was in decline: many Americans, by no means just conservatives, believed that their divisions were sharpening. Their perceptions had a basis in social and cultural conditions. "New" immigrants often found it difficult to assimilate into a dominant culture (or could not even be certain what that culture was), although that was a familiar problem for immigrants, for whom children usually complete the task. Racial, ethnic, and gender groups emphasized their autonomous cultures. Perhaps the biggest cultural shift came from the religious revival among champions of "traditional" values. Corporations reflected and magnified the shifts, as they now aimed their products to "niche" markets rather than a generalized national audience.

Changes in America's social composition did not just happen, however; they were partly driven by the nation's militarized history, at times by the very people who now bewailed the resulting social changes. Immigration into the United States, for example, was stirred by hot and cold wars abroad, with American responses to them serving as the sieve excluding some and inviting others. Those responses were undertaken for strategic, political, and humanitarian (or guilt-ridden) reasons, but war and America's perceived needs in it were often paramount. Johnson had made that clear when he signed the 1965 Immigration Act abolishing most old racial quotas: in the Vietnam War men were dying "named Fernandez and Zajac and Zelinko and Mariano and Mc-

Cormick. Neither the enemy who killed them nor the people whose independence they have fought to save ever asked them where they or their parents
came from. They were all Americans."[72] Europeans fleeing repression and
World War II constituted the first great wave, climaxed by the entry of Hungarians after their abortive revolt against Soviet rule in 1956, with a slower
trickle of Soviet Jews following in the 1970s and 1980s. When center stage in the
Cold War moved to Latin America and Asia, sources of immigration also
shifted—Cubans leaving Castro's regime, Koreans after their war cemented
South Korea's bond with the United States, a tide of Southeast Asian refugees,
and in the 1980s Central Americans fleeing that region's bloody struggles.
Much immigration—many Latinos, Pakistanis, and Asian Indians, for
example—sprang from other sources, and much of it was illegal or unwanted
by Americans already here (even by some recent immigrants). But indirect connections between immigration and America's militarized past were also powerful: many emigrating Filipinos had lived in the shadow of American military
bases, served as messboys in the American navy, given birth to the offspring of
American servicemen, or otherwise experienced the intense Filipino-American
bond.

Their influx did help to change America, but measured against a longer slice
of America's turbulent past, cultural disarray in the 1980s was less a new phenomenon than a return to an old one obscured by war and militarization. In the
1940s, 1950s, and 1960s, political, professional, and corporate elites had championed uniform values and systems in their quest to mobilize national power,
asking Americans to subordinate their particular identities, aspirations, and
grievances to that quest. Although in retrospect the jagged edges of a polyglot
culture remained beneath the surface of those values and systems, the latter
were nonetheless pervasive enough to shape a widespread sense of a common
national culture. When agreement about that culture began eroding in the
1960s, the resulting disarray was less something new than a return to the rich,
seething cluster of cultures evident early in the century. For sure, some fault
lines in the 1980s were new, and even familiar ones got expressed in new ways,
reworked as they had been in part by decades of militarization. The *fact* of cultural discord, however, as opposed to its particulars, was not new. What advocates of "traditional" values sought to reconstitute was not a timeless American
culture but by and large one invented in the 1940s and 1950s, as they sometimes
made clear in their nostalgia for that era. Hence, too, they tried to reconstitute
the militarized policies that had buttressed that invented culture.

Despite their efforts, the foundations of remilitarization were crumbling by
1988. Shaky even at the start of the decade, they weakened further as Reagan
emerged as more interested in its forms than its substance, as worries deepened
about its cultural and economic foundations, and as the agendas of various
Americans became increasingly detached from the quest for military might. Although conservatives had forged the ideological foundation for remilitariza-

tion, they divided over competing agendas: as figures like Goldwater moved to the margins, the ascendant wing simultaneously praised the cultural cohesion they presumably had achieved, bemoaned its apparent dissolution, and pursued it as a goal in itself, one apart from the nation's military power in the world. The Cold War's end speeded the erosion of these foundations but did not cause it; the fissures among Americans would have continued to widen even without its end.

By the same token, the Cold War's end was not the death knell of militarization. Cultural cohesion had earlier been sustained in part by pointing to external enemies hard to identify after the mid-1980s, yet the habit of seeing things in militarized terms was ingrained, and not only among conservatives. Old enemies were fading, but new ones could be located outside or within the nation. Above all, many Americans, as they had intermittently since the 1960s, found those enemies among each other and thus continued to reconceive war in a fundamental fashion—as something waged within America rather than as international struggle.

A FAREWELL TO MILITARIZATION?
1988-1995

Declaring New Wars

Sounding a bit like another Texan—LBJ waging war on poverty a quarter-century earlier—President George Bush deployed the full arsenal of military metaphors when he declared his drug war. He announced a "comprehensive strategy," warned that "if we fight the war as a divided nation, then the war is lost," asserted that "victory over drugs is our cause," and seemed to make all Americans suspect as the enemy. "Who's responsible?" he asked. "Everyone who uses drugs. Everyone who sells drugs. And everyone who looks the other way."[1]

When he spoke in 1989, the "war on drugs" was becoming a ubiquitous metaphor, used by the media, politicians, and citizens in everyday talk and elaborated floridly in references to "battle plans," "fronts," and "enemies." Such language was typical of the times: Americans were finding "wars" to wage all over their political and cultural agenda. As they did so, they marked the completion of the inward turn of militarization, though also perhaps its impending dead-end. By the same token, they waged another war abroad that ironically undercut the state's militarized policies. Those developments moved militarization into another phase, one of notable, if also contingent, contraction.

Pyrrhic Victories

The 1980s closed with apparent victories—for capitalist democracy over Soviet communism, for peace over the militarization that had dominated the century, for George Bush over his political opponents. Those victories proved short-lived, unsatisfying, or contested, however—sufficient to shake the old order but not to define a new one. The Cold War's end did not halt militarization, never caused in the first place by the Cold War alone, but it did destroy the most prominent rationale for militarization, and no sure replacement emerged. Looking outward, Americans saw an untidy world which provided only flickering points of reference. Looking inward, they saw war's passions surging at home, but there too the reference points were unstable. The age of militarization was ending, but in a distinctly fitful, rancorous, uncertain fashion.

George Bush did not invent that fashion, rooted as it was in deeper forces, but he revealed it and on occasion shamelessly abetted it. It was fine by him to make the Pledge of Allegiance a centerpiece of his 1988 campaign and to parade his grandchild before the GOP convention to lead its recitation. Reagan had exploited the symbols of America's militarized age in a guileless, almost benign fashion. Bush turned to them with a vengeance.

Prepared to be America's commander in chief in the Cold War, Bush lacked the training and temperament to rethink his role and the nation's. He grew up in an affluent family isolated from the realities of depression and fascism in the 1930s, someone who "never rocked any boats" in prep school, a teacher recalled—trained to serve the nation, not to scrutinize its mission. The resumé he boasted was extensive but, like the man, oddly unfocused. Texas congressman, failed senatorial candidate in the 1960s, ambassador to the United Nations, envoy to Beijing, CIA director—each of these duties was brief and none quite in the inner circles of power; together they comprised almost random assignments rather than a coherent package. As Reagan's vice president he was again the executor of others' wills. Never had he achieved an intellectual or political breakthrough in national policy. He had the same virtue that his 1988 opponent, Massachusetts governor Michael Dukakis, claimed—competence. "The vision thing," as Bush called it by 1988, puzzled him.[2]

World War II, in which he served as a young navy pilot, imprinted on him what war should be, a grand allied effort against evil. No President after FDR so ably forged a coalition for war. Vietnam, however, shaped his sense of war's domestic politics. GOP National Committee chairman during the Watergate crisis, he stayed loyal to Nixon and learned from him. Despite different social backgrounds, Bush resembled Nixon in his instinct (sharpened by rough-and-tumble Texas politics) to exploit the divisions that war produces, and in his abrupt rhetorical shifts—one moment reaching unconvincingly for an uplifting vision ("a kinder, gentler America" was his famous phrasing), at another bearing down viciously on presumed enemies at home, with the two styles oddly juxtaposed, joined only by Bush's "celebrated no-subject-pronoun cadences." Bush commented early in the 1988 campaign, "It'll be like the Nixon-McGovern race in '72 as far as the breadth of differences on issues." In fact, those differences were murky in 1988. His comment only revealed that he would reprise Nixon's focus on symbols of cultural and social division rather than on policy issues. Both Nixon and Bush also equated strong leadership with bellicose mean-spiritedness. When Bush "tries to show that he is tough," reporter Elizabeth Drew noticed in 1988, "he often gets it wrong," not realizing "that in most cases tough equals calm: Clint Eastwood, Gary Cooper, Ronald Reagan." Moreover, Bush, like Nixon, lacked any vision for the nation out of the grooves cut by decades of hot and cold war. "Frankly," commented Bush's chief of staff John Sununu in 1990, "this President doesn't need another single piece of legislation, unless it's absolutely right. . . . In fact, if Congress wants to come together, adjourn, and leave, it's all right with us." Bush shared Nixon's contempt for "domestic" issues and for Congress, with which he had to work to address them. What views he did have on such issues were often quixotic—as vice president he embraced the "voodoo economics" and anti-abortion ortho-doxy he had condemned in running for the 1980 GOP nomination.[3]

Nor did he have a settled, coherent identity: New England patrician, Texas plunger, able bureaucrat—his juggling of these roles was transparently awk-ward, especially when he played populist outsider against arrogant eastern in-tellectuals. Dukakis's allegedly soft-on-defense views were "born in Harvard Yard's boutique," he claimed in 1988;[4] in 1992 he tried to make Bill Clinton's time at England's Oxford University sound menacing. From a Yale man with impeccable patrician credentials, Bush's insinuations of his opponents' effete privilege rarely rang true.

Like a character in a Kurt Vonnegut novel, Bush had floated out of time. Had he entered the Oval Office in 1981, when remilitarization was in high gear, he might have served ably, if not inspirationally. Instead, he had to preside over military retrenchment and the Cold War's end, less opposed to them than sim-ply baffled by them, lacking a moral or ideological compass by which to track their course. Unlike Eisenhower, Carter, even Reagan in his way, Bush had no grasp—or no way to articulate it—of militarization's historical course and dan-gers. His attempt to cope with change was prudent—a real virtue, as Bush boasted; "Must be prudent!" ran comedian Dana Carvey's dead-on impersonation—but also grudging, as he applied a lifetime's unquestioned memories, views, and habits to a new era. Trained to be a war President, not because he relished war but because it seemed his duty and his arena, he searched for the real thing or its substitute, but "his natural state without war was political collapse," which he met repeatedly, then catastrophically.[5]

Bush failed to adapt to change in America's militarization. His roots lay in the older form of militarization based on America's armed preeminence in the world. Politics pushed him to exploit the newer form in which Americans went to "war" with each other. He tried his hand at both, but gained only temporary successes and lost touch with the economic issues now dominant.

Bush's 1988 campaign foreshadowed his choices and difficulties as Presi-dent. Reporters sensed voters' "lurking fear that America was slipping"—the October 1987 stock market crash and more talk of educational and scientific decline stoked that fear—and believed that "the public wanted to hear these themes addressed." They were "the campaign's hidden issue," according to one account, though less hidden than poorly addressed. Dukakis made a stab at tackling them, urging that several weapons programs be axed, but he seemed paralyzed by Bush's attacks and by the example of Mondale's failed liberalism in 1984. Lacking conviction on other issues and facing mounting anxiety about the economic foundations of national power, Bush reasserted its cultural foundations. He was following Reagan's example—"spiritual values *alone* are essential to our nation's health and vigor," Reagan announced in January 1988—but in an edgier fashion shaped by his insecurities and the gutter tactics of aides like Lee Atwater. "We have to change this whole culture," Bush said, and stop the "deterioration of values." By "change" Bush largely meant reviving the rituals, like prayer in public schools, of a vaguely defined past. What he meant by "culture" was less striking than his emphasis on it.[6]

Bush made patriotism the foundation of his campaign. He assailed Dukakis's veto eleven years earlier of a Massachusetts law requiring students to recite the Pledge of Allegiance, recited it himself "constantly," and visited a factory making American flags, monster versions of which framed his public appearances (and soon Dukakis's as well), even if campaign workers had to "scratch the 'Made in Taiwan' imprint off the handles." Under Carter, one senator told the GOP convention, "the American flag drooped in shame," but flag sales, Bush boasted, flourished under Reagan. Bush and his campaign ads condemned Dukakis as a "card-carrying member of the ACLU [American Civil Liberties Union]," phrasing that equated membership in that group with joining the Communist Party. A photograph of Dukakis awkwardly riding a tank was rendered as an image of his laughable discomfort with military issues and weapons. Implied, too, was his unfitness as a mere governor to grasp such issues—like another governor, Carter (Reagan was another matter)—while Bush boasted a long record on them. Claiming that Dukakis would imperil national defense, Bush made him seem a man of failed moral character, lacking patriotism itself. Wrapping sex, disloyalty, Vietnam, and incompetence into one smarmy package, Bush suggested that Dukakis "thinks a naval exercise is something you find in Jane Fonda's workout book," linking Dukakis to the anti–Vietnam-War-activist-turned-exercise-guru. His choice of running mate—Indiana senator Dan Quayle, viewed within his own party as a lightweight—compromised his claim to take the nation's issues seriously but did no fatal damage. GOP strategists fended off attacks on Quayle's patriotic ardor—family connections had helped him get into the National Guard and avoid duty in Vietnam—by equating them with attacks on the Guard itself. So went the party's general strategy as well, as in 1984. Questioning the nation's economic strength and global destiny was portrayed as America-bashing. "America stands tall again," Bush announced in a debate, repeating a Reagan line.[7]

Once again, the GOP line had been foreshadowed by conservative intellectuals. The Committee for the Free World complained in 1987 that "never have we been more beset by tempters" (like the "shrewd and formidable" Gorbachev), and warned against those who "blame ourselves for whatever goes wrong in the world. . . . We must more than anything else learn not to listen to them." Their warning added more pressure on Bush to embrace strident nationalism. Conservatives were clashing over Reagan's embrace of Gorbachev, their dominant voices warning Bush not to be fooled: Reagan's visit to Moscow in June 1988 marked "a sad week for the free world" in which "the chief thug" (Gorbachev) got the upper hand, admonished the *Manchester Union Leader;* William Buckley, though admitting that "something wildly exciting is going on in the Soviet Union," warned that "to greet it [the USSR] as if it were no longer evil is on the order of changing our entire position toward Adolf Hitler on receiving the news that he has abolished one extermination camp."[8]

By temperament cautious and by experience a Cold Warrior, Bush was not going to rock the conservative boat by contesting such claims or advancing a new agenda. Nor did political forces compel him to do so. The nation's economic challenges prompted gnawing anxiety, not consensus on how to tackle them. The Cold War's end was apparent but poorly acknowledged—more by Reagan than by those around him in 1988: Bush "took issue with Reagan's generous new view of the Soviet Union"; Defense Secretary Frank Carlucci argued "that helping the Soviet Union modernize may be 'an enormous miscalculation,' and warned against emulating the detente of the nineteen-seventies."[9]

Observers, wondering if the winner could even govern effectively, noted the vapidness of the 1988 campaign and the meanness of Bush's assault on liberalism. Though winning an ample 54 percent of the popular vote, he had barely addressed the problems that pundits thought important (Goldwater, again the GOP maverick, had urged him publicly "to start talking about the issues") and sometimes mangled his thoughts when he did ("I stand for anti-bigotry, anti-Semitism, anti-racism," he once announced).[10]

Although the campaign's vapidness was real, from another perspective Bush's effort marked a final defense of America's militarized course. It was a curious defense, however, since Bush laid out no coherent military or economic strategy for the nation and cited no credible foreign threat (Manuel Noriega, Panama's drug-running ruler, was a pale substitute in campaign politics). He emphasized symbols of moral revival and cultural unity but made them seem detached from the material conditions of power, as if flag waving alone made the nation strong. Bush campaigned amid the twilight's last gleaming of Reagan-era militarization, which led Americans to expect military displays done on the cheap—the glamor of arms, the heart tugging of the flag, not body bags and tough decisions.

There was disturbing irony, too, in how the GOP pried open the very divisions of race and culture it claimed were out of place in the unified nation it celebrated, as if unity rested on no firm basis, or was not even what it wanted. The GOP used a furlough that Massachusetts had granted Willie Horton (a convicted black murderer) as evidence that Dukakis was soft on crime (and by implication, on communism and defense). Many conservatives had long insisted that national power rested on shared values, and once had seemed confident that their values were triumphing: "We are the dominant faction within the world of ideas—the most influential—the most powerful," Norman Podhoretz proclaimed in 1983.[11] In 1988, however, their confidence in cultural unity sagged even as they proclaimed it, the cultural base of power seeming as decayed to them as its economic foundations did to their critics.

The start of Bush's presidency showed it adrift without a crisis, at least one it recognized. Bush's inaugural, brief and visionary in his "kinder" mode, only hinted that he might use military force. He offered "a renewed vow" to the world "to protect the peace," adding that "the offered hand is a reluctant fist; once made—strong, and can be used with great effect." His nomination of Senator John Tower as defense secretary found Republicans dividing badly without the Cold War—conservatives torpedoed the nomination, arguing moral turpitude on Tower's part—and showed the administration resistant to rethinking defense policies. Richard Cheney's ascension to the defense post marked no changes in policy. Meanwhile, the administration labored long to produce a new national security policy, then announced one that a spokesman proudly defended as "status quo plus."[12]

Such caution reflected and reinforced the often joyless and uncertain response of Americans to the Cold War's conclusion. An apparently triumphal end to this titanic struggle might have seemed bound to unleash patriotism, self-satisfaction, and optimism. At moments such emotions did surge: at Reagan's visit to Moscow in 1988; in waves of "Gorby-mania" about the new Soviet leader; when the East German regime collapsed in 1989 and the Berlin wall, one of the Cold War's most odious symbols, crumbled; and again in 1991, when Boris Yeltsin's forces defeated a countercoup and the Soviet Union itself dissolved. Yet no sustained euphoria seemed to connect the dots of these discrete moments.

Circumstances accounted partly for the uncertain moods. The end of the Soviet-American Cold War was marked by a series of moves, some initially ambiguous in import and together strung out over several years, rather than one cathartic moment. As the enslaved gained freedom, they often failed to embrace what most Americans understood freedom to mean. Instead of plunging into American-style capitalism, many looked elsewhere for models of political economy, met resistance from former communist authorities still in key positions, or lamented the loss of the old system's threadbare but reliable social welfare programs. Their new politics proved chaotic, their internal antagonisms ugly, their military forces dangerously unstable (as when the Soviet Union's collapse scattered its nuclear weapons into the control of several new countries), their new leaders tin-eared (as Gorbachev seemed to become), bullying (as Boris Yeltsin was often portrayed), or overwhelmed (as Poland's Lech Walesa seemed to be). A familiar paternalism did let Americans make allowances

Fig. 10. While earlier themes in America's militarization lingered, emphases shifted: by the 1980s, war was depicted less as an external threat, more as a reference point for Americans' anxieties and conflicts with each other. This 1989 political cartoon used the anniversary of Pearl Harbor to highlight their fears for their economic future—and to suggest, by use of nearly identical wording, typeface, and layout for both putative headlines, that World War II and the "trade war" were parts of the same timeless conflict with Japan. (By permission of Mike Luckovich and Creators Syndicate)

Fig. 11. Although many "wars" of the 1980s were short-lived, the "trade wars" persisted, restoked in imagination by fiftieth-year anniversaries of World War II events. Like the preceding cartoon, this one (appearing in the *Chicago Tribune,* Jan. 9, 1992) conveyed both the sense of a timeless conflict with Japan and the fear that the United States was losing its current version. It also appealed to older Americans—few younger ones likely recognized this as showing the battleship *Missouri* on which Japanese officials surrendered in 1945. (Reprinted by permission of Tribune Media Services)

Fig. 12. In the "wars" of the Reagan-Bush era, government propaganda never achieved the visibility and volume that it had in World War II, but it still appeared, sometimes in strange forms. The "drug war" yielded this 1991 Drug Enforcement Administration poster (the original in a mix of lurid greens and reds), which bizarrely conflated drug use with male homosexuality as the caricatured athletes inject each other in the buttocks.

Fig. 13. Even amid euphoria about the Gulf War, doubt set in that the triumph of America's war machine (shown here as huge and lumbering) would suffice to jumpstart the nation's economy and Americans' confidence in it, or that Bush (here rendered as a bit befuddled) had the strength to make the connection. The cartoon's internally referential content is also notable: focus on enemies abroad was fleeting, attention to the nation's internal sense of self and destiny more sustained. (*Chicago Tribune,* March 17, 1991; reprinted by permission of Tribune Media Services)

Fig. 14. The dense web of connections among war, gender, sexuality, and citizenship surfaced in the 1993 debate over lesbians and gay men in the armed forces. As suggested by this political cartoon, appearing after an April 1993 gay rights march in Washington and depicting the Vietnam War memorial there, war figured in that debate more as a reference point from the past than as an ongoing threat. Political cartoonists highlighted what political leaders in the end refused to acknowledge—that gay men and women had long served and sacrificed. (By permission of Chris Britt and Copley News Service)

Fig. 15. In the wake of the gays-in-the-military debate, this October 1993 political cartoon rendered a feminized, big-bosomed President Clinton feyly and fecklessly leading the troops, implying that his effort to change the military's gay "ban" revealed his womanly nature and his incapacity to lead the nation in war. But it also suggests that what troubled Americans most was not crises abroad—noted only in the background—but their sense of themselves. (Reprinted by permission of Tribune Media Services)

Fig. 16. Although the paradigm of war weakened in debates on public policy in the 1990s, it persisted in the so-called culture wars. It appears obliquely in this July 1994 political cartoon about the role of Catholic bishops in debate on Clinton's health care program, whose provisions for coverage of abortion services were much at issue. (Reprinted by permission of Tribune Media Services)

Fig. 17. Seen by millions of motorists traveling interstate highways during the autumn of 1994, billboards like this one tersely summarized an era's felt connections between war abroad and challenges at home. Although weakening at mid-decade, the pursuit of war's moral equivalents still possessed emotive and political power. (By permission of Robert Kwait for the Elizabeth Taylor AIDS Foundation; photo by James M. Beal)

for growing pains; like Germany and Japan after 1945, ex-communist nations were seen as children struggling to learn the mature ways of capitalist democracy. But the growing pains seemed maddeningly protracted. And unlike the case in 1945, Americans lacked the ability, will, and circumstances to control the process.

As usual, social factors also shaped the varied reactions that pundits shamelessly lump into a "public opinion." African-Americans, less invested ideologically in the Cold War in the first place, were now less invested in victory (those who saw military service as an avenue of upward mobility wondered whether a downsized military would become another dead-end). Americans of Soviet and Eastern European extraction usually cheered communism's fall but also jostled against each other, reflecting rising ethnic and religious tensions within and among their homelands. The rise of Catholic authority in Poland, the most-watched former Soviet satellite, alarmed abortion-rights feminists and gay activists, who wondered if the church's ugly hostility was preferable to the communist state's gray repression that had nonetheless guaranteed some rights. Cultural conservatives could cheer the church's role there but remained more inclined to worry about moral rot at home.

Partisan and ideological politics also kept the brakes on celebration. Cold War conservatives, though inclined to gloat because their man was in power at the decisive moment, were also candid about feeling bereft of the anticommunist cause that had served them so well. Democrats and liberals nagged Bush to recognize the Cold War's end but exerted little pressure on him, remembering Dukakis's fate in 1988, and pushed lamely for a "peace dividend" that would reap victory's rewards and turn resources to other ends. Leftists remained scattered, some excited and some bewildered by communism's collapse, many more attuned to race and gender politics at home, and collectively a marginal force.

Nor did the Bush administration sound much of a celebratory note. Though it handled diplomacy efficiently, its attempts to take credit for victory sometimes sounded provincial or mean—Democrats wanted to share the glory and Europeans who had struggled against communist rule were incredulous—rather than triumphal. Reporters sensed something missing: as the Berlin wall fell, one noted that in Bush's talk "of great victory for our side in the big East-West battle, . . . you don't seem elated. And I'm wondering if you're thinking of the problems." "I am not an emotional kind of guy," Bush acknowledged, making another pitch for prudence.[13]

Soon Bush and others warned so often of new, perhaps worse, dangers coming after the Cold War that they offered little reason for Americans to savor the moment. "Global conditions," argued GOP senator John McCain in January 1990, made use of military force "likely to be even more important in the future," American power remaining "the free world's insurance policy." The United States, argued the army chief of staff in April, faced "an increasingly turbulent world" and must remain able "to defeat potential threats wherever they occur." "Notwithstanding the alteration in the Soviet threat," Bush added on the eve of the Gulf crisis, "the world remains a dangerous place with serious threats to important U.S. interests." Victory's spoils already seemed sour.[14]

Other struggles, certainly World War II, had ended with messy results, ominous implications, and uninspired Presidents, yet also allowed euphoria to mingle with apprehension. Neither the complex circumstances nor the modest presidential leadership at the end of the Cold War alone accounted for the muted reactions. They were also rooted in Americans' understandings of what war and victory should mean. The great struggle had been called the Cold *War*, and though Americans knew that this "war" was different, the term shaped expectations rooted in the example of World War II: the enemy's brutal defeat at American hands, punishment of its war criminals, pride in American accomplishment, and visions of a better tomorrow. If only by counterexample, the Vietnam War reminded younger Americans of those expectations: victory had been denied, returning troops had not paraded, and the enemy (at least in POW/MIA myth) continued to humiliate the United States. Americans were supposed to humiliate *their* enemies—though afterwards to act generously.

In muted forms, hints of America's triumph and the enemy's humiliation occasionally surfaced. In 1987, the media presented the dramatic spectacle of a young German, Matthias Rust, outfoxing Soviet air defenses to land his tiny airplane on Red Square—a humbling moment for the Soviets if there ever was one. For a few seasons, commercial advertisements featured clever scenes in which wide-eyed Russian peasants or blockheaded communist bureaucrats—the totalitarian genius turned into dumb brute—encountered wondrous Western products. Disenchanted Soviets and Western reporters exposed the old regime's brutalities and follies. And the outstretched hand of Gorbachev and Yeltsin seeking Western aid revealed the momentous fall taken by America's archenemy.

Yet the pity-the-poor-Russians mood was rarely the triumphalism associated with victory, and the uncertain response of American (and other Western) leaders to the old enemy's edgy begging—its leaders all but threatened a renewed Cold War if their needs were not met—also lacked the triumphal element evident at the end of World War II. No invasion, no atomic bomb, no war crimes trials, no Marshall Plan, no MacArthur—gratitude that such things were not required mingled with regret about what their absence meant.

The Cold War's end brought few chances to inflict the final punishing blow, even imaginatively or symbolically. American responsibility for victory was itself in doubt, since it came at the hands of restive forces within the Soviet empire, catching most Americans by surprise. They might take pride in making the upheaval *possible,* in some abstract way—the West had preserved freedom, held up a model, and exhausted the enemy by its very staying power. But the dirty work of change had been carried out by others—Sakharov, Gorbachev,

Havel, Walesa, and thousands more. In any event, Soviet politics were so delicate after 1987 that American leaders hardly dared heap scorn on the failed Soviet experiment. A war ending with a whimper did not provide a fully satisfying conclusion, one that many Americans may have sought instead in Middle Eastern deserts.

War's meaning had long been mediated for Americans through the rituals of consumer culture and economic progress. In 1941, booming factories and fattened paychecks signaled entry into a militarized age as much as headlines about Poland or maps with menacing arrows; in the 1970s, defeat in Vietnam seemed linked to gasoline lines. The correlations were less clear at the Cold War's close. Victory initially brought few tangible changes—no flood of troops home, no surge of inflation or geyser of consumer goods—only upheavals in far-off lands to view on the screen. Tangible signs of victory emerged slowly. By the early 1990s, shuttered factories, closed bases, mothballed ships, and regional economic troubles, especially California's, offered delayed signals that victory was real and an era was passing. Even then, it was hard to see how the underlying economic changes were "connected to whether the mini-mall at the corner made it or went under."[15]

The signals were not only vivid but depressing. Victory's bounty seemed thin, if there at all. A "peace dividend" might show it, but the metaphor was awkward—if the federal government was a nearly bankrupt enterprise, as many charged, how could it declare a dividend?—and it spoke to fiscal issues, not to consumers' daily pleasures. Claims were made—now in daily newspapers, not just learned journals—that the Cold War had inflicted economic harm on the United States, and though debated they were sufficiently plausible to steal more of victory's pleasures.

Finding victory hard to savor, Americans also had trouble imagining what was to follow. World War II had excited hopes or fears of returning to a recent past. That bell-curve model of history did not always aid foresight, but at least it provided a framework in which to imagine, a sense of a past to reach back for, or to avoid in the case of the Depression. Even in the Vietnam War's wake, conservatives yearned nostalgically for the 1950s.

No remembered past served as benchmark or foil for imagining the post–Cold War world, however—perhaps one reason that State Department official Francis Fukuyama wrongly foresaw "the end of history" in a much-discussed 1989 essay.[16] The Cold War comprised too big an arc of history. It had lasted so long that it defined "normalcy" for most Americans, and at its end the American agenda was too changed to see the relevance of some pre–Cold War past. In any event, since the 1940s and 1950s marked the peak of American power and affluence, there simply was no better era prior to it to invoke. Earlier American wars had involved a short effort, after which an imagined past was readily available. The Cold War had made obsolete that way of finding meaning in war's end.

Nor was the imaginative problem confined to Joe Six-Pack, plodding politicians, or event-oriented journalists. Assembling essays by twenty-six distinguished figures (only one a woman), the editors of *Rethinking America's Security* were "struck . . . by just how uncomfortable Americans find the challenge of rethinking. . . . This applies to foreign policy experts and establishmentarians, perhaps especially so." The ensuing essays largely confirmed that judgment. Though varied and intelligent, they tended to view future policies as updated versions of familiar ones, only with the Cold War subtracted and economic challenges added. Commerce, affluence, and social justice seemed less like goals in themselves than means to enhance a familiar "national security," whose dominance as term paid homage to the past half-century. After all, argued one academic, "there have been no fundamental changes in the nature of international politics since 1945." By comparison, speculative literature at the close of World War II was bold, shaped as it was by sharp memories of the prewar past, sharp reactions to the war's climactic revelations, and the suddenness of its end.[17]

This structure of memory, experience, and imagination accounted in part for the shifting, dyspeptic mood apparent in everything from cartoons to novels to learned commentaries on the public pulse. Comic-strip Congressman Bob Forehead gave his wife so much trouble that she took him to a "perestroichiatrist," who opined, "The fading of the Cold War has left a terrible void inside him. He'll need a lot of care until he finds a new enemy," one the *New Yorker* saw many Americans finding in drugs. Novelist John Updike put his long-time character Rabbit to rest in 1990, having him muse, "The cold war. It gave you a reason to get up in the morning," and lament, "Without the cold war, what's the point of being an American?" Updike explained that Rabbit's "sense of being useless" had "this political dimension. . . . Like me, he has lived his adult life in the context of the cold war," and Rabbit had a "concept of freedom, of America, that took sharpness from contrast with Communism."[18]

The renewed popularity in 1990 of a predictive literature of American decline also measured the sour mood. To be sure, noted Paul Kennedy, a "revivalist" literature also blossomed but, as he observed, its creators seemed to be paddling upstream. For those conservatives clinging to the cultural agenda and toasting Cold War victory, dark musings from their own ranks were especially startling. Interrupting his cultural jeremiads, columnist George Will unleashed a barrage of depressing statistics about America's economic and medical status—"a boy born in Harlem today has a lower life expectancy than a boy born in Bangladesh." In a 1990 bestseller, *The Politics of Rich and Poor*, Kevin Phillips warned that "the triumph of upper America" in the Reagan era posed grave danger to the Republican Party and to the nation, blamed growing social inequalities in part on Reagan's defense spending, and pointed out that "human resources" spending, as opposed to the middle-class entitlements usually cited, had declined sharply relative to defense in the 1980s.[19]

From a different vantage point, former Commerce Secretary Peter Peterson complained in 1991 that Americans "sleepwalked, choicelessly, through critical years," just as journalist Haynes Johnson thought that "sleepwalking through history" defined the Reagan era. Americans, Peterson claimed, had clung greedily to entitlements, fought the taxes to pay for them, deadlocked on making decisive changes, and, through monstrous public and private debt, squandered their economic legacy to their children. "No generation in living memory has come of age sensing how little adults care about their fate," he charged. Political gridlock, economy folly, social fragmentation—his list of ills was long, and common to them all was a " 'have-it-all-today mentality," argued Peterson, reprising the lament about "narcissism" in the 1970s, that earlier moment when the Cold War had seemed about to end.[20]

Such complaints revealed Americans' uncertainty more than their failures. Even if real, the ills described had causes. Insofar as Americans "rose" to challenges in the 1940s in a united and self-sacrificing spirit, it was because the threats they faced had been sufficiently big, plausible, and external to mobilize them, not because they had been a more virtuous people. If they now seemed crabby and greedy, they had not forfeited virtue but faced challenges that seemed more complex, diffuse, and internal. And if they did not march boldly into the future, or even see one into which to march, it was because the age of militarization had drained the reservoirs of imagination and resources.

These constrictions on imagination played into the caution with which Americans approached the vast institutional and attitudinal apparatus acquired over the previous half-century. Bold proposals to dismantle that apparatus were few, usually at the margins of national debate. Even old foes of dominant policies were often careful; in 1990, the *Bulletin of the Atomic Scientists* featured defense analyst William Kaufmann's plan to cut defense funds by just 3 percent per year in the early 1990s (but in half by 2000). Others offered faster but still carefully graduated timetables. The sharp increases of 1941, 1950, 1961, and 1981—one model for what might now be done—were not to be matched in reverse. The nation's spy and police agencies had a disturbing record of inept forecasting, infiltrating political groups, hounding homosexuals in the military, and working in a secrecy inimical to democracy. Yet the summons to dismantle these institutions were few. New missions for them were imagined, although the *Chicago Tribune*, in a critique of the Cold War legacy notably harsh for the mainstream media, doubted that tasks like monitoring enemies in the trade war were "worth the scrutiny of a massive spy system or the propaganda of a vast government information system."[21]

Part of the problem was that Americans had long assumed that the Cold War alone had given rise to militarized institutions, so that the former's demise somehow guaranteed the latter's. The other roots of those institutions, less often grasped, were less easily ripped out. Those roots involved old perceptions, confirmed more than caused by fascism and communism, that evolving technological, economic, and political systems created a closed world posing permanent peril for the United States. The "Cold War," historian Walter LaFeber noted, included "confrontations that were at times only faintly, if at all, related to the U.S.-Soviet struggle." It had also subsumed impulses—to contain Germany and Japan as well as Russia, to control the global economy, to turn America "into a consensual, secret, militaristic, international force" (as LaFeber put it)—that had sustained militarization.[22] Hence there was a certain logic in arguing, as administration officials did, that Soviet decline did not warrant a corresponding decrease in American vigilance. As the Cold War's superstructure crumbled, a less visible substructure surfaced in calls to resist demilitarization. Unfortunately, the substructure dated to the world of the 1930s and 1940s, and clinging to it arrested efforts to adapt to a new era.

Other obstacles to faster liquidation of militarization loomed: fear of the economic damage that might result; residual anxieties about the Soviets and new ones about other threats; desires to bend old institutions to new purposes—often newly imagined "wars" of drugs, trade, and crime—and the interests that stood behind those desires. Put another way, those obstacles revealed that militarized institutions were so familiar that foreseeing—or remembering—an America without them was nearly impossible. No wonder George Bush had problems.

The best he could do was find new wars to wage. It was striking that his first televised address to the nation, just after Labor Day 1989, was his occasion to declare a war, this time on drugs. He and Reagan had already made similar declarations, and a Gallup poll established that Americans were in "a wartime mode" regarding drugs (while noting that "fear of war" had declined sharply, as if the drug war replaced it). "All of us agree that the gravest domestic threat facing our nation today is drugs," Bush announced, though many Americans rated other threats higher. Drugs alone did not occupy Bush that autumn; he continued his cautious efforts to support Gorbachev and nudge along arms control. But even those efforts were sometimes drenched in war's symbols. In December, the two leaders met at Malta, site of a major Anglo-American meeting during World War II (preparatory to the Yalta Conference), and convened on warships of each country, with a studied effort to maintain warship "parity" between the two superpowers. Secretary of State James Baker had acknowledged that "the world has clearly outgrown the clash between the superpowers that dominated world politics after World War II." Still, the Malta summit's symbolism looked back to that war, not forward.[23]

Bush quickly followed metaphorical war with a real one, an invasion of Panama in December 1989, with the deaths of likely hundreds of Panamanians, followed by antics worthy of a Gilbert-and-Sullivan war to secure the kidnapping of Manuel Noriega and his incarceration in the United States on drug charges. That was the logical outcome of Bush's September declaration: given a war on drugs, should not military action follow? It did, not only in Panama but in South America, along the Mexican border, and elsewhere, as the administration expanded military assistance to governments facing the drug trade and drafted a reluctant Pentagon into the cause. Familiar notions of the unbounded nature of national security were also reapplied: threats abroad and at home are indistinguishable, the tools to meet one can address the other, and American law applies to a foreign leader (Noriega, with whom the Reagan administration had probably colluded in illegal activities in return for his help against the Sandinistas). This was not the Cold War redux, however—the episode in Panama was too farcical and fleeting, too reminiscent of Reagan-era militarization, with its fondness for big guns in little wars.

Nor did it extinguish Bush's "wimp" image, as "his first real war was followed rapidly by his first [political] collapse—a harbinger of his fate after the Gulf War." Collapse was due in part to renewed anxieties about economic and fiscal problems. Bush compounded those problems by embracing Reagan's legacy, pledging to fight new taxes and declining seriously to engage Congress, itself squeamish about bold action. Nor would he or Congress wring savings from defense spending, which declined only at the 1-to-2-percent-a-year pace set in Reagan's last years. Vast bureaucracies and overseas deployments stayed intact and big-ticket weapons programs continued, though nuclear arsenals contracted to 10,500 American and 15,000 Soviet/Russian warheads by early 1993 (thousands more awaited dismantlement). By autumn, Bush did accept a budget deal that included new taxes, but he did so "almost passively ('Looks O.K. to me')," soon "repeatedly calling it all a 'mistake.'" Only war seemed to offer a way out of this muddle, although an earnest Bush may not have calculated the political payoff.[24]

His resistance to demilitarization played out against another critique of war, one informed by an end-of-the-Cold-War sense of how damaging militarization had been but focused on the futility of war itself. "War has fallen upon hard times," announced Robert O'Connell, a historian and civilian analyst for army intelligence. The "venerable institution" of war had become "virtually incapable of performing any of the roles classically assigned to it." John Mueller made a bracing case that major war among "developed" powers was moving, like dueling and slavery had, "toward terminal disrepute," in part "because of its perceived repulsiveness and futility." War, he claimed, had not troubled Europe since the 1940s, and many developing nations were also withdrawing from the "war system." "Conventional war" between massively armed states "may be at its last gasp," Martin van Creveld suggested. The "utility of fighting wars has sharply declined," argued Richard Barnet. Like earlier critics, the new ones hardly ruled out war's renewed eruption: "There is still accident and madness" to cause it, O'Connell noted; pandemic terrorism would elicit a military response from major powers, van Creveld observed; "Politicians are still tempted to use a splendid little war as a piece of political theatre," noted Barnet after Panama's invasion, "provided the risks appear minor"; Mueller saw "the obsolescence of major war," not of lesser versions. Offering the most somber prediction, van Creveld thought that national states and their wars would "wither away," displaced by "low-intensity conflict" waged by terrorist groups, private security forces, and rogue governments: "It will be a war of listening devices and of car-bombs, of men killing each other at close quarters, and of women using their purses to carry explosives and the drugs to pay for them. It will be protracted, bloody, and horrible." But even that sort of war, he suggested, made America's technologically top-heavy military establishment obsolete—or counterproductive. In any event, as a rational act of the state carried out on a large scale—"A mere continuation of policy by other means," as Clausewitz put it—war was folly.[25]

This outlook hardly generated universal acceptance. Its reappearance coincided with fiftieth-year observances of the start of World War II and with publication of Paul Fussell's caustic memoir/history of that struggle, *Wartime*. Both events elicited defenses of American efforts in World War II: it was "the good war," the *New York Times* asserted, if only because it "had to be fought and had to be won." Fussell thought "anyone who had fought in the war should be ashamed," noted the *Nation*'s reviewer, but "most of the Allied participants have been cagey about their lunacy" and "remain perversely convinced that they did something significant."[26] Bush articulated that unsurprising view, which served, not always intentionally, to reaffirm war's utility, or at least its occasional necessity. Still, World War II was long in the past, and recalling it was now an act of nostalgia. A sense of war's obsolescence, whatever its past necessity, was widespread.

It was even echoed by military leaders. Duty, self-interest, presidential policy, and institutional stodginess kept them from repudiating war's utility, much less its inevitability. Still, the caution evident since Vietnam persisted, despite their demands to shore up military budgets. Even amid Reagan's rearmament, Defense Secretary Weinberger had loudly announced so many preconditions to use of American armed force as virtually to preclude it. At least bad wars, if not all wars, were to be avoided, the message ran. Strategic doctrine also shaped caution: deterring rather than waging war long had been the military's priority, though some chafed under it. Caution was evident before both Panama's invasion and the Gulf War. "Patience," retired JCS chairman Adm. William Crowe reportedly believed on the eve of the Gulf War, "had paid off handsomely in the Cold War. Waiting out the Soviet Union for 40 years would be marked as one of the great victories of all time. Why can't we think in the long term?" His successor, Gen. Colin Powell, apparently agreed.[27]

Prudence was a virtue George Bush often claimed; patience, it seems, was another matter. War's obsolescence was a debatable theory; he would test it. Demilitarization had barely begun; its course remained fitful indeed.

Moral Equivalents of War

When George Bush declared a drug war, he was no innovator. The Jamesian search for a moral equivalent of war was an old tradition in America, one renewed by Reagan among others, especially when he addressed drugs and crime. In 1981, Reagan praised police chiefs "who command the front lines in America's battle for public order" and "the thin blue line that holds back a jungle which threatens to reclaim the clearing we call civilization," language evoking frontier mythology about whites conquering and civilizing the American West. "This administration hereby declares an all-out war on big-time organized crime and the drug racketeers," he announced in his 1983 State of the Union address. "The war against drugs is a war of individual battles," he added in 1988.[28] Indeed, by the time of Bush's 1989 announcement, the drug war had been so often and loudly declared that citizens might wonder when it began or might end. The search for war's equivalent thus preceded Bush's presidency, but climaxed during it in part because of his more acerbic and uneven leadership and because of the Cold War's end.

Use of the war metaphor was also now more diverse in sources and promiscuous in application than in the 1960s, when it had emanated primarily from the White House. Presidents now had limited control over it. They might jump-start it in specific cases, as with drugs, but ignore it in others, as in the "war on AIDS," or find it turned against them. No single political force conceived it; Reagan and Bush simply revealed one way to exploit it. Although the rhetoric sometimes proclaimed a campaign *by* Americans against some national problem, it more often signaled, sometimes intentionally, conflict *among* Americans. As such it traced and propelled the continuing inward turn of militarization, as its energies and institutions shifted toward Americans' conflicts with each other and away from the Soviet-American struggle. To be sure, that formulation is maddeningly vague about causation—no sentient being, militarization could not "turn" anywhere. As at its start, so too now: many forces and circumstances redirected it.

Among those was the outlook of many conservatives in the Reagan era. Since they presented the sources of national strength as more cultural than military and economic—a matter of internal cohesion more than power abroad—they raised the premium on fighting out and overcoming internal divisions. The decisive war was at home; once won, victory abroad would follow. By the same token, as prospects for serious war abroad receded, the search for a substitute at home intensified among a people so accustomed to war of some sort that its cessation seemed almost unimaginable, to conservatives and to many other Americans. The "wars" that ensued were varied, fascinating, and often baleful in their consequences.

One waged early in the decade was against terrorism. The Iran hostage affair had highlighted it; other incidents, usually in the Middle East, followed. This war proved hard for Reagan to declare and sustain, however, despite likening himself to cinema's Rambo. In 1981, he compared the struggle against terrorism to the Allied effort against Nazi genocide but admitted that terrorism, "scattered through the world," was "not quite large enough in dimension for us to rally behind as we once did in that war."[29] Lack of victory was also a reason not to trumpet this war. Instead it became a secret war waged by the illegal methods exposed as the Iran-Contra affair. In the end, Reagan surrendered rather than wage this war; bribery to get hostages released was not a bellicose policy. There was another reason this war was a nonstarter: it drew too little on the passions Americans felt about each other.

This feckless war, like the long war on drugs, indicated that the line between real and metaphorical wars was blurry, since the latter did embrace elements of real war: guns were fired, troops deployed, and people killed in such causes, in alarming numbers as the drug war went on. Blurry, the line was still recognizable. Few people argued (although Reagan did try) that these wars were the literal equivalent of others the United States had waged—World War II, for example—or current wars raging elsewhere, as in Afghanistan, where thousands died in combat.

At the same time, however, metaphorical wars with staying power had to partake *something* of war's death and passion. Not every public issue would qualify. No war was declared in behalf of education, although Education Secretary Terrel Bell argued that "if an unfriendly foreign power had attempted to impose on America the mediocre educational performance that exists today, we might have viewed it as an act of war." Reagan presumably waged a "war on waste" in government, as a presidential commission chaired by Peter Grace titled its report, but the enemy was too abstract.[30] Too, the notion was an oxymoron: since by nature war is a wasteful activity that enlarges government, to wage war on governmental waste was silly. By the same token, no "war on the federal deficit" emerged, although politicians of all stripes labeled the deficit a major problem. Not only was the enemy again abstract, few politicians seriously sought to defeat it. Metaphorical wars required political payoff if politicians were to declare them.

At first glance, America's "trade war" confronted similar obstacles: "trade" was an abstraction, and the dull complexities of economics did not easily generate public passion. Still, this label stuck; the metaphor was ubiquitous, its implications and imagery widely elaborated. In part it stuck because America's trade deficit seemed to have more obvious results than the fiscal deficit: shuttered factories, ruined cities, discarded workers, and foreign goods were the visible casualties and weapons. More than that, it was closely associated with Japan, America's old *war* enemy and racial competitor. Trade with many countries—including West Germany, another wartime enemy—swelled the trade deficit, just as other nations' investors, British and Dutch for example, bought up

American properties as aggressively, if more quietly. But Japan loomed largest in that deficit—the singular enemy in most renderings of the "trade war."

Given its resonance with World War II and that war's racial antagonisms, the trade war readily took passionate form. In political rhetoric, everyday complaints, and media culture, an acute sense emerged that the United States and Japan really *were* at war, even if no guns were yet fired. Thus Howard Baker, a leading Republican, used the fortieth anniversary of the end of World War II to insist that "we're still at war with Japan" and "we're losing"; a senator characterized Japan's export of cars to the United States as "an economic Pearl Harbor"; and a White House staffer urged that "the next time B-52s fly over Tokyo . . . we better make sure they carry bombs." Desperate American competitors exploited that outlook. Buick featured a photograph of MacArthur's receipt of Japan's surrender on the battleship *Missouri* above the words: "ONCE AGAIN, THE JAPANESE MUST COME TO TERMS WITH AN AMERICAN LEADER." (The imagery probably meant little to younger Americans, but they were not Buick's target market.) After 1989, a string of fiftieth-year anniversaries of World War II events supplied new opportunities to attach war's imagery and ugliness to Japanese-American economic relations, giving the trade war life into the 1990s when other metaphorical wars faded away. Freer in form and content, political cartoons exposed this outlook baldly. The *Atlanta Constitution* equated "Japan Bombs Pearl Harbor" with "Japan Buys Pearl Harbor" by keeping the typeface and words of its mock 1941 and 1989 front pages almost identical, as if World War II still raged, with only a minor change in wording (see fig. 10). Such cartoons suggested that Japan was an unchanging enemy, that only its devious tactics had altered, and that it again earned American vengeance, though how to inflict it remained elusive. They set up reassuring expectations—America would triumph in this war as in the last one—but also undercut them: maybe this time the United States was surrendering.[31]

As in World War II, Americans did not alone set the tone of the interchange. For many Japanese, too, talk of trade war reawakened images of real war, prompted renewed claims about America's sloth and racial impurity, and stirred dreams of redeeming Japan's humiliation in 1945. Japanese competed better, argued one official in 1982, because they "are a race of completely pure blood, not a mongrelized race as in the United States." The military balance between the two nations was far different than in 1941, to the point that during the Gulf War one American expert derided Japan's "infantile fear of war"—a remarkable criticism given American insistence on Japan's demilitarization after 1945—and Japanese conservatives praised "Americans for possessing a 'samurai spirit' lacking in Japan." But such language still drew on the images of World War II, simply inverting them—Japan now soft and squeamish about war, the United States "a war-loving, sloganeering, extremist country" fitting, John Dower noted, America's "World War II images of Japan." No wonder,

James Fallows reported, that "Japan's opinion-making class," eyeing Pearl Harbor's fiftieth anniversary, "prepared the public to cringe in dread of U.S. outbursts this month."[32]

The old war entwined with the new one in other ways. In Hawaii, some Americans (usually tourists, not Hawaiians) continued to resent the presence of numerous Japanese investors and tourists, regarding it as a sign that Japan had won the war by other means or threatened the "physical defilement" of the sacred site of Pearl Harbor. Other Americans met Japanese there in a spirit of reconciliation but, sensing ugly feelings, the National Park Service's acting director thought an official invitation for Japan's participation in the fiftieth-anniversary commemoration of the Pearl Harbor attack would be "inappropriate, possibly offensive, and fraught with problems and incalculable indelicacies." The president of the Pearl Harbor Survivors Association had a cruder response: "Would you expect the Jews to invite the Nazis to an event where they were talking about the Holocaust?" That anniversary stirred up more images linking the old war of combat with the new one of trade. The *Chicago Tribune*'s dissonant treatment caught the conflicting emotions: on December 7, 1991, it featured a cartoon of a sunken battleship at Pearl Harbor with the words "we remember"—above an editorial captioned "Looking Beyond Pearl Harbor." Months later, fifty years after internment camps for Japanese-Americans opened, one cartoonist compared Japan-bashing in 1992 to wartime American attitudes.[33]

This was such volatile stuff that national leaders usually tiptoed around the war metaphor, lest they disrupt the delicate ballet of Japanese-American negotiations on a host of matters. In the drug war, Presidents issued ringing calls to arms. In the trade war, the metaphor bubbled up more from below—from aspirants to rather than holders of high office (despite some indelicate remarks), from middling politicians exploiting the plight of congressional districts losing the war, from ad agencies and cartoonists who sensed the popular passions involved, from ordinary Americans, however many Japanese products they bought.

The trade war revealed another source of the metaphorical wars: the continuing hold of World War II on Americans' imaginations. Only the Civil War's grip had lingered so long, until weakened by World War I. No comparable event (although the Cold War's end came close) came fifty years after Pearl Harbor. Overwhelmingly, the images, reference points, and models cited for war's moral equivalents of the 1980s ran back to World War II, or to its aftermath and its legacy of nuclear weapons. It was as if Americans had no other benchmark against which to measure themselves and their challenges, their militarized culture looking more to past triumphs than to future glories.

World War II did not alone account for Japanese and American images of each other. "Why," an American once asked, "do so many Americans, after witnessing the devastation and futility of war, continue to think of Japan and the

Japanese in terms of war? Why have so many Japanese a similar mental attitude toward the United States?" Franklin Roosevelt raised those questions in 1923. "It is natural for the language of war to be applied to the battlefields of commerce," John Dower has argued. "There is not, after all, an infinite variety of lively words to go around." In fact, others were imaginable—from sports, for example, which had long supplied Americans' metaphors for war—but the trade war's language was "historically specific . . . the rhetoric of World War II," albeit set in a longer record of Japanese-American hostility.[34]

That war's hold, remarkable in longevity, was in other ways unsurprising. World War II ushered in the peak of America's global power and domestic affluence. Since America's ensuing wars in Korea and Vietnam were hardly attractive replacements—and since any imaginable big war in the future would be a nuclear conflict—World War II was left as "the only appropriate model for 'all-out' war metaphors." Among past and prospective wars, it alone offered the attractive combination of giant scale, moral clarity, American unity, and total American victory. Beneath the surface of 1980s rhetoric, other wars did rumble. Like Vietnam, the drug war lacked clear battlefronts, bled America slowly, and saw victory promised but never achieved. As the *Nation* noted, "Sending advisers to Peru recalls widening the war into Cambodia; stressing the number of people put behind bars sounds like body counts." Or in the different comparison to the Vietnam War offered by *Soldier of Fortune* magazine, the drug war is one "in which Bleeding Hearts pity the drug dealers and gang members. . . . It's a war where the police, as the soldiers of the streets, aren't given the opportunity to win." Vietnam's undertow was one reason that the metaphorical wars of the 1980s, especially those proclaimed by Presidents, often came to seem dispiriting and divisive. It was also a reason to keep drawing from the deep wells of World War II.[35]

Despite the trade war, the greatest passions were usually reserved for "wars" that engaged Americans' feelings about each other, not distant enemies. The drug war did so. It did occasionally feature external foes like Cuba's Castro, Panama's Noriega, and mysterious Columbian cartels. But more alarming for many Americans were the enemies in their midst: briefly in the 1980s, cocaine-snorting white "yuppies"; more often, inner-city black and Hispanic men, the urban gangs they joined, and the addicted mothers they failed to marry, with their drug-crippled or AIDS-infected babies. On occasion, conservatives drew wider circles encompassing all those defeatists who did not see a rosy future emerging from America's military and moral revival. "The same people who winked at us about drugs also told us that America's future was bleak," Reagan told Americans in 1988, and "said that the traditional values of family and community were old fashioned and out of date. It was as if they'd lost faith in the future and wanted the rest of us to lose it, too."[36] The harder divisions, however, involved race, ethnicity, and social class.

As with the war metaphor generally, drug war rhetoric was ostensibly designed to unite Americans. "As in World War II, I am convinced that the war on drugs will not be won until we mobilize the American public," argued one congressman wanting "drug war bonds" to finance the cause (the Bush White House demurred).[37] That reasoning drew on powerful memories of war as a unifying force, but the memories were rose-tinted: Americans had had some of their ugliest internal conflicts, especially racial ones, during and right after their wars, even World War II. The unifying purposes of war metaphors could never stick anyway when the enemy included fellow Americans. All were to unite against drugs and "just say no," as Nancy and Ronald Reagan put it, but Bush defined the enemy as "everyone who uses drugs" or "sells drugs" or just "looks the other way." That included many Americans. And war required visible enemies. So the impulse to unify that stimulated pursuit of war's moral equivalent yielded divisive consequences—in the drug war, above all of white against black.

Those consequences were enhanced by the repressive course that a warlike stance sanctioned. Insofar as it arises, wartime unity derives not only from shared purpose but from clubbing war's dissidents and outsiders into conformity or invisibility; many Americans did prison or concentration-camp time in the two world wars. War sanctions the suspension of civil liberties in order to achieve unity, just as the Cold War did amid nominal peace. In the drug war, leaders highlighted the war metaphor's unifying thrust more than its repressive implications, but those surfaced in police actions, court decisions, legislative changes, property seizures, sentencing rules, the record number of men (especially African-Americans) in prison, the routine drug-testing of military personnel and much of the labor force, and the mothers of crack babies embraced by the law's long arm. They also emerged in schemes for "prisoner-of-war camps" (to be located in "large tracts of federal properties in the West" where Japanese-Americans were interned, proposed one professor; Americans can "make all the necessary adjustments. . . . We did it after Pearl Harbor"). Nor was a war mentality limited to official agencies, any more than in wartime. Private institutions also enlisted in this war. The cover of the *Yale Alumni Magazine* proclaimed "Yale's war on drugs"—a "war on a number of fronts" and involving "battlefield" conditions.[38]

Criticism of these repressive consequences, and how the war metaphor served them, did ensue. Bush's "war on drugs has become a war against the poor," complained columnist Clarence Page, "an ever-mounting assault on those"—largely black—"easiest to arrest and prosecute," even though most cocaine users were white. An "incredible pressure on the military" to wage the drug war marks "the road of militarization," worried another commentator: "It's likely to fail of a solution" and "to corrode a pillar of our democratic way of life." Stephen Chapman, conservative columnist and dogged critic of the drug war, argued that "the first casualty of war . . . is the truth. . . . The ominous images of war and plague obscure the essential fact: Drug use, unlike most crimes, is not a form of aggression against others." Bush's "military model," the *New Yorker* lamented, "identifies many millions of Americans as the enemy, dismissing them in fundamental ways from our national life." "Bellicose rhetoric," added the *Nation*, leads to a "dehumanization of the enemy," with drug dealers portrayed as "subhuman life forms," as the Japanese were in wartime propaganda. Betty Ford regretted that phrasing "our number one public health problem as a 'war on drugs' has allowed a return to the strictly punitive approach to dealing with people who are, in fact, sick." With a war presumably on, however, such criticism went mostly unheeded.[39]

The contests in the 1980s over women and abortion revealed many of the dynamics evident in the drug war. Those contests had been phrased in war's terminology long before the eighties, but its use now intensified. Reagan and Bush rarely employed it. Instead it emerged from anti-abortion forces, and then, partly in reaction, from their pro-choice opponents. Groups like Operation Rescue, founded in 1986 by ex-car salesman Randall Terry, took the rhetorical offensive in these matters. In these male-dominated organizations—women in Operation Rescue seemed to comprise a submissive "female auxiliary"—members often saw themselves as "warriors" and spun out military analogies. Planned Parenthood, in their view, was "an institution that dwarfs the Pentagon." Activist Father Norman Weslin had once been a "commander in charge of nuclear weapons" but thought "that was bush league" compared to the enemies he now faced. Terry saw feminists as "diehard enemies" and operated from "command-central" in upstate New York. Anti-abortionists' imagery, wrote critic Susan Faludi, lay in a "war-torn psychological landscape" on which "the enemy was feminism, the weapon was aggressively moralistic rhetoric, and the strategy for reclaiming the offensive was largely semantic."[40]

Pro-choice feminists sometimes dipped into the same linguistic well. Responding to the Supreme Court's 1989 decision allowing restrictions on abortion services, angry editors of *Ms.* magazine offered a cover emblazoned, "IT'S WAR!" Faludi herself, in a widely discussed book, was unsure whether to reject or embrace the war metaphor. She criticized "imagining the conflict as two battalions neatly arrayed on either side of the line," but thought "the metaphor of combat is not without its merits" and titled her account *Backlash: The Undeclared War Against American Women.* Others echoed this language in other causes: lesbian activist Susie Bright lectured on "sex wars" in which officials squashed free speech rights to sell and buy pornography; historian Lillian Faderman surveyed the "lesbian sex wars" of the 1980s; antiporn feminist Andrea Dworkin penned *Letters from a War Zone.* In matters of gender, the war metaphor knew few political boundaries.[41]

These rhetorical parries were less telling and imaginative, however, than a newer one—the antifeminists' claim that abortion constituted a crime comparable to the Nazi Holocaust, its murdered millions equivalent to the Jews and others slaughtered under Hitler. While comparisons between abortion clinics and "Nazi ovens" were apparently "commonplace" from 1960 on, they swelled in volume and authority during the 1980s, spurred partly by the abortion politics swirling around Geraldine Ferraro's nomination for the vice presidency in 1984. That year New York City Archbishop John J. O'Connor commented, "I always compare the killing of 4,000 babies a day in the United States to the Holocaust." Other bishops saw such killing as foreshadowing a nuclear holocaust. In 1983, Interior Secretary James Watt, viewing photographs of death camp corpses shown at a Holocaust conference, explained how they reminded him of aborted fetuses.[42]

These comparisons seemed bizarre: abortion was a timeless if varied practice, not a discrete and concerted event like the Holocaust, and it usually arose from individual decisions, not government mandate. Moreover, the abortion-as-genocide claim arose from elements of the religious Right and the Catholic church not noted for their concern about the fate of Jews in the Holocaust, perhaps one reason why *Christian Century* objected that the claim risked the "trivialization" of the Holocaust itself.[43] Anti-abortionists had their own reasoning, however—*Roe v. Wade* and federal policy made government at the least complicit in genocide—and the war metaphor rarely rested on users' compelling logic.

And anti-abortionists were indeed using a war metaphor, if an unusual one. To be sure, genocide sometimes occurred outside of war (as under Stalin in the 1930s), and anti-abortionists saw themselves not as dabbling in metaphor but as speaking the literal truth. Still, it was the Nazi Holocaust, not other incidents of genocide, that they usually cited. And that Holocaust was an inextricable part of World War II, both when it occurred and as Americans, with their flickering cinematic images of that war, now recalled it. Its use indicated again how World War II remained the touchstone of political imagination—a still expanding one in that Holocaust imagery was relatively new to political culture. The further Americans got from World War II, the more meaning they seemed to see in it.

Doing so in the anti-abortion crusade exposed anew the corrosive potential of the war metaphor—the vehicle it provided to express ugly emotions. Anti-abortionists did tap the urge to unify; all Americans were told to defeat an evil equivalent to that faced in World War II, when they had also united in common cause. But with the casualties so "innocent" and "human," the enemy so visible, and the divisions over gender so longstanding, the Holocaust metaphor for abortion only divided people further. No wonder that the popular radio commentator Rush Limbaugh fulminated against pro-choice "femi-Nazis"—if abortion was like *the* Holocaust, pro-choice feminists loomed as latter-day Nazis (anti-abortionists were themselves occasionally condemned as latter-day fascists).

Of course, German Nazis mostly had been men. Limbaugh's jaunty tirades exposed not only the obvious gender politics of the abortion issue but the subtler ones of the war metaphor. Seeing feminists as waging war on fetuses, and on men—many anti-abortionists insisted that women were trampling on male privilege—inverted standard notions of gender roles in warfare. It also sanctioned some men to adopt military poses and, on occasion involving abortion, violent methods. Feminists did employ the war metaphor, but less often, and usually from a defensive posture, as if responding to a war already waged on them.

It was no coincidence that the war metaphor surged in the 1980s, when anti-feminism also flourished. Despite women's growing role in the armed forces, war was still with reason regarded as a male activity. Most metaphorical wars were male-defined in inspiration and male-led in action. To frame causes as "wars," especially if women were blamed for starting them, was to see them in male terms and to place them under men's control. Many men took that logic a step further in the flourishing paramilitary culture of the 1980s, imagining a "New War" to reverse America's humiliation in Vietnam and redeem its manhood. In fantasy or simulation, paramilitary warriors fought "the battles of Vietnam a thousand times, each time winning decisively," saw "terrorists and drug dealers . . . blasted into oblivion," put illegal aliens at home and non-whites abroad in "their proper place," got Jews "herded into canyons and shot," found that women had "to be mastered, avoided, or terminated," or wiped out homosexuals. Paramilitary culture was understandably seen as on the lunatic fringe, given the apocalyptic visions, hateful views, gun-loving mentality, and mass-murder binges accompanying it, but it overlapped mainstream culture in imagery and ideology. Restoration of "warrior dreams" and repudiation of post-Vietnam self-doubt were central to Reagan-Bush politics, to the adulation given Oliver North, and to Hollywood films of the Rambo variety that sought to replace the "soft bodies" of the 1970s (Jimmy Carter was "a 'woman' president" according to the *Wall Street Journal*) with "hard bodies" performing warrior deeds. (By the same token, Hollywood sometimes portrayed single career women as knife-wielding murderers compelling male resort to violence, as in *Fatal Attraction* [1987].) Paramilitary culture, like urban gang culture, simply offered a more striking example of how militarization was turning inward, in its case in a quite literal way that showed how the eruption of "war" among Americans was a gendered phenomenon.[44]

Gender was at issue in another "war" at the end of the 1980s, over culture and the federal government's funding of it. Backed by private lobbies, congressional conservatives like Sen. Jesse Helms inveighed against funding by the National Endowment for the Arts of artists like photographer Robert Mapplethorpe and exhibits they deemed pornographic or obscene. In many ways, this was another variant in the long struggle to contain the feminist and gay presence; most artists singled out were women (often lesbians) or gay men. Critics, and sometimes conservatives themselves, indicated that the Right had just discovered such people as new enemies to replace disappearing communists, but while cynical calculation was indeed involved, no new discovery was at work. Homosexuality and feminism long had been linked to communism, which was one reason why the new assault on them worked to the degree it did, although it worked in the ironic ways that had long marked such campaigns: to highlight further the presence of gays in the arts (and to make sales of Mapplethorpe's photographs soar).

Again, common phrasing of the struggle was as telling as the struggle itself. This was "a full-scale war between religious fundamentalists and the arts and museum communities," one observer noted. John Frohnmayer, the NEA chair who endured the wrath of artists for defending them weakly and of the White House for attacking them halfheartedly, subtitled his memoirs *Confessions of an Arts Warrior*. Americans were told they were waging "culture wars" whose fronts extended far beyond NEA policies. Even scholars like James Davison Hunter used the terminology literally, though admitting that America "is neither Belfast nor Beirut. (Not yet anyway.)" Just as the NEA furor peaked in 1989, another erupted over a Supreme Court decision (as it was oversimplified) protecting flag burning. No war was proclaimed—the flag was too much a war symbol to warrant such a declaration—but the passions, politics, and posturings were linked to those in the NEA struggle and the 1988 campaign: were not some artists exploiting the flag or trampling it in their exhibits?[45]

Most themes in the decade's metaphorical wars emerged in the most complex "war" of all, the one on, by, over, or against (it was hard to tell which) AIDS. War was not the sole framework enfolding AIDS, and disease had long been described in military metaphors, just as now the infectious agent HIV was seen as an "invader" which "attacks" the body's "defenses," as if a war *by* AIDS was ongoing.[46] But many uses of the war metaphor were novel and inflammatory.

They derived in part from the high rate of AIDS among gay men when the disease appeared in the early 1980s. Indeed, medical experts initially dubbed it "Gay Related Immune Deficiency" and the notion of it as a "gay plague" stuck despite its appearance among drug users, hemophiliacs, heterosexuals, and others. A decade later, the Manchester, New Hampshire, *Union Leader* still insisted that "homosexual intercourse is the genesis of every single case of AIDS" and that "anal intercourse by sodomites is the fundamental point of origin."[47]

That notion stuck because moral conservatives saw in AIDS a chance to resume the anti-gay offensive begun in the 1970s. Gay men, however, also expressed a keen sense of vulnerability to—and, as some saw it, responsibility for—the disease, and their strenuous efforts to rally their own communities and the nation tightened the association between them and AIDS, one that revived older notions of homosexuality as a medical problem. Meanwhile, other affected groups, millions of Africans for example, often lacked the political clout or even minimal respectability to command attention. A familiar American habit of finding people responsible for their own health problems also played a role in efforts to stigmatize people with AIDS; the 1970s had seen much speculation about how "Type A" personalities or "lifestyle" habits caused cancer or heart trouble. A stubborn distinction between AIDS' "innocent" and other victims further fastened on gay men the stigma of culpability. They occupied exposed ground—politically strong enough to call attention to their plight but not to control the forms that attention took.

Given the dread and the politics involved, war's metaphors issued easily, from conservatives in particular at first. As Pat Buchanan railed in 1983: "The poor homosexuals—they have declared war upon Nature, and now Nature is exacting an awful retribution." That war metaphor implied another: although "Nature" presumably had the upper hand anyway, Americans should take up arms against homosexuals. William F. Buckley called for tattooing infected people on the buttocks—reminding some of how death-camp inmates were marked in World War II—and others for locking them up. Responding to those calls, some gay men wondered if they would be incarcerated like Japanese-Americans in 1942 or worried about the "Dachau scenario," and "it was virtually an article of faith among homosexuals that they would somehow end up in concentration camps." "Out of the Baths, Into the Ovens," read a 1984 San Francisco protest sign; a gay reporter asked if officials were "preparing the boxcars for relocation."[48]

World War II, the Holocaust particularly, had found another lodgment in political culture, in a striking demonstration of how its use transcended political categories. Desperate gay men and righteous anti-abortionists had nothing in common politically—they hated each other for the most part—but they now drew from the common well of the Holocaust's example and its rising visibility in American culture. For gay men, the way had been prepared in the 1970s with the rediscovery of the mass death of gays under Nazi rule; the pink triangle worn by the Nazis' gay prisoners then emerged as a symbol of gay militancy. As metaphor or analogy, the Holocaust carried ominous and diverse implications, including prolific use by gay activists of "fascist" and "Nazi" to characterize malign politicians, health officials, or corporate leaders who presumably permitted AIDS to work its genocide, but also to assail as "sexual fascists" those gay men who supported closing San Francisco's bathhouses as a way to curb the disease.[49]

The most sustained use of the Holocaust came from writer Larry Kramer, the decade's best-known AIDS polemicist. Kramer cited the Holocaust occasionally early in the 1980s and systematically by its close—a trajectory matching the increasing scale of the disease and despair over it. Gay and Jewish, he used the Holocaust variously as metaphor, model, analog, and prophecy, in a rich and strident fashion, but above all to describe what was done *to* gay men by a homophobic society and its genocidal leaders. "AIDS is our holocaust and Reagan is our Hitler. New York City is our Auschwitz," he asserted in 1987. The Holocaust also illuminated for Kramer what was done *by* gay men, as he decried a "participation in your own genocide" analogous to Jews' presumed complicity in their own destruction. He pulled these thoughts together in *Reports from the Holocaust*. Others, some influenced by Kramer, offered a similar outlook. ACT-UP helped popularize the logo "Silence = Death," one of many references to the Holocaust.[50]

Kramer's angry polemics indicated how richly gay men developed war's metaphors for AIDS. In contrast, the many lesbians in this struggle rarely did, indicating gender differences again, while conservatives, less inventive and personally invested in the struggle (though closeted brethren like Terry Dolan and Roy Cohn died of AIDS), relied on rhetorical stock-in-trade. The Nazi Holocaust was only the most conspicuous among war's horrors that gay men cited, however. One used nuclear holocaust—AIDS was like an atomic bomb that fell at the "ground zero" of Manhattan, where many gay men lived. Another elaborately compared "the experience of the gay community to that of survivors of Hiroshima" in an essay "AIDS and A-Bomb Disease." Most writers evoked World War II, the Holocaust, nuclear attack or other forms of aerial war, or a potent mixture of them all—those forms of war most associated in the modern imagination with mass carnage. The film *Longtime Companion* (1990) ended by equating the joy imagined when a cure for AIDS arrived with the emotions felt at the end of World War II; the fitting title of one review was "A People at War." Or sometimes war in a generic sense was summoned up—Randy Shilts's account of the disease described "battle lines" and "the butcher's bill"—or World War I, or a third world war. Too, war language was not confined to gay men or writing about them: "Fear in the Foxholes" was an article about the burdens on health workers.[51]

Such language also appeared in memoir and fiction as well as political polemics, indicating how the war mentality was a cultural as well as political phenomenon (if that distinction held regarding AIDS). Its use by gay writers confronting AIDS was seemingly casual but in fact pointed. So Paul Monette noted in passing that "in a jerkoff scene it was very bad form to bring up one's [dead] lover, let alone the holocaust." Prefacing his poems, he wrote of "a warrior burying a warrior." Describing a dying lover, he asked, "Is this how a Jew feels when he hears 'holocaust' appropriated to some other calamity?" and speculated that "if AIDS had struck boy scouts first rather than gay men, or St. Louis rather than Kinshasha, it would have been covered like nuclear war."[52]

As with other uses of the war metaphor, those about AIDS had their share of internal contradictions, unforeseen results, and pure silliness. To write that "the bomb" of AIDS "fell without anyone's knowing the bomb had fallen" was awkward at best (few bomb explosions go unnoticed!). Kramer's assertion that "Reagan is our Hitler" did not work: Reagan lacked the necessary menace and control over his own government. Kramer's backtracking—he soon spoke of "unintentional" holocausts for which it was "not possible to locate one

Hitler"—only blurred his analogy to the Nazi Holocaust. Of course, metaphors rarely meet rigid tests of historical accuracy. Their use testified to the grief and the stakes involved for gay men, and to a political culture which, despite their marginality and radicalism, they shared, one in which war metaphors were now promiscuously used.

The most pervasive metaphor regarding the disease—of a "war on AIDS"— emerged at mid-decade in efforts to galvanize federal action and spread as those efforts met a cold shoulder from the Reagan and Bush administrations. Nearer the mainstream of American rhetoric, it became commonplace in media reporting and commentary, among politicians and medical officials, and among many gay activists. "Finally tonight," Charlayne Hunter-Gault began the last segment of a *MacNeil/Lehrer Newshour* in November 1986, "we look at the latest development in the war on AIDS." That metaphor seemed especially inviting in media treatment of uniformed officials: Surgeon General Koop "makes waves in his war on AIDS," announced *Newsweek;* retired Adm. James Watkins, chair of a presidential commission on AIDS, was "drawing the battle lines on AIDS," according to another magazine.[53]

Such language reflected the pressure on government to mobilize with the energy and fiscal abandon it presumably showed in wartime. Again, World War II, and sometimes the Cold War, defined the imagination. Larry Kramer, echoing scientist David Baltimore, proposed "a Manhattan Project to deal with AIDS." Two sociologists, sidestepping the federal government's long record on health problems, offered the 1950s crash development of Polaris nuclear submarines as a model.[54]

Reagan recognized that war rhetoric sanctioned federal action on AIDS—by refusing to use it. To him, "primary responsibility for avoiding AIDS lies with the individual," whose duty was "to abstain from sex until marriage" (as if gay men should now marry, although legally they could not). Since Reagan wanted government's role in AIDS to be minimal, war rhetoric to mobilize it made no sense. Addressing the United Nations in 1988, Reagan made that clear. He saw AIDS as a "grave crisis," but regarding drugs: "We will not tolerate the drug traffickers. We mean to make war on them, and we believe this is one war the United Nations can endorse and participate in." His choices about when to use and not use the war metaphor clearly reflected his priorities.[55]

Reagan's comments, the arguments about the "war on AIDS," and the larger pursuit of war's moral equivalents all reflected the antistatist tradition of hostility toward powerful government and concerted social action. As so often before, war as analog and metaphor served to justify governmental efforts. Reluctant to defend forceful government in the interest of social or economic welfare—as if that would coddle the drug user, burden the taxpayer, reward the AIDS carrier, throttle free enterprise—Americans wrapped their demands for action in war rhetoric. Doing so, they made viable an otherwise politically untenable claim on resources and placed their demands in the one arena of national action where expense was deemed incidental, politics suspended, unity compelled, and hostility to taxation and central authority overridden. Their political culture remained remarkably like the one during the New Deal that "had yet to find a way to organize collective action save in war or its surrogate."[56]

Indeed, that was especially so in the 1980s, since Reaganism further undercut appeals for federal action grounded in social justice and economic welfare. If, after all, government was the problem, not the solution, as Reagan argued, what could justify mobilizing it into action? Only war, which presumably suspended Reagan's rule, just as national security was one item for which he refused to recognize limits. Reagan himself paid homage to that reasoning by his drug war rhetoric. As critic Susan Sontag noted:

> The transformation of war-making into an occasion for mass ideological mobilization has made the notion of war useful as a metaphor for all sorts of ameliorative campaigns. . . . Abuse of the military metaphor may be inevitable in a capitalist society . . . that increasingly restricts the scope and credibility of appeals to ethical principle, in which it is thought foolish not to subject one's actions to the calculus of self-interest and profitability. War-making is one of the few activities that people are not supposed to view 'realistically'; that is, with an eye to expense and practical outcome. In all-out war, expenditure is all-out, unprudent—war being defined as an emergency in which no sacrifice is excessive.[57]

After all, in the previous half-century, most sustained, successful actions by national government were war-related. It made sense then that new campaigns against AIDS, drugs, or other perceived threats were justified in the language of the only crusades that had proved enduring. Hence advocates of those campaigns invoked not only war generally but specific models of America's most shining success in war, like the Manhattan Project. And if models of success were drawn from war, models of catastrophe also had to be—hence the Holocaust as a model for gay men's fate.

To be sure, such uses of "war" provided cosmetic cover for political agendas quite divorced from war and national security, but their persistence was nonetheless telling. For liberals, conservatives, radicals, and reactionaries, war served to legitimate the powerful government Americans feared to admit they wanted and the huge bureaucracies they claimed to hate. Just how powerfully this distrust of government operated was suggested by Kramer's accusation that the National Institutes of Health "is drowning in waste, fraud, corruption and mismanagement. They are, in fact, pissing one billion dollars down the toilet."[58] Aside from "pissing," his rhetoric was similar to decades of conservative denunciations of national government.

The impulse to invoke war operated with special force for gays and lesbians. Their politics had been localized in the 1970s, and they lacked close ties to (much less trust in) national government and a long political tradition of their own. Their war metaphors thus served to mobilize both government and their own community, and likewise to express distrust of the bureaucratic results at both levels. Kramer hurled the same invective of spinelessness and waste at agencies formed by his brethren, like the Gay Men's Health Crisis, as he did against the federal government, while groups like ACT-UP thrived on an anti-bureaucratic and antihierarchical ethos. Use of war to summon "collective action" operated both externally vis-à-vis government and internally within the gay community.

How much it galvanized action was hard to measure, since it was not the only impetus to collective effort. It also had no guaranteed effect. Reagan, vetoing a 1983 bill providing a "drug czar," showed how the war metaphor could serve different purposes: "The war on crime and drugs does not need more bureaucracy in Washington" but instead "more action in the field."[59] Still, federal funds for AIDS research, education, and treatment, like monies for the drug war, did rise sharply in the late 1980s, as did repressive actions, especially at the state level, where laws were passed or proposed to mandate tracing of sexual partners, shut gay bathhouses, permit doctors to test patients without their permission, and prosecute under criminal charges those who transmitted the disease. A lively debate, like that during war, ensued about whether to restrict individual civil liberties in order to stop the spread of AIDS. Despite their war rhetoric, most gay activists and medical experts rejected such restrictions as doomed to make HIV-infected people hide their disease and thereby impede efforts to staunch its spread. At the federal level, the trend was less coercive. Surgeon General Koop denounced punitive measures. Congress and the courts gradually applied to people with AIDS the laws and rules protecting handicapped persons in housing, employment, and health insurance. Nonetheless, coercive measures, like mandatory testing of military recruits, did emerge, as predictably did the impulse to find enemies in war. Gay activists often found them in the higher reaches of government; homophobes like Senator Helms regarded gay men as the enemy.

Though designed in part to counter distrust of government, war metaphors also showed this distrust to be deepening in the 1980s. The uses made of the Holocaust suggested that the war metaphor was becoming "appropriated by those who view themselves as victims of the state instead of its beneficiaries." No longer serving only those who wanted to mobilize the state, it now also acquired a "counter-hegemonic function." Propelling that shift were much-observed trends—a "victim" culture and a loss of faith in national government. But more may have been involved. For decades Americans had seen their government accrue in secrecy the ultimate means of destruction and had learned to fear a nuclear war in which victimization awaited the whole world. In the Vietnam War, many came to see themselves as suffering from secretive, dishonest leadership, a theme first nourished on the left but sustained by the Right, especially by those who saw a conspiracy to cover up the plight of POWs in Vietnam. "It is not surprising, therefore, that Americans who feel that they are not being served by their government have determined the state has secretly declared war against them." The bitter legacy of a militarized age shaped the apocalyptic uses of the war metaphor now evident.[60]

Revealing growing distrust of government, the search for war's moral equivalent also deepened that distrust. "War on AIDS," for example, provided a frail basis for mobilizing government or the gay community. Crusades grounded in war's metaphors and models, whether against poverty in the 1960s or drugs in the 1980s, tended to have limited life. Like wars themselves, they bristled with activity and then flamed out, leaving behind a substantial and often repressive bureaucratic and legal residue, and frustration that lofty goals were not met. Talk of war, after all, presumed that victory (or defeat) would follow, and in fairly short order. By 1990 Kramer was giving a lecture called "AIDS: The War Is Lost." Given his model of AIDS as war and holocaust its outcome, he had to make the story end like World War II, when victory or defeat were the only alternatives; he could hardly claim victory. As Sontag noted, the "end-of-the-world rhetoric" about AIDS "offers a stoic, finally numbing contemplation of catastrophe," just as similar rhetoric after the atomic bomb's advent had numbed the citizens that it was supposed to arouse. That a "war on AIDS" might have a different outcome (the stalemate of Korea? the futility of Vietnam?), or might just be a bad metaphor, was hard to conceive.[61]

The search for war's moral equivalent had invited government to pursue quick solutions to chronic problems resistent to speedy resolution. When the inevitable failure, waste, and repression surfaced, many Americans bewailed government's ineffectiveness, finding confirmation of the very weaknesses that had initially inspired their rhetoric. It was a cycle of raised hopes, calls for action, and ensuing disappointment that accounted for much of the cynicism about politics expressed by Americans in the Bush years.

For sure, by then war metaphors displayed such a range of sources, meaning, and gravity, however, that they seemed drained of real content, more thoughtlessly habitual than meaningful. An account of the defeat of Robert Bork's nomination to the Supreme Court was titled *Battle for Justice;* Bork himself referred to "the war to control the legal culture." Chicago mayor Richard Daley proclaimed a "war on rats," and New York mayor David Dinkins proclaimed a "war on fear"—an odd notion, since war usually stokes fear. In that vein, the *Chicago Tribune* claimed that President Bush, after a wave of bombings against civil rights leaders, "vows war on hate," although it never quoted Bush using such words. Health-related war metaphors also continued to spread: columnist Anna Quindlen scoffed at how Bush's health and human services secretary was "waging his war" on tobacco and declared herself "in favor of a War on Cigs, but a real one, with teeth." No wonder that Garrison Keillor imagined the arrest of America's last five cigarette smokers by federal agents who call in "members of a crack anti-smokers jogging unit." War metaphors were applied to a dizzying range of issues and occasions: on its five hundredth anniversary, Columbus's landing in the Americas seemed comparable to the detonation of the first atomic bomb and a steppingstone on "the road to Auschwitz," according to historian David Stannard in *American Holocaust*. In economic affairs, too, experts found their benchmarks in war itself or its aftermath: they proposed a new Marshall Plan to rebuild East European nations freed from Soviet rule, or argued that instead "the U.S. needs a domestic Marshall Plan first."[62] Even sustained metaphors lost clarity: Were Americans waging war on AIDS, or AIDS on them? Was the enemy the virus, the politicians, the doctors, the drug companies, or the people with the disease?

Still, even thoughtless or internally contradictory uses of the war metaphor indicated how ingrained the habit had become of seeing all sorts of causes and crusades as wars. Its use could be thoughtless because no thought seemed necessary to make it work—because the assumption was automatic that "war" was the best way to mobilize Americans and to capture their problems and conflicts. At the least, such language expressed an intensity (or a longing for it) that critics overlooked when they regretted the stale character of politics: many Americans still cared fiercely about politics and government. A politics stripped of metaphor would have expressed little of that intensity. Yet political culture was hardly so uniform that alternatives to war rhetoric were unimaginable—the quilt stitched to memorialize victims of AIDS evoked images of family and folk culture quite different from those embedded in talk of war. Facing their problems, Americans did have recourse to more than the war metaphor.

That it stuck revealed how political culture remained militarized even as war itself seemed to recede. Indeed, war's remoteness to Americans was probably one reason they talked glibly of finding a substitute for it. They had little knowledge of the real thing and, as Soviet-American conflict diminished, less reason to fear it. The slippage of "war" in discourse—signifying international conflict less and less, domestic struggle more and more—was also mirrored in the reluctance of American leadership and media to designate military action abroad as war. Intervention in Lebanon, invasion of Grenada, naval action in the Persian Gulf, invasion of Panama, and the Gulf War itself usually received other labels—Desert Shield/Storm for the biggest of those actions. Almost anything was called a "war," it seemed, except war itself.

Yet even as the war metaphor reflected war's remoteness, it had the potential to make war real and viable again. The search for war's moral equivalent privileged the arena of war itself. It posited something good in war to be extracted from it and applied to other endeavors. It presumed that Americans found purpose only in war, that their state functioned effectively only in a warlike mode, and that the nation knew triumph only in warfare, with World War II still their model in that regard. But if there was something good about war, why should Americans settle for a substitute—why not the real thing, which would mobilize and rejuvenate Americans even more? That was the implicit logic of the war metaphor, one that worked powerfully because it was unspoken. Soon, Americans would have a real war.

War's Last Hurrah?

President Bush did not articulate the war metaphor's logic, but instead the more familiar rules of domestic and international politics. Facing the 1990 Mideast crisis, he thought that a military solution to it would redress a grievous wrong, reaffirm America's global hegemony, reinstate war's utility for the United States, and rescue his political fortunes. As a patrician patriot, he probably thought less about his own fortunes, but "a short, successful war would be pure political gold," his aide John Sununu reportedly believed; it "would guarantee his reelection."[63] In the end, however, the Gulf War served Bush's fortunes badly and his other goals at best partially.

Hardly his doing alone, that war arose out of the Mideast's complex politics and the many American interests there that Washington's leaders perceived. Iraqi ruler Saddam Hussein was a tyrant, ruthless in suppressing minorities like the rebellious Kurds. Still, under Reagan and Bush, the United States (and others, including Britain and West Germany) had allowed economic and military resources to be given or sold to Hussein in order to reap the economic rewards involved and to have Iraq offset Syria and Iran. The Bush administration also sent Hussein ambiguous signals about his designs on the oil-rich kingdom of Kuwait, not foreseeing the form those designs would take and not wanting to antagonize a skittish ally. Iraq's invasion of Kuwait on August 2, 1990, came as a shock but also indicated that misjudgments were widespread: Kuwait had not grasped the danger; Hussein did not foresee the reaction his conquest would elicit.

Such misjudgments, the familiar prelude to war, led to a crisis involving familiar elements of power and interest. Iraq's threat to the flow of Mideast oil was real though exaggerated: to capitalize on his booty Hussein would have to sell Kuwait's oil, and only if he advanced into Saudi Arabia (a remote possibility) would he really control the region's oil. Kuwait's rich and well-placed refugee rulers and their oil-state allies leaned hard on Washington to act. So did Israel's government, long fearful of Hussein. Kuwait's regime hardly deserved rescue as a means to defend democracy, Americans' favorite reason to act, but Iraq had committed aggression across international borders, plus real and alleged atrocities in Kuwait that stirred Bush's indignation.

These familiar interests and arguments emerged, however, in a new environment. Islamic fundamentalism, though never a unitary force, made other Arab leaders nervous about confronting Hussein, who suddenly laid claim to Islamic virtue, and nervous about not confronting him. The Cold War's end neutralized the Soviet Union, long a player in the Mideast, freeing *both* Hussein and Bush to act in ways that would have been unlikely a few years earlier. The Israeli-Palestinian conflict seemed to demand resolution, which American officials argued would be advanced by humbling Hussein.

Of all those factors, the implications of the Cold War's end most influenced Washington's leaders. They feared the loss of American hegemony now that economic power seemed more decisive than military might and that Soviet retreat undercut America's apparent need to lead its allies and to sustain its military superiority. As JCS chairman Gen. Colin Powell reportedly argued in 1989, "We have to put a shingle outside our door saying 'Superpower Lives Here,' no matter what the Soviets do, even if they evacuate from Eastern Europe." As Democratic senator David Boren worried in April 1990, "I don't think that we fully understand [that] the decline of the Soviet Union might lead to our decline as well," because other nations no longer depended on the United States to protect them. That danger seemed especially grave for Bush since he lacked a plan to revive American economic power. "I would not call [the United States] the world's policeman," he said after the Gulf crisis began, and it would not be able "to act or want to act" everywhere. "But we have a disproportionate responsibility for the freedom and the security of various countries." In fact, Bush wanted his nation to remain "the world's policeman," although he was wary of the term. Thus while American interests triggered alarm about Hussein, a deeper concern was to reassert America's role as military superpower— perhaps why Bush offhandedly told reporters, in a remark no one pursued, that he wanted the military draft renewed.[64]

Bush's concern for America's status abroad was strengthened by his wobbly political fortunes at home, where pollsters still detected pessimism about the future, and by his intuitive sense that his destiny lay abroad as America's— indeed all good nations'—commander in chief. He quickly decided to confront Hussein with military force. "This [the invasion of Kuwait] will not stand," he announced on August 5, reaching that conclusion after little consultation (apparently Powell learned of it by watching CNN news). Deployment of American forces to the Mideast went forward, though its objectives remained unclear: perhaps, in concert with economic sanctions against Iraq, it alone would force Hussein to retreat; perhaps war to dislodge him would be necessary. Arguments over which scenario should emerge dominated debate in the fall, but so too did fear that war was inevitable. Bush's "advisers say that he hasn't made a decision to go to war," one journalist reported, "but, of course, that is what they would say." Insiders leaked word that "some officials saw sanctions and diplomacy as the necessary precursors of war," with each only " 'a box to check.' "[65]

Bush had announced on August 20 that "peace is more than just the absence of war." He did not spell out the "more"—the "vision thing" still eluded him— but apparently peace itself might require war. His boast after the war—"By God, we've kicked the Vietnam syndrome once and for all"—came closer to the mark. He meant that Americans were no longer afraid of going to war and military prowess might again be the country's defining feature. He also hinted at another value in war in his many homilies and anecdotes (echoed in media coverage) about the nation's troops: war revealed the virtue and advanced the unity of Americans. To be sure, unity was usually treated by politicians and the media as a means rather than an end—needed so that Americans not again be divided in war. "It's time for America to stand together," declared Sen. Sam Nunn in January, though he opposed Congress's grant of authority to Bush to go to war. But means and ends are hard to distinguish in war: soon Bush celebrated unity as victory's product, not just its instrument.[66]

More striking than his decision to square off against Hussein was his use of World War II analogies to justify it. With Prime Minister Thatcher urging him to be Churchillian, Bush insisted that Hussein's regime, character, and threat were similar to those of Hitler before and during World War II. He often described Iraq's forces as engaged in "blitzkrieg" warfare and repeatedly cited the lessons of the 1930s: "Appeasement does not work," he told the nation; "As was the case in the 1930s, we see in Saddam Hussein an aggressive dictator threatening his neighbors," he claimed; "We're not about to make that same mistake twice," he added on August 15. Implicitly citing Hitler, he saw the world facing "another threat made by . . . a man of evil standing against human life itself." By November he was explicit: Iraqi forces did things "that even Adolf Hitler didn't do," he said, adding days later that "we do not need another Hitler in this time of our century." Hussein's fulminations about Jews added plausibility to comparisons of him to Hitler, ones also made by columnists. "If we don't check this aggression," Bush said in December, "a chance for lasting peace and for stability and security in the Gulf and a new world order will have been . . . forgone. It's that big. It's that important. Nothing like this since World War II. Nothing of this moral importance since World War II."[67]

Overestimates of Hussein's military might—especially his prospects for developing nuclear weapons—flowed logically from Bush's World War II analogy, although Bush's antiwar opponents also exaggerated Hussein's military prowess (and America's weakness). The analogy seemed to foreclose a peaceful end to the crisis—war had been necessary to stop Hitler. It also obscured the role of other nations in making Hussein a menace. His efforts to acquire nuclear weapons, like those of other nations, would have been impossible if nuclear powers had not produced such weapons in obscene volume and sold or given away much of the technology involved.

Bush's historical analogy was strained at best. It made him seem oddly naive—if Hussein was like Hitler, why had Bush failed to recognize earlier his monstrous evil? It clashed with indications that Bush might not seek to destroy Hussein's regime lest Syria or Iran rush into the vacuum—a compromise peace with Hitler was unimaginable. It did violence to the Mideast's complex politics. And it granted Hussein a historical stature that he did not warrant. Mussolini, another serious but second-rate menace with a blustery style, was a more credible analogy.

Part of the problem was that Hussein's invasion was atypical of the post-1945 world, in which aggression across international boundaries (although not civil war) had been rare, leaving World War II a plausible touchstone. Even North Korea's invasion of the South in 1950, which Bush also mentioned, occurred in a divided nation. Closer in nature, politics, and geography to Hussein's action were the various wars involving Israel or the Iran-Iraq war, but those lacked the moral or military gravity Bush wanted to see, and analogies to them were politically impossible since many of the nations involved now willingly or reluctantly joined Bush's coalition. Past wars by China against Tibet and the Soviet Union against Afghanistan were also out of bounds, since Bush sought to enlist Beijing and Moscow in his cause and Gorbachev's government was too fragile to play games with his country's history. For a man who wanted history's sanction and felt his destiny guided by it, it offered few options other than Hitler and World War II.

Strained as it was, Bush's Hitler analogy was unpersuasive to many Americans. His notion that "Saddam Hussein is worse than Hitler," reported Elizabeth Drew, "gave a number of his own advisors a headache. That Bush, a veteran of the Second World War, doesn't get it about Hitler and the feelings he still causes is puzzling."[68] Still, the analogy guided Bush, revealed his worldview, and adhered to the history of American militarization, so tied to World War II. With the Cold War's added layers peeled away, a return to the founding moment made sense.

Trying to recreate the grand alliance of World War II, Bush displayed his greatest skill in assembling a coalition to challenge Hussein. Not only did NATO allies join up, but at greater political risk Egypt, Saudi Arabia, and others, many sending major contingents to the allied force. (Israel, whose military involvement would have inflamed its neighbors, had to be kept on a short leash.) Even the Soviet Union and China said the right things, or avoided saying the wrong ones. Knitting them together was Bush himself, tireless on the telephone and in *Air Force One,* and Secretary of State James Baker, doing what he knew best, calming tempers and brokering deals. The United Nations added legal and political stature to the coalition, although it could not eliminate resentment about America playing cop on the world beat.

But this was not a repeat of the grand coalition of World War II, when the United States had footed much of the bill. Bush knew that few Americans, amid their nation's budget crisis, welcomed spending billions on war. Rich allies (Germany, Japan, exiled Kuwaitis) were tapped for the costs, which in the end they mostly covered, but the undertone of these deals was sour. Allies were treated as if cash were the price they paid for being militarily timid or incompetent, while America's armed forces seemed like mercenaries who might even accrue a profit for America's empty treasury. Bush's success in money raising underlined America's economic weakness. Its gun was to its shoulder, but its hat was in hand.

Bush pressed on, despite problems. Persuasive with allied leaders, at home he erratically articulated his policy for stopping Hussein. "The problem isn't that he hasn't stated some reasons," Drew commented; "the problem is that he jumps about among the reasons"—oil, aggression, Hitler, and, from Baker, "jobs." "He's dealt in slogans; he's campaigned rather than explained." His image of being "steady" in international matters seemed belied, and in his campaign mode for the 1990 elections, he was again "shrill and silly," while many GOP candidates kept their distance from him. Crude outbursts—Hussein is "going to get his ass kicked"—diminished his dignity, feeding speculation that he personalized grave issues and still worried about his "wimp" image. The criticism was premature—Bush got the action against Hussein he wanted and he was "a dogged, resilient figure"—but it did speak to a brittle side of Bush that, doggedly, kept reemerging.[69]

He also pressed on despite the reluctance of seemingly natural allies. Though most conservatives rallied around Bush, they divided sharply. They split over Israel—it was "goading us to attack," fumed Pat Buchanan. The Cold War's end revealed a bigger division, as people like Buchanan lost their taste for global interventionism and decried it in some of the terms the antiwar Left a generation earlier had used. They also seemed to revert to a pre–Cold War "isolationism," though as always the term was simplistic. Many were more unilateralist than isolationist, wary of the entangling alliances Bush assembled. Buchanan heard "the Wilsonian gobbledygook we followed into the trenches of World War I—when, all the time, the hidden agenda was to pull Britain's chestnuts out of the fire." Too, many conservatives doubted Bush's fidelity to their cultural agenda, whose wars they were more eager to wage.[70]

Other conservatives assailed not only the war's necessity but its politics. Columnist Stephen Chapman condemned the conflation of "patriotism" with "militarism," the coercive belief "that the only way to support our troops is to endorse the policies that put them there," and the insistence that dissent stop once war starts: "A war that was stupid the day before it started has not become suddenly wise through the dropping of bombs and the shedding of blood. Anyone in search of the miracle of transubstantiation should look in the Catholic mass, not the Pentagon. . . . Fighting the Vietnam War would have been easier, too, without critics. Without the critics, we might still be fighting it."[71] Similar sentiments were expressed by liberals and leftists, but their emergence at the other end of the political spectrum showed how political alignments of the Cold War era were shifting.

In liberal and leftist circles, opposition was quick to emerge and substantial but also politically isolated (few could see linking arms with the likes of Pat Buchanan), offset by the fear some felt for Israel's fate, and limited by the rush of events. Its thrust was also sometimes wobbly. In their peace marches, students and older citizens (the latter bulked larger than in Vietnam protests) denounced war on Iraq and urged instead "war" on AIDS, homelessness, and poverty, unwittingly reaffirming war's utility. AIDS seemed "the forgotten war" to the *Village Voice* in February; "how can the silent, gray war in the clinic compete with TV cameras built into the heads of missiles?"[72]

That, however, was not the line usually taken by mainstream politicians who supported sanctions but criticized the rush to war. For some, the Iraq-Kuwait conflict lacked moral clarity—"A nasty little country invaded a littler but just as nasty country," said Sen. Daniel Patrick Moynihan—and the benefits of an American victory seemed murky. Moynihan also detected a subtle regression to Cold War thinking, as if "our institutions" were saying, " 'Oh, my God, we missed World War III. Maybe we can have it now here.' . . . Dr. Strangelove, where are you now that we need you?" In contrast, columnist Barbara Ehrenreich foresaw not the Cold War redux but a Panama invasion writ large— which "could be in the long term just about as bad," she added, noting how the Panama operation had failed to dent the drug trade or democratize the liberated land.[73]

Even those supporting military action often condemned Bush's methods and sense of proportion. For strategist Edward Luttwak, Hussein was a "village ruffian" and "Mafia boss" typical of his region's rulers, not deserving "the wild hyperbole" of Bush's "Hitler comparison." Bush, eager to forget mounting fiscal and banking woes, operated "very much in the manner of the aristocrat still disdainful of the tradesmen pleading bills at his door as he sells yet more of the family's broad acres." Hussein's conquest of Kuwait, Luttwak argued, posed a modest problem that Bush should have liquidated by an ultimatum to withdraw, followed by bombing Iraq, rather than by assembling "an army of reconquest."[74]

Luttwak added his voice to the doubt most consistently expressed about Bush's course—not that his effort to corral Hussein was wrong but that his obsession with it, his moralizing about it, and his determination to settle it by a big war were grossly out of proportion to the issues involved and dangerously neglectful of economic problems the nation faced. "War against Iraq will be the most unnecessary war in American history," opined Arthur Schlesinger, Jr.[75] Others saw a different sign of Bush's disproportionate, or hypocritical, policy: he claimed to operate under United Nations mandate but ignored the mandates that applied to Israel's occupation of territory it had seized in war.

Among military officials, doubts about Bush's course were more muted, expressed in the measured ways expected of them. Still, by one account, the Pentagon was "the most cautious player in the Gulf policy mix" and Bush "the most hard-line." In October, JCS Chairman Powell reportedly wanted a "containment or strangulation policy," but Bush responded, "I don't think there's time politically for that strategy." War would resolve the matter; "strangulation" of Iraq might take years, although as it turned out, "strangulation" resumed once war ended. Nearly every recent defense secretary and a parade of retired officers—including former JCS chairs Adm. William Crowe and Gen. David Jones—voiced reluctance to go to war. And Gen. Norman Schwarzkopf, who would lead the troops, publicly castigated the rush to war: given "evidence that the sanctions are pinching, . . . why should we say, 'Okay, gave 'em two months, didn't work. Let's get on with it and kill a whole bunch of people?' That's crazy."[76]

To be sure, officers' reluctance was in part a tactic to leverage a large armed force and a strong political mandate so that they could avoid Vietnam's trap and gain a sure victory. Resistance to war making often arises from specific considerations as well as flat-out principles, however, and with the military it also went beyond the moment. Powell reputedly admired Eisenhower's caution as President about making war. In pointed words for an officer who had served Reagan and Bush, Crowe publicly doubted that the question to ask was "whether Saddam Hussein is brutal, deceitful, or as Barbara Bush would put it, a dreadful man," and thought "it would be a sad commentary if Saddam Hussein, a two-bit tyrant, . . . proved to be more patient than the United States, the world's most affluent and powerful nation."[77] There was also a generational difference. World War II shaped Bush's view of war. For most military officials, Vietnam loomed larger.

It also loomed large in December and January as debate intensified about a war that now seemed inevitable. Particularly in Congress, debate was both insightful and irrelevant. It came too late, after war's engines already had been fueled, to affect the outcome, especially since Bush made it clear that he sought Congress's sanction for political reasons—to avoid a repetition of Vietnam's divisions—rather than constitutional ones, feeling free to wave aside the much-disputed War Powers Act and to make war without Congress. For their part, many Congressmen were reluctant to be counted, chiding Bush for not "consulting" them but eager to have him bear the decision-making burden. Moreover, their debate often focused on whether the circumstances for waging war against Iraq resembled those in Vietnam—"This will not be another Vietnam," Bush had promised on November 30[78]—but those circumstances were so different that this focus made it hard to address what now was at stake. And as in the Vietnam era, debate focused on whether this war could be, rather than needed to be, won. Even the striking rhetorical and substantive flair of Congress's debate seemed to lubricate the path to war, as if by being high-toned and troubled about it, Americans proved their maturity, their readiness to take on this serious burden.

The unsurprising outcome was a resolution (not a declaration of war) authorizing Bush to use force. It passed by small margins on January 12, with Congress dividing largely on partisan lines, but with Democrats like Les Aspin and Al Gore providing key support. Still, no congressional debate about going to war of this depth and division had taken place since 1917, indicating that the President no longer had quite the free hand his predecessors had wielded and that war was too serious for the nation to inch its way into it.

More often than not, however, Bush seemed simply to ignore the doubts raised, perhaps in part because the objection most persuasive to a politician—that he risked political peril—was hardly offered. Almost everyone agreed that he would profit politically from war, at least from a quick, victorious one (a forgotten voice, George McGovern's, warned that Churchill's electoral defeat at the end of World War II "could happen to Bush").[79] It was a curious assumption given the fate of modern war Presidents, not one of whom survived politically the waging of major war (FDR, of course, died before war's surly aftermath set in). It was tied to another dated assumption—that "a President has a better chance of influencing events abroad than at home," whereas (so two political scientists argued after the Gulf War) declining "American hegemony" now meant that "other nations have the capacity to exchange influence with the White House."[80] But of course it was such decline that Bush hoped to arrest.

On January 16, 1991, allied warplanes began attacking Iraq and its positions in Kuwait, beginning what Hussein called "the mother of all battles." "The liberation of Kuwait has begun," announced the President's press secretary; this was not even to be called a "war," though if it was, Bush insisted it "started August 2," since he took no responsibility for initiating it.[81]

Allied—primarily American—aerial action dominated the war's opening weeks, and its sensational fireworks, as portrayed for and perceived by Americans at home, did much to erase the grave mood felt on war's eve. The spectacle on television of cruise missiles racing toward Baghdad, of "smart" bombs with nose cameras homing in on their targets, of Stealth bombers going into action, imparted a glitzy, high-tech dimension to the war; the formidable destruction unleashed by older B-52s rarely made it to the screen. The advent of Iraqi Scud missile attacks on Israel and Saudi Arabia was worrisome since allied forces had trouble stopping them, but they added to the video spectacular and provided a welcome touch of parity to the aerial contest—it would not be so one-sided as to render victory meaningless. The Scud attacks (and Iraq's firing and dumping of oil in and offshore Kuwait) also seemed to right the moral scales just when they threatened to tip over, offsetting criticism that allied bombing was inflicting heavy casualties on Iraqi civilians. So too did media and official complaints, recalling World War II notions of Japanese trickery, that Hussein played nasty games—piling bodies before the cameras, disguising a strategic factory as "Baby Milk Plant," billeting commanders in schools—as if propaganda and deception were outside war's rules and unknown to American war making.

Long the first resort for the United States in war, air power's use reawakened familiar themes: it would eliminate the costly ground war many feared, display anew America's superior technology, and reveal its moral superiority by securing quick victory with minimal damage. Bush stirred many of these themes in a flag-bedecked appearance before Raytheon workers who made the Patriot missiles that intercepted Scuds—patriotism, divine blessing, and technological prowess were parts of the same whole: "Thank God for the Patriot missile.

Thank God for that missile."[82] Star Wars was vindicated, he added (a judgment few experts shared).

Air power also kept war at a satisfying psychic distance for Americans, but that distance was troubling if Americans felt no sense of risk and involvement: war that was *too* easy and mechanical would be drained of the peril and passion that made it meaningful. Here, too, the Scud attacks played a vital role. As they rained down on Israel, most of them traced by television cameras, many Americans evinced a sense of vicarious participation in war, as if they were on the front lines—Tel Aviv playing in 1991 the role London had played in 1941. Stateside Americans could erase the distance and still maintain it: war's enduring remoteness was overcome in imagination even as it was sustained in reality. Not only was television coverage of the war extensive, so was the talk about it, complete with claims that this was the first television war. Since similar claims had been made about the Vietnam War, they revealed—as in that war—a need to express a closeness to war that in fact was eerily mediated by television and made strangely ephemeral by it.

The old dream of swift, sanitary, satisfying victory through air power was vindicated, according to many observers. Vengeance was wreaked on the enemy—yet not so brutally, they thought, that consciences had to be troubled, and with stunningly little loss of American lives. At times, it hardly seemed to be war but instead, as the *Chicago Tribune* described the opening aerial assaults, "the largest military air show ever displayed." "High technology," claimed reporter R. W. Apple, "sets this war apart from Vietnam," even though such technology had been celebrated in that war. When allied ground forces gained a quick victory, the stock of air power soared still higher. It was now "the *determinant of victory* in war," one cheerleading historian soon argued.[83]

But final pronouncements on its vindication were unwarranted. Allied air forces operated ably but in ideal circumstances—with overwhelming superiority, in desirable climatic and strategic conditions, against a politically isolated second-rate power, not against the Warsaw Pact armada once imagined as the enemy. For all his bluster, Hussein may never intended to wage a do-or-die war but to put up a good show and position himself as Arab martyr, although, to be sure, that may have been because allied sanctions and military power kept him from waging extended war. Lavish assessments of bombing's surgical accuracy diminished under later scrutiny, the superiority of newer weapons like the B-1 bomber over older ones like the B-52 receded, and the toll for Iraqi civilians—from direct destruction, and even more because the bombing degraded their economic, medical, and sanitary systems—was large despite the war's brevity. Too, a ground war still had to be fought and Hussein stayed in power—because the allies hesitated to topple him, but also because the bombs did not scare him away or set most of his people after him.

One war proved relatively little for—or for that matter against—air power. Still, pundits soon proclaimed the advent of "postmodern" war in which high-tech weaponry "could minimize the shedding of American blood while maximizing the destruction on the other side"; war "now consists of short, quick actions that take days to complete, not months or years."[84] Such predictions reflected the old dream that American hegemony could proceed effortlessly. Soon, Yugoslavia's war showed distressingly few "postmodern" features. The Gulf War could be a model for future American military action only if the nation avoided most wars.

More astonishing than the air war was the triumph of allied ground forces at the end of February (though no one claimed that ground war was now ascendant). They rolled through Iraqi defenses in and near Kuwait with stunning ease, and American casualties, numbering in the dozens, had not been so light since the Spanish-American War. Indeed, the war threatened to become an unseemly massacre of Iraqis—American soldiers' descriptions of a "turkey shoot" and "shooting fish in a barrel" (phrases used to describe American action against the Japanese late in World War II) also expressed their unease.[85] The skill of Schwarzkopf and his forces, and the use of tactical air power— overlooked at the time, but more critical to victory than bombs on Baghdad— did much to account for success. So did the state of the Iraqi army, battle-tested but also badly bled after its long war with Iran; the administration's designation of it as the world's fourth-largest had been misleading (size alone hardly determines fighting ability). High-level decisions on both sides also kept the ground war short: Hussein chose not to let his army bleed long, and Bush chose not to pursue it far.

Pride, relief, and jubilation—sincere, media-stoked, and commercially exploited—washed over America after the "hundred-hour war" on the ground, as it was often called. Much of the mood involved sheer reveling in war and victory; "Desert Storm" was already becoming "Desert Party" before it was over, worried one columnist. Occasionally that included crude sentiments about the enemy; one political cartoon featured "Stormin' Norman's 4 Star Extermination" truck, with General Schwarzkopf depositing a rat into a garbage can. But the war was too short, and perhaps the memory of ugly sentiments in earlier wars too keen, to foster many dehumanizing portrayals of the enemy.[86]

The dominant mood was more diffuse and upbeat. "Bush was Caesar," Sidney Blumenthal later noted; "his popularity rating hit ninety per cent, the highest ever recorded for a President." In Washington he saluted General Schwarzkopf, "marching before thousands of lockstepping troops," while "Independence Mall was a theme park of military technology." A corollary to the celebration of military prowess was its extrapolation into the future. With the ghost of Vietnam vanquished ("It's Vietnam revisited as it should have been— Vietnam: The Movie, Part II, and this time it comes out right," commented one historian), Americans would resume their rightful place as the world's supreme warriors. Confusingly, Bush both confirmed and challenged that expectation. America's "reestablished credibility" would deter future wars, he claimed, but added that it was "time to turn away from the temptation to protect unneeded weapons systems and obsolete bases" and noted that "even the new world order cannot guarantee an era of perpetual peace."[87]

Americans, however, rarely had gloried in military prowess as an end in itself, insisting instead that it serve higher purposes. Two seemed obvious to the war's champions in March 1991. Americans had "fought for the just and moral cause of freeing the enslaved, brutalized people of a helpless country," argued one columnist. "We came here," a serviceman wrote from Saudi Arabia, "to protect the freedom of the people of Kuwait and Saudi Arabia. Freedom is for everyone around the world, not just Americans." "Who says wars never solve anything?" asked another columnist—not those who now foresee "a new, Saddam-free Iraq," a "new Middle East order," and "real peace between Israel and her neighbors."[88]

More insistently, however, celebrants cheered what the war revealed for and about Americans rather than its benefits for other people. "In 100 hours," claimed columnist Ann McFeatters, "George Bush and his band of able assistants," and the "young men and women" abroad she applauded, "restored America's can-do spirit. . . . It felt good to win." "It is as if all the confusion and pain of recent decades have melted," noted the *New York Times*, "leaving the nation with its reassuring images from World War II intact." Conservatives who embraced the war felt vindicated: it proved the wisdom of Reagan's weapons programs. "The moral chasm between us and our enemy couldn't be a wider," a columnist added, and moral rearmament had succeeded: "We sure are doing something very right in the moral education department. We are raising men and women who are not too soft to fight when necessary, but who do not take unseemly pleasure in the suffering they must inflict."[89]

It spoke volumes about their moods that many Americans thought it took war to restore and reveal "America's can-do spirit." It exposed anew the driving element of American war making since the Vietnam era—to address Americans' sense of themselves more than their place in the world or the evils in it they sought to combat. And it revealed again how they saw their nation as able to act purposefully and effectively only in war. To be sure, policymakers also calculated power and interest, but there was no mistaking Bush's sincerity when he proclaimed on March 6 that "the brave men and women of Desert Storm . . . set out to confront an enemy abroad, and in the process, they transformed a nation at home. . . . Think about their sense of duty, about all they taught us about our values, about ourselves."[90]

Along with critics' marginalization, the war's remoteness facilitated the rush of such claims. Since "we don't have direct experience" of war, historian Robert Dallek remarked, "there's an openness about the meanings we give to it," making it "a blank slate." "We have lost some sense of the true reality of war," another expert noted, so Americans can "talk very blithely about war."[91] Of course, war's "true reality" is not necessarily combat but whatever people experience—for most Americans, the Gulf War's reality had been the charged emotions and images it elicited. That was so less for the reasons often noted at the time—the advance of media technology or the vise of official censorship—than because of the war's brevity and ease. No new taxes or war-bond drives, no vexing inflation or shortages, no wearisome political debate or troublesome news intervened to connect stateside experience to events abroad. Only words and images remained, with which the imagination had free play.

Since war had shown America's "can-do" spirit, the process of tapping that spirit for peacetime purposes resumed. Chicago mayor Richard Daley asked President Bush to put General Schwarzkopf in charge of a renewed war on drugs: "The general would bring an attitude of 'Forget all the politicians because we're going to protect Americans first,'" Daley argued. Others soon proposed using the demobilized troops in campaigns against crime, drugs, illiteracy, or poverty. Democratic senator Tom Daschle had "this dream," as the *New York Times* paraphrased it: "Now that the war is over, the Government and the news media begin to focus on domestic problems with the same intensity they gave the Persian Gulf." Economist Robert Reich, soon to join Bill Clinton's Cabinet, urged a "vast investment" in America's work force: "It needs the political equivalent of a warrior like Gen. Norman Schwarzkopf to propose a plan for rebuilding America, as Gen. George Marshall did 44 years ago for rebuilding Western Europe."[92]

Bush seized this line of reasoning as avidly as anyone, though bending it to different purposes. Noting the Gulf War's "clear-cut objectives" and "overriding imperative to achieve results," on March 6 he lectured the cheering luminaries assembled in Congress and the millions of Americans watching on television: "We must bring that same sense of self-discipline, that same sense of urgency, to the way we meet challenges here at home." He urged passage of his major domestic initiatives, a crime bill and funding for road construction: "If our forces could win the ground war in 100 hours, then surely the Congress can pass this legislation in 100 days." If Americans could "selflessly confront evil" abroad, he added, "then surely we can make this land all it should be."[93]

Yet by April the euphoria—and Bush's popularity—were dissipating. Even at the moment of victory, Bush had seemed out of focus—eager to celebrate but also at loose ends, as he had been at the end of the Cold War. Reporters again noticed that he seemed "somber," and Bush admitted, "I haven't yet felt this wonderfully euphoric feeling that many of the American people feel." He was pleased by "a new, wonderful sense of patriotism" and happy that "there isn't any antiwar movement out there." But sensing something missing, he pointed to "World War II; there was a definitive end to that conflict."[94] He had in mind the Mideast's unresolved problems but also seemed restless without a war to wage.

His immediate problem was that war's achievements turned out to be limited and his leadership again lackluster. His decision to let Hussein stay in power and to backpedal from noisily urging Iraqis to overthrow him mocked his earlier claim that Hussein was Hitler's moral equal. His reluctance to intervene on behalf of Shiites and Kurds, who had rebelled against Hussein and suffered mightily at the hands of his army, raised the same problem (similar to Eisenhower's when he sat out the 1956 Hungarian revolution). Bush's inaction unleashed a torrent of moral indignation against him and suggested that the man who had "kicked the Vietnam syndrome" now was gripped by it himself. The spectacle of Kuwait's returning rulers casting out thousands of Palestinian and other guest workers tarnished his claim to have liberated that country. No "new world order" took shape and it was unclear whether Bush had any idea what it would entail, beyond continued American hegemony; he soon discarded the phrase. The promise that victory would help resolve Israeli-Arab conflict also seemed exaggerated. The Iraqis had been thrown out of Kuwait, but other than that this moral equivalent of World War II had ambiguous results.

The ensuing letdown was in good part Bush's fault. His World War II analogy set up Americans to expect total victory, something he was unable or unwilling to deliver. Perhaps admirable by other criteria, his caution regarding further intervention in Iraq—soon continued under United Nations aegis, but only to protect Kurds in a northern enclave—failed the test of his own rhetoric.

The presumed moral and military efficacy of America's war making also receded in the spring. Bush's pre-August policy of appeasing Hussein met tough criticism. Reassessment also focused on the necessity of slaughtering so many Iraqi soldiers—one hundred thousand dead and three hundred thousand wounded by Defense Intelligence Agency estimates—and on the damage to conditions for Iraqi civilians (it was clear they were not liberated). Praise for American weaponry also became more muted. Most of the bombs, it turned out, had not been the precision-guided ordnance featured in media coverage, and some glitzy weapons like the Patriot (actually an older technology) had performed less ably than thought. This was no "antiseptic Nintendo game" or "surgical war," concluded one early review; "it was a slaughter." Meanwhile, some of Hussein's atrocities were verified but others turned out to be trumped up, by the propaganda machine of Kuwait's exiled rulers, among others. Nor did the carping come only from the antiwar Left. The war's conservative opponents weighed in again, and NBC's low-key John Chancellor, writing in the *New York Times*, acidly commented on earlier predictions that "Iraq might actually use fuel-air explosives, a horrible weapon of almost nuclear potency. When the fighting began, the country that did use fuel-air explosives was the U.S., and nobody complained."[95]

Reassessment usually follows wars; whether it discredited this war was in the eye of the beholder. But because praise of American war making had soared so high and then the war ended so quickly, reappraisal rubbed the luster off this victory more quickly than after most wars. A squabble between Bush and his generals dulled it more. Bush was reportedly pounding the table in fury at reports that they had resisted his recourse to war and that he had halted their march through Iraq short of the final blow to Hussein's forces. Schwarzkopf, in a celebrated television interview, claimed that his "recommendation had been . . . continue the march. I mean, we had them in a rout," though in February Powell had apparently regarded a further rout as "unchivalrous."[96] Vietnam still echoed: once more, it seemed, a civilian had denied the generals victory.

Indeed, the demise of the "Vietnam syndrome" seemed prematurely declared. The POW/MIA mythology continued to fester, with Bush himself accused by an angry crowd of not doing enough to find Americans in Vietnam (and, as CIA director, of participating in the alleged cover-up). More than that, the Gulf War had been too unlike the Vietnam War to prove much; brevity was both its virtue and its limitation in that regard. Bush himself had noted before it began that if it were long, "I think support would erode, as it did in the Vietnam conquest—I mean, conflict."[97] Aside from that notable slip of the tongue, Bush indicated the limits of burying Vietnam—what if protracted war occurred again? Just such a war seemed to loom with Hussein still dealing out misery to Kurds and others, and soon when Americans considered intervention in Yugoslavia's civil war. Like most of them, Bush was gun-shy.

There was more to Bush's problems than war's murky aftermath and his ineptitude dealing with it, however. The very elements of this war that elicited jubilation also robbed it of lasting satisfaction and significance. The ease of victory, against an enemy seemingly reluctant to fight and incompetent when it did, stripped the war of that gravity of sacrifice and achievement that embeds a war in language and memory and establishes it as a model of concerted national action. The war soon seemed transient, forgettable—not *substantial* enough to change the course of the nation and the world. Bush had asked Americans to see it like World War II, but it lacked such meaning for them. It was a fantasy war seen on television, with all the staying power of a television show—vivid as long as the screen flickered, gone once the television sets were turned off. It lacked legs—in politics, diplomacy, economics, even the imagination.

So the language and analogies it spawned turned out to be few and fleeting. Hussein's phrase "the mother of all battles" sparked a flood of jokes, then vanished. One of many products keyed to the war, Desert Shield Condoms ("designed with the hardened veteran in mind") lacked commercial staying power.[98] By the summer of 1991, the calls (never numerous anyway) to turn the Gulf War's spirit toward stateside problems faded, although Bush persisted with them. The war metaphor itself was oddly absent, at least its inspirational form calling for governmental action, not so much dispelled as bankrupted by real war. The Gulf War was sufficient to debase its old currency but insufficient to issue a new one.

The war's unifying effects also proved transient. Bush and others celebrated those effects, especially among American soldiers, but unity dissolved as soon as war ended. Bush himself was deaf to the social issues involved. Asked in December 1990 whether "a disproportionate number of U.S. troops stationed on the front line hail from minorities and the working class," he had given an angry, incomprehensible answer.[99] Even buoyed by victory, he only uttered platitudes about not hating each other.

Again, the fault was not his alone: war is a bad healer. In this case, conservatives took the lead in rubbing old wounds, either resenting how the war had set aside their cultural agenda or emboldened by the war to advance it anew. They resumed their attack on abortion, the NEA, gay rights, and "political correctness." In April, columnist George Will captured the thrust of this attack when he linked the Gulf War to the "low visibility, high-intensity war" against the Left waged by Lynne Cheney, the NEA chair and defense secretary's spouse. She "is secretary of domestic defense. The foreign adversaries her husband, Dick, must keep at bay are less dangerous, in the long run, than the domestic forces with which she must deal. Those forces are fighting against the conservation of the common culture that is the nation's social cement."[100] Precisely the attitude that Barry Goldwater had long feared seemed more baldly than ever at the surface of American life.

The new fury over political correctness was rich with history, irony, and obfuscation. A struggle over "PC" activism had gone on for years, another skirmish in the supposed "culture wars" of the 1980s. If political correctness had any meaning, it involved efforts to develop multicultural curricula in schools and to ban "hate speech" at some college campuses. To its critics, it comprised the sweeping agenda of a monolithic, feminist-dominated Left, although in few places was it a decisive force, since those deemed to be on the left disagreed mightily with each other.

Nonetheless, Bush condemned the Left's "boring politics of division and derision," the very politics he had practiced, and conservatives saw their backs to the wall after a decade of Republican rule and a war many had championed. They inveighed against the Left's ideological rigidity after years of hardening their own test of politicians' views on abortion and other issues, and just when the Left was in disarray. Though "really a marginal movement," political correctness was "treated as if it's what universities are all about," one university official correctly noted, and despite its alleged power, it met attack from mainstream media and liberal intellectuals as well as conservatives. Critics were also humorless, failing to recognize that "political correctness" was an in-joke used by liberals and leftists to chide each other and lament their differences.[101]

But this struggle had long confounded all parties. Few in 1991 recognized that its renewal was partly linked to the Gulf War: to its passions and sour aftermath; to the return of rituals like flag waving and homecoming parades evoking an earlier era of white male dominance; to victory over an Arab enemy and by implication over non-Western values; and to the Left's marginality during the war. Operation Desert Storm preceded "Operation Campus Storm," noted one of the few astute observers of the controversy, arguing that the Western culture defended by conservatives as timeless and apolitical was in part a product of ideological mobilization during the world wars. Failing to see such things, all parties paid homage to the Gulf War's curious transience—they talked as if the war had never happened, but acted very much as if it had.[102]

To be sure, war's satisfactions did not immediately vanish. In June 1991, victorious troops marched down Manhattan's streets, greeted by "a magnificent blizzard of ticker tape, patriotism and affection." *Time* took that occasion to reaffirm that even if "the gulf still burns," what was important was not how the war changed the Mideast but how it changed "the way Americans think about themselves and what their country has achieved by war." Perhaps "the great postwar party now in progress is more a mark of national maturity than of smugness and jingoism." As *Time* defined it, "maturity" included Americans' willingness to go to war, leavened by their "healthy cynicism about the chance of bringing lasting peace to an ancient war zone." Above all, the celebrants cheered "the return of American competence." The war, according to one public opinion expert, banished Americans' doubt about their economic and technological prowess "in a profound way that will be long lasting, well past the year 2000." Yet coverage of the "postwar party" was strained. *Time*'s editors felt enjoined to explain why the party lasted longer than the war itself, which "didn't amount to a bad weekend in Vietnam," one veteran of that war noted. Covering his city's parade, a *New York Times* reporter alternated purple prose about the exultation with acid comments—that, for example, "many Americans could not find triumph in the conquest of a nation with the gross national product of Kentucky."[103]

June's celebrations were faded memories when the next furor broke out, this one pitting two black Yale Law School graduates against each other. Bush's nomination of Clarence Thomas to the Supreme Court was under fire but apparently destined to prevail until Thomas's former subordinate, Anita Hill, reluctantly brought charges of sexual harassment against him. The Senate Judiciary Committee's hearings in October stirred a potent brew of racial, gender, and sexual issues. The following spring saw much of Los Angeles aflame in a riot triggered by the acquittal of policemen accused of assaulting black motorist Rodney King. The riots raised the specter of "race war," though most Americans, having used war as a metaphor for other issues, avoided it with regard to their deepest social division. Moreover, that division seemed more complex, no longer a simple black-white fissure as rioters displayed many colors and blacks and Latinos took after Asian-Americans as well as whites.

Both ugly moments were treated, wrongly, as detached from the Gulf War and militarization's course. The war had colored gender relations, yielding familiar renderings of war as a male arena. During autumn's build-up of forces, the media had noted the role of women in the armed forces and as expert commentators, but once "the serious business of combat had begun," women "slid further off the page; only their yellow ribbons caught the public eye." (In a big *Chicago Tribune* photo wrap-up on the war, only three military women, one cradling a teddy bear, appeared among the pictures of heroic men, and no women on the enemy's side.) The victory celebrations were largely a male affair, focused on the American potency presumably shown in the war. No direct line ran between those moods and events to follow—the Hill-Thomas hearings and the Tailhook affair, in which male navy personnel assaulted fellow servicewomen. Yet every modern American war had strengthened proscriptions on or hostilities to women. It seems unlikely that this war was an exception, though its brevity limited its force in that regard. The war did lead to another expansion of women's roles in the armed forces, but the military's goal seemingly was "to absorb just enough of the changes in women's expectations and influence to permit it to use women without drastically altering its own political mission"— or gender inequalities generally.[104]

Connections to the Gulf War were more obvious in the case of the Los Angeles riots. The area was reeling from defense cutbacks that soured the outlook of many social groups. Lakewood's white middle-class residents had rested their livelihoods and their sense of purpose and place on McDonnell Douglas ("It's a town on the plantation model," one local noted, "Douglas being the big house"). In the shadow of corporate "cathedrals of the Cold War," they "believed their companies to be consecrated to what they construed as the national interest, and to deserve, in turn, the nation's unequivocal support." When the defense boom went bust, "it was their adolescent males, only recently the community's most valued asset, who were most visibly left with nowhere to go" and found a substitute in the Spur Posse gang that terrorized local children and abused girls sexually.[105]

Most black Angelenos had less far to fall but also less to cushion the blow, and even more reason to contrast their plight to the triumphal mood unleashed by the war. True, General Powell was hailed as showing what black men could achieve. President Bush asked West Point cadets to look around them: "People divided by race and religion? No." In fact "the military," Powell showed, was "the greatest equal opportunity employer around."[106] But beyond the hint of tokenism in that statement, as the military shrank, it offered fewer opportunities for poor and minority men and women, and its example no longer guided other institutions—what had once been a mighty beachhead for racial progress now seemed a remote outpost. That American leaders extolled racial equality in the military still sent the disturbing message that equality counted there because it served national power, and elsewhere was less important. And of course race riots had accompanied most American wars, each heightening the tension between the declared pursuit of freedom abroad and tolerance of inequalities at home. Now, however, that tension arose in straitened fiscal and political circumstances, whereas post–World War II abundance had underwritten racial reform. The fortunes of African-Americans were troubled for many reasons, but among them was the dissolution of the Cold War that had provided them political and ideological leverage. The result was the spectacle of billions spent to free Kuwait's rulers from exile, while pockets were declared empty for Americans' mounting problems—a contrast pointed out by some Los Angeles rioters and victims (and again when Hurricane Andrew devastated Florida in 1992 and floods swept the upper Mississippi valley in 1993).

Yet the connections between war and Americans' internal difficulties were fewer, thinner, and briefer after the Gulf War than in the aftermath of earlier wars, and not only because of its brevity. Despite the war, militarization—as state policy if not state of mind—was slowly contracting, no longer providing an arena of the size it once had for making such linkages. The Gulf War's aftermath thus exposed the autonomy of issues of race, gender, and other social divisions—as issues in themselves, not just as matters to settle in order to strengthen national power. Those issues always had that autonomy, of course, just as their connections—being ones of perception as much as reality—to militarization hardly disappeared in 1991. Still, the overriding framework that national security once provided—for Truman's order desegregating the armed forces, for example, or even for conflict over feminism in the 1970s—was not there. Insofar as militarization still defined Americans' internal conflicts, it did so less because of its dominating presence than because of its distasteful residue—of emotions, words, and, especially for regions that once thrived on militarization, economic woes.

The Gulf War also exposed Bush's political weakness: He "was a war President unlike any other since Polk; all the rest, from Lincoln through Nixon, had consistently believed in the efficacy of government." Bush's Reaganesque denial of that efficacy at home "after deploying the military abroad was the very soul of contradiction," and one reason that the war brought him "a victory from which he never recovered." His popularity collapsed when he seemed to have no idea what to do without a war. A mission was not hard for many Americans to envision—solutions to problems of debt, competitiveness, and health care were often mentioned—but Bush could not engage these issues. As recession continued and trade and budget deficits swelled, he floundered. Since the war had established him as a strong leader, critics asked why he did not lead at home. As an administration official said after the 1992 election: "Voters thought he was very effective" in foreign policy. "If he wanted to, he could solve their problems. When he didn't, it made them resentful." Bush came across as callous; clearly he had the capacity to lead (look at the war!) but did not care to do so at home. War had "inflated the illusion of omnipotence—and then punctured it."[107]

He kept trying, but his State of the Union address in January 1992, billed as the occasion to restart his presidency, failed to do so. He issued familiar injunctions to remain strong: "We cannot repeat the mistakes made twice in this century, when armistice was followed by recklessness and defense was purged as if the world were permanently safe." Continued if more prudent militarization was his opening theme. Then, in an oddly indifferent way—"And now to our troubles at home"—he shifted to the nation's economic troubles but could not leave war behind: "I know we're in hard times. But I know something else. This will not stand," the last phrase being his line after Iraq's invasion of Kuwait (he repeated it near the end of the address). He tried to use the Gulf War to build support for his economic programs: "We can bring the same courage and sense of common purpose to the economy that we brought to Desert Storm. And we can defeat hard times together." If Congress failed to pass his legislation by March 20, then "the battle is joined." But invoking the Gulf War did not work. That war seemed almost forgotten, and many Americans, accurately or not, thought Bush had no program for dealing with economic problems.[108]

Those troubles involved a mild, meandering recession which the war's confidence-building victory did not halt. In the long run, they were also global— other Western economies were faltering, many more than America's—and structural, tied to ebbing defense outlays. The war strengthened the Pentagon's claim on the defense budget, whose decline after the mid-1980s was slower than after the Second, Korean, and Vietnam Wars, but dependence on defense monies was now more entrenched and regionally concentrated, so that the cumulative effects of even modest declines mounted, above all in California. Politicians and regional interests accepted the broad drift of demilitarization but sought damage control for their districts, so that politics focused on redistributing the pain, not on underlying dynamics. In 1992, Bill Clinton and billionaire independent candidate Ross Perot addressed those dynamics, but cautiously in Clinton's case, erratically in Perot's. Bush added to his problems by pretending there was no issue, leaving him in a political no-man's land: he could hardly blame economic woes whose existence he denied on a course of demilitarization he refused to admit was being taken.

All he could do was assail Democrats for fiscal imprudence and failure to pass his legislation, and return to the "culture war." That meant an awkward alliance with Pat Buchanan, his foe in the GOP primaries. "All the institutions of the Cold War," Buchanan had said in announcing his candidacy, "must be reexamined," a bolder declaration than any Democrat made. As for Bush, "He is yesterday." But Buchanan wanted to redeploy those institutions to the culture war as much as dismantle them. In May he heard the sounds of the Los Angeles rioters as "the authentic laughter of the barbarian"—comparable to noises once made by Nazi "Brown Shirts" and communist "Red Guards"—and charged that privileged forces sought to destroy "Judeo-Christian culture." He admired General Schwarzkopf and his troops, but "as America's imperial troops guard frontiers all over the world, our own frontiers are open, and the barbarian is inside the gates." At the GOP convention in August, Bush operatives desperate for allies gave Buchanan a national stage. He proclaimed "a religious war" and "a cultural war, as critical to the kind of nation we shall be as the Cold War itself, for this war is for the soul of America." In it, Bill and Hillary Clinton "are on the other side, and George Bush is on our side." Just as troops had retaken Los Angeles's streets after the riots, "we must take back *our* cities, and take back *our* culture and take back *our* country." Others were no less pointed: keynoter Phil Gramm and evangelist Pat Robertson compared Clinton and the Democrats to communists; denunciations of gay rights and paeans to "family values" were routine (but music from Broadway's gay-themed *La Cage aux Folles* swelled as the Bush and Quayle families marched to the podium).[109]

"By virtue of his political weakness," Bush "found himself waging a Kulturkampf that autumn," despite evidence that it had backfired at the convention. Since Buchanan was a poisonous figure, Bush made Dan and Marilyn Quayle his deputy commanders. "The only combat Dan Quayle ever experienced was in the Kulturkampf," but in it "he proved a hero." Like other Republicans, the Quayles worked a vague but charged divide: foes of the Vietnam War, gays and feminists and single mothers, and the "cultural elite" (though Quayle's publishing family belonged to it) were responsible for everything from economic decline to the poverty of children to Los Angeles's racial cauldron. Despite his own office and twelve years of GOP rule, Quayle saw himself as "playing David to the Goliath of the dominant cultural elite." The thrust of conservatism was never more evident: war abroad was for show, war at home was serious; enemies abroad were secondary, those at home more dangerous; American decline was a fiction pedaled by America-bashers, though they were also responsible for it; needed was "not just economic, not just political, but cultural change," as Quayle put it. In retirement, Barry Goldwater, backing a gay-rights law for Phoenix and women's right to abortions (they have "been going on ever since man and woman have lived together"), saw his estrangement from conservatism's dominant wing deepen.[110]

As part of their "Kulturkampf," Bush and his allies "waged generational war." He "used the Second World War and the Cold War as his reservoirs of experience for attacking Clinton as draft dodger and Moscow tourist." On occasion he pulled from those wars something positive, offering a "G.I. bill for kids" to help families pay for children to attend private schools, awkwardly comparing it to the 1944 GI Bill (only if kids were veterans of the "culture war" could this analogy work). More often those reservoirs spewed poison. One Bush friend on the campaign trail, tapping Cold War images of homosexuality (and canceling out Clinton's image as womanizer), called Clinton "a sissy. . . . You can tell how he walks. . . . Watch as he kind of swishes his rear end."[111] Bush raised the specter of a future war—though all candidates dealt gingerly with the ongoing one in Yugoslavia—to charge that Clinton lacked the experience and manliness to be president.

Finally, Bush ran as commander in chief. His television ads late in October featured scenes from the Gulf War and his leadership in it, and ended, in white letters against an ominous dark background: *"President Bush, Commander in Chief."* But commander in chief of what? The ad did not specify the armed forces, as if he were commander in chief of all Americans, who were obligated to follow his orders. And against whom? With no enemy abroad, at least none he wanted to engage, this was a hollow image. He had no war to wage except against Clinton and all he presumably stood for—and against Perot, whom Bush hated even more. Bush got 38 percent of the popular vote, less than any sitting President since Taft, though with Perot seizing a big chunk, Clinton fell far short of a majority. "Family values" sometimes did better—Oregon nearly ratified an anti-gay amendment and Colorado ratified a milder one, although even the GOP was divided on these matters.

The election over, Bush tried again to be commander in chief. In December he sent American troops as part of a United Nations force to feed and impose order on Somalia, ravaged by famine and civil war. Billed as a humanitarian action, this was not quite war (though it soon turned ugly), but it was notable that Bush's final act as President was to call American forces into action again, and that his first major appearance as ex-President was a trip to Kuwait, the scene of his greatest glory. Even in retirement, he remained the war President.

No other Western power had such an extensive recent record of military action—four wars in five decades, plus countless deployments, incursions, interventions, and confrontations. Would Bush's retirement break the pattern? Had the Gulf War's fickle impact already done so?

The Persisting Primacy of War

Taking office, Bill Clinton promised to "force the spring" of "American renewal." The metaphor was notable: invoking the natural rhythms of the seasons rather than the harsh logic of war marked a major change in presidential rhetoric. Unfortunately, spring's renewal soon seemed stuck in March's turbulent winds.

Clinton's challenge to militarization seemed obvious. The first President since FDR to have done no military service, as well as the first to have been born after World War II and to have significant roots in antiwar politics and culture, he had pledged economic renewal. Though chiding Bush for failing to halt the bloodshed among Yugoslavia's warring remnants, he had made it clear that foreign policy and the projection of military power abroad were not his major interests. Other Presidents had seen America as an exemplary rather than muscular city on a hill to the world, but, like Carter, Clinton seemed to mean it more ("Our greatest strength is the power of our ideas, which are still new in many lands," he announced), and he indicated that he would discard at least some relics of militarization. Although he heard "a call to service" and "the trumpets" sounding it, this was martial rhetoric in soft focus. His plan for national service, giving youngsters educational benefits in return for community service, drew on the system of duty and rewards available for military service but recognized that the latter now offered such rewards to fewer Americans.

Like his substantive positions, his style marked a change. As his seasonal metaphor indicated, it was noncombative, displaying little martial toughness, ideological rigidity, personal meanness, or partisan sharpness. He seemed the nation's patient schoolteacher, not its strutting commander in chief. Though undoubtedly at times grudging, his willingness to work with—even to be over-shadowed by—Republican moderates, conservative Democrats, and ex-President Carter indicated a lack of personal vanity or a grasp of the presi-dency's scaled-down nature in the absence of war. Most notably, he departed from his predecessors in choosing not to present war, either in the abstract or in specific instance, as a model for tackling the nation's problems. He did not re-pudiate that model; like most politicians in 1993, he simply ignored it.

But if obvious, Clinton's challenge to militarization was also largely implicit, an effort to outflank it rather than attack it head-on. He had an agenda of "re-newal," but neither he nor most other national figures firmly proposed to dis-card the old agenda, perhaps assuming it would wither on its own or under the pressure of mounting fiscal and economic problems. It did not wither on its own, however, at least not rapidly. The disadvantage of Clinton's attempt to outflank it was that he mobilized no constituency and fervor that would arrest the historical momentum of militarization. Of course, to take on its entire leg-acy was a daunting task in a political system that works incrementally, issue by issue, agency by agency—especially for Clinton, who, given his beliefs and ex-perience as governor of Arkansas, had little feel for the politics and apparatus of militarization. Yet to strike only at a few parts left the legacy largely intact and allowed its advocates to concentrate their defenses, as Clinton imme-diately found out.

There were advantages to ignoring it—let the beast slumber and slip away rather than provoke it—but they hinged in part on the vigor and savvy, neither initially notable, with which Clinton pursued the alternatives. Perhaps Ameri-cans were so out of practice articulating any mission disconnected from war or national security that they, including Clinton, lacked the vocabulary and values for doing so. "Domestic reform without a background of overwhelming for-eign crisis has not been attempted in sixty years," noted Sidney Blumenthal, but "war cannot be Clinton's paradigm."[112] Like Carter, Clinton was often ac-cused of lacking focus—of taking on too many causes and failing to mobilize support for a few he prized highly—but as with Carter this was shallow criti-cism. Often it came from opponents who simply disliked the focus Clinton did have, as when they scorned him for addressing the "ban" on gays in the armed forces, much as they had Carter for granting amnesty to draft-resisters. Both also governed at transitional, postwar moments when older agendas were re-ceding and newer ones contested, and when the presidency's power usually recedes and Congress's surges. Appropriately, Clinton rarely tried to bully

Congress, yielded to its byzantine law-making processes, and avoided the veto, while Republicans increased their use of old devices like the filibuster. His problem was less lack of focus than the fact that he entered office with "no mandate, no war, no party."[113] Critics assailed his low-key leadership, as if they longed for the war years when Presidents boldly exercised power. They might better have welcomed the invigorated roles now played by Congress and other institutions—and Clinton's deference to them.

The "focus" charge bore down especially on Clinton's foreign and military policy, said to betray "a general bankruptcy . . . unparalleled in recent American history." Richard Nixon's death in April 1994 provided one of many occasions for such charges. Nixon was hailed as a master "realist" and a "foreign policy genius," in apparent contrast to a feckless Clinton.[114] Such praise testified more to a sour nostalgia for a mythic muscular America than to Clinton's failures: the "genius" had taken five years to extricate his nation from a disastrous war, failed to build a lasting consensus for detente, and poisoned the political culture on which national strength rests. Nor did Clinton's meandering course look bad compared to Bush's vapid generalities and foolish embrace of Saddam Hussein's regime before the Gulf War. Clinton's priorities were consistent if uninspired, and plausibly in tune with the preferences of most Americans: America's economic revival and a prudent contraction in its military power, its use confined to low-risk actions whose burdens would be spread among many nations. If Clinton acted on his priorities unsteadily, so have most American Presidents.

Clinton's problem was less one of focus than of leadership on those issues he did address, about which he said little of a grand, public nature. Deference to other institutions was one thing, failure to clarify what he wanted from them was something else. Able in press conferences, he held almost none. Skilled to a fault in the arts of compromise, he lacked a sense of which problems deserved compromise and which required tougher positions for political, moral, or other reasons. He seemed to regard matters of moral import—the fate of Bosnian Muslims, the rights of gay soldiers, the appointment of black officials, the thuggery of Haiti's regime—as subject to the same process of compromise that governed fiscal policy or pork-barrel legislation, as if compromise were a virtue in itself. "The man is like a big fat cushion," one critic complained. "He bears the impression of whoever last sat upon him."[115] That approach to governance distinguished him from Carter, a notably if inconsistently stubborn leader. It still left many Americans unsure what, if anything, Clinton really believed.

Their uncertainty sprang as much from their own confusion, however, as from Clinton's leadership, bearing down on him in somewhat the same way it had on Bush, and on Carter at an earlier transitional moment. His harshest critics, usually but not always zealous conservatives, portrayed him as both a rigid liberal ideologue and a spineless compromiser—it was hard to see how he could be both. On health care, they assailed him for grasping for too much and settling for too little. When military intervention abroad loomed, they condemned him for considering action and then for backing away from it—and then for invoking presidential war-making powers that many of the same critics had eagerly yielded to Reagan and Bush. While Clinton was ineffectual in challenging them, these criticisms—and their contradictions—seemed more intense than the usual routine carping of American politics, reflecting the state of political culture as much as the vagaries of Clinton's leadership. That was the case, too, with the extraordinarily vicious attacks on Hillary Rodham Clinton.

Despite Clinton's caution, Congress's divisions, and Americans' uncertainties, his presidency did see steps away from a militarized agenda. New social initiatives emerged (as they had under Bush, including legislation protecting Americans with disabilities). Congress passed a Family Leave Act giving many workers limited rights to take leave of their jobs to deal with childrearing or illness among family members. Clinton and Congress scaled back restrictions on federal support of abortion. The Clintons formulated reforms for a troubled health-care system. Clinton and congressional Democrats also devised a federal budget designed to curb the swelling deficit accumulated in part because of Reagan's remilitarization. Though not much bolder than the 1990 budget deal—a mix of modest tax increases and cuts in projected spending increases—the 1993 deal differed by reversing a bit the regressive tilt of the tax system under Reagan and Bush and by receiving Clinton's full-scale support, whereas Bush had obviously looked for burden and glory abroad.

Clinton's approach to his first major opportunity for military intervention indicated the virtues and drawbacks of his ambiguous challenge to militarization. During the spring of 1993, Serbs and Croats bore down ruthlessly on beleaguered Bosnian Muslims, while in Washington the opening of the Holocaust Memorial Museum prompted renewed analogies between Yugoslavia's horrors and those of the Nazi era. Again, the analogies were strained—missing was the populous, powerful nation-state that carried out the Nazi Holocaust—and how much they moved Clinton was unclear. In any event, his response echoed Eisenhower's to the Dien Bien Phu 1954 crisis—a bold call for military intervention, hedged by so many conditions (again of assent by Europe's major powers) that action was destined to be limited, if it occurred at all. Like Ike, Clinton was faulted for temporizing leadership, but whether because he fumbled or calculated shrewdly, he avoided a risky initiative and followed precisely the oft-proclaimed lessons of the Vietnam War (as Ike had followed the Korean War's similar lessons): military action abroad was out of bounds without resounding support from allies and Americans, who were divided or indifferent about Bosnia.

Later controversies—over Bosnia's carnage, American deaths in Somalia, intervention in Haiti's civil war, North Korea's alleged nuclear threat—sometimes found the administration echoing Cold War rhetoric about America's credibility abroad. But they also found military leaders squeamish about action and Congress skittish about American deaths abroad—as if military intervention could be cost-free. With the unilateralist mood in Congress also intense, the chance diminished that the United Nations would provide pretext or genuine reason for the American cop to go back on the world beat. "Globo-Cop: Does America Have the Will to Fight?" asked *Newsweek* on its August 23, 1993, cover. Americans' differences about the answer seemed less significant than their lack of interest in the question. Given all those constraints, Clinton's modest success in the spring of 1994—in concert with the UN and NATO and Moscow—in curbing the Bosnian war by threatening Serb forces with NATO air power was notable. By the same token, what looked to some like hopeless waffling over Haiti and North Korea—the latter saw strident talk of war coming from his critics—more likely indicated Clinton's inclination, like that of Eisenhower and Carter, to refuse to see and define "crises" and go to war over them.

But Clinton was as cautious about dismantling militarization as he was about acting on its claims. Defense Secretary Les Aspin's initial military budget only accelerated slightly the modest cuts Bush proposed and preserved most weapons systems Bush bequeathed. In fact, defense budgets were shrinking only relative to the peak levels of the 1980s—simply returning to their late-1970s levels, and projected by the administration to rise again late in the 1990s. Aspin was, in his words, "very cautious," and "treading water on two accounts: research and development and procurement." That bureaucratic mumbo-jumbo meant that an old pattern continued: when budgets were squeezed, personnel went first, weapons last. The number of American troops in Europe was scheduled to slide from 304,000 in fiscal 1990 to 133,700 in the 1994 budget, and of forces overall to 1.4 million at the decade's end, but costly, troubled programs like the C-17 transport and the B-1 bomber lumbered along. The armed forces were slowly shrinking, but their technological top-heaviness endured. Nor did Clinton's caution result only from economic and congressional pressures, though men like Senate Armed Services Committee Chair Sam Nunn worked hard to retard demilitarization. Neither Clinton nor Aspin issued a bold call for change in the first place.[116]

More diffuse forms of militarization also persisted. The summons to take up arms in various "culture wars" was still heard, unleashed, as earlier, not only by moral conservatives. "We are today indeed engaged in a cultural war," announced Eugene Genovese, once a leading leftist historian. Troubled by "the deepening racial crisis in America," he took time to condemn "the arrogant pretensions to newly invented constitutional protections as envisaged, for example, in the program of the gay and lesbian movement." As usual, declaration of a "cultural war" fit oddly with the search for unity—with "our common willingness to overcome ancient hostilities and hear each other's voices," as Genovese put it. His war rhetoric, if not his politics, was echoed in tirades by figures like conservative radio host Rush Limbaugh, in academic struggles over curriculum, and in local and state conflicts over immigration, race, abortion, and gay rights. "We are keepers of what is right and what is wrong," asserted Lou Sheldon of the Traditional Values Coalition, one of many groups for whom, wrote a critic accurately capturing its rhetoric, politics was now "a post-millennialist battle for ultimate dominion over America." It was unclear whether that rhetoric was only a residue of an earlier style for expressing conflict—as its failure in the 1992 election and Clinton's avoidance of it as President might indicate—or a sign of that style's continued vitality.[117]

But another issue most vividly illustrated the persisting primacy of war—not as an activity Americans sought but as a framework in which they defined themselves. As campaigner, Clinton had promised to end the military's "ban" on gay men and lesbians in the armed forces, as if he could do so with the stroke of a pen (since the ban was only a Pentagon policy, it indeed was revocable by executive order—unless Congress stepped in). That ban had done little to prevent gay people's presence, but it had subjected them to intimidation and expulsion. The mainstream media paid little attention to Clinton's promise before the election, but during the interregnum it consumed media attention. By January 1993, television news featured sensational footage, with soft-porn overtones, of naked men in barracks showers presumably subject to the lustful gaze and predatory intentions of soon-to-liberated gay soldiers.

An uncommonly ferocious and silly debate ensued about whether to "let" gays and lesbians into the armed forces, as if they were not already there. Military leaders, reported the *New York Times*, "concede that there are now and always have been thousands of homosexuals in the military. But they say that to acknowledge that fact would inject an element of sexual tension and anxiety," so they defended a policy that denied the reality they conceded. Few military authorities trotted out the old reasons for expelling homosexuals—reasons involving competence to serve that every suppressed Pentagon study of the matter had undercut—instead emphasizing their supposed threat to order and discipline, that is, the disorder straight servicemen would manifest if faced with identifiably gay personnel. The military, a RAND Corporation study solemnly declared, "is no place to flaunt one sexual's identity or orientation," though it was hard to think of an institution where sexual bravado and boasting were more endemic and honored, at least among straight men. Many arguments were bizarrely contradictory: open homosexuality was intolerable because men have no privacy in barracks, argued the ban's defenders, who then asserted straight soldiers' right to precisely such privacy vis-à-vis gay men. Asserted too was the military's right to define its own values: Clinton's proposed change "threatens the strong, conservative, moralistic tradition of the troops," argued a retired marine general. That tradition, Russell Baker wryly noted, had included during his World War II service "manly vomiting" and "sexual boasting rites" that could not "possibly . . . have helped wrest the Pacific from the Japanese."[118]

Gender, male privilege, and their place in the armed forces were as much at issue as sexual orientation. Straight men dominated the debate. The voices of gay people were curiously silenced, while Sen. Sam Nunn, Colin Powell, and Les Aspin suddenly became experts on them. Women, who in and out of the armed forces were less opposed to the change, rarely surfaced as experts, potential victims of gay lust if the ban were lifted, or real victims of straight male lust. Hovering ominously in the background was the 1991 Tailhook incident, in which male navy personnel celebrating victory in the Gulf War sexually harassed female personnel, producing a scandal not just about the event, where top brass had been in attendance, but about the navy's botched investigation into it. While given much attention as a women's issue (unlike other evidence of violence and sexual assault against military women), Tailhook went mostly unmentioned in the debate on gays in the military, although Clinton briefly raised it.

Nonetheless, women's surging presence in the armed forces did much to drive the debate. Their presence was far more novel and disturbing to military traditionalists than the old if officially taboo presence of gay men, just as traditionalists used lesbian-baiting to curb women's power and beat back accusations of sexual harassment and exploitation by men. Ending the "ban" jeopardized that tool of control. The result was the seeming "contradiction" whereby "the military *acts* as if lesbians are the chief threat to its culture, whereas military and civilian policymakers *talk* as if lesbians aren't an issue and gay men are the threat." A crude remark by a key advisor to Nunn and the Pentagon revealed how much male-female rather than gay-straight relations were at issue: straight soldiers should not have to endure gay men's "sexual barbarics" in the showers, Northwestern University professor Charles Moskos said, "until I get to shower with Hillary Clinton."[119] Also heard in military circles was the notion that Hillary Clinton had to be a lesbian if her husband was promoting this change. Such were the defenses of the military as a bastion of male privilege.

And as a sacred institution which civilian authority dared not challenge. Extraordinary criticism of Clinton arose, as if, having done no military service, he had no right to be commander in chief (although lifelong civilians Woodrow Wilson and Franklin Roosevelt had commanded the armed forces in two great wars). Usually off the record, officers muttered threats to resign or mutinous remarks about Clinton, while sailors openly mocked Clinton in his presence. In turn, his diffident response seemed to invite more defiance: He "must," pled the *Chicago Tribune*, banish the appearance of being "a marshmallow."[120] Obscene remarks by male personnel made about—or faxed right to—Rep. Pat Schroeder, a leading voice in Congress on these matters, joined two themes: defiance of civilian authority and disgust with women's power.

Nonetheless, beneath the surface of this ugly debate, change was evident. However lurid, the specter of predatory gay men further buried stereotypes of limp-wristed sissies (and asexual lesbians), and debate pivoted less on the failings of gay men than on the fears of straight soldiers, rendered as in a nervous panic at the mere thought they might shower with homosexuals. "There are predictions of off-duty Marines in pearls and pumps, and red-blooded boys being importuned for perversions," noted Anna Quindlen, who advised: "Just say no, guys—female soldiers have had to do it for years." Fearful straight men, noted Allan Bérubé, seemed engaged in an act of "female impersonation," presenting themselves as like women—subject to the sexual desire of men and needing protection from them. However disingenuous that posture, it stripped old images of military manhood of their strutting, macho character, as if men were being "feminized" while military women showed "masculine" characteristics. "Being the oglee instead of, say, the ogler" upset the men who wrote to columnist Ellen Goodman; suddenly they were "worrying about male sexual aggression."[121]

Contests over gender, rarely confined to relations between men and women, also involve struggles over what it means to be a man or a woman. In the struggles of 1993, military manhood seemed fragile in the images purveyed by the ban's defenders (behavioral reality in the armed forces being another matter). Thus the debate reflected crazily the changes in gender relations at work in the military and in American life generally. In addition, as Clinton ineffectually but rightly noted, the mere fact that national leaders engaged in sustained debate about homosexuality marked a change—less the much-touted power of gay lobbies than the underlying social dynamics that made those lobbies possible.

Clinton himself fumbled the issue, never making a case for the change he proposed and trying to placate opponents, who only seized on his temporizing to scorn him more. He and gay Congressman Barney Frank reasoned that Congress would override any bold order and rejected the argument that an override would at least leave him on high moral ground. So he compromised, only to have Congress override him anyway. His later decision to fight court orders overturning anti-gay policies suggested that his temporizing reflected his mushy beliefs, not just Congress's power.

The resulting "don't ask, don't tell" policy ended questioning about a recruit's sexuality, but otherwise reinstated the military closet, albeit on murkier terms: gay men and women might serve, but only if they kept their identity secret, precisely the condition under which many had long tacitly served. The Pentagon no longer even offered reasons for expelling homosexuals, as if homophobia needed no justification. Clinton presented the new policy as an "honorable compromise," and pundits saw it as an inevitable one between "liberals" and "conservatives" on this issue. But as Barry Goldwater's thundering call for abolition of the ban indicated, Clinton had elbow room on this issue that he refused to exercise. Support for decisive action had surged in the spring, from the gay community but also from middle-of-the-road media like the *Chicago Tribune*. "Is it too much to hope," asked one columnist aware of the military's many closeted gay officers, "that the military will rethink its obsolete code before some general is found trying to squeeze into a size 14 at Saks?"[122]

The ugly debate revealed how resistant many Americans were to change in their military institutions, exposed anew the belief that the military retained pride of place among their institutions, and reaffirmed that citizenship was secured above all by military service. Gay organizations had not even made abolition of the military's policies a high priority. They did so only after being caught in a complex political process that made military service the test of citizenship. Win this test and the full citizenship of gay Americans would be assured—that became the rallying cry for gay groups and the evil that their opponents feared. At a time when homosexuality was at issue in many facets of American life, its place in the armed forces seized attention. Just when politicians agreed that economic challenges were top priority, they expended enormous energy on the place of gay men and lesbians in the military. Many Americans apparently still regarded the armed forces as the institution on whose composition and policies hinged much of the nation's fate.

Real and apparent analogies to the fate of black Americans in the 1940s also revealed the backward-looking focus. Sen. Strom Thurmond, who had bolted the Democratic Party when Truman ordered integration of the armed forces, now thundered that homosexuality was not "normal" (neither was it normal to have a ninety-year-old senator who had married two different Miss South Carolinas half his age) and joined the congressional charge, in which Southerners provided much of the muscle, against Clinton. Exponents of change spotted prejudice in 1993 similar to what Truman had tackled in 1948, when most military leaders had resisted racial integration and open defiance had rumbled through the ranks. Traditionalists presented Colin Powell, who opposed letting gays "in," to rebut that charge—how could a black general be accused of prejudice? Common to debate in both 1948 and 1993 was the assumption that military service validated and expanded citizenship, and indeed Truman's 1948 order had emboldened the civil rights movement. Meanwhile, some black Americans debated whether gays faced an oppression comparable to what they had experienced before 1948, as if one form of oppression had to be like another to warrant condemnation. The odd claim also emerged that discrimination was bad only if it involved inherited traits like color or gender, as if the law never barred it when based on chosen attributes like religious affiliation.

But the 1948 debate had erupted when the military was an ascendant, expanding institution. The Cold War had made it essential to national leaders that the armed forces not appear discriminatory to millions abroad or to minority Americans forced to share freedom's burdens under conscription. Racial integration had facilitated the military's role as showcase of American liberty and protector of freedom. Indeed, Truman could not have intervened as forcefully in the Korean War with segregated forces—the political backlash from African-

Americans would have been intense, and desperate commanders in Korea needed authority to use forces of whatever color in whatever combination.

Too blatantly unrepresentative of the American people, the military became an alien institution unfit to enforce the people's will. As a representative institution, it was empowered to act. Change in its social make-up had long served— in the 1940s regarding race, in the 1970s and 1980s regarding gender—to legitimate the military when its mission was in question. Marginal people gained fuller citizenship; in return, the military's charter as the people's force was renewed.

Against that background, the failure to make a decisive change in the "ban" indicated something besides, although linked to, the persisting homophobia. Perhaps the military was no longer important enough as an instrument of power abroad to require that its social charter be renewed. No global struggle framed this debate and justified reform—no millions of homosexuals elsewhere who would judge America's fitness to lead the world (though the Pentagon policy received considerable mockery abroad); no grand battle looming to justify more equitable use of military personnel. And insofar as action abroad was anticipated as part of United Nations peacekeeping forces, those forces were often reviled as weak-kneed and incapable of real war making—seen as vaguely feminine by American skeptics, often the same people who saw women and homosexuals as weakening the United States armed forces.

Serious proponents of military power and martial virtue, on the other hand, might have welcomed the formal inclusion of another group, so that they could return to the main business of preparing to fight wars. And so some voices argued. "The strength of our military depends ultimately upon its bonds to the people," wrote military historian Richard Kohn, who had close ties to the armed forces; "the armed forces will be stronger the more they reflect the values and ideals of the society they serve." "Gay rights mean a bolstering of the military's legitimacy," argued the *New Yorker*, "not an undermining of their morale: not a weakness, but a new strength." Or, as Goldwater put it in his pithier fashion, "You don't have to be straight to shoot straight"; the retired air force general would happily fly with a gay airman "as long as the son of a bitch could fly." In fact, fear of enhancing "the military's legitimacy" led many gay activists, often steeped in the antiwar culture of the 1970s, to look askance at the effort to lift the "ban" on gays. But Clinton's "compromise" left the ban largely in place. Only if the courts overturned it (its proscriptions on speech made it vulnerable) would the military's charter be renewed.[123]

The military would remain an important institution, but more as a fun-house mirror of American society than as a forward-looking force. Given the assumption that the nation's fate hinged on its outcome, the 1993 debate attested to the persisting primacy of military institutions, but also to their eclipse— diminishing as instruments of American power abroad, they no longer warranted the social renewal undergone earlier. Nineteen ninety-three would not recapitulate 1948, when the imperatives of American hegemony seemed to demand change. This time, the inefficiencies and hypocrisies of discrimination would stand, even more easily because a shrinking military system had the luxury of being choosier, by its lights, about whom it purportedly allowed to serve. It was enough that the armed forces replicate rather than contest widely felt prejudices, since few anticipated their use in some major assignment abroad. The ugly outcome of this ugly debate revealed that militarization—at least as it had operated over the previous half-century—was in decline.

Agitation about immigration in 1993 revealed much the same. Though long voiced, the demand—from Pat Buchanan and California governor Pete Wilson, among others—mounted that the United States literally fence off its borders, patrol them with troops, and (Wilson proposed) change the Constitution to deny automatic citizenship to anyone born on American soil. These proposals did address a rising problem—the movement of millions of people across borders—to which few countries were finding solutions. They also had ironic and ugly dimensions, however. After decades of moralizing about how the "Iron Curtain" blocked the movement of people across borders, many Americans now wanted their own barriers, venting nativist impulses with deep roots in American history. No one seriously argued that California, already irrevocably polyglot, could attain some ethnically purified status, but the move to fence off southern borders showed sharp lines of class, color, and culture still operating—it was aimed largely at Latin Americans, especially if poor and dark-skinned. In the Northeast, where Irish and Italians comprised the biggest groups of illegal immigrants, no comparable agitation arose.

These proposals were also tied to militarization's changing fortunes. They arose most vigorously in California, reeling from defense cutbacks. And they echoed a concept of security that predated the militarized era, one focused on continental defense rather than global hegemony, on America as island fortress rather than world cop, on its purity at home rather than its power abroad. The notion that America's borders were key to its survival had a quaint ring to it. In the great age of militarization, leaders had asked Americans to imagine a borderless globe on which geography meant nothing and threats to America could arise from the remotest places. Emanating from many of the folks who demanded exclusion of homosexuals from the armed forces, the nativists' call to arm American borders constituted another implicit rejection of the assumptions that had guided America's militarization.

To be sure, leaders continued to see an unbounded world, but now in economic more than military terms. Clinton made the shift clear, emphasizing that "our place in the world will be determined as much by the skills of our workers as by the strength of our weapons, as much by our ability to pull down foreign trade barriers as our ability to breach distant ramparts." Those were finely balanced words. "The new world order," the *New York Times* noted about Clinton's vision, "seamlessly integrates security and economics." The "ability to breach distant ramparts" was hardly repudiated, and the ability "to pull down foreign trade barriers" had a familiar aggressive ring.[124] Still, at least for the moment, coveted jobs and competitive products, rather than dangerous weapons and subversive ideas, filled this President's vision of a world without borders.

The ambiguities of a contracting militarization surfaced again when the administration intervened in Haiti in the autumn of 1994. A continental rather than global view of borders and defense needs defined Clinton's case for intervention—needed, he said, to keep Haitians out of the United States. The operation smacked of gunboat diplomacy before the 1930s—of a time when American intervention was imperialist but not fully militarized, regional rather than global in focus, and overtly racist in motive. As then, racism informed not just imperialism but often the resistance to it—Perot decried "Haitians as a people that practices voodoo, likes dictators, is too illiterate to participate in a meaningful democracy and lacks the 'Spirit of '76' necessary to achieve their own freedom from a small army," as his views were summarized. "Is Haiti worth fighting and dying for?" Perot asked. "No!" his audience replied.[125] Whatever their views on Haiti, most Americans, after two decades of memorializing their dead and missing in war, seemed to regard no foreseeable mess abroad as worth the loss of American lives. Clinton, who probably felt the same way, sensed their mood, using Jimmy Carter, Sam Nunn, and Colin Powell to broker a deal with Haiti's regime that obviated a contested invasion; the Haitian army could hardly have resisted anyway, but not one American life was to be lost if conflict was avoidable.

For his part, Clinton's case for intervention echoed themes from America's militarized age. Like some of his predecessors, he seemed to seek redemption abroad for his failures in domestic policy, as if the Haiti operation could restore (or create) an image of him as a decisive leader, at a time when his (and everyone else's) proposal on health care was in shambles. By August 3, 1994, he was citing earlier war Presidents to assert his right to invade Haiti without Congress's assent. Haiti marked the third time he had spoken to Americans about matters of "national security" from the Oval Office—the place he rarely used in addressing his presumably weightier goals of health-care reform and economic revitalization. It was if the presidency remained above all "Supreme Headquarters," as David Broder commented, rather than the "less grandiose office" it had become (merely "part of a governmental system that is barely able to cope"). His words on the eve of Haiti's invasion were uncannily like Bush's on the eve of the Gulf War: "I know that the United States cannot, indeed we should not be, the world's policeman," he said in the shop-worn manner by which Presidents renounce a course about to be taken anyway, "but when brutality occurs close to our shores, it affects our national interests."[126]

Yet his caveat—"close to our shores"—was as important as the familiar claim. Unlike Bush, Clinton still hesitated to see a global writ for American power. Indeed, he seemed trapped. When he tried to act as commander in chief at "Supreme Headquarters," he was assailed as an imposter defying the wishes of Congress and most Americans. When he tried to don a different hat, he was assailed for neglecting his duties as commander. That pattern of criticism suggested how much pundits and critics continued to judge Presidents on their perceived performance in the arena of war, even in a nation with little evident taste for going to war—as if the arena still held primacy even though the act of war making did not. Part of Clinton's problem was his reluctance to state his reasons for setting aside older visions of a muscular, militarized America—as in the gays-in-the-military debate, he wrongly thought he could appease the forces of patriotic ardor, who in turn only ridiculed him each time he bowed to them. Moreover, phrases like America's "sacred mission" abroad—used by Clinton before the United Nations on September 26—were fraught with Wilsonian peril. Still, when he did state his vision, his intelligent attention to the complexities of the post–Cold War world got lost in blithe media summaries.

Clearly, not all of this was Clinton's doing. The fact that questions of steadiness, resolve, and manliness had also dogged Bush (the "wimp" factor)—a very different politician and personality—suggested that such questions reflected less the individual than the state of political culture. In that culture, desire to put aside America's militarized past clashed with bewilderment about what would replace it. The resulting frictions tore away at Clinton as they had at Bush, even though Clinton could boast a reasonable economic recovery, long regarded as the necessary precondition for any President's reelection. In both cases, feckless leadership aggravated the frictions but did not create them. The cliché—that Americans deserve the Presidents they get—may well apply. Indecisive Americans—or more accurately, a political culture whose internal tensions produced indecision—got indecisive leaders.

The outcome of the gays-in-the-military debate, like Haiti and other developments in Clinton's presidency, was ambiguous enough to defeat firm conclusions about its meaning. On their own, such moments did not set the pace of America's exit from its militarized age, which would be determined also by Clinton's success with alternative agendas. The mere fact that Americans vigorously debated health care and the North American Free Trade Agreement hinted at success in that regard—the dull if vital matter of tariff and trade legislation (as opposed to the heated but substantively thin "trade war" talk of the 1980s) had not stirred many Americans since the musty days of the Smoot-Hawley tariff debate sixty years earlier. Yet progress on many of those matters was remote, and no issue at the start of Clinton's presidency generated the fire of gays-in-the-military. The episode suggested how heatedly the contraction of militarization would be contested—but, ironically, advanced as well—by presumed defenders of American martial power.

Politics at mid-decade revealed anew how ragged and ugly contraction would be. Clinton, refashioning himself as diplomatic and military leader, often simply disappeared from the scene of domestic policy debate—and from the nation itself—late in 1994. That move shored up his personal popularity a bit and yielded some specific accomplishments—in places like Haiti, where the United States operated with a free hand, and in bipartisan initiatives like the General Agreement on Tariffs and Trade (GATT), though not in Bosnia, where the decisions were tougher. But it also left him offering a pale imitation of the older model of President as commander in chief—one insufficient to quell conservative furor at him but adequate to liquidate any challenge on his part to the nation's militarized legacy.

For their part, many Republicans, gloating about retaking Congress and offering antistatist rhetoric scarcely changed from a half-century earlier, said little about what government might do, except keep the nation militarily strong and morally virtuous. They—and sometimes Clinton administration leaders as well—spoke and acted as if the federal government, in the absence of war as an immediate threat or a compelling paradigm, should simply shut down: there was little other business it could legitimately or competently perform. Elements of the far-right fringe took that premise to bizarre extremes in the gruesome April 1995 bombing of a federal building in Oklahoma City. For its part, Congress tried to act on that premise as it was embodied in the GOP's "Contract with America," by cutting programs that benefited poorer or politically marginal Americans. Fittingly, measures like federal funding of school lunches, initiated in the 1940s to make poor youth more fit to serve the nation in an age of peril, were among those under assault, even as disparities of wealth and income among Americans reached levels unmatched in other Western nations. The dissolution of national security as a dominant framework revealed how much social welfare programs, like much else the federal government did, had owed to that framework.

Mid-1990s politics also revealed how much the presidency itself owed to that framework. Not since early in the century had Congress appeared so dominant, with Speaker of the House Newt Gingrich treated almost like a rival President. At times Clinton seemed almost irrelevant, but although his low profile was attributed to failings in his own leadership, it owed more, as Bush's fate after the Gulf War had already suggested, to the shrinkage of national security as an arena for vigorous presidential leadership. By the same token, Clinton seemed most passionate and significant when he could redefine that arena by serving as the nation's "commander in chief" for domestic disaster and violence. He pushed a crime bill through Congress in 1994, pled for gun control, energized federal relief efforts in the wake of natural and man-made disasters, and, especially after the Oklahoma City bombing, seized the media bully pulpit to insist that national government still had a role to play in the realm of domestic security. Indeed, one form of growth in federal action that most politicians supported was efforts to curb violence and terrorism at home and overseas, with the United States exporting its crime-fighting apparatus while its warfighting apparatus abroad contracted. Those efforts indicated both the continued salience of national security as rationale for federal activism and its much-altered terms—in its new, more inward form, criminals and terrorists at home supplanted communists and other threats abroad.

Given that shift in terms, what government might do in a more conventional military mode seemed unclear. Republicans' calls for increased defense spending rang hollow, probably irrelevant to their success in the 1994 elections. Clinton had barely been cutting such spending anyway—and moved after the elections to raise it—and leading Republicans opposed every move on his part to use American forces abroad, leaving them to champion a larger defense force for which they outlined almost no practical purpose. The rising tide of anti-immigrant sentiment, shared by some Democrats and disavowed by some Republicans, indicated that national security continued to be reconceived as a matter of guarding America's borders rather than patrolling far-flung outposts.

The priorities of patriotic conservatives also emerged in their defeat of the National Air and Space Museum's plan to display the *Enola Gay* bomber that had attacked Hiroshima. In that fracas, they stressed that the atomic bombs of 1945 had saved American soldiers' lives, just as they demanded that no such lives be lost abroad in 1995. Intent on celebrating past military glory, they also indicated that such glory belonged in a museum rather than in future battlefields. Patriotic poses, that is, served to disguise rather than to arrest martial decline.

Some Republicans even worked to discredit the very authority they deemed necessary for the muscular nation they claimed to espouse. North Carolina GOP senator Jesse Helms declared that Clinton was unfit to be commander in chief and that he had "better have a bodyguard" if he visited Helms's state because the President had "serious problems with his record of draft avoidance, with his stand on homosexuals in the military and with the declining defense capability of America's armed forces."[127] Those comments—close to inviting Clinton's resignation, or violence against him—suggested that America's power in the world now was hardly even at issue. Instead, as Helms's reference to "homosexuals" made clear, cultural politics, though never inseparable from questions of power abroad, ruled.

Indeed, many conservatives sought to revive and intensify the "cultural wars" of the 1980s. As Irving Kristol, one of their intellectual godfathers, put it in 1993: "There is no 'after the Cold War' for me. So far from having ended, my cold war has increased in intensity, as sector after sector of American life has been ruthlessly corrupted by the liberal ethos . . . . Now that the other 'Cold War,' is over, the real cold war has begun," one for which "we are far less prepared" and in which we are "far more vulnerable."[128] Such statements made clear that raising the defense budget was irrelevant to the agenda of many conservatives—except as another means to wage the "real cold war," a telling phrase that called into question how much the Cold War of the past had actually had to do with the global clash of armaments and ideologies.

Clear, too, was how much the apocalyptic outlook of a militarized era now defined Americans' views of each other rather than their sense of threats abroad. The real "war" raged at home, at least in the sensibilities of many Americans. In it, conservatives now sounded the triumphal note that had seemed so feeble at the end of the Cold War abroad in the 1980s—for now they sensed real victory in the "real cold war," against their presumed domestic foes. Liberals, although they too mostly had been Cold Warriors (often more zealous ones than professed conservatives), were treated—and often seemed to act—like defeated enemies, driven from the battlefield of politics. How long that particular political outcome would last was uncertain at mid-decade—American politics seemed more mercurial than ever, and Clinton was a resilient if not always purposeful figure. Still, at mid-decade the most intractable legacy of the age of militarization was not so much armies and defense budgets but the warlike states of mind that many Americans indulged about one another.

CONCLUSION

The future of America's militarization hinged on the politics of Clinton's presidency, but even more on patterns set over a much longer arc of history. As with industrialization, the United States rode the historical wave of militarization rather than setting it in motion, but became by the mid-twentieth century its primary motor, triumphant practitioner, and chief beneficiary, as much as one nation could be. Its most unsullied success came in World War II, when it did much, if with more Allied help than most Americans acknowledged, to secure victory over the Axis powers.

A more ambiguous achievement emerged out of the Cold War. It was unclear how much the military power of the United States and its allies contained or, conversely, provoked their Cold War opponents. Most likely, it did both. By the same token, it probably helped both to perpetuate the Soviet regime (which depended even more than the American version on having an enemy to legitimate it) and to increase the strains on it that caused its demise. It was also likely that victory owed more to America's economic, ideological, and cultural strength than to its technological and military supremacy—although those forms of power are closely linked—in part because war as a usable tool of power for great nations was in decline. The ambiguity of victory was compounded by how much it cost the United States: militarization sapped its economic power, its political system's responsiveness, its freedom from coercive state power, and its ability to resolve or finesse internal conflicts.

However the necessity and efficacy of America's military power in the Cold War are assessed—matters about which historians appear doomed to disagree for a long time—it is also clearer now that external threats were not the only precipitant to America's militarization. Otherwise, its military power might not have assumed such gargantuan, baroque, menacing, and often useless dimensions. America's militarization derived as much from impulses within the nation as from forces impinging on it (insofar as the two can be distinguished, since each shaped perceptions of the other and both were generally subsumed under, though not always beholden to, the framework of the Cold War).

Historians are, it is true, rightly wary of grand generalizing about such impulses, lest they obscure Americans' many differences with each other—and their many similarities to other nations. Still, American political culture featured persistent if not unique moods—distrust of powerful government except when war validates it, longing for the unity and progress that war seems to entail, aspirations for military power and global hegemony, and anxieties about the costs incurred in attaining them. To highlight those impulses need not obscure differences among Americans. Instead, it suggests how those differences were accommodated, channeled, or on occasion crushed. Indeed, subordinate groups often (if reluctantly) hitched their fortunes to war specifically or militarization generally—most strikingly among African-Americans in the 1940s and 1950s, in a process still ongoing judged by the stature of someone like Gen. Colin Powell. To be sure, corporate and political elites and their junior partners generally controlled such processes, but they could do so in part because those processes also tapped the aspirations and anxieties of most Americans. Arising from many sources, the urge to marshal an effective state, indeed a prosperous and powerful nation, imparted much of the energy and character of America's militarization.

The result was the peculiarly ragged, quixotic course of its militarization. Large chunks of the nation's ecology, economy, politics, cultural life, and social relations—everything that defines a nation—became annexed to this historical process. Yet America's militarization never took the totalizing, singleminded course associated with Nazi Germany, Imperial Japan, or Stalinist Soviet Union. Lacking total control (or even coherent direction) at the top, the tool more than the objective of diverse interests, the means for marshaling the state more than its overriding goal, militarization in the American instance was a diffuse phenomenon.

There were other reasons, too, that the American version worked out in partial and uneven ways. By nature, militarization, like industrialization, was complex and multifaceted: individuals and interests could grasp one aspect of it and resist another. Just as nineteenth-century workers could flock to factory jobs and cling to pre-industrial work rhythms, or business moguls could forge organizational discipline and celebrate heroic individualism, so in the twentieth century liberals could yearn for the triumph of America's mechanized army over fascist enemies and bewail its racist and dehumanizing ways, southern politicians could embrace the Cold War but turn a blind eye to its implications for their own racial ideology, and Lyndon Johnson could declare his commitment to peace and wage "war" at home and abroad. If a measure of myopia or hypocrisy was involved in these discordant postures, so too was the sheer complexity of the historical process. There never was a single, unitary "militarization" either to embrace or reject.

Then too, Americans rarely admitted that they were engaged in militarizing their nation. They defined or responded to crises at home and abroad, but few conceptualized a grand historical process. Arthur Schlesinger, Jr.'s 1949 notion of a "permanent crisis" captured their uncertainty: "crisis" suggested an emergency demanding sudden improvisation, "permanent" something else indeed.[1] In the dominant American view, militarization was something that warlike or totalitarian nations embraced, not the United States. By denying their nation's engagement in it, Americans imparted to it much of its feverish, capricious nature—the sudden plunge into action abroad, the crash program to build a new weapon, the hysterical witch-hunt, the emergency effort to tackle poverty or AIDS or drugs. At the same time, however, they curtailed the process. Insofar as they denied its existence, it lacked a permanent ideological foundation. Seen as an emergency response to others' threats, it had legitimacy only as long as such threats remained plausible. Especially after the mid-1960s, an odd assortment of groups—moral conservatives, troubled liberals, impassioned radicals, worried ecologists, prophets of economic doom—challenged (not always consciously) that plausibility and championed, albeit often in warlike terms, agendas of domestic renewal that pushed external threats to the side.

The nation's economic and political characteristics also limited the scale and disrupted the course of its militarization. When American abundance seemed almost limitless, as in the 1940s and 1950s, militarization had seemed almost painlessly affordable, even economically beneficial, with both guns and butter readily attainable. When abundance appeared imperiled after the mid-1960s, growing numbers of Americans questioned militarization. Tolerance for its encroachments on Americans' liberties was also limited—sufficient to permit gross abuses but hardly to destroy all constraints on the state's power.

Perhaps most of all, but hardest to prove, militarization was quixotic, capricious, and contingent because war itself, in the sense of bombs and bullets and destruction, remained a shadowy presence in the lives of most Americans. They imagined war floridly, they transposed its words and images and emotions to their own struggles in striking ways, and they worried greatly and sincerely about its outbreak in the final cataclysm. But war remained largely an arena not of experience but of imagination, where it could be played out and acted on in lavish ways. In their hearts, Americans longed for war's spirit more than its substance, even though the line between real and imaginary wars often blurred.

That longing contributed in turn to their difficulty in explaining the internal quarrels that increasingly beset them. They did have explanations. By the 1990s, various Americans pointed to the aspirations, often couched in a language of victimhood, of marginal social groups, or to the resistance those aspirations met; to the rise of interest-group politics and the decay of a common culture; to the crumbling foundations of American prosperity, and to the social conflict that hard times presumably yield. All these explanations had validity, but some described symptoms more than causes and most got couched in a persistent but misleading language of war.

The history of militarization offered another explanation for Americans' internal quarrels. World War II and the Cold War had given most Americans common symbols, enemies, and purposes, a unity both real and fictive but sufficient to obscure or contain many of the conflicts simmering among them. After the 1960s, the United States went through the throes of a postwar era, of the sort that commonly opens the floodgates of internal conflict for nations, just as it encourages challenges to centralized authority and a more disorderly politics. But because the decline of warlike unity, like the process of demilitarization itself, was so ragged, partial, and protracted—a twenty-five year process—it lacked the clarity, the preciseness of moment, evident in the aftermath of earlier wars, making it hard to see Americans' internal struggles as, at least in part, the downside of war's end. Only with the final demise of the Cold War in the 1980s did that explanation gain some credence, and even then other explanations plausibly competed with it, while the recurrence of real war abroad in the Gulf and supposed wars at home further confused the matter. But it was no wonder that Americans set about redefining what the nation was and quarreled over the competing definitions offered—a superpower, a queer nation, a multicultural nation, a Christian nation (perhaps under "the Christian flag" to which Dan Quayle pledged allegiance in 1994)?[2] Such quarrels always seem raw and fresh, and indeed their terms had changed, but they were hardly new—they erupted after all of America's wars.

Grasping the historical breadth and depth of militarization also encourages caution about judging Americans harshly for their puzzled responses to their quarrels. That process dominated American life for a half-century, and played a major role in it for even longer. Disengaging from it—or, more modestly, moving it from the center to the periphery of American life—would plausibly take as long as engaging it did, especially in a still strife-torn world. To expect that Americans would disengage with few convulsions and little confusion was silly. We may lament feverish moments like the Gulf War when leaders clung desperately to the past and lurched blindly into the future, but we need not be surprised by them or think that they indicate that change is simply not happening at all.

Whether the great age of militarization was ending for the United States in the mid-1990s also depended on forces over which it had seemingly declining control: national, ethnic, and religious conflict abroad, and the migrations set loose by it; the continuing spread of military technologies, now furthered by ex-communist countries desperate to sell the few worthwhile products they had; the planetary reach of corporations and communications; and global ecological problems, economic rivalries, and disparities between "have" and "have-not" nations. Indeed, so immense were these forces and problems that, as staple commentary had it, nations and governments no longer had much control over them. "The balance of power in world politics has shifted in recent years from territorially bound governments to companies than can roam the world," Richard Barnet asserted. "The next world war, if there is one," predicted scholar Samuel P. Huntington, "will be a war between civilizations," not nations.[3]

Predictions about the decline of nations and their wars had appeared throughout the century, however—along with the ritual claim that "the world is becoming smaller," as Huntington put it—only to recede before the forces of national power and identity. Likewise, the century's national wars had always featured transnational elements of cultural, racial, ideological, and economic hostility. No definitive change in that mix was likely in the next century: nations would remain important and Americans could still try to define themselves in a troubled world.

They were not doing so imaginatively in the 1990s. President Clinton, Senator Moynihan complained in 1993, "hasn't gone near those institutions" like the CIA that arose under militarization. With the Cold War's end he should ask, "'what do I need this for? And what do I need that for?'" By and large, most leaders were not asking. Reactions to various fiftieth anniversaries of the momentous events of World War II both displayed and exacerbated the backward-looking focus. Understandably proud and patriotic, the celebration of D-Day's fiftieth anniversary in 1994 was also disturbingly nostalgic—and provincial as well, carried on as if the Soviet Union had hardly even participated in Germany's defeat. A chorus of protest arose against an effort by the National Air and Space Museum to present America's use of the atomic bomb against Japan as something more complex than an act of righteous and necessary vengeance. No wonder Paul Kennedy worried that Americans, like the British in decline a century earlier, thought it "better to 'muddle' through'" than to chart a new course.[4]

Americans would likely drift away from their militarized past. By some measures, they had been doing so since the end of the Vietnam War, and by the 1990s the forces pulling them away were substantial: the absence of a formidable enemy, the dubious utility of resorting to war, the rise of economic challenges, the swelling burden of other responsibilities (health care alone now seized 14 percent of GNP, over twice that devoted to defense), and the unhappy outcome of the many "wars" they had waged among each other. But they would drift away from that past fitfully, without repudiating it, or even much acknowledging that it had existed. In the take-off phase of militarization, Franklin Roosevelt had offered a grandly reasoned if not always honest rationale in its behalf. In its waning hours, few leaders spoke in behalf of its liquidation. There were good reasons for the difference: war, World War II in FDR's case, concentrates the mind; peace rarely does, especially when it emerges raggedly and partially. Still, one hoped for more celebration of peace alongside the wariness about its staying power, and for more deliberation about the opportunities it offered to wriggle free of a militarized past.

Those opportunities could take several forms. None involved a complete break from the past, but the United States might become a residually militarized nation, using a scaled-down military force in circumspect fashion. It might keep militarized institutions but bend them to new purposes, as in efforts of the 1990s to redeploy weapons labs and procurement agencies to the struggle for economic vitality, to use Pentagon money to "convert" defense industries to civilian production (and thereby retain an industrial base for producing weapons), to enlarge the military's role in the "war" against drugs, to swell police forces with ex-soldiers, and to dispatch military officers to inner-city schools in order to teach "at-risk" youth (usually nonwhite) "discipline and life skills."[5] War and militarization themselves might diverge further from each other, as they already had in the 1970s and 1980s. Nations can, after all, be war-like but not very militarized—like the United States when it rushed into the Mexican-American War—or be militarized but not very warlike, like the Soviet Union after 1945.

Predicting the fate of America's militarization is difficult, however, not only for the obvious reason that historians are poor at prediction, but because of the paucity of instructive examples among other nations. When other modern na-tions have repudiated or drifted away from a militarized course, war, internal dissolution, or both has usually catalyzed the change. France, Great Britain, Germany, and other Western European powers underwent that change after 1945, in good part because two world wars, regardless of whether they were victorious, left them exhausted and partially destroyed, diminishing their will and capacity to sustain their armed might and imperial ambitions. The Soviet Union's course was disrupted by different circumstances—the dissolution of its political order—but also hastened by war (in Afghanistan in its case) and accompanied by the collapse of empire.

No comparable trauma befell the United States (at least not after the Vietnam War), leaving the record of other nations a poor guide to its fate in this regard, and making questionable whether the force of circumstances in its case was sufficient to compel great change. To be sure, as Paul Kennedy argued, eco-nomic decline also shaped the fate of militarization in these nations, but its role in America's fate is uncertain because the extent of its economic decline is argu-able and because such decline does not always (and certainly not quickly) com-pel a nation to demilitarize. Facing no stark economic crisis, no large-scale di-saster in war, and no sudden demise of the interests and politics that long had sustained militarization, the United States likely would continue to drift only fitfully and partially away from its militarized past, as actual and projected de-fense budgets for the 1990s indicated. The strategic, ideological, and economic foundations of militarization—never as solid anyway as its champions had maintained—had eroded to the point of disappearing, but its historical mo-mentum persisted.

What would most likely trace the path taken were Americans' attitudes to-ward national government and governance itself. Aside from their engage-ment with the global process of militarization, the most persistent impulse be-hind militarization in the United States was its leaders' and citizens' inability to trust and justify collective national action except when it occurred in war or a warlike mode. Usually wanting their government to do more, while claiming they did not, they repeatedly looked to war or its surrogate to overcome their own distrust of governmental action.

The wobbly start of Clinton's presidency, though explainable in many ways, suggested that this old problem endured. Setting aside war as metaphor, paradigm, and course of action, he often seemed bereft of any alternative framework for justifying his initiatives. Meanwhile, efforts like health care reform were assailed as socialism in stridently antistatist rhetoric—as if anything the state did outside a militarized arena was suspect and bound to be bungled. The enduring problem was also evident in talk by the media late in 1993, amid a wave of sensational murders and legislative initiatives to combat violence, of a new "war on crime," in which Americans were nearing their "Pearl Harbor," as one official claimed. Subsequent passage in 1994 of a crime bill was accompanied by similar talk. By then, Clinton himself had begun slipping into the familiar mode, rejecting further cuts in defense and justifying his health care plan by arguing that rising medical costs drained money from the defense budget, constituted "the biggest long-term threat to defense readiness," and jeopardized national security.[6] The persistent distrust of state action was flammable kindling that might restoke the fires of militarization.

The irony was that if militarization had made possible an end-run around antistatism, it also aggravated distrust of the state. Decades of colossal spending on useless armaments, lavish subsidies to corporations, failed or fickle military actions, capricious state repression, inattention to nagging problems or warlike fervor when addressing them—that troubled history left many Americans further suspicious about, or simply indifferent to, the state's wisdom and efficacy. That point was little noted in political debates of the 1990s. Americans instead located their distrust of the state elsewhere—in everything from the inefficiencies of the post office, to the outrages of the National Endowment for the Arts, to the failures of welfare programs, to the follies of politicians, to the burdens of taxes, and so on.

But most likely, their distrust also arose from experiencing what the state had done in America's great age of militarization.

ENDNOTES

Most sources cited here are given in abbreviated form, with full information about them appearing in the bibliography. A small number of sources—those less helpful or cited only a few times in one chapter—appear only in citations. Citations are used primarily to indicate sources for quotations. Where a single endnote gives citations for several quotations, brief parenthetical indications link the citations to specific passages in my text. Citations to newspapers usually do not include page numbers, since the newsstand editions I often used differ in pagination from the official record on microfilm. Only rarely do I offer citations to indicate sources for statistics (most used here can readily be found in sources like *Statistical Abstracts of the United States*) or to engage scholarly debates.

The following abbreviations are frequently used:

FDR PP   *Public Papers and Addresses of Franklin D. Roosevelt.* New York, 1938–1950.

HST PP   *Public Papers of the Presidents of the United States: Harry S. Truman.* Washington, 1961–1966.

Ike PP   *Public Papers of the Presidents of the United States: Dwight D. Eisenhower.* Washington, 1958–1961.

JFK PP   *Public Papers of the Presidents of the United States: John F. Kennedy.* Washington, 1962–1964.

LBJ PP   *Public Papers of the Presidents of the United States: Lyndon B. Johnson.* Washington, 1965–1970.

Nixon PP   *Public Papers of the Presidents of the United States: Richard Nixon.* Washington, 1971–1975.

Ford PP   *Public Papers of the Presidents of the United States: Gerald R. Ford.* Washington, 1975–1979.

Carter PP   *Public Papers of the Presidents of the United States: Jimmy Carter.* Washington, 1977–1982.

Reagan PP   *Public Papers of the Presidents of the United States: Ronald Reagan.* Washington, 1982–1991.

Bush PP   *Public Papers of the Presidents of the United States: George Bush.* Washington, 1990–1993.

Preface

1. John R. Gillis, employing Michael Geyer's definition, in Gillis, *Militarization of the Western World*, 1.
2. Ibid., 3 (Gillis's words).

Prologue

1. Weigley, *American Way,* 5.
2. See ibid.
3. Royster, *Destructive War,* 241.
4. Franklin, *War Stars,* 5, 13.
5. Peter Karsten, "Militarization and Rationalization in the United States, 1870–1914," in Gillis, *Militarization,* 33 (Holmes), 36 ("militarism"); Frederickson, *Inner Civil War,* 209 (on "the ideal"), 215 (on "vice and poverty"), 235 ("army of," "get the"). On the war metaphor regarding science and religion, see George M. Marsden, *Religion and American Culture* (New York, 1990), 126.
6. Lincoln quoted in Smith, *Thinking the Unthinkable,* 110.
7. Leonard, *Above the Battle,* 148.
8. Vinovskis, "Have Social Historians Lost the Civil War?" 53 (on veterans' aid). Merritt Roe Smith, "Military Arsenals and Industry Before World War I," in Cooling, *War,* 41 ("the day"). McNeill, *Pursuit,* 269f., applies the term "military-industrial complex" to Britain; "keel" from Karsten, "Militarization," 31. Millis, *Arms and Men,* 148 (Cleveland).
9. Calculations from U.S. Bureau of the Census, *Historical Statistics of the United States, Colonial Times to 1970* (Washington, D.C., 1975), 224, 1114–16, and M. S. Kendrick, *A Century and a Half of Federal Expenditures* (New York, 1955).
10. On force levels, see *Historical Statistics,* 8, 1140–42, and Kendrick, *Century and a Half,* 43–44; for comparisons to European forces, Kennedy, *Rise and Fall,* 203; on deaths, Vinovskis, "Have Social Historians Lost the Civil War?"
11. Millis, *Arms and Men,* 166 ("organic"); Challener, *Admirals,* 12 ("or we"); Leonard, *Above the Battle,* 91 ("were thought").
12. Kennedy, *Over Here,* 22 ("If you"), 150.
13. Ibid., 50.
14. Ibid., 52.
15. See Lotchin, *Fortress California* (on "metropolitan-military complex"), and Vander Meulen, *Politics,* 6.
16. Alonso, *Peace,* 86.
17. Kennedy, *Over Here,* 227; see also 222 for comments by Alfred Kazin paraphrased here.
18. Quoted in Sherry, *Rise,* 28, 44.
19. Millis, *Arms and Men,* 239.

Chapter 1

1. Arthur Krock, *New York Times,* March 5, 1933, in Leuchtenburg, "New Deal," 104. FDR inaugural: *FDR PP,* 2 (1933): 11–16. For crowd reaction and Eleanor Roosevelt's comments, see Garraty, *Great Depression,* 205.
2. Levine, "Hollywood's Washington," 236.
3. Leuchtenburg, "New Deal," 143.
4. Ibid., 130.

5. Ibid., 90.

6. For Chase and the *Nation,* see Richard Pells, *Radical Visions and American Dreams* (New York, 1973), 73, 78. Other quotations from Leuchtenburg, "New Deal," 82–83.

7. See Leuchtenburg, "New Deal," 92–100.

8. Ibid., 100 (on Hoover); see also 100, 127–28.

9. Ibid., 96–97, 101.

10. Ibid., 107–09.

11. Ibid., 109–13, 123–24.

12. Ibid., 118 (for quotation); see generally 117–21.

13. Ibid., 121 (Johnson); see generally 120–21. Other quotations and material from Arthur Schlesinger, Jr., *The Coming of the New Deal* (Boston, 1958), 116–18.

14. The $824 million figure is from Garraty, *Great Depression,* 188; U.S. Public Works Administration, *America Builds: The Record of the PWA* (Washington, D.C., 1939), 290–91, suggests a lower figure.

15. See John A. Salmond, *The Civilian Conservation Corps, 1933–1942* (Durham, 1967), generally, and for "Americanizing influence," 130.

16. Ibid., chap. 5 on the corps and race relations; for "political dynamite," 98.

17. Ibid., 117, 193.

18. *FDR PP,* 5 (1936): 407.

19. *FDR PP,* 8 (1939): 5–6.

20. Louis Wirth, "The Urban Community," in Ogburn, *American Society,* 66; Wecter, *When Johnny Comes Marching Home,* 481.

21. Susman, *Culture as History,* 153, 154, 157.

22. Ibid., 158, 159.

23. Ibid., 157; Alexander, *Nationalism,* 23.

24. See Novick, *That Noble Dream,* 237–38.

25. See Eileen Eagan, *Class, Culture and the Classroom: The Student Peace Movement of the 1930s* (Philadelphia, 1981).

26. White, quoted in Wittner, *Rebels Against War,* 3.

27. On the Ludlow Amendment, see Kyle Smith, "War and the Ballot Box: The Debate over the Ludlow Amendment," M.A. thesis, Northwestern University, 1988; FDR quotation in Elliot Roosevelt, ed., *F.D.R.: His Personal Letters, 1928–1945* (New York, 1947–50), 2: 751.

28. Susan Gubar, " 'This Is My Rifle, This Is My Gun': World War II and the Blitz on Women," in Higonnet et al., *Behind the Lines,* 240.

29. Brogan, *American Character,* xiv, 91, xv; Wittner, *Rebels Against War,* 26 ("belligerent").

30. Sherry, *Rise,* 62.

31. Robert and Helen Lynd, *Middletown in Transition* (1937; New York, 1965), 120, 142.

32. "Sea of troubles" is the title of chap. 10, William E. Leuchtenburg, *Franklin D. Roosevelt and the New Deal, 1932–1940* (New York, 1963); characterization of the reorganization struggle is Leuchtenburg's, 279.

33. Quotation from Sherry, *Rise*, 76–77 (emphasis in original). See also Donald Cameron Watt, *How War Came: The Immediate Origins of the Second World War, 1938–1939* (New York, 1989), 30.

34. Sherry, *Rise*, 76, 89–80.

35. *FDR PP*, 7 (1938): 492.

36. *FDR PP*, 8 (1939): 2, 4, 3, 7.

37. *FDR PP*, 8 (1939): 5, 6.

38. Sherry, *Rise*, 81; *FDR PP*, 8 (1939): 516.

39. See McCormick, *America's Half-Century*, 28–33, and Hearden, *Roosevelt Confronts Hitler*, 159, which argues flatly that "the Roosevelt administration regarded Nazi Germany as a formidable economic threat rather than a dangerous military menace."

40. Herring, *Impact of War*, 239.

41. *FDR PP*, 8 (1939): 3, 156; Sherry, *Rise*, 78–79.

42. *FDR PP*, 8 (1939): 461–62; 9 (1940): 186, 199, 319–20, 198, 289.

43. *FDR PP*, 9 (1940): 434; see also 387–90, 431–34.

44. Ibid., 543, 546, 636, 663.

45. Susman, *Culture as History*, 266.

46. *FDR PP*, 9 (1940): 241, 375. On "phonoscope," see Murphy, "Lonely Battle," 92.

47. Bland, *Marshall Papers*, 1: 644, 621 and 2: 309 (emphasis in original). Other quotations from Sherry, *Rise*, 88–89.

48. Quotations from Edward Mead Earle, "National Security and Foreign Policy," *Yale Review* 29 (March 1940): 458; *Against This Torrent* (Princeton, 1941), 4; "The Threat to American Security," *Yale Review* 30 (March 1941): 455. For a similar outlook, see Herring, *Impact of War*, esp. chap. 1. See also Robert Osgood, *Ideals and Self-Interest in American Foreign Relations* (Chicago, 1953), 391–400.

49. Wittner, *Rebels Against War*, 16 ("now renounced"); Alexander, *Nationalism*, 180 (Mumford); see Novick, *That Noble Dream*, 281–82, 287, for other quotations from the period and his characterizations.

50. Quoted in Novick, *That Noble Dream*, 287.

51. Schneider, *Should America Go to War?* 105.

52. Henrikson, "Map," 28, 30, 31–32, 38–39, 50; nn. 22, 29, 47. See also Joseph Corn, *The Winged Gospel: America's Romance with Aviation, 1900–1950* (New York, 1983), 122–24.

53. Characterizations of radio journalists by Steele, in *Propaganda*, 135, and Culbert, in *News for Everyman*, 206. MacLeish quoted in Culbert, 194; characterization of Murrow by Culbert, 207.

54. Culbert, *News for Everyman*, 73, 24.

55. Newspapers as quoted in Schneider, *Should America Go to War?* 1; Schneider's characterization, 13.

56. Quoted in Steele, *Propaganda*, 122.

57. Schneider, *Should America Go to War?* 88 (emphasis in original), 98; Roosevelt, in *FDR PP*, 9 (1940): 487–88.

58. Murphy, "Lonely Battle," 114–16 ("penetration of"), 83 (Thurber). For other quotations on "War of the Worlds" and his speculations at the time, Hadley

Cantril, *The Invasion from Mars* (Princeton, 1940), esp. 189–205. Weart, *Nuclear Fear*, 81 ("a probe").

59. Hearden, *Roosevelt Confronts Hitler*, 243, 244; Herring, *Impact of War*, 12.

60. Bland, *Marshall Papers*, 2: 308–09 (emphasis in the original); Herring, *Impact of War*, title of chap. 8.

61. *FDR PP*, 8 (1939): 521.

62. Gardner, *Covenant with Power*, 48.

63. Sherry, *Rise*, 98.

64. Ibid., 97–98, 143; Bland, *Marshall Papers*, 2: 609 (emphasis in original).

65. Gregory, *America 1941*, 55.

66. Ibid., 80; Herring, *Impact of War*, 251.

67. Gregory, *America 1941*, 81; Herring, *Impact of War*, 9.

68. See Gregory, *America 1941*, 81.

69. Herring, *Impact of War*, 273.

70. Gregory, *America 1941*, 27.

71. Bland, *Marshall Papers*, 2: 387; Sherry, *Rise*, 134 (Steinbeck); Gregory, *America 1941*, 32; Herring, *Impact of War*, 22–23, 19, 21.

72. Gregory, *America 1941*, 43 ("carnival"); *FDR PP*, 10 (1941): 416.

73. Gregory, *America 1941*, 218.

74. *FDR PP*, 10 (1941): 216; see also 233–37.

75. Millis, *Arms and Men*, 268–69.

76. *FDR PP*, 9 (1940): 238, 239.

77. Ribuffo, *Old Christian Right*, chap. 5, and Ribuffo, "Brown Scare."

78. Ribuffo, "Brown Scare," 9 (Chase); *Old Christian Right*, 181 ("there was no").

79. Ribuffo, *Old Christian Right*, 183, 184; Herring, *Impact of War*, 236 ("mass hysteria," etc.).

80. Ribuffo, "Brown Scare," 41. See also Athan G. Theoharis and John Stuart Cox, *The Boss: J. Edgar Hoover and the Great American Inquisition* (Philadelphia, 1988), chaps. 8–9.

81. Harold Lasswell, "The Garrison State," *American Journal of Sociology* 46 (January 1941): 455–68; quotations on 455, 458, 459, 461.

82. Koppes and Black, *Hollywood*, 22, 36.

83. Ibid., 29.

84. Gregory, *America 1941*, 264, 77.

85. Koppes and Black, *Hollywood*, 40, 43.

86. Gregory, *America 1941*, 20.

87. Schneider, *Should America Go to War?* 103.

88. Henry Luce, "The American Century," *Life*, Feb. 19, 1941: 61–65; Gregory, *America 1941*, 20.

89. Alexander, *Nationalism*, 177; Schneider, *Should America Go to War?* 153 ("In a"), 154 ("had ceased"); Steele, *Propaganda*, 172; Luce, "American Century."

90. *FDR PP*, 10 (1941): 278.

91. Mead, *And Keep Your Powder Dry*, 139, 150–51, 157.

92. Reynolds, *Creation*, 288.

93. Harold Ickes, *The Secret Diary of Harold L. Ickes*, vol. 3 (New York, 1954), 523. Heinrichs, *Threshold of War*, 68 (on FDR's dream).

94. Quoted in Ellen Nore, *Charles A. Beard: An Intellectual Biography* (Carbondale, 1983), 186.

95. Beard and Beard, *America in Midpassage*, 455. Charles Beard on lend-lease, quoted in Nore, *Beard*, 185.

96. *FDR PP*, 10 (1941): 385, 390 (on *Greer*); 438 (on *Kearny*).

97. See Sherry, *Rise*, 107–09.

98. On polls and *Life*, see O'Neill, *Democracy at War*, 73.

99. Schneider, *Should America Go to War?* 216 (*Tribune*); Samuel Grafton, *An American Diary* (Garden City, 1943), 144 (entry of Dec. 31, 1941).

Chapter 2

1. Kennett, *For the Duration*, 59.

2. *FDR PP*, 11 (1942): 32 (Jan. 6 State of the Union Address).

3. I. F. Stone, *Nation*, Dec. 13, 1941, repr. in Stone, *The War Years, 1939–1945* (Boston, 1988), 92; Sherry, *Rise*, 116.

4. "Betrayal of the peace": Mead, *And Keep Your Powder Dry*, 119.

5. *FDR PP*, 10 (1941): 528–29 (Dec. 9, 1941, Fireside Chat); see also 11: 105ff.

6. *FDR PP*, 10: 526; 11: 103; see also 11: 40. Warner, *Democracy in Jonesville*, 268–69; Tuttle, *"Daddy's Gone to War,"* 7.

7. Blum, *V Was for Victory*, 16 ("imagination"); *FDR PP*, 11: 35.

8. Kennett, *For the Duration*, 81.

9. Dower, *War Without Mercy*, 92.

10. Ibid., 176 ("By the"); Isaiah Berlin, *Washington Despatches, 1941–1946*, ed. H. G. Nicholas (Chicago, 1981), 67, 108.

11. Mead, *And Keep Your Powder Dry*, 213; Stuart Chase, *The Road We Are Traveling, 1914–1942* (New York, 1942), 5, 100; Wylie, *Generation*, 75, 315.

12. T. R. B., *New Republic*, Aug. 2, 1943, as quoted in Ross, *Preparing for Ulysses*, 34 ("suffer"); Doherty, *Projections of War*, 73 ("not a"); Consolidated ad, *Life*, Sept. 6, 1943, 74; Blum, *V Was for Victory*, 16.

13. Brogan, *American Character*, 163–64.

14. *FDR PP*, 12 (1943): 329.

15. Kennett, *For the Duration*, 107.

16. Ibid., 104 (Catton); Kennedy, *Rise and Fall*, 350 ("polycratic").

17. Nash, *American West*, 25, vii, 17; White, *"It's Your Misfortune,"* 496.

18. Peter Daniel, "Going Among Strangers: Southern Reactions to World War II," *Journal of American History* 77 (December 1990): 909, 886; Allan Clive, *State of War: Michigan in World War II* (Ann Arbor, 1979), 237.

19. Kennedy, *Rise and Fall*, 361.

20. Blum, *V Was for Victory*, 120, 122 (Stimson).

21. My characterization in *Rise*, 192.

22. O'Neill, *A Democracy at War*, 209 ("approaching"), 202 ("saved"); *FDR PP*, 13 (1944–45): 37.

23. Vander Meulen, *Politics of Aircraft*, 211, 215.

24. Vagts, *History of Militarism*, 463.

25. Lekachman, *Age of Keynes*, 153.

26. Michael Geyer, "The Militarization of Europe, 1914–1945," in Gillis, *Militarization*, 71.

27. U.S. Chamber of Commerce, *Bulletin 8: Deficit Spending and Private Enterprise* (1944), 12–13. Galambos and Pratt, *Rise of the Corporate Commonwealth*, 131, 157.

28. *FDR PP*, 13 (1944–45): 34, 42, 503; Stuart Chase, *For This We Fought* (New York, 1946), 49.

29. Polenberg, *War and Society*, 219, 236.

30. Blum, *V Was for Victory*, 276, 115.

31. Polenberg, *War and Society*, 86.

32. *FDR PP*, 13 (1944–45): 42, 41, 33, 317; on compulsory service, see 228–231; on campaign rhetoric, see 396, 400, 406.

33. Blum, *V Was for Victory*, 256.

34. Sherry, *Rise*, 192.

35. Sherry, *Preparing*, 129.

36. Quotations from Sherry, *Rise*, 210, 290, 350, 162; on "technological fanaticism," see chap. 8.

37. O'Neill, *Democracy at War*, 114 (on MacArthur). On "strategies of annihilation," see Weigley, *American Way of War*.

38. Fussell, *Wartime*, 16; Sherrod, *Tarawa*, 40.

39. Sherry, *Preparing*, 86.

40. Ibid., 88.

41. Brogan, *American Character*, 156. Walter Lippmann, *U.S. War Aims* (Boston, 1944), 197. Other quotations: Sherry, *Preparing*, 133, 55, 56–57, 47, 131.

42. Sherry, *Preparing*, 51; Sherry, *Rise*, 185.

43. Divine, *Second Chance*, 84.

44. Wecter, *When Johnny Comes Marching Home*, 553.

45. Ibid., 6.

46. Art Gallaher, *Plainville: Fifteen Years Later* (New York, 1961), 227; Mead, *And Keep Your Powder Dry*, 16–17.

47. Wecter, *When Johnny Comes Marching Home*, 485, 482.

48. Koppes and Black, *Hollywood Goes to War*, 59, 71.

49. Ibid., 61 (Tarzan); Westbrook, "Fighting for the American Family," 198 (Westbrook's emphasis); Brogan, *American Character*, 147; Blum, *V Was for Victory*, 17 (Morgenthau).

50. Blum, *V Was for Victory*, 39.

51. Wecter, *When Johnny Comes Marching Home*, 482 ("that power"), 493 ("far less"); Blum, *V Was for Victory*, 70 ("were dragons"); Ellis, *Sharp End*, 315 ("microcosmic"); Warner, *Democracy*, 282–84 (on allies, "saw," "knew"); Brogan, *American Character*, 168; Abzug, *Inside the Vicious Heart*, 30 (Eisenhower).

52. Leslie Epstein, "Blue Skies: Reflections on Hollywood and the Holocaust," *Tikkun* Sept.-Oct. 1989: 11–14, 84–90; Wecter, *When Johnny Comes Marching Home*, 484–85;

53. Ralph Ingersoll, quoted in Sherry, *Rise*, 118.

54. Fussell, *Wartime*, 138; Dower, *War Without Mercy*, 185.

55. Sherrod, *Tarawa*, 151; Wecter, *When Johnny Comes Marching Home*, 505; Fussell, *Wartime*, 116, 270.

56. Ellis, *Sharp End*, 53.

57. Hynes, *Flights of Passage*, 180, 209.

58. Quoted in Sherry, *Rise*, 211.

59. Bernstein, *American Indians*, 175; Hynes, *Flights of Passage*, 162.

60. Fussell, *Wartime*, chap. 7 ("Chickenshit, An Anatomy"); Wecter, *When Johnny Comes Marching Home*, 482 ("prone to"); Kennett, *For the Duration*, 96; Samuel Stouffer, in Ogburn, *American Society*, 105.

61. Fussell, *Wartime*, 70, 38, 36, 95.

62. Ibid., 294 (Fussell's characterization and Sledge quotation), 285 (Eisenhower). Ellis, *Sharp End*, 103 ("literal truth").

63. See Fussell, *Wartime*, esp. 66–67.

64. "Survivor's guilt" quoted in Sherry, *Rise*, 206; Hynes, *Flights of Passage*, 208, 209.

65. As George Roeder phrased it in the manuscript, used with his permission, for *The Censored War;* see p. 3 of that book for different phrasing.

66. Fussell, *Wartime*, 127.

67. Miller, *Irony*, 195; Warner, *Democracy*, 287, 288 ("In simple," etc.).

68. Wecter, *When Johnny Comes Marching Home*, 483.

69. Herbert Blumer, in Ogburn, *American Society*, 229–30; Wecter, *When Johnny Comes Marching Home*, 19, 558.

70. Ralph David Abernathy, *And the Walls Came Tumbling Down: An Autobiography* (New York, 1989), 49.

71. Quoted in Nalty, *Strength for the Fight*, 176.

72. Blum, *V Was for Victory*, 210, 217–18; Doherty, *Projections of War*, 206 ("Deutschland"), 214 ("the racist"); Polenberg, *One Nation Divisible*, 70 .

73. Reed, *Seedtime*, 345; Norrell, "Caste in Steel," 680 ("Devil's," "be called"); Nelson, "Organized Labor," 955 ("faced"); Blum, *V Was for Victory*, 220.

74. White, *"It's Your Misfortune,"* 504 (FDR Columbus Day 1942 speech); 506.

75. Kelley, " 'We Are Not What We Seem,' " 76; Fass, *Outside In*, 144.

76. Polenberg, *One Nation Divisible*, 53 ("the idea"), 78 ("Where"); Doherty, *Projections*, 50 ("foreigners").

77. Diggins, *Mussolini and Fascism*, 352, 351, 366; Polenberg, *One Nation Divisible*, 60 ("a lot").

78. Takaki, *Strangers*, 358, 368–69, 377, 359–60.

79. Wylie, *Generation of Vipers*, 68, 61.

80. D'Emilio, *Sexual Politics*, 26.

81. Bérubé, *Coming Out Under Fire*, 253.

82. Hartmann, *Home Front*, 42 (quotations from female commanders), 24 (on job segregation); Tuttle, *"Daddy's Gone to War,"* 69 ("latchkey").

83. Tuttle, *"Daddy's Gone to War,"* 26.

84. Hartmann, *Home Front*, 157.

85. Kennett, *For the Duration*, 162.

86. Wecter, *When Johnny Comes Marching Home*, 498.

87. Kennett, *For the Duration*, 127, 187; Susan Gubar, " 'This Is My Rifle, This Is My Gun,' " in Higonnet et al., *Behind the Lines*, 251 (on Hersey).

88. Gubar, "'This Is My Rifle,'" 248 ("The fat wife"), 250 ("O war"); Wecter, *When Johnny Comes Marching Home*, 497 ("beginning to"); Hartmann, *Home Front*, 202.

89. Hartmann, *Home Front*, 36; Richard Polenberg, ed., *America at War: The Home Front, 1941–1945* (Englewood Cliffs, 1969), 2–3 (Daniels); Thomas Hart Benton, "Death of Grant Wood," *University Review* Spring 1942: 148.

90. Gubar, "'This Is My Rifle,'" 258, 253; Campbell, *Women at War*.

91. See George Mosse, *Nationalism and Sexuality: Middle-Class Morality and Sexual Norms in Modern Europe* (Madison, 1985), and Higonnet et al., *Behind the Lines*.

92. Journalist Virginius Dabney, quoted in Tuttle, *"Daddy's Gone to War,"* 175.

93. Janann Sherman, "'They either need these women or they do not': Margaret Chase Smith and the Fight for Regular Status for Women in the Military," *Journal of Military History* 54 (January 1990): 61; Bernstein, *American Indians*, 54.

94. FDR PP, 13 (1944–1945): 181; Ross, *Preparing for Ulysses*, 70.

95. Wecter, *When Johnny Comes Marching Home*, 522, 523; Ross, *Preparing for Ulysses*, 123 ("New Deal"); Vatter, *U.S. Economy*, 136; Amenta and Skocpol, "Redefining the New Deal," 94 ("a special").

96. Prediction on women by Ernest W. Burgess, in Ogburn, *American Society*, 31. See also Modell et al., "World War II in the Lives of Black Americans" and Reed, *Seedtime*, esp. Epilogue.

97. Masuo Kato, quoted in Sherry, *Rise*, 281.

98. Fenrich, "Imagining Holocaust," xii.

99. *Time*, June 11, 1945 (emphasis in original), quoted in Perrett, *Days of Sadness*, 421.

100. Sherry, *Rise*, 349 (Truman); Boyer, *By the Bomb's Early Light*, 6 (*Herald Tribune*).

101. Boyer, *By the Bomb's Early Light*, 76 (*One World*), 68 (song), 5 ("mammalian"), 14 ("sole"); Wuthnow, *Restructuring*, 39 ("haunted," etc.); Sherry, *Rise*, 353 ("world of").

102. Quoted in Sherry, *Rise*, 349.

103. Gardner, *Covenant with Power*, 73.

104. Sherry, *Preparing*, 210.

105. Perrett, *Days of Sadness*, 416, 418; Dallek, *American Style*, 129.

106. Polenberg, *War and Society*, 208; *Life*, July 30, 1945, quoted in Perrett, *Days of Sadness*, 423; Fried, *Nightmare in Red*, 57.

107. Ross, *Preparing for Ulysses*, 176–77, 187.

108. Boyer, *By the Bomb's Early Light*, 11.

109. Chase, *For This We Fought*, 117; Boyer, *By the Bomb's Early Light*, 9, 3.

110. Sherry, *Rise*, 349.

111. Sherry, *Preparing*, 213.

112. Mark Priceman, "No World War III to Stop," *Bulletin of the Atomic Scientists* December 1989: 49–50 ("the premise"); Wuthnow, *Restructuring*, 46.

113. Fenrich, "Imagining Holocaust," 103 (quoting Chase, *For This We Fought*), 109.

114. Gillis, *Militarization*, 7.

Chapter 3

1. John Gunther, *Inside U.S.A* (New York, 1947), xii.

2. Donovan, *Conflict and Crisis*, 212–13.

3. Garry Wills, "Keeper of the Seal," *New York Review of Books* July 18, 1991: 19 (Clifford); Donovan, *Conflict and Crisis,* 125 (AMA), 216 (Roosevelt).

4. Charles S. Maier, "Alliance and Autonomy: European Identity and U.S. Foreign Policy Objectives in the Truman Years," in Lacey, *Truman Presidency,* 276; the first term is Maier's, the second is John Lewis Gaddis's. On the American–West German relationship, see Schwartz, *America's Germany,* 305. Leffler, *Preponderance,* 19.

5. Maier, "Alliance and Autonomy," 274, n. 2.

6. Rosenberg, "Cold War," 281.

7. Walter Millis, ed., *The Forrestal Diaries* (New York, 1951), 134; Donovan, *Conflict and Crisis,* 187.

8. Donovan, *Conflict and Crisis,* 189 (Vandenberg); Ambrose, *Rise to Globalism,* 73 (Churchill).

9. Ambrose, *Rise to Globalism,* 80; May, *"Lessons" of the Past,* 37 (Truman).

10. Schwartz, *America's Germany,* 299 ("dual," etc,), 308 ("to a deplorable"); Gimbel, "Project Paperclip," 355 ("we have").

11. Ambrose, *Rise to Globalism,* 85, 78.

12. Ibid., 78.

13. Barnet, *By the Rockets' Red Glare,* 252 (poll and Forrestal); 267 (State Department); 276 (Barnet summarizing 1948 poll).

14. Ibid., 269 (Barnet's brackets), 271, 288.

15. Emily S. Rosenberg, "Gender," *Journal of American History* 77 (June 1990): 119 ("emotional"); on Dulles and images of Indians, Andrew Rotter, "Gender, Foreign Relations: The United States and South Asia, 1947–1964," *Journal of American History* 81 (September 1994): 525, 532.

16. McCormick, *America's Half-Century,* 70 (Taft); Paterson, *On Every Front,* 119 (Muste).

17. Boyer, *By the Bomb's Early Light,* 34 (Lerner), 339, 349.

18. Ambrose, *Rise to Globalism,* 105; Brodie, *Strategy in the Missile Age,* 272.

19. Herken, *Winning Weapon,* 316–17.

20. Ambrose, *Rise to Globalism,* 113 ("America's"); Gaddis, *Strategies of Containment,* 92 ("to depend").

21. Gaddis, *Strategies of Containment,* 93.

22. DuBoff, *Accumulation and Power,* 99.

23. Robert Ferrell, *Off the Record: The Private Papers of Harry S. Truman* (New York, 1980), 47; Donovan, *Conflict and Crisis,* 143 (Forrestal).

24. Hughes, *American Genesis,* 425.

25. Donovan, *Conflict and Crisis,* 201.

26. Schwartz, *America's Germany,* 302 (quoting Charles Maier on "transnational"), 303 ("whose"); Barnet, *By the Rockets' Red Glare,* 255 ("populist").

27. Paul K. Hoch, "The Crystallization of a Strategic Alliance: The American Physics Elite and the Military in the 1940s," in Mendelsohn et al., *Science, Technology, and the Military,* 1: 88 ("would"); Greenberg, *Politics of Pure Science,* 134–35 (Ridenour); Geiger, *Research and Relevant Knowledge,* 332 ("chiefly"); Leslie, *Cold War and American Science,* 5 ("at best"), 9 ("defined," etc).

28. Mills, *Power Elite*, 214.

29. Quoted in Pach, *Presidency of Dwight D. Eisenhower*, 35.

30. Galambos and Pratt, *Rise of the Corporate Commonwealth*, 137 ("increased"), 140 ("defense"); DuBoff, *Accumulation and Power*, 102 ("indirect"); I. Bernard Cohen, "The Computer: A Case Study of Support by Government, Especially the Military, of a New Science and Technology," in Mendelsohn et al., *Science, Technology, and the Military*, 1: 199 ("exceeded"); Wittner, *Cold War America*, 117 (Hofstadter).

31. Galambos and Pratt, *Rise of the Corporate Commonwealth*, 139–39; Charles S. Maier, "American Visions and British Interests: Hogan's Marshall Plan," *Reviews in American History* 18 (March 1990): 109.

32. Markusen et al., *Rise of the Gunbelt*, 40.

33. Lotchin, *Fortress California*, 353.

34. Galambos and Pratt, *Rise of the Corporate Commonwealth*, 180–82.

35. Boyer, *By the Bomb's Early Light*, 109, 111, 107 (chapter title), 112 (Hutchins), 113 (*PM* and *Nation*).

36. Ibid., 123, 127 (Boyer's description of illustration), 124 (emphasis in original); Hughes, *American Genesis*, 441 (AEC commissioner).

37. Nef, *Western Civilization*, 377. For a brief, updated challenge to the claim that "military needs stimulate and inspire technological growth," see Joel Mokyr, *The Lever of Riches: Technological Creativity and Economic Progress* (New York, 1990), 183–86.

38. Nalty, *Strength for the Fight*, 204–05.

39. Ibid., 233.

40. Polenberg, *One Nation Divisible*, 112.

41. Nalty, *Strength for the Fight*, 242.

42. Roosevelt quoted in Joanna Schneider Zangrando and Robert L. Zangrando, "ER and Black Civil Rights," in Joan-Hoff Wilson and Marjorie Lightman, eds., *Without Precedent: The Life and Career of Eleanor Roosevelt* (Bloomington, 1984), 102; Polenberg, *One Nation Divisible*, 108 (Acheson); Stephen Lawson, *Running for Freedom: Civil Rights and Black Politics in America since 1941* (Philadelphia, 1991), 34 (President's Commission); Donovan, *Conflict and Crisis*, 334 (Truman); Dalfiume, *Desegregation*, 139 (Truman); Pemberton, *Harry S. Truman*, 114 ("top dog").

43. Polenberg, *One Nation Divisible*, 112; Duberman, *Robeson*, 342.

44. Polenberg, *One Nation Divisible*, 113, 114; Berman, *Politics*, 232. Regarding the Eisenhower quotation, I must beg the reader's indulgence: I have long had it in lecture notes but cannot retrieve the published source from which it came. But in tone and substance it sounds like Eisenhower, who said much the same thing, if in more pallid form, several times in 1952, as in South Carolina: "And neither at home nor in the eyes of the world can Americans risk the weakness which inevitably results when any group of people are ranked—politically and economically—as second-class citizens." See "Text of Eisenhower's Address in South Carolina," *New York Times* Oct. 1, 1952.

45. Burk, *Eisenhower Administration*, 24.

46. Polenberg, *One Nation Divisible*, 109, 110.

47. Ibid., 113 ("Stalin"); Duberman, *Robeson*, 389, 344, 357. See also Mary L. Dudziak, "Josephine Baker, Racial Protest, and the Cold War," *Journal of American History* 81 (September 1994): 543–70.

48. Polenberg, *One Nation Divisible*, 101, 103, 107.

49. Ibid., 107.

50. Janann Sherman, " 'They Either Need These Women or They Do Not': Margaret Chase Smith and the Fight for Regular Status for Women in the Military," *Journal of Military History* 54 (January 1990): 68, 71.

51. Smith, "Commentary," 86, n. 16; Hartmann, *Home Front*, 155 (Truman).

52. Boyer, *By the Bomb's Early Light*, 11–12; Elaine Tyler May, "Explosive Issues: Sex, Women, and the Bomb," in May, *Recasting America*, 160, 161, 163; Rosenberg, " 'Foreign Affairs' After World War II," 66 ("ideology"), 69 ("patriotism"); Carter, *Another Part of the 50s*, 86, 91 (Stevenson).

53. Jack Lait and Lee Mortimer, *Washington Confidential* (New York, 1951), 96.

54. Jack Lait and Lee Mortimer, *U.S.A. Confidential* (New York, 1952), 42, 44–45.

55. D'Emilio, *Sexual Politics*, 43 ("outward"); Ehrenreich, *Hearts of Men*, 24 ("They cannot"); Lewes, *Psychoanalytic Theory*, 151, 115, 136–37.

56. Quoted in Robert Griffith, "Harry S Truman and the Burden of Modernity," *Reviews in American History* 9 (September 1981): 298 (my thanks to David Johnson for bringing this to my attention).

57. Polenberg, *One Nation Divisible*, 120, 121.

58. Pemberton, *Harry S. Truman*, 148; Takaki, *Strangers*, 416.

59. For "remapping" and "gunbelt," see Markusen et al., *Rise of the Gunbelt*.

60. Ibid., chap. 2; quotation, p. 4

61. Lotchin, *Fortress California*, 156.

62. Markusen et al., *Rise of the Gunbelt*, 7. See also Polenberg, *One Nation Divisible*, 163.

63. Jane De Hart Mathews, "Art and Politics in Cold War America," *American Historical Review* 81 (October 1976): 777, 772; Fried, *Nightmare in Red*, 31 ("because"); Erika Doss, "The Art of Cultural Politics: From Regionalism to Abstract Expressionism," in May, *Recasting America*, 216.

64. Whitfield, *Culture of the Cold War*.

65. See Graebner, *Age of Doubt*, esp. chap. 3.

66. Polenberg, *One Nation Divisible*, 127.

67. See Jane Smith, *Patenting the Sun: Polio and the Salk Vaccine* (New York, 1990), esp. 158–60 and the posters opposite 256.

68. This is my reading of *High Noon;* Whitfield, *Culture of the Cold War*, 146–49, sees a more subversive message in it. On Ford, see Slotkin, *Gunfighter Nation*, 334, 343.

69. Joel Carpenter, "Youth for Christ and the New Evangelicals' Place in the Life of the Nation," in Sherrill, *Religion and the Life of the Nation*, 129, 133; Whitfield, *Culture of the Cold War*, 86–87 ("not so much").

70. Carpenter, "Youth for Christ," 139 ("Visions"); Wuthnow, *Restructuring*, 38 ("new beginnings," Dulles, Truman); Whitfield, *Culture of the Cold War*, 77 (Graham), 87 ("America must").

71. Whitfield, *Culture of the Cold War*, 92–99 (on Spellman and the church); Wittner, *Cold War America*, 89 ("Long the," "Communist floodings"); Wuthnow, *Restructuring*, 75 ("as blind").

72. Boyer, *By the Bomb's Early Light*, 25, 31; Weart, *Nuclear Fear*, 192 ("filled a"); Novick, *That Noble Dream*, 314, 315.

73. Fried, *Nightmare in Red*, 98 ("garnered"), 99 ("pageants").

74. Warren Susman, "Did Success Spoil the United States? Dual Representations in Postwar America," in May, *Recasting America*, 30; Goldman, *Crucial Decade*, 218 ("We have").

75. Susman, "Did Success Spoil the United States?" 26.

76. Novick, *That Noble Dream*, 314, 318, see also 312. On MIT and Morison, see Alan Needell, "'Truth Is Our Weapon': Project TROY, Political Warfare, and Government-Academic Relations in the National Security State," *Diplomatic History* 17 (Summer 1993): 418–19.

77. In Douglas and Sylvia Angus, eds., *Contemporary American Short Stories* (New York, 1967), 254.

78. Schlesinger, *Vital Center*, 1, 2, 9, 98.

79. Ibid., 219, 3, 4, 100, 9, 236.

80. Ibid., 4, 160, 50, 36, 40, 151 ("perverts politics"), 127, 210, 150, titles of chaps. 7 and 11, 245, 255.

81. Hofstadter, *Age of Reform* (1955), as quoted in David W. Noble, "The Reconstruction of Progress: Charles Beard, Richard Hofstadter, and Postwar Historical Thought," in May, *Recasting America*, 72.

82. Schlesinger, *Vital Center*, 2.

83. Millis, *Arms and Men*, 307. Mills, *Power Elite*, 222.

84. Thomas P. Hughes and Agatha C. Hughes, eds., *Lewis Mumford: Public Intellectual* (New York, 1990); see Hughes's introduction and essays by Everett Mendelsohn and Michael Zuckerman. Quotations: 343 (from "Gentlemen: You are Mad!" in *Saturday Review of Literature* March 2, 1946), 372 (Zuckerman's words), 8 (Hughes's).

85. Novick, *That Noble Dream*, 299, 300, 295, 294.

86. Ibid., 304.

87. Marling and Wetenhall, *Iwo Jima*, 125, 160.

88. Ibid., 136, 137. On *The Caine Mutiny*, see Whitfield, *Culture of the Cold War*, 60–62.

89. Lipsitz, *Class and Culture*, 218; Lipsitz's context for this comment is primarily class relations rather than foreign and military policy.

90. May, *Homeward Bound*, 16–18 (on Nixon), 168; Novick, *That Noble Dream*, 307 (Bemis).

91. Carter, *Another Part of the Fifties*, 114–16.

92. Fried, *Nightmare in Red*, 76, 75, 76.

93. Ibid., 67.

94. Polenberg, *One Nation Divisible*, 124–25.

95. Wittner, *Cold War America*, 108 ("Adlai"); Griffith, *Politics of Fear*, 115–16, 145.

96. Fried, *Nightmare in Red*, 115–116.

97. Carter, *Another Part of the Fifties*, 272; Fried, *Nightmare in Red*, 167 ("the Red"); Griffith, *Politics of Fear*, 89 ("Communists," "prancing mimics").

98. Fried, *Nightmare in Red*, 68; Wittner, *Cold War America*, 86–87 (McGrath), 90 (Rankin); Carter, *Another Part of the Fifties*, 13 (Stevenson).

99. Fried, *Nightmare in Red*, 69, 22; Whitfield, *The Culture of the Cold War*, 19 (Nixon); Griffith, *Politics of Fear*, 73.

100. Fried, *Nightmare in Red*, 99, 198.

101. Novick, *That Noble Dream*, 331, 332; Schrecker, *No Ivory Tower*, 111 (Yale's Charles Seymour; Conant); Diamond, *Compromised Campus*, 25; Wittner, *Cold War America*, 122 (Commager); Pells, *Liberal Mind*, 343 (on Oppenheimer, etc.), 339.

102. Goldman, *Crucial Decade*, 177.

103. May, *"Lessons" of the Past*, 62.

104. Ibid., 79.

105. Barton Bernstein, "The Truman Administration and the Korean War," in Lacey, *Truman Presidency*, 420 ("clear-cut" and "absolutely"), 423 ("We had to"); other quotations from May, *"Lessons" of the Past*, 81–83.

106. Ambrose, *Rise to Globalism*, 118.

107. Bernstein, "Truman Administration and the Korean War," 425.

108. On this point generally, see Garry Wills, "Keeper of the Seal," *The New York Review of Books* July 18, 1991: 19–22.

109. Kaufman, *Korean War*, 37.

110. Bernstein, "Truman Administration," 434 ("atomic bombardment"), 436 ("12:30"); Ambrose, *Rise to Globalism*, 129 ("to receive"); Weigley, *American Way of War*, 390 (Bradley).

111. Ambrose, *Rise to Globalism*, 129.

112. Cumings, *Origins of the Korean War*, 2: 750 (Gore); 748 (estimate of two million).

113. I. F. Stone, *The Hidden History of the Korean War* (New York, 1952), 258; Cumings, *Origins of the Korean War*, 2: 755.

114. Quoted in "Truman, in 1952 Memos, Considered Nuclear Strike," *New York Times* Aug. 3, 1980. See also Pemberton, *Harry S. Truman*, 158; Cumings, *Origins of the Korean War*, 2: 747–53.

115. Pach, *Arming the Free World*, 231.

116. Daniel Hirsch and William G. Mathews, "The H-Bomb: Who Really Gave Away the Secret?" *Bulletin of the Atomic Scientists* January–February 1990: 22–30.

117. Freedman, *Evolution of Nuclear Strategy*, 69.

118. Gaddis, *Strategies of Containment*, 126.

119. Hixson, *George F. Kennan*, 101; Bernstein, "Truman Administration," 424 (quoting a paraphrase of comments by Kennan).

120. Pemberton, *Harry S. Truman*, 151.

121. HST PP, 1952–1953: 189.

122. *Life* editorial, Jan. 15, 1951: 24; Hodgson, *America in Our Time*, 103.

123. Cumings, *Origins of the Korean War*, 2: 760, 763.

124. Kaufman, *Korean War*, 50

125. Friedan, *Feminine Mystique*, 286, 275–76. My analysis, and "appalling girl-lessness," are taken from Lane Fenrich, "Their Mothers' Sons: Maternal Pathology and the Problem of Defection, 1953–63," paper delivered at the 1993 Berkshire Conference on the History of Women.

Chapter 4

1. Goldman, *Crucial Decade*, 212.
2. Ibid., 221.
3. Carter, *Another Part of the Fifties*, 15 (Carter), 12 (Truman, Carter summarizing Stevenson).
4. Eisenhower speeches, July 3 and Oct. 29, 1952, both in D.D.E Papers as President 1953–61 (Speech Series), Boxes 1 and 2, respectively, Dwight D. Eisenhower Library, as quoted in Matthew Olson, "Dwight D. Eisenhower's 1952 Campaign Strategy" (unpublished senior thesis, Northwestern University, 1991); Goldman, *Crucial Decade*, 234 ("red hot," etc).
5. Pach, *Presidency of Eisenhower*, 12 ("strengthening"); *Peace with Justice: Selected Addresses of Dwight D. Eisenhower* (New York, 1961), 11, 12 (1950 remarks).
6. Ambrose, *Eisenhower*, 89.
7. Ibid., 118 (on Knowland), 114 (Kennan), 240 ("Don't worry); Hughes, *Ordeal of Power*, 218 (on Dulles); Murray Kempton, "The Underestimation of Dwight D. Eisenhower," *Esquire* September 1967: 108 ("I would").
8. Fred Greenstein, *The Hidden-Hand Presidency: Eisenhower as Leader* (New York, 1982); Kempton, "Underestimation," 156; Hughes, *Ordeal of Power*, 279.
9. *Ike PP*, 1953: 4–5, 7; Hughes, *Ordeal of Power*, 51.
10. See Gaddis, *Strategies of Containment*, esp. chaps. 4–5.
11. *Ike PP*, 1953: 34, 17; Gaddis, *Strategies of Containment*, 146.
12. Gaddis, *Strategies of Containment*, 130 (Ike), 147 (Dulles); Pach, *Presidency of Eisenhower*, 80 (NSC); Weigley, *American Way of War*, 400 (Weigley's words).
13. Pach, *Presidency of Eisenhower*, 77, 31.
14. Ibid., 76 ("permanent state"); Hughes, *Ordeal of Power*, 217 ("If we"); Gaddis, *Strategies of Containment*, 136 ("Should we").
15. Ambrose, *Eisenhower*, 89, 100.
16. Ibid., 88–89 ("damn tired," "We pulverized"); Gaddis, *Strategies of Containment*, 135 ("Gain such"), 173 ("If the"); Hughes, *Ordeal of Power*, 88 ("notion that"); *Ike PP*, 1953: 817, 820 (UN speech).
17. Gaddis, *Strategies of Containment*, 149, 151.
18. *Ike PP*, 1953: 182, 186.
19. Gaddis, *Strategies of Containment*, 128.
20. Ambrose, *Eisenhower*, 87.
21. Ibid., 35, 99.
22. Ibid., 52, 107.
23. See Marling and Wetenhall, *Iwo Jima*, 10–16.
24. Ambrose, *Eisenhower*, 180.
25. Ibid., 177. But Eisenhower's role in this crisis is much contested. For a different view, see George C. Herring and Richard H. Immerman, 'Eisenhower, Dulles, and Dienbienphu: 'The Day We Didn't Go to War' Revisited," *Journal of American History* 71 (September 1984): 343–63.

26. Herring, *America's Longest War*, 43 (Kennedy); Ambrose, *Eisenhower*, 176 (paraphrase of Eisenhower comments), 177 ("tradition," etc.), 184.

27. Ambrose, *Eisenhower*, 240 ("aggressive fanaticism"); Gaddis, *Strategies of Containment*, 170, 173; Hughes, *Ordeal of Power*, 182 (Dulles's boast).

28. Carter, *Another Part of the Fifties*, 72, 73.

29. Ambrose, *Eisenhower*, 227 (Doolittle), 197; Carter, *Another Part of the Fifties*, 287.

30. Carter, *Another Part of the Fifties*, 79.

31. Broadwater, *Eisenhower*, 106.

32. Gary W. Reichard, "The Domestic Politics of National Security," in Norman Graebner, ed., *The National Security: Its Theory and Practice, 1945–1960* (New York, 1986), 267.

33. Pach, *Presidency of Eisenhower*, 59.

34. Ibid., 59–60.

35. Ibid., 62.

36. Ambrose, *Eisenhower*, 264.

37. Ibid., 260 ("appeasement"); Hughes, *Ordeal of Power*, 148.

38. Brands, "Age of Vulnerability," 987 (Humphrey); Ambrose, *Eisenhower*, 150. On megatonnage, see *Bulletin of the Atomic Scientists* December 1989: 52.

39. Brands, "Age of Vulnerability," 989.

40. Ambrose, *Eisenhower*, 168, 170.

41. Ibid., 135.

42. Ibid., 348.

43. Stone, "The Liberals and the Military Budget," May 27, 1957, in Stone, *Haunted Fifties*, 210–14.

44. Hughes, *Ordeal of Power*, 122–24.

45. Ibid., 165; Ambrose, *Eisenhower*, 115, 116.

46. *Ike PP*, 1953: 186.

47. *Peace with Justice* (cited in n. 5), 12; *Ike PP*, 1953: 2.

48. See Griffith, "Dwight D. Eisenhower"; for Eisenhower quotation, see p. 105.

49. Eisenhower, *Mandate for Change*, 549 ("sprout up"); *Ike PP*, 1955: 276; Pach, *Presidency of Eisenhower*, 123.

50. Pach, *Presidency of Eisenhower*, 123; Eisenhower, *Mandate for Change*, 548.

51. *Architectural Forum* July 1957, quoted in Mark Gelfand, *A Nation of Cities* (New York, 1975), 227.

52. William H. Chafe, "The Civil Rights Revolution, 1945–1960," in Bremner and Reichard, *Reshaping America*, 85.

53. *Congressional Digest* 36 (April 1957): 116, 118. Burk, *Eisenhower Administration*, 257 (Nixon).

54. Branch, *Parting the Waters*, 218.

55. Martin Luther King, Jr., *Why We Can't Wait* (New York, 1964), 39 ("brutality," etc.; "nonviolent army"); "The Sword That Heals," title of chap. 2; 21 ("Throughout the"); see also pp. x, 84. Branch, *Parting the Waters*, 273 (on Woolworth's demonstrations).

56. Pach, *Presidency of Eisenhower*, 140 ("prejudices"), 137 ("first-class"); Hughes, *Ordeal of Power*, 176 ("We can't").

57. Eisenhower, *Mandate for Change*, 230; Ambrose, *Eisenhower*, 412, 274.

58. Ambrose, *Eisenhower*, 426 ("policy of"); Polenberg, *One Nation Divisible*, 153.

59. Ambrose, *Eisenhower*, 200; Branch, *Parting the Waters*, 213 (King).

60. Pach, *Presidency of Eisenhower*, 150; Chafe, "Civil Rights Revolution," 87 (on "military code").

61. Branch, *Parting the Waters*, 224 ("Well, if"); Hughes, *Ordeal of Power*, 213; Pach, *Presidency of Eisenhower*, 154 ("occupied," "compared"); Ambrose, *Eisenhower*, 421. See also Ambrose, 417.

62. *Ike PP*, 1957: 694; Hughes, *Ordeal of Power*, 213.

63. *Ike PP*, 1960–1961: 927.

64. Ambrose, *Eisenhower*, 277, 278, 283 (emphasis in Ambrose); *Ike PP*, 1955: 55.

65. Ronald Lora, "Education: Schools as Crucible in Cold War America," in Bremner and Reichard, eds., *Reshaping America*, 243 (characterizing and quoting Rickover), 245 (on Conant).

66. Quoted in Kenneth Jones, "The Government-Science Complex," in Bremner and Reichard, eds., *Reshaping America*, 330.

67. Beschloss, *Mayday*, 148 (Jackson, NBC); *Congressional Digest*, February 1958, 36 (LBJ); Aliano, *American Defense Policy*, 210 (Flood), 193 (Kissinger).

68. Newhouse, *War and Peace*, 118 (Teller); on Manhattan Project, see Ambrose, *Eisenhower*, 438, and Jones, "Government-Science Complex," 331.

69. 1958 speech, quoted in Miroff, *Pragmatic Illusions*, 37.

70. MacDougall, *Heavens*, 137, 142.

71. Dyson, *Disturbing the Universe*, 109, 111; Stone, *Haunted Fifties*, 255–56.

72. Koppes, *JPL*, 111 ("'When do'"); Newhouse, *War and Peace*, 117.

73. Ambrose, *Eisenhower*, 435.

74. Ibid., 495 "how many"), 493 ("into an"), 494 ("there just"), 568 ("Why don't"); Beschloss, *Mayday*, 154 ("sanctimonious").

75. Ambrose, *Eisenhower*, 561 ("damn near"); Newhouse, *War and Peace*, 120 ("I'm not," "you can't"); Dyson, *Disturbing the Universe*, 115.

76. *Ike PP*, 1957: 229–30 ("there is"); Ambrose, *Eisenhower*, 433 ("We face," etc); Pach, *Presidency of Eisenhower*, 171; Hughes, *Ordeal of Power*, 235.

77. Ambrose, *Eisenhower*, 491, 516, 567.

78. Ibid., 433.

79. Arthur von Hippel, quoted in Leslie, *Cold War and American Science*, 211 ("What"). MacDougall, *Heavens*, 140, argues that Sputnik ushered in an "age of technocracy."

80. Ambrose, *Eisenhower*, 432, 450.

81. Ibid., 451 ("This"); Adam Ulam, *The Rivals: America and Russia since World War II* (New York, 1971), 230 ("Every Russian").

82. Dan O'Neill, "Project Chariot: How Alaska Escaped Nuclear Excavation," *Bulletin of the Atomic Scientists* December 1989: 28–37.

83. Weart, *Nuclear Fear*, 212; Divine, *Blowing in the Wind*, 323.

84. Brodie, *Strategy in the Missile Age*, 292; Thomas Schelling, quoted in Freedman, *Evolution of Nuclear Strategy*, 164.

85. Stone, *Haunted Fifties*, 320–21.

86. Weigley, *American Way of War*, 430; Freedman, *Evolution of Nuclear Strategy*, 156 (Freedman on "exaggerated"), 162–63 (Kissinger).

87. Weigley, *American Way of War*, 414 (Kissinger), 412 ("the only"), 434–35 (Brodie).

88. Freedman, *Evolution of Nuclear Strategy*, 180–81 ("It was"); Weigley, *American Way of War*, 440 ("grim jocularity").

89. Kaplan, *Wizards of Armageddon*, 134 (LeMay); Ford, *Button*, 107 ("If there").

90. Stone, *Haunted Fifties*, 273 ("the pets"); Pach, *Presidency of Eisenhower*, 200 ("West," etc.).

91. Pach, *Presidency of Eisenhower*, 200–204; Ambrose, *Eisenhower*, 519 ("Where").

92. Pach, *Presidency of Eisenhower*, 207, 208.

93. *Ike PP*, 1958: 2, 3.

94. Wolfe, *Right Stuff*, 120, 157.

95. See *United States at Large, 1958* (Washington 1959), vol. 72, part 1, 1580-1605.

96. Goldman, *Rendezvous with Destiny*, 314.

97. MacDougall, *Heavens*, 161 (on technocracy); Ambrose, *Eisenhower*, 459.

98. Barry Goldwater, *The Conscience of a Conservative* (New York, 1960), 108, 90, 20.

99. Peter Drucker, Delbert C. Miller, and Robert A. Dahl, *Power and Democracy in America* (Notre Dame, 1961); D. W. Brogan, *America in the Modern World* (Rutgers, 1960), 74, 112.

100. Pells, *Liberal Mind*, 213 (characterizing Goodman); Paul Goodman, *Growing up Absurd: Problems of Youth in the Organized System* (New York, 1960), 109, 13.

101. Jules Henry, *Culture Against Man* (New York, 1963, 1965), 123, 102, 103, 104, 110.

102. Novick, *That Noble Dream*, 415, 418. John Lukacs, *The History of the Cold War* (New York, 1961, 1962), xi, 272, 339.

103. Marling and Wetenhall, *Iwo Jima*, chap. 9; quotations: 172, 176–77, 184.

104. Weart, *Nuclear Fear*, 218.

105. Whitfield, *Culture of the Cold War*, 213 (on *The Manchurian Candidate*). See also Lane Fenrich, "Mommies, Commies, and Queers," paper delivered at the Lesbian and Gay Studies Conference, Rutgers University, November 1991.

106. Weart, *Nuclear Fear*, 218.

107. *Ike PP*, 1960–1961: 690.

108. *JFK PP*, 1961: 1.

109. Fred I. Greenstein and Richard H. Immerman, "What Did Eisenhower Tell Kennedy about Indochina? The Politics of Misperception," *Journal of American History* 79 (September 1992): 568–87. See also Ambrose, *Eisenhower*, 614–15.

110. *Ike PP*, 1960–1961: 1035–40.

111. Ibid., 1045. Comments from 1953 quoted in Aliano, *American Defense Policy*, 34–35.

112. Schlesinger, *Thousand Days*, 317n.

113. *Nation*, quoted in Pach, *Presidency of Eisenhower*, 230; *New Republic* Jan. 30, 1961: 2; Schlesinger, *Thousand Days*, 312.

114. *Ike PP*, 1960–1961: 1047; Pach, *Presidency of Eisenhower*, 233 (Pach's characterizations), 235 (Eisenhower).

115. Richard M. Nixon, *RN: The Memoirs of Richard Nixon* (New York, 1978), 235; *JFK*

PP, 1961: 1–2; *Ike PP*, 1960–1961: 1037; Ambrose, *Eisenhower*, 89 (1953 statement).

Chapter 5

1. Kennedy before Massachusetts state legislature, quoted in *Time* Jan. 20, 1961: 15; Stone, *Haunted Fifties*, 313.
2. *Life* Feb. 10: 1961, 17, 21.
3. On the April 14 meeting, see Hugh Sidey, *John F. Kennedy, President* (New York, 1964), 120–23; Sidey, "How the News Hit Washington—With Some Reactions Overseas," *Life* April 21, 1961: 26–27, and *Life* editorial, 35. *JFK PP*, 1961: 397, 404; 1962: 669.
4. MacDougall, *Heavens*, 322; Koppes, *JPL and the American Space Program*, 111 (T. Keith Glennan on Khrushchev).
5. MacDougall, *Heavens*, 323.
6. Beschloss, *Crisis Years*, 166.
7. Wolfe, *Right Stuff*, 122–23.
8. Henry W. Cooper, "Annals of Space," *New Yorker* Sept. 2, 1991: 63.
9. Smith, "Selling the Moon," 178 ("to differentiate," etc.); MacDougall, *Heavens*, 305 ("the greatest"). On William Leuchtenburg's phrase "save war or its surrogate," see Chap. 1 above.
10. *Life* March 3, 1961: 26.
11. Smith, "Selling the Moon," 200.
12. *JFK PP*, 1961: 535; Baritz, *Backfire*, 117 ("shared").
13. Gaddis, *Strategies of Containment*, 212.
14. Daniel Bell, "The Dispossessed" (1962), in Bell, ed., *The Radical Right: The New American Right, Expanded and Updated* (1963; Garden City, 1964), 1, 32, 16, 15, 40. John A. Stormer, *None Dare Call It Treason* (Florissant, Mo., 1964), 10.
15. Students for a Democratic Society, "The Port Huron Statement," excerpts in William H. Chafe and Harvard Sitkoff, eds., *A History of Our Time*, 3d ed. (New York, 1991), 345–50.
16. Memorandum, LBJ to JFK, May 23, 1961, in New York Times, *Pentagon Papers*, 129; Ambrose, *Rise to Globalism*, 191; Bell, "Dispossessed," 44, 45.
17. Cook, *Warfare State*, 15.
18. *JFK PP*, 1961: 306 ("convinced"), 534 ("Bastogne"); Miroff, *Pragmatic Illusions*, 14 (1958).
19. Miroff, *Pragmatic Illusions*, 75 ("that Khrushchev"); Parmet, *JFK*, 196 ("the U.S.," Parmet's words); *JFK PP*, 1961: 536–37; Burner, *John F. Kennedy*, 77 ("empty gesture").
20. *Life* Sept. 15, 1961: 96; Sept. 29, 1961, 57. Stone, *Haunted Fifties*, 317.
21. Eugene Burdick and Harvey Wheeler, *Fail-Safe* (New York, 1962), 151.
22. *JFK PP*, 1962: 808 ; Robert F. Kennedy, *Thirteen Days: A Memoir of the Cuban Missile Crisis* (New York, 1969), 108.
23. Newhouse, *War and Peace*, 172 ("What difference"); *JFK PP*, 1962: 806, 807; Theodore Sorensen, *Kennedy* (New York, 1965), 678 (Sorensen's emphasis).

24. George Ball, "JFK's Big Moment," *New York Review of Books* Feb. 13, 1992: 18.

25. Beschloss, *Crisis Years*, 509. *JFK PP*, 1962: 807. *Life* Nov. 2, 1962: 35, for quotation; Nov. 9, 38–39, for air-raid drills. *U.S. News and World Report* Nov. 5, 1962: 41 (map), 120 (Lawrence).

26. Beschloss, *Crisis Years*, 477, 501.

27. Ibid., 544 (emphasis in Beschloss).

28. Boyer, *By the Bomb's Early Light*, 357.

29. Newhouse, *War and Peace*, 184.

30. *JFK PP*, 1962: 895. Newhouse, *War and Peace*, 198 ("strangest"). Beschloss, *Crisis Years*, 549 ("I cut"). Memorandum, Walt Whitman Rostow to Secretary of State Dean Rusk, Nov. 23, 1964, in New York Times, *Pentagon Papers*, 421. "Coming Tests and Opportunity in Cold War," editorial, *Life* Nov. 9, 1962, 4 (*Life*'s emphasis).

31. Adam Yarmolinsky, quoted in Charlton and Moncrieff, *Many Reasons Why*, 60–61.

32. FitzGerald, *Fire in the Lake*, 124.

33. Halberstam, *Best and Brightest*, 503.

34. Herring, *America's Longest War*, 79.

35. Schlesinger, *Thousand Days*, 547 (JFK); Baritz, *Backfire*, 103 (Bundy). Other quotations from New York Times, *Pentagon Papers*, 129 (Memorandum, LBJ to JFK, May 23, 1961), 422 (Memorandum, Rostow to Rusk, May 23, 1964), 372 (Taylor, briefing at Washington meeting, Nov. 27, 1964).

36. Gaddis, *Strategies of Containment*, 211 (LBJ), 248 (Rusk); New York Times, *Pentagon Papers*, 276 (JCS); Baritz, *Backfire*, 89 ("muscular realists," Baritz's phrase).

37. Henry Steele Commager, ed., *Documents in American History*, vol. 2 (New York, 1968), 711; Charlton and Moncrieff, *Many Reasons Why*, 136 (Westmoreland); Gaddis, *Strategies of Containment*, 244 (JCS and Lansdale); Curtis E. LeMay, with MacKinlay Kantor, *Mission with LeMay* (Garden City, 1965), 565.

38. David Halberstam, *The Making of a Quagmire: American and Vietnam During the Kennedy Era*, rev. by Daniel J. Singal (New York, 1988), 155; Halberstam, *Best and Brightest*, 200–201 (Halberstam's emphasis).

39. Singal, xix, in Halberstam, *Making of a Quagmire*; Baritz, *Backfire*, 104.

40. Westmoreland, *Soldier Reports*, 119; *LBJ PP*, 1966 (I): 496.

41. Baritz, *Backfire*, 126.

42. August Meier, Elliot Rudwick, and Francis L. Broderick, eds., *Black Protest Thought in the Twentieth Century*, 2d ed. (Indianapolis, 1971), 319 (emphasis in original); King, *Why We Can't Wait*, 21; *JFK PP*, 1963: 488.

43. Appy, *Working-Class War*, 21.

44. Stephen Lawson, "Civil Rights," in Divine, ed., *Johnson Years*, 1: 109, 122 (n. 51); *LBJ PP*, 1967 (vol. 1): 194.

45. D'Emilio, *Sexual Politics*, 151.

46. Rosenberg, *Divided Lives*, 162–67 (quotations are Rosenberg's paraphrases).

47. Rustin, "The Meaning of Birmingham" (1963), in Meier et al., *Black Protest Thought*, 339, 340. Carmichael, "What We Want," *New York Review of Books* Sept. 22, 1966, excerpted in Richard Hofstadter, *Great Issues in American History: From Reconstruction to the Present Day, 1864–1969* (New York, 1969), 499.

48. Baldwin, from *The Fire Next Time* (1963), excerpts in Howard, *Sixties*, 115.

49. Polenberg, *One Nation Divisible*, 175.

50. Michael Harrington, *The Other America: Poverty in America* (1962; Baltimore, 1971), 179.

51. Friedan, *Feminine Mystique*, 17, 338, 339, 182; on camps, see chap. 12.

52. Novick, *That Noble Dream*, 377, 375, 376, 366; Woodward, "The Age of Reinterpretation," 3.

53. Cook, *Warfare State*, 19, 65, 16; Stone, *Haunted Fifties*, 323.

54. *LBJ PP*, 1963–1964 (I): 114 ("This administration"), 376 ("a national war"), 380 ("If we now," "in a few months"). Other quotations from Lyndon B. Johnson, *My Hope for America* (New York, 1964), 41, 42, 44.

55. Zarefsky, *President Johnson's War on Poverty*, 29, 31; James Q. Wilson, "The War on Cities" (1966), repr. in Thomas R. Dye, *American Public Policy* (Columbus, 1969), 373.

56. Zarefsky, *President Johnson's War on Poverty*, 36; Lyndon Baines Johnson, *Vantage Point: Perspectives of the Presidency, 1963–69* (New York, 1971), 79; Leuchtenburg, "New Deal," 143.

57. Film, *The American Experience: LBJ* (PBS, 1991).

58. Conkin, *Big Daddy*, 222 ("was only"); Zarefsky, *President Johnson's War on Poverty*, 43 (Shriver).

59. *LBJ PP*, 1967 (I): 517; Conkin, *Big Daddy*, 214 (Conkin on "class rhetoric"); Zarefsky, *President Johnson's War on Poverty*, 98 (congressman); Rosenberg and Rosenberg, *In Our Times*, 129; Rorabaugh, *Berkeley at War*, 61 (emphasis in Rorabaugh).

60. Zarefsky, *President Johnson's War on Poverty*, 29.

61. *LBJ PP*, 1966 (I): 232 (Peace Corps), 291, 293, 296 (emphasis in original).

62. All quotations and much of the analysis here are from Clarence G. Lasby, "The War on Disease," in Divine, *Johnson Years*, 2: 183–216.

63. *LBJ PP*, 1966 (I): 163 ("I propose," emphasis in original; "There can"); *LBJ PP*, 1966 (II): 1266.

64. Appy, *Working-Class War*, 31–33.

65. Conkin, *Big Daddy*, 209.

66. *LBJ PP*, 1966 (I): 48; Polenberg, *One Nation Divisible*, 175.

67. Conkin, *Big Daddy*, 237; Small, *Johnson, Nixon, and the Doves*, 46. For an early depiction of LBJ's outlook, see Doris Kearns, *Lyndon Johnson and the American Dream* (New York, 1976), esp. chap. 11.

68. Schell, *Village of Ben Suc*, 56; Schell, *Real War*, 9–10.

69. *Time*, quoted in Pisor, *End of the Line*, 43; Schell, *Village of Ben Suc*, 31, 46, 47.

70. Schell, *Village of Ben Suc*, 94, 103, 86, 132.

71. Herring, *America's Longest War*, 156 ("was like"); Appy, *Working-Class War*, 197 ("military policy").

72. Conkin, *Big Daddy*, 196.

73. Ibid., 243–44.

74. Berman, *Planning a Tragedy*, 20 (LBJ); Herring, *America's Longest War*, 137; Guenter Lewy, *America in Vietnam* (New York, 1978), 73 ("We'll"); Westmoreland, *Soldier Reports*, 334.

75. Galluci, *Neither Peace Nor Honor*, 94.

76. Clodfelter, *Limits of Air Power*, 100, 65.

77. Ibid., 101, 135; Galluci, *Neither Peace Nor Honor*, 83 ("if you"), 84.

78. Westmoreland, *Soldier Reports*, 261; Clodfelter, *Limits of Air Power*, 145.

79. Hodgson, *America in Our Time*, 274.

80. *LBJ PP*, 1965 (I): 395–96.

81. LBJ quoted in Robert Divine, "The Johnson Revival," in Divine, *Johnson Years*, 2: 18.

82. Herring, *America's Longest War*, 170 ("Win"); Hixson, *George F. Kennan*, 247; Rorabaugh, *Berkeley at War*, 115, 110.

83. Rorabaugh, *Berkeley at War*, x.

84. Hodgson, *America in Our Time*, 275.

85. Charles DeBenedetti, "Lyndon Johnson and the Antiwar Opposition," in Divine, *Johnson Years*, 2: 23.

86. William Appleman Williams et al., eds., *America in Vietnam: A Documentary History* (Garden City, 1985), 256, 258–59; David M. Shoup, "The New American Militarism," *Atlantic* April 1969: 56.

87. King, "Beyond Vietnam," in Joanne Grant, ed., *Black Protest: History, Documents, and Analyses* (New York, 1968), 418–25; Martin Luther King, Jr., *Where Do We Go from Here: Chaos or Community?* (New York, 1967), 174 ("Nothing").

88. Rosenberg, *Divided Lives*, 197 ("is often"); Sara Evans, *Personal Politics*, 160, 185.

89. Barry Commoner, *Science and Survival* (New York, 1966), chap. 1 title; 10 ("greenhouse"); 132.

90. Matusow, *Unraveling of America*, 386, 387.

91. Grant McConnell, *Private Power and American Democracy* (New York, 1966), 337, 255; Paul Baran and Paul Sweezy, *Monopoly Capital: An Essay on the American Economic and Social Order* (New York, 1966), 187, 211, 210, 186. See also Christopher Lasch, *The New Radicalism in America, 1889–1963* (New York, 1965); *The Agony of the American Left* (New York, 1966–68).

92. Markusen et al., *Rise of the Gunbelt*, 14.

Chapter 6

1. Herring, *America's Longest War*, 178.

2. Pisor, *End of the Line*, 56-58.

3. Ibid., 47, 41; Herring, *America's Longest War*, 151 ("The solution").

4. Gibson, *Perfect War*, 99.

5. Pisor, *End of the Line*, 59.

6. Ambrose, *Nixon: Triumph*, 195.

7. Ibid., 11, 12, 48, 49, 61.

8. Ibid., 73, 77, 81.

9. Heineman, *Campus Wars*, 49, 251; Ambrose, *Nixon: Triumph*, 104.

10. Lt. Gen. Philip B. Davidson (U.S. Army, Ret.), *Vietnam at War* (1988), quoted in Hammond, "Press in Vietnam," 312; Hallin, *"Uncensored War,"* 3 (Nixon).

11. Hammond, "Press in Vietnam," 316; Tuttle, *"Daddy's Gone to War,"* 153 (on *Life*). See also Ambrose, *Nixon: Triumph*, 135.

12. Hammond, "Press in Vietnam," 317, 319.

13. Michael Arlen, *Living Room War* (1969), as excerpted in Howard, *Sixties*, 435–36, 438,

14. Herring, *America's Longest War*, 191, 192.

15. Quoted in Young, *Vietnam Wars*, 223.

16. Herring, *America's Longest War*, 194.

17. Schell, *Real War*, 37, 39.

18. Ibid., 205, 206.

19. Kutler, *Wars of Watergate*, 29.

20. Mailer, *Armies of the Night*, 38.

21. Ibid., 117, 228, 86, 88.

22. Ibid., 90, 92, 280; Matusow, *Unraveling*, 388 (Lowell).

23. Matusow, *Unraveling*, 328.

24. Ibid., 421.

25. Ibid., 318 (Rubin); Ambrose, *Nixon: Triumph*, 126.

26. Reich, *Greening*, 295; Hodgson, *America in Our Time*, 349–51, 341; *Atlantic* October 1968: 56 and February 1969: 450.

27. Heineman, *Campus Wars*, 30, 38.

28. Appy, *Working-Class War*, 41, 42.

29. Hodgson, *America in Our Time*, 311.

30. Mailer, *Armies of the Night*, 270, 271.

31. Kenneth Kenniston, *Youth and Dissent: The Rise of a New Opposition* (New York, 1971), 154 (Kenniston's emphasis).

32. Heineman, *Campus Wars*, 25.

33. Marling and Wetenhall, *Iwo Jima*, 199–204.

34. Levy, *Debate Over Vietnam*, 117.

35. Reich, *Greening*, 213 ("curious," etc.); Levy, *Debate Over Vietnam*, 119 (Hope); Ambrose, *Nixon: Triumph*, 480.

36. Address, Oct. 30, 1969, "Impudence in the Streets," in Spiro T. Agnew, *Frankly Speaking: A Collection of Extraordinary Speeches* (Washington, 1970), 44.

37. Ambrose, *Nixon: Triumph*, 310.

38. *LBJ PP*, 1966 (I): 20 (Jan. 13, 1966).

39. For 1964 quotations and analysis of them, see Lee Edelman, "Tearooms and Sympathy, or, The Epistemology of the Water Closet," in Andrew Parker, Mary Russo, Doris Sommer, and Patricia Yaeger, eds., *Nationalisms and Sexualities* (New York, 1991), 263–84. *LBJ PP*, 1966 (I): 519 ("Nervous"); Smith, "Commentary," 87 ("Hell"); Herring, *America's Longest War*, 181 ("frustrated"); Small, *Johnson, Nixon, and the Doves*, 65.

40. Agnew, *Frankly Speaking*, "Impudence," 44–51 (Agnew's emphasis) and "Rationality and Effetism," 18.

41. Ambrose, *Nixon: Triumph*, 348, 317, 496, 529.

42. Gibson, *Perfect War*, 329 (LBJ); Levy, *Debate Over Vietnam*, 109 (Daly); Carroll, *It Seemed Like Nothing Happened*, 34 (Friedan).

43. Mailer, *Armies of the Night*, 38, 171; Ambrose, *Nixon: Triumph*, 334; Evans, *Personal Politics*, 200. See also Jeffords, *Remasculinization*, esp. 47.

44. Ehrenreich, *Hearts of Men*, 105; Jeffords, *Remasculinization*, xii.

45. Evans, *Personal Politics*, 189–90 ("on the cover"), 215 ("intimacy"); Karla Jay and Allen Young, *Out of the Closets: Voices of Gay Liberation* (1972; New York, 1992), 197 (Brown), 253 ("translated").

46. Vonnegut, *Slaughterhouse-Five*, 74–75.

49. Catton, *Waiting for the Morning Train*, 232, 176, 220, 222, 245–46, 219.

48. Ambrose, *Nixon: Triumph*, 203, 142, 207.

49. Ibid., 323.

50. Ibid., 150, 292, 406, 394.

51. *Nixon PP*, 1970: 940–41 (on pornography); 12 ("overblown," etc.).

52. Ambrose, *Nixon: Triumph*, 432, 433, 657.

53. Ibid., 267, 27; Kutler, *Wars of Watergate*, 46 ("'togetherness'").

54. Ambrose, *Nixon: Triumph*, 404–05.

55. Kutler, *Wars of Watergate*, 69 ("There's"); Ambrose, *Nixon: Triumph*, 144, 168, 167, 195.

56. *Nixon PP*, 1969: 696–97.

57. Ibid., 699.

58. Gibson, *Perfect War*, 434.

59. Ambrose, *Nixon: Triumph*, 252.

60. Ibid., 224, 281, 282.

61. Ibid., 299, 342.

62. Ibid., 278.

63. Ambrose, *Nixon: Ruin and Recovery*, 42, 41, 50.

64. D. Michael Schafer, "The Vietnam Combat Experience," in Schafer, *Legacy*, 89.

65. Gen. William R. Peers, *The May Lai Inquiry* (New York, 1979), 254–55; Ambrose, *Nixon: Triumph*, 429.

66. Ambrose, *Nixon: Triumph*, 186, 172.

67. Ibid., 229, 409, 250.

68. Ibid., 361.

69. Ibid., 609.

70. William Safire, *Before the Fall: An Inside View of the Pre-Watergate White House* (Garden City, 1975), 377; H. R. Haldeman, *The Ends of Power* (New York, 1978), 110 ("shows"). For sources and analysis here, I also benefited from Gary Friedman, "Nixon, the Madman Theory, and the Roots of Watergate" (M.A. thesis, Northwestern University, 1988).

71. Ambrose, *Nixon: Triumph*, 239, 611; Kutler, *Wars of Watergate*, 97 (Huston).

72. See Ambrose, *Nixon: Triumph*, 659.

73. Ambrose, *Nixon: Ruin and Recovery*, 58.

74. George McGovern, *An American Journey: The Presidential Campaign Speeches of George McGovern* (New York, 1974), 103, 86, 21, 26; Ambrose, *Nixon: Triumph*, 605 (Scott).

75. Ambrose, *Nixon: Triumph*, 556, 588.

76. Ibid., 623, 624, 637; Ambrose, *Nixon: Ruin and Recovery*, 12.

77. Ambrose, *Nixon: Triumph*, 660; *Nixon: Ruin and Recovery*, 14, 15, 44.

78. Weigley, *American Way of War*, 476–77.

79. Bernard Brodie, *War and Politics* (New York, 1973), 222, 275.

80. Louis J. Halle, "Does War Have a Future?" *Foreign Affairs* 52 (October 1973): 34. For views of guerrilla warfare, see Walter Laqueur, *Guerrilla: A Historical and Critical Study* (Boston, 1976).

81. A. Ernest Fitzgerald, *The High Priests of Waste* (New York, 1972), chap. 1 title; Seymour Melman, *The Permanent War Economy: American Capitalism in Decline* (New York, 1974), 11; Wiesner, quoted in Freedman, *Evolution of Nuclear Strategy*, 338.

82. Quoted in Freedman, *Evolution of Nuclear Strategy*, 360.

83. Ambrose, *Nixon: Ruin and Recovery*, 320.

84. Ibid., 303; on "sufficiency," see Freedman, *Evolution of Nuclear Strategy*, 341.

85. Ambrose, *Nixon: Ruin and Recovery*, 99, 95.

86. Gaddis, *Strategies of Containment*, 321.

87. Carroll, *It Seemed Like Nothing Happened*, 97, 99.

88. Ambrose, *Nixon: Ruin and Recovery*, 95, 380; on "pitiful, helpless giant," see Ambrose, *Nixon: Triumph*, 345.

89. Polenberg, *One Nation Divisible*, chap. 7 title; Robert Wiebe, *The Segmented Society: An Introduction to the Meaning of America* (New York, 1975).

90. See FitzGerald, *Cities on a Hill*.

91. Carroll, *It Seemed Like Nothing Happened*, 31.

92. Ibid., 81.

93. Ambrose, *Nixon: Ruin and Recovery*, 55-56, 587 (Ambrose on Nixon); *Newsweek* Sept. 10, 1973: 18.

94. "Arabs' Final Weapon," *Time* Sept. 17, 1973: 29; James Burnham, "Choose Your Weapons, Gentlemen," *National Review* Dec. 21, 1973: 1401 (Burnham's emphasis).

95. Carroll, *It Seemed Like Nothing Happened*, 129.

96. Ibid., 131 ("Women"), 118.

97. *Nixon PP*, 1973: 920.

98. Ambrose, *Nixon: Ruin and Recovery*, 84, 127, 419.

99. Ibid., 106.

100. Ibid., 157, 250.

101. Ibid., 48, 68, 88.

102. Ibid., 149.

103. Ibid., 248.

104. This paragraph draws on Garry Wills, "Keeper of the Seal," *New York Review of Books* July 18, 1991: 19-22, which includes the Haig quotation. The characterization of Nixon is Bernard Brodie's, in *War and Politics* (cited in n. 79), 216.

105. Ambrose, *Nixon: Ruin and Recovery*, 507.

106. Ibid., 597.

107. Ibid., 323; Newhouse, *War and Peace*, 245; Gaddis, *Strategies of Containment*, 321 (Reagan).

108. Gaddis, *Strategies of Containment*, 320.

109. Ambrose, *Nixon: Ruin and Recovery*, 530-32 (emphasis in Ambrose).

110. *Ford PP*, 1975: 482-83.

111. Carroll, *It Seemed Like Nothing Happened*, x ("pervasive"); *Ford PP*, 1975: 498, 641; Herring, *America's Longest War*, 273-74.

Chapter 7

1. "A Strong but Risky Show of Force," *Time* May 26, 1975: 9.
2. Ibid. Other quotations: Carroll, *It Seemed Like Nothing Happened*, 168.
3. *Time* May 26, 1975: 10; Sidey, "An Old-Fashioned Kind of Crisis," 18.
4. See Schell, *Observing the Nixon Years*, 268–72.
5. Vagts, *History of Militarism*, 15.
6. Ribuffo, *Right, Center, Left*, 190, 189 (Ford), 200 (Reagan), 204 (on Carter "as a"); Carroll, *It Seemed Like Nothing Happened*, 189 ("Lon Chaney").
7. Ribuffo, *Right, Center, Left*, 201 (paraphrasing LBJ).
8. *Carter PP*, 1977 (I): 2–3.
9. Ribuffo, *Right, Center, Left*, 222 ("weirdo"); see also chap. 10 generally.
10. Ibid., 217; *Carter PP*, 1977 (I): 956.
11. *Carter PP*, 1977 (I): 955, 545, 3, 77.
12. Carroll, *It Seemed Like Nothing Happened*, 213.
13. *Carter PP*, 1977 (I): 500 ("we still"), 501 ("the destruction"); other quotations from Notre Dame speech, 954–62.
14. Ibid., 958.
15. Ibid., 498.
16. Ambrose, *Rise to Globalism*, 298.
17. Newhouse, *War and Peace*, 310.
18. Ibid., 278.
19. Ibid., 332.
20. Ibid., 258. Moynihan on CBS News, *Face the Nation*, June 17, 1979 (CBS transcript).
21. *Carter PP*, 1977 (II): 1716. On comparing slavery and nuclear weapons, see Smith, *Thinking the Unthinkable*.
22. Ribuffo, *Right, Center, Left*, 246; Carter memoirs, as quoted in Smith, *Morality, Reason, and Power*, 83.
23. *Carter PP*, 1977 (I): 656; (II): 1783.
24. Carroll, *It Seemed Like Nothing Happened*, 216 (brackets in Carroll), 217.
25. Smith, *Morality, Reason, and Power*, 57, 58.
26. Linenthal, *Sacred Ground*, 185–86; "courageous" and "make all" quotations from Confederate Air Force, "Narration of the World War II Air Power Demonstration" [n.d.], provided courtesy Linenthal.
27. Linenthal, *Sacred Ground*, 189, 182, 188, 185.
28. Marling and Wetenhall, *Iwo Jima*, 207; more generally, see chaps. 10–11.
29. Linenthal, "War and Sacrifice," 23, 25, 28–29; Richard Pipes, "Why the Soviet Union Thinks It Could Fight and Win a Nuclear War," *Commentary* July 1977: 21–34; Falwell, *Listen America!* 98.
30. Linenthal, "War and Sacrifice," 22, 24, 25, 27; Vance in *New York Times* June 6, 1980.
31. *Star Wars* (George Lucas, 1977); Hellmann, *American Myth*, 214; see also Hellmann's discussion of the rest of the trilogy.
32. See generally Linenthal, "Restoring America: Political Revivalism in the Nuclear Age," in Sherrill, *Religion;* for "fierce," see p. 42.

33. Weart, *Nuclear Fear*, 320.

34. "A Republic of Insects and Grass," title of section 1, Schell, *Fate of the Earth;* Kevin Lewis, "The Prompt and Delayed Effects of Nuclear War," *Scientific American* July 1979: 47.

35. Linenthal, "Restoring America," in Sherrill, *Religion,* 36 (Linenthal's words), 37 (Caldicott); Schell, *Fate of the Earth,* 359.

36. Boyer, *By the Bomb's Early Light,* 362; see more generally Boyer's epilogue.

37. Ibid. 364.

38. Dyson, *Disturbing the Universe,* 30.

39. Jeanine Basinger, *The World War Two Combat Film: Anatomy of a Genre* (New York, 1986), 332.

40. Judith E. Doneson, *The Holocaust in American Film* (New York, 1987), 188, 196.

41. Here I draw loosely, with no claim to hold them accountable for the results, on comments by Lane Fenrich and Marilyn Young.

42. Falwell, *Listen America!* 11. On the "cult of the superweapon," see Franklin, *War Stars.*

43. See Leonard, *Above the Battle,* for this theme at earlier points in American history.

44. Hal Lindsey, *The Late Great Planet Earth* (1970; New York, 1973), 165, 170, 155.

45. Boyer, *When Time Shall Be No More,* 145, 142, 144.

46. Ibid., 138, 128, 139 (Graham), 148.

47. Bruce Taylor, "The Vietnam War Movie," in Shafer, *Legacy,* 191 (quoting Gilbert Adair), 198.

48. Basinger, *World War II Combat Film,* 212 ("about combat"); Taylor, "Vietnam War Movie," 192 ("metaphor," etc.). See also Hellmann, *American Myth,* chap. 7.

49. Taylor, "Vietnam War Movie," 194–96.

50. I draw here on Taylor, as cited in preceding notes, on my own reading of these films, and on suggestions by Leo Ribuffo.

51. Franklin, *M.I.A.,* 75, 133, 136, 156.

52. Ibid., 142.

53. The quotation and some of the analysis here come from Thomas Laqueur, "Bodies, Names, Memory," paper delivered at Northwestern University, May 1993.

54. Carroll, *It Seemed Like Nothing Happened,* 250; Lasch, *The Culture of Narcissism: American Life in an Age of Diminishing Expectations* (New York, 1978), xv.

55. *Carter PP,* 1979 (II): 1237.

56. Lasch, *Culture of Narcissism,* 199, 4; Carroll, *It Seemed Like Nothing Happened,* x. See also Falwell, *Listen America!* 57.

57. *Carter PP,* 1979 (II): 1239; general, quoted in Edward Linenthal, "'A Reservoir of Spiritual Faith': Patriotic Faith at the Alamo in the Twentieth Century," *Southwestern Historical Quarterly* 91 (April 1988): 517.

58. Polenberg, *One Nation Divisible,* 236.

59. Nalty, *Strength for the Fight,* 340–41.

60. Graphic accompanying Raymond Coffey, "U.S. Youth: Farewell to Arms," *Chicago Tribune* Dec. 17, 1978.

61. Sociologist Charles Moskos, quoted in ibid.; Nalty, *Strength for the Fight,* 343 ("to fulfill").

62. *Time* July 19, 1976: 74; "Of Arms and the Woman," *Newsweek* Jan. 26, 1976: 60; Holm, *Women in the Military,* 311, 333.

63. *Time* cover, Sept. 8, 1975; "Homosexual Sergeant," *Time* June 9, 1975: 18. See also Shilts, *Conduct Unbecoming.*

64. Pentagon 1982 policy, in Mary Ann Humphrey, *My Country, My Right to Serve: Experiences of Gay Men and Women in the Military, World War II to the Present* (New York, 1990), 262.

65. Dennis Altman (1982), quoted in Ehrenreich, *Hearts of Men,* 130.

66. Ruth Rosen, "The Day They Buried Traditional Womanhood: Women and the Vietnam Experience," in Shafer, *Legacy,* 246–47, 249.

67. George F. Will, "How Far out of the Closet?" *Newsweek* May 30, 1977: 92; Falwell, *Listen America!* 181, 183, 185; FitzGerald, *Cities on a Hill,* 164 ("the church").

68. Linenthal, "War and Sacrifice," 24–25; Midge Decter, "The Boys on the Beach," *Commentary* September 1980: 43, 37, 46; letters, *Commentary* December 1980: 12, 13.

69. Felsenthal, *Sweetheart,* 237. See also Phyllis Schlafly and Chester Ward, *Ambush at Vladivostok* (Alton, Ill., 1976).

70. Felsenthal, *Sweetheart,* 238 (paraphrasing Schlafly), 317–18; Holm, *Women in the Military,* 264 (Ervin).

71. Ehrenreich, *Hearts of Men,* 148 (Schlafly), 152, 162, 163.

72. Ibid., 156, 157 (Schmitz), 157; Wuthnow, *Restructuring,* 203 (Falwell).

73. Wuthnow, *Restructuring,* 201.

74. Falwell, *Listen America!* 106.

75. "A Stunning Show, After All," *Time* March 3, 1980: 30; "U.S. Skaters Put the Gold on Ice," *Newsweek* March 3, 1980: 81, 85; "The Talk of the Town," *New Yorker* March 10, 1980: 37.

76. *Carter PP,* 1980–1981 (I): 106 ("powerful"); Smith, *Morality, Reason, and Power,* 226 (Vance), 227–28 (Mondale).

77. Smith, *Morality, Reason, and Power,* 182 (on shah); *Carter PP,* 1980–1981 (I): 109; Edward Luttwak, "After Afghanistan, What?" *Commentary* April 1980: 49; Raymond Coffey, "U.S. Military," *Chicago Tribune* Aug. 24, 1980.

78. *Carter PP,* 1980–1981 (I): 108; (III): 2891.

79. Smith, *Morality, Reason, and Power,* 209, 90; Carroll, *It Seemed Like Nothing Happened,* 343 (Reagan); George Will, "Reaping the Whirlwind," *Newsweek* Jan. 21, 1980: 92; "Talk of the Town," *New Yorker* April 28, 1980: 33; *Carter PP,* 1979 (II): 2233.

80. Ambrose, *Rise to Globalism,* 308 (bracketed comments Sherry's); *Carter PP,* 1980–1981 (I): 197.

81. Scheer, *With Enough Shovels,* 66.

82. Newhouse, *War and Peace,* 291; Smith, *Morality, Reason, and Power,* 82.

83. Scheer, *With Enough Shovels,* 21, 23.

84. Newhouse, *War and Peace,* 286, 289, 286.

85. Scheer, *With Enough Shovels,* 29, 31.

86. Newhouse, *War and Peace,* 321, 322; James Coates, "Lake Michigan Missile Subs Eyed," *Chicago Tribune* April 6, 1980 ("man's"); Bill Keller, "Attack of the Atomic Tidal Wave," *Washington Monthly* May 1980: 55 ("Put").

87. "The Talk of the Town," *New Yorker,* Feb. 25, 1980; George Will, "Reaping the Whirlwind," 92; Alexander Solzhenitsyn, "Misconceptions about Russia Are a Threat to America," *Foreign Affairs* Spring 1980: 833.

88. Newhouse, *War and Peace,* 359; Gregg Herken, *Cardinal Choices: Presidential Science Advising from the Atomic Bomb to SDI* (New York, 1992), 195.

89. *Carter PP,* 1980–1981 (I): 289 ("to increase"); 1979 (II): 2240 ("that a").

90. "The Talk of the Town," *New Yorker* March 10, 1980: 37 and Feb. 25, 1980: 31.

91. Smith, *Morality, Reason, and Power,* 204–05.

92. Meg Greenfield, "Let's Avoid Scapegoats," *Newsweek* May 5, 1980: 104; "Talking Loudly, with a Small Stick," *Newsweek* May 12, 1980: 47; "Valiant Try—or Bad Faith?" *Newsweek* May 5, 1980: 40; "Can U.S. Weapons Take the Heat?" *Business Week* May 12, 1980: 27.

93. Richard A. Gabriel and Paul L. Savage, *Crisis in Command: Mismanagement in the Army* (New York, 1978), 7, 131, 9, 118, 9.

94. James Fallows, *National Defense* (New York, 1981), 171, 35, 62, 68. See also Mary Kaldor, *The Baroque Arsenal* (New York, 1981).

95. Len Ackland, "Doomsday by a Short-Circuit?" *Chicago Tribune* June 20, 1980; "The Talk of the Town," *New Yorker* June 30, 1980: 26; Ford, *Button,* 15, 240.

96. Fallows, *National Defense,* xvi, xvii, 73.

97. Richard J. Barnet, *Real Security: Restoring American Power in a Dangerous Decade* (New York, 1981), 11–12, 19, 39, 97, 90, 109, 111.

98. Duboff, *Accumulation and Power,* 117.

99. Kennedy, *Rise and Fall,* 443 (quoting the Worldwatch Institute).

100. Duboff, *Accumulation and Power,* 117, 118.

101. John Updike, *Rabbit Is Rich* (1981; New York, 1982), 1, 31, 435, 436.

Chapter 8

1. Wills, *Reagan's America,* 406.

2. *Reagan PP,* 1981: 2–4.

3. *Reagan PP,* 1986 (I): 808.

4. Schaller, *Reckoning with Reagan,* 14.

5. Johnson, *Sleepwalking,* 50 ("preferred"); Deborah Silverman, *Selling Culture: Bloomingdale's, Diana Vreeland, and the New Aristocracy of Taste in Reagan's America* (New York, 1986), 158, 9.

6. Frances FitzGerald, "A Critic at Large," *New Yorker* Jan. 16, 1989: 75 (Haig), 88; Ignatius, "Reagan's Foreign Policy," 180 ("this inability").

7. Ignatius, "Reagan's Foreign Policy," 174.

8. Ibid., 174, 183.

9. Ibid., 174–75; Stanley Hoffmann, "Semidetached Politics," *New York Review of Books* Nov. 8, 1984: 36.

10. *Reagan PP,* 1983 (I): 364.

11. Ignatius, "Reagan's Foreign Policy," 177; Newhouse, *War and Peace,* 334.

12. Johnson, *Sleepwalking,* 45, 49; Wills, *Reagan's America,* 420.

13. Wills, *Reagan's America,* 489.

14. Quotations from James J. Kilpatrick, *Nation's Business* January 1983, repr. in Boyer, *Reagan as President,* 43.

15. Blumenthal, "Reaganism and the Neokitsch Aesthetic," 288, 289. On Clancy, see Hixson, "Red Storm Rising," 613.

16. *Reagan PP,* 1981: 164, 194, 168. On Churchill, see Linenthal, "Restoring America," 41; on Weinberger, Schaller, *Reckoning,* 48.

17. Quoted in Lafeber, *America, Russia, and the Cold War,* 302.

18. Schaller, *Reckoning with Reagan,* 47.

19. Ann Markusen, "Cold War Economics," *Bulletin of the Atomic Scientists* January–February 1989: 42; Brands, *The Devil We Knew,* 176.

20. "Disaster Agency Focus: Plan for Surviving Nuclear War," *Chicago Tribune* Feb. 24, 1993.

21. Kennedy, *Rise and Fall,* 522; Nick Kotz, *Wild Blue Yonder: Money, Politics, and the B-1 Bomber* (Princeton, 1989), 229, 227.

22. Wills, *Reagan's America,* 423.

23. *Reagan PP,* 1983 (I): 384 ("evil empire"); (II): 1223–25.

24. Newhouse, *War and Peace,* 335.

25. Ibid., 348.

26. Ibid., 355.

27. Ibid., 343, 344, 375.

28. Ibid., 351.

29. Malcolm W. Browne, *New York Times* Dec.4, 1978.

30. Baucom, *Origins of SDI,* 192 ("Wouldn't"); Franklin, *War Stars,* 202 ("a new"); *Reagan PP,* 1983 (I): 443 ("could"), and 1986 (I): 810.

31. Newhouse, *War and Peace,* 361 ("stunned"); *Reagan PP,* 1983 (I): 438, 442–43.

32. Boyer, *Reagan as President,* 212 (*National Review* April 15, 1983); *Reagan PP,* 1983 (I): 443; Linenthal, *Symbolic Defense,* 13 ("cruel"), 14 (on Buchwald); Wills, *Reagan's America,* 447.

33. Brands, *The Devil We Knew,* 177; Newhouse, *War and Peace,* 363.

34. Smith, *Unthinking the Unthinkable,* 116 ("SDI sought," etc.; emphasis in Smith); Linenthal, *Symbolic Defense,* 67 ("a restored").

35. Linenthal, *Symbolic Defense,* 65 ("striking"); *Reagan PP,* 1986 (II): 950.

36. Ambrose, *Rise to Globalism,* 337 ("most"); Newhouse, *War and Peace,* 367 ("febrile").

37. Bushnell, *Moscow Graffiti,* 120–21, 231.

38. *Reagan PP,* 1983 (I): 364.

39. *Reagan PP,* 1985 (I): 229.

40. Ambrose, *Rise to Globalism,* 339.

41. Newhouse, *War and Peace,* 373.

42. Ibid., 381 ("that Reagan"); Baucom, *Origins of SDI,* 200.

43. Ignatius, "Reagan's Foreign Policy," 177; Newhouse, *War and Peace,* 376 ("Moscow").

44. Newhouse, *War and Peace*, 408, 405, 408, 409.

45. Ibid., 339, 382.

46. Ibid., 401.

47. Sidney Weintraub, "The Budget: Guns Up, People Down," *New Leader* Feb. 22, 1982, in Boyer, *Reagan as President*, 116.

48. Amitai Etzioni quoted in Joseph Finkelstein, *The American Economy: From the Great Crash to the Third Industrial Revolution* (Arlington Heights, Ill., 1992), 172 (brackets in Finkelstein); Johnson, *Sleepwalking*, 192 (Volcker).

49. Elizabeth Drew, "Letter from Washington," *New Yorker* Oct. 31, 1988: 92 (Bentsen); Uwe E. Reinhardt, "Reaganomics, R.I.P.," *New Republic* April 20, 1987, in Boyer, *Reagan as President*, 122, 125.

50. Didion, "Trouble in Lakewood," 62.

51. Quoted in DuBoff, *Accumulation and Power*, 118.

52. *Christian Science Monitor* Feb. 26, 1988: 20.

53. Kennedy, *Rise and Fall*, 417, 435.

54. Ibid., 432, 444, 445.

55. Ibid., 515, xxiii, 532, 533.

56. John Barry, "Is It Twilight for America?" *Newsweek* Jan. 25, 1988: 21.

57. Samuel T. Francis, "Managing Decline," *National Review* April 1, 1988: 47–48.

58. William Nekirk, "Reagan's a Liberal in Right-wing Garb," *Chicago Tribune* Sept. 11, 1988.

59. Johnson, *Sleepwalking*, 209 ("Christians"); Schaller, *Reckoning with Reagan*, 61 ("bad news," "blame," "untested," "promoted," etc., "raise taxes"); Jumonville, *Critical Crossings*, 231 (Epstein); John McLaughlin, "The New Nationalism," *National Review* Sept. 21, 1984, in Boyer, *Reagan as President*, 89; Andrew Kopkind, "The Age of Reaganism," *Nation* Nov. 3, 1984, in Boyer, *Reagan as President*, 94 ("appropriate," etc.).

60. On "affirmers," see Jumonville, *Critical Crossings*, chap. 6.

61. Goldwater, "To Be Conservative," Sept. 15, 1981, *Congressional Record*, 97th Congress, 1st sess., 20589–90.

62. Jerome Himmelstein, in Liebman and Wuthnow, *New Christian Right*, 20 (n. 4).

63. Linenthal, *Sacred Ground*, 215, 159, 144, 161.

64. Jumonville, *Critical Crossings*, 233 ("led"); Fass, *Outside In*, 235 ("the success," etc.); Lawrence W. Levine, *Highbrow/Lowbrow: The Emergence of Cultural Hierarchy in America* (Cambridge, Mass., 1988), 250–51 ("the same"); Allan Bloom, *The Closing of the American Mind* (New York, 1987), 51.

65. E. D. Hirsch, *Cultural Literacy: What Every American Needs to Know* (Boston, 1987), 3.

66. Novick, *That Noble Dream*, 523, 565, 593.

67. Ibid., 577, 584 (Woodward), 628.

68. Koop characterized by Shilts in *And the Band Played On*, 588.

69. "Backlash," title of chap. 10, Ehrenreich, *Hearts of Men*.

70. Rosenberg, *Divided Lives*, 233, 242, 232, 235.

71. "New Conservative Index Will Chart Moral Decline," *Chicago Tribune* March 3, 1993.

72. Polenberg, *One Nation Divisible*, 207.

Chapter 9

1. *Bush PP*, 1989 (II): 136–40.
2. PBS *Frontline*, "The Choice" (1988), with commentary by Garry Wills (teacher's recollection); Drew, "Letter from Washington," *New Yorker* July 4, 1988: 75.
3. Joan Didion, "Insider Baseball," *New York Review of Books* Oct. 27, 1988: 25 (on Bush's cadences); Drew, "Letter," 71 (Bush), 76 (Drew on Bush); Blumenthal, "Letter from Washington," 68–69 (Sununu).
4. Drew, "Letter," 76.
5. Blumenthal, "Letter," 63.
6. Johnson, *Sleepwalking*, 392, 393 ("lurking," etc.); Benjamin Friedman, "The Campaign's Hidden Issue," *New York Review of Books* Oct. 13, 1988: 26–38; *Reagan PP*, 1988 (I): 88 (emphasis added); Didion, "Insider Baseball," 25 (Bush).
7. Johnson, *Sleepwalking*, 398 ("constantly," "card-carrying"); Drew, "Letter from Washington," *New Yorker* Oct.10, 1988: 97 ("scratch," Dukakis "thinks"); Drew, "Letter from Washington," *New Yorker* Sept. 12, 1988: 102 ("the American flag"); Drew, "Letter from Washington," *New Yorker* Oct. 31, 1988: 100 ("America stands").
8. Jumonville, *Critical Crossings*, 233 ("never," etc.); "No More Evil," *Manchester Union Leader* June 5, 1988, and William F. Buckley, "So Long, Evil Empire," *National Review* July 8, 1988, both in Boyer, *Reagan as President*, 249, 251.
9. Drew, "Letter from Washington," *New Yorker* July 4, 1988: 77.
10. Drew, "Letter from Washington," *New Yorker* Oct.10, 1988: 100 (Goldwater), 96 (Bush).
11. Jumonville, *Critical Crossings*, 231.
12. *Bush PP*, 1989 (I): 3; Blumenthal, "Letter," 66.
13. *Bush PP*, 1989 (II): 1489 (Nov. 9).
14. All quotations from Michael T. Klare, "Policing the Gulf—and the World," *Nation* Oct. 15, 1990: 416–18, 418, 420.
15. Didion, "Trouble in Lakewood," 60.
16. Francis Fukuyama, "The End of History?" *National Interest* Summer 1989: 3–18.
17. Graham Allison and Gregory F. Treverton, eds., *Rethinking America's Security: Beyond Cold War to New World Order* (New York, 1992), 31 (the editors), 214 (John Mearsheimer).
18. "The Talk of the Town," *New Yorker* Jan. 1, 1990: 21; John Updike, *Rabbit at Rest* (New York, 1990), 353, 442–43; John Updike, "Why Rabbit Had to Go," *New York Times Book Review* Aug. 5, 1990: 27.
19. Paul Kennedy, "Fin-de-Siècle America," *New York Review of Books* June 28, 1990: 31–38; George F. Will, "Who Will Stoke the Fires?" *Newsweek* April 9, 1990, quoted in Kennedy's piece, 31; Kevin Phillips, *The Politics of Rich and Poor* (1990; New York, 1991), xvii, 87.
20. Peter Peterson, "The Primacy of the Domestic Agenda," in Allison and Treverton, *Rethinking America's Security*, 92, 85.
21. William Kaufmann, "A Plan to Cut Military Spending in Half," *Bulletin of the Atomic Scientists* March 1990: 35–39; Nicholas M. Horrock, "As Cold War Ebbs, a Crisis of Peace Arises," *Chicago Tribune* July 30, 1989: 1, 14.

22. Walter LaFeber, "An End to *Which* Cold War?" in Hogan, *End of the Cold War*, 13, 17–18.

23. *Chicago Tribune* Aug. 15, 1989: 6 (Gallup); *Bush PP*, 1989 (II): 136–40; LaFeber, *America, Russia, and the Cold War*, 327 (Baker).

24. Blumenthal, "Letter," 67, 68. On nuclear arsenals, see *Bulletin of the Atomic Scientists* May 1993: 48.

25. Robert O'Connell, *Of Arms and Men: A History of War, Weapons, and Aggression* (New York, 1989), 3; John Mueller, *Retreat from Doomsday: The Obsolescence of Major War* (New York, 1989), 3–4, 245; Martin van Creveld, *The Transformation of War* (New York 1991), 205, 207, 212; Richard Barnet, "Reflections (After the Cold War)," *New Yorker* Jan. 1, 1990: 72.

26. *New York Times* editorial, Aug. 31, 1990; Frederic Paul Smoler, "Fighting the Bad Fight," *Nation* Oct. 23, 1989: 464.

27. Woodward, *Commanders*, 37.

28. *Reagan PP*, 1981: 839, 846; 1983 (I): 107; 1988 (I): 88.

29. *Reagan PP*, 1981: 396 (April 30).

30. Schaller, *Reckoning with Reagan*, 89 (Bell); President's Private Sector Survey on Cost Control, *War on Waste* (New York,1984).

31. Dower, *War Without Mercy*, 314 (Baker, etc.); Buick ad in *Chicago Tribune* Feb. 23, 1990; *Atlanta Constitution* political cartoon by Mike Lukovich, repr. *Chicago Tribune* Nov. 9, 1989.

32. Dower, *War Without Mercy*, 315 (1982 quotation); John Dower, "Japan and the U.S. Samurai Spirit," *Bulletin of the Atomic Scientists* June 1991: 29–30; James Fallows, "Remember Pearl Harbor How?" *Atlantic* December 1991: 22.

33. Linenthal, *Sacred Ground*, chap. 5 (quotations: 192, 204); Ian Buruma, "Ghosts of Pearl Harbor," *New York Review of Books* Dec. 19, 1991: 9 ("Would you"); *Chicago Tribune* Dec. 7, 1991, and March 12, 1992 (on camps, a cartoon originally appearing in the *Cincinnati Enquirer*).

34. FDR, in the magazine *Asia*, as quoted in Buruma, "Ghosts of Pearl Harbor," 9; Dower, *War Without Mercy*, 313–14.

35. Bruce Boyden, seminar paper, Northwestern University, June 1992 ("the only"); Robert Brauer, "The Drug War of Words," *Nation* May 21, 1990: 706; Gibson, *Warrior Dreams*, 290.

36. *Reagan PP*, 1988 (I): 47.

37. " 'Drug war bond' proposal for kids meets resistance," *Chicago Tribune* April 26, 1990.

38. Joseph Small, "POW Camps for the Drug War of '89," *Chicago Tribune,* May 17, 1989; *Yale Alumni Magazine* November 1989: cover, table of contents, 46.

39. Clarence Page, "America's War on Those Easiest to Bust for Drugs," *Chicago Tribune* May 2, 1990; Kenneth E. Sharpe, "What If Soldiers Become Antidrug Cops in the U.S.?" *Chicago Tribune* Jan. 16, 1990; Stephen Chapman, "The Dishonesty of Bush's War on Drugs," *Chicago Tribune* Sept. 7, 1989; "The Talk of the Town," *New Yorker* Sept. 18, 1989: 34; Ralph Brauer, "The Drug War of Words," *Nation* May 21, 1990: 705; "Betty Ford: Alcoholism Overlooked," *Chicago Tribune* March 26, 1991.

40. Faludi, *Backlash*, 400, 405, 408, 405 (Faludi).

41. *Ms.* July–August 1989 cover; Faludi, *Backlash*, xx–xxi; Susie Bright lecturing at the Fourth Annual Lesbian, Bisexual, and Gay Studies Conference, Harvard University, Oct. 27, 1990; Lillian Faderman, *Odd Girls and Twilight Lovers* (New York, 1991), chap. 10 title; Andrew Dworkin, *Letters from a War Zone: Writings, 1976–1989* (New York, 1989).

42. Celeste Michelle Condit, *Decoding Abortion Rhetoric: Communicating Social Change* (Urbana, 1990) offers the "commonplace" characterization but does not explore this rhetoric at length. On O'Connor and Watt, see Robert McAfee Brown, "Abortion and the Holocaust," *Christian Century* Oct. 31, 1984: 1004.

43. Brown, "Abortion and the Holocaust," 1005.

44. Gibson, *Warrior Dreams*, 11–12, 223; Jeffords, *Hard Bodies*, 10.

45. Michael Killian, "Culture's Costs: NEA Chief Fights for Funding in 'Obscenity Battle,'" *Chicago Tribune* April 15, 1990, Arts Section: 14; John Frohnmayer, *Leaving Town Alive: Confessions of an Arts Warrior* (Boston, 1993); Hunter, *Culture Wars*, 316.

46. See Sontag, *AIDS and Its Metaphors*, esp. 16–19.

47. Quoted in Lee Edelman, "The Mirror and the Tank," in Murphy and Poirier, *Writing AIDS*, 14.

48. Buchanan's syndicated column, May 1983, quoted in Robert A. Padgug, "Gay Villain, Gay Hero: Homosexuality and the Social Construction of AIDS," in Kathy Peiss and Christine Simmons, with Robert A. Padgug, *Passion and Power: Sexuality in History* (Philadelphia, 1989), 297. Other quotations from Shilts, *And the Band Played On*, 220, 228, 442, 447.

49. Shilts, *And the Band Played On*, 305.

50. Kramer, *Reports from the Holocaust*, 173, 163.

51. Andrew Holleran, *Ground Zero* (New York, 1988); Chris Glaser, "AIDS and the A-Bomb Disease," original in *Christianity and Crisis*, as summarized in George S. Buse, "Chris Glaser Talks About Gays, Lesbians and Presbyterians," *Windy City Times* Nov. 8, 1990: 20; R. Woodward, "A People at War," *Cleveland Edition* June 28, 1990: 16; Shilts, *And the Band Played On*, 217, 505; L. Scott, "Fear in the Foxholes: Health Workers' Alarm About Telling AIDS Patients," *New York* Jan. 4, 1988: 30–38. See also Mike Hippler, "Battlefields Revisited: AIDS and World War I," *Windy City Times* March16, 1989: 10; Michael Bronski, "Between the Lines," *Guide* October 1990: 18; Emmanuel Dreuilhe, *Mortal Embrace: Living with AIDS* (New York, 1988.

52. Paul Monette, *Afterlife* (New York, 1990), 51; Monette quoted in Padgug, "Gay Villain, Gay Hero," 310; Monette, *Borrowed Time: An AIDS Memoir* (New York, 1988), 85, 110.

53. PBS, *MacNeil/Lehrer Newshour* Nov. 21, 1986; *Newsweek* March 2, 1987: 31; "Drawing the Battle Lines on AIDS," *Saturday Evening Post* May–June 1988: 50–57.

54. Kramer, *Reports from the Holocaust*, 189, and Kramer, "A 'Manhattan Project' for AIDS," *New York Times* July 16, 1990; Charles Perrow and Mauro F. Guillen, *The AIDS Disaster: The Failure of Organizations in New York and the Nation* (New Haven, 1990), 181–83.

55. *Reagan PP,* 1988–89 (I): 109; (II): 1225.

56. Leuchtenburg, "New Deal," 143.

57. Sontag, *AIDS and Its Metaphors,* 10–11.

58. Kramer, "A Call to Riot: Part II," *Outlines* May 1990: 38.

59. *Reagan PP,* 1983 (I): 49–50.

60. Derek Johnson, "Metaphors and Their Victims," graduate seminar paper, Northwestern University, June 1991.

61. Larry Kramer, "A Call to Riot: Part II," *Outlines* May 1990: 38; Sontag, *AIDS and Its Metaphors,* 86.

62. On Bork, see Stanley Kutler reviewing *Battle for Justice, Chicago Tribune* Sunday Book Review, Oct. 22, 1989; "Daley Latest to Declare War on Rats," *Chicago Tribune* April 4, 1990; "N.Y. Mayor Plans 'War on Fear,'" *Chicago Tribune* Oct. 3, 1990; "Bush Praises King, Vows War on Hate," *Chicago Tribune* Jan. 10, 1990; Anna Quindlen, "A War on Cigs: Better Censure Than Cancer," *Chicago Tribune* May 6, 1990 (original in *New York Times*); Clarence Petersen, review of Keillor, *We Are Still Married, Chicago Tribune* Sunday Book Review, March 25, 1990. On Stannard, see Rockwell Gray review, *Chicago Tribune* Sunday Book Review, May 2, 1993: 5; "The U.S. Needs a Domestic Marshall Plan First" (title given three letters to the editor), *New York Times,* May 27, 1990.

63. Drew, "Letter from Washington," *New Yorker* Feb. 4, 1991: 83 (paraphrasing Sununu).

64. Powell and Boren quoted in Michael T. Klare, "Policing the Gulf—and the World," *Nation* Oct. 15, 1990: 401, 416 (Klare's brackets); Bush quoted in "The Talk of the Town," *New Yorker* Jan. 21, 1991: 23. On draft, see *Bush PP,* 1990 (II): 1725.

65. *Bush PP,* 1990 (II): 1102; Drew, "Letter from Washington," *New Yorker* Dec. 3, 1990: 176 and Feb. 4, 1991: 82.

66. *Bush PP,* 1990 (II): 1154; 1991 (I): 197; Nunn, as quoted in Stephen Chapman, "The War and Its Critics: Should We All Close Ranks?" *Chicago Tribune* Jan. 31, 1991.

67. *Bush PP,* 1990 (II): 1107, 1113 (on "blitzkrieg"), 1107, 1108, 1137 (on "appeasement"), 1155 ("another"), 1509, 1541 (on Hitler); Bush quoted in "The Talk of the Town," *New Yorker* Jan. 21, 1991: 23.

68. Drew, "Letter from Washington," *New Yorker* Dec. 3, 1990: 180.

69. Ibid., 182, 187; Bush, quoted in Drew, "Letter from Washington," *New Yorker* Feb. 4, 1991: 83.

70. Pat Buchanan, "Have the Neocons Thought This Through?" Aug. 25, 1990, as in Sifry and Cerf, *Gulf War Reader,* 213–15.

71. Chapman, "War and Its Critics."

72. Robert Massa, "The Forgotten War," *Village Voice* Feb. 12, 1991, as in Sifry and Cerf, *Gulf War Reader,* 323–25.

73. Moynihan, Jan. 10, 1991, speech, as in Sifry and Cerf, *Gulf War Reader,* 284–86; Ehrenreich, *Time* essay, Jan. 21, 1991, as in *Gulf War Reader,* 299–301.

74. Edward Luttwak, "Agencies of Disorder," *Times Literary Supplement* Jan. 18, 1991, as in Sifry and Cerf, *Gulf War Reader,* 290–98.

75. Arthur Schlesinger, Jr., "White Slaves in the Persian Gulf," *Wall Street Journal* Jan. 7, 1991, as in Sifry and Cerf, *Gulf War Reader*, 265–68.

76. Drew, "Letter from Washington," *New Yorker* Dec. 3, 1990: 178 ("the most," etc.). Other quotations: Woodward, *Commanders*, 42, 313.

77. Crowe's testimony before the Senate Armed Services Committee, Nov. 28, 1990, as in Sifry and Cerf, *Gulf War Reader*, 236, 237.

78. *Bush PP*, 1990 (II): 1720.

79. Quoted in Alan Pell Crawford, "A Republican Vote for McGovern," *Chicago Tribune* March 15, 1991.

80. Richard Rose and Robert J. Thomson, "The President in a Changing International System," *Presidential Studies Quarterly* Fall 1991: 751.

81. *Bush PP*, 1991 (I): 42.

82. *Bush PP*, 1991 (I): 150.

83. *Chicago Tribune* Jan. 20, 1991, sec. 1: 4; R. W. Apple, "Hueys and Scuds: Vietnam and Gulf Are Wars Apart," *New York Times* Jan. 23, 1991; Hallion, *Storm Over Iraq*, 264 (his emphasis).

84. Markusen and Yudken, *Dismantling the Cold War Economy*, 14, 31.

85. Drew, "Letter from Washington," *New Yorker* May 6, 1991: 101.

86. Colman McCarthy, "Top Gun War," *Washington Post* Feb. 17, 1991, as in Sifry and Cerf, *Gulf War Reader*, 334; cartoon in *Chicago Tribune* March 5, 1991.

87. Blumenthal, "Letter," 68; Peter Applebome, "Sense of Pride Outweighs Fears of War," *New York Times* Feb. 25, 1991, sec. 4: 3 ("It's"); *Bush PP*, 1991 (I): 201, 220, 221.

88. Ann McFeatters, "The Good Guys Won, and America's Can-do Spirit Was Restored," *Chicago Tribune* March 1, 1991 ("fought for," "In 100"); letter to the editor, "Thanks, America," *Chicago Tribune* March 5, 1991; Mona Charen, "Mixed with Fear, a Deep Sense of Pride," *Chicago Tribune* Jan. 21, 1991 ("Who").

89. McFeatters ("In 100") and Charen ("the moral") as cited in n. 88; Applebome, "Sense of Pride," *New York Times* Feb. 24, 1991, sec. 4: 1.

90. *Bush PP*, 1991 (I): 221.

91. Quoted in Applebome, "Sense of Pride," 1, 3.

92. "Let Schwarzkopf Run Drug War, Daley Suggests," *Chicago Tribune* March 29, 1991; on Daschle, see David E. Rosenbaum, "Wanted in Home Agenda: Unity the U.S. Had in War," *New York Times* March 20, 1991; Robert B. Reich, "Who Champions the Working Class?" *New York Times* May 26, 1991.

93. *Bush PP*, 1991 (I): 221.

94. *Bush PP*, 1991 (I): 201 (March 1 news conference).

95. Paul F. Walker and Eric Stambler, " . . . And the Dirty Little Weapons," *Bulletin of the Atomic Scientists* May 1991: 24; John Chancellor, "War Stories," *New York Times* April 1, 1991.

96. Drew, "Letter from Washington," *New Yorker* May 6, 1991: 101.

97. *Bush PP*, 1990 (II): 1805.

98. Gibson, *Warrior Dreams*, 295.

99. *Bush PP*, 1990 (II): 1808.

100. George Will, "Literary Politics," *Newsweek* April 22, 1991: 72.

101. *Bush PP,* 1991 (I): 471; university official quoted in "Reeling from Harsh Attacks, Educators Weigh How to Respond to 'Politically Correct' Label," *Chronicle of Higher Education* June 12, 1991.

102. For "Operation Campus Storm" and fine analysis of the PC debate, see Evan Carton, "The Self Besieged: American Identity on Campus and in the Gulf," *Tikkun* July–August 1991: 40–47.

103. "Millions on Broadway Roar a 'Well Done' to Gulf Veterans, *New York Times* June 11, 1991 ("a magnificent," "many Americans"); "Sense of the Storm," *Time* June 17, 1991: 24–26.

104. Cynthia Enloe, "The Gendered Gulf," in Peters, *Collateral Damage,* 95, 110; "Storm in the Desert," *Chicago Tribune* March 20, 1991.

105. Didion, "Trouble in Lakewood," 65, 60, 64.

106. *Bush PP,* 1991 (I): 590.

107. Blumenthal, "Letter," 68, 70.

108. *Bush PP,* 1992–93 (I): 158, 160.

109. Blumenthal, "Letter," 70 ("All the"). For other quotations and a shrewd analysis, see Garry Wills, "The Born-Again Republicans," *New York Review of Books* Sept. 24, 1992: 9–14 (Wills's emphases).

110. Blumenthal, "Letter," 70, 71 (on Bush and Quayle); Quayle, "Prepared Remarks by the Vice President for the National Right to Life Convention," June 11, 1992, press release from the vice president's office; Goldwater quoted in *Washington Post* July 7, 1992: 12, as cited in Max Heerman, "The Changing Conscience of a Conservative," senior thesis, Northwestern University, May 1993.

111. Blumenthal, "Letter," 71, 72; "Bush Slams Media, Draws Closer in Polls," *Chicago Tribune* Oct. 25, 1992 ("sissy").

112. Sidney Blumenthal, "Rendezvous with Destiny," *New Yorker* March 8, 1993: 44.

113. Alan Brinkley, "The 43% President," *New York Times Magazine* July 4, 1993: 22.

114. See *Chicago Tribune* May 1, 1994, for Ray Moseley, "U.S. Foreign Policy Fails with Clinton" ("a general"), and for the perceptive dissents from the praise of Nixon in columns by Stephen Chapman, William Pfaff, and Steve Daley.

115. Christopher Hitchens, "Minority Report," *Nation* July 5, 1993: 6.

116. "Aspin: 'Very Cautious' Defense Cuts for1994," *Chicago Tribune* March 28, 1993. For long-term trends in the defense budget, see "Times Have Changed; Pentagon Budget Hasn't," *Detroit Free Press* Aug. 16, 1993.

117. Eugene D. Genovese, "Voices Unite for Victory in the Cultural War," *Chicago Tribune* Dec. 22, 1993; Sidney Blumenthal, "Letter from Washington: Christian Soldiers," *New Yorker* July 18, 1994: 31 (quoting Sheldon in 1993; Blumenthal's comment).

118. *New York Times:* "Military Cites Wide Range of Reasons for Its Gay Ban," Jan. 27, 1993 ("concede"); "Pentagon Remains Silent on Rejected Gay Troop Plan," July 23, 1993 (RAND); "The Odd Place of Homosexuality in the Military," April 18, 1993 ("threatens"); Russell Baker, "By Sex Obsessed," Nov. 17, 1992.

119. Enloe, *Morning After,* 93 (her emphasis); Moskos quoted in *Summer Northwestern,* "NU Prof Plays Major Role in Lift of Gay Ban," July 22, 1993.

120. Editorial, "Let the Chief Command," *Chicago Tribune* March 29, 1993.

121. Anna Quindlen, "Phone Democracy Is Tyranny of the Stereotype," *Chicago Tribune* Feb. 2, 1993 (original in *New York Times*); Allan Bérubé discussed "female impersonation" on National Public Radio, *Fresh Air* March 31, 1993; Ellen Goodman, "Now It's Men Worrying About Male Sexual Aggression," *Chicago Tribune* Jan. 31, 1993.

122. Frank Rich, "Men in Uniform," *New York Times Magazine* April 11, 1993: 54.

123. Richard H. Kohn, "Women in Combat, Homosexuals in Uniform: The Challenge of Military Leadership," *Parameters: Journal of the U.S. Army War College* 23 (Spring 1993): 2–4; "Comment: A Democratic Army," *New Yorker* June 28, 1993: 6; Chris Bull, "Right Turn," *Advocate* Sept. 7, 1993: 35 (Goldwater).

124. David E. Sanger, "Clinton Puts a Foot in the Opening Door of the Global Market," *New York Times* Nov. 21, 1993, sec. 4: 1.

125. "Perot Still Preaching, But Does He Pack Same Punch?" *Chicago Tribune* Sept. 23, 1994.

126. David Broder, "Boomers Bungle White House 'Trust Factor,'" *Chicago Tribune* Sept. 14, 1994; "Clinton Steps to Brink of Invasion," ibid., Sept. 16, 1994.

127. "Helms Is at Center of Storm After New Clinton Criticism," *New York Times*, Nov. 23, 1994.

128. Quoted in David Remnick, "Lost in Space," *New Yorker*, Dec. 5, 1994: 86.

Conclusion

1. Schlesinger, *Vital Center*, 9.

2. Sidney Blumenthal, "Letter from Washington: Christian Soldiers," *New Yorker* July 18, 1994: 37.

3. Richard J. Barnet and John Cavanagh, *Global Dreams: Imperial Corporations and the New World Order,* as quoted in R. C. Longworth, "Multinational Firms Forge Ahead with the New World Order," *Chicago Tribune* March 27, 1994; Samuel P. Huntington, "The Coming Clash of Civilizations—Or, the West Against the Rest," *New York Times* June 6, 1993.

4. Moynihan quoted in Sidney Blumenthal, "Letter from Washington," *New Yorker* July 5, 1993: 38; Paul Kennedy, "The American Prospect," *New York Review of Books* March 4, 1993: 52.

5. On the last of these possibilities, see Linda Rocawich, "Education Infiltration: The Pentagon Targets High Schools," *Progressive* February 1994: 24.

6. *NBC Evening News* Dec. 9, 1993 (on crime); "Clinton Hails Defense, Raises Funds," *Chicago Tribune* May 22, 1994.

ESSAY ON SOURCES

Although generally keyed to sources for my quotations, many citations also reflect my debts to a work as a whole as well. For the most part, I have avoided using notes to engage or refer to disputes among scholars, since such disputes are not my major focus; citations and this essay indicate most of my preferences among sources that involve disputed matters. Regarding quotations, my usual rule has been to cite the sources where I first found them, since the context those sources provide is important. Thus, when I found a primary source quoted in a secondary source, I have usually cited the latter.

This discussion and the accompanying bibliography do not provide a comprehensive guide to all scholarship on recent United States history, or all that may be relevant to my focus, or all the "best" scholarship on that history. The scholarship on war and foreign policy alone is far too immense to discuss in detail here. Much fine scholarship goes unmentioned here because its focus lies elsewhere, because it is redundant of works I have cited, or because I have not read it, especially if it appeared in the last years of this book's preparation. This, then, is a guide to those sources I find most useful. Moreover, historians of recent America also draw—more than they usually acknowledge—on memories, words, images, and emotions that they have experienced or accumulated. I cannot reconstruct the often unconscious process by which I filtered out some of those and called upon others in writing this book, but it seems right to acknowledge that process.

My preface discusses in a general way how I understand my work in relation to other scholarship. Most of that scholarship is overly confined, as I see it, by the boundaries of the Cold War and thus bears only implicitly or indirectly on militarization, which I regard as the more fundamental, underlying dynamic of this era. Often that distinction involves hair-splitting, however, and scholarship may lack my conceptual apparatus but be rich on its own terms and invaluable for my work. In general, I have relied on secondary sources where they cover subjects well, and have sought to supplement them with primary sources where they do not.

For the sake of convenience, scholarship can be divided into familiar categories, although most works in one category speak to others as well. Following a review of scholarship in those categories is a survey of sources pertinent to specific periods.

I first read a few grand, older accounts of the history of warfare so long ago, and have revisited them so often, that they have influenced this book more than citations will indicate. Although in varying ways angry about the course that warfare had taken, the authors of these accounts anchored their dismay in broad scholarship and shrewd analysis, and each account plays a double role as both primary and secondary source for my work. Nef, *War and Human Progress* (1950)—later reprinted under the title *Western Civilization,* the version cited here—and Vagts, *A History of Militarism* (1937, 1959) have enormous scope. Millis, *Arms and Men* (1956) remains the best introduction to American military history. Although lacking the length and reach of those works, Leuchtenburg's 1964 essay "The New Deal and the Analogue of War," provided insights that I have applied, with substantial modifications, to the whole period.

Although necessarily brief and sketchy, Gillis, ed., *The Militarization of the Western World* is the best single introduction to the subject and concept of militarization, and to the large literature on it. Markusen et al., *The Rise of the Gunbelt* is the best single guide to the economic and institutional bases of America's militarization. Lotchin, *Fortress California* is a quirkier though more imaginative alternative.

Broad surveys of this period, although often fine on their own terms, deal little with my themes—one reason I wrote this book. Although now dated in coverage and scholarship, Wittner, *Cold War America,* Polenberg, *One Nation Divisible,* and Hodgson, *America in Our Time* were very valuable, more so than most recent surveys, among which I found the most useful to be Rosenberg and Rosenberg, *In Our Times.* On the other hand, many broad studies with a thematic or topical approach were essential.

Scholarship on Presidents and presidencies, despite its reputation among some historians for being old-fashioned in topic and methodology, is essential to a study like this, and often of high quality. Its pertinence to my interests varies widely, however, so that with some Presidents I could rely heavily on it, but with others I found primary sources, especially the *Public Papers* series, my main base; with all Presidents, that series was essential at least to supplement the scholarship. Partly because of their quality, partly because of their proximity to my themes, Stephen Ambrose's magisterial studies of Eisenhower and Nixon were the most important to me. On Roosevelt, I relied heavily on my own previous scholarship, a variety of secondary sources, and extensive use of the *Public Papers.* On Truman, Kennedy, and Johnson, I have relied on an eclectic mix of primary and secondary sources. After Nixon, the secondary scholarship trails off and I depended more on the *Public Papers* series and on journalistic comment. Although infrequently cited, Garry Wills's several studies of recent Presidents have strongly influenced me.

On war and foreign policy, in addition to sources already noted, the scholarship is rich despite complaints among historians in recent years about its limits. Numerous and fashionable, critiques of the historiography of American foreign relations as parochial in methodology and perspective were well summarized, explored, and themselves sometimes criticized in three forums at the close of the decade: "Writing the History of U.S. Foreign Relations: A Sympo-sium," *Diplomatic History* 14 (Fall 1990): 553–605; "A Round Table: Explaining the History of American Foreign Relations," *Journal of American History* 77 (June 1990): 93–180; and "Culture, Gender, and Foreign Policy: A Symposium," *Diplomatic History* 18 (Winter 1994): 47–124. Rosenberg, "The Cold War and the Discourse of National Security," is a valuable start at historicizing a critical term.

As for the scholarship itself, Ambrose, *Rise to Globalism* and LaFeber, *America, Russia, and the Cold War* are the best surveys, despite their origins in their earlier editions as studies of the Cold War. Gaddis, *Strategies of Containment* rigorously traces the grand strategies of successive presidencies, even if it finds more or-der and logic to their shifts than many historians see; his later account, *The Long Peace*, provocatively explores sources of stability during the Cold War. Though appearing after most of this book was written, Brands's smart, breezy survey, *The Devil We Knew*, parallels this study in some of its tone and arguments. Dal-lek, *The American Style of Foreign Policy* is a pioneering attempt to trace the inter-nal, often psychological impulses behind American foreign and military policy. May, *"Lessons" of the Past* is a dated, short, but essential study of how policy-makers used history. Although primarily about World War II, Dower, *War Without Mercy* is far broader in its utility. On international dimensions and per-spectives, see especially McNeill, *The Pursuit of Power* and Kennedy, *The Rise and Fall of the Great Powers*. On the forces promoting American hegemony in the world economic order, Thomas J. McCormick, *America's Half-Century* offers a cogent argument pulling together much literature. Although dated, Weigley, *The American Way of War* remains the best guide to and interpretation of Ameri-can military strategy and war making; my use of his title and his account in many other ways indicates my debt. Freedman, *The Evolution of Nuclear Strategy* expertly charts the often hyperbolic or arcane course of that story. Newhouse, *War and Peace in the Nuclear Age* is broader and better than many scholarly ac-counts concerning nuclear weapons and diplomacy.

Although much of the scholarship noted elsewhere in this essay speaks to political history, many ways in which that history pertains to militarization are as yet poorly examined by historians. The treatment of Congress, the courts, and political parties, as opposed to the presidency, is thin in the literature, and various milestones have been neglected: scholars of America's "welfare state" generally have little to say about the GI Bill, Veterans Administration pro-grams, and the broader possibility that defense spending has provided a wel-fare system for many—hardly all—Americans. The literature on specific insti-tutions of the "national security state" tends to be dull, although richer on relationships among science, universities, corporations, and the state; for the Defense Department and many other governmental agencies, I found policy and presidential studies more useful.

In the history of political culture, on the other hand, the literature is rich, though not yet synthesized. Marling and Wetenhall, *Iwo Jima* was the single most useful source in this category. Although it came to my attention too late for full use in this book, Slotkin, *Gunfighter Nation* is valuable. Franklin, *War Stars*, Weart, *Nuclear Fear*, and Sherry, *The Rise of American Air Power* examine fantasies among Americans (and others) of technological mastery and the relationships between fantasy and weapons development. Whitfield, *The Culture of the Cold War*, although using the "cold war" framework, is smart and informative. Several essays in May, ed., *Recasting America* are useful on the 1940s and 1950s. For the 1970s and 1980s, especially for the return of overtly religious themes in political discourse, the books and essays by Edward Linenthal that I cite were essential.

Much other work in cultural and intellectual history bears on political culture in a militarized age even when not specifically billed as doing so. Novick, *That Noble Dream*, though focused on the evolution and agonies of the historical profession, is also a fine guide to recent intellectual history generally. Additional sources on religion include Wuthnow, *The Restructuring of American Religion* and Boyer, *When Time Shall Be No More*, on apocalyptic thought.

A host of recent work on women, gender, and sexuality bears on political culture and indeed on most of the categories used here, although much of that work comes in the form of monographic articles and books too numerous to mention here. Higonnet et al., *Behind the Lines* is a pioneering introduction to the field. Although dated and essayistic, Ehrenreich, *The Hearts of Men* effectively addresses the anxieties about gender I emphasize. Rosenberg, *Divided Lives* is a recent survey with much useful background and information. Since lesbian and gay history and the modern gay identity itself are bound up with militarization, much work in that field has been useful: see, in addition to numerous articles, Berube, *Coming Out Under Fire*, D'Emilio, *Sexual Politics, Sexual Communities*, and Shilts, *Conduct Unbecoming*.

In the closely related fields of social, racial, and ethnic history, the relevant scholarship has been less forthcoming. Polenberg, *One Nation Divisible* is a valuable overview necessarily lacking depth on many specifics. Usually screeching to a halt before World War II, most histories of ethnicity and immigration do not engage in a broad way the story I tell here, but some are valuable on particular elements of it: Takaki, *Strangers from a Different Shore* is rich on Asian-Americans; Nalty, *Strength for the Fight* is colorless but informative on the place of African-Americans in the armed forces; Fass, *Outside In* is valuable on education and minorities. Much of my material and observations about these fields, however, is teased out of scholarship not primarily focused on those fields.

On economic history, and the intimately related fields of science, technology, and education, the scholarship is much richer. Markusen et al., *The Rise of the Gunbelt*, and Lotchin, *Fortress America* are essential starting points. While standard surveys of American economic history often neglect militarization, two are very useful: Galambos and Pratt, *The Rise of the Corporate Commonwealth* and

Duboff, *Accumulation and Power*. On science and its relationship to other militarized institutions, see several of the essays in Mendelsohn, Smith, and Weingart, eds., *Science, Technology, and the Military;* Hughes, *American Genesis;* Geiger, *Research and Relevant Knowledge;* and Leslie, *The Cold War and American Science,* a fine synthesis. Regional studies are also valuable in this field, especially Nash, *The American West Transformed.* Vander Meulen, *The Politics of Aircraft* is provocative on a critical industry.

In addition to the scholarship noted above, other sources on particular periods of this study were important.

For my Prologue, I also relied on Royster, *A Revolutionary People at War;* on Royster, *The Destructive War,* for the Civil War and its aftermath; and on a large literature in military history not specifically cited for this section. On the "military-industrial complex" (the much-disputed term Dwight Eisenhower used in 1961), see many of the broad studies cited above. On demographic and other consequences of the Civil War, Vinovskis, "Have Social Historians Lost the Civil War?" is very useful. On cultural and imaginative anticipations of and responses to war, see also Leonard, *Above the Battle* and Frederickson, *The Inner Civil War.* Challener, *Admirals, Generals, and American Foreign Policy, 1898–1914,* is useful on its subject. On World War I and its aftermath, Kennedy, *Over Here* and Cohen, *Empire Without Tears,* are valuable.

On the 1930s and the coming of World War II, Levine, "Hollywood's Washington" helped me to extend the themes in Leuchtenburg, "The New Deal and the Analogue of War." Karl, *The Uneasy State* is background for interpretation. Garraty, *The Great Depression* helps place American developments within a world context. Charles and Mary Beard, *America in Midpassage* (1939) is marvelous as both contemporary source and historical commentary.

The notion of a "construction of national security" is mine. Most scholarship on this period focuses less on that longer-term development than on debate about American intervention in the world crisis. On military and foreign policy, I have relied heavily on my earlier study, *The Rise of American Air Power,* on Reynolds, *The Creation of the Anglo-American Alliance,* and on my own reading of Roosevelt. The economic wellsprings of American policy are effectively argued in McCormick, *America's Half-Century* and Hearden, *Roosevelt Confronts Hitler.* Heinrichs, *Threshold of War* is a vivid narrative of 1941 sympathetic to Roosevelt. Gregory, *America 1941* sensitively presents a wealth of information.

On political culture, the relevant essays in Susman, *Culture as History* are suggestive, while Alexander, *Nationalism in American Thought,* and Wittner, *Rebels Against War* traverse more specific currents of intellect and opinion. Henrikson, "The Map as an 'Idea'" is far more valuable than its brevity would suggest. The most sympathetic treatment of the Nye Committee can be found in Paul Koistinen, "Toward a Warfare State: Militarization in America During the Period of the World Wars," in Gillis, ed., *The Militarization of the Western World* and in Koistinen, *The Military-Industrial Complex.* Murphy, "The Lonely Battle" analyzes contemporary anxieties about war. On relationships among opinion, the media, and the Roosevelt administration, the following are valuable and suggest similar conclusions: Koppes and Black, *Hollywood Goes to War;* Culbert, *News for Everyman,* Steele, *Propaganda in an Open Society,* and Schneider, *Should America Go to War?.* Ribuffo, *The Old Christian Right* is the best source on its subject and many related ones, and on what Ribuffo calls the "Brown Scare."

In the vast literature on World War II, in addition to which most of the sources already noted also apply, three older general accounts remain remarkably fresh and rich: Blum, *V Was for Victory;* Perrett, *Days of Sadness, Years of Triumph;* and Polenberg, *War and Society.* Dower, *War Without Mercy* was the most influential among more recent sources; in that category, O'Neill, *A Democracy at War* offers no grand reinterpretation but many fresh (and occasionally wrongheaded) insights. Once again, I have relied heavily on my earlier works, *Preparing for the Next War* and *The Rise of American Air Power,* and on FDR's public statements. Among many wartime commentaries, several retain special vitality: Wylie, *A Generation of Vipers;* Mead, *And Keep Your Powder Dry;* Wecter, *When Johnny Comes Marching Home,* far broader than its apparent focus on veterans would suggest; Sherrod, *Tarawa,* a classic of war reporting; and Brogan, *The American Character.*

For early reactions to Pearl Harbor and American entry into the war, Kennett, *For the Duration* is rich and compact. In a large literature on economic mobilization, the broader sources noted above met most of my needs. Valuable on liberal thought is Brinkley, "The New Deal and the Idea of the State"; see also Lekachman, *The Age of Keynes,* and Amenta and Skocpol, "Redefining the New Deal." A good survey is Vatter, *The U.S. Economy in World War II.* Many sources touch on organized labor, but see O'Neill, *A Democracy at War* for a valuable overview.

On wartime strategies, an excellent introduction can be found in Weigley, *The American Way of War.* On the plans and objectives of American elites for the postwar world, see also McCormick, *America's Half-Century,* which emphasizes hegemonic designs; Dallek, *The American Style of Foreign Policy,* which emphasizes the outward projection of American ideals and anxieties; and Divine, *Second Chance.* Walker, "The Decision to Use the Bomb," is a fair-minded review of the scholarship on that issue.

On wartime experiences of civilians, I relied heavily on other sources noted here. On those in uniform, Ellis, *The Sharp End* is insightful and balanced, while Fussell, *Wartime* is jaundiced but provocative. Both largely ignore minority and women's experience. Several fine recent studies generally uphold, but refine and alter, Blum's earlier treatment of how Americans were asked to view the war. Westbrook, "Fighting for the American Family" is insightful. Koppes and Black, *Hollywood Goes to War* is comprehensive. Doherty, *Projections of War* shows convincingly how film shaped a common wartime culture. Roeder, *The Censored War* shrewdly explains how wartime circumstances and censorship narrowed American's visual grasp of the war. For reactions to the carnage of World War II, I rely heavily on Fenrich, "Imagining Holocaust."

On social change, in addition to Polenberg's *One Nation Divisible* and Nalty's *Strength for the Fight*, there is a growing literature on race and labor: Reed, *Seedtime for the Modern Civil Rights Movement* is a careful institutional study; Norrell, "Caste in Steel," and Nelson, "Organized Labor and the Struggle for Black Equality in Mobile During World War II" probe conditions in the South. Modell et al., "World War II in the Lives of Black Americans," and Kelley, " 'We Are Not What We Seem' " are highly suggestive. Bernstein, *American Indians and World War II* traces a record substantially different from that of black Americans. Tuttle, *"Daddy's Gone to War"* is a rich social and political history of children and much else in the war. On women, Hartmann, *The Home Front and Beyond*, and Campbell, *Women at War with America* are important general studies; in Higonnet et al., *Behind the Lines*, see especially the essay by Susan Gubar. Bérubé, *Coming Out Under Fire* and D'Emilio, *Sexual Politics, Sexual Communities* are essential on gays and lesbians. On veterans and the GI Bill, an older study, Ross, *Preparing for Ulysses* remains the best source, along with Wecter's contemporary analysis. Miller, *The Irony of Victory* is the most recent of several local and state studies.

A rich body of scholarship has also developed for the Truman era, to which many of the broad studies noted above provide valuable introductions. Pemberton, *Harry S. Truman* is a brief, savage synthesis; Lacey, ed., *The Truman Presidency* offers provocative essays reflecting recent scholarship on a wide range of subjects. C. Wright Mills, *The Power Elite* (1956) is vital as both primary and secondary source.

The early Cold War has drawn much attention from historians. Broad theoretical and interpretive issues are ably reviewed in Leffler, "National Security." Barnet, *The Rockets' Red Glare* views policy elites critically. Paterson, *On Every Front*, is a fine, brief synthesis that moves beyond the usual categories. Leffler, *Preponderance of Power* is more exhaustive and up-to-date on the Truman administration, but not fully convincing. In addition to the broader studies on strategy and nuclear weapons already noted, Herken, *The Winning Weapon* focuses on this period. On the much-examined figure of George Kennan, Hixson, *George F. Kennan* is excellent. A nuanced study of both policy and an elite figure guiding it is Schwartz, *America's Germany*, on John J. McCloy. On the Korean War, the most compelling and debated account is Cumings, *The Origins of the Korean War*, with valuable insights as well into the broader course of American policy and the international system. No general study of the "homefront" during the Korean War has appeared, but Goldman, *The Crucial Decade and After* offers the flavor of the period.

On social relations, Polenberg, *One Nation Divisible* remains valuable, though it tends to attribute to the Cold War what I attribute to broader processes. Duberman, *Paul Robeson* superbly illuminates relationships among race, politics, and culture. For federal policy on race relations, Dalfiume, *Desegregation of the Armed Forces* is a rich older source; Berman, *The Politics of Civil Rights in the Truman Administration* is also useful.

In a swelling literature on women, gender, and sexuality, see, in addition to sources already noted, May, *Homeward Bound*, an important study. Despite its title, Lewes, *The Psychoanalytic Theory of Male Homosexuality* offers much about intellectual currents during this period. Rupp and Taylor, *Survival in the Doldrums* shaped my sense of women's experiences. On changing "sexual regimes," Chauncey, *Gay New York*, introduces arguments bearing on the 1940s and 1950s.

On culture and intellectual life, I relied heavily on the broad studies listed above, but Boyer, *By the Bomb's Early Light* is also essential, and Graebner, *The Age of Doubt* is a rich synthesis employing a framework very different from mine. Pells, *The Liberal Mind in a Conservative Age* is broad but less useful to my purposes. Many other studies noted here touch on scientists, but see also the affecting memoir, Dyson, *Disturbing the Universe*.

Most sources noted above deal with the Red Scare. In addition, Fried, *Nightmare in Red* is a balanced synthesis. Schrecker, *No Ivory Tower* is valuable. Diamond, *Compromised Campus* is personal and angry but revealing. Griffith, *The Politics of Fear* remains the best study of the Red Scare's politics.

In terms of the presidency, in some ways Eisenhower has yielded a richer secondary literature than his predecessor. Ambrose, *Eisenhower: The President* is masterful and deeply informed. Pach and Richardson, *The Presidency of Dwight D. Eisenhower*, more compact and current, adds additional insights. Carter, *Another Part of the Fifties*, offers acute, idiosyncratic observations on Eisenhower and the whole decade, the myths about which Carter effectively challenges. Beschloss's accounts of superpower confrontation, *Mayday* and *The Crisis Years*, are richly informative on details. Hughes, *The Ordeal of Power* was an insider's sharp account that anticipated the "postrevisionist" synthesis on Ike emerging in the 1980s and 1990s. Critical contemporary commentary is in Stone, *The Haunted Fifties*.

On more specialized issues of national security, see the sober study of Korean War armistice talks, Foot, *A Substitute for Victory*. The start of American intervention in Indochina is the object of a whole cottage industry, but for introductions see Baritz, *Backfire: A History of How American Culture Led Us into Vietnam and Made Us Fight the Way We Did*, his subtitle indicating his approach; the more dispassionate but also damning synthesis, Herring, *America's Longest War*; and Young, *The Vietnam Wars*, a survey especially attuned to Vietnamese and Asian history. Nuclear strategy and policy have produced a rich historiography mirroring the complexities of the original debates. In addition to the broader accounts already noted, Kaplan, *The Wizards of Armageddon* is a sharp account of civilian theorists, while Trachtenberg, *History and Strategy* offers a more sympathetic and scholarly examination of them and other issues. Ford,

The Button: The Pentagon's Command and Control System is broader than its title indicates. Divine, *Blowing on the Wind: The Nuclear Test Ban Debate, 1954–1960* and Aliano, *American Defense Policy from Eisenhower to Kennedy* are solid and informative. On Sputnik and the space race, MacDougall, . . . *The Heavens and the Earth: A Political History of the Space Age* is tendentious but monumental; Koppes, *JPL and the American Space Program* focuses precisely on one institution. Wolfe, *The Right Stuff* is insightful popular history. Smith, "Selling the Moon" shrewdly reveals the values ascribed to and manipulated in the space program.

On cultural, intellectual, and social history in the 1950s, I have generally relied on sources already noted, but on race relations, see also Branch, *Parting the Waters: America in the King Years,* which is shrewd and monumental. Morris, in *The Origins of the Civil Rights Movement,* recovers the movement's heterogeneity and indigenous roots. Burk, *The Eisenhower Administration and Black Civil Rights* is detailed, precise, often damning.

The best general interpretations of the 1960s are two older ones: Hodgson, *American In Our Time* and Matusow, *The Unraveling of America.* Two older revisionist accounts are fine on the real and perceived differences between Kennedy and Eisenhower and on the impulses behind Kennedy's Cold War policies: Miroff, *Pragmatic Illusions* and Wills, *The Kennedy Imprisonment.* Parmet, *JFK* is solid and informative; Burner, *John F. Kennedy and a New Generation* is short and uninspired. Among many books on Johnson, Conkin, *Big Daddy from the Pedernales* is singularly brief, balanced, yet judgmental. Zarefsky, *President Johnson's War on Poverty: Rhetoric and History* is essential on its subject, though some of the conclusions I draw from the story are not Zarefsky's. Two volumes edited by Divine, *Exploring the Johnson Years* and *The Johnson Years,* contain valuable essays.

Much of the best insight into the Vietnam War emerged during the early, angry phase of retrospection—more recent scholarship has tended to recycle earlier insights in pallid ways. I have relied on several sources in addition to those by Baritz, Herring, and Young. The most probing contemporary journalism was by Jonathan Schell, especially in *The Village of Ben Suc;* equally valuable are his later reflections that introduce *The Real War.* Berman, *Planning a Tragedy,* is useful on Johnson's administration. Galluci, *Neither Peace Nor Honor* is an older study effectively exposing the irrationalities of American war making. Among more recent studies, Gibson, *The Perfect War* is convincingly damning; Hess, *Vietnam and the United States* is bland but attentive to recent scholarship, especially about the Asian and international dimensions of the story; Clodfelter, *The Limits of Air Power* is the best single book on its subject. Small, *Johnson, Nixon, and the Doves* offers more common sense than many studies of the antiwar movement and its relationship to presidential policy. Levy, *The Debate Over Vietnam* is uninspired in analysis but informative. On the media's role, Hammond, "The Press in Vietnam as Agent of Defeat: A Critical Examination" summarizes a wealth of other studies, including a lengthier one by Hammond, while Hallin, *The "Uncensored War"* is balanced. Appy, *Working-Class War* relies heavily on disgruntled veterans for its sources but sensitively both confirms and contests standard myths about the war, as does Heineman, *Campus Wars* on its subject. Shafer, ed., *The Legacy: The Vietnam War in the American Imagination* is the best of many scholarly anthologies, and Charlton and Moncrieff, *Many Reasons Why* is one of the best oral histories. Pisor, *The End of the Line*, is excellent journalistic history of the war at its peak.

On women, gender, sexuality, and the Vietnam War, I found the existing scholarship largely inadequate to my purposes and arrived at my own judgments, but Evans, *Personal Politics* is valuable. Jeffords, *The Remasculinization of America* offers a bold if strained argument; Ehrenreich, *The Hearts of Men* captures some of the period's mood and arguments. A fine study with broad utility despite the community's uniqueness is Rorabough, *Berkeley at War.*

The late 1960s and early 1970s—better thought of as one period, rather than separating the "sixties" from the "seventies"—have yielded surprisingly rich scholarship in political history because the legal and political turmoil over the war and Nixon's presidency forced early declassification or exposure of official documentation and encouraged participants to rush rapidly into print. Most of the sources previously noted for Vietnam remain applicable to this period. Among general treatments, the best remains one written very close to the 1970s, Carroll, *It Seemed Like Nothing Happened.* On Nixon and politics preceding, during, and after his presidency, the two volumes of Ambrose, *Nixon* are superb. Kutler, *The Wars of Watergate* provides more detail and a different analysis on that subject. Still, for Nixon there is no substitute for his own words, even when public utterances, which I draw from his *Public Papers* as well as secondary sources.

The politics and culture of opposition to the war are revealed in many sources cited here and for the previous and following chapters. Among primary sources revealing radical ferment, most used here are well known: Mailer, *The Armies of the Night*; Reich, *The Greening of America*; Vonnegut, *Slaughter-House Five.* Unknown but equally revealing is the memoir by Catton, *Waiting for the Morning Train.* The travails of patriotic culture have received much less attention but can be glimpsed in Marling and Wetenhall, *Iwo Jima*; Anderegg, ed., *Inventing Vietnam: The War in Film and Television*; and Shafer, ed., *The Legacy.*

The late 1970s have been neglected by historians with big reputations and a synthetic approach, despite rich scholarship on many particulars, and for that reason the interpretations offered here are more particularly mine than for earlier chapters in this study. The periodization here is also looser: I see many historical currents sliding over the divide that Reagan's ascent to the presidency presumably marked, and thus Chapter 7, although mostly on the 1970s, traces some of those currents into the 1980s.

The best general source remains Carroll, *It Seemed Like Nothing Happened.*

Ford's presidency has received no strong general treatment, while Carter has seemed such an anomaly that historians have largely discarded him, just as voters did in 1980. Still, two shrewd essays by Leo Ribuffo, done in preparation for a full study by him, provide excellent starting points: both are in Ribuffo, *Right, Center, Left*. And Smith, *Morality, Reason, and Power* is comprehensive and insightful on Carter-era foreign policy. The Afterword to Schell, *Observing the Nixon Years* offers a broad understanding of how the Vietnam War affected politics and foreign policy in the 1970s and 1980s. On nuclear weapons, strategy, and arms control, the best general source remains Newhouse, *War and Peace in the Nuclear Age*. Scheer, *With Enough Shovels: Reagan, Bush and Nuclear War* is a biting contemporary account. But for Carter more than his predecessors, I relied on his public papers and other primary sources. Among those, the *New Yorker* was at its most perceptive during these years.

For Americans' conflicting understandings of war in the 1970s, Edward Linenthal has provided probing insights; see "War and Sacrifice in the Nuclear Age"; "Restoring America: Political Revivalism in the Nuclear Age," in Sherrill, ed., *Religion and the Life of the Nation;* and *Sacred Ground.* Equally valuable are Hellmann, *American Myth and the Legacy of Vietnam;* Franklin, *M.I.A.;* essays in Shafer, ed., *The Legacy;* Boyer, *When Time Shall Be No More;* and broad treatments of cultural history already noted.

In contrast, historians' work is weak on the overlapping conflicts over social relations and the armed forces' demographics. The final chapter of Weigley, *History of the United States Army* does, however, provide a superb overview, while Nalty, *Strength for the Fight* remains useful. Focusing on women's opposition to national policies on war and foreign relations, the literature of women's history is astonishingly silent on women's place in the armed forces in the 1970s and the battles over it, but see Holm, *Women in the Military.* On lesbians and gays in the military, Shilts, *Conduct Unbecoming*, provides an impassioned, persuasive critique of official policies.

On opposition to ERA and gay rights, Ehrenreich, *The Hearts of Men* is the best single study. Felsenthal, *The Sweetheart of the Silent Majority* is useful journalism. On moral conservatism, Young, *God's Bullies* provides rich if unflattering detail; scholarly appraisals include Wuthnow, *The Restructuring of American Religion* and Wuthnow and Liebman, eds., *The New Christian Right.* Shilts, *The Mayor of Castro Street* captures California's struggles over homosexuality. FitzGerald, *Cities on a Hill* informs my broader sense of cultural politics and social segmentation.

For the 1980s and 1990s, I have relied heavily on the rather random gleaning of popular media, instant intellectual analysis, and other contemporary sources on which any historian of recent events depends, and heavily as well on the *Public Papers* of the Presidents involved as available through the time of this writing (the final volume of Bush's papers only became available as this book went to press), although, as with other Presidents, some off-hand statements by Bush and Reagan never made it to these official volumes and are cited instead to contemporary reporting. But Reagan and his presidency, even before the latter ended, yielded a richer body of commentary and scholarship than had Jimmy Carter. Moreover, contemporary reporting and commentary are always history's first draft, and for the period covered here, much of it was sharp and energetic, and wittingly or unwittingly revealing.

On Reagan, Wills, *Reagan's America* is the best single account. Schaller, *Reckoning with Reagan* is a brief, less imaginative, but useful survey. Johnson, *Sleepwalking through History* is solid journalism. Newhouse, *War and Peace in the Nuclear Age* is even more essential for this period since scholars provide less coverage, but Linenthal, *Symbolic Defense* is a marvelous study of reactions to SDI; Smith, *Thinking the Unthinkable* is also insightful on SDI; while Baucom, *The Origins of SDI* is informative about but overly enamored with SDI. Boyer, ed., *Reagan as President,* is a useful collection.

For Bush, especially for the 1988 campaign and the Gulf War, I found the extensive reporting for the *New Yorker* by Elizabeth Drew, though often tedious, also detailed, informative, and reliable. Though brief, the best single portrait of Bush pertinent to my themes is Blumenthal, "Letter from Washington: All the President's Wars." Sifry and Cerf, eds., *The Gulf War Reader* is a valuable collection of contemporary reporting, commentary, and testimony, and Peters, ed., *Collateral Damage* adds later evidence and reflections. Hallion, *Storm Over Iraq* celebrates the Reagan and Bush administrations and air power's role in the Gulf War. Woodward, *The Commanders,* although weakly documented, is a useful account of military leaders in the Bush administration. Enloe, *The Morning After* is valuable on a wide range of issues involving gender and national defense. Among many works on this subject, Hogan, ed., *The End of the Cold War* is a strong collection. In addition to the standard literature already noted on Soviet-American relations, Bushnell, *Moscow Graffiti* especially informed my interpretation of developments within the Soviet Union.

The uncertain economic foundations for remilitarization are reviewed in many primary and secondary sources, though often with little attention to relationships between economic patterns and defense policy. I have relied particularly on Duboff, *Accumulation and Power* and Kennedy, *The Rise and Fall of the Great Powers,* which at this point in my story serves as both a primary and a secondary account. Didion, "Trouble in Lakewood" beautifully chronicles southern California's defense-based culture and its bewildered response to defense retrenchment.

On popular culture and its relationship to politics, see especially Jeffords, *Hard Bodies;* Gibson, *Warrior Dreams;* and Hixson, " 'Red Storm Rising.' " On intellectual currents, Jumonville, *Critical Crossings* is particularly useful for this period. On the supposed "culture wars," Hunter, *Culture Wars* is insufficiently sensitive to language but a solid chronicle of its subject. Most of the analysis of war's metaphors and moral equivalents is mine, derived in part from an earlier essay of mine, "The Language of War in AIDS DIscourse," in Murphy and Poirier, eds., *Writing AIDS,* a volume of rich critical reflections. Also on AIDS, Shilts, *And the Band Played On* is the standard journalistic account. Sontag, *AIDS and Its Metaphors,* differs from my analysis in many ways but is useful on contemporary attitudes toward the state. On the debate on lesbians and gays in the military, I largely drew my own conclusions based on following the media circus that accompanied it, but I also gained from advice from Allan Bérubé, George Chauncey, Lane Fenrich, and Leisa Meyer.

BIBLIOGRAPHY

Abzug, Robert H. *Inside the Vicious Heart: Americans and the Liberation of Nazi Concentration Camps.* New York, 1985.

Adler, Les K., and Thomas Paterson. "Red Fascism: The Merger of Nazi Germany and Soviet Russia in the American Image of Totalitarianism." *American Historical Review* 75 (April 1970): 1046–64.

Alexander, Charles. *Nationalism in American Thought, 1930–1945.* Chicago, 1969.

Aliano, Richard A. *American Defense Policy from Eisenhower to Kennedy: The Politics of Changing Military Requirements, 1957–1961.* Athens, Ohio, 1975.

Alonso, Harriet Hyman. *Peace as a Women's Issue: A History of the U.S. Movement for World Peace and Women's Rights.* Syracuse, 1993.

Ambrose, Stephen. *Eisenhower: The President.* New York, 1984.

——. *Nixon: The Triumph of a Politician, 1962–1972.* New York, 1989.

——. *Nixon: Ruin and Recovery, 1973–1990.* New York, 1991.

——. *Rise to Globalism: American Foreign Policy since 1938.* 5th ed. New York, 1988.

Amenta, Edwin, and Theda Skocpol. "Redefining the New Deal: World War II and the Development of Social Provision in the United States." In *The Politics of Social Policy in the United States.* Edited by Margaret Weir, Ann Shola Orloff, and Theda Skocpol. Princeton, 1988.

Anderegg, Michael, ed. *Inventing Vietnam: The War in Film and Television.* Philadelphia, 1991.

Appy, Christian G. *Working-Class War: American Combat Soldiers and Vietnam.* Chapel Hill, 1993.

Baritz, Loren. *Backfire: A History of How American Culture Led Us into Vietnam and Made Us Fight the Way We Did.* New York, 1985.

Barnet, Richard J. *The Rockets' Red Glare: When America Goes to War, the Presidents and the People.* New York, 1990.

Baucom, Donald R. *Origins of SDI, 1944–1983.* Lawrence, Kan., 1992.

Beard, Charles and Mary. *America in Midpassage.* New York, 1939.

Berman, Larry. *Planning a Tragedy: The Americanization of the War in Vietnam.* New York, 1982.

Berman, William. *The Politics of Civil Rights in the Truman Administration.* Columbus, 1970.

Bernstein, Alison R. *American Indians and World War II: Toward a New Era in Indian Affairs.* Norman, Okla., 1991.

Bérubé, Allan. *Coming Out Under Fire: The History of Gay Men and Women in World War Two.* New York, 1990.

Beschloss, Michael. *The Crisis Years: Kennedy and Khrushchev, 1960–1963.* New York, 1991.

————. *Mayday: Eisenhower, Khrushchev, and the U-2 Affair.* New York, 1986.

Bland, Larry, ed. *The Papers of George Catlett Marshall.* 2 vols. Baltimore, 1981, 1986.

Blum, John Morton. *V Was for Victory: Politics and American Culture During World War II.* New York, 1976.

Blumenthal, Sidney. "Letter from Washington: All the President's Wars." *New Yorker* Dec. 28, 1992 / Jan. 4, 1993: 62–72.

————. "Reaganism and the Neokitsch Aesthetic." In *The Reagan Legacy.* Edited by Sidney Blumenthal and Thomas Byrne Edsall. New York, 1988.

Boyer, Paul. *By the Bomb's Early Light: American Thought and Culture at the Dawn of the Atomic Age.* New York, 1985.

————. *When Time Shall Be No More: Prophecy Belief in Modern American Culture.* Cambridge, Mass, 1992.

Boyer, Paul, ed. *Reagan as President: Contemporary Views of the Man, His Politics, and His Policies.* Chicago, 1990.

Branch, Taylor. *Parting the Waters: America in the King Years, 1954–63.* New York 1988, 1989.

Brands, H. W. *The Devil We Knew: Americans and the Cold War.* New York, 1993.

————. "The Age of Vulnerability: Eisenhower and the National Insecurity State." *American Historical Review* 94 (October 1989): 963–89.

Bremner, Robert H., and Gary W. Reichard, eds. *Reshaping America: Society and Institutions, 1945–60.* Columbus, 1982.

Brinkley, Alan. "The New Deal and the Idea of the State." In *The Rise and Fall of the New Deal Order, 1930–1980.* Edited by Steve Fraser and Gary Gerstle. Princeton, 1989.

Broadwater, Jeff. *Eisenhower and the Anti-Communist Crusade.* Chapel Hill, 1992.

Brodie, Bernard. *Strategy in the Missile Age.* Princeton, 1959, 1965.

Brogan, D. W. *The American Character.* New York, 1944.

Burk, Frederick. *The Eisenhower Administration and Black Civil Rights.* Knoxville, 1984.

Burner, David. *John F. Kennedy and A New Generation.* Glenview, Ill., 1988.

Bushnell, John. *Moscow Graffiti: Language and Subculture.* Boston, 1990.

Campbell, D'Ann. *Women at War with America: Private Lives in a Patriotic Era.* Cambridge, Mass., 1984.

Carroll, Peter. *It Seemed Like Nothing Happened: America in the 1970s.* 1982; New Brunswick, 1990.

Carter, Paul. *Another Part of the Fifties.* New York, 1983.

Catton, Bruce. *Waiting for the Morning Train: An American Boyhood.* 1972; Detroit, 1987.

Challener, Richard D. *Admirals, Generals, and American Foreign Policy, 1898–1914.* Princeton, 1973.

Chang, Gordan H. "JFK, China, and the Bomb." *Journal of American History* 74 (March 1988): 1287–1310.

Charlton, Michael, and Anthony Moncrieff. *Many Reasons Why: The American Involvement in Vietnam.* New York, 1978.

Chauncey, George. *Gay New York: Gender, Urban Culture, and the Making of the Gay Male World, 1890–1940.* New York, 1994.

Clodfelter, Mark. *The Limits of Air Power: The American Bombing of North Vietnam.* New York, 1989.

Cohen, Warren. *Empire Without Tears: America's Foreign Relations, 1921–1933.* New York, 1987.

Conkin, Paul K. *Big Daddy from the Pedernales: Lyndon Baines Johnson.* Boston, 1986.

Cook, Fred J. *The Warfare State.* New York, 1962.

Cooling, Benjamin Franklin, ed. *War, Business, and American Society: Historical Perspectives on the Military-Industrial Complex.* Port Washington, N.Y., 1977.

Culbert, David. *News for Everyman: Radio and Foreign Affairs in Thirties America.* Westport, Conn., 1976.

Cumings, Bruce. *The Origins of the Korean War.* 2 vols. Princeton, 1981, 1990.

Dalfiume, Richard. *Desegregation of the Armed Forces: Fighting on Two Fronts, 1939–1953.* Columbia, Mo., 1969.

Dallek, Robert. *The American Style of Foreign Policy: Cultural Politics and Foreign Affairs.* New York, 1983.

D'Emilio, John. *Sexual Politics, Sexual Communities: The Making of a Homosexual Minority in the United States, 1940–1970.* Chicago, 1983.

D'Emilio, John, and Estelle Freedman. *Intimate Matters: A History of Sexuality in America.* New York, 1988.

Diamond, Sigmund. *Compromised Campus: The Collaboration of Universities with the Intelligence Community, 1945–1955.* New York, 1992.

Didion, Joan. "Trouble in Lakewood." *New Yorker* July 26, 1993: 46–65.

Diggins, John P. *Mussolini and Fascism: The View from America.* Princeton, 1972.

Divine, Robert A. *Blowing on the Wind: The Nuclear Test Ban Debate, 1954–1960.* New York, 1978.

———. *Second Chance: The Triumph of Internationalism in the United States During World War II.* New York, 1967.

Divine, Robert A., ed. *Exploring the Johnson Years: Foreign Policy, the Great Society, and the White House.* Austin 1981.

———. *The Johnson Years: Vietnam, the Environment, and Science.* Lawrence, Kan., 1987.

Doherty, Thomas. *Projections of War: Hollywood, American Culture, and World War II.* New York, 1993.

Donovan, Robert. *Conflict and Crisis: The Presidency of Harry S Truman, 1945–1948.* New York, 1976.

Dower, John. *War Without Mercy: Race and Power in the Pacific War.* New York, 1986.

Drew, Elizabeth. "Letter from Washington." *New Yorker,* various dates, 1988–91, cited in endnotes by date of *New Yorker* issue.

Duberman, Martin Bauml. *Paul Robeson: A Biography.* New York, 1988.

Duboff, Richard B. *Accumulation and Power: An Economic History of the United States.* Armonk, N.Y., 1989.

Dyson, Freeman. *Disturbing the Universe.* 1979; New York, 1981.

Ehrenreich, Barbara. *The Hearts of Men: American Dreams and the Flight from Commitment.* New York, 1983.

Eisenhower, Dwight D. *Mandate for Change, 1953–1956.* New York, 1963.

Ellis, John. *The Sharp End: The Fighting Man in World War II.* New York, 1980.

Enloe, Cynthia. *The Morning After: Sexual Politics at the End of the Cold War.* Berkeley, 1993.

Evans, Sara. *Personal Politics: The Roots of Women's Liberation in the Civil Rights Movement and the New Left.* New York, 1980.

Faludi, Susan. *Backlash: The Undeclared War Against American Women.* New York, 1991.

Falwell, Jerry. *Listen America!* Garden City, 1980.

Fass, Paula S. *Outside In: Minorities and the Transformation of American Education.* New York, 1989.

Felsenthal, Carol. *The Sweetheart of the Silent Majority: The Biography of Phyllis Schlafly.* Garden City, 1981.

Fenrich, Robert Lane. "Imagining Holocaust: Mass Death and American Consciousness at the End of World War II." Ph.D. diss., Northwestern University, 1992.

FitzGerald, Frances. *Cities on a Hill: A Journey through Contemporary American Cultures.* New York, 1986.

——. *Fire in the Lake: The Vietnamese and the Americans in Vietnam.* 1972; New York, 1973.

Foot, Rosemary. *A Substitute for Victory: The Politics of Peacemaking at the Korean Armistice Talks.* Ithaca, 1990.

——. "Where Are the Women? The Gender Dimension in the Study of International Relations." *Diplomatic History* 14 (Fall 1990): 615–22.

Ford, Daniel. *The Button: The Pentagon's Command and Control System.* New York, 1985.

Franklin, H. Bruce. *M.I.A. or Mythmaking in America.* 1992; revised and expanded edition, New Brunswick, 1993.

——. *War Stars: The Superweapon and the American Imagination.* New York, 1988.

Frederickson, George. *The Inner Civil War: Northern Intellectuals and the Crisis of the Union.* 1965; New York, 1968.

Freedman, Lawrence. *The Evolution of Nuclear Strategy.* 2d ed. New York, 1989.

Fried, Richard M. *Nightmare in Red: The McCarthy Era in Perspective.* New York, 1990.

Friedan, Betty. *The Feminine Mystique.* New York, 1963.

Fussell, Paul. *Wartime: Understanding and Behavior in the Second World War.* New York, 1989.

Gaddis, John Lewis. *The Long Peace: Inquiries into the History of the Cold War.* New York, 1987.

——. *Strategies of Containment: A Critical Appraisal of Postwar American National Security Policy.* New York, 1982.

Galambos, Louis, and Joseph Pratt. *The Rise of the Corporate Commonwealth: U.S. Business and Public Policy in the Twentieth Century.* New York, 1988.

Galluci, Robert. *Neither Peace Nor Honor: The Politics of American Military Policy in Viet-Nam.* Baltimore, 1975.

Gardner, Lloyd. *A Covenant with Power: America and World Order from Wilson to Reagan.* New York, 1984.

Garraty, John. *The Great Depression: An Inquiry into the Causes, Course, and Consequences of the Worldwide Depression of the Nineteen-Thirties, as Seen by Contemporaries and in the Light of History.* Garden City, 1987.

Geiger, Roger L. *Research and Relevant Knowledge: American Research Universities since World War II.* New York, 1993.

Gibson, James William. *The Perfect War: Technowar in Vietnam.* Boston, 1986.

———. *Warrior Dreams: Paramilitary Culture in Post-Vietnam America.* New York, 1994.

Gillis, John, ed. *The Militarization of the Western World.* New Brunswick, 1989.

Gimbel, John. "Project Paperclip: German Scientists, American Policy, and the Cold War." *Diplomatic History* 14 (Summer 1990): 343–65.

Goldman, Eric. *The Crucial Decade and After, 1945–1960.* New York, 1960.

Graebner, William. *The Age of Doubt: American Thought and Culture in the 1940s.* Boston, 1991.

Greenberg, Daniel. *The Politics of Pure Science.* New York, 1967.

Gregory, Ross. *America 1941: A Nation at the Crossroads.* New York, 1989.

Griffith, Robert. "Dwight D. Eisenhower and the Corporate Commonwealth." *American Historical Review* 87 (February 1982): 87–122.

———. *The Politics of Fear: Joseph R. McCarthy and the Senate.* Lexington, Ky., 1970.

Halberstam, David. *The Best and the Brightest.* Greenwich, Conn., 1972.

Hallin, Daniel C. *The "Uncensored War": The Media and Vietnam.* New York, 1986.

Hallion, Richard P. *Storm Over Iraq: Air Power and the Gulf War.* Washington, 1993.

Hammond, William M. "The Press in Vietnam as Agent of Defeat: A Critical Examination." *Reviews in American History* 17 (June 1989): 312–23.

Hartmann, Susan. *The Home Front and Beyond: American Women in the 1940s.* Boston, 1982.

Hearden, Patrick. *Roosevelt Confronts Hitler: America's Entry into World War II.* DeKalb, Ill., 1987.

Heineman, Kenneth J. *Campus Wars: The Peace Movement at American State Universities in the Vietnam Era.* New York, 1993.

Heinrichs, Waldo. *Threshold of War: Franklin D. Roosevelt and American Entry into World War II.* New York, 1988.

Hellmann, John. *American Myth and the Legacy of Vietnam.* New York, 1986.

Henrikson, Alan. "The Map as an 'Idea': The Role of Cartographic Imagery During the Second World War." *American Cartographer* 2 (April 1975): 19–53.

Herken, Gregg. *The Winning Weapon: The Atomic Bomb in the Cold War, 1945–1950.* New York, 1980.

Herring, George C. *America's Longest War: The United States and Vietnam, 1950–1975.* New York, 1986.

Herring, Pendleton. *The Impact of War: Our American Democracy Under Arms*. New York, 1941.

Hess, Gary D. *Vietnam and the United States: Origins and Legacy of War*. Boston, 1990.

Higonnet, Margaret Randolph, et al., eds. *Behind the Lines: Gender and the Two World Wars*. New Haven, 1987.

Hixson, Walter L. *George F. Kennan: Cold War Iconoclast*. New York, 1989.

———. "'Red Storm Rising': Tom Clancy's Novels and the Cult of National Security." *Diplomatic History* 17 (Fall 1993): 599–613.

Hodgson, Godfrey. *America in Our Time*. New York, 1976, 1978.

Hogan, Michael J., ed. *The End of the Cold War: Its Meaning and Implications*. Cambridge, 1992.

Holm, Jeanne. *Women in the Military: An Unfinished Revolution*. Novato, Cal., 1982.

Howard, Gerald, ed. *The Sixties: Art, Politics and Media of Our Most Explosive Decade*. New York, 1991.

Hughes, Emmet John. *The Ordeal of Power: A Political Memoir of the Eisenhower Years*. New York, 1962, 1963.

Hughes, Thomas Parke. *American Genesis: A Century of Invention and Technological Enthusiasm, 1870–1970*. New York, 1989.

Hunter, James Davison. *Culture Wars: The Struggle to Define America*. New York, 1991.

Hynes, Samuel. *Flights of Passage: Reflections of a World War II Aviator*. New York and Indianapolis, 1988.

Ignatius, David. "Reagan's Foreign Policy." In *The Reagan Legacy*. Edited by Sidney Blumenthal and Thomas Byrne Edsall. New York, 1988.

Jeffords, Susan. *Hard Bodies: Hollywood Masculinity in the Reagan Era*. New Brunswick, 1994.

———. *The Remasculinization of America: Gender and the Vietnam War*. Bloomington, 1989.

Johnson, Haynes. *Sleepwalking through History: America in the Reagan Years*. New York, 1991.

Jumonville, Neil. *Critical Crossings: The New York Intellectuals in Postwar America*. Berkeley, 1991.

Kaplan, Fred. *The Wizards of Armageddon*. New York, 1983, 1984.

Karl, Barry. *The Uneasy State: The United States from 1915 to 1945*. Chicago, 1983.

Kaufman, Burton I. *The Korean War: Challenges in Crisis, Credibility, and Command*. New York, 1986.

Kelley, Robin D. G. "'We Are Not What We Seem': Rethinking Black Working-Class Opposition in the Jim Crow South." *Journal of American History* 80 (June 1993): 75–112.

Kennedy, David. *Over Here: The First World War and American Society*. New York, 1980.

Kennedy, Paul. *The Rise and Fall of the Great Powers: Economic Change and Military Conflict from 1500 to 2000*. New York, 1987.

Kennett, Lee. *For the Duration . . . The United States Goes to War * Pearl Harbor-1942**. New York, 1985.

Koistinen, Paul A. C. *The Military-Industrial Complex: A Historical Perspective.* New York, 1980.

Koppes, Clayton. *JPL and the American Space Program: A History of the Jet Propulsion Laboratory.* New Haven, 1982.

Koppes, Clayton R., and Gregory D. Black. *Hollywood Goes to War: How Politics, Profits, and Propaganda Shaped World War II Movies.* New York, 1987.

Kramer, Larry. *Reports from the Holocaust: The Making of an AIDS Activist.* New York, 1989.

Kutler, Stanley. *The Wars of Watergate: The Last Crisis of Richard Nixon.* New York, 1990.

Lacey, Michael, ed. *The Truman Presidency.* New York, 1989.

Leffler, Melvyn P. *A Preponderance of Power: National Security, the Truman Administration, and the Cold War.* Stanford, 1992.

———. "National Security." *Journal of American History* 77 (June 1990): 143–52.

Lekachman, Robert. *The Age of Keynes.* New York, 1966.

Leonard, Thomas C. *Above the Battle: War-Making in America from Appomattox to Versailles.* New York, 1978.

Leslie, Stuart W. *The Cold War and American Science: The Military-Industrial-Academic Complex at MIT and Stanford.* New York, 1993.

Leuchtenburg, William. "The New Deal and the Analogue of War." In *Change and Continuity in Twentieth-Century America.* Edited by John Braeman et al. Columbus, 1964.

Levine, Lawrence W. "Hollywood's Washington: Film Images of National Politics During the Great Depression." In Lawrence Levine, *The Unpredictable Past: Explorations in American Cultural History.* New York, 1993.

Levy, David W. *The Debate Over Vietnam.* Baltimore, 1991.

Lewes, Kenneth. *The Psychoanalytic Theory of Male Homosexuality.* New York, 1988.

Linenthal, Edward Tabor. *Sacred Ground: Americans and Their Battlefields.* Urbana, 1991.

———. *Symbolic Defense: The Cultural Significance of the Strategic Defense Initiative.* Urbana, 1989.

———. "War and Sacrifice in the Nuclear Age: The Committee on the Present Danger and the Renewal of Martial Enthusiasm." In *A Shuddering Dawn: Religious Studies and the Nuclear Age.* Edited by Ira Chernus and Edward Tabor Linenthal. Albany, 1989.

Lipsitz, George. *Class and Culture in Cold War America: A Rainbow at Midnight.* South Hadley, Mass., 1982.

Lotchin, Roger W. *Fortress California, 1910–1961: From Warfare to Welfare.* New York, 1992.

MacDougall, Walter. . . . *The Heavens and the Earth: A Political History of the Space Age.* New York, 1985.

McCormick, Thomas. *America's Half-Century: United States Foreign Policy in the Cold War.* Baltimore, 1989.

McNeill, William Hardy. *The Pursuit of Power: Technology, Armed Force, and Society since A.D. 1000.* Chicago, 1982.

Mailer, Norman. *The Armies of the Night: History as a Novel, the Novel as History.* New York, 1968.

Markusen, Ann, Scott Campbell, Peter Hall, and Sabina Deitrick. *The Rise of the Gunbelt: The Military Remapping of Industrial America.* New York, 1991.

Markusen, Ann, and Joel Yudken. *Dismantling the Cold War Economy.* New York, 1992.

Marling, Karal Ann, and John Wetenhall. *Iwo Jima: Monuments, Memories, and the American Hero.* Cambridge, Mass., 1991.

Matusow, Allen J. *The Unraveling of America: A History of Liberalism in the 1960s.* New York, 1984.

May, Elaine Tyler. *Homeward Bound: American Families in the Cold War Era.* New York, 1988.

May, Ernest R. *"Lessons" of the Past: The Use and Misuse of History in American Foreign Policy.* New York, 1973.

May, Lary, ed. *Recasting America: Culture and Politics in the Age of Cold War.* Chicago, 1989.

Mead, Margaret. *And Keep Your Powder Dry: An Anthropologist Looks at America.* New York, 1942.

Mendelsohn, Everett, Merritt Roe Smith, and Peter Weingart, eds. *Science, Technology, and the Military.* 2 vols. Boston, 1988.

Miller, Marc Scott. *The Irony of Victory: World War II and Lowell, Massachusetts.* Urbana, 1988.

Millis, Walter. *Arms and Men: A Study of American Military History.* New York, 1956.

Mills, C. Wright. *The Power Elite.* New York, 1956, 1959.

Miroff, Bruce. *Pragmatic Illusions: The Presidential Politics of John F. Kennedy.* New York, 1976.

Modell, John, et al. "World War II in the Lives of Black Americans: Some Findings and an Interpretation." *Journal of American History* 76 (December 1989): 838–48.

Morris, Aldon D. *The Origins of the Civil Rights Movement: Black Communities Organizing for Change.* New York, 1984.

Murphy, Daniel. "The Lonely Battle: American Dreams and Nightmares and the Debate Over Intervention in the Second World War." Ph.D. diss., Northwestern University, 1988.

Murphy, Timothy F., and Suzanne Poirier, eds. *Writing AIDS: Gay Literature, Language, and Analysis.* New York, 1993.

Nalty, Bernard. *Strength for the Fight: A History of Black Americans in the Military.* New York, 1986.

Nash, Gerald D. *The American West Transformed: The Impact of the Second World War.* Bloomington, 1985.

Nef, John U. *War and Human Progress* (1950). Reprinted as *Western Civilization since the Renaissance: Peace, War, Industry and the Arts.* New York, 1963.

Nelson, Bruce. "Organized Labor and the Struggle for Black Equality in Mobile During World War II." *Journal of American History* 80 (December 1993): 952–88.

Newhouse, John. *War and Peace in the Nuclear Age.* New York, 1989.

New York Times. *The Pentagon Papers.* New York, 1971.

Norrell, Robert J. "Caste in Steel: Jim Crow Careers in Birmingham, Alabama." *Journal of American History* 73 (December 1986): 669–94.

Novick, Peter. *That Noble Dream: The "Objectivity Question" and the American Historical Profession.* New York, 1988.

Ogburn, William Fielding, ed. *American Society in Wartime.* Chicago, 1943.

O'Neill, William L. *A Democracy at War: America's Fight at Home and Abroad in World War II.* New York, 1993.

Pach, Chester J. *Arming the Free World: The Origins of the United States Military Assistance Program, 1945–1950.* Chapel Hill, 1991.

Pach, Chester J., and Elmo Richardson. *The Presidency of Dwight D. Eisenhower.* Lawrence, Kan., 1991.

Parmet, Herbert S. *JFK: The Presidency of John F. Kennedy.* 1983; New York, 1984.

Paterson, Thomas G. *On Every Front: The Making of the Cold War.* New York, 1979.

Pells, Richard H. *The Liberal Mind in a Conservative Age: American Intellectuals in the 1940s and 1950s.* New York, 1985.

Pemberton, William E. *Harry S. Truman: Fair Dealer and Cold Warrior.* Boston, 1989.

Perrett, Geoffrey. *Days of Sadness, Years of Triumph: The American People, 1939–1945.* 1973; Baltimore, 1974.

Peters, Cynthia, ed. *Collateral Damage: The New World Order at Home and Abroad.* Boston, 1992.

Pisor, Robert. *The End of the Line: The Siege of Khe Sanh.* New York, 1982.

Polenberg, Richard. *One Nation Divisible: Class, Race, and Ethnicity in the United States Since 1938.* New York, 1980.

———. *War and Society: The United States, 1941-1945.* Philadelphia, 1972.

Reed, Merl E. *Seedtime for the Modern Civil Rights Movement: The President's Committee on Fair Employment Practice.* Baton Rouge, 1991.

Reich, Charles. *The Greening of America: How the Youth Revolution Is Trying to Make America Livable.* New York, 1970.

Reynolds, David. *The Creation of the Anglo-American Alliance, 1937–1941: A Study in Competitive Co-operation.* London, 1981.

Ribuffo, Leo P. "The Brown Scare: A 'Paranoid Style' in American Politics." Unpublished paper.

———. *The Old Christian Right: The Protestant Far Right from the Great Depression to the Cold War.* Philadelphia, 1983.

———. *Right, Center, Left: Essays in American History.* New Brunswick, 1992.

Roeder, George. *The Censored War: American Visual Experience During World War Two.* New Haven, 1993.

Rorabough, William. *Berkeley at War: The 1960s.* New York, 1989.

Rosenberg, Emily S. "Commentary: The Cold War and the Discourse of National Security." *Diplomatic History* 17 (Spring 1993): 277–84.

———. " 'Foreign Affairs' After World War II: Connecting Sexual and International Politics." *Diplomatic History* 18 (Winter 1994): 59–70.

Rosenberg, Norman L. and Emily S. *In Our Times: America since World War II.* 4th ed. Englewood Cliffs, N.J., 1991.

Rosenberg, Rosalind. *Divided Lives: American Women in the Twentieth Century.* New York, 1992.

Ross, Davis R. B. *Preparing for Ulysses: Politics and Veterans During World War II.* New York, 1969.

Royster, Charles. *The Destructive War: William Tecumseh Sherman, Stonewall Jackson, and the Americans.* New York, 1991.

———. *A Revolutionary People at War: The Continental Army and American Character, 1775–1783.* 1979; New York, 1981.

Rupp, Leila, and Verta Taylor. *Survival in the Doldrums: The American Women's Rights Movement, 1945 to the 1960s.* New York, 1987.

Schaller, Michael. *Reckoning with Reagan: America and Its President in the 1980s.* New York, 1992.

Scheer, Robert. *With Enough Shovels: Reagan, Bush and Nuclear War.* 1982; New York, 1983.

Schell, Jonathan. *The Fate of the Earth.* New York, 1982.

———. *Observing the Nixon Years: "Notes and Comment" from the* New Yorker *on the Vietnam War and the Watergate Crisis, 1969–1975.* New York, 1989.

———. *The Real War: The Classic Reporting of the Vietnam War.* New York, 1988.

———. *The Village of Ben Suc.* New York, 1967.

Schlesinger, Arthur, Jr. *The Vital Center: The Politics of Freedom.* Boston, 1949.

———. *A Thousand Days: John F. Kennedy in the White House.* Boston, 1965.

Schneider, James. *Should America Go to War? The Debate Over Foreign Policy in Chicago, 1939–1941.* Chapel Hill, 1989.

Schrecker, Ellen. *No Ivory Tower: McCarthyism and the Universities.* New York, 1986.

Schwartz, Thomas Alan. *America's Germany: John J. McCloy and the Federal Republic of Germany.* Cambridge, Mass., 1991.

Shafer, D. Michael, ed. *The Legacy: The Vietnam War in the American Imagination.* Boston, 1990.

Sherrill, Rowland A., ed. *Religion and the Life of the Nation.* Urbana, 1990.

Sherrod, Robert. *Tarawa.* 1944; Fredericksburg, Tex., 1973.

Sherry, Michael S. *Preparing for the Next War: American Plans for Postwar Defense, 1941–1945.* New Haven, 1977.

———. *The Rise of American Air Power: The Creation of Armageddon.* New Haven, 1987.

Shilts, Randy. *And the Band Played On: Politics, People, and the AIDS Epidemic.* 1987; New York, 1988.

———. *Conduct Unbecoming: Lesbians and Gays in the U.S. Military, Vietnam to the Persian Gulf.* New York, 1993.

———. *The Mayor of Castro Street: The Life and Times of Harvey Milk.* New York, 1982.

Sifry, Micah L., and Christopher Cerf, eds. *The Gulf War Reader: History, Documents, Opinion.* New York, 1991.

Slotkin, Richard. *Gunfighter Nation: The Myth of the Frontier in Twentieth-Century America.* New York, 1992.

Small, Melvin. *Johnson, Nixon, and the Doves.* New Brunswick, 1988.

Smith, Gaddis. *Morality, Reason, and Power: American Diplomacy in the Carter Years.* New York, 1986.

Smith, Geoffrey S. "Commentary: Security, Gender, and the Historical Process." *Diplomatic History* 18 (Winter 1994): 79–90.

Smith, Jeff. *Thinking the Unthinkable: Nuclear Weapons and Western Culture.* Bloomington, 1989.

Smith, Michael L. "Selling the Moon: The U.S. Manned Space Program and the Triumph of Commodity Scientism." In *The Culture of Consumption: Critical Essays in American History, 1880–1990.* Edited by Richard Wightman Fox and T. J. Jackson Lears. New York, 1983.

Sontag, Susan. *AIDS and Its Metaphors.* New York, 1989.

Steele, Richard. *Propaganda in an Open Society: The Roosevelt Administration and the Media, 1933–1941.* Westport, Conn., 1985.

Stone, I. F. *The Haunted Fifties.* 1963; New York, 1969.

Susman, Warren. *Culture as History: The Transformation of American Society in the Twentieth Century.* New York, 1984.

Takaki, Ronald. *Strangers from a Different Shore: A History of Asian Americans.* Boston, 1989.

Trachtenberg, Marc. *History and Strategy.* Princeton, 1991.

Tuttle, William M., Jr. *"Daddy's Gone to War": The Second World War in the Lives of America's Children.* New York, 1993.

Vagts, Alfred. *A History of Militarism, Civilian and Military.* 1937; 1959 revised edition, New York, 1967.

Vander Meulen, Jacob. *The Politics of Aircraft: Building an American Military Industry.* Lawrence, Kan., 1991.

Vatter, Harold. *The U.S. Economy in World War II.* New York, 1985.

Vinovskis, Maris A. "Have Social Historians Lost the Civil War? Some Preliminary Demographic Speculations." *Journal of American History* 76 (June 1989): 34–58.

Vonnegut, Kurt, Jr. *Slaughterhouse-Five, or The Children's Crusade: A Duty-Dance with Death.* New York, 1968, 1969.

Walker, J. Samuel. "The Decision to Use the Bomb: A Historiographical Update." *Diplomatic History* 14 (Winter 1990): 97–114.

Ware, Susan. *Holding Their Own: American Women in the 1930s.* Boston, 1982.

Warner, W. Lloyd. *Democracy in Jonesville: A Study in Quality and Inequality.* New York, 1949.

Weart, Spencer. *Nuclear Fear: A History of Images.* Cambridge, Mass., 1988.

Wecter, Dixon. *When Johnny Comes Marching Home.* Cambridge, Mass., 1944.

Weigley, Russell. *The American Way of War: A History of United States Military Strategy and Policy.* New York, 1973.

———. *History of the United States Army.* Enlarged edition. Bloomington, 1984.

Westbrook, Robert B. "Fighting for the American Family: Private Interests and Political Obligations in World War II." In *The Power of Culture: Critical Essays in American History.* Edited by Richard Wightman Fox and T. J. Jackson Lears. Chicago, 1993.

Westmoreland, William. *A Soldier Reports.* 1976; New York, 1989.

White, Richard. *"It's Your Misfortune and None of My Own": A History of the American West*. Norman, Okla., 1991.

Whitfield, Stephen J. *The Culture of the Cold War*. Baltimore, 1991.

Wills, Garry. *The Kennedy Imprisonment: A Meditation on Power*. Boston, 1981, 1982.

———. *Reagan's America*. 1987; New York, 1988.

Wittner, Lawrence. *Cold War America: From Hiroshima to Watergate*. New York, 1974.

———. *Rebels Against War: The American Peace Movement, 1941–1960*. New York, 1969.

Wolfe, Tom. *The Right Stuff*. New York, 1979.

Woodward, Bob. *The Commanders*. New York, 1991.

Woodward, C. Vann. "The Age of Reinterpretation." *American Historical Review* 66 (October 1960): 1–19.

Wuthnow, Robert. *The Restructuring of American Religion: Society and Faith since World War II*. Princeton, 1988.

Wuthnow, Robert, and Robert Liebman, eds. *The New Christian Right: Mobilization and Legitimation*. New York, 1983.

Wylie, Philip. *A Generation of Vipers*. New York, 1942.

Young, Marilyn. *The Vietnam Wars: 1945–1990*. New York, 1991.

Young, Perry Deane. *God's Bullies: Native Reflections on Preachers and Politics*. New York, 1982.

Zarefsky, David. *President Johnson's War on Poverty: Rhetoric and History*. University, Ala., 1986.

INDEX